The Rolls of the Freemen of the City of Chester.

1700-1 [12-13 W. iii.] RICHARD OULTON, Esquire, Mayor.

Oct. 12 James s. of Edward Hammond, yeoman, and p. of Charles Shale, butcher.
,, 18 *Sir Henry Bunbury, baronet.
,, 26 John s. of John Finchett of Chester, brewer, and p. of Samuel Taylor of Chester, barber chirurgeon.
Nov. 2 William Ellis p. of William Harrison of Chester, cordwainer.
,, 14 *John Grosvenor, esquire.
,, 14 *Andrew Betty, tailor.
,, 14 *Richard Lawrence, tailor.
,, 20 *Samuel Simpson, merchant.
Dec. 20 George s. of John Shone, husbandman, and p. of Richard Calley of Chester, weaver.
,, 24 Ralph Pickmore, butcher, s. of Randle Pickmore of Chester, butcher, defunct.
,, 24 William Wiswall, silkweaver, s. of William Wiswall of Chester, labourer, defunct, and p. of George Fernall of Chester, silkweaver.
Jan. 1 Thomas s. of Ralph Cotgreave of Sutton, co. Chester, yeoman, and p. of John Kelsall of Chester, confectioner.
,, 1 William s. of Geoffrey Chears of Barrow, co. Chester, yeoman, and p. of Edward Croughton of Chester, tanner.
,, 6 John s. of John Smith of Waverham, co. Chester, defunct, and p. of Henry Hall of Chester, tanner.
,, 8 *James Kenna [Kennay, M.B.], innholder.
Mar. 8 Samuel Crane, silkweaver, s. of William Crane of Chester, barber, defunct.
Apl. 12 Thomas s. of Samuel Gerrad of Chester, tailor, and p. of Charles Gerrard, linen-draper.

1701 [13 W. iii.] HUGH STARKEY, Esquire, Mayor.

May 10   John s. of Joseph Clubb of Huntington, co. Chester, yeoman, and p. of Nathan Bradburn of Chester, ironmonger.
„   17   *Thomas Smith, sawyer.
June 14 *Randle Stanway [Stannaway, M.B.], gardener.
July 26 Josiah s. of John Richardson of Clotton, co. Chester, yeoman, and p. of Gerrard Jones of Chester, skinner.
Aug. 2 William s. of Laurence Gaulter of Chester, joiner, and p. of Thomas Bavand of Chester, turner.
„   16   Richard s. of William Witter of Chester, ironmonger, defunct, and p. of John Bingley, chandler.
„   18   *William Jones, yeoman.
„   19   Robert Winnington, plasterer, s. of Thomas Winnington of Chester, plasterer.
„   23   John s. of John Elcock of Chester, tailor, defunct.
„   28   *John Key, gentleman.
Sep. 20 Benjamin s. of John Davyes of Chester, brewer, defunct, and p. of Isaac Warmingham of Chester, saddler.
„   20   Richard s. of Richard Mitchell of Newton, co. Chester, yeoman, and p. of John Millington, currier.
„   23   *Samuel Coleclough, carpenter.
Oct. 6 Thomas s. of Thomas Watmough, late of Chester, barber chirurgeon.
„   6   Thomas Coe, cordwainer, s. of Thomas Coe of Chester, cordwainer.
„   6   Robert Hankey, cordwainer, s. of John Hankey of Chester, cordwainer.
„   6   Richard Griffith, glover, s. of John Griffith of Chester, glover, defunct.
„   9   Richard Bathoe, bricklayer, s. of Nathaniel Bathoe of Chester, bricklayer.
„   9   Joseph Davyes, baker, s. of Ralph Davyes of Chester, baker.
„   9   Adam Kemp, baker, s. of Adam Kemp of Chester, baker, defunct.
„   9   Thomas Withers, yeoman.

The Rolls Of The Freemen Of The City Of Chester (Part II) 1700-1805

Editor: J. H. E. Bennett

Alpha Editions

This Edition Published in 2020

ISBN: 9789354364099

Design and Setting By
Alpha Editions
www.alphaedis.com
Email – info@alphaedis.com

As per information held with us this book is in Public Domain.
This book is a reproduction of an important historical work. Alpha Editions uses the best technology to reproduce historical work in the same manner it was first published to preserve its original nature. Any marks or number seen are left intentionally to preserve its true form.

1701-2 [13 W. iii.–1 Anne] THOMAS HAND, Esquire, Mayor.

Oct. 11 Thomas Totty p. of Richard Gamon, late of Chester, chandler.
„ 15 Thomas s. of Thomas Ledsham, late of Chester, feltmaker, and p. of Samuel Pyke of Chester, tailor, defunct.
„ 15 John s. of Edward Croughton of Chester, cordwainer, defunct, and p. of Thomas Deane of Chester, cordwainer.
Nov. 1 Richard Smith, skinner, s. of Richard Smith of Chester, tanner, defunct.
„ 15 Charles Moulson, tanner, s. of Charles Moulson of Chester, tanner.
„ 22 John Crosse, joiner, s. of Isaac Crosse of Chester, joiner, defunct.
„ 28 George s. of Robert Hickson of Overton, yeoman, and p. of John Thomason of Chester, brewer.
„ 29 Matthew s. of Matthew Brown of Chester, bricklayer.
Dec. 6 John Knight, bricklayer, s. of John Knight of Chester, bricklayer, defunct.
„ 6 John s. of William Langdale of Bredford, co. Derby, yeoman, and p. of John Woodward of Chester, bricklayer.
Jan. 5 Calveley Speed p. of Thomas Parnell of Chester, ironmonger.
„ 5 Richard s. of Richard Wright of Chester, clerk, and p. of Charles Warmingham of Chester, barber chirurgeon.
„ 5 William s. of Richard Bridge of Chester, dyer, defunct, and p. of Timothy Deane of Chester, ironmonger.
„ 5 Moses s. of Moses Marsh of Chester, upholsterer.
„ 5 Joseph Alcott, smith, s. of Thomas Alcott of Chester, smith.
„ 5 Joseph s. of John Dutton, late of Rossett, co. Denbigh, yeoman, and p. of John Bevan of Chester, butcher.
Feb. 14 Robert s. of George Pyke of Manley, co. Chester, yeoman, and p. of Hugh Holliwell of Chester, baker.
Apr. 28 John s. of Charles Boswell of Chester, paver, defunct, and p. of Randle Annion of Chester, baker, defunct.
Mar. 23 *Charles Hurleston, esquire.
„ 21 *John Carter, mason, s. of John Carter of Flookers Brook, mason.

Apr. 4 *Daniel Peck, merchant.
„ 4 *Thomas Sampson, periwigmaker.
„ 11 *William Gamull, esquire.
„ 11 *Thomas Tynsdale, gentleman.
„ 25 Peter Horton, tailor, p. of Thomas French, tailor, defunct.
May 2 George s. of George Guest of Pulford, co. Chester, clerk, and p. of Giles Reece, barber, defunct.
„ 9 William s. and p. of William Coker of Chester, cheesefactor.
„ 9 John s. of John Potter of Chester, tailor, defunct, and p. of William Mercer, chandler.
„ 9 John s. of John Calcott of Chester, turner, and p. of John Annion, joiner.
„ 23 *Ralph Lightfoot, yeoman.
June 5 *George Griffith, plumber.
„ 5 *Joseph Dunstan.
„ 6 Edward Walton, baker, s. of Thomas Walton of Chester, baker.
„ 6 *Samuel Deane, yeoman.
„ 6 *Robert Brice.
„ 20 John Thornley, smith, s. of John Thornley of Chester, smith, defunct.
„ 20 Robert s. of John Thornley, defunct, and p. of William Huntington of Chester, baker.
July 11 *James Comberbach, merchant.
„ 11 Thomas s. of Edward Twanbrook of Walbank, gentleman, and p. of Samuel Heath of Chester, confectioner.
„ 18 Thomas s. of John Harrison the elder, yeoman, and p. of John Harrison the younger, tailor.
„ 18 Charles s. of Charles Banner of Chester, brewer, defunct, and p. of William Woodfin of Chester, slater, defunct.
Aug. 15 Joseph s. of John Woodworth of Chester, husbandman, and p. of William Lytherland of Chester, joiner.
„ 19 Josiah Kenrick p. of Randle Pickmore of Chester, butcher, defunct.
„ 22 *Samuel Filkin of Boughton, yeoman.
Sep. 5 *Joseph Harding, yeoman.
„ 14 *John Piers, yeoman.
Oct. 6 John Brett, clerk, s. of Richard Brett of Chester, merchant, defunct.
Sep. 19 *Richard Bowcock.
Oct. 10 John s. of George Brown of Chester, ironmonger, defunct, and p. of Henry Jones of Chester, saddler.

[1702-3]   THE CITY OF CHESTER   211

Oct. 16 James Gilbert, chandler, s. of James Gilbert of Chester, tallowchandler, defunct.
„ 16 *Richard Key, yeoman.
„ 26 William s. of John Hancock, late of Chester, joiner.

1702-3 [1-2 A.] [WILLIAM, EARL OF DERBY, DIED NOV. 5] MICHAEL JOHNSON, ESQUIRE [SUCC.], MAYOR[S].

Nov. 7 Randle Bathoe, tanner, s. of Daniel Bathoe of Chester, tanner, defunct.
Jan. 6 Randle Minshull, stationer, ⎱ ss. of John Minshull of Chester, stationer, and
„ 6 Richard Minshull, stationer, ⎰ one of the Sheriffs of the city.
„ 6 William Dicas s. and p. of Richard Dicas of Chester, tailor.
„ 16 Thomas s. of Thomas Young of Chester, brewer, and p. of John Gaulter of Chester, joiner.
Mar. 6 Thomas s. of Thomas Crooks, miller, and p. of Thomas White of Chester, carpenter.
„ 27 Hugh s. of Rowland Hughes of Llandaniell, com. Anglesey, ironmonger, and p. of John Yeaman of Chester, ironmonger.
Apr. 3 Richard s. of John Richardson and p. of Ralph Walley of Chester, goldsmith.
„ 10 William s. of Daniel Hickman of Farne, co. Somerset, turner, and p. of Alban Gray of Chester, bricklayer.
May 1 Edward s. of Edward Oulton of Chester, alderman, defunct.
„ 1 *Thomas Cranwall.
„ 5 William Clayton, merchant.
„ 8 Jonathan s. of Mary Minshull of Mollington, widow, and p. of John Dob, glover.
„ 8 John Fithian p. of Thomas Thomason of Chester, cordwainer.
„ 8 Robert s. of Robert Gregg, yeoman, and p. of John Lockit of Chester, cordwainer.
„ 22 *Bernard Feilding, yeoman.
June 26 William s. of Edward Daxon of Coddington, clerk, and p. of Charles Warmingham of Chester, chirurgeon.
„ 26 Samuel s. of John Malbone of Chester, defunct, and p. of Robert Young of Chester, cutler.
July 2 John s. of John Worrall of Backford, yeoman, and p. of William Smith of Chester, tallowchandler.

July 3 Joseph Dyson, tinplate-worker, } ss. of Joseph Dyson
 ,,   3 Thomas Dyson, tinplate-worker, } of Chester, tinplate-worker.
 ,, 17 Trafford s. of Roger Massey, late of Clutton, gentleman, and p. of William Cockayn of Chester, ironmonger.
 ,, 24 Ambrose Whawell, ironmonger, s. of John Whawell, yeoman, and p. of Henry Colson of Chester, barber.
Aug. 19 Robert Williams, carpenter, s. of Robert Williams of Wrexham, co. Denbigh, carpenter.
 ,, 19 John Cawley p. of John Clayton of Chester, feltmaker.
 ,, 19 *Hugh, Lord Cholmondeley.
 ,, 19 *John Egerton, esquire.
 ,, 21 *William Meales, ship carpenter.
Sep. 4 Henry s. of Henry Frodsham of Thornton, gentleman, and p. of Thomas Chapman of Chester, barber chirurgeon.
 ,, 25 *William Pennington, gentleman.
 ,, 25 William Morgell, gentleman, s. of Ralph Morgell, draper, defunct.
Oct. 2 Thomas s. of Thomas Bolland, late of Chester, joiner, and p. of Hugh Starkey, alderman, barber chirurgeon.
 ,, 11 George Wilcock, gentleman, s. of Thomas Wilcock of Chester, alderman, defunct.
 ,, 11 Robert Helley s. of William Helley of Upton, co. Chester, yeoman, and p. of Robert Jones, dyer.
 ,, 14 Peter s. of Peter Bennett of Chester, alderman.
 ,, 14 Matthew Oulton, merchant, s. of Richard Oulton of Chester, alderman, defunct.
 ,, 14 Daniel Taylor, merchant, s. of Samuel Taylor of Chester, gentleman.
 ,, 14 Thomas s. of Thomas Reece of Chester, defunct.
 ,, 14 Robert Oulf, feltmaker, s. of John Oulf of Chester, baker.
 ,, 14 John Oliver p. of Samuel Deane of Chester, cordwainer.
 ,, 14 William Pemberton, merchant, s. of Peter Pemberton of Chester, goldsmith.
 ,, 14 Richard Owens p. of John Pugh of Chester, ironmonger.
 ,, 14 Peter Leaconby, ironmonger, p. of Robert Murrey of Chester, alderman.
 ,, 14 Charles Howard p. of William Carter of Chester, mason.
 ,, 14 Charles Bailey } pp. of Robert Crosby of Chester,
 ,, 14 Thomas Hampton } cordwainer.

| 1703-4] | THE CITY OF CHESTER | 213 |

Oct. 14 Joseph   ⎫ ss. of William Witter of Chester, iron-
„ 14   William ⎭   monger, defunct.
„ 14   John Acton p. of Thomas Thomason of Chester, cordwainer.
„ 14   Thomas Hutchins p. of John Harrison of Chester, tailor.
„ 14   Richard Price, tobacconist, s. of Thomas Price of Chester, butcher, defunct.
„ 14   John Ormes, pipemaker, s. of Thomas Ormes of Chester, pipemaker.
„ 14   Thomas Jones, pipemaker, s. of Thomas Jones of Chester, pipemaker.
„ 14   Francis Ormes, pipemaker, s. of Thomas Ormes of Chester, pipemaker.
„ 14   Thomas s. of William Moor of Chester, cooper, defunct.
„ 14   Samuel Meadows, chandler, s. of John Meadows, and p. of John Roberts of Chester, chandler, defunct.
„ 14   George s. of William Warmingham of Chester, tailor, defunct.
„ 14   John s. of Richard Stubbs of Chester, tanner, defunct.
„ 14   John s. of John Witter of Chester, apothecary, defunct.
„ 14   Thomas Shone p. of Thomas Bridge of Chester, feltmaker.
„ 14   Robert Denteth, merchant, s. of Robert Denteth of Chester, merchant, defunct.
„ 14   Simon Oliver p. of George Tunnall of Chester, cordwainer.
„ 14   Elias Rylance, baker, s. of Joseph Rylance of Chester, silkweaver.
„ 14   Jonathan Tapley, cordwainer, s. of Jonathan Tapley of Chester, cooper, defunct.
„ 14   John Tunnall, cordwainer, s. of George Tunnall of Chester, cordwainer.

1703-4 [2-3 A.] NATHANIEL ANDERTON, Esquire, Mayor.

Nov. 26 Arthur s. of Richard Mercer of Croton, co. Chester, yeoman, and p. of Arthur Bolland of Chester, brewer.
Dec. 20 *John Hurleston, gentleman.
Jan. 10 Richard s. of Thomas Holland of Tiverton, *alias* Tereton, co. Chester, yeoman, and p. of John Holland, draper.

Jan. 10 Joseph s. of Joseph Smith of Saighton, co. Chester, husbandman, and p. of Peter Woods of Chester, feltmaker.
Feb. 5 James s. of Robert Whitfield of West Derby, co. Lanc., watchmaker, and p. of William Bellis of Chester, ironmonger.
„ 8 *Jonathan Bruen, esquire.
„ 29 James Hutchinson, merchant, s. of James Hutchinson of Chester, ironmonger, defunct.
Mar. 25 *William Francis, periwigmaker.
Apr. 22 John s. and p. of Elias Massey of Chester, pipemaker.
„ 27 William s. of Richard King of Chester, chandler, defunct.
„ 29 *Thomas Morris.
May 6 *Richard Myers.
„ 6 *Timothy Challoner.
„ 6 Phillip s. of Richard Cooper of Chester, gardener, and p. of Thomas Davies, carver.
„ 13 *Rosingreave Okyll, innholder.
July 1 William Briscoe, smith, s. of William Briscoe of Chester, blacksmith.
„ 22 David Jones p. of Randle Foulkes of Chester, clothworker.
„ 29 Edward s. of Edward Walmesley, late of Chester, slater, and p. of Joseph Hatton, chandler.
„ 29 Richard Doe p. of Edward Starkey of Chester, brewer, defunct.
Aug. 19 Randle Burrowes, cutler, s. of Isaac Burrowes of Chester, brewer, defunct.
„ 26 Edward s. of William Briscoe of Chester, smith.
Sep. 2 George s. of George Taylor of Chester, feltmaker, and p. of John Bromfeild of Boughton, co. Chester, tailor.
„ 2 *Thomas Coppock, apothecary.
„ 2 *William Cotton, yeoman.
„ 19 *Cuthbert Ogle, gentleman.
„ 23 Henry Bibby p. of Richard Yates ot Chester, slater, defunct.
Oct. 5 John Rider, tailor, s. of William Rider of Chester, tailor, defunct.
„ 5 Joshua s. of John Yockson of Higher Bebbington, yeoman, and p. of John Wrench of Chester, watchmaker.

1704–5 [3–4 A.] EDWARD PARTINGTON, Esquire, Mayor.

William Witcherley.
Thomas Jellicoe, cordwainer.
William Throp, tailor.
William Platt, tanner.
John Adshead.
William Bennett, cordwainer.
Griffith Williams, bricklayer.
Richard Woodfin.
Thomas Davies, slater.
Ormson Calley, slater.
Randle Young, bricklayer.
Robert Taylor.
Thomas Williams.
John Mason, glazier.
John Yowd, feltmaker.
William Briscoe, baker.
John Briscoe, baker.
John Platt, tailor.
John Smith.
Hugh Thornley.
Francis [Asley ?], smith.
Hugh Jones, labourer.
John Stephens, feltmaker.
Henry Harpur, linendraper.
John Valentine, ironmonger.
Ambrose Evans, innholder.
William Stockton, innholder.
John Smith, feltmaker.
Thomas Woodfin, feltmaker.
James Bummer, slater.
William Barrett, cordwainer.
William Moreton.
George Hewett, slater.
John Hancock.
Daniel Jones.
William Traver, wetglover.
John Amery, merchant.
Samuel Randle, brewer.
Robert Fletcher.
John Barnett, brewer.
Hugh Jordan.
George Hunt.

216 THE ROLLS OF THE FREEMEN OF [1704-5

        Jonathan Haswell, cooper.
        Richard Golding, tailor.
        John Birkenhead, esquire.
        John Rea, tailor.
        John Sparke.
        Thomas Whittney, cooper and fishmonger.
        Thomas Bolland, joiner.
        George Taylor, tailor.
        Robert Millington.
        William Bromley.
        Christopher Carre, spurrier.
        John Warrington, carpenter.
        Samuel Greasty, feltmaker.
        John Jones, tanner.
        William Smith, plasterer.
        George Boswell.
        Thomas Walton, glazier.
        John Parker, apothecary.
        Thomas Roughley, joiner.
        George Holliwell.
        John Davies, bricklayer.
        John Vause, linendraper.
        Phillip Bateman.
        James Clews, chirurgeon.
        William Tomlinson.
        Edward Lytherland.
        Thomas Fisher, yeoman.
July 5 *Hugh Brandred, yeoman.
Aug. 7 *William Bunbury, esquire.
  „   7 John s. of William Mercer of Chester, tallowchandler.
  „ 18 *John Darlington, mariner.
  „ 18 *Richard Wilkinson.
  „ 18 *John Dandey.
  „ 18 *Robert Hughes.
Sep. 15 Thomas s. of John Hughes of Bringriffith, gentleman, and p. of Thomas Walmsley of Chester, ironmonger.
  „ 19 Hugh Patten of Liverpool, merchant, s. of William Patten, late of Chester, and afterwards of Warrington, co. Lanc., draper.
Oct. 6 William s. of John Hayes of Willaston, co. Chester, yeoman.
  „   6 Daniel s. of William Hayes of Willaston, co. Chester, and p. of Ellis Lewis of Chester, draper.
  „   6 Owen s. of Lewis Parry of Chester, ironmonger.
  „   6 William s. of Richard Owen of Whitchurch, gentleman, defunct, and p. of John Pugh, ironmonger.

[1705-6]   THE CITY OF CHESTER   217

Oct.   6   Richard s. of Mark Griffith of Broadlane, co. Flint, yeoman, and p. of Nathaniel Smith, baker.
  "   8   William s. of William Qua of Isle of Man, and p. of Christopher Park of Chester, tailor.
  "   8   William s. of Peter Bostock of Chester, mason, defunct.
  "   12   *Thomas Ley, barber chirurgeon.

1705-6 [4-5 A.] EDWARD PULESTON, Esquire, Mayor.

Oct. 19   Richard Leving, esquire, s. of Sir Richard Leving, Knight, alderman of the city of Chester.
  "   20   *John Ball, mariner.
Nov. 3   William s. of Richard Bird of Chester, tanner, defunct.
  "   3   William s. of Jabez Bathoe of Chester, tanner.
  "   19   James s. of James Lem of Chester, distiller, defunct.
  "   13   *Thomas Brown, mariner.
  "   17   *John Briscoe, mariner.
Dec. 15   Thomas s. of Hugh Usher of Burton, co. Denbigh, defunct, and p. of Laurence Gother of Chester, joiner, defunct.
  "   8   John Harvie, tallowchandler, s. of John Harvie, late of Tarvin, co. Chester, tallowchandler.
  "   13   Perry s. of Perry Dawson of Chester, glover, and p. of John Bellinge, glover.
  "   15   Paul s. of Paul Maddock of Chester, cordwainer.
  "   15   Thomas s. of Alice Soreton of Chester, widow, and p. of Nathaniel Bather, bricklayer.
  "   19   Richard s. of Henry Boulton of Chester, feltmaker.
  "   22   George s. of George Hinkley, late of Chester, vintner.
  "   22   Thomas s. of Joseph Rylance of Chester, silkweaver.
  "   22   *Rice s. of Rice Symon.
  "   22   James s. of John Prince, maltster, and p. of George Tunnell of Chester, cordwainer.
  "   22   James Ratcliffe, mason, p. of John Shettles of Chester, mason.
  "   28   *Richard Thompson, mariner.
  "   29   Robert Lea p. of John Dewsbury, feltmaker.
  "   29   *David Jones.
Jan.   2   Richard s. of Joseph Sefton of Chester, dyer, defunct.
  "   12   Thomas s. of Edward Edge of Chester, dyer, defunct.
  "   12   *Hugh Piggott, gentleman.
  "   12   *Samuel Aires, gardener.
  "   26   John s. of John Kirkes of Chester, tailor.
Feb.   2   William s. of William Yewd of Aston, co. Flint, and p. of Thomas Whitasse of Chester, carpenter.

218   THE ROLLS OF THE FREEMEN OF [1706

Feb.   2 *Laurence Clifton, mariner.
  ,,   15 Richard s. of Thomas Stevenson of Peele, co. Stafford, gentleman, and p. of John Buckley of Chester, apothecary, defunct.
  ,,   23 William s. of Robert Higginson of Chester, innholder, defunct.
Mar. 19 *Jonathan Gilbody, confectioner.
  ,,   19 Joseph s. of Joseph Whittle of Chester, clerk, defunct.
  ,,   26 Peter s. of James Key, slater, and p. of Thomas Cowdock of Chester, slater.
Apr.   2 John s. of William Bristow of Chester, tanner, defunct, and p. of John Kynaston, alderman.
  ,,   5 Roger s. of Roger Massie, gentleman, defunct, and p. of Robert Sparke, linendraper.
  ,,   9 William s. of William Throp of Chester, stationer, defunct.
May   4 John s. of Robert Wilding of Chester, combmaker.
  ,,   8 *Charles Walley, esquire.
  ,,   11 *William Haswell, yeoman.
June   1 *Stephen Urmston, mariner.
  ,,   11 William s. of Henry Baforn of Chester, brewer, defunct.
  ,,   15 *Andrew Potter, mariner.
  ,,   15 Ralph s. of Henry Mason of Chester, clothworker, defunct, and p. of Charles Shale, butcher.
Aug. 17 Thomas s. of Thomas Deane of Chester, cordwainer, defunct, and p. of Samuel Smith, cooper.
  ,,   31 Thomas s. of Thomas Alcott of Chester, smith.
Sep.   5 William ⎫ ss. of William Fernihaugh of Chester,
  ,,   5 John   ⎭   ironmonger.
  ,,   5 Robert s. of Thomas Wrench of Chester, carpenter, defunct, and p. of Thomas Fernihaugh, draper.
  ,,   14 Richard s. of Thomas Dewsbury of Chester, feltmaker, defunct.
  ,,   24 James s. of John Roberts of Wrexham, innholder, defunct, and p. of Richard Penket, ironmonger.
Oct.   5 John s. of Robert Roberts, mason, and p. of Thomas Biggins of Chester, tailor, defunct.
  ,,   7 John s. of John Johnson of Chester, innholder, defunct.
  ,,   11 Richard Cowdock, smith, s. of Robert Cowdock of Chester, smith.
  ,,   11 Thomas Hiccocke, barber, s. of Richard Hiccocke, baker.
  ,,   11 *Robert Lawson.
  ,,   11 *Robert Cowles.
  ,,   11 Thomas s. of Phillip Plumb, late of Chester, carpenter.

1706-7 [5-6 A.] PULESTON PARTINGTON, Esquire,
                     Mayor.

Oct. 21 William s. of Ephraim Bennett, brewer, and p. of
           Thomas Holland of Chester, barber.
Nov. 2 *John Wettenhall.
  ,, 9 Samuel s. of Richard Bushell of Thornton, co. Chester,
           yeoman, and p. of John Clayton of Chester, tailor.
  ,, 26 *William Frost, periwigmaker.
  ,, 26 *Michael Wood.
Dec. 2 James s. of Robert Pool of Hatherton, yeoman, and p.
           of Matthew Buckley of Chester, linendraper.
  ,, 21 *John Johnson.
  ,, 21 *Thomas Adams.
  ,, 21 *John Bowen.
  ,, 28 *Stephan Sone, periwigmaker.
Jan. 6 *Robert Withers.
  ,, 27 Thomas s. of John Wright of Chester, gardener, and
           p. of Richard Ledsham, slater.
  ,, 29 William s. of Thomas Warmingham of Chester, cord-
           wainer.
  ,, 30 John s. of John Cotgreave of Chester, brewer.
  ,, 30 William s. of Roger Yewd of Chester, clothworker.
Feb. 1 Benjamin s. of Nicholas Williams of Chester, tailor.
  ,, 1 Robert s. of Richard Neal of Chester, mason, and p. of
           Peter Bostock.
  ,, 1 Edward s. of William Higginson of Chester, butcher,
           defunct.
  ,, 15 John Jellicoe p. of Richard Blease of Chester, cord-
           wainer, defunct.
  ,, 22 Robert Nield p. of Jabez Bathoe of Chester, tanner.
Mar. 1 *Samuel Bennett, gentleman.
  ,, 15 Thomas s. of Edward Davies of Chester, husbandman,
           and p. of John Bentley, innholder.
  ,, 15 Benjamin s. of Mary Price of Boles, co. Flint, widow,
           and p. of John Dewsbury, feltmaker.
  ,, 15 *Francis Massie.
May   3 Thomas s. of Charles Moulson, tanner, and p. of
           Richard Ords, barber.
  ,, 22 James s. of John Burroughs of Chester, alderman,
           defunct.
  ,, 22 Thomas s. of David Williams of Chester, brewer,
           defunct.
June 28 Thomas Carter p. of James Usher of Chester, cord-
           wainer.

220 THE ROLLS OF THE FREEMEN OF [1707-8

July 16 Randle s. of Randle Poynton of Aldford, co. Chester, husbandman, and p. of Charles Jellicoe, baker.
Aug. 9 *Thomas Lewis the younger.
Sep. 20 *Matthew Trueman.
May 20 *Joseph Avern, corkcutter.
Oct. 6 *Thomas Deane.
,, 8 Thomas s. of Robert Murrey of Chester, alderman.
,, 8 Phillip Buckley, linendraper, s. of Matthew Buckley of Chester, alderman.

1707-8 [6-7 A.] HUMPHREY PAGE, Esquire, Mayor.

Dec. 6 Samuel Orange p. of David Williams of Chester, brewer, defunct.
,, 20 *Edward Davies, yeoman.
Jan. 10 William s. of Richard Bavin of Chester, smith, defunct.
,, 10 John Maddock, slater, s. of John Maddock of Chester, slater.
,, 17 Thomas Wright, tailor, s. of Thomas Wright of Chester, tailor.
,, 31 Samuel Potter, tailor, s. of John Potter of Chester, tailor, defunct.
Feb. 7 Peter s. of Peter Parry of Chester, ropier, and p. of John Pemberton, ropier.
,, 7 Joseph s. of Joseph Maddock of Chester, ropier, and p. of Thomas Kennion, carpenter.
,, 9 William Holland, barber, s. of Thomas Holland of Chester, barber.
,, 21 Charles Drinkwater p. of William Woods, mason.
,, 21 John s. of John Wright, labourer, and p. of Nathaniel Weld of Chester, cordwainer.
,, 28 Samuel Walton, chandler, s. of Thomas Walton of Chester, baker.
,, 28 Henry s. of Arthur Godwin of Saughall Massie, co. Chester, defunct, and p. of Thomas Gill, joiner.
Mar. 1 *Ralph Fenton.
,, 1 Edmund Parker, mercer, s. of John Parker of Chester, mercer.
,, 1 Thomas s. of Samuel Cooke of Chester, ironmonger.
,, 3 John s. of Robert Joynson of Chester, cordwainer, defunct.
,, 11 John Johnson, cordwainer, s. of William Johnson of Chester, cordwainer, defunct.

Mar.	12	Obadiah s. of George Johnson of Great Saughall, in Wirrall, husbandman, and p. of George Johnson, glazier.
,,	12	Edward s. of Edward Avans of Chester, husbandman, and p. of Thomas Dunbabin, glazier.
,,	12	Edmund s. of Thomas Kennerley of Chester, labourer, and p. of William Jackson, bricklayer.
,,	12	John s. of William Green of Willaston, co. Chester, yeoman, and p. of Samuel Pyke, tailor.
,,	12	Peter s. of Reginald Whittaker of Chester, butcher.
,,	12	Samuel Moulson, tanner, s. of Robert Moulson of Chester, tanner, defunct.
,,	12	Randle Wilson, dyer, s. of Randle Wilson of Chester, dyer, defunct.
,,	12	Humphrey s. of Thomas Williams of Hope, co. Flint, labourer, and p. of Thomas Bennett, feltmaker.
,,	12	John s. of Peter Meredith of Chester, brewer, defunct.
,,	16	George s. of George Fearnall of Chester, silkweaver.
,,	16	Peter s. of Robert Robinson of Chester, tanner.
,,	16	Samuel s. of Samuel Nicholls of Chester, butcher.
,,	16	John s. of John Rothwell of Chester, cordwainer.
,,	16	Peter s. of Charles Moulson of Chester, tanner.
,,	16	Peter s. of Peter Potter of Chester, skinner, defunct.
,,	16	William s. of Edward Lytherland of Chester, tailor, defunct.
,,	16	Robert s. of John Bennett of Chester, cordwainer, defunct.
,,	16	Phillip s. of Phillip Plumb of Chester, carpenter, defunct.
,,	16	William Darwell, glover, s. of Charles Darwell of Chester, glover.
,,	16	Samuel s. of Joseph Presbury of Chester, glover.
,,	16	Samuel s. of Benjamin Maddock of Chester, tailor.
,,	16	Benjamin Hall, chandler, s. of Benjamin Hall of Chester, chandler.
,,	16	Francis Jordan, slater, s. of Gerrard Jordan of Chester, innholder, defunct.
,,	16	John s. of Ralph Done of Chester, cooper, defunct.
,,	16	John s. of William Harrison of Chester, cordwainer.
,,	16	Samuel Braddock p. of Thomas Hancock of Chester, mason, defunct.
,,	16	Peter s. of John Darwell of Preston on the Hill, and p. of Richard Dewsbury, feltmaker.
,,	16	William s. of Thomas Ledsham, ropemaker, and p. of Alban Gray of Chester, bricklayer.
,,	16	Thomas Roberts p. of William Woods, mason.

Mar.	16	William s. of William Crue of Chester, ironmonger, defunct.
,,	16	Richard s. of Gregory Heylin of Chester, cordwainer, defunct.
,,	17	*Samuel Weld.
,,	17	*Ralph Griffith, gardener.
,,	17	*John Almond.
,,	17	*John Price, tobacco-cutter.
,,	17	*Anthony Brown.
,,	17	*John Whittbey.
,,	17	*Robert Batchelor.
,,	17	*Thomas Jones.
,,	17	*Richard Carre, flaxdresser.
,,	17	*Joseph Hallett.
,,	17	*John Wetherbey, tobacco-cutter.
,,	17	*James Lawrenson.
,,	17	*Samuel Dennall, mason.
,,	17	*William Odcroft.
,,	17	*Thomas Posnett, shoemaker.
,,	17	John s. of Samuel Dicas, brewer, and p. of Ambrose Whawell of Chester, barber.
,,	17	Richard s. of Richard Bavand of Chester, smith, defunct.
,,	17	John Young p. of Edmund Mathews of Chester, cordwainer.
,,	17	James s. of William Hickson of Chester, tailor.
,,	18	Randle } ss. of Randle Pickmore of Chester, butcher,
,,	18	William } defunct.
,,	18	Edward s. of William Woodfen of Chester, slater.
,,	18	Henry s. of Samuel Brandred of Chester, tailor.
,,	18	Jonathan s. of John Dob of Chester, glover.
,,	20	Edward s. of Richard Johnson of Chester, feltmaker, and p. of John Dewsbury, feltmaker.
,,	20	Valentine Ley p. of William Huntington of Chester, baker.
,,	20	John Axon p. of Peter Woods of Chester, feltmaker.
,,	20	George Griffith p. of James Walley of Chester, feltmaker.
,,	20	William s. of William Ryder, late of Chester, tailor.
,,	20	John Crane, cordwainer, s. of William Crane, late of Chester, painter.
,,	20	Joseph s. of William Bryan of Churton, butcher, and p. of Nathaniel Selby of Chester, butcher, defunct.
,,	20	Richard s. and p. of Richard Humphreys of Chester, hornbreaker.
,,	23	Daniel Davies p. of Samuel Leenes of Chester, joiner.

Mar.	23	Richard Holland p. of William Jackson, late of Chester, bricklayer.
,,	24	Thomas s. of Thomas Winnington of Chester, plasterer, and p. of Henry Coulson, barber.
,,	24	*Thomas Mulleney, cordwainer.
,,	24	*Samuel Davies, cordwainer.
,,	24	*George Whittaker.
,,	24	*Samuel Maddock, hornbreaker.
,,	24	*John Waterwoods, periwigmaker.
,,	24	*John Jones, yeoman.
,,	26	*Richard Pratchett, silk stocking weaver.
,,	27	Thomas s. and p. of John Conway of Chester.
,,	26	William s. of Jonathan Dawson, and p. of Joseph Wright the elder of Chester, tanner.
,,	27	Daniel s. of Thomas Pemberton, cordwainer, and p. of Thomas Jones of Chester, carpenter.
,,	26	Daniel s. of John Craven of Peckforton, and p. of John Ollerhead of Chester, tanner.
Apr.	3	John Thomason p. of Richard Bridge of Chester, dyer, defunct.
,,	10	Thomas son of John Jennion of Chester, feltmaker.
,,	10	John s. of William Hall of Mostyn, co. Flint, and p. of John Tilston, carver.
,,	10	John s. of William Heycock of Chester, innholder, defunct.
,,	17	Robert s. of Samuel Sudlow of Chester, dyer, defunct.
,,	17	Robert s. of Thomas Walley of Chester, feltmaker, defunct.
May	1	*Owen Edwards, labourer.
,,	6	Thomas s. of Thomas Bulkley of Bulkley, co. Chester, gentleman, defunct, and p. of Robert Bulkley of Chester, ironmonger.
,,	8	Thomas ⎫ ss. of William Allen the elder of Chester,
,,	8	John ⎭ alderman.
June	5	Richard s. of William Briscow of Chester, smith, defunct.
,,	14	Arthur s. of Roger Trevor, gentleman, and p. of George Bennion of Chester, ironmonger, defunct.
,,	21	*John Brown, merchant.
,,	26	*Samuel Rylance.
July	3	Thomas s. of William Grice of Chester, labourer, and p. of Alban Gray, bricklayer.
,,	17	*Thomas Chamberlain, yeoman.
,,	17	*Edward Parsonage.
,,	18	John s. of Sarah Dod of Lea, and p. of Randle Annion of Chester, baker.

224 THE ROLLS OF THE FREEMEN OF [1708-9

Sep. 4 John Riscoe p. of William Davies of Chester, cordwainer.
Oct. 7 John s. of Thomas Hewitt of Northwich, co. Chester, yeoman, defunct, and p. of William Hewitt, ironmonger.
„ 8 *Thomas Charleton, gentleman.
„ 8 Thomas Bradbury p. of Isaac Warmingham, tailor.
„ 9 John s. of Thomas Barrow of Aldford, co. Chester, yeoman, and p. of Jonathan Goldson, feltmaker.
„ 14 Robert s. of John Low of Salop, clerk, and p. of Robert Carrington of Chester, apothecary.
„ 14 Daniel s. of William Whitaker of Chester, tanner, and p. of William Welshman, baker.

1708-9 [7-8 A.] JAMES MAINWARING, Esquire, Mayor.

Oct. 16 Charles ⎱ ss. of Henry Salisbury of Chester, periwig-
„ 16 George ⎰ maker, defunct.
„ 26 Thomas s. of Daniel Crosse of Chester, joiner.
„ 26 John s. of Roger Wilbraham of Chester, chandler, defunct.
„ 26 Joseph s. of Robert Ellis of Chester, glover.
„ 30 Thomas s. of Isaac Holcroft, labourer, and p. of Thomas Harvey of Chester, bricklayer.
„ 30 Joseph s. of Robert Price of Chester, porter, defunct.
Nov. 13 John s. of Richard Hamnett of Chester, clothworker, and p. of Griffith Trygarn of Chester, saddler, defunct.
Dec. 18 *Robert Rogers p. of William Sherman, cabinetmaker.
„ 18 James s. of William Farrington of Chester, vintner, defunct, and p. of Thomas Bowers, gardener.
„ 27 Thomas s. of Thomas Critchley of Chester, draper.
Jan. 15 Richard Alleby p. of Ralph Blagg of Chester, innholder, defunct.
„ 22 John s. of John Beigh of Chester, tanner, and p. of James Dewsbury, feltmaker.
„ 22 Robert s. of Richard Pulford of Farndon, co. Chester, yeoman, and p. of Thomas Pate of Chester, butcher.
„ 29 Isaac s. of William Powell of Chester, minstrel.
Feb. 5 Josiah s. of William Crook of Broughton, co. Flint, yeoman, defunct, and p. of Jonathan Bostock of Chester, ironmonger.
„ 19 Roger s. of Roger Yewd of Chester, clothworker.
„ 19 John s. of John Davies of Chester, joiner, defunct.

Mar.	7	Ellis Gateley p. of John Lockett of Chester, cordwainer.
,,	7	William s. of Thomas Roberts of Chester, labourer, and p. of William Bolland, joiner.
,,	12	Peter s. of Thomas Gibbons of Chester, feltmaker, and p. of Michael Bromley, chandler.
,,	19	Henry Bennett, merchant, s. of Henry Bennett of Chester, alderman, defunct.
,,	26	James s. of James Allcock of Chester, tailor, defunct.
,,	26	John Dewsbury, chandler, s. of Richard Dewsbury of Chester, barber, defunct.
,,	26	James s. of Ralph Suthern, feltmaker, and p. of Thomas Winnington of Chester, plasterer.
,,	26	Bryan s. of Bryan Bolland.
Apr.	2	John Roberts s. of Robert Price of Cargurley, co. Flint, yeoman, and p. of Thomas Bavand of Chester, turner.
,,	16	John s. and p. of Henry Hall of Chester, tanner, defunct.
,,	20	John Kemp, cutler, s. of Adam Kemp of Chester, baker, defunct.
,,	21	Thomas Wright p. of John Hiccocke of Chester, baker, defunct.
May	14	Robert s. of William Barratt [Barret, M.B.], tailor, and p. of John Hiccocke of Chester, baker.
June	23	Thomas s. of Samuel Urmston of Seacomb, mariner, defunct, and p. of Samuel Smith of Chester, cooper.
July	30	Thomas s. of Thomas Water, and p. of Titus Dewsbury of Chester, tailor.
Aug.	12	Thomas Wilson, gentleman, s. of William Wilson of Chester, alderman, defunct.
,,	20	Thomas Bellin, cooper, s. of Ralph Bellin of Chester, cooper and fishmonger, defunct.
Oct.	7	Samuel Bradburn, ironmonger, s. of Nathan Bradburn of Chester, ironmonger, defunct.
,,	8	*John Powell, labourer.
,,	8	John s. of Moses Dannatt of Chester, beerbrewer, defunct.
,,	10	*Thomas Chaddock.
,,	13	Gabriel s. of John Bingley of Chester, chandler.
,,	13	Peter s. of Peter Nicholls of Chester, tanner.
,,	13	*John Griffith, plumber.

226 THE ROLLS OF THE FREEMEN OF [1709-10

1709-10 [8-9 A.] WILLIAM ALLEN, Esquire, Mayor.

Oct. 17 Herbert Simpson, gentleman, s. of Thomas Simpson of Chester, alderman, defunct.
Nov. 5 Joseph Walley, skinner, s. of Thomas Walley of Chester, haberdasher, defunct.
  „ 26 *Thomas Sexton, dancing master.
  „ 26 Edward s. of Randle Ince of Chester, smith, defunct.
Dec. 3 John Larden, feltmaker, s. of John Larden, late of Chester, and now of Tattenhall, co. Chester, feltmaker.
  „ 3 Thomas s. of Roger Jones of Chester, and p. of Thomas Gibbons, feltmaker.
Jan. 6 John s. of Andrew Leigh of Saighton, yeoman, and p. of John Thomason of Chester, brewer.
  „ 6 Samuel s. of John Fearnall of Chester, buttonmaker.
  „ 6 Henry s. of Nathaniel Bathoe of Chester, tanner, defunct, and p. of Robert Crosby, cordwainer.
  „ 6 John Greenholgh p. of Thomas Williams of Chester, wetglover.
Feb. 2 John s. of William Elson of Tarporley, co. Chester, husbandman, and p. of Nicholas Williams of Chester, tailor.
  „ 6 Sir Richard Grosvenor, baronet, s. of Sir Thomas Grosvenor, baronet, defunct.
  „ 12 Peter s. of Catherine Yates, widow, and p. of Thomas Billinge of Chester, glover.
Mar. 25 William s. of David Griffith of Chester, inkhorn maker, and p. of John Edwards, butcher.
Apr. 19 Benjamin s. of John Smith of Saighton, co. Chester, yeoman, and p. of Robert Sparke of Chester, linen-draper.
  „ 22 Richard s. of Richard Ledsham of Chester, slater.
  „ 22 James s. of Thomas Mottershead of Chester, innholder, and p. of Samuel Maddock, baker.
May 6 *Henry Jackson.
  „ 20 Edward s. of William Glegg of Whitbey, co. Chester, gentleman, and p. of Thomas Jackson of Chester, skinner, defunct.
  „ 20 George s. of Thomas Pulford of Chester, and p. of Henry Crosby, shoemaker.
  „ 26 *William Whitear.
  „ 29 *John Allen, gentleman.
June 8 *Thomas Mather, esquire.
  „ 8 *Edward Foulkes, gentleman.

June	14	William s. of Roger Jennings of Pudleston, co. Salop, gentleman, and p. of Thomas Jackson of Chester, glover, defunct.
July	1	William s. of John Wilkinson of Chester, barber chirurgeon.
,,	11	William s. of William Plumbley of Chester, merchant, defunct.
,,	29	Randle s. of Joseph Bulkley of Chester, smith, defunct.
Aug.	21	Edward s. of Thomas Ley of Chester, cordwainer, defunct, and p. of Thomas Moulson, barber chirurgeon.
,,	26	*Thomas Lloyd, gentleman.
,,	26	*George Massie.
Sep.	9	*Charles Nicholls, vintner.
,,	23	William s. of William Starkey of Chester, alderman.
,,	23	Robert Orme, pipemaker, s. of Thomas Orme of Chester, pipemaker.
Oct.	9	Peter s. of Peter Ellames of Lostock, co. Chester, glasier, and p. of Ralph Brown, apothecary.

1710-1 [9-10 A.] THOMAS PARTINGTON, Esquire, Mayor.

Oct.	21	Thomas s. of John Maddock of Chester, slater.
,,	21	Edward s. of Thomas Harvey of Chester, bricklayer.
Dec.	2	Thomas s. of Josiah Cook of Chester, dyer, defunct, and p. of George Crooks, tailor.
,,	5	Nathan s. of John Wright of Elton, co. Chester, gentleman, defunct, and p. of Randle Bingley of Chester, ironmonger, defunct.
Jan.	1	Edward Hammond p. of Robert Pike of Chester, baker.
,,	1	William Perry p. of William Knot of Chester, bricklayer.
,,	6	Joseph s. of Daniel Birch of Handbridge, within the liberties of the city of Chester, husbandman, and p. of Charles Jackson, smith.
,,	6	Noah s. of Richard Golborn, tailor, and p. of Humphrey Sharpe of Chester, pipemaker.
,,	6	Francis s. of Francis Richardson of Manchester, tailor, defunct, and p. of John Harrison of Chester, tailor.
,,	6	Samuel s. of Hugh Hughes, cutler, defunct, and p. of John Kirkes of Chester, tailor.
,,	6	James Cappur p. of George Hastings of Chester, carpenter.

228 THE ROLLS OF THE FREEMEN OF [1711

Jan. 6 Thomas Nixson, cordwainer, s. of Edward Nixson of Chester, mason, defunct.
,, 9 Charles s. of John Ryley, plasterer, and p. of Thomas Fletcher of Chester, pipemaker.
,, 10 ‡Thomas s. of Isaac Warmingham of Chester, saddler.
,, 10 Peter Weigh p. of Richard Thomason of Chester, currier.
,, 10 William Whitaker p. of John Jones of Chester, shoemaker.
,, 10 William s. of William Poynton of Chester, ironmonger.
,, 20 *John Povall.
,, 20 William s. of Thomas Hatton of Newton, yeoman, and p. of John Jennings of Chester, feltmaker, defunct.
,, 26 *Ralph Bridge, gentleman.
Feb. 3 William Johnson, glover, s. of John Johnson of Chester, innholder, defunct.
,, 3 Thomas s. of Thomas Duke, defunct, and p. of Joseph Soreton of Chester, glover.
,, 3 John s. of Ralph Cotgreave of Guilden Sutton, co. Chester, yeoman, and p. of Griffith Knowles of Chester, cordwainer.
,, 3 *Ralph Wood.
,, 17 Samuel s. of Samuel Finlow of Chester, glover, defunct.
,, 19 *Thomas Vincent.
,, 19 Edward s. of Jabez Bathoe of Chester, tanner.
,, 26 Owen Hughes s. of Hugh Roberts [sic] of Trebwell, co. Denbigh, gentleman, and p. of Edward Croughton of Chester, tanner.
Mar. 3 *Robert Hayward, gentleman.
,, 3 *Richard Wrench, gentleman.
,, 17 *Hugh Nicholls, yeoman.
,, 17 *James Kent.
,, 28 Josiah s. of John Leigh of Lyme, co. Chester, yeoman, and p. of Charles Warmingham of Chester, barber chirurgeon, defunct.
,, 31 John s. and p. of Thomas Wheawell of Boughton, co. Chester, bricklayer, defunct.
Apr. 2 Charles Bingley, chandler, s. of John Bingley of Chester, chandler, defunct.
,, 2 Edward s. of Edward Leadbeater, ironmonger, defunct, and p. of John Sparrow of Chester, barber chirurgeon.
,, 7 *Thomas Tagg, gentleman.
June 16 William s. of Samuel Farrington of Chester, gentleman, defunct.

June 16 William s. of John Johnson of West Houghton, co. Lanc., gentleman, and p. of Randle Aston of Chester, glover.
„ 16 Thomas s. of John Bagnall of Bromboro, co. Chester, yeoman, and p. of John Yeamon of Chester, ironmonger.
„ 30 John s. of Jonathan Newton, defunct, and p. of John Salisbury of Chester, periwigmaker, defunct.
„ 30 Samuel s. of Samuel Dannald of Chester, barber chirurgeon, defunct.
„ 30 John Meacock, weaver, s. of John Meacock of Chester, weaver.
„ 30 William s. of John Barton, and p. of William Blundell of Chester, tailor, defunct.
July 7 Samuel s. of William Woodfin of Chester, slater.
„ 9 William s. of William Jones, rector of " Llanymonthy," co. Merioneth, clerk, and p. of Trafford Massie of Chester, ironmonger.
„ 19 John s. of Joseph Wright of Chester, tanner.
Dec. 27 *Sir Richard Vernon, baronet.[1]
Oct. 6 *Richard Cottingham, gentleman.
„ 11 *Leonard Grantham, gentleman.
„ 12 Richard s. of Eleanor Mathews, late of Wrexham, co. Denbigh, widow, and p. of William Wilbraham of Chester, chandler.

1711-2 [10-11 A.] JOHN MINSHULL, Esquire, Mayor.

Oct. 20 Richard s. of Richard Edwards, late of Chester, drover, defunct, and p. of Thomas Hale of Chester, butcher.
Nov. 3 John s. of John Wright of Ashton, co. Chester, and p. of Peter Leadbeater of Chester, brewer.
„ 24 *Thomas Davies, mariner.
Dec. 15 John s. of George Hastings, carpenter, and p. of Thomas Bevand of Chester, turner.
„ 17 William s. of Josiah Cooke of Chester, dyer, defunct, and p. of Thomas Whitaffe, carpenter.
„ 17 Joseph Dennell p. of Humphrey Collins of Chester, glazier.
„ 26 John s. of William Colecligh [Colecliffe, M.B.] of Chester, yeoman, and p. of Thomas Crookes, carpenter.

---

[1] This admission took place in 1711, *i.e.* in John Minshull's mayoralty, and is entered out of date order on the Roll.

Dec. 26 Thomas s. of William Colecligh [Colecliffe, M.B.] of Chester, yeoman, and p. of Thomas Coe of Chester, cordwainer.
Jan. 7 Thomas Winstanley, vintner, s. of William Winstanley of Chester, vintner, defunct.
,, 7 Peter s. of John Bostock of Chester, mason, and p. of Thomas Hiccocke, tanner.
,, 8 Edward s. of Fulke Panton of Chester, tanner, defunct, and p. of John Palin, tanner.
,, 12 Edward s. of Richard Calley of Chester, weaver.
,, 12 Thomas s. of Hugh Bennett of Bretton, and p. of Charles Jellicoe of Chester, baker.
,, 26 Peter Adamson p. of Hugh Maddock of Chester, tanner.
Feb. 2 John Wilkinson, tanner, s. of John Wilkinson of Chester, barber chirurgeon.
,, 2 John s. of Ralph Wilson, late of Chester, pewterer, defunct.
,, 4 Robert s. of Robert Martin of Chester, clothworker.
,, 4 Samuel Coleclough [carpenter, M.B.] p. of Thomas Dunbabin of Chester, glazier.
,, 16 Roger Wilbraham, chandler, s. of Roger Wilbraham, late of Chester, chandler, defunct.
,, 16 Randle Joynson, tailor, s. of Peter Joynson of Chester, shoemaker.
,, 23 Richard Oulton, brewer, s. of Richard Oulton of Chester, alderman, defunct.
Mar. 22 *Joseph Bradshaw.
Apr. 5 John s. of Thomas Bennett, late of Willaston, defunct, and p. of John Palin of Chester, tanner.
,, 15 Joseph s. of John Bowker of Bickerton, co. Chester, clerk, and p. of Alexander Denton of Chester, draper.
,, 26 John s. of John Robertson of Chester, watchmaker, and p. of Thomas Ledsham, tailor.
May 21 *John s. and p. of Samuel Coleclough of Chester, carpenter.
June 12 Phillip s. of Sarah Downes of Salop, widow, and p. of John Maddock of Chester, tanner.
,, 28 Collins Pendlebury p. of Thomas Williams of Chester, wetglover.
,, 28 William Milton p. of Thomas Billinge of Chester, wetglover.
Sep. 20 *Francis Bassano, gentleman.
,, 24 *Edward Davies, tailor.
Oct. 9 John s. and p. of Francis Sayer of Chester, alderman.
,, 10 William s. of Peter Meredith of Chester, brewer, defunct, and p. of Thomas Smith, sawyer.

1712-3 [11-12 A.] JOHN THOMASON, Esquire, Mayor.

Nov. 24 Roger Comberbach, gentleman, s. of Roger Comberbach, Recorder of Chester.
,,   29 Edward Hulton of Chester, glover.
Dec. 30 *Ralph Wynne.
,,   27 John s. of Henry Woodcock of Guilden Sutton, co. Chester, yeoman, defunct, and p. of Joseph Smith of Chester, feltmaker.
Jan. 29 William s. of Samuel Revington the younger of Chester, cordwainer, and p. of Nathaniel Smith, baker.
,,   31 William s. of Thomas Yewd of Aston, co. Flint, yeoman, and p. of Thomas Whitaff of Chester, carpenter, defunct.
Feb. 11 John s. of Charles Walley of Trafford, co. Chester, yeoman, and p. of John Smith of Chester, tanner.
,,   14 John Haworth, haberdasher, s. of Charles Haworth, late of Litchfeild, co. Staff., mercer, and p. of John Stringer of Chester, alderman.
,,   28 William s. of William Goodwin of Northwich, co. Chester, innholder, and p. of Richard Penkett of Chester, ironmonger.
Mar. 7   Samuel s. of Samuel Tonna of Aldersey, co. Chester, yeoman, and p. of Thomas Pate of Chester, butcher.
Apr. 18 John s. of Peter Linford of Lea, co. Chester, yeoman, and p. of Paul Wilcock of Chester, fishmonger.
,,   18 Thomas Young, ropier.
,,   28 John s. of Sarah Tristram of Shrewsbury, co. Salop, widow, and p. of Ralph Sudlow of Chester, apothecary.
May 5   William Croughton, linendraper, s. of Charles Croughton of Chester, silkweaver.
,,   23 Joseph s. of John Parker of Barton, co. Chester, gentleman, and p. of Randle Bingley of Chester, upholsterer.
June 20 John s. of John Nevitt of Stanlow House, co. Chester, yeoman, and p. of John Worrall of Chester, tallowchandler.
,,   25 Thomas s. of Anne Ravenscroft of Foulke Stapleford, co. Chester, widow, and p. of Jabez Bathoe of Chester, tanner.
,,   27 John s. of Sarah Haylin [Heylin, M.B.] of Chester, widow, and p. of James Whitfeild of Chester, ironmonger.

232 THE ROLLS OF THE FREEMEN OF [1713

June 27 Robert s. of Robert Scaisbrook, defunct, and p. of Edward Hiccock of Chester, barber.
Aug. 7 William s. of Thomas Selby of Chester, baker, defunct, and p. of Henry Gill of Chester, barber.
„ 7 John Poole, barber, s. of John Poole of Chester, haberdasher, defunct.
„ 18 Charles Oulton, clerk, s. of Edward Oulton of Chester, alderman.
„ 18 Thomas Williams, cordwainer, s. of John Williams of Chester, brewer, defunct.
„ 29 Randle s. of Peter Wrench of Middlewich, co. Chester, carpenter, defunct, and p. of Ralph Pickmore of Chester, butcher.
Sep. 2 John Whitbey, innholder, s. of Jonathan Whitbey of Chester, ironmonger.
„ 2 John Shard the younger, apothecary, s. of John Shard of Chester, apothecary.
„ 5 William s. of William Smith, defunct, and p. of George Johnson, chandler.
„ 5 Thomas Cooper, tailor, s. of Nicholas Cooper of Chester, silkweaver.
„ 10 John s. and p. of Thomas Biggins of Chester, innholder.
„ 19 Thomas Whitehead, tailor, s. of Thomas Whitehead of Chester, slater.
Oct. 10 William Wilson, butcher, s. of Thomas Wilson of Chester, butcher.

1713-4 [12-13 A.-1 G. i.] JOHN STRINGER, Esquire, Mayor.

Oct. 24 Randle Dicas, chandler, s. of Samuel Dicas of Chester, brewer.
„ 24 Ednevett s. of John Jones of Chester, labourer, and p. of John Tunnall, cordwainer.
Nov. 3 George Brereton, ironmonger, s. of Richard Brereton of Chester, ironmonger, defunct.
„ 3 Peter s. of John Bristow of Dublin in Ireland, merchant, defunct, and p. of Thomas Parnell of Chester, ironmonger, defunct.
„ 3 John s. of Joseph Dyson of Chester, tinplateworker.
Dec. 2 John Nicholls, butcher, s. of Samuel Nicholls of Chester, butcher.
„ 18 *John Marsden, merchant.
„ 29 *Thomas Ashton, esquire.

Jan.	9	*James Smith, yeoman.
,,	30	Charles Vernon, chandler, s. of Richard Vernon of Chester, gentleman.
,,	30	Thomas Litler, cordwainer, ⎫ ss. of James Litler of
,,	30	James Litler, cordwainer, ⎬ Chester, cordwainer.
,,	30	Richard Rylance, cordwainer, s. of Joseph Rylance of Chester, cordwainer.
Feb.	20	*Roger Adams, printer.
,,	27	John s. of George Buckley of Kingsley, co. Chester, yeoman, and p. of Arthur Mercer, brewer.
Mar.	7	Griffith Williams, currier, s. of John Williams of Chester, currier.
Apr.	3	Thomas Hall, cordwainer, s. of Andrew Hall of Chester, cordwainer.
May	1	John Moulson, ironmonger, s. of Thomas Moulson, late of Chester, tanner.
,,	1	Joseph Basnett, ironmonger, s. of Joseph Basnett, ironmonger, defunct.
,,	1	William Guile, cooper, s. of Thomas Guile of Westkerby, co. Chester, yeoman.
,,	29	John Minshull p. of John Thomas of Chester, saddler.
June	17	*William Chetwode, " in Medicin' Doctor."
,,	19	John Jones, dyer, s. of Robert Jones of Chester, dyer.
,,	19	Randle s. of Nicholas Reece of Chester, and p. of Hugh Thornley, smith.
,,	29	Charles s. of Thomas Buckley of Chester, defunct, and p. of Henry Cousson of Chester, barber.
,,	29	William s. of George Millington of co. Flint, yeoman, and p. of Robert Wrench, joiner.
July	3	‡Samuel s. of Samuel Smith of Cotton Edmunds, defunct, and p. of John Clubb of Chester, ironmonger.
,,	23	Thomas s. of James Powell of Chester, labourer, and p. of John Carter the younger, mason.
,,	27	Robert s. of Edward Griffith of Aston, co. Flint, husbandman, and p. of Thomas Bennett of Chester, feltmaker.
,,	27	John s. of Hugh Brandritt of Chester, cheesemonger, and p. of Thomas Moulson of Chester, barber.
,,	31	John Barton, silkweaver, s. of Thomas Barton of Chester, silkweaver.
,,	31	William Shepherd, weaver, s. of William Shepherd of Chester, weaver.
,,	31	Thomas Minshull, silkweaver, s. of Thomas Minshull of Chester, silkweaver, defunct.
Aug.	21	*Stephan Rose, vintner.

234 THE ROLLS OF THE FREEMEN OF [1714–5

Sep. 2 Thomas Grosvenor, esquire, s. of Sir Thomas Grosvenor, baronet, defunct.
,, 11 *Isaac Faulkner.
,, 13 *George Ball, gentleman.
,, 13 *Thomas Stringer, gentleman.
,, 18 Samuel Cooke the younger, ironmonger, s. of Samuel Cooke of Chester, ironmonger.
,, 18 Samuel Jervis the younger, silkweaver, s. of Samuel Jervis of Chester, silkweaver.
,, 25 Joseph s. of Nathaniel Bruen, late of Rushton, co. Staff., gentleman, and p. of Robert Young of Chester, cutler, defunct.
Oct. 2 Thomas Partington, gentleman, s. of Thomas Partington of Chester, alderman.
,, 22 *Sir Thomas Cotton, baronet.
,, 22 Hugh s. of Thomas Topping of Warrington, innholder, and p. of Thomas Cottingham of Chester, barber, defunct.
,, 25 John s. of Humphrey Parry of Estin, co. Flint, defunct, and p. of Peter Parry of Chester, feltmaker.
,, 25 Piercy Pigot p. of Alexander Pulford late of Chester, goldsmith.

1714–5 [1–2 G. i.] FRANCIS SAYER, Esquire, Mayor.

Oct. 30 Henry Pemberton, tailor, s. of Jonathan Pemberton of Chester, silkweaver.
,, 30 John Calley, weaver, s. of Richard Calley of Chester, weaver.
Nov. 2 Isaac Croughton, tanner, s. of Charles Croughton of Chester, silkweaver.
,, 2 Samuel s. of John Bagnall of Bromborough, co. Chester, yeoman, and p. of Randle Bathoe of Chester, tanner.
,, 5 Thomas Knowles, cooper and fishmonger, s. of Thomas Knowles of Simons Woods, co. Lanc., husbandman, and p. of Paul Wilcock of Chester, cooper.
,, 24 William Seller, brewer, s. of William Seller of Chester, brewer.
Dec. 11 Benjamin s. of Richard Ledsham of Chester, slater.
,, 11 William s. of Thomas Biggins, late of Chester, tailor.
Jan. 7 Hamnett s. of Samuel Kirkes of Chester, upholsterer.
,, 10 John s. and p. of Richard Golding of Chester, pipemaker.
,, 14 John s. of Thomas Lewis of Chester, "musitioner," and p. of Richard Goulding of Chester, pipemaker.

[1715] THE CITY OF CHESTER

Jan. 15 Richard s. of Richard Clerkson of Chester, carpenter.
„ 15 *Benjamin Perrin, gentleman.
„ 15 Joshua s. of Charles Dod of Upton, co. Chester, yeoman, and p. of Thomas Walton, baker.
„ 15 *John Oliver, clerk.
„ 15 Roger s. of Thomas Cliffe of Chester, labourer, and p. of Peter Wrench of Chester, feltmaker.
„ 15 Thomas s. of Thomas Fletcher of Chester, pipemaker.
„ 17 Richard Leadbeater, brewer, s. of Peter Leadbeater of Chester, sheriff.
„ 17 *William Langton, merchant.
„ 17 Robert s. of William Warmingham of Chester, tailor, defunct.
„ 17 Richard Moulson, chandler, s. of Thomas Moulson of Chester, tanner, defunct.
„ 17 Thomas s. of Thomas Yates of Chester, bricklayer, defunct.
„ 17 Edward Bromley, cabinet-maker,
„ 17 Roger Bromley, tailor, } ss. of Edward Bromley of Chester, baker.
„ 17 Elisha Massey, pipemaker, s. of Elias Massey, late of Chester, pipemaker.
„ 17 Hugh Hands, joiner, s. of Hugh Hands of Chester, joiner.
„ 17 Peter s. of Thomas Jones of Chester, pipemaker.
„ 17 John s. of Robert Farrington of Chester, innholder, defunct.
„ 17 Edward Powell, feltmaker, s. of John Powell of Chester, pipemaker.
„ 17 John s. of Thomas Mullenex, and p. of Hugh Rodes of Chester, cordwainer, defunct.
„ 17 Randle s. of Alexander Matchell of Chester, shoemaker, and p. of Edmund Mathews of Chester, cordwainer.
„ 17 Samuel Walmsley, slater, s. of Samuel Walmsley of Chester, slater.
„ 17 Thomas Oulton p. of William Coker of Chester, alderman.
„ 17 Thomas s. of Richard Borden of Eccleston, co. Chester, defunct, and p. of Thomas Gill of Chester, joiner.
„ 19 Samuel Whitehead, tailor, s. of Thomas Whitehead of Chester, slater.
„ 22 John Davies, slater, s. of John Davies of Chester, slater.
Feb. 15 Edward s. of Edward Warrington of Sutton, co. Chester, yeoman, and p. of Thomas Jones of Chester, carpenter.

Feb. 17 Joseph s. of Thomas Linager of Chester, cooper, and p. of William Knott of Chester, bricklayer.
" 14 John Partington, merchant, s. of Thomas Partington of Chester, alderman.
" 14 Jonathan Ridge, goldsmith, s. of Jonathan Ridge of Altrincham, co. Chester, surgeon.
" 15 *Jonathan Robinson, gentleman.
" 15 Owen Hughes s. of Hugh Owen [sic] of Dolgan, co. Merioneth, and p. of John Thomas of Chester, saddler.
" 15 Arthur s. of Arthur Davenport of Chester, cordwainer, defunct, and p. of Nathaniel Batho of Chester, bricklayer, defunct.
" 15 Edward Parry p. of John Pemberton of Chester, ropier.
Mar. 19 John s. of John Weatherby of Chester, tobacconist, and p. of John Lockett, late of Chester, cordwainer.
Apr. 9 Joseph s. of Samuel Holland of Chester, labourer, and p. of Richard Carr of Chester, flaxdresser.
" 30 Benjamin Bridge, gentleman, s. of Edward Bridge of Chester, innholder, defunct.
May 3 Henry Bathoe, cordwainer, s. of Jabez Bathoe of Chester, tanner.
" 3 John s. of Peter Ravenscroft of Brereton Park, defunct, and p. of Thomas Thomason of Chester, cordwainer.
" 21 John s. of John Williams of Chester, beerbrewer, and p. of Ambrose Whawell of Chester, barber.
June 11 Charles s. of John Mason of Chester, yeoman, and p. of William Ellis of Chester, cordwainer.
" 16 Henry s. of John Meacock of Chester, weaver.
" 16 Peter s. of Peter Holbrook of Chester, clothworker, and p. of John Meacock of Chester, weaver.
July 2 Josiah s. of Charles Haworth, gentleman, and p. of George Johnson of Chester, chandler.
" 2 John Cross, barber, s. of Daniel Cross of Chester, barber.
" 2 John s. of Benjamin Davies of Wrexham, and p. of Randle Aston of Chester, wetglover.
" 30 Thomas s. of William Hand of Chester, mariner, and p. of Uriah Woodfin, slater.
Aug. 5 *William Massie, gentleman.
" 5 Samuel s. of Joseph Weld of Chester, cordwainer.
" 20 Peter s. and p. of Peter Wrench of Chester, feltmaker.
Sep. 3 *John Spurstow, merchant.
Oct. 1 Robert Harvey, bricklayer, s. of Thomas Harvey of Chester, bricklayer.

[1715-6] THE CITY OF CHESTER 237

Oct. 1 John s. of Jonathan Huxley of Tarvin, co. Chester, husbandman, and p. of Phillip Bateman of Chester, butcher, defunct.
„ 4 *Cornelius Hignett, gentleman.
„ 8 William s. of Peter Gatcliffe of Mickle Trafford, co. Chester, yeoman, and p. of Jonathan Pickering of Chester, carpenter.
„ 10 *John Jackson.
„ 13 Nathaniel s. of William Bolton [Boulton, M.B.] of Chester, bricklayer.
„ 14 Oliver s. of Oliver Battrich of Waverton, co. Chester, gentleman, defunct, and p. of John Mathews of Chester, baker.
„ 14 Richard s. of John Conway of Burton, co. Denbigh, and p. of Josiah Jackson of Chester, wetglover, defunct.

1715-6 [2-3 G. i.] SIR RICHARD GROSVENOR, BARONET, MAYOR.

Oct. 15 George Morris, goldsmith, s. of Thomas Morris of Chester, bricklayer, defunct.
„ 29 Thomas Moulson, tanner, s. of Thomas Moulson of Chester, tanner, defunct.
Nov. 5 Thomas Price, joiner, s. of Thomas Price of Chester, clothworker, defunct.
„ 5 Edward s. of Edward Price of Chester, gardener, and p. of Robert Glegg of Chester, cordwainer.
„ 19 John s. of Joseph Maddock of Chester, tanner.
„ 26 John s. of Daniel Smith of Huxley, co. Chester, shoemaker, and p. of Maurice Briscoe of Chester, smith.
Dec. 3 James s. of Thomas Bateman of Chester, husbandman, and p. of John Valentine of Chester, ironmonger, defunct.
Jan. 6 Isaac s. of Isaac Warmingham of Chester, slater, defunct, and p. of Robert Young of Chester, cutler, defunct.
Mar. 12 Bartholomew s. of Thomas Duke of Neither Leigh, within the liberties of the city of Chester, and p. of Nathaniel Bullen, goldsmith, defunct.
„ 19 Henry Bennion, cooper, s. of Thomas Bennion of Chester, cooper.
„ 19 Joseph Royden, bricklayer, s. of Alexander Royden of Chester, bricklayer.
Apr. 2 William s. of William Jackson of Chester, bricklayer, defunct, and p. of Humphrey Collins, glazier.

Apr. 21   John s. of Richard Lea [Ley, M.B.] of the parish of Tarvin, co. Chester, and p. of William Welshman of Chester, barber, defunct.
May 18   Samuel s. of Richard Mercer of Croughton, co. Chester, yeoman, and p. of Thomas Cross of Chester, joiner, defunct.
„ 18   Charles s. of Charles Hutchins [Hitchins, M.B.] of Tattenhall, co. Chester, yeoman, and p. of Joseph Dutton of Chester, butcher.
„ 25   Zacheus Nicholls, cordwainer, s. of John Nicholls of Chester, cordwainer.
„ 19   *William Calkin, mariner.
„ 19   *William Adshead, labourer.
„ 19   *William Griffith, labourer.
„ 19   William s. of John Venables of Chester, cordwainer, and p. of William Knott, bricklayer.
June 1   Samuel s. of Samuel Davies of Chester, carver, and p. of George Johnson of Chester, glazier, defunct.
„ 4   Thomas Bathoe, barber chirurgeon, s. of Jabez Bathoe of Chester, tanner.
„ 18   *James Percivall.
„ 27   Jonathan s. of George Grason of Chester, pipemaker, and p. of Thomas Fletcher, pipemaker.
July 4   *George Prescott, cheesefactor.
„ 16   Robert Grosvenor, esquire, s. of Sir Thomas Grosvenor, baronet.
Aug. 1   James s. of Richard Wright of Chester, innholder, defunct.
„ 6   Thomas s. and p. of John Sarratt of Chester, tailor.
Sep. 1   Samuel Fletcher, cordwainer, s. of John Fletcher of Chester, cordwainer.
Oct. 6   *Hugh Davies, labourer.
„ 6   John Sudlow, tailor, s. of William Sudlow of Chester, apothecary, defunct.
„ 6   Robert Bowyer, baker, s. of Phillip Bowyer of Chester, gardener.
„ 8‡*Thomas Coplands, mason.
„ 12‡*Daniel Porter, innholder.
„ 12‡*Thomas Fox, pipemaker, of Hawarden, co. Flint, s. of Thomas Fox of Hawarden, baker, defunct.

1716-7 [3-4 G. i.] HENRY BENNETT, Esquire, Mayor.

Nov. 3   ‡John s. of John Millington of Chester, currier, defunct, and p. of Joseph Weld, cordwainer.

Dec.	1	‡William s. of John Rogers, late of Wrexham, co. Denbigh, butcher, and p. of Ralph Pickmore of Chester, butcher.
,,	8	Robert Bellin, cooper, s. of Robert Bellin, late of Chester, cooper.
Jan.	12	George s. of Moses Marsh, late of Chester, upholsterer.
,,	12	William s. of Thomas Bulkeley of Bulkeley, co. Chester, gentleman, defunct, and p. of Robert Bulkeley of Chester, ironmonger.
,,	31	Watkin s. of John Lloyd of Kailin, co. Merioneth, gentleman, and p. of Trafford Massy of Chester, ironmonger.
Feb.	9	*William Gerrard.
,,	16	*George Rider, mariner.
Mar.	2	Andrew s. of Thomas Duke of Chester, yeoman, defunct, and p. of William Witter of Chester, wet-glover.
,,	16	*Francis Blakemore.
,,	16	Benjamin Critchley, goldsmith, s. of Thomas Critchley of Chester, draper.
,,	23	*Leonard Pointon, yeoman.
,,	30	John s. of Thomas Shrigley of Chester, feltmaker, defunct, and p. of William Gibbons of Chester, feltmaker.
,,	30	Thomas Davies, draper, s. of Thomas Davies of Chester, carver, defunct.
April	8	William Wrench, watchmaker, s. of John Wrench of Chester, watchmaker.
,,	8	Thomas Gother, ironmonger, s. of Laurence Gother of Chester, ironmonger.
May	18	Henry Gill, apothecary, s. of Henry Gill of Chester, barber.
,,	23	*John Comberbach of Namptwich, co. Chester, gentleman.
,,	23	*Foster Cunliffe, merchant.
June	22	Thomas Selby, butcher, s. of Nathaniel Selby of Chester, butcher, defunct.
,,	29	Thomas Hope s. of Samuel Hope of Renbury, co. Chester, and p. of Robert Crosley of Chester, cordwainer.
July	2	William Francis, gentleman, s. of William Francis of Chester, alderman, defunct.
,,	22	*Jonathan Bramwell, yeoman.
,,	27	*John Hancocke, mariner.
,,	27	*William Brackley, mariner.
,,	27	John s. of Richard Street of Stanney, and late of Chester, glover.

240   THE ROLLS OF THE FREEMEN OF [1717-8

Aug. 16   Joseph Hincks, mariner, s. of Joseph Hincks of Chester, silkweaver, defunct.
„ 31   *John Leche [Lach, M.B.].
Sep. 7   James s. of James Eason of Chester, weaver, defunct, and p. of John Dicas of Chester, barber.
„ 17   William Panton, tanner, s. of Fulke Panton of Chester, innholder, defunct.
Oct. 15   *Peter Rider, mariner.
„ 10   Edward s. of Edward Puleston of Chester, alderman.

1717-8 [4-5 G. i.] JOSEPH HODGSON, Esquire, Mayor.

Oct. 19   Daniel s. of Peter Ravenscroft of Foulke Stapleford, co. Chester, defunct, and p. of Thomas Billinge of Chester, glover.
„ 24   Watkin Williams, esquire, s. of Sir William Williams, baronet.
Nov. 5   William Edwards, linendraper, s. of Thomas Edwards of Chester, alderman.
„ 23   Thomas s. of David Murrey, merchant, and p. of John Yeamon of Chester, ironmonger.
Jan. 18   John s. of John Jones of Chester, mason, and p. of James Ratcliffe of Chester, mason, defunct.
Feb. 9   *Thomas Rowley, yeoman.
„ 22   John s. of John Trevor of Chester, wetglover, and p. of William Witter of Chester, wetglover.
„ 27   Joseph Hodgson, bookseller, s. of Joseph Hodgson, esquire, mayor of the city.
Apr. 12   ‡William Davies, cordwainer, s. of John Davies of Chester, clothmaker, defunct.
„ 12   John s. of John Meredith of Hawarden, co. Flint, labourer, defunct, and p. of Thomas Harvey of Chester, bricklayer.
May 3   William s. of William Wirrall of Chester, and p. of Thomas Coe of Chester, cordwainer.
Charles Dicas, barber chirurgeon.
Daniel Aldersey, draper.
Laurence Gother, gentleman.
John Thomas, clerk.
Davies Gerrard, gentleman.
Timothy Ormes, pipemaker.
Thomas Walley.
Peter Murrey, clerk.
Samuel Croughton, barber chirurgeon.
John Leigh.

Edward Pickford, bricklayer.
Edmund Mathews, cordwainer.
Daniel Cross, tailor.
Richard Ordes, cordwainer.
John Nicholls, merchant.
Richard Gough, carpenter.
John Francis.

1718-9 [5-6 G. i.] ALEXANDER DENTON, Esquire, Mayor.

Nov. 4   John s. and p. of John Woodworth of Chester, bricklayer.
,, 19   Joseph s. of Peter Wright of Tattenhall, co. Chester, cordwainer, and p. of Joseph Wright of Chester, tanner.
Dec. 20   Peter s. of John Hickson of Chester, tailor, and p. of Robert Gregg of Chester, cordwainer.
,, 23   *Edmund Glover, corkcutter.
Jan. 10   William s. of Daniel Cross of Chester, joiner, and p. of Thomas Manning of Chester, cordwainer.
,, 14   Thomas s. and p. of Thomas Smith of Chester, carpenter and sawyer.
,, 30   Michael s. of Edward Bromley of Ashton, co. Chester, brewer, and p. of James Almond of Chester, butcher.
Feb. 7   Ralph Suthern, weaver, s. of Ralph Suthern of Chester, feltmaker.
,, 21   Robert Cooke, feltmaker, s. of Josiah Cooke of Chester, dyer, defunct.
Mar. 5   Philip Willoughby, brewer, s. of William Willoughby of Chester, brewer.
,, 7   John Starkey, wetglover, s. of Peter Starkey of Chester, brewer, defunct.
,, 21   *John Melling, watchmaker.
,, 21   *John Coughton, innholder.
,, 28   *William Griffith, labourer.
,, 28   Enoch s. of Arthur Bennett of Chester, cordwainer, and p. of Henry Crosby, cordwainer.
Apr. 6   Charles s. of Charles Gerrard of Chester, linendraper, and p. of Hugh Wooley of Chester, barber.
,, 15   *Thomas Jones, esquire.
May 2   John Johnson p. of Robert Davies of Chester, brewer.
June 15   Ralph s. of Frances Tushingham of Hatton, co. Chester, widow, and p. of Ralph Pickmore of Chester, butcher.

242 THE ROLLS OF THE FREEMEN OF [1719-20

June 18 Samuel s. of Robert Harvey of Mannor, in the parish of Hawarden, co. Flint, defunct, and p. of John Davies of Chester, joiner.
„ 22 Hugh s. of Hugh Jones of Chester, joiner, defunct, and p. of Thomas Young of Chester, joiner.
„ 20‡*Michael Hiccocke.
„ 29 Thomas Wilkinson, chandler, s. of John Wilkinson of Chester, chirurgeon, defunct.
July 1 John s. of John Francis of Childer Thornton, co. Chester, schoolmaster, and p. of Thomas Bagnall of Chester, ironmonger.
„ 10 *John Powell, sawyer.
„ 25 George Bennion, chandler, s. of George Bennion of Chester, ironmonger, defunct.
Aug. 22 John Parry, carpenter, s. of Henry Parry of Chester, carpenter, defunct.
Oct. 6 Richard s. of John Ormes of Chester, tailor.
„ 7 John Hale, butcher, s. of William Hale of Chester, butcher, defunct.
„ 8 Samuel Ashbrooke, tailor, s. of Samuel Ashbrooke of Chester, tailor.
„ 10 William Ball, baker, s. of William Ball of Chester, wetglover, defunct.
„ 13 Peter s. of Peter Leadbeater, brewer, and p. of Thomas Billinge of Chester, glover.
„ 15 Leigh Page, gentleman, s. of Humphrey Page of Chester, alderman, defunct.

1719-20 [6-7 G. i.] RANDLE BINGLEY, Esquire, Mayor.

Oct. 17 *Thomas Munk, innholder.
„ 20 Ralph Bingley, upholsterer, s. of John Bingley of Chester, chandler, defunct.
„ 20 Thomas Richards, cordwainer, s. of William Richards of Chester, cordwainer.
„ 31 Ephraim Bardsley, baker, s. of Ephraim Bardsley of Chester, baker.
Nov. 4 *Thomas Wilkinson, wheelwright.
„ 25 John s. of William Gamon of Chester, and now of Bridge Trafford, co. Chester, baker.
Dec. 5 John s. of John Johnson of Chester, slater.
„ 10 William s. of Frances Jones, widow, and p. of Samuel Selby of Chester, baker, defunct.
Jan. 9 Richard Snead, cooper, s. of Richard Snead of Chester, fletcher, defunct.

1720]   THE CITY OF CHESTER   243

Jan. 29 Humphrey Kynaston, mercer, s. of John Kynaston of Chester, alderman.
Feb. 20 John Cockayne, apothecary, s. of Benjamin Cockayne of Chester, apothecary.
Mar. 26 Richard s. of John Backarn of Broughton, co. Flint, yeoman, and p. of Thomas Crooks of Chester, carpenter.
Apr. 4   William s. of William Holland of Siverfield, co. Chester, yeoman, and p. of William Briscoe of Chester, baker.
,, 12   *John Lyon, gardener.
,, 23   John s. of John Hughes of Wrexham, co. Denbigh, brazier, and p. of Ellis Hughes of Chester, pewterer and brazier.
         Walter Pigot, gentleman.
,, 26   *William Glegg, gentleman.
May 7   Richard s. of William Litler of Tarvin, co. Chester, yeoman, and p. of John Calley of Chester, feltmaker.
,, 12   Ralph s. of Randle Bagnall of Handley, gentleman, and p. of Thomas Croughton of Chester, linendraper.
June 7   Francis Sayer the younger, tinplateworker, s. of Francis Sayer of Chester, alderman.
,, 7   Jonathan Gouldson, feltmaker, s. of Jonathan Gouldson of Chester, feltmaker, defunct.
July 2   George Taylor, yeoman, s. of George Taylor of Chester, slater, defunct.
,, 2   John s. of William Smith of Chester, labourer, and p. of John Tunnall of Chester, cordwainer.
Aug. 6   Richard Brock, brazier, s. of Richard Brock of Chester, brazier.
,, 6   Thomas Cowper, esquire, s. of Thomas Cowper of Chester, esquire, defunct.
,, 6   Thomas Brereton, esquire, s. of Edward Brereton of Chester, defunct.
,, 6   Thomas Pigot, gentleman, s. of Robert Pigot of Eaton, co. Chester.
,, 13   Charles Whitehead, mason, s. of Richard Whitehead of Chester, silkweaver, defunct.
,, 15   Gabriel Nicholls, bridlecutter, s. of Peter Nicholls of Chester, tanner.
,, 20   John s. of William Lawton of Chester, yeoman, and p. of William Hughes of Chester, innholder.
,, 20   Daniel s. of Rosingreave Okell of Chester, innholder, and p. of Thomas Deane of Chester, cooper, defunct.

Aug. 20 Jonathan s. of John Prestbury of Chester, wheelwright, defunct, and p. of Charles Jackson, smith, defunct.
„ 20 *William Anderton.
„ 20 *Martin Rose.
„ 20 *Hugh Roberts.
„ 20 William Hale, butcher, s. of William Hale of Chester, butcher, defunct.
„ 20 Samuel Davies, mason, s. of Samuel Davies of Chester, mason, defunct.
„ 20 *Francis Roberts.
„ 20 Edward s. of Alice Williams of Allington, in the parish of Gresford, co. Denbigh, widow, and p. of Thomas Gill of Chester, joiner.
„ 27 John s. of Thomas Pate of Chester, butcher.
Sep. 1 *Charles Aldcroft, clerk.
„ 1 William Hughes, gentleman, s. of William Hughes of Chester, innholder.
„ 9 Thomas Witcherley, wetglover, s. of William Witcherley of Chester, wetglover.
„ 9 Richard s. of William Witcherley.
„ 14 *John Peeres the younger.
Oct. 4 Samuel Minshull, esquire, s. of Richard Minshull of Chester, esquire, defunct.
„ 8 Thomas Warmingham, cordwainer, s. of Charles Warmingham of Chester, surgeon, defunct.
„ 8 John Welsh, feltmaker, s. of Robert Welsh of Chester, maltster.
„ 8 John s. of Roger Jones of Chester, gardener, and p. of John Croughton of Chester, cordwainer.
„ 11 ‡Thomas s. of John Stringer of Chester, alderman, defunct.
„ 12 John s. of John Moreton of Barrow, co. Chester, cordwainer, defunct.
John Edwards.
Thomas Maddock, goldsmith.
Richard Lee, upholsterer.
Ralph Probert, feltmaker.
Richard Parker, cheesefactor.
James Silvester, cheesefactor.
Robert Philpot.
John Philpot.
Joseph Philpot.
Thomas Maddock.
Thomas Mulleney, cordwainer.
Samuel Humphreys.
John Meredith.

Charles Orme, tobacconist.
Thomas Vause, barber.
Stephen Burchett, painter.
Richard Dewsbury, feltmaker.

1720-1 [7–8 G. i.] THOMAS EDWARDS, Esquire, Mayor.

Charles Foulkes, gentleman.
John Dannald, barber chirurgeon.
Edward Partington, gentleman.
George Reece, butcher.
George Wilson, ironmonger.
Hugh Foulkes, esquire.
John Kendrick, gentleman.
William Crachley, ironmonger.
Joseph Sorton.
William Nicholls, tanner.
Thomas Rayne, glazier.
Robert Davies, mercer.
John Briscoe, barber.
George Whitbey, yeoman.
William Richardson, goldsmith.
Thomas Paynton, cooper.
Peter Woodward, yeoman.
Christopher Eakins.
William Stones, saddler.
John Lloyd, gentleman.
Thomas Vernon, apothecary.
William Vernon, glover.
Daniel Shone, mariner.
Samuel Jennions.
Charles Price, joiner.
Edward Wrench, chandler.
Ralph Gorst, apothecary.
Simon Young, mariner.
William Ball, mariner.
Robert Williams, esquire.
Richard Williams, esquire.
Hugh Williams, esquire.
Kyffin Williams, gentleman.
John Williams, gentleman.
Johnson Mainwaring, esquire.
Richard Lee, weaver.
Robert Leivesley, barber.
Roger Maddock, cordwainer.

Paul Maddock, cordwainer.
John Nicholls, tanner.
Simon Maddock, cordwainer.
Ralph Moss, butcher.
William Richards, cordwainer.
Joseph Richards, cooper.
Hamnett Dobb, cordwainer.
Joseph Stout, butcher.
Ralph Bulkeley, cordwainer.

Sep. 21 Richard Jennions, feltmaker, s. of John Jennions of Chester, feltmaker, defunct.
,, 21 Moses Nicholls, butcher, s. of Samuel Nicholls of Chester, butcher.
,, 21 William Skellington, tailor, s. of William Skellington of Chester, cordwainer.
,, 21 William s. of Peter Jones of Chester, labourer, and p. of Urian Woodfin of Chester, slater, defunct.
,, 21 William s. of William Carter, defunct, and p. of Thomas Carter of Chester, cordwainer.
,, 22 William s. of Abel Payton of Catspole, co. Warwick, gentleman, and p. of Edward Hincks of Chester, linendraper.
,, 23 Samuel Maddock, tanner, s. of Joseph Maddock of Chester, tanner.
,, 23 Hugh s. of Hugh Maddock of Chester, tanner.
,, 23 Richard Dunbabin, glazier, s. of Peter Dunbabin of Chester, glazier, defunct.
,, 23 James Walley, cordwainer, s. of John Walley of Chester, wetglover, defunct.
,, 23 John Sarratt, tailor, s. of John Sarratt of Chester, tailor.
,, 23 Thomas Kelley, tailor, s. of William Kelley of Chester, tailor.
,, 23 William Plumbley, flaxdresser, s. of Thomas Plumbley of Chester, flaxdresser.
,, 23 John Hough, cordwainer, s. of Gilbert Hough of Chester, yeoman.
,, 23 Thomas Stringer, baker, s. of Thomas Stringer of Chester, turner.
,, 23 John Gother, weaver, s. of John Gother of Chester, joiner.
,, 23 Thomas Suthern, plasterer, s. of Ralph Suthern of Chester, feltmaker.
,, 23 William Ratcliffe, barber, s. of Benjamin Ratcliffe of Chester, ironmonger, defunct.
,, 23 Joseph Cook, chandler, s. of Samuel Cook of Chester, ironmonger.

[1721]   THE CITY OF CHESTER   247

Sep. 23 William s. of Richard Neale, mason, and p. of Robert Neale of Chester, mason.
„ 23 William Clayton, feltmaker, s. of John Clayton of Chester, feltmaker.
„ 23 John Ellis, joiner, s. of Robert Ellis of Chester, wetglover, defunct.
„ 23 John s. of George Wright of Chester, brewer, defunct.
„ 23 Joseph Wright, tailor, s. of George Wright of Chester, brewer, defunct.
„ 23 John Hickson, tailor, s. of John Hickson of Chester.
„ 23 Esau Andrew, slater, s. of Esau Andrew of Chester, carpenter, defunct.
„ 23 Joseph Warmingham, tailor, s. of Robert Warmingham of Chester, tailor.
„ 23 Thomas Davies, mason, s. of Samuel Davies of Chester, mason, defunct.
„ 23 Edward Davies, turner, ⎫ ss. of Edward Davies of
„ 23 John Davies, cordwainer, ⎭ Chester, turner, defunct.
„ 23 John Page, chandler, s. of John Page of Chester, smith, defunct.
„ 23 James Calveley, flaxdresser, ⎫
„ 23 Hugh Calveley, joiner, ⎬ ss. of Hugh Calveley of Chester, joiner.
„ 23 Calveley Calveley, joiner, ⎭
„ 23 Benjamin Powell, barber, s. of William Powell of Chester.
„ 23 George Harvey, bricklayer, s. of William Harvey of Chester, bricklayer.
„ 23 James Hand, corkcutter, s. of Hugh Hand of Chester, joiner.
„ 23 Stephen Hand, smith, s. of Stephen Hand of Chester, turner, defunct.
„ 23 Hamnett s. of Thomas Ley of Chester, cordwainer.
„ 23 Thomas Ellis, tailor, s. of Thomas Ellis of Chester, brewer, defunct.
„ 23 William Selby, butcher, s. of Nathaniel Selby of Chester, butcher, defunct.
„ 23 Thomas Strettwell, mason, s. of John Strettwell of Chester, mason.
„ 23 Peter Starkey, butcher, s. of Peter Starkey of Chester, brewer, defunct.
„ 23 John Walley, cordwainer, s. of John Walley of Chester, wetglover, defunct.
„ 23 John Williams ["baker" crossed out in M.B. and "corkcutter" inserted] s. of John Williams of Chester, baker.

Sep. 23 Charles Nicholls, mason, s. of John Nicholls of Chester, mason.
„ 23 Robert Gardner, corkcutter, s. of Timothy Gardner of Chester, goldsmith, defunct.
„ 23 Robert Griffith, cordwainer, s. of Laurence Griffith of Chester, cordwainer.
„ 23 Benjamin Maddock, tailor, s. of Benjamin Maddock of Chester, tailor.
„ 23 Thomas Maddock, cordwainer, s. of Paul Maddock of Chester, cordwainer, defunct.
„ 23 John Witcherley, wetglover, s. of William Witcherley of Chester, wetglover.
  John Woodfin, feltmaker, "disfranchised"? [No entry in M.B.]
„ 23 Thomas Leivesley, tailor, s. of Robert Leivesley of Chester, barber.
„ 23 Thomas Wrench, feltmaker, s. of Peter Wrench of Chester, feltmaker.
„ 23 John s. of George Taylor of Chester, slater, defunct.
„ 23 Thomas Farrington, papermaker, s. of Robert Farrington of Chester.
„ 23 James Doe, corkcutter, s. of Richard Doe of Chester, innholder.
„ 23 Thomas s. of Thomas Higginson of Chester, ironmonger, defunct.
„ 23 Thomas s. of John Calley of Chester, yeoman.
  †William Neal, mason.
„ 25 Thomas Bevan, turner, s. of Richard Bevan of Chester, smith, defunct.
„ 25 Thomas Peers, tailor, s. of Thomas Peers of Chester, plumber, defunct.
„ 25 John Bennion, cordwainer, s. of John Bennion of Chester, cordwainer.
„ 25 John Fletcher, carpenter, s. of John Fletcher of Chester, carpenter.
„ 25 William Speed, ironmonger, s. of Calveley Speed of Chester, ironmonger, defunct.
„ 25 William Croughton, cordwainer, s. of William Croughton of Chester, cordwainer, defunct.
„ 25 Thomas s. of Charles Broster of Chester, tanner.
„ 25 James s. of Zachary Wright of Chester, ironmonger, defunct.
„ 25 John Whitehead, feltmaker, s. of Thomas Whitehead of Chester, slater.
„ 25 John Shone, weaver, s. of John Shone of Chester, weaver.

| 1721] | THE CITY OF CHESTER | 249 |

Sep. 25 John Thornley, baker, s. of Robert Thornley of Chester, baker, defunct.

,, 25 Richard s. of Richard Brock of Chester, yeoman, defunct.

,, 25 Henry Bulkeley, linendraper, s. of Matthew Bulkeley of Chester, linendraper, defunct.

,, 25 Robert Maddock, tanner, s. of Joseph Maddock of Chester, tanner.

,, 25 Thomas Crookes, tailor, ⎫ ss. of George Crookes of
,, 25 George Crookes, tailor, ⎭ Chester, tailor, defunct.

,, 25 William Whitehead, cord- ⎫ ss. of Richard White-
wainer,   ⎬ head of Chester, silk-
,, 25 Josiah Whitehead, mason, ⎭ weaver, defunct.

,, 25 Thomas Hancock, mason, s. of Thomas Hancock of Chester, mason, defunct.

,, 25 Andrew Middleton, ironmonger, s. of Andrew Middleton of Chester, distiller, defunct.

,, 25 William Warmingham, cooper, s. of William Warmingham of Chester, tailor, defunct.

,, 25 Richard s. of Richard Carden of Chester, brewer.

,, 25 Richard Parsons, mariner, s. of Robert Parsons of Chester, mariner, defunct.

,, 25 Thomas Bulkeley, barber, s. of John Bulkeley of Chester, silkweaver, defunct.

,, 25 Elnathan s. of Jonathan Pemberton of Chester, silkweaver, defunct.

,, 25 George Powell, gunsmith, s. of John Powell of Chester, pipemaker.

,, 25 Thomas Calley, weaver, s. of Edward Calley of Chester, weaver.

,, 25 Henry Hancocke, tailor, s. of Thomas Hancocke of Chester, mason, defunct.

,, 25 John Venables, carpenter, s. of John Venables of Chester, cordwainer.

,, 25 Charles Rushton, shipwright, s. of James Rushton of Chester, bricklayer.

,, 25 Thomas Ball, carpenter, s. of Thomas Ball of Chester, carpenter.

,, 25 Thomas s. of John Maddocke of Chester, defunct.

,, 25 Joseph s. of John Maddocke, late of Chester.

,, 25 George Denson, baker, s. of Thomas Denson of Chester, baker.

,, 25 John Sproston, cooper, s. of John Sproston of Chester, cooper, defunct.

,, 25 George Dicas, tailor, s. of Richard Dicas of Chester, tailor, defunct.

250   THE ROLLS OF THE FREEMEN OF [1721

Sep. 25   Jonathan Coleclough, carpenter, s. of Samuel Coleclough of Chester, carpenter.
,, 25   Joseph Bennet, slater, s. of John Bennet of Chester, plasterer, defunct.
,, 25   Thomas Bolland, joiner, s. of William Bolland of Chester, joiner.
,, 25   John Davies, mason, s. of Thomas Davies of Chester, cordwainer.
,, 25   Joseph Rylance, baker, s. of Ellis Rylance of Chester, baker.
,, 25   Thomas Croxton, cordwainer, s. of William Croxton of Chester, upholsterer.
,, 25   John Sherman, jeweller, s. of William Sherman of Chester, cabinetmaker.
,, 25   Ralph Bellen of Thornton Hough, co. Chester, s. of Joseph Bellen of Thornton Hough, gentleman, defunct.
,, 25   John Cowdock, slater, s. of Thomas Cowdock of Chester, slater.
,, 25   Thomas Shone, collier, s. of John Shone of Chester, weaver.
,, 25   John Calley, weaver, s. of Edward Calley of Chester, weaver.
,, 25   Thomas s. of John Hickson of Chester, tailor.
,, 25   Shedrach s. of William Ball of Chester, wetglover, defunct.
,, 25   John Ellcocke, combmaker, s. of John Ellcocke of Chester, combmaker.
,, 25   John Foulkes of Hope s. of Ellis Foulkes of Chester, wetglover.
,, 25   John Allcocke, tailor, s. of Peter Allcocke of Chester, smith.
,, 25   Thomas Plumbley, tailor, s. of Thomas Plumbley of Chester, carpenter.
,, 25   Richard Cottingham, cabinetmaker, s. of Thomas Cottingham of Chester, barber, defunct.
,, 25   William Brock, carpenter, } ss. of Robert Brock of
,, 25   Robert Brock, smith,   }   Chester, carpenter.
,, 25   John Ledsham, tailor, s. of Thomas Ledsham of Chester, tailor.
,, 25   Thomas Tapley, cooper, s. of Henry Tapley of Chester, cooper.
,, 25   Richard Parsons, baker, s. of Richard Parsons of Chester, mariner, defunct.
,, 25   Edward Jones, cordwainer, s. of Thomas Jones of Chester, tanner, defunct.

Sep.	25	Thomas Hutchinson, brewer, s. of James Hutchinson of Chester, merchant.
,,	25	Richard Wilkinson, barber, s. of Richard Wilkinson of Chester, maltster.
,,	25	Joseph Cawley, feltmaker, s. of John Cawley of Chester, feltmaker.
,,	25	John Jones, pipemaker, s. of Thomas Jones of Chester, pipemaker.
,,	25	William Jones, pipemaker, s. of Thomas Jones of Chester, pipemaker, defunct.
,,	25	John ⎫
,,	25	Thomas ⎬ ss. of Randle Bennion of Stretton, co.
,,	25	George ⎭ Chester, soapmaker.
,,	25	Charles Johnson, dyer, s. of Thomas Johnson of Hawarden, co. Flint, dyer.
,,	25	Richard Reece, mariner, s. of Thomas Reece of Chester, innholder.
,,	25	John Price, butcher, s. of Richard Price of Chester, butcher.
,,	25	Joseph Fisher, butcher, s. of Edward Fisher of Hawarden, co. Flint, butcher, defunct.
,,	25	Matthew Heycocke, yeoman, s. of William Heycocke of Chester, defunct.
,,	25	John Porter, turner, s. of Richard Porter of Chester, turner.
,,	25	Thomas Bennion, cooper, s. of Thomas Bennion of Chester, brewer, defunct.
,,	25	John Harrison, cordwainer, s. of Joseph Harrison of Chester, tailor.
,,	25	John Smith of Ince, yeoman, ⎫ ss. of John Smith of
,,	25	William Smith, yeoman, ⎭ Chester, silkweaver.
,,	25	William Smith, carpenter, s. of William Smith of Chester, sawyer, defunct.
,,	25	Paul Whittaker, butcher, s. of Reginald Whittaker of Chester, butcher, defunct.
,,	25	Thomas ⎫ ss. of John Turner of Hawarden, co. Flint,
,,	25	William ⎭ victualler, defunct.
,,	25	Randle Foulkes, cordwainer, s. of Thomas Foulkes of Chester, carpenter.
,,	25	George Bridge, joiner, s. of Thomas Bridge of Holt, co. Denbigh, joiner.
,,	25	Peter Whawell, tailor, s. of John Whawell of Chester, baker, defunct.
,,	25	James Finchatt, barber, s. of John Finchatt of Chester, brewer, defunct.
,,	25	William Billinge, weaver, ⎫ ss. of William Billinge of
,,	25	Benjamin Billinge, weaver, ⎭ Chester, defunct.

Sep. 25 Seth Harrison, cordwainer, s. of Samuel Harrison of Chester, joiner.
"   25 John Minshull, gentleman, s. of William Minshull of Chester, ironmonger, defunct.
"   25 Joseph Pritchard, bricklayer, } ss. of John Pritchard of
"   25 John Pritchard, yeoman,   }   Chester, mason.
"   25 William s. of William Hughes of Chester, bricklayer.
"   26 Benjamin Pemberton, goldsmith, s. of Peter Pemberton of Chester, goldsmith, defunct.
"   25 Thomas Horton, cordwainer, s. of Peter Horton of Chester, tailor.
"   25 John s. of John Finchatt of Chester, barber.
"   25 Jonathan Taylor, combmaker, s. of George Taylor of Chester, slater, defunct.
"   25 Michael Powell, pipemaker, s. of Edward Powell of Chester, defunct.
"   25 Thomas s. of Thomas Bowers of Poulton, co. Chester, gardener, defunct.
"   25 Thomas s. of John Smith of Chester, feltmaker.
"   25 George Brock, brazier, s. of Richard Brock of Chester, brazier.
"   25 John Woodfin, slater, s. of William Woodfin of Chester, slater.
"   25 William Hewitt, cordwainer, s. of George Hewitt of Chester, slater.
"   25 John Johnson, gentleman, son of Thomas Johnson of Hawarden, co. Flint, dyer.
"   25 Robert Moreton, yeoman, s. of John Moreton of Chester, cordwainer.
"   25 Joshua Shone, weaver, s. of George Shone of Chester, weaver.
"   25 Matthew Walley of Tarporley s. of John Walley of Chester, tanner, defunct.
"   25 James Wilkinson, baker, s. of John Wilkinson of Chester, chirurgeon, defunct.
"   25 Thomas Smith, smith, s. of Thomas Smith of Aston, co. Flint, smith, defunct.
"   25 William s. of John Corbin of Broadlane, co. Flint, defunct.
"   25 William Street of Hawarden, co. Flint, s. of William Street of Chester, feltmaker.
"   25 James Ords, silkweaver, s. of Richard Ords of Chester, barber, defunct.
"   25 Thomas Heath, cordwainer, s. of George Heath of Chester, cardmaker.

1721]   THE CITY OF CHESTER   253

Sep. 25 Thomas Warmingham, weaver, s. of William Warmingham of Chester, cordwainer, defunct.
,, 25 Charles Harvey, bricklayer, s. of William Harvey of Chester, bricklayer.
,, 25 Henry Grantham, brewer, s. of Henry Grantham of Tarvin, co. Chester, gentleman, defunct.
,, 25 John s. of Phillip Bore of Chester, gardener, defunct.
,, 25 Richard Adams, bricklayer, s. of Joseph Adams of Chester, smith.
,, 25 Thomas Moyle, saddler, s. of John Moyle of Chester, woollendraper, defunct.
,, 25 John Dutton, butcher, s. of Joseph Dutton of Chester, butcher, defunct.
,, 25 James s. of James Hutchinson of Chester, merchant.
,, 25 Randle s. of Richard Oulton of Chester, alderman, defunct.
,, 25 Phillip Prestbury, wetglover, s. of Joseph Prestbury of Chester, wetglover, defunct.
,, 25 George Heath, cordwainer, s. of George Heath of Chester, cardmaker.
,, 25 John Gouldson, cordwainer, s. of Jonathan Gouldson of Chester, feltmaker, defunct.
,, 25 John Taylor, cordwainer, s. of Joshua Taylor of Chester, cordwainer.
,, 25 Thomas Moores, cooper, s. of Theodore Moores of Chester, cooper.
,, 25 John Holliwell, baker, s. of Hugh Holliwell of Chester, baker.
,, 25 John Wrench, butcher, s. of Peter Wrench of Chester, feltmaker.
,, 25 John Orme, tailor, s. of John Orme of Chester, tailor.
,, 25 Richard s. of Hugh Whickstead of Chester, glover.
,, 25 Timothy Taylor, ropemaker, s. of Daniel Taylor of Chester, ironmonger, defunct.
,, 25 John Briscoe, smith, s. of Maurice Briscoe of Chester, smith.
,, 25 Matthew Sharp, pipemaker, s. of Humphrey Sharp of Chester, pipemaker.
,, 25 George Woods, pipemaker, s. of George Woods of Chester, cordwainer.
,, 25 John King, baker, s. of William King of Chester, baker.
,, 25 William Peck, glazier, s. of Christopher Peck of Chester, tailor, defunct.
,, 25 John s. of Richard Burrowes of Chester, baker.

Sep.	25	Thomas s. of Thomas Skellern of Barrow, co. Chester, tobacconist.
,,	25	John Heath, cordwainer, s. of George Heath of Chester, cardmaker.
,,	25	Richard Wrench, feltmaker, s. of Peter Wrench of Chester, feltmaker.
,,	25	John Sharp, pipemaker, s. of Humphrey Sharp of Chester, pipemaker.
,,	25	Thomas Harrison, cooper, s. of William Harrison of Chester, cooper.
,,	25	John Bennet of Willaston s. of John Bennett of Little Nesson, yeoman.
,,	25	Joseph Maddock, slater, s. of John Maddock of Chester, slater.
,,	25	George Hilton, bricklayer, s. of Ralph Hilton of Chester, cordwainer, defunct.
,,	25	John Simmons, cordwainer, s. of John Simmons of Chester, barber.
,,	25	Charles Adshead, barber, s. of William Adshead of Chester, cordwainer, defunct.
,,	25	William Percivall, yeoman, } ss. of John Percivall of Chester, feltmaker, defunct.
,,	25	Peter Percivall, yeoman,
,,	25	Thomas Johnson, carpenter, s. of John Johnson of Chester, slater.
,,	25	Henry Harpur, cordwainer, s. of Henry Harpur of Chester, dyer, defunct.
,,	25	John Hand, corkcutter, s. of Stephen Hand of Chester, turner, defunct.
,,	25	William Cotton, carpenter, s. of William Cotton of Chester, yeoman.
,,	25	John Johnson, barber chirurgeon, s. of John Johnson of Chester, defunct.
,,	25	Simon s. of Simon Oliver of Chester, cordwainer.
,,	25	Thomas Skellington, cordwainer, s. of William Skellington of Chester.
,,	25	John Hatton, mariner, s. of Joseph Hatton of Chester, chandler.
,,	25	William Heycock, fisherman, s. of William Heycock of Chester, brewer, defunct.
,,	25	William Walton, baker, s. of Thomas Walton of Chester, baker.
,,	26	Randle Bennion, yeoman, s. of Randle Bennion of Stretton, co. Chester, yeoman.
,,	26	Adonijah Brooke, gentleman, s. of Richard Brooke of Chester, draper, defunct.

Sep.	26	Samuel s. of Richard Lee of Chester, gardener, defunct.
,,	26	Robert Welsh, feltmaker, s. of Robert Welsh of Chester, maltster.
,,	26	Thomas s. of George Bennion, late of Chester.
,,	26	John Stubbs, bricklayer, s. of John Stubbs of Chester, bricklayer.
,,	26	Arthur Wilson, cordwainer, s. of William Wilson of Chester, cordwainer, defunct.
,,	26	William Calley, weaver, s. of Richard Calley of Chester, weaver.
,,	26	Thomas Briscoe, smith, s. of William Briscoe of Chester, smith, defunct.
,,	26	James Jennings, joiner, s. of Samuel Jennings of Chester, joiner, defunct.
,,	26	Thomas s. of Alexander Emley, tailor, and p. of Richard Golding of Chester, tailor.
,,	26	John Bedward p. of Joseph Meredith of Chester, mason, defunct.
,,	26	John s. of Timothy Chaloner, yeoman, and p. of Stephen Soane of Chester, periwigmaker.
,,	26	Samuel s. of Daniel Hostage, and p. of Maurice Briscoe of Chester, smith.
,,	26	William s. of William Wright, labourer, and p. of John Dewsbury of Chester, feltmaker.
,,	26	William s. of Thomas Holt, tailor, and p. of John Pemberton of Chester, ropier.
,,	26	Samuel s. of Daniel Foxley, joiner, defunct, and p. of John Gaulter of Chester, joiner, defunct.
,,	26	Samuel s. of William Smith, sawyer, defunct, and p. of Edward Twanbrook of Chester, cabinetmaker.
,,	26	William Pollatt p. of Jonathan Gouldson of Chester, feltmaker, defunct.
,,	26	Robert Jones of Flint, grocer, p. of James Wright of Chester, ironmonger, defunct.
,,	26	Thomas Evans p. of Peter Parry of Chester, feltmaker.
,,	26	Thomas Tilley p. of James Dewsbury of Chester, feltmaker.
,,	26	Richard s. of Samuel Parsonage, and p. of John Hollewell of Chester, baker, defunct.
,,	26	William s. of William Cooke, and p. of Richard Bather of Chester, bricklayer.
,,	26	John s. of William Billington, and p. of Thomas Thropp of Chester, cordwainer.
,,	26	Henry s. of John Rogers of Burton, co. Denbigh, and p. of Thomas Morris of Chester, cordwainer.

Sep. 26 John s. of John Boden, gardener, and p. of Thomas Cowdocke of Chester, slater.
,, 26 Ralph Boden p. of John Fletcher of Chester, cordwainer.
,, 26 Henry s. of Henry Boxley, cordwainer, and p. of Thomas Winnington of Chester, plasterer.
,, 26 Samuel s. of Samuel Randle, and p. of James Litler of Chester, cordwainer.
,, 26 Thomas s. of Thomas Lamb, and p. of John Sutton of Chester, cordwainer.
,, 26 Thomas s. of Duncan Steward, and p. of Thomas Harrison of Chester, tailor.
,, 26 Matthew s. of Thomas Gethley, and p. of John Usher of Chester, mason.
,, 26 Joseph s. of Azariah Sharp, and p. of Edward Calley of Chester, weaver.
,, 26 Thomas s. of Edward Crew, and p. of John Davies of Chester, slater, defunct.
,, 26 Henry s. of John Carey, and p. of William Knot of Chester, bricklayer.
,, 26 John s. of John Price, tobacconist, and p. of Richard Carre of Chester, flaxdresser.
,, 26 Paul s. and p. of Richard Carre of Chester, flaxdresser.
,, 26 William s. of Margaret Prescott, and p. of John Davies of Chester, slater, defunct.
,, 26 John s. of Thomas Smith, and p. of Hugh Jordan of Chester, bricklayer.
,, 26 John s. of John Rathbone, and p. of Thomas Stringer of Chester, turner.
,, 26 Richard Spencer p. of William Woods of Chester, mason, defunct.
,, 26 Thomas Bodon p. of Thomas Warmingham of Chester, cordwainer, defunct.
,, 26 William s. of Henry Price, labourer, defunct, and p. of Thomas Hancocke of Chester, mason, defunct.
,, 26 George s. of George Price, yeoman, and p. of Samuel Dennill of Chester, mason.
,, 26 John s. of John Griffith, labourer, and p. of John Hankey of Chester, cordwainer, defunct.
,, 26 William Almond p. of Laurence Griffith of Chester, cordwainer.
,, 26 Benjamin s. of Daniel Burch, and p. of William Johnson of Chester, cordwainer.
,, 26 George s. of George Perkins of Chester, ropier, and p. of John Crane of Chester, cordwainer.

Sep.	26	John s. of Edward Shone, labourer, and p. of Roger Maddock of Chester, cordwainer.
,,	26	George s. of Richard Golborne, defunct, and p. of Francis Ormes of Chester, pipemaker.
,,	26	Peter s. of John Bowden, and p. of Richard Bathoe of Chester, bricklayer.
,,	26	John s. of Jane Towsey, widow, and p. of Thomas Bridge of Chester, feltmaker, defunct.
,,	26	Richard s. of Margaret Roberts, and p. of Thomas Cowdock of Chester, slater.
,,	26	Thomas s. of Hugh Sant, and p. of Maurice Briscoe of Chester, smith.
,,	26	Rowland s. of Roger Mostyn, husbandman, and p. of Joseph Hallett of Chester, jerseycomber.
,,	26	Richard s. of Richard Golborn, and p. of John Dobb of Chester, cordwainer.
,,	26	Thomas s. of Thomas Wetherell, glover, and p. of John Lewis of Chester, glover.
,,	26	Thomas s. of Jonathan Drinkwater, and p. of Thomas Kenion of Chester, carpenter, defunct.
,,	26	Richard s. of Peter Jones, labourer, and p. of Thomas Kennion of Chester, carpenter, defunct.
,,	26	Edward Orum p. of James Litler of Chester, cordwainer.
,,	26	John s. of Roland Rowley, and p. of William Briscoe of Chester, smith.
,,	26	Peter s. of John Locket, labourer, defunct, and p. of John Jones of Chester, cordwainer.
,,	26	Edward s. of Edward Hewitt, and p. of Edmund Matthews of Chester, cordwainer, defunct.
,,	26	James s. of Catherine Bailey, widow, and p. of Joseph Smith of Chester, feltmaker.
,,	26	John s. of John Jones, labourer, and p. of John Jones of Chester, cordwainer.
,,	26	Robert s. of Thomas Sproston, and p. of Richard Humphreys of Chester, hornbreaker.
,,	26	James s. of John Suthern, and p. of Samuel Nicholls of Chester, butcher.
,,	26	Thomas s. of Catherine Nayle, widow, and p. of Richard Ormes of Chester, pipemaker.
,,	26	Thomas s. of Martha Williams, and p. of William Johnson of Chester, cordwainer.
,,	27	Henry Hankey, mariner, s. of John Hankey of Chester, cordwainer.
,,	27	James Maddock, glazier, s. of Thomas Maddock of Chester, mariner.

Sep. 27 John Hall, cordwainer, s. of Andrew Hall of Chester, cordwainer.
" 27 Thomas s. of George Taylor of Chester, slater, defunct.
" 27 Edward Howard, butcher, s. of Charles Howard of Chester, mason, defunct.
" 27 Laurence Smith, cooper, s. of George Smith of Chester, cooper, defunct.
" 27 William Bromley of Tarvin s. of Edward Bromley of Chester, baker, defunct.
" 27 Richard Broster, feltmaker, s. of Richard Broster of Chester, saddler, defunct.
" 27 John Lightfoot, joiner, s. of Ralph Lightfoot of Chester, yeoman.
" 27 Samuel Bennett of Little Neston s. of John Bennet of Little Neston, co. Chester, yeoman.
" 27 Samuel Bennett of Soughall s. of Samuel Bennet of Soughall, co. Chester, yeoman.
" 27 Peter Shaw, feltmaker, s. of Peter Shaw of Chester, feltmaker.
" 27 Roger s. of Thomas Jones, and p. of John Williams of Chester, innholder, defunct.
" 27 Thomas s. of Thomas Bell, gardener, and p. of Alexander Roden of Chester, bricklayer, defunct.
" 27 George s. of John Sconce, feltmaker, and p. of Elisha Massey of Chester, pipemaker, defunct.
" 27 Owen s. of Owen Dod of Sutton, and p. of Parry Dawson of Chester, wetglover.
" 27 John Williams s. of William Jones [sic], and p. of Samuel Aspinall of Chester, brewer, defunct.
" 27 George s. of William Massey of Burton, co. Chester, and p. of Richard Massey of Chester, cordwainer.
" 27 Samuel s. of Daniel Peires of Ridley, co. Denbigh, and p. of Jonathan Gouldson of Chester, feltmaker, defunct.
" 27 Randle s. of William Soreton, clerk, and p. of Joseph Soreton of Chester, wetglover.
" 27 Stephen s. of Thomas Wilkinson, mariner, and p. of George Smith of Chester, joiner, defunct.
" 27 John Conway, plasterer, s. and p. of Thomas Conway of Chester, slater.
" 27 John Davies p. of Thomas Bridge of Chester, feltmaker.
" 27 Richard Holme p. of Peter Wood of Chester, feltmaker, defunct.

Sep.	27	Thomas Hughes, pavier, p. of George Boswell of Chester, paver.
,,	27	Edward s. of John Jackson, tobacco-cutter, and p. of Daniel Woods of Chester, slater.
,,	27	James s. of Susan Macquien, widow, and p. of John Massey of Chester, pipemaker.
,,	27	Edward Lloyd of Prenton s. of William Lloyd, labourer, and p. of Thomas Morris of Chester, cordwainer, defunct.
,,	27	Thomas s. of Elizabeth Walker, widow, and p. of Daniel Woods of Chester, slater.
,,	27	Thomas s. of Michael Crane, and p. of Charles Banner of Chester, slater.
,,	27	Samuel Marsh of Tattenhall, co. Chester, brewer, p. of Arthur Bolland of Chester, brewer, defunct.
,,	27	Thomas Wilkinson ⎫ pp. of Thomas Winnington of
,,	27	William Holland ⎭ Chester, plasterer, defunct.
,,	27	John s. of Thomas Holt, and p. of Joseph Maddock of Chester, carpenter.
,,	27	William s. of Simon Tompson, and p. of John Locket of Chester, cordwainer, defunct.
,,	27	Robert s. of John Williamson, and p. of Edward Matthew of Chester, cordwainer, defunct.
,,	27	Samuel s. of George Pike, and p. of Robert Pike of Chester, baker.
,,	27	John s. of Humphrey Oulton, and p. of John Crane of Chester, cordwainer.
,,	27	John Dobb p. of John Palin of Chester, cordwainer.
,,	27	Thomas s. of Edward Wall, cordwainer, and p. of Edward Tompson of Chester, pipemaker.
,,	27	Thomas Griffith p. of Randle Aston of Chester, wetglover, defunct.
,,	27	Henry s. of Roger Mostyn, and p. of William Warmingham of Chester, cordwainer, defunct.
,,	27	Robert Downes p. of Timothy Gardner of Chester, goldsmith, defunct.
,,	27	Edward Bellis p. of Thomas Reece of Chester, hornbreaker.
,,	27	Randle s. of John Meakin, and p. of Richard Golding of Chester, pipemaker.
,,	27	George Bennion of Hawarden parish p. of Randle Bennion of Chester, dyer, defunct.
,,	27	William s. of Elizabeth Starkey of Wimbles Trafford, and p. of John Rothwell of Chester, patternmaker, defunct.

Sep. 27 Thomas Booth p. of Richard Blease of Chester, cordwainer, defunct.
,, 27 Peter Horton p. of John Lockett of Chester, cordwainer, defunct.
,, 27 Samuel Horton s. of Peter Horton, labourer, and p. of Richard Bathoe of Chester, bricklayer.
,, 27 John s. of James Percivall, flaxdresser, and p. of Moses Dolbey of Chester, glazier.
,, 27 Lewis s. of Jane Vaughan, defunct, and p. of Thomas Reece of Chester, hornbreaker, defunct.
,, 27 Robert s. of Joseph Rutter, labourer, and p. of John Woodworth of Chester, bricklayer.
,, 27 William s. of Simon Oliver, and p. of Thomas Carter of Chester, cordwainer.
,, 27 Laurence Corles p. of William Johnson of Chester, wetglover, defunct.
,, 27 Edward s. of Thomas Griffith of Mollington, and p. of John Brock of Chester, ironmonger.
,, 27 Gawen s. of Joseph Richardson, defunct, and p. of Richard Golding of Chester, pipemaker, defunct.
,, 27 Peter s. of Peter Belward, brewer, and p. of Edward Litherland of Chester, tailor.
,, 27 Thomas s. of Hans Brown, and p. of Francis Ireland of Chester, cordwainer, defunct.
,, 27 Benjamin s. of Samuel Maddock, labourer, and p. of John Maddock of Chester, slater.
,, 27 John Seddon p. of Henry Parry of Chester, carpenter, defunct.
,, 27 Thomas s. of Thomas Roberts, defunct, and p. of John Dobb of Chester, cordwainer.
,, 27 Samuel s. of Randle Stanway, and p. of William Moreton of Chester, wetglover.
,, 27 Hugh s. of Hugh Cowdock, and p. of John Davies of Chester, cordwainer.
Oct. 2 John Sellers, tanner, s. of William Sellers of Chester, brewer, defunct.
,, 7 Thomas Whitaff, mercer, s. of Thomas Whitaff of Chester, carpenter, defunct.
,, 7 Thomas Bennett, yeoman, s. of Joseph Bennett of Elton, co. Chester, baker, defunct.
,, 7 Nathaniel Deane of Doddleston s. of Nathaniel Deane of Chester, cordwainer, defunct.
,, 7 Thomas Gill of Manchester, slater, s. of Peter Gill of Chester, feltmaker, defunct.
,, 7 John Whittaker, butcher, s. of Reginald Whittaker of Chester, butcher, defunct.

Oct.	7	Charles Cottingham, wetglover, s. of Thomas Cottingham of Chester, barber, defunct.
,,	7	John Kirkes of Liverpool, mariner, s. of Robert Kirkes of Chester, ironmonger, defunct.
,,	7	Richard Coleson of Oulton, yeoman, s. of Samuel Coleson of Chester, barber, defunct.
,,	7	John Bellin, mariner, s. of Joseph Bellin of Thornton Hough, gentleman, defunct.
,,	7	Richard Gamon of Bridge Trafford s. of William Gamon of Chester, baker.
,,	7	Griffin Edwards of Whitchurch, mercer, s. of Peter Edwards of Chester, goldsmith, defunct.
,,	7	John Brock of Tarvin, co. Chester, mariner,
,,	7	Thomas Brock of Tarvin, co. Chester, mariner,

ss. of Richard Brock of Chester, defunct.

,,	7	Joseph Whawell, yeoman, s. of Thomas Whawell of Chester, bricklayer, defunct.
,,	7	Samuel Hayes, mariner, s. of John Hayes of Willaston, co. Chester, yeoman.
,,	7	Edward ap Ellis of Poulton, yeoman, s. of John ap Ellis of Chester, defunct.
,,	7	George Warrington, gentleman, s. of John Warrington of Chester, alderman.
,,	7	James Litler, barber, s. of Thomas Litler of Chester, cordwainer.
,,	7	Thomas Gardner, goldsmith, s. of Timothy Gardner of Chester, goldsmith, defunct.
,,	7	Ottiwald Shawcross, tailor, s. of Robert Shawcross of Chester, tailor, defunct.
,,	7	Peter Griffith of Liverpool, nailer, s. of Peter Griffith of Chester, labourer, defunct.
,,	7	John Poynton of Alkington, yeoman, s. of William Poynton of Chester, ironmonger.
,,	7	William Griffies, plumber, s. of George Griffies of Chester, plumber, defunct.
,,	7	Thomas Wynne, gentleman, p. of Thomas Robinson of Chester, goldsmith.
,,	7	Ralph Wright of Tiverton, co. Chester, tanner, p. of Hugh Maddock of Chester, tanner.
,,	7	Ralph Williams of Utkinton, weaver, p. of John Meacock of Chester, weaver.
,,	7	Samuel s. of John Adamson of Alvanley, and p. of Owen Ellis of Chester, mercer.
,,	7	Thomas Maddock of Flint, bricklayer, p. of Peter Platt of Chester, bricklayer, defunct.

Oct.	7	Timothy Davies of Tarvin, p. of Thomas Harvey of Chester, bricklayer.
,,	7	Richard s. of Thomas Poole, and p. of John Dewsbury of Chester, feltmaker.
,,	7	Robert s. of George Mainwaring, cordwainer, and p. of Thomas Thomason of Chester, cordwainer.
,,	7	Thomas Moores of Beeston, co. Chester, and p. of Thomas Moores of Chester, cordwainer, defunct.
,,	7	Henry s. of Richard Jones, and p. of Arthur Mercer of Chester, brewer.
,,	7	Roger Jones p. of Richard Eminall of Chester, feltmaker, defunct.
,,	7	Thomas s. of Thomas Cliffe, labourer, defunct, and p. of Richard Golding of Chester, pipemaker.
,,	7	Thomas s. of Samuel Withers, and p. of John Rothwell of Chester, pattenmaker, defunct.
,,	7	John Wright of Hawarden p. of David Evans of Chester, carpenter, defunct.
,,	7	John s. of Hugh Leadbeater, and p. of William Jackson of Chester, plasterer, defunct.
,,	7	John s. of Thomas Almond, labourer, and p. of Thomas Litler of Chester, cordwainer.
,,	7	William s. of Elizabeth Taylor, widow, and p. of John Davies of Chester, slater, defunct.
,,	7	Thomas s. of John All, and p. of Jonathan Goldson of Chester, feltmaker.
,,	9	Henry Crosby, clerk, s. of Robert Crosby of Chester, alderman.
,,	9	William Davies, gentleman, s. of William Davies of Chester, cordwainer, defunct.
,,	11	William Ince, mariner, s. of Nicholas Ince of Chester, gentleman.
,,	11	Richard Dewsbury, feltmaker, s. of John Dewsbury of Chester, feltmaker.
,,	11	Edward Forshall of Bebington, clerk, s. of William Forshall of Willaston, cordwainer, defunct.
,,	11	Charles s. of Samuel Coleclough of Chester, carpenter.
,,	11	Randle Moyle of Shocklach, co. Chester, gentleman, s. of Randle Moyle of Chester, mercer.
,,	11	John Minshull of Barton, gentleman, ss. of John Minshull of Coddington.
,,	11	Henry Minshull of Coddington, gentleman,
,,	11	Charles s. of Robert Farrington of Chester, innholder, defunct.

Oct.	11	Thomas Bingley, ironmonger, s. of Randle Bingley of Chester, ironmonger.
,,	11	Samuel Pemberton of Grisby in Wirrall, goldsmith, } ss. of Peter Pemberton of Chester, goldsmith.
,,	11	Peter Pemberton of Grisby in Wirrall, goldsmith,
,,	11	William Foster, cordwainer, s. of Elias Foster of Chester, feltmaker.
,,	11	Peter Bellis of Mickle Trafford s. of William Bellis of Chester, ironmonger, defunct.
,,	11	William Pickmore, gentleman, s. of Thomas Pickmore of Chester, innholder, defunct.
,,	11	Samuel Bolland, gentleman, s. of Samuel Bolland of Chester, brewer, defunct.
,,	11	John Davies, wetglover, s. of Samuel Davies of Chester, carver.
,,	11	Samuel Jackson of Higher Bebington, co. Chester, joiner, p. of John Dutton of Chester, joiner.
,,	11	John s. of Thomas Roberts, defunct, and p. of William Warmingham of Chester, cordwainer, defunct.
,,	11	Samuel Briscoe of Mould, co. Flint, p. of Nicholas Ollerhead of Chester, feltmaker.
,,	11	Josiah s. of Samuel Coleclough, and p. of Humphrey Collins of Chester, glazier.
,,	11	John Ashton p. of Nathaniel Bathoe of Chester, bricklayer, defunct.
,,	11	Ralph Dutton p. of John Minshull of Chester, saddler, defunct.
,,	11	John Michael of Whitford, co. Flint, smith, p. of Robert Cowdock of Chester, blacksmith, defunct.
,,	11	Richard Redrope of Wrexham p. of Thomas Gibbons of Chester, feltmaker, defunct.
,,	11	Peter Cartwright p. of John Johnson of Chester, cordwainer, defunct.
,,	12	William Anderton, gentleman, s. of Matthew Anderton of Chester, alderman, defunct.
,,	12	Gerrard Parker, gentleman, s. of Richard Parker of Chester, gentleman, defunct.
,,	12	William Maddock, gentleman, s. of Richard Maddock of Chester, innholder, defunct.
,,	12	John s. of Richard Maddock of Chester, innholder, defunct.
,,	12	Henry s. of William Winstanley of Chester, vintner, defunct.
"	12	Randle s. of Randle Bingley of Chester, ironmonger, defunct.

Oct. 12 Thomas Bennett, upholsterer, s. of Joseph Bennett of Chester, surgeon, defunct.
,, 12 Jonathan Bostock, ironmonger, } ss. of Jonathan Bostock of Chester, ironmonger.
,, 12 Richard Bostock, ironmonger,
,, 12 Thomas Kirkes of Kinnerton, co. Chester, s. of Thomas Kirkes of Chester, tanner, defunct.
,, 12 George Hibbert of Moore in Hawarden parish, yeoman, s. of William Hibbert of Chester, shoemaker, defunct.
,, 12 John Ridge of Knutsford, periwigmaker, s. of Jonathan Ridge of Chester, surgeon.
,, 12 John Woods of Hodnett, plasterer, s. of John Woods of Chester, plasterer.
,, 12 Thomas Hutchins, mariner, s. of Thomas Hutchins of Chester, tailor, defunct.
,, 12 Hugh Holliwell of Manchester, cordwainer, s. of Hugh Holliwell of Chester, baker.
,, 12 Charles Kirkes of Chester, tapemaker, s. of Robert Kirkes of Chester.
,, 12 Francis Fearnall of Crew, yeoman, s. of Robert Fearnall of Chester, butcher, defunct.
,, 12 Robert Hiccocke, brewer, s. of Thomas Hiccocke of Chester, tanner.
,, 12 Hugh Bennett of Little Neston s. of John Bennett of Little Neston, yeoman.
,, 12 William Blakemore of Sandbach, plumber, s. of William Blakemore of Sandbach, plumber.
,, 12 Thomas Dewsbury of Liverpool, feltmaker, s. of James Dewsbury of Chester, feltmaker.
,, 12 Edward Wilkinson, surgeon, s. of John Wilkinson, late of Chester, surgeon, defunct.
,, 12 Samuel Hinton, apothecary, } ss. of Samuel Hinton of Chester, apothecary.
Robert Hinton, ironmonger,
,, 12 William s. of John Speed of Coughall, co. Chester, yeoman, and p. of Hugh Smith of Chester, surgeon, defunct.
,, 12 James Dobb of Gadlis, co. Flint, p. of John Woodworth of Chester, bricklayer.
,, 12 John Davies of Caerwys, p. of Edward Burrowes of Chester, feltmaker, defunct.
,, 12 John s. of Robert Griffith, and p. of William Bathoe of Chester, tanner.
,, 12 John Littlehales of Ellesmere, co. Salop, feltmaker.
,, 12 Roger Williams, mariner, p. of Alban Gray of Chester, bricklayer, defunct.

1721]   THE CITY OF CHESTER   265

Oct. 12 John Monkes of Haswell in Wirrall and p. of Samuel Dennill, mason.
 „   12 James Arnett of Liverpool p. of William Litherland of Chester, joiner.
 „   12 Lewis Hughes of Ruthin, mercer, p. of Charles Croughton of Chester, silkweaver.
 „   12 Thomas Moores, labourer, p. of Richard Bathoe of Chester, bricklayer.
 „   12 Isaac s. of John Prestbury, wheelwright, defunct, and p. of Titus Dewsbury of Chester, tailor.
 „   12 Robert ap Owen, labourer, p. of William Harvey of Chester, bricklayer.
 „   12 John Tilston, merchant, s. of John Tilston, "in Medicina Doctor," defunct.
 „   12 *Robert Edwards of Kelsterton, gentleman. .
 „   12 *Daniel Shore, yeoman.
 „   12 *Joseph Porter, maltster.
 „   13 Joseph Goodacre, gentleman, s. of William Goodacre of Chester, gentleman, defunct.
 „   13 Roger Eaton of Manley, yeoman, s. of Richard Eaton of Chester, defunct.
 „   13 Thomas Moreton of Barrow, yeoman, s. of John Moreton of Chester, defunct.
 „   13 John Denson, baker, s. of John Denson, late of Chester, baker, defunct.
 „   13 William Dutton, baker, s. of Jonathan Dutton of Chester, baker, defunct.

1721-2 [8-9 G. i.] THOMAS WILSON, Esquire, Mayor.

Nov. 11 George Calveley, gentleman, s. of Hugh Calveley of Chester, joiner.
Dec. 2 Samuel Revington, cordwainer, s. of Samuel Revington of Chester, cordwainer, defunct.
 „   2 John s. of John Rivers, defunct, and p. of John Green of Chester, tailor.
 „   2 William s. of Thomas Ratcliffe of Chester, labourer, and p. of Richard Rylance of Chester, cordwainer.
 „   2 Francis Falkner p. of John Crane of Chester, cordwainer.
 „   16 Benjamin s. of Richard Francis of Chester, and p. of Thomas Whitney of Chester, cooper.
 „   16 John s. of Elizabeth Walker, widow, and p. of Bryan Bolland of Chester, joiner, defunct.

266 THE ROLLS OF THE FREEMEN OF [1721-2

Dec. 19   Thomas s. of Charles Travers, defunct, and p. of Samuel Potter of Chester, tailor.

,, 23   James s. of John Olliver of Chester, cordwainer, and p. of Thomas Morris, cordwainer.

,, 23   William Done, mariner, s. of Samuel Done of Chester, feltmaker.

Jan. 1   John s. of John Peacock of Lower Kinnerton, co. Chester, yeoman, and p. of Hugh Thornley of Chester, smith.

,, 1   James s. of Jonathan Williamson of Sandiway, co. Chester, yeoman, and p. of John Totty of Chester, smith.

,, 2   John Pulford, gentleman,   ⎫ ss. of Alexander Pulford,
,, 2   Thomas Pulford, gentleman, ⎭ goldsmith, defunct.

,, 6   Phillip s. of Samuel Adams of Chester, silkweaver, defunct, and p. of Robert Gregg of Chester, cordwainer.

,, 8   John Hand, corkcutter, s. of Hugh Hand the elder of Chester, joiner.

,, 13   Wareing Croxton, corkcutter, s. of William Croxton of Chester, upholsterer.

,, 15   George Moreton, glazier and plumber, s. of John Moreton of Barrow, co. Chester, cordwainer, defunct.

,, 20   Samuel s. of Edward Huet of Chester, tobacco-cutter, defunct.

,, 26   William Boulton, weaver, s. of Henry Boulton of Chester, feltmaker.

,, 27   George s. of Hans Brown of Chester, tailor, and p. of John Adshead of Chester, cordwainer.

,, 27   *Griffith Roberts, maltmaker.

,, 31   *Robert Davies, esquire.

Feb. 3   *Christopher Gill, cordwainer.

,, 3   Samuel Young of Baddeley, co. Chester, clockmaker, s. of Peter Young of Bunbury, co. Chester, brewer.

,, 3   Daniel Young of Bunbury, co. Chester, yeoman, s. of Peter Young of Bunbury, co. Chester, brewer.

,, 10   William Griffith of Aston, co. Flint, p. of Richard Price of Chester, butcher.

,, 10   *Benjamin Glover of Chester, gardener.

,, 10   John Phillipps of Chester, yeoman, s. of Cornelius Phillipps of Chester, defunct.

,, 12   Phillip Brock, brazier, s. of Richard Brock of Chester, brazier.

,, 12   John Gaulter, gentleman, s. of William Gaulter of Chester, innholder.

Feb.	17	John s. of Thomas Woodfin of Chester, feltmaker, and p. of Henry Burrowes of Chester, feltmaker.
,,	17	William Anwill p. of Jonathan Pickering of Chester, carpenter, defunct.
,,	19	*John Spencer, esquire.
,,	24	John Smith of Bangor, co. Flint, yeoman, s. of Thomas Smith of Chester, dyer.
,,	24	George Eaton of Over, co. Chester, p. of William Warmingham of Chester, tailor, defunct.
,,	26	*Richard Manley, gentleman.
,,	26	John Kelsall, mercer, } ss. of John Kelsall, late of
,,	26	Thomas Kelsall, mercer, } Chester, ironmonger.
,,	26	John Jones of Warrington, co. Chester [sic], p. of John Rothwell of Chester, pattenmaker, defunct.
,,	28	John Tompkins of Liverpool, co. Lanc., yeoman, s. of Thomas Tompkins of Malpas, co. Chester, yeoman, and p. of Thomas Gibbons of Chester, feltmaker, defunct.
Mar.	1	Peter Sadler, gentleman, s. of Thomas Sadler of Chester, ironmonger, defunct.
,,	3	*Adam Cluff of Eaton, co. Chester, yeoman [innholder, M.B.].
,,	3	*William Smith of Whitchurch, co. Salop, yeoman.
,,	3	Richard Dobb, cordwainer, s. of Samuel Dobb of Chester, tailor.
,,	3	Abner Scoles the younger, upholsterer, s. of Abner Scoles of Chester, upholsterer.
,,	3	Charles Croughton of Chester, apothecary, s. of Charles Croughton of Chester, silkweaver.
,,	3	*William Littleton, gardener.
,,	3	William Simpson, clerk, s. of Thomas Simpson of Chester, alderman, defunct.
,,	5	*William Bethell, yeoman.
,,	5	William s. of Thomas Patten of Warrington, co. Lanc., merchant.
,,	12	John s. of William Ledsham, bricklayer, and p. of Alban Gray of Chester, bricklayer, defunct.
,,	12	William s. of Thomas Lewis of Chester, and p. of William Ravenscroft of Chester, tailor, defunct.
,,	14	John Pemberton the younger, merchant, s. of John Pemberton of Liverpool, co. Lanc., merchant.
,,	15	Sir Thomas Mainwaring, baronet, s. of Sir John Mainwaring of Peover, co. Chester, baronet, defunct.
,,	16	John Myers the younger s. of John Myers of Chester, clothworker, and p. of John Golding of Chester, pipemaker.

Mar. 17 Ralph Wilson of Wiggan, co. Lanc., pewterer, s. of Ralph Wilson of Chester, pewterer, defunct.

" 17 Robert s. of George Postons of Hawarden, co. Flint, labourer, defunct, and p. of Peter Platt of Chester, bricklayer, defunct.

" 17 Robert Wilbraham, mariner, s. of Richard Wilbraham of Chester, chandler, defunct.

" 24 William Maxfield of Over, co. Chester, gentleman, s. of William Maxfield of Chester, innholder, defunct.

" 24 William s. of Laurence Bridgewood of Chester, and p. of Robert Hankey of Chester, cordwainer, defunct.

" 26 Thomas Wilcock, clerk, s. of Thomas Wilcock of Chester, alderman, defunct.

" 29 William Hulton, esquire, s. of John Hulton of Chester, gentleman, defunct.

" 29 John Bardsley of Sandbach, co. Chester, glazier and plumber, s. of Ephraim Bardsley of Chester, baker.

" 31 Peter Dewsbury, tailor, s. of Titus Dewsbury of Chester, tailor, defunct.

" 31 Samuel Billingham of Dublin, cordwainer, s. of Fabian Billingham of Chester, cordwainer.

" 31 John Bennett, feltmaker, s. of Thomas Bennett of Chester, feltmaker.

" 31 Thomas Taylor, pipemaker, s. of Joshua Taylor of Chester, cordwainer, defunct.

" 31 George s. of Edward Totty of Brinford, co. Flint, yeoman, and p. of John Totty of Chester, smith.

" 31 William Kelsall of Little Hassall, co. Chester, yeoman, s. of John Kelsall of Chester, linendraper.

" 31 John Denson, baker, s. of Thomas Denson of Chester, baker.

Apr. 2 Thomas Ince, gentleman, s. of Nicholas Ince of Chester, gentleman.

" 2 Edward Price of Dymerchion, co. Flint, gentleman, s. of Thomas Price of Chester, merchant, defunct.

" 2 John Bridge of Holt, co. Denbigh, joiner, s. of Richard Bridge of Holt, joiner.

" 2 John Bellis of Liverpool, co. Lanc., barber, s. of William Bellis of Chester, ironmonger, defunct.

" 2 John Aldcroft of Manchester, co. Lanc., fustianmaker, s. of Theodore Aldcroft of Chester, merchant, defunct.

" 2 Thomas Rogers of Farndon, co. Chester, smith, s. of John Rogers of Chester, smith, defunct.

Apr.	3	*The most noble James, Earl Barrymore in the kingdom of Ireland.
,,	3	Edward Roberts, gentleman, s. of John Roberts of Chester, ironmonger, defunct.
,,	3	Robert Holland, linendraper, s. of Thomas Holland of Chester, barber.
,,	3	William s. of Robert Williams of Roe, co. Carnarvon, and p. of Thomas Williams of Chester, wetglover.
,,	3	Edward Bellis the younger s. of Edward Bellis of Chester, hornbreaker, and p. of Richard Humphreys of Chester, hornbreaker.
,,	3	Henry Mainwaring, esquire, s. of Sir John Mainwaring of Peover, co. Chester, baronet, defunct.
,,	3	Richard Bird of Northwich, smith, s. of Richard Bird of Chester, tanner, defunct.
,,	3	Richard Boswell, pavier, s. of Charles Boswell of Chester, pavier, defunct.
,,	3	William s. of Robert Farrington of Chester, innholder, defunct.
,,	3	William Wrench, joiner, s. of Robert Wrench of Chester, joiner.
,,	3	John s. of Elizabeth Baker of Chester, widow, and p. of Joseph Meredith of Chester, mason, defunct.
,,	3	Thomas Davies p. of Abraham Heathley of Chester, slater, defunct.
,,	3	John Swinton of Knutsford, co. Chester, gentleman, s. of John Swinton of Chester, ironmonger.
,,	3	Joseph Jennion p. of John Brandrett of Chester, barber.
,,	4	*William Brock, esquire.
Sep.	11	William Cowper, gentleman, s. of John Cooper [*sic*] of Chester, clerk, defunct.
,,	11	John Cowper, gentleman, s. of John Cowper of Chester, clerk, defunct.
,,	11	*Reginald Clay.

1722-3 [9–10 G. i.] LAURENCE GOTHER, Esquire, Mayor.

Jan.	5	*John Beech, silkdyer.
,,	19	Thomas s. of William Usher of Burton, co. Denbigh, yeoman, and p. of John Kemp of Chester, cutler.
Feb.	4	Robert s. of Joseph Ogdain of Hawarden, co. Flint, smith, and p. of Richard Bathoe of Chester, bricklayer, defunct.

Apr. 9 Samuel Wilcock of Woodchurch, co. Chester, p. of Thomas Knowles of Chester, cooper, defunct.
,, 13 Thomas s. of John Oliver of Chester, clerk, and p. of William Croughton of Chester, linendraper.
May 8 *Samuel Young, cordwainer.
,, 24 William Page, smith, s. of John Page of Chester, smith, defunct.
June 8 Charles s. of Charles Howard of Chester, mason, and p. of John Huxley of Chester, butcher.
July 27 Henry Croughton, wetglover, s. of Charles Croughton of Chester, silkweaver.
Sep. 2 *William Fisher, yeoman.
Oct. 5 Henry s. of Henry Ridley of Namptwich, co. Chester, and p. of Alexander Denton of Chester, draper, defunct.
,, 9 *Perseus Griffith, gentleman.
,, 9 *John Price, mariner.
,, 10 *William Lawson, mariner.
,, 10 *Ralph Hutchins, yeoman.
,, 10 *John Sempole, yeoman.
,, 10 *Randle Hackney, glass grinder.

1723-4 [10-11 G. i.] ROBERT PIGOT, Esquire, Mayor.

Oct. 26 Ralph s. of John Wilkinson of Great Sutton in Wirrall, and p. of Thomas Billinge of Chester, glover.
,, 26 Thomas s. of William Dutton of Waverton, yeoman, and p. of John Thomason of Chester, brewer, defunct.
Nov. 5 Thomas s. of Hugh Jones of Wrexham, co. Denbigh, defunct, and p. of Thomas Birkhened, an alderman of the art or mystery of the Butchers.
Feb. 29 William Williams, wetglover, s. of William Thomas [*sic*] of Rhyding, co. Flint, and p. of Thomas Williams of Chester, wetglover.
,, 29 Jonathan Litler, mariner, s. of James Litler of Chester, cordwainer.
Mar. 7 John s. of Thomas Egerton of Cotton, and p. of Arthur Mercer of Chester, brewer.
,, 24 *Joseph Sewell the younger, gentleman.
,, 24 *Simon Young the younger, confectioner.
Apr. 27 *Samuel Mathews, mariner.
May 11 Edward s. of Mary Nicholls of Chester, widow, and

		p. of William Rimmer of Chester, apothecary, defunct.
May	11	Henry s. of George Bushell of Great Sutton, co. Chester, and p. of William Witter of Chester, wetglover.
„	11	Samuel s. of Richard Price of Chester, labourer, defunct, and p. of Hugh Jordan of Chester, bricklayer.
June	8	John s. of William Buckley of Chester, gardener, and p. of John Crosse of Chester, barber.
„	9	John s. of John Lloyd of Chester, tailor, defunct, and p. of Griffith Knowles of Chester, cordwainer.
July	4	Thomas Hankey, saddler, s. of Thomas Hankey of Chester, innholder.
„	4	Thomas Sayer, cutler, s. of Francis Sayer of Chester, alderman.
Aug.	22	*Thomas Beeby, corkcutter.
„	29	*Richard Platt, gentleman.
„	29	*Joseph Wilkinson, wheelwright.
Sep.	17	*Sir George Warburton, baronet.
„	18	Peter s. of Andrew Hughes of Kelston, co. Flint, mariner, defunct, and p. of Laurence Gother of Chester, ironmonger.
„	18	*Francis Price, yeoman.
„	19	*Ignatius Fox, gentleman.
Oct.	15	*Joseph Sewell, esquire.
„	15	*Richard Barnard, gardener.
„	15	*Henry Wynne, yeoman.
„	15	Thomas Willoughby, wetglover, s. of Willoughby [sic] of Chester, brewer.
„	16	*Edward Harwood, gentleman.

1724-5 [11-12 G. i.] JOHN PARKER, Esquire, Mayor.

Oct.	24	*Benjamin Aldersey, surgeon.
Nov.	21	Daniel Maddocks p. of Richard Holliwell of Chester, tailor.
„	28	William s. of William Owen of Flixton, co. Lanc., gentleman, and p. of John Yeamon of Chester, ironmonger.
Dec.	8	Nathaniel s. of Thomas Price of Chester, clothworker.
Jan.	4	Robert s. of Adam Cluff, late of Eaton, co. Chester, cook, and p. of Thomas Gill of Eaton, joiner.
„	30	Matthew Robinson, painter, s. of William Robinson of Chester, painter, defunct.
„	30	*John Porter, innholder.

272   THE ROLLS OF THE FREEMEN OF [1725

Feb.   1 *Lucas Gawen, gentleman.
  ,,   1 *Hockenhull Short, mariner.
  ,,   2   Edward s. of Robert Yearsley of Sandbach, co. Chester, skinner, defunct, and p. of John Parker of Chester, mercer.
  ,,   2   Peter s. of Thomas Jones of Kelin, co. Flint, gentleman, and p. of Edward Parker of Chester, mercer.
  ,,   6 *Joseph Young.
April 3   William s. of Robert Phillipps of Chester, and p. of John Tilston of Chester, carver, defunct.
  ,,   3   John s. of Mary Bostock of Allostock, co. Chester, widow, and p. of William Farrington of Chester, merchant.
  ,, 17   John s. of Samuel Nicholas of Chester, pattenmaker, defunct, and p. of John Phithian of Chester, cordwainer.
  ,, .24 William Fielding, barber, s. of Bernard Fielding of Chester, innholder, defunct.
May   1   Richard s. of John Rogers of Chester, yeoman, and p. of George Smith of Chester, joiner.
July 19   Joseph Denson, baker, s. of Richard Denson of Chester, baker.
  ,, 31 *Thomas Povall.
  ,, 31 *Richard Hughes, yeoman.
Aug.   6   John s. of John Preece of Tattenhall, co. Chester, yeoman, and p. of James Almond of Chester, butcher.
  ,, 12 *Edward Morgan, esquire.
  ,, 12 *James Croxton, gentleman.
  ,, 21   Samuel Seller, brewer, s. of William Seller of Chester, brewer, defunct.
  ,, 28 *Thomas France.
Sep.   8 *Philip Fernihough, "in medicin doctor."
  ,, 20 *The most honourable George, Earl Cholmondeley.
  ,, 20 *The most honourable George, Lord Malpas.
Oct.   9   Charles Malbon, gunsmith, s. of Charles Malbon of Chester, gunsmith.
  ,, 14 *Joseph Snow the younger, weaver.
  ,, 14 *John Anderton.
  ,, 15 *Thomas Rippington, yeoman.

1725-6 [12-13 G. i.] THOMAS BOLLAND, Esquire, Mayor.

Oct. 30 *Thomas Hales.
Nov. 13   William s. of Evan Roberts of Gloverstone, co. Chester, tailor, and p. of Richard Lawrence of Chester, tailor.

Nov. 20 John s. of John Troughton of Liverpool, co. Lanc., gentleman, and p. of Richard Stevenson of Chester, apothecary.

„ 20 Ebenezer s. of Sarah Tristram of Whitchurch, co. Salop, widow, and p. of John Tristram of Chester, apothecary, defunct.

Dec. 29 *George Robertson, corkcutter.

Jan. 6 Thomas Weigh, late of Great Saughall, and p. of Peter Weigh of Chester, currier.

Feb. 2 Joseph s. of Jonathan Cawley of Chester, coachman, and p. of Ormson Kelley of Chester, slater.

„ 2 Roger s. of Edmund Massey of Chester, and p. of Thomas Deane of Chester, cooper.

„ 5 William Throp, tailor, s. of William Throp of Chester, tailor, defunct.

„ 12 John Reece, butcher, s. of Nicholas Reece of Chester, smith.

„ 19 John Pemberton, chandler, s. of John Pemberton of Chester, ropier.

„ 19 John s. of Josiah Richardson of Chester, furrier, defunct, and p. of William Selby, barber, defunct.

„ 28 John Hankey, mariner, s. of Thomas Hankey of Chester, feltmaker, defunct.

Mar. 2 George s. of George Whittaker of Chester, yeoman.

April 9 Humphrey s. of Edward Wynne, late of Bangor, co. Flint, defunct, and p. of Joseph Basnett of Chester, ironmonger, defunct.

„ 13 Robert Croughton, clerk, s. of Charles Croughton of Chester, linendraper.

„ 13 Thomas Bennett the younger, linendraper, s. of Thomas Bennett of Chester, feltmaker.

„ 18 James s. of James Walley of Chester, feltmaker.

„ 19 *John Cooper.

„ 29 Thomas Crookes, carpenter, s. of Thomas Crookes of Chester, carpenter, defunct.

May 4 William s. of Jonathan Hill of Chester, carpenter, and p. of John Foulkes of Chester, carpenter.

„ 7 Thomas s. and p. of Richard Pratchett of Chester, silkstocking-weaver.

June 1 Thomas Bolland, surgeon, s. of Thomas Bolland, esquire, mayor of Chester.

„ 1 Samuel Sayer, tinplateworker, s. of Francis Sayer of Chester, alderman.

„ 6 Barton s. of Roger Davies of Dongray, co. Flint, esquire, and p. of John Parker of Chester, apothecary.

„ 9 *Peter Daniel, merchant.

274 THE ROLLS OF THE FREEMEN OF [1726-7

June 9 *Daniel Porter, gentleman.
„ 9 *Thomas Sudlow, gentleman.
July 5 Robert s. of Hugh Roberts of Chester, labourer, and p. of John Hastings of Chester, turner.
„ 9 John Singleton of Chester, p. of Daniel Pemberton of Chester, carpenter.
Aug. 15 John Tudor, glover, s. of John Tudor of Chester, tinplateworker, defunct.
Sep. 5 *Robert Patrick, yeoman.
„ 24 John Leadbeater, brewer, s. of Peter Leadbeater of Chester, brewer.
„ 27 *Joshua Small.
Oct. 3 *John Townsend, esquire.
„ 8 Marmaduke s. of Peter Moulson of Coddington, co. Chester, gentleman, defunct, and p. of Samuel Walton of Chester, chandler.
„ 10 *Thomas Williams, gentleman.

1726-7 [13 G. i.–1 G. ii.] JOHN PARKER, Esquire, Mayor.

Nov. 22 Thomas s. of Thomas Gerrard of Chester, linendraper, defunct.
Dec. 3 Thomas s. of Charles Griffith of Chester, innholder, defunct.
Jan. 3 Abraham s. of Reece Jones of Gresford, co. Denbigh, blacksmith, and p. of William Revington of Chester, baker.
„ 7 Andrew s. of John Bruen of Chester, surgeon, defunct, and p. of Richard Stevenson of Chester, apothecary.
„ 11 Samuel s. of John Rogers, late of Wrexham, co. Denbigh, butcher, and p. of William Rogers of Chester, butcher.
„ 21 William s. of Jane Povey of Shocklidge, co. Chester, and p. of Randle Poynton of Chester, baker.
„ 21 James Fletcher, cordwainer, s. of Robert Fletcher of Chester, cordwainer, defunct.
Nov. 12 Richard s. of John Golborne of Chester, gentleman, defunct, and p. of William Bennett of Chester, baker, defunct.
Jan. 24 Thomas Walton, baker, s. of Edward Walton of Chester, baker, defunct.
„ 24 Gilbert s. of Gilbert Newton of Chester, upholsterer, defunct, and p. of William Johnson of Chester, cordwainer.
„ 28 William Calley, tailor, s. of William Calley of Chester, tailor, defunct.

1727]

Mar.	4	*Charles Price, maltster.
"	8	*Wilfrid Grantham, innholder.
"	11	John s. of Richard Wixstead of Chester, defunct, and p. of Thomas Hope of Chester, cordwainer.
"	25	Thomas Wrench, joiner, s. of Robert Wrench of Chester, joiner.
"	22	Richard s. of Thomas Cawley of Neither Poole, co. Chester, yeoman, and p. of Daniel Aldersey of Chester, draper.
"	29	Thomas Woodfin, ironmonger, s. of Uriah Woodfin of Chester, slater, defunct.
May	4	Nathaniel Bathoe, glazier, s. of Richard Bathoe of Chester, bricklayer, defunct.
"	14	Thomas Evans, glazier, s. of Edward Evans of Chester, glazier, defunct.
"	29	Edward s. of Edward Ralph of Llay in Gresford parish, co. Denbigh, and p. of James Comberbach of Chester, timber merchant.
July	8	*George Bennion, butcher.
"	8	*Thomas Lloyd, labourer.

John Bruce, innholder.
James Comberbach, gentleman.
William Weld.
Joseph Clubb, joiner.
Edward Vizar, gentleman.
Robert Roberts, cooper.
Edward Hawkins, upholsterer.
Charles Buckley, barber.
Thomas Shrigley, weaver.
Henry Orandale, slater.
Samuel Crew, gentleman.
John Hayes, baker.
John Rogers, pipemaker.
James Mainwaring the younger, esquire.
Thomas Hall, gentleman.
Robert Higginson.
William Trevor, wetglover.
William Ollerhead, brewer.
Joseph Butler, bricklayer.
John Thomason Hickson [sic].
John Williams, carpenter.
Joseph Tellett, slater.
John Brown, mariner.
James Underwood, gentleman.
Samuel Denton.

1727–8 [1–2 G. ii.] JAMES COMBERBACH, Esquire, Mayor.

        Edward Bingley, mariner.
        William Holt, gardener.
        Laurence Fogg, merchant.
        Thomas Gamul, merchant.
        Thomas Welchman.
        Edward Evans, yeoman.
        Henry Perkins, ropier.
        Robert Cawley, watchmaker.
        Robert Bowers, linendraper.
        Joseph Ridgway, glover.
        Daniel Kirkes, goldsmith.
        Thomas Hatfield, barber.
        John Wilbraham, feltmaker.
        Robert Cowdock.
        Richard Pratchett, silkstocking-weaver.
        John Betley.
        Edward Middlehurst, barber.
        Benjamin Perrin, gentleman.
        Peter Stringer.
        John Golborne, cordwainer.
        Joseph Burrowes, cabinetmaker.
        Robert Meacock, yeoman.
        John Johnson, glazier.
Sep. 18 *John Crew, esquire.
,, 18 *John Crew the younger, gentleman.
,, 18 Charles Bunbury, esquire, s. of Sir Henry Bunbury of Chester, baronet.
,, 21 Nathaniel s. of Thomas Smith of Chester, sawyer, and p. of Peter Parry of Chester, feltmaker.
,, 21 Thomas s. of Thomas Wright of Chester, defunct, and p. of Laurence Griffith of Chester, cordwainer.
Oct. 5 John s. of Joseph Snow of Chester, weaver, and p. of Robert Jones of Chester, dyer.
,, 11 *Thomas Sefton, mariner.

1728–9 [2–3 G. ii.] WILLIAM HUGHES, Esquire, Mayor.

Oct. 14 Edward Bateman, butcher, s. of Philip Bateman of Chester, yeoman, defunct.
Nov. 1 Thomas s. of John Dutton of Waverton, co. Chester, yeoman, defunct, and p. of Thomas Harrison of Chester, tailor.

Dec. 7 William s. of John Peeres of Chester, hosier, and p. of Charles Gerrard of Chester, barber.
„   14 *Samuel Gerrard.
„   21 *John Edwards, gentleman.
„   27 Ralph Ords, wetglover, s. of Richard Ords of Chester, barber, defunct.
„   8 George Brown, barber, s. of John Brown of Chester, saddler, defunct.
„   22 John Kelsall, corkcutter, s. of William Kelsall of Chester, tailor.
„   22 Peter s. of Thomas Frodsham of Elton, co. Chester, esquire, defunct, and p. of Thomas Davies of Chester, draper.
Apr. 26 *George Burghall, yeoman.
May 8 John Woodfin, tinplateworker, s. of Uriah Woodfin of Chester, slater, defunct.
June 18 William Cockayne, ironmonger, s. of Benjamin Cockayne of Chester, apothecary.
„   18 William s. of Mary Speed of Chester, widow, and p. of Thomas Bagnall of Chester, ironmonger.
Aug. 9 John Dutton, baker, s. of Jonathan Dutton of Chester, baker, defunct.
„   23 *Joseph Margarey, pipemaker.
„   23 *James Lumber.

1729 30 [3-4 G. ii.] THOMAS BROOK, Esquire, Mayor.

Oct. 14 *Charles Mytton, merchant.
Nov. 1 Sefton Carter, cordwainer, s. of Thomas Carter of Chester, cordwainer.
„   1 Peter Platt, cordwainer, s. of Peter Platt of Chester, cordwainer, defunct.
„   5 John Ords, cordwainer, s. of Richard Ords of Chester, barber, defunct.
„   5 William Adshead the younger, cordwainer, s. of John Adshead of Chester, cordwainer.
„   5 John s. of John Jones of Chester, cordwainer, and p. of John Croughton of Chester, cordwainer.
„   8 John Beckett, s. of Martha Kerfoot of Stretton, co. Chester, widow, and p. of Robert Barrett of Chester, baker.
Jan. 6 Thomas Reece, joiner, s. of Thomas Reece of Chester, mariner, defunct.
„   31 John Gough p. of Richard Gough of Chester, carpenter.

Feb. 7 Robert Cotton, cordwainer, s. of William Cotton of Chester, innholder.
„ 28 Cornelius s. of Cornelius Hobrow of Chester, dyer, and p. of Peter Parry of Chester, feltmaker.
Mar. 7 James s. of James Dobb of Chester, bricklayer, defunct, and p. of Randle Wrench of Chester, butcher.
„ 21 Richard Ralphson p. of William Goodwin of Chester, ironmonger.
„ 28 Thomas Corbin, joiner, s. of John Corbin of Broad-lane, co. Flint, yeoman, defunct.
Apr. 25 Griffith s. of Hugh Williams, late of Conway, co. Carnarvon, gentleman, and p. of Joseph Parker of Chester, upholsterer.
„ 25 John s. of Peter Cornelius of Chester, tailor, and p. of Thomas Powell of Chester, mason.
May 2 Charles s. of Thomas Rowe, late of Hartford, co. Chester, gentleman, and p. of Thomas Golborne of Chester, apothecary, defunct.
„ 9 Robert Pyke, goldsmith, s. of Robert Pyke of Chester, baker, defunct.
„ 9 John s. of William Bowker of Bickerton, co. Chester, gentleman, defunct, and p. of Joseph Bowker of Chester, draper, defunct.
„ 18 *David Williams.
July 1 Charles Moulson, chandler, s. of Thomas Moulson of Chester, barber, defunct.
„ 8 William Moss the younger, butcher, s. of William Moss of Chester, butcher.
„ 8 Samuel Nicholls the younger, butcher, s. of John Nicholls of Chester, butcher, defunct.
„ 10 James s. of John Wilkinson of Great Sutton, co. Chester, yeoman, and p. of John Moulson of Chester, ironmonger.
„ 11 John Jones p. of John Melling of Chester, watchmaker.
Aug. 22 John s. of William Edwards of Chester, cooper, and p. of Thomas Wright of Chester, tailor.
Sep. 26 *William Sherman, tailor.
Oct. 10 James s. of James Brodrick of Chester, joiner, defunct, and p. of Thomas Gill of Eaton, co. Chester, joiner.
„ 13 *Thomas Puleston, esquire.
„ 14 Thomas Burrowes, gentleman, s. of Edward Burrowes of Chester, alderman, defunct.
„ 14 *Elias Williams.
„ 16 John Willoughby, apothecary, s. of William Willoughby of Chester, brewer.

Oct. 16 *Maurice Mathews, vintner.
„ 16 William s. of William Coy of Chester, p. of John Tilston of Chester, carver and mason, defunct.

1730-1 [4-5 G. ii.] JOHN PEMBERTON, Esquire, Mayor.

Nov. 2 John s. of John Green of Chester, yeoman, and p. of Nathaniel Smith of Chester, baker, defunct.
„ 7 James s. of Elizabeth Hesketh of Capenhurst, co. Chester, widow, and p. of Ephraim Bardsley of Chester, baker.
„ 11 George s. of George Robinson of Chester, tailor, and p. of William Qua of Chester, tailor.
„ 14 William Reece, butcher, s. of Thomas Reece, late of Chester, innholder, defunct.
„ 21 William Huntington, smith, s. of William Huntington of Chester, baker.
Dec. 30 Mathew Hinton, apothecary, s. of Samuel Hinton of Chester, apothecary, defunct.
Feb. 2 John Posnett, cordwainer, s. of Thomas Posnett of Chester, cordwainer.
„ 13 Joseph Hatton, barber, s. of Joseph Hatton of Chester, chandler.
„ 15 John s. of Ralph Wilkinson of Great Sutton, co. Chester, gentleman, and p. of Charles Croughton of Chester, apothecary.
„ 15 John s. of Thomas Halwood of Whitby, co. Chester, gentleman, defunct, and p. of Andrew Middleton of Chester, ironmonger.
„ 20 Joseph s. of James Ratcliffe of Chester, mason, defunct, and p. of Nathan Maddock of Chester, flaxdresser, defunct.
Mar. 6 Richard Whittingham p. of Samuel Jenyons of Chester, joiner.
Apr. 3 Thomas s. of Robert Williams of Roe, co. Carnarvon, yeoman, and p. of William Milton of Chester, wetglover.
„ 6 John s. and p. of John Warrington of Chester, carpenter.
„ 4 John Mason, butcher, s. of Ralph Mason of Chester, butcher.
„ 30 John Kirkes, upholsterer, s. of Samuel Kirkes of Chester, upholsterer.
May 1 James s. of John Mottershead of Aldersey, co. Chester, yeoman, and p. of William Frost of Chester, barber.

280   THE ROLLS OF THE FREEMEN OF   [1731

May   3   John s. of Jonathan Hill of Chester, carpenter, and p. of William Wilson of Chester, butcher, defunct.
„   8   Peter s. of Peter Cornelius of Chester, and p. of Daniel Pemberton of Chester, carpenter.
„   15   John s. of William Tyrer of Chester, labourer, and p. of John Fithian of Chester, cordwainer.
June   5   Matthew Owens of Churton, co. Chester, p. of Benjamin Davies of Chester, saddler, defunct.
„   12   William Bennett, barber, s. of William Bennett of Chester, barber, defunct.
„   12   John s. of Thomas Finchett of Kelsall, co. Chester, gentleman, and p. of Thomas Billinge of Chester, glover.
„   22   Humphrey s. of Thomas Davies of Chester, merchant, defunct, and p. of Laurence Gother of Chester, alderman, ironmonger.
„   26   Charles s. of Joseph Cotterill of Chester, miller, and p. of Thomas Barton of Chester, weaver, defunct.
July   3   Richard s. and p. of Richard Carr of Chester, flax-dresser, defunct.
„   31   *Richard Ellames, plumber.
„   31   *John Pemberton, tailor.
„   31   *John Thomas.
Aug. 25   *Thomas Jones, yeoman.
„   28   William Francis the younger, hosier, s. of William Francis of Chester, periwigmaker.
Sep.   10   George s. of John Glover, late of Chester, gentleman, and p. of John Shard of Chester, apothecary, defunct.
„   11   John Mottershead, yeoman, s. of Thomas Mottershead of Chester, innholder, defunct.
„   13   *Thomas Barker, gentleman.
Oct.   13   Christopher s. of Christopher Gill of Chester, cordwainer, and p. of Nicholas Williams of Chester, tailor, defunct.

1731–2 [5–6 G. ii.] TRAFFORD MASSIE, Esquire, Mayor.

Nov.   6   Joseph Meredith, wetglover, s. of Joseph Meredith, late of Chester, mason.
„   9   Robert Townsend, gentleman, s. of Gerard Townsend, late of Christleton, co. Chester, esquire.
„   13   William Bunbury, esquire, s. of Sir Henry Bunbury of Chester, baronet.
„   13   Arthur Williams, clerk, s. of John Williams of Chester, esquire.

Nov.	20	Thomas Davies, tailor, s. of Edward Davies of Chester, turner, defunct.
Dec.	10	Charles s. of Samuel Deane of Chester, yeoman, defunct, and p. of Thomas Manning of Chester, cordwainer, defunct.
,,	18	John s. of Joshua French of Chester, saddler, and p. of Stephen Sone of Chester, periwigmaker.
Jan.	3	Phillip s. of Phillip Chevers of Chester, mariner, and p. of Richard Edwards of Chester, butcher.
,,	8	Thomas s. and p. of Samuel Braddock of Chester, mason, defunct.
,,	10	Roger Massie, ironmonger, s. of Trafford Massie, esquire, mayor of Chester.
,,	12	Robert s. of John Tapley, late of Boughton, co. Chester, saddler, and p. of Samuel Coleclough of Chester, glazier, defunct.
,,	15	*George Leigh, gentleman.
,,	15	*George Buckton, yeoman.
,,	15	*Edward Davies, yeoman.
,,	18	John Brereton, innholder, s. of Edward Brereton of Chester, innholder, defunct.
,,	22	Thomas s. of Thomas Hughes of Caervallough, in Northop parish, co. Flint, yeoman, defunct.
,,	22	David Hughes, yeoman, s. of above Thomas Hughes.
,,	29	Thomas s. of Samuel Sadler, late of Tarvin, co. Chester, ironmonger.
Feb.	5	*Robert s. of Thomas Jackson of Chester, gentleman, defunct, and p. of John Lloyd of Chester, merchant, defunct.
,,	12	George Croxton of Manchester, co. Salop [*sic*], merchant, s. of Hugh Croxton of Chester, ironmonger, defunct.
,,	12	Ralph s. of John Kerkham of Stapleford, co. Chester, yeoman, and p. of Thomas Stringer of Chester, turner.
,,	16	John Bafarn, brewer, s. of William Bafarn of Chester, brewer, defunct.
Mar.	11	Richard Jennings, wetglover, s. of William Jennings of Chester, wetglover, defunct.
,,	24	Daniel Taylor, mercer, s. of Thomas Taylor of Chester, barber.
Apr.	22	George s. of Richard Smith of Chester, tanner, defunct.
,,	24	John Ollerhead, tanner, s. of John Ollerhead of Chester, tanner.
,,	24	Jabez Bathoe, tanner, s. of William Bathoe of Chester, tanner.

May	20	Thomas s. of John Jones of Northop, co. Flint, gentleman, defunct, and p. of Peter Parry of Chester, feltmaker.
June	10	George Marsh, brewer, s. of Moses Marsh of Chester, toyman, defunct.
,,	30	John s. of John Bennet of Pickton, co. Chester, yeoman, and p. of John Buckley of Chester, barber.
July	8	John s. of Robert Shelley of Chester, labourer, defunct, and p. of James Litler the elder of Chester, cordwainer.
,,	8	George s. of George Cowley of Chester, pavier, and p. of Randle Hackney of Chester, glassgrinder.
,,	19	Henry Roughley, joiner, s. of Thomas Roughley of Chester, joiner.
,,	22	Humphrey Walley, wetglover, s. of Joseph Walley of Chester, wetglover, defunct.
,,	22	*Michael Fisher, corkcutter.
,,	22	Thomas Allcock the younger, smith, s. of Thomas Allcock of Chester, smith.
,,	22	Henry Bolland, joiner, s. of Thomas Bolland of Chester, joiner.
,,	22	John Chapman, baker, s. of John Chapman of Chester, baker, defunct.
,,	22	Thomas Carter, feltmaker, s. of John Carter of Chester, mason, defunct.
,,	22	George Griffies, plumber, s. of John Griffies of Chester, plumber.
,,	24	William Hughes, ironmonger, ⎫ ss. of Owen Hughes of
,,	24	John Hughes, mercer, ⎬ Oswestry, co. Salop,
,,	24	Owen Hughes, apothecary, ⎭ barber, defunct.
,,	25	Stephen s. of Stephen Palin of Chester, tailor, and p. of John Platt of Chester, tailor, defunct.
,,	25	*Robert Crachley the elder, gentleman.
,,	25	*Robert Crachley the younger, gentleman.
,,	28	Jonathan Whittle, ropier, s. of Joseph Whittle of Chester, draper, defunct.
,,	29	John s. and p. of Joseph Wilkinson of Chester, wheelwright.
,,	29	James Mottershead the younger, baker, s. of James Mottershead of Chester, draper.
,,	29	Randle s. of Elizabeth Key of Whitchurch, co. Salop, and p. of John Clubb of Chester, ironmonger, defunct.
Aug.	1	Thomas Massey, linendraper, s. of Roger Massey of Chester, alderman.

Aug.	1	Richard Richardson, goldsmith, s. of Richard Richardson of Chester, goldsmith, defunct.
,,	1	Thomas Coy, tailor, } ss. of William Coy of Chester,
,,	1	Samuel Coy, tailor, } tailor.
,,	2	Robert Walley, cooper, s. of Ralph Walley of Chester, goldsmith, defunct.
,,	2	Richard s. of Samuel Parsonage of Aldersey, co. Chester, yeoman, and p. of Joseph Dyson of Chester, merchant.
,,	2	John s. of Thomas Pownall of Chester, sawyer, and p. of Richard Humphreys of Chester, hornbreaker.
,,	5	Edward Ellis of Cornist, co. Flint, gentleman, and s. of Edward Ellis of Chester, ironmonger, defunct.
,,	5	Thomas Cowper, gentleman, s. of John Cowper of Middlewich, co. Chester, clerk, defunct.
,,	5	Daniel s. of Randle Bathoe of Chester, tanner, defunct.
,,	5	John Hughes of Caervallough, co. Flint, yeoman, s. of Thomas Hughes of Caervallough, in Northop parish, co. Flint, yeoman.
,,	5	Richard s. of Mary Basseen, widow, and p. of Samuel Mercer of Chester, joiner, defunct.
,,	5	John s. of Hugh Sant of Bolin, co. Chester, yeoman, defunct, and p. of Joseph Dennil of Chester, glazier.
,,	5	Richard s. of Thomas Payne of Chester, pipemaker, and p. of Thomas Cliffe of Chester, pipemaker.
,,	5	Aquila s. of Aquila Davenport of Chester, labourer, and p. of Thomas Wright of Chester, tailor.
,,	5	Thomas Wakefield the younger, slater, s. of Thomas Wakefield of Chester, slater.
,,	5	Samuel s. of Robert Foulkes, and p. of William Jennings of Chester, wetglover, defunct.
,,	5	Joseph s. of Charles Stanton of Chester, defunct, and p. of Thomas Hale of Chester, butcher, defunct.
,,	5	Richard s. of Richard Baker of Chester, cordwainer, defunct, and p. of John Warrington of Chester, carpenter.
,,	7	John s. of John Gough of Christleton, co. Chester, carpenter, and p. of William Gatcliffe of Chester, carpenter, defunct.
,,	7	James Rimmer, carpenter, s. of James Rimmer of Chester, slater.
,,	7	Thomas Bakern of Ewloe, co. Flint, p. of Thomas Crookes of Chester, carpenter, defunct.
,,	7	William Harrison, cordwainer, s. of Joseph Harrison of Chester, tailor.

Aug.	7	Henry Salisbury of Boughton, co. Chester, nailor, s. of Henry Salisbury of Chester, periwigmaker, defunct.
,,	7	Richard Darwell, periwigmaker, s. of Richard Darwell of Chester, glover, defunct.
,,	7	Samuel s. of Aquila Davenport of Chester, labourer, and p. of Ormeson Calley of Chester, slater.
,,	7	George s. of Nathan Maddock of Chester, flaxdresser, defunct.
,,	7	George s. of Peter Wareing of Chester, gardener, and p. of John Millington of Chester, cordwainer, defunct.
,,	7	John s. of Abraham Ernshaw, defunct, and p. of John Thomason of Chester, brewer, defunct.
,,	7	John Ryley of Nantwich s. of Walter Ryley of Chester, labourer, and p. of Samuel Harvey of Chester, joiner.
,,	7	Josiah s. of William Brethwood of Chester, husbandman, and p. of John Jones of Chester, mason.
,,	7	John s. of Elizabeth Reece, widow, and p. of John Jones of Chester, mason.
,,	7	John Walker p. of John Johnson the younger of Chester, slater.
,,	7	John s. of Randle Brookes, defunct, and p. of James Dewsbury of Chester, feltmaker.
,,	7	Richard s. of George Sconce of Chester, fisherman, and p. of Edward Warrington of Chester, carpenter.
,,	7	Richard Bathoe, tailor, s. of Richard Bathoe of Chester, bricklayer, defunct.
,,	7	Samuel Prichard, slater, s. of John Prichard of Chester, mason, defunct.
,,	7	William s. of Jeremy Sellers of Chester, periwigmaker, and p. of Laurence Griffith of Chester, cordwainer.
,,	7	Thomas s. of Edward Lewis of Chester, labourer, and p. of James Littler of Chester, cordwainer.
,,	7	William Boulton, bricklayer, s. of Nathaniel Boulton of Chester, bricklayer.
,,	7	Mathew Brown the younger, } ss. of Mathew Brown of Chester, bricklayer.
,,	7	John Brown,
,,	7	John Ormes, pipemaker, } ss. of Francis Ormes of Chester, pipemaker.
,,	7	James Ormes, pipemaker,
,,	7	Richard Stubbs, bricklayer, s. of John Stubbs of Chester, bricklayer.
,,	7	Ralph s. of John Lockett of Chester, labourer, defunct, and p. of Richard Bathoe of Chester, bricklayer, defunct.

1732]   THE CITY OF CHESTER   285

Aug. 7 William Bevan p. of John Langdale of Chester, bricklayer.
"   7 William Jones, cordwainer, s. of David Jones of Chester, labourer.
"   7 Ralph s. of Ralph Walley of Chester, goldsmith, defunct.
"   7 William s. of Robert Edwards of Chester, smith, and p. of Laurence Griffiths of Chester, cordwainer.
"   7 Joseph s. of William Waterwoods of Chester, labourer, and p. of Thomas Whitehead of Chester, slater.
"   7 Roger s. of Roger Mostyn of Chester, labourer, and p. of John Smith of Chester, smith.
"   7 William Gill p. of Charles Whitehead of Chester, mason.
"   7 James s. of Thomas Ridley of Chester, innholder, defunct.
"   7 Thomas Tylston, cordwainer, s. of Thomas Tylston of Chester, bricklayer.
"   7 Thomas s. of Richard Rogers of Chester, labourer, and p. of John Mulleney of Chester, cordwainer.
"   7 Edward Price, feltmaker, s. of Richard Price of Chester, tobacconist.
"   7 John s. of Robert Rutter of Chester, labourer, and p. of Samuel Price of Chester, bricklayer.
"   7 Edward Powell, mason, s. of Thomas Powell of Chester, mason.
"   7 Edward s. and p. of Edward Pickford of Chester, bricklayer, defunct.
"   7 John Baker of Malpas, co. Ches., p. of John Hastings of Chester, turner.
"   7 William Griffith p. of Thomas Roberts of Chester, mason.
"   7 Thomas Carter the younger, cordwainer, s. of Thomas Carter of Chester, cordwainer.
"   7 Samuel Thomlinson of Mickle Trafford, co. Ches., husbandman, s. of Benjamin Thomlinson of Chester, cordwainer, defunct.
"   7 William Haswell, cordwainer, } ss. of Jonathan Haswell of Chester, cooper.
"   7 George Haswell, staymaker,
"   7 Arthur s. of John Culm of Chester, leatherseller, and p. of Richard Golding of Chester, pipemaker, defunct.
"   7 John s. of Robert Holcroft of Chester, yeoman, and p. of John Palin of Chester, cordwainer.

Aug. 7 Joseph Davies p. of John Harrison of Chester, cordwainer.
,, 7 William s. of Thomas Ridley of Chester, apothecary, defunct.
,, 7 John Lindford, cooper, s. of John Lindford of Chester, cooper, defunct.
,, 7 James Bathoe, bricklayer, s. of Richard Bathoe of Chester, bricklayer, defunct.
,, 7 John Bennett, bricklayer, s. of John Bennett of Chester, baker.
,, 7 Hector Cotton, cordwainer, s. of William Cotton of Chester, innholder.
,, 7 Henry Cowduck, slater, s. of Thomas Cowduck of Chester, slater.
,, 7 Charles Hiccocke, tailor, } ss. of Edward Hiccocke of Chester, barber, defunct.
,, 7 Edward Hiccocke, cordwainer,
,, 8 William Ellison p. of Thomas Maddock of Chester, slater.
,, 8 Charles Fletcher, cordwainer, } ss. of Robert Fletcher of Chester, cordwainer, defunct.
,, 8 John Fletcher, cordwainer,
,, 8 John Meadowes, wetglover, s. of Samuel Meadowes of Chester, chandler, defunct.
,, 8 William Shone, silkweaver, s. of Thomas Shone of Chester, feltmaker, defunct.
,, 8 John Smith, feltmaker, s. of John Smith of Chester, feltmaker.
,, 8 John Urmston of Parkgate, co. Ches., periwigmaker, s. of Thomas Urmston of Chester, cooper, defunct.
,, 8 Joseph Peeres of Wrexham, co. Denbigh, cordwainer, s. of John Peeres of Chester, labourer.
,, 8 Hugh Jones, flaxdresser, s. of David Jones of Chester, flaxdresser.
,, 8 William Almond, silkweaver, s. of John Almond of Chester, yeoman, defunct.
,, 8 Thomas Minshull, barber, s. of John Minshull of Chester, saddler, defunct.
,, 8 Robert s. of Robert Lawrence of Chester, tailor, and p. of Richard Orme of Chester, tailor.
,, 8 John s. of Archibald Forrester of Chester, and p. of Jonathan Goldson of Chester, feltmaker.
,, 8 Thomas s. of Charles Orbistone of Chester, defunct, and p. of Thomas Cooper of Chester, tailor, defunct.
,, 8 Paul Roberts p. of Robert Bellin of Chester, cooper.

Aug. 8 Samuel Whitney, cooper, s. of Thomas Whitney of Chester, cooper, defunct.
,, 8 Thomas s. of Thomas Durbar of Chester, and p. of Hugh Jordan of Chester, bricklayer.
,, 8 William Harrison, cordwainer, s. of William Harrison of Chester, cooper, defunct.
,, 8 Daniel s. of John Partridge of Chester, carpenter, and p. of Richard Carr of Chester, flaxdresser, defunct.
,, 8 John Kessack p. of Daniel Woods of Chester, slater.
,, 8 Thomas s. of John Speed of Chester, labourer, defunct, and p. of John Maddock of Chester, slater.
,, 8 John Tottey, mercer, } ss. of Thomas Tottey of Holywell, co. Flint, chandler.
,, 8 Robert Tottey, apothecary,
,, 8 William Roberts, carpenter, s. of William Roberts of Chester, cabinetmaker.
,, 8 William s. of Josiah Crooke of Broughton, co. Flint, yeoman.
,, 8 William s. of William Seller of Milton Green, co. Chester, and p. of Samuel Davies of Chester, mason.
,, 8 William s. of Roger Mostyn of Handbridge, within the liberties of the city of Chester, labourer, and p. of Charles Whitehead of Chester, mason.
,, 8 William s. of William Tyrer of Chester, and p. of James Hickson of Chester, tailor.
,, 8 Richard Burroughs, flaxdresser, } ss. of Richard Burroughs of Chester, baker, defunct.
,, 8 Samuel Burroughs, baker,
,, 8 John Thornley, smith, s. of Hugh Thornley of Chester, smith, defunct.
,, 8 John s. of Thomas Jones of Handbridge, labourer, defunct, and p. of William Hickman of Chester, bricklayer, defunct.
,, 8 John s. of Ellen Hughes of Chester, widow, and p. of Hugh Jordan of Chester, bricklayer.
,, 8 Joseph Grice p. of William Harvey of Chester, bricklayer.
,, 8 John Meacock the younger s. of John Meacock of Chester, weaver.
,, 8 Thomas s. of Thomas Whitehead of Chester, husbandman, and p. of Thomas Maddock of Chester, slater.
,, 8 Samuel s. of Ralph Edge of Chester, husbandman, and p. of George Reece of Chester, butcher.

Aug. 8 James Hinckley, corkcutter, } ss. of George Hinckley of Chester, mason, defunct.
,, 8 George Hinckley, cooper,
,, 8 Thomas s. of Humphrey Edge of Handbridge, and p. of Thomas Harvey of Chester, bricklayer.
,, 8 Alexander s. of Alexander Mitchell of Chester, cordwainer, defunct, and p. of John Fletcher of Chester, cordwainer.
,, 8 Ralph Griffith, smith, s. of Peter Griffith of Chester, yeoman, defunct.
,, 8 John s. of William Griffith of Chester, mason, and p. of Thomas Cooke of Chester, tailor.
,, 8 Edward s. of George Cowley of Chester, labourer, and p. of Samuel Maddock of Chester, tailor.
,, 8 Henry Bayley p. of Thomas Bridge of Chester, feltmaker, defunct.
,, 8 Richard s. of Richard Wickstead of Macclesfield, co. Ches., glazier, defunct, and p. of John Davies of Chester, cordwainer.
†Robert Lucas, weaver.
,, 8 William s. of John Jones of Chester, cordwainer, and p. of John Croughton of Chester, cordwainer.
,, 8 Nicholas Cooper, cooper, s. of Nicholas Cooper of Chester, silkweaver, defunct.
,, 8 John s. and p. of Thomas Wilkinson of Chester, wheelwright.
,, 8 John Dutton the younger, joiner, s. of John Dutton of Chester, joiner.
,, 8 Edward s. of Thomas Edge of Chester, dyer, defunct.
,, 8 Peter Lee of Chester, corkcutter, p. of John Revington of Chester, tailor.
,, 8 John Calley, tailor, s. of William Calley of Chester, tailor, defunct.
,, 8 Robert s. of Thomas Lamb of Chester, ironmonger, and p. of Peter Darwell of Chester, feltmaker.
,, 8 Hugh Thornley, combmaker, s. of Hugh Thornley of Chester, smith, defunct.
,, 8 William s. of William Pemberton of Chester, yeoman, defunct, and p. of James Dewsbury of Chester, feltmaker, defunct.
,, 8 Thomas s. of Henry Clutton of Whitchurch, co. Salop, and p. of John Elcock of Chester, combmaker, defunct.
,, 8 Richard Woodfin, slater, s. of William Woodfin of Chester, slater, defunct.

Aug.	8	George Hunt, joiner, s. of George Hunt of Chester, yeoman, defunct.
,,	8	William Woodfin, joiner, s. of William Woodfin of Chester, slater, defunct.
,,	8	Roger s. of Charles Dawson of Coddington, co. Ches., smith, defunct, and p. of Thomas Briscoe, of Chester, smith.
,,	8	Roger s. of Roger Williams of Chester, mariner, defunct, and p. of Richard Humphreys of Chester, hornbreaker.
		Robert Lucas, weaver.[1]
,,	8	Randle Whittle, mariner, s. of Joseph Whittle of Chester, barber, defunct.
,,	8	Charles s. of Charles Roston of Eccleston, co. Ches., husbandman, defunct, and p. of Richard Dewsbury of Chester, feltmaker, defunct.
,,	8	Samuel Kelsall, corkcutter, s. of William Kelsall of Chester, tailor.
,,	8	George Vincent, smith, s. of Thomas Vincent of Chester, surgeon, defunct.
,,	8	Edward Burroughs, currier, s. of Richard Burroughs of Chester, baker, defunct.
,,	8	Thomas s. of Thomas Ellis of Chester, defunct, and p. of Richard Calley of Chester, weaver, defunct.
,,	8	Richard Golding, pipemaker, s. of John Golding of Chester, pipemaker.
,,	8	John Peeres, cordwainer, s. of John Peeres of Chester, labourer.
,,	9	Peter Griffith of Handbridge, husbandman, s. of John Griffith of Chester, cordwainer, defunct.
,,	9	Thomas s. of John Magarey, and p. of Henry Meacock of Chester, weaver.
,,	9	Samuel Woodfin, slater, } ss. of Edward Woodfin of
,,	9	Uriah Woodfin } Chester, slater.
,,	9	Edward Hughes of Wrexham, co. Denbigh, barber, p. of John Johnson of Chester, barber.
,,	9	John Lewis, pipemaker, s. of John Lewis of Chester, pipemaker.
,,	9	John Greenholgh, cordwainer, } ss. of John Greenholgh of Chester,
,,	9	Benjamin Greenholgh } wetglover.
,,	9	John Moore, cordwainer, s. of Theodore Moore of Chester, cooper.

[1] Duplicate entry; see earlier admission among those for August 8.

Aug. 9 John Heycock, feltmaker, s. of John Heycock of Chester, yeoman, defunct.
,, 9 Thomas Wilson, butcher, s. of William Wilson of Chester, butcher, defunct.
,, 9 John Joynson p. of Robert Gregge of Chester, cordwainer.
,, 9 Robert Skellington, tailor, s. of William Skellington of Chester, cordwainer.
,, 9 John Wakefield, slater, s. of Thomas Wakefield of Chester, slater.
,, 9 Peter Jones, pipemaker, s. of Peter Jones of Chester, woolcomber.
,, 9 Peter Oulfe, cordwainer, s. of Joseph Oulfe of Chester, baker, defunct.
,, 9 Thomas Foulkes, pipemaker, s. of Thomas Foulkes of Chester, carpenter.
,, 9 John Prince, cordwainer, } ss. of James Prince of
,, 9 George Prince } Chester, cordwainer.
,, 9 Samuel s. of Samuel Robinson of Little Neston, co. Ches., tailor, and p. of John Cotgreave of Chester, cordwainer.
,, 9 Samuel Jackson p. of John Platt of Chester, tailor, defunct.
,, 9 John s. of John Bavand of Gresford parish, co. Denbigh, yeoman, defunct, and p. of Robert Ogdain of Chester, bricklayer.
,, 9 Richard s. of Andrew Archer of Chester, and p. of John Pemberton of Chester, ropier.
,, 9 Thomas Crane, cordwainer, s. of John Crane of Chester, cordwainer.
,, 9 Thomas s. of John Kell of Chester, wheelwright, and p. of John Palin of Chester, cordwainer.
,, 9 Edward Calcott of Bangor, co. Flint, dyer, s. of John Calcott of Chester, joiner, defunct.
,, 9 Charles Panton, goldsmith, s. of Edward Panton of Chester, innholder.
,, 9 John Tylston, mason, s. of Thomas Tylston of Chester, bricklayer.
,, 9 Samuel s. of John Sparke of Broadlane, co. Flint, yeoman, defunct.
,, 9 Samuel Welsh, cordwainer, s. of Robert Welsh of Chester, maltster, defunct.
,, 9 Richard Calley, weaver, s. of Edward Calley of Chester, weaver.
,, 9 Christopher s. of Christopher Foreackers of Chester, yeoman, defunct, and p. of Joseph Sorton of Chester, wetglover.

Aug. 9 Joshua Dobb, glover, s. of John Dobb of Chester, glover, defunct.
„ 9 William s. of William Wathew of Willaston, co. Ches., yeoman, and p. of Robert Pyke of Chester, baker, defunct.
„ 9 John Adshead, barber, s. of John Adshead of Chester, cordwainer.
„ 9 Peter Hale, butcher, s. of William Hale of Chester, butcher, defunct.
„ 9 Thomas Golborn, pipemaker, s. of Noah Golborn of Chester, pipemaker.
„ 9 John s. of Thomas Sharrat of Chester, mason, defunct, and p. of John Dobb of Chester, cordwainer.
„ 9 John Lloyd p. of Zacheus Nicholls of Chester, cordwainer.
„ 9 Peter Shone, carpenter, s. of John Shone of Chester, weaver, defunct.
„ 9 John Warmingham, tailor, s. of William Warmingham of Chester, cordwainer, defunct.
„ 9 Henry Bennett, barber, s. of Samuel Bennet of Chester, maltster.
„ 9 Robert Gregg, gardener, s. of Robert Gregg of Chester, cordwainer.
„ 9 William s. of John Coddington, and p. of Thomas Sarratt of Chester, tailor.
„ 9 Thomas Thornley, smith, s. of Hugh Thornley of Chester, smith, defunct.
„ 9 Samuel s. of Randle Brookes of Handbridge, miller, defunct, and p. of William Ledsham of Chester, bricklayer.
„ 9 John Thomlinson, wheelwright, s. of William Thomlinson of Chester, yeoman, defunct.
„ 9 Samuel Mottershead, feltmaker, s. of Thomas Mottershead of Chester, innholder, defunct.
„ 9 Ralph Cotgreave, cordwainer, s. of John Cotgreave of Chester, cordwainer.
„ 9 Thomas Whitehead p. of Josiah Whitehead of Chester, mason.
„ 9 John s. of Thomas Pickmore of Chester, innholder, defunct.
„ 9 John Colecliffe, carpenter, s. of John Colecliffe of Chester, carpenter, defunct.
„ 9 John Palin p. of John Boswell of Chester, baker.
„ 9 Robert Barrat, barber, s. of William Barrat of Chester, cordwainer, defunct.

Aug. 9 Crispin Johnson, cordwainer, } ss. of William Johnson of Chester, cordwainer.
„ 9 William Johnson, cordwainer,
„ 9 Samuel Pickmore, weaver, s. of Thomas Pickmore of Chester, innholder, defunct.
„ 9 George Shone p. of Richard Clarkson of Chester, carpenter.
„ 9 John Oulfe, yeoman, s. of Robert Oulfe of Chester, feltmaker.
„ 9 Robert s. of John Griffies of Chester, plumber.
„ 9 John Maddock, cordwainer, s. of Paul Maddock of Chester, cordwainer, defunct.
„ 9 Thomas s. of John Burton of Nantwich, co. Ches., defunct, and p. of Richard Wrench of Chester, feltmaker.
„ 9 Daniel Potter, tailor, s. of Daniel Potter of Chester, tailor.
„ 9 William Yewd, joiner, s. of William Yewd of Chester, carpenter, defunct.
„ 9 Richard King, tobacconist.
„ 9 William Young, bricklayer, s. of Randle Young of Chester, bricklayer, defunct.
„ 9 Thomas Jordan, carpenter, s. of Francis Jordan of Chester, slater.
„ 9 Samuel Brock, brassfounder, s. of Richard Brock of Chester, carpenter.
„ 9 William Sherman, watchmaker, s. of William Sherman of Chester, cabinetmaker, defunct.
„ 9 Arthur Harvey, bricklayer, s. of Edward Harvey of Chester, bricklayer.
„ 9 Thomas Aires, gardener, } ss. of Samuel Aires of Chester, gardener.
„ 9 William Aires, baker,
„ 9 Richard Almond, feltmaker, s. of John Almond of Chester, yeoman, defunct, and p. of Peter Wrench, feltmaker.
„ 9 William Crookes, cutler, s. of Thomas Crookes of Chester, carpenter, defunct.
„ 9 Thomas s. of John Midless of Hawarden, co. Flint, yeoman, and p. of John Nevitt of Chester, chandler, defunct.
„ 9 Peter Trevor, wetglover, } ss. of William Trevor of Chester, wetglover, defunct.
„ 9 John Trevor, barber,
„ 9 Thomas Hampton, yeoman, s. of Thomas Hampton of Handley, co. Chester, cordwainer.
„ 9 Philip s. of Jonathan Bostock of Chester, ironmonger.

[1732] THE CITY OF CHESTER

Aug. 9 Josiah Richardson, watchmaker, s. of Josiah Richardson of Chester, farrier, defunct.
,, 9 Thomas Brown, wheelwright, s. of Anthony Brown of Chester, yeoman.
,, 9 Thomas s. of John Kemp of Chester, cutler, defunct.
,, 9 Peter s. of Peter Joynson of Aldford, co. Ches., and p. of William Cooke of Chester, printer.
,, 9 Richard Shone, ironmonger, s. of John Shone of Chester, weaver, defunct.
,, 9 Joseph Buckley, butcher, s. of Edward Buckley of Chester, smith, defunct.
,, 9 John Johnson, cordwainer, s. of William Johnson of Chester, cordwainer.
,, 9 Thomas Collins, baker, s. of Humphrey Collins of Chester, glazier.
,, 9 Peter s. of Thomas Waters of Chester, tailor.
,, 9 John Adams, printer, s. of Roger Adams of Chester, printer.
,, 9 Edward Walmsey, barber, s. of Edward Walmsey of Chester, slater, defunct.
,, 9 William Prestbury, wetglover, s. of Samuel Prestbury of Chester, wetglover, defunct.
,, 9 John Meredith, tinplateworker, s. of John Meredith of Chester, sawyer.
,, 9 William Crane, cordwainer, } ss. of John Crane of
,, 9 Edward Crane, cordwainer, } Chester, cordwainer.
,, 9 Thomas s. of William Higginson of Chester, innholder.
,, 9 Thomas Ledsham, bookseller, s. of Thomas Ledsham of Chester, tailor.
,, 9 John } ss. of Robert Pulford of Chester, butcher.
,, 9 Robert }
,, 9 John Darwell, feltmaker, s. of Peter Darwell of Chester, feltmaker.
  †John Boswell the younger.
,, 9 John Wright, tailor, s. of Thomas Wright of Chester, tailor.
,, 9 William s. of William Crue of Chester, ironmonger.
  †John Kelley, cordwainer.
,, 9 Thomas s. of William Yewd of Chester, carpenter, defunct.
,, 9 William s. of Isaac Faulkner of Chester, warehouse-keeper.
,, 9 William Tapley, cooper, s. of Henry Tapley of Chester, cooper, defunct.
,, 9 Thomas Hickson, tailor, s. of James Hickson of Chester, tailor.

Aug. 9 Robert Finchatt, vintner, s. of John Finchatt of Chester, barber, defunct.
,, 9 George Crookes, watchmaker, s. of Thomas Crookes of Chester, carpenter, defunct.
,, 12 Richard Griffies of Middlewich, co. Ches., smith, s. of John Griffies of Chester, plumber.
,, 12 William Ellis of Cornist, co. Flint, gentleman, s. of Edward Ellis of Chester, ironmonger, defunct.
,, 12 Thomas Wallworth, tailor, s. of Thomas Wallworth of Puddington, co. Ches., tanner.
,, 12 William s. and p. of Samuel Dennil of Chester, mason, defunct.
,, 12 Robert Hammond of Ness, co. Ches., and s. of Edward Hammond of Chester, baker.
,, 9 Joseph Bellin of Thornton Hough, co. Ches., gentleman, s. of Joseph Bellin of Chester, ironmonger, defunct.
,, 12 Thomas Smith of Ince, s. of John Ince [sic] of Chester, silkweaver.
,, 12 Samuel Smith of Stanney, s. of the above John Smith.
,, 12 Roger Sadler, baker, s. of Samuel Sadler of Tarvin, co. Ches., ironmonger, defunct.
,, 12 Joseph s. of Michael Atkinson of Chester, husbandman, and p. of William Johnson of Chester, wetglover, defunct.
,, 12 Thomas Roberts, mason, s. of Thomas Roberts of Chester, mason, defunct.
,, 12 Samuel Maddock of Mould, co. Flint, flaxdresser, s. of Nathan Maddock of Chester, flaxdresser, defunct.
,, 12 John Craven, tanner, s. of Daniel Craven of Bunbury, co. Ches., tanner.
,, 12 John Hiccocks, barber, s. of Thomas Hiccocks of Chester, barber, defunct.
,, 12 James Maddock of Holt, } ss. of John Maddock of
,, 12 Edward Maddock of Holt, } Chester, tanner, defunct.
,, 12 Samuel Collins, glazier, s. of Humphrey Collins of Chester, glazier.
,, 18 James s. of John Goolding, pipemaker, and p. of Richard Golding of Chester, pipemaker, defunct.
,, 18 Thomas Jellicoe, cordwainer, s. of John Jellicoe of Chester, cordwainer.
,, 18 John Hand, cordwainer, s. of John Hand of Chester, cordwainer, defunct.
,, 18 Thomas Jones of Manchester p. of Joseph Smith of Chester, feltmaker.

Aug.	18	Thomas s. of John Porter, defunct, and p. of Andrew Duke of Chester, wetglover.
„	18	Peter Hall of Holme, co. Ches., and p. of Joseph Sorton the elder of Chester, wetglover.
„	18	Joseph Skellern of Frodsham, co. Ches., yeoman, s. of Thomas Skellern of Barrow, co. Ches., defunct.
„	18	Samuel Spruce of Manchester s. of Samuel Spruce, defunct, and p. of William Johnson of Chester, cordwainer.
„	18	Richard s. of Roger Parker of Barton, co. Ches., butcher, and p. of Michael Bromley of Chester, butcher.
„	19	James Gilbert, yeoman, ⎫ ss. of James Gilbert of Shot-
„	19	Thomas Gilbert, glover, ⎭ wick, co. Ches., chandler.
„	19	Paul Nicholls, corkcutter, ⎫ ss. of John Nicholls of
„	19	Peter Nicholls, corkcutter, ⎭ Chester, chandler, defunct.
„	19	John Dannat of Poolton, co. Ches., yeoman, s. of John Dannat of Kinnerton, co. Ches., yeoman, defunct.
„	19	John Massie, pipemaker, s. of John Massie of Chester, pipemaker.
„	19	Ralph Dutton, joiner, s. of John Dutton of Chester, joiner.
„	19	Richard Griffith of Chester p. of George Boswell of Chester, pavier.
„	19	John s. of John Ashton, bricklayer, and p. of Benjamin Maddock of Chester, tailor.
„	19	John Tapley, tailor, s. of Jonathan Tapley of Chester, cordwainer, defunct.
„	19	Robert Johnson of Hawarden, co. Flint, s. of Thomas Johnson of the same, dyer, defunct.
„	19	Thomas Watmough of Brimstage, co. Ches., s. of Thomas Watmough of Beckett, co. Ches., yeoman, defunct.
„	19	Daniel s. of Nathaniel Ashbrooke of Chester, wheelwright, and p. of William Ball of Chester, baker.
„	19	Samuel Kerfoot p. of Samuel Tonna of Chester, butcher.
„	19	William Thomlinson of Neston, co. Ches., saddler, s. of William Thomlinson of Chester, yeoman, defunct.
„	19	Charles Walley of Belgreave, co. Ches., yeoman, s. of John Walley of Chester, tanner.
„	19	George s. and p. of Edward Pickford of Chester, bricklayer, defunct.
„	19	Joseph Wright, woolcomber, s. of Joseph Wright of Chester, tanner, defunct.

Aug. 19 Edward s. of William Parry of Holywell, co. Flint, bricklayer.
„ 19 Owen s. of Owen Hughes of Holywell, co. Flint, saddler, defunct.
„ 19 Francis Massie of Aldford, co. Chester, s. of Francis Massie of Chester, yeoman, defunct.
„ 19 Henry Mostyn of Mould, co. Flint, p. of John Thomas of Chester, saddler, defunct.
„ 19 Thomas Thomason, brewer, s. of Richard Thomason of Chester, glazier, defunct.
„ 19 Ambrose Evans, glass-grinder, s. of Edward Evans of Chester, glazier, defunct.
„ 21 Thomas Poole of Northwich, co. Ches., p. of John Dewsbury of Chester, feltmaker, defunct.
„ 21 John Johnson of Liverpool, feltmaker, s. of Edward Johnson of Chester, feltmaker.
„ 23 John Massie, gentleman, s. of Trafford Massie, esquire, mayor of Chester.
„ 23 Thomas Parker, apothecary, s. of John Parker of Chester, apothecary and alderman.
„ 23 Thomas } ss. of Thomas Brock of Chester, alderman.
„ 23 John
„ 29 Henry s. of John Pemberton of Chester, alderman.
„ 29 William s. of Nathan Wright of Chester, ironmonger.
„ 23 John Pyke, baker, s. of Robert Pyke of Chester, baker, defunct.
„ 23 Edward Burrowes, feltmaker, s. of Henry Burrowes of Chester, feltmaker.
„ 23 John Johnson, apothecary, s. of William Johnson of Chester, wetglover, defunct.
„ 23 James Bromley, apothecary, s. of Edward Bromley of Chester, baker, defunct.
„ 23 Simon Lloyd of Broughton, co. Flint, s. of Edward Lloyd of Chester, linendraper, defunct.
„ 23 Samuel s. of Collins Pendlebury of Chester, wetglover, defunct.
„ 26 John Richardson, cordwainer, s. of Thomas Richardson of Broadlane, co. Flint, yeoman, defunct.
„ 26 John s. of Thomas Ley of Chester, cordwainer, defunct.
„ 26 George Hewitt, pipemaker, s. of George Hewitt of Chester, slater, defunct.
„ 26 Thomas Buckley, cordwainer, s. of Francis Buckley of Chester, cordwainer, defunct.
„ 26 William s. of Benjamin Sudlow, defunct, and p. of Richard Humphreys of Chester, hornbreaker.

[1732] THE CITY OF CHESTER 297

Aug. 26 Charles Dod, baker, s. of Joshua Dod of Chester, baker, defunct.
,, 26 Roger Woodfin p. of Peter Woods of Chester, feltmaker, defunct.
,, 26 Thomas Wright, tailor, s. of Thomas Wright of Chester, tailor.
,, 26 George Walley of Tarpourley, co. Ches., cooper, s. of John Walley of Chester, tanner, defunct.
,, 28 Robert s. of Roger Fisher of Plimyard in Wirrall, co. Ches., yeoman, and p. of John Briscoe of Chester, barber.
,, 30 Thomas s. of Mary Gough, widow, defunct, and p. of Thomas Roughley of Chester, joiner.
,, 31 John s. of John Lockett of Chester, labourer, defunct, and p. of Richard Bathoe of Chester, bricklayer, defunct.
Sep. 1 Robert Massie, clerk, s. of Trafford Massie, esquire, mayor of the city.
,, 1 *Peter Leigh, gentleman.
,, 1 *Robert Pace.
,, 1 *Gilbert Rimmer.
,, 1 *Edward Williams.
,, 1 Josiah Moores p. of George Taylor of Gloverstone, co. Ches., tailor.
,, 2 *Thomas s. and p. of Henry Meacock of Chester, weaver.
,, 2 Jonathan Haswell of Kinnerton, locksmith, s. of Jonathan Haswell of Chester, cooper.
,, 2 Francis Buckley, smith, s of Francis Buckley of Chester, cordwainer, defunct.
,, 2 William Moyle, milner, of Wrexham parish, co. Denbigh, s. of Randle Moyle of Shocklach, co. Chester, gentleman, defunct.
,, 2 Thomas Sampson of Middlewich, co. Ches., surgeon, s. and p. of Thomas Sampson of Chester, periwigmaker, defunct.
,, 2 John s. of John Almond, defunct, and p. of Thomas Littler the younger, of Chester, cordwainer.
,, 2 William Morris of Gadlis, co. Flint, p. of William Jackson of Chester, bricklayer, defunct.
,, 2 Edward Bridge, gentleman, ⎫ ss. of Thomas Bridge
,, 2 Thomas Bridge, feltmaker, ⎬ of Chester, feltmaker,
,, 2 John Bridge, upholsterer, ⎭ defunct.
,, 2 Charles Broster, goldsmith, s. of Charles Broster of Chester, gentleman, defunct.

Sep. 2 John Price of Llangollen, co. Denbigh, p. of John Thomas of Chester, saddler, defunct.
,, 2 *Jonathan Hill, carpenter.
,, 2 Thomas Pate of Gresford parish, co. Denbigh, s. of Thomas Pate of Chester, butcher, defunct.
,, 2 Gilbert Reynolds of Middlewich, co. Ches., cordwainer,
,, 2 Humphrey Reynolds of Middlewich, co. Ches., tailor,
} ss. of Gilbert Reynolds of Chester, shoemaker, defunct.
,, 9 Thomas Wilbraham, barber, s. of Roger Wilbraham of Chester, chandler.
,, 9 John Rea, tailor, s. of John Rea of Bromboro, co. Ches., tailor.
,, 9 Robert Robinson, tanner, s. of Peter Robinson of Chester, tanner.
,, 9 John Robinson of Frodsham, co. Ches., cordwainer, p. of John Usher of Chester, cordwainer.
,, 9 John Stretch of Whitchurch, co. Salop, p. of James Baguley of Chester, turner.
,, 9 Robert Clarkson, carpenter, s. of Richard Clarkson of Chester, carpenter.
,, 9 Richard Lloyd, gentleman,
,, 9 Thomas Lloyd,
} ss. of Thomas Lloyd, clerk of the Prentice.
,, 9 Collins Pendlebury of Liverpool, cabinetmaker, s. of Collins Pendlebury of Chester, wetglover, defunct.
,, 14 George Mainwaring, gentleman,
,, 14 Robert Mainwaring,
} ss. of James Mainwaring of Chester, alderman.
,, 14 Edmund Bolland, mercer, s. of Thomas Bolland of Chester, alderman.
,, 14 William Warrington, gentleman, s. of John Warrington, of Chester, alderman.
,, 14 Thomas Hinckes, merchant, s. of Edward Hinckes of Chester, linendraper.
,, 14 John Wrench, watchmaker, s. of Richard Wrench of Chester, gentleman.
,, 14 Richard Bowcock, gentleman, s. of Richard Bowcock of Chester, yeoman, defunct.
,, 14 Nathaniel
,, 14 William
} ss. of Joseph Philpott of Chester, silkweaver, defunct.
,, 14 Joseph Chamberlain, ironmonger, s. of Thomas Chamberlain of Saughall, co. Ches., gentleman.
,, 14 Henry Leckonby, merchant,
,, 14 Peter Leckonby, merchant,
} ss. of Peter Leckonby of Chester, merchant.

[1732] THE CITY OF CHESTER 299

Sep. 14 John s. of Richard Penkett of Chester, ironmonger.
,, 14 John Orange, linendraper, s. of Samuel Orange of Chester, gentleman.
,, 14 William Whitfield, ironmonger, s. of James Whitfield of Chester, ironmonger, defunct.
,, 14 John Witter, apothecary, } ss. of William Witter of Chester, wetglover.
,, 14 William Witter, wetglover,
,, 14 Thomas Witter,
,, 14 William s. of John Bristoe of Chester, maltster.
,, 14 Joseph Clubb, ironmonger, s. of John Clubb of Chester, ironmonger, defunct.
,, 14 Thomas Bolland, joiner, s. of Thomas Bolland of Chester, joiner.
,, 14 John Davies, baker, } ss. of Edward Davies of Chester, yeoman.
,, 14 Joseph Davies,
,, 14 Charles Moyle, yeoman, s. of Randle Moyle of Shocklach, co. Ches., yeoman, defunct.
,, 14 Joseph } ss. of Joseph Smith of Chester, feltmaker.
,, 14 William
,, 14 Griffith Biggins, upholsterer, s. of John Biggins of Chester, innholder, defunct.
,, 14 William Litherland, tailor, s. of Edward Litherland of Chester, tailor, defunct.
,, 14 John s. of John Barrow of Ma———, feltmaker.
,, 14 William Barrow ———.
,, 14 William Wrench, feltmaker, s. of ——— feltmaker, defunct.
,, 14 William Rathbone p. of John Francis of Chester, ironmonger.
,, 14 Edward Williams of Liverpool p. of William Shephard of Chester, weaver.
,, 14 Richard Ward, gentleman, s. of Richard Ward of Chester, gentleman.
,, 16 Robert Patton of Warrington, co. Lanc., grocer, s. of Thomas Patton of ———ington in the same county, grocer.
,, 16 John Hampton, cordwainer, ——— of ———n Green, co. Ches., cordwainer.
,, 16 Thomas Linneall [s. of] ——— Lyneall of Farndon, co. Ches., yeoman, and [p. of] William Briscoe of Chester, baker.
,, 16 William Tristram, apothecary, s. of John Tristram of Chester, apothecary.
,, 18 Samuel Kirkes, upholsterer, s. of Samuel Kirkes of Chester, upholsterer.

Sep. 18 Thomas Almond, butcher, s. of James Almond of Chester, butcher.
„ 19 William Woods, mason, s. of William Woods.
Thomas Edwards, gentleman.
Robert [Battrick ?] gentleman.
Joseph [Carter ?] cordwainer.
Thomas Wilbraham, surgeon.
William Almond, butcher.
John Roberts, watchmaker.
Joseph Bennet, yeoman.
Hugh Thomason, gentleman.
Robert Millington, joiner.
John Page.
Thomas Roberts, mercer.
Charles Boswell, pavier.
„ 30 Ralph Holland, draper, s. of Ralph Holland, late of Chester and now of Hull, co. ——, draper.
„ 30 Thomas Hiccocke, mariner, s. of Thomas Hiccocke of Chester, barber, defunct.
„ 30 Ralph Williams, cordwainer, s. of Thomas Williams of Barrow, co. Chester, cordwainer.
„ 30 Charles Salisbury, mariner, s. of Charles Salisbury of Parkgate, co. Chester, defunct.
„ 30 Fulk Salisbury of Parkgate, co. Chester, mariner, s. of George Salisbury of Parkgate, mariner, defunct.
„ 30 Richard s. of Patrick Fitzgerrald, and p. of Griffith Knowles of Chester, cordwainer.
„ 30 William s. of William Usher of Burton, co. Denbigh, yeoman, defunct, and p. of John Sparrow of Chester, surgeon, defunct.
Oct. 2 Thomas s. of Joseph Spencer of Whitegate parish, co. Chester, yeoman, and p. of John Revington of Chester, tailor.
„ 2 Samuel Anley of London, tailor, p. of Thomas Harrison of Chester, tailor.
„ 3 Joseph Allcock, smith, s. of Joseph Allcock of Chester, smith.
„ 3 Robert Harvey, barber, s. of Edward Harvey of Chester, bricklayer.
„ 3 Thomas s. of Thomas Posnett of Chester, cordwainer, and p. of John Ravenscroft of Chester, cordwainer, defunct.
„ 3 Thomas s. of Thomas Smith, defunct, and p. of Thomas Molyneux of Chester, cordwainer.
„ 3 Richard Hughes, bricklayer, s. of William Hughes of Chester, bricklayer.

Oct.	3	James Grundy of London, leatherseller, s. of Richard Grundy of Chester, smith, defunct.
,,	4	Alexander } ss. of Alexander Denton of Chester, alder-
,,	4	Arthur } man, defunct.
,,	4	Samuel Cotgreave of London, cordwainer, s. of Jonathan Cotgreave of Chester, brewer, defunct.
,,	4	Hugh Diason of London, tailor, } ss. of Samuel Diason of Chester, glover, defunct.
,,	4	John Diason of London, cabinetmaker.
,,	4	Mathias Clayton of London, tailor, s. of John Clayton of Chester, tailor.
,,	4	Hugh Farrington, mariner, s. of Robert Farrington of Chester, innholder, defunct.
,,	4	Thomas Stapleton, mariner, s. of Thomas Stapleton of Chester, gentleman, defunct.
,,	4	William Higginson, glazier, s. of William Higginson of Chester, innholder.
,,	4	John Rider, barber, s. of John Rider of Chester, tailor.
,,	4	John Parks of Manchester, weaver, s. of Josiah Parks of Chester, weaver.
,,	4	John s. of William Usher of Burton, co. Denbigh, yeoman, defunct, and p. of William Cowper of Chester, surgeon.
,,	4	Thomas Reece of London, barber, s. of Giles Reece of Chester, barber, defunct.
,,	4	Richard Phillips of London s. of Thomas Phillips, defunct, and p. of Robert Pyke of Chester, barber, defunct.
,,	4	Alexander s. of Thomas Ridley of Chester, apothecary, defunct.
,,	4	William Wall of London p. of Francis Ireland of Chester, cordwainer, defunct.
,,	4	James Betty of Liverpool, co. Lanc., tailor, s. of Andrew Betty of Chester, tailor, defunct.
,,	5	Edward Walton, chandler, s. of Samuel Walton of Chester, chandler, defunct.
,,	5	William s. of John Poval of Chester, yeoman, defunct, and p. of John Tunnall of Chester, cordwainer, defunct.
,,	5	Aaron Andrew of London, cordwainer, s. of Abel Andrew of Chester, carpenter, defunct.
,,	5	Joseph Whittle, barber, s. of Joseph Whittle of Chester, barber, defunct.
,,	5	Richard Johnson of London, gentleman, s. of George Johnson of Chester, glazier, defunct.

Oct. 5 John Potter, mercer, s. of Samuel Potter of Chester, tailor, defunct.

„ 5 Thomas Hatton, feltmaker, s. of William Hatton of Chester, feltmaker.

„ 5 Richard Barlow of London s. of Richard Barlow, defunct, and p. of William Adshead of Chester, cordwainer.

„ 5 Thomas Kelsall of Liverpool, co. Lanc., cooper, s. of John Kelsall of Chester, linendraper, defunct.

„ 5 James s. of James Kennant of Chester, innholder, defunct.

„ 5 John Sadler of Tarvin, co. Chester, periwigmaker, s. of Samuel Sadler of Tarvin, grocer, defunct.

„ 5 John Davies of Nantwich, co. Chester, ironmonger, s. of David Davies of Chester, vintner, defunct.

„ 5 William Rice of London p. of Stephen Sone of Chester, ironmonger.

„ 5 Charles Ince, gentleman, s. of William Ince of Chester, gentleman.

„ 5 John Revington, corkcutter, s. of John Revington of Chester, tailor.

„ 5 James Ewede of London p. of Stephen Sone of Chester, periwigmaker.

„ 6 John Golborn, gentleman, s. of John Golborne of Chester, alderman, defunct.

„ 6 Edward William [sic] of London, gentleman, s. of John Williams of Chester.

„ 6 Hugh s. of Owen Hughes, late of Holywell, co. Flint, saddler.

„ 6 John Beeby of Chelsea s. of Thomas Beeby of Chester, labourer, defunct.

„ 6 Robert Foulkes, mariner, s. of Randle Foulkes, late of Chester, clothworker.

„ 6 Samuel Griffith of London, periwigmaker, s. of Thomas Griffith of Chester, vintner, defunct.

„ 6 Thomas Ley, surgeon,
„ 6 Samuel Ley, periwig- } ss. of Edward Ley of Chester, maker, surgeon.

„ 6 Robert Key of Dublin, weaver, s. of Robert Key of Chester, brewer, defunct.

„ 6 William Goodacre of London, gentleman, s. of William Goodacre of Chester, gentleman, defunct.

„ 6 John Darlington, mariner, s. of John Darlington of Chester, mariner, defunct.

„ 6 Samuel Farrington of London, feltmaker, s. of Robert Farrington of Chester, innholder, defunct.

Oct.	6	Thomas s. of Richard Stevenson of Chester, apothecary.
,,	6	William Wilson, butcher, s. of William Wilson of Chester, butcher, defunct.
,,	6	John Anderson of London p. of Edward Davies of Chester, turner, defunct.
,,	6	Roland Carden of London p. of Thomas Bridge of Chester, feltmaker, defunct.
,,	6	Thomas Orme of London p. of Thomas Orme of Chester, tobacco cutter, defunct.
,,	6	John Parry of Newcastle, co. Staffs., p. of John Jennions of Chester, feltmaker, defunct.
,,	6	Aston } ss. of William Johnson of Chester, wetglover,
,,	6	John } defunct.
,,	7	Thomas Thomason of Middlewich, co. Chester, gentleman, s. of John Thomason of the same, gentleman, defunct.
,,	7	Thomas Nicholls of London, cordwainer, s. of Samuel Nicholls of Chester, butcher.
,,	7	Robert Oulfe of London, whipmaker, s. of Robert Oulfe of Chester, feltmaker.
,,	7	Samuel Lowndes of London s. of Robert Lowndes of Chester, mercer, defunct.
,,	7	Richard s. of John Jones of Mould, co. Flint, tanner.
,,	7	Richard } ss. of Thomas Duke of Chester, wetglover.
,,	7	Thomas }
,,	7	James Bushell of London, cordwainer, } ss. of Richard Bushell, late of Chester and now of London, cordwainer.
,,	7	Richard Bushell of London, cordwainer, }
,,	7	Richard Jones of Beumaris p. of Henry Jones of Chester, saddler, defunct.
,,	7	Samuel Haynes of Newcastle-on-Tyne s. of Samuel Haynes of Wrexham, and p. of John Tunnall of Chester, cordwainer, defunct.
,,	7	Edward s. of Edward Powell of Stretton, co. Chester, yeoman, and p. of Robert Bowyer of Chester, baker.
,,	7	William Briscoe, smith, s. of Richard Briscoe of Chester, smith.
,,	7	Joseph Witter, wetglover, s. of William Witter of Chester, wetglover.
,,	7	John Maddock of Shrewsbury, co. Salop, goldsmith, s. of John Maddock of Chester, tanner, defunct.
,,	7	James Kennerley of Nantwich, co. Chester, mercer, p. of John Holland of Chester, draper, defunct.
,,	7	Mathias Hayes of London, cordwainer, s. of Mathias Hayes of Chester, cordwainer, defunct.

Oct. 7 Thomas Meredith of Daresbury, co. Chester, yeoman, s. of John Meredith of Chester, mason, defunct.
,, 9 Philip Bryen of London p. of Edmund Mathews of Chester, cordwainer, defunct.
,, 9 John Whittle of London, silk dyer, s. of Joseph Whittle of Chester, barber, defunct.
,, 9 Edward Dod of London, upholsterer, s. of Thomas Dod of Chester, brewer.
,, 9 Thomas Woodward of London, joiner, s. of Joseph Woodward of Chester, joiner.
,, 9 Francis Shawcross of London, tailor, s. of Robert Shawcross, late of Chester and now of London, tailor.
,, 9 John Ratcliffe of Plimouth, mariner, s. of Benjamin Ratcliffe of Chester, ironmonger, defunct.
,, 9 Robert Hankey of London s. of Thomas Hankey of Chester, innholder.
,, 9 Benjamin Maddock of Elsmere, flaxdresser, s. of Nathan Maddock of Chester, flaxdresser, defunct.
,, 9 John Newton of Warwick p. of Richard Rylands of Chester, cordwainer.
,, 9 Joseph Dennil, barber, s. of Joseph Dennil of Chester, glazier.
,, 9 George Johnson of Plimouth, mariner, s. of John Johnson of Chester, chandler, defunct.
,, 10 Gerrard Jordan of Chester p. of Richard Ledsham of Chester, slater, defunct.
,, 10 Salusbury Lloyd of London, esquire, s. of John Lloyd of Chester, esquire, defunct.
,, 10 Samuel Leche, gentleman, s. of Charles Leche of Chester, mercer, defunct.
,, 10 John Rogers of Preston, cabinetmaker,
,, 10 Richard Rogers of Preston, buttonmaker,
} ss. of Robert Rogers of Preston, co. Lanc., cabinetmaker.
,, 10 Robert Ingham of Dublin, cabinetmaker, s. of William Ingham of Chester, cabinetmaker, defunct.
,, 10 Thomas s. of John Finchatt, yeoman, defunct, and p. of Richard Thomason of Chester, currier, defunct.
,, 10 John }
,, 10 Peter } ss. of Charles Warmingham of Chester, surgeon, defunct.
,, 10 William Shelley of London p. of Nathaniel Smith of Chester, baker, defunct.
,, 10 Henry Hough of Chester p. of Peter Wrench of Chester, feltmaker, defunct.

Oct.	10	Edward Davies of London, barber, s. of Edward Davies of Chester, clothworker.
,,	10	Thomas Morris of London, periwigmaker, s. of Thomas Morris of Chester, yeoman, defunct.
,,	10	Thomas Bromley of London, baker, s. of Edward Bromley of Chester, baker, defunct.
,,	10	Timothy Gardner of London, stockingweaver, s. of Timothy Gardner of Chester, goldsmith, defunct.
,,	10	Edward Foulkes, gentleman, s. of Edward Foulkes of Chester, gentleman, defunct.
,,	10	Hamlet Gilbody of Manchester, fustianmaker, s. of Jonathan Gilbody of Chester, confectioner, defunct.
,,	10	William Wilkinson of London p. of John Tunnall of Chester, cordwainer, defunct.
,,	12	William Gamull, esquire, s. of William Gamull of Chester, esquire, defunct.
,,	12	Peter Cowper, clerk, } ss. of John Cooper of Middlewich, co. Chester, clerk, defunct.
,,	12	Edmund Cooper, gentleman,
,,	12	Thomas Hodgskinson, mercer, s. of John Mercer [sic] of Eccleston, co. Lanc., clerk.
,,	12	Abner Gilbody of Manchester s. of Jonathan Gilbody of Chester, confectioner, defunct.
,,	12	Henry Walley of Pemberton, co. Lanc., s. of Ralph Walley of Chester, goldsmith, defunct.
,,	12	Thomas s. of John Tylston of Chester, carver, defunct.
,,	12	John Townsend, gentleman, s. of Gerrard Townsend of Christleton, co. Chester, esquire, defunct.
,,	12	Joseph Pownall p. of John Towsey of Chester, feltmaker.
,,	12	John s. of John Whitbey of Chester, innholder.
,,	12	Peter s. of William Rimmer, labourer, defunct, and p. of Joseph Roydon of Chester, bricklayer, defunct.
,,	12	Samuel Swinton of Liverpool, merchant, s. of John Swinton of Knutsford, co. Chester, gentleman, defunct.
,,	12	Samuel Leconby of London, jeweller, s. of Peter Leconby of Chester, merchant.
,,	12	Peter Nicholls of London, leather seller, } ss. of William Nicholls of Chester, clothworker, defunct.
,,	12	Samuel Nicholls of London, leather seller,
,,	12	John Ingham of Dublin, cabinetmaker, s. of William Ingham of Chester, cabinetmaker, defunct.
,,	12	Richard Williamson of Liverpool, watchmaker, s. of Richard Williamson of Chester, barber chirurgeon, defunct.

Oct. 12 Randle Hallet, dyer, s. of Joseph Hallet of Chester, jerseycomber.
„ 12 Robert s. of Thomas Dutton of Willaston, co. Chester, yeoman, and p. of Thomas Jones of Chester, butcher.
„ 12 John s. of Thomas Middlehurst of Christleton, co. Chester, and p. of Peter Leadbeater of Chester, brewer, defunct.
„ 12 Richard Pigot of Bristol, merchant, s. of Robert Pigot of Chester, alderman.
„ 12 Ralph Holland, painter, s. of Thomas Holland of Chester, barber.
„ 12 Richard Porter of London p. of Thomas Holland of Chester, barber.
„ 12 William Cranwell of London, periwigmaker, p. of Stephen Sone of Chester, periwigmaker.
„ 12 Isaac Thomas, hornbreaker, s. of Isaac Thomas of Chester, carpenter, defunct.
„ 12 John Craven of London, grocer, p. of William Cockayne of Chester, ironmonger, defunct.
„ 12 John Williams of Holyhead, co. Anglesey, p. of William Goodwin of Chester, ironmonger.
„ 12 John Foulkes of Wedgebury, co. Staffs., nailer, s. of Randle Foulkes of Chester, clothworker, defunct.
„ 12 Richard Lawrence of Bristol, upholsterer, s. of Richard Lawrence of Chester, tailor.
„ 12 George Brown of London, barber, s. of Charles Brown of Chester, draper, defunct.
„ 12 John Wilkinson, mariner, s. of Stephen Wilkinson of Chester, mariner.
„ 12 Thomas s. of Thomas Ley of Chester, cordwainer, defunct.
„ 12 John s. of Samuel Walmsley of Chester, slater.
„ 12 Charles Fletcher of Shrewsbury, clothworker, s. of William Fletcher of Chester, mason, defunct.
„ 12 William Hadley of Birmingham p. of Francis Sayer of Chester, plumber, defunct.
„ 12 Michael Jones of London p. of James Mottershead of Chester, barber.
„ 12 Roger s. of Thomas Woods of Broughton, co. Lanc., yeoman, and p. of William Clayton of Liverpool, merchant.
„ 12 Prenton Hancock, apothecary, s. of William Hancock of Parkgate, co. Chester, mariner, defunct.
„ 12 John Dyason of Birmingham, whitesmith, s. of Richard Dyason of Chester, turner, defunct.

Oct. 12 William Dyason of Warden, co. Warwick, yeoman, s. of Samuel Dyason of Chester, wetglover, defunct.
,, 12 Robert Frodsham, clerk, s. of Henry Frodsham of Chester, surgeon.
,, 12 William Lee of Birmingham p. of Jonathan Goldson of Chester, feltmaker, defunct.
,, 12 William Bellin, mariner, s. of Joseph Bellin of Thornton Hough, co. Chester, yeoman, defunct.
,, 12 Samuel Marsh of Bristol, glassgrinder, s. of Moses Marsh of Chester, haberdasher, defunct.
,, 12 Thomas Scott of Bristol, cordwainer, s. of Richard Scott of Chester, carpenter.
,, 12 John Cotgreave of Stone, co. Staffs., butcher, s. of Benjamin Cotgreave of Chester, chandler, defunct.
,, 12 Thomas Davies of Church Minshull, co. Chester, yeoman, s. of John Davies of Chester, yeoman, defunct.
,, 12 William Croughton of Bristol, joiner, s. of Michael Croughton of Chester, joiner, defunct.
,, 12 Hugh Hand of Bristol, corkcutter, s. of Stephen Hand of Chester, turner, defunct.
,, 12 Richard Bevan, weaver, s. of William Bevan of Chester, maltster, defunct.
,, 12 Thomas Moreton of Wenlock, co. Salop, mercer, p. of Samuel Bradburn of Chester, ironmonger.
,, 12 Samuel Rylance of Knutsford, co. Chester, yeoman, s. of Samuel Rylance of Chester, yeoman, defunct.
Robert Bellin, cooper, s. of Robert Bellin of Chester, cooper.
Thomas Gerrard, flaxdresser.
Thomas Robinson, mariner.
Robert Whittle, mariner.
Anthony Harrison, gentleman.
John Durbar, cabinetmaker.
William Briscoe.
Aquila Davenport, brewer.
William Williams, wetglover.
Richard Porter, barber.
Thomas Adshead, mariner.
George Salusbury, mariner.
John Blakemore, saddler.

1732-3 [6-7 G. ii.] GEORGE JOHNSON, Esquire, Mayor.

Jan. 20 Thomas s. of ——— Calkin of Waverton, co. Chester, gentleman, and p. of Edward ——— of Chester, cabinetmaker, defunct.
,, 20 Matthew s. of James Bayley of Wistaston, co. Chester, esquire, and p. of Henry Bennett of Chester, alderman.
,, 23 Benjamin s. of John Wilson of Over Kellett, co. Lanc., gentleman, defunct, and p. of John Marsden of Chester, merchant.
,, 26 Thomas Davies, silkweaver, s. of Samuel Davies of Chester, gentleman.
Mar. 17 Thomas s. of William Harrison of Chester, ropier, and p. of Richard Carr of Chester, flaxdresser, defunct.
,, 20 Phillip Cooper, baker, s. of Phillip Cooper of Chester, carver, defunct.
,, 20 John Bullock p. of Peter Parry of Chester, feltmaker.
May 28 Thomas s. of Thomas Harvey of Hargrave, co. Chester, defunct, and p. of Edward Griffith of Chester, ironmonger.
June 26 *Sir Thomas Brooke, baronet.
,, 26 *Roger Wilbraham, esquire.
,, 26 *John Prescott, clerk.
,, 26 *Peregrine Gastrell, esquire.
,, 26 *Bagot Read, esquire.
,, 26 *Foote Gower, doctor of physick.
,, 26 *William Falconer, esquire.
,, 29 *John Oliver, clerk.
,, 29 *Tobias Cooke.
,, 29 *George French.
,, 29 *Robert Foulkes, esquire.
,, 29 *John Cottingham, gentleman.
,, 29 *Thomas Robinson, gentleman.
,, 29 *Thomas Prescott, merchant.
,, 29 *William Vizer.
,, 29 *Edward Peregrine Gastrell, gentleman [esquire, M.B.].
,, 29 *William Mercer, mariner.
July 7 *Peter Capper, yeoman.
,, 7 Robert Nicholls, cabinetmaker, s. of John Nicholls of Chester, butcher, defunct.
,, 11 *Isaac Fawlkner the younger.
,, 11 *Thomas Ellis, mariner.
,, 11 *Edward Jones, mariner.
,, 13 *Thomas Carrington, gentleman.

THE CITY OF CHESTER

July 13 *Mathias Bolland.
" 13 William Wright p. of Joseph Holland of Chester, flaxdresser.
" 13 Thomas s. and p. of Benjamin Glover of Chester, gardener.
" 13 *Thomas Vernon, gardener.
" 13 *Edward Williams, mariner.
" 21 James s. of James Newell, carpenter, and p. of Samuel Dennill, mason, defunct.
" 21 *Charles Cholmondeley, esquire.
" 21 *John Myddleton, esquire.
" 21 *Thomas Lloyd, esquire.
" 21 *Peter Brooke, esquire.
" 21 *Peter Leigh the younger of Lyme, esquire.
" 21 *Philip Egerton, esquire.
" 21 *Thomas Eyton, esquire.
" 21 *Broughton Whitehall, esquire.
" 21 *Edward Williams of Ystin Colwyn, esquire.
" 21 *Amos Meredith, esquire.
" 21 *Edward Mainwaring, esquire.
" 21 *Edward Williams of Nerquis, esquire.
" 21 *Peter Pennant, esquire.
" 21 *Edward Kynaston, esquire.
" 21 *John Mapletoff, clerk.
" 21 *John Egerton of Tatton, esquire.
" 21 *Thomas Booth, esquire.
" 21 *Thomas Aubrey, clerk.
" 21 *Richard Davenport, esquire.
" 21 *John Daniel, esquire.
" 21 *Charles Crew, esquire.
" 21 *Hugh Poole, clerk.
" 21 *John Egerton of Broxton, esquire.
" 21 *Edward Green, esquire.
" 21 *Robert Hyde, esquire.
" 21 *William Dod of Edge, esquire.
" 21 *William Dod of Hampton, esquire.
" 21 *Eubule Lloyd, esquire.
" 21 *William Edwards, esquire.
" 21 *Edward Dod, gentleman.
" 21 *John Lloyd, gentleman.
" 21 *Gabriel Wettenhall, esquire.
" 21 *John Newman, yeoman.
" 28 *Edward Pennant, esquire.
Aug. 9 *William Taylor, yeoman.
" 18 *Phillip Henry Warburton, esquire.
" 18 *Lawrence Booth, gentleman.

Aug. 23 *George Eaton, esquire.
,, 23 *Ralph Barrow, gentleman.
,, 23 *Benjamin Culm, clerk.
,, 25 *John Brookes, merchant.
,, 25 *Thomas Groves, gentleman.
,, 30 *James Foulkes, gentleman.
Sep. 1 *David Pennant, esquire.
,, 1 *Hugh Whishaw, gentleman.
,, 1 *John Stones, clerk.
,, 1 *Francis Elcock, esquire.
,, 11 *John Lloyd of Pentrehobin, esquire.
,, 11 *Samuel Mostyn, esquire.
,, 11 *Thomas Walley, gentleman.
,, 11 *Robert Herbert, gentleman.
,, 11 *Thomas Aldersey, esquire, doctor in physick.
,, 11 *Sir John Glynne, baronet.
,, 11 *John Fletcher, clerk.
,, 12 *John Parker, esquire.
,, 12 *James Edge, gentleman.
,, 13 *William Bankes, esquire.
,, 13 *Charles Lloyd, esquire.
,, 17 *John Morgan, doctor in physick.
,, 25 William s. of James Kent of Chester, maltster.
,, 29 *John Hopley, gentleman.
Oct. 1 *Richard Massie, esquire.
,, 2 *John Pennant, gentleman.
,, 3 *Thomas Hesketh, esquire.
,, 3 *William Evered, merchant.
,, 9 *George Hope the younger, esquire.
,, 9 *Thomas Chrachley,[1] gentleman [of Daniel's Ash].
,, 9 *John Crachley, gentleman [of Broad Lane].
,, 11 *John Bennet, gentleman.
,, 11 Robert Moores of London, cabinetmaker, s. of Thomas Moores of Chester, cordwainer, defunct.
,, 12 *The Honourable and Reverend Doctor Henry Moore.
,, 12 *Sir Rowland Hill, baronet.
,, 12 *Thomas Whitley, esquire.
,, 12 *John Puleston the younger, esquire.
,, 12 *Arthur Owen, esquire.
,, 12 *Richard Puleston, gentleman.

[1] In addition to these, the names of Richard Crachley of Dig Lane, gentleman, and William Crachley of Broad Lane, gentleman, were "recommended" by the Mayor, *vide* Mayor's Files (MS.).

1733-4 [7-8 G. ii.] PETER ELLAMES, Esquire, Mayor.

Oct.	13	*Thomas Mostyn, esquire.
,,	13	*Randle Wilbraham, esquire.
,,	20	William s. of William Wilbraham of Marlston cum Lach, co. Chester, yeoman, defunct, and p. of William Stones of Chester, saddler.
,,	27	*Legh Master, esquire.
Nov.	6	Jonathan s. of Jonathan Gamon of Stanney, co. Chester, yeoman, and p. of Daniel Aldersey of Chester, woollendraper, defunct.
Dec.	19	*Humphrey Parry, esquire.
Jan.	28	*Peter Shakerley, esquire.
,,	28	*Colley Humberston Colley, esquire.
Mar.	2	Richard Chevers s. of Philip Chester [sic] of Chester, mariner, defunct, and p. of Randle Joynson of Chester, tailor, defunct.
,,	16	John s. of Elizabeth Peers of Chester, widow, and p. of Michael Hiccocke of Chester, silkdyer, defunct.
,,	21	*Robert Williams, mercer.
May	9	*Thomas Patton, merchant.
,,	11	Thomas s. of Samuel Maddock of Chester, tailor.
,,	11	James s. of Robert Walley of Chester, carpenter, and p. of William Hickman of Chester, bricklayer, defunct.
,,	11	Mathias s. of Samuel Ireland of Chester, silkweaver, defunct, and p. of James Littler the younger of Chester, cordwainer.
,,	11	Thomas s. of John Waterwoods of Chester, periwigmaker.
,,	11	Thomas Hall p. of Peter Hickson of Chester, cordwainer.
,,	11	John s. of John Jackson of Chester, tobacco cutter, and p. of John Gouldson of Chester, cordwainer.
,,	11	Joseph s. of Joseph Crosbie, cordwainer, defunct, and p. of John Dobb of Chester, cordwainer.

Richard Shewton, bricklayer.
William Crachley, gentleman.
William Maddock, feltmaker.
Samuel Davies the younger.
John White, barber.
Richard Coytmore, gentleman.
Thomas Price, esquire.
William Brown, cordwainer.
John Percival, joiner.

312 THE ROLLS OF THE FREEMEN OF [1734-5

    William Vaughan, esquire.
    Sir Francis Edwards, baronet.
    John Rowlands, clerk.
    Geoffrey Williams, clerk.
    Thomas Davies, cooper.
    Thomas Smith, joiner.
    Samuel Brown, cordwainer.
    Corbet Kynaston, esquire.
    Robert Day, saddler.
    Paul Patton, gentleman.
    John Mytton, esquire.
    Samuel Hill, currier.
    John Croxton, merchant.
    John Eccles, watchmaker.
    Robert Bulkeley, ironmonger.
    Thomas Humphreys, joiner.

1734-5 [8-9 G. ii.] ROGER MASSEY, Esquire, Mayor.

    Thomas Sidebotham, innholder.
    Richard Cooper, mariner.
    Thomas Davies.
    Roger Gill, cordwainer.
    John Wheawell.
    George Griffies.
—   —   Samuel Ansdell, linendraper.
—   2   Thomas s. of William Buckley of Chester, gardener, and p. of William ——— of Chester, bricklayer.[1]
—   29   Thomas s. of Hugh Maddock of Chester, tanner, defunct.
Aug. 2   John s. of John Shard of Chester, apothecary, defunct.
Sep. 27   *John Bethell, yeoman.
Oct. 3   John s. of John Sant of Stoke in Acton parish, co. Chester, yeoman, and p. of Randle Wrench of Chester, butcher.
,,   —   *Edward Dutton.
,,   7   *John Williams, gentleman.

1735-6 [9-10 G. ii.] JOHN COTGREAVE, Esquire, Mayor.

Oct. 25   Robert s. of Pickering Lamb of Chester, butcher, and p. of John Hale of Chester, butcher.
Dec. 13   Samuel s. of Samuel Jones of Chester, tailor, and p. of William Frost of Chester, barber.

    [1] "Disfranchised" written against this admission on the Roll.

1736]   THE CITY OF CHESTER   313

Jan.   5   Ralph Whittingham stepson of Joshua Nicholson, mariner, and p. of John Robertson of Chester, tailor, defunct.
  „   10   William s. of Thomas Calkin of Waverton, co. Chester, yeoman, and p. of Thomas Dunbabin of Chester, glazier, defunct.
  „   10   John Evans son-in-law of Thomas Hulton of Golborn David, co. Chester, smith, and p. of Samuel Harvey of Chester, joiner.
  „   10   John s. of Henry Roughley of Liverpool, co. Lanc., and p. of Samuel Bradburn of Chester, ironmonger.
Apr. 16   *James Rowe of York, druggist.
May   5   John s. of John Hickson of Parkgate, co. Chester, defunct, and p. of William Willoughby of Chester, brewer, defunct.
Aug. 14   *James Stephenson.
  „   14   *John Evans.
  „   14   *John Lampkin.
  „   14   *Robert Whitehead.
  „   21   *John Harrison, carpenter.
Sep.   1   Samuel s. of John Warrington of Chester, carpenter.
  „   14   John s. of Henry Horner of Tamworth, co. Staffs., clothier, and p. of Edward Nicholls of Chester, apothecary.
  „   29   *Thomas Hall, gentleman.
Oct.   6   *Randle Pickmore, gentleman.
  „   9   Harwar s. of Lucretia Harvie, widow, and p. of Abner Scoles, upholsterer, defunct.
  „   13   *John Cartwright, cook.
  „   14   John s. of Thomas Lloyd of Chester, gentleman, clerk of the pentice.
  „   14   *John Wright, woolcomber.
  „   14   *Robert Walley, esquire.
  „   15   *John Egerton, esquire.
  „   15   *Richard Lister, esquire.
  „   15   Roger Mather, gentleman, s. of Thomas Mather of Chester, esquire, recorder of the city.

1736-7 [10-11 G. ii.] WATKIN WILLIAMS WYNNE, Esquire, Mayor.

Oct. 16   *Thomas Booth, esquire.
  „   20   *Sir Walter Wagstaff Bagot, baronet.
  „   20   *Sir Robert Williams, baronet.
  „   20   *Thomas Bootle, esquire.

314 THE ROLLS OF THE FREEMEN OF [1736-7

Oct. 20 *Charles Bagot, esquire.
„ 20 *William Owen, esquire.
„ 20 *Edward Mainwaring, esquire.
„ 20 *Richard Davenport, esquire.
„ 20 *Peter Shakerley, esquire.
„ 20 *Robert Davies, esquire.
„ 20 *John Townshend, esquire.
„ 20 *Giwn Lloyd, esquire.
Nov. 5 *John Dimmock, gentleman.
„ 5 *John Spencer, esquire.
Jan. 11 *Richard Massie, esquire.
James Apperley, doctor of physick.
James Morgan, gentleman.
Thomas Lloyd, yeoman.
James Price, barber.
The Rt. Hon. John Lord Gower.
The Hon. William Leveson Gower, esquire.
Sir John Hind Cotton, baronet.
Thomas Rowney, esquire.
Walter Powell, gentleman.
Robert Davies.
Samuel Sidebotham.
Thomas Jones.
Edward Lindsey.
John Cary.
Samuel Wilkinson.
Edward Prichard.
Robert Bradbury.
John Amery.
Peter Golding.
Richard Williams, clerk.
John Griffith, butcher.
Joseph Jordan.
Thomas Warre, esquire.
Joseph Newport.

1737-8 [11-12 G. ii.] Sir ROBERT GROSVENOR,
BARONET, MAYOR.

Thomas Palin, ironmonger.
Richard Sidebotham.
John Sidebotham.
Henry Aspinwall, chandler.
Peter Parry the younger.
John Chrichley, clerk.

[1737–8]   THE CITY OF CHESTER   315

        John Biggins, cordwainer.
        William Parker, butcher.
        James Richards, butcher.
        Randle Townsend, ironmonger.
        Thomas Nevett, chandler.
        Samuel Kennerley, cooper.
        Philip Egerton, esquire.
        George Coppock, slater and plasterer.
        John Hollins, flaxdresser.
        Joseph Wilson, butcher.
        John Barton, silkweaver.
        William Painter, plumber.
        John Easom, barber.
        Joseph Meredith, bricklayer.
        Thomas Pemberton, tailor.

Aug. 17 Thomas s. of Thomas Parker of Malpas, defunct, and p. of Joseph Dennill of Chester, glazier.
,, 17 Elias s. of John Hope of Chester, labourer, and p. of John Jones of Chester, cordwainer.
,, 18 *William Dod, esquire.
,, 19 James s. of John Powell of Chester, sawyer.
,, 19 *Henry Vigars.
,, 19 *John Fossey.
,, 19 *Daniel Gorton.
,, 19 *Thomas Wright.
,, 19 *Sir John Werden, baronet.
,, 21 James s. of Owen Jones of Chester, labourer, defunct, and p. of John Woodward of Chester, bricklayer.
Sep. 16 George s. of George Geary of Edgemont, co. Salop, victualler, and p. of William Littleton of Chester, gardener.
,, 18 *Timothy Lelfwiche, gentleman.
,, 18 *John Kelsall, gentleman.
,, 18 *Nathaniel Barber, gentleman.
,, 30 William Johnson, wetglover, s. of William Johnson of Chester, wetglover, defunct.
Oct. 2 *Peter Morgan, gentleman [this word is underlined on the Roll], s. of Edward Morgan, esquire.
,, 12 *Peter Legh, esquire.
,, 13 *Bagot Read, esquire.
,, 13 *Edward Green, esquire.
,, 13 *Thomas Bird.

1738-9 [12-13 G. ii.] NATHANIEL WRIGHT, Esquire,
Mayor.

Oct. 14   *Thomas Ormes, gentleman.
Nov. 18   John s. of John Peck of Northwich, co. Chester, and
          p. of Matthew Owens of Chester, saddler.
Jan. 31   Richard Bather, barber, s. of George Bather of Nampt-
          wich, co. Ches., barber and periwigmaker, defunct,
          and p. of Thomas Halfeild of Chester, barber and
          periwigmaker.
— —   Thomas Gough, carpenter, s. of Richard Gough of
          Chester, carpenter, defunct.
Feb. 9   William Cartwright, butcher, s. of Richard Cartwright
          of Hawarden, co. Flint, weaver, defunct, and p. of
          Charles Hitchins of Chester.
 ,, 19   Robert Prichard, merchant, s. of Thomas Prichard of
          Rhuabon, co. Denbigh, yeoman, and p. of Henry
          Bennett of Chester.
—   12   Robert s. of Roger Barnston of Chester, esquire, and
          p. of Alderman H——— of Chester, merchant.
—   6   Thomas Stanton, cooper, s. of Abraham Stanton of
          Chester, and p. of Henry Bennion of Chester, fish-
          monger.
— —   Thomas Spencer, mason, s. and p. of Richard Spencer.
July 24   William s. of William Prescott of Chester, slater, and
          p. of John Davies of Chester, slater.
 ,, 24   Richard Walley, brickmaker, s. of Thomas Walley of
          Chester, labourer, defunct.
Aug. 18   Hohme [sic] Burrowes, cutler, s. of Randle Burrowes
          of Chester, cutler, defunct.
Oct. 2   John Jones, wheelwright, ⎫ ss. of John Jones of
 ,,   2   Thomas Jones, mason,   ⎭   Chester, mason.
 ,, 10   *Thomas Doe the younger, gentleman.

1739-40 [13-14 G. ii.] JOHN MARSDEN, Esquire,
Mayor.

Oct. 20   Thomas Palin, tailor, s. of Stephen Palin, tailor,
          deceased, and p. of John Hixon.
Nov. 1   Joseph Prestbury, wetglover, s. of Samuel Prestbury of
          Chester, wetglover, deceased.
 ,,   1   John Waters, cordwainer, s. of Thomas Waters of
          Chester, tailor.

	15	William s. of John Parry of ———, co. Flint, weaver, deceased, and p. of ——— Jones of Chester, butcher.
—	5	Charles Poynton, yeoman, s. of Ran——— ——— of Chester, baker, deceased.
,,	—	Robert Salisbury, brother of J——— ——— of ———, co. Denbigh, gentleman, and p. of ——— ——— of Chester, tinplateworker.
,,	29	Randle Wilbraham, s. of Roger Wilbraham of Chester, chandler.
—	29	Thomas s. of William Golborne of Chester, gentleman, deceased, and p. of Richard ——— of Chester, barber and periwigmaker.
Apr.	12	Robert s. of Robert Maddock of Sandbach, co. Chester, gentleman, and p. of Thomas Oliver of Chester, linendraper.
May	10	Proby s. and p. of Thomas Vause of Chester, barber.
June	21	Charles Barker, joiner, brother of Robert Barker of Northwich, co. Ches., mercer, and p. of Robert Wrench of Chester, joiner.
July	5	Thomas Porter, brazier and pewterer, s. of Daniel Porter of Wrexham, co. Denbigh, innholder, deceased.
,,	5	Ralph Mercer, joiner, s. of James Mercer of Chester, joiner, deceased.
,,	13	Thomas Patton, currier, s. of Edward Patton of Chester, innholder, deceased.
,,	23	*James Trelford.
,,	23	*Edward Smith.
,,	23	*Abel Rowlinson.
Aug.	23	*Thomas Golding.
Sep.	3	John s. of John Beech of Chester, yeoman, and p. of John Mason, butcher.
,,	6	*John Baldwin, clerk.
,,	6	James s. of Allen Jopson of Chester, distiller, deceased, and p. of William Cooke, stationer.
,,	6	*Ellis Cunliffe, merchant.
Oct.	8	*John Conner.

1740–1 [14–15 G. ii.] THOMAS DUKE, Esquire, Mayor.

Oct. 18 William Coleclough [Colecliffe, M.B.], tobacco cutter, s. of Thomas Colecliffe of Chester, carpenter, deceased.

Nov. 5 John s. of John Humphreys, deceased, and p. of James Mottershead of Chester, baker.

318 THE ROLLS OF THE FREEMEN OF [1740-2

Dec. 6 John s. of John Davies of Chester, wetglover.
„ 10 William Dicas, barber, } ss. of John Dicas of
„ 10 ‡Samuel Dicas, staymaker, } Chester, barber.
„ 10 Charles Dicas, chandler, s. of Randle Dicas of Chester, chandler.
„ 13 Peter s. of Samuel Hall of Frodsham, co. Ches., gentleman, and p. of James Wilkinson of Chester, ironmonger.
Jan. 31 John Crooke, yeoman, s. of Josiah Crook of Broughton, co. Flint, ironmonger.
Feb. 16 Samuel s. of John Taylor of Marple, co. Ches., yeoman, and p. of John Beech of Chester, silkdyer.
„ 21 John s. of Richard Hayes of Middlewich, co. Ches., innholder, and p. of John Dicas of Chester, barber.
Mar. 13 John s. and p. of John Boden of Chester, slater.
Richard Billington, cooper.
—— Francis, baker.
Samuel ———, slater.
Thomas Dutton, ironmonger.
Richard Massey, baker.
Thomas Minshull, baker.
John Wilkinson, mariner.
Richard Ford, tallowchandler and soapboiler.
Nathaniel Gough.
—— ———, ———.

1741-2 [15-16 G. ii.] CHARLES BINGLEY, ESQUIRE, MAYOR.

William Wright, ironmonger.
Thomas Allcock, whitesmith.
Joseph Wilkinson, cabinetmaker.
Joseph Wilkinson, baker.
Joseph Lawton, yeoman.
John Elrington, upholsterer.
William Craven, gentleman.
Edward Bromley, saddler.
Arthur Darlington, brewer.
Samuel Brown, tailor.
Samuel Chapman, baker.
Daniel Ledsham, baker.
Humphrey Jones, bricklayer.
Charles Whittle, cordwainer.
May 15 Robert s. of Robert Fearnall of Lea, co. Ches., yeoman, and p. of Thomas Jones, butcher.

1742]   THE CITY OF CHESTER   319

May 19   William Hale, butcher, s. of John Hale of Chester, butcher.
„   19   John Hale the younger, butcher, s. of John Hale of Chester, butcher.
June 2   Richard Tonna, druggist,⎫ ss. of Samuel Tonna of
„   2   John Tonna, butcher,   ⎭ Chester, butcher.
„   2   John Bromley, butcher, s. of Michael Bromley of Chester, butcher.
„   8   John Bennion, chandler, s. of Thomas Bennion of Chester, innholder, deceased.
„   8   Ralph s. of Ralph Joyns of Hoole, co. Ches., yeoman, deceased, and p. of Michael Bromley, butcher.
„   12   William s. of William Seller of Chester, brewer, deceased.
July 13 William Jones p. of George Heath of Chester, cordwainer.
„   13   George Heath the younger, cordwainer, s. of George Heath the elder, cordwainer.
Aug. 20 *Thomas Staut.
Sep. 4   Robert Maddock, corkcutter, s. of Paul Maddock of Chester, cordwainer, deceased.
„   10   *Edward Thomas.
„   15   John Rowley, bookseller, s. of Thomas Rowley of Chester, yeoman, deceased.
„   16   James Percival, watchmaker, s. of James Percival, swordbearer of the city of Chester.
„   16   Thomas Richards, brewer, s. of Thomas Richards of Chester, innholder.
„   20   Joseph Wright, staymaker, s. of Joseph Wright of Chester, tailor.
„   25   Peter s. of John Platt of Great Barrow, yeoman, deceased, and p. of Charles Hitchins of Chester, butcher.
„   25   Robert s. of Thomas Yoxall of Great Boughton, co. Ches., glover, and p. of Thomas Briscoe of Chester, smith.
Oct. 9   Thomas Hickman p. of Thomas Davies of Chester, "comon brewer," deceased.

1742-3 [16-17 G. ii.] SAMUEL JARVIS, Esquire, Mayor.

         Thomas Jones, periwigmaker.
Oct. 30 Matthew Jones, tailor, s. of Peter Jones of Chester, woolcomber.

II.   H

Nov. 6 Roger Parry, merchant, s. of Edward Parry of Mostyn, co. Flint, gentleman, deceased, and p. of Charles Mytton of Chester, merchant.
„ 13 *John Hesketh, merchant.
„ 15 John Nevett, chandler, s. of John Nevitt of Chester, chandler, deceased.
Jan. 6 Thomas Bayley, bricklayer, s. of Thomas Bayley of Handbridge, labourer, and p. of Hugh Jordan of Chester, bricklayer.
„ 8 John Jordan, mason, stepson of William Williams of Chester, skinner, and p. of John Cornelious of Chester, mason.
„ 31 Peter Weigh the younger, currier, s. of Peter Weigh of Chester, currier.
Apr. 3 Thomas Price, hosier, s. of Richard Price of Chester, tobacconist, deceased.
„ 9 John Warrington, watchmaker, s. of Edward Warrington of Chester, carpenter.
June 18 William Griffith, gentleman, s. of William Griffith of Chester, innholder.
„ 27 James Walker, joiner, s. of John Walker of Chester, joiner.
July 4 John Gratrex, chandler, s. of John Gratrex of Pentre, co. Flint, yeoman, and p. of Charles Bingley of Chester, chandler.
„ 7 Thomas Cotgreave, linendraper, s. of John Cotgreave of Chester, alderman.
„ 7 James Briscoe, silkweaver, s. of John Briscoe late of Chester, and now of Ledsham, co. Chester, baker.
„ 9 John Evans, plasterer, s. of David Evans of Chester, deceased, and p. of James Suddons of Chester, plasterer.
„ 12 John Porter, surgeon barber, son-in-law and p. of Edward Wilkinson of Chester, surgeon-barber, wax and tallowchandler, and innholder, deceased.
Aug. 13 Thomas Avern, corkcutter, s. of Joseph Avern of Chester, corkcutter.
„ 20 Thomas Woodfin, bricklayer, s. of Thomas Woodfin of Chester, labourer, deceased, and p. of Hugh Jordan of Chester, bricklayer.
„ 20 Richard Ollerhead, apothecary, s. of John Ollerhead of Chester, tanner, deceased.
Sep. 23 *Thomas Hart, innholder.
„ 24 *Matthew Fitchett, yeoman.
„ 24 *John Starkey, yeoman.
„ 24 Samuel Dob, gardener, s. and p. of Hamnet Dob of Chester, gardener.

1743-4 [17-18 G. ii.] THOMAS DAVIES, Esquire, Mayor.

Oct. 29 Peter Hickson the younger, cordwainer, s. of Peter Hickson of Chester, cordwainer.

„ 29 Richard Briscoe, smith, s. of Richard Briscoe of Chester, smith, deceased.

Nov. 2 *Thomas Blower, yeoman.

Dec. 17 William Davies, joiner, s. of Robert Davies of Leeswood, co. Flint, yeoman, and p. of Thomas Humphreys of Chester, joiner.

Feb. 4 John Neild, carpenter, s. of Martha Neil of Hollinwood, co. Lanc., widow, and p. of William Yewd of Chester, carpenter, deceased.

„ 18 Robert Vernon, baker, stepson of Richard Gamon of Thornton in the Moores, co. Ches., yeoman, and p. of William Briscoe of Chester, baker.

„ 20 John Craven, ironmonger, s. of John Craven of Pulford, co. Ches., gentleman, deceased, and p. of Thomas Bingley of Chester, ironmonger.

„ 20 John s. of Thomas Pratchitt of Chester, stockingweaver.

Mar. 19 Samuel Tylston, slater, s. of Thomas Tylston of [Chester ?], bricklayer, deceased.

„ 19 Robert Scarsbrocke, barber, s. of Robert Scarsbrocke of Chester, barber.

„ 19 Robert Robinson, baker, s. of Thomas Robinson of Little Sutton, co. Ches., yeoman, deceased, and p. of James Hesketh of Chester, baker, deceased.

„ 24 John Hatton, feltmaker, s. of Thomas Hatton of Chester, feltmaker.

Apr. 3 William Boyle, cordwainer, s. of William Boyle of Chester, gardener, and p. of Thomas Wright of Chester, cordwainer.

„ 4 George Hollins, cordwainer, s. of George Hollins of Chester, yeoman, and p. of Thomas Hope of Chester, cordwainer.

„ 4 Thomas Spence, barber, s. of Andrew Spence, late of Chester, yeoman, and p. of Robert Fisher of Chester, barber.

„ 4 John Bevan, cordwainer, s. of Thomas Bevan of Chester, turner, deceased.

„ 4 Aldersey Fletcher, cordwainer, s. of Samuel Fletcher of Chester, cordwainer.

„ 4 James Stewart, tailor, s. of Thomas Stewart of Chester, tailor.

Apr. 4 Henry Ellis, cordwainer, s. of Robert Ellis, late of Chester, husbandman, and p. of John Harrison of Chester, cordwainer.

,, 4 Charles Barton, wine cooper, s. of George Barton of Adlington, co. Chester, yeoman, and p. of William Tapley of Chester, wine cooper.

,, 4 William Colecliffe, tobacconist, s. of Thomas Colecliffe of Chester, cordwainer.

,, 4 Richard Humphreys the younger, hornbreaker and combmaker, s. of Richard Humphreys of Chester, hornbreaker and combmaker.

,, 4 James Suddons, butcher, s. of James Suddons of Chester, plasterer.

,, 5 Richard Suddons, writing master, s. of Ralph Suddons of Chester, weaver.

,, 6 Hugh Hastings, turner, s. of John Hastings of Chester, turner.

,, 6 Paul Maddock, tailor, s. of Paul Maddock of Chester, lastmaker, deceased.

,, 6 Edward Hamilton, stuffweaver, stepson of Robert Gregg of Chester, cordwainer, and p. of Joseph Snow of Chester, stuffweaver.

,, 6 William Brown, coachmaker, s. of Anthony Brown of Chester, yeoman.

,, 6 William Howard, butcher, s. of Charles Howard of Chester, butcher, deceased.

,, 7 William Hei, cordwainer, s. of Matthew Hei late of Dublin, mariner, and p. of John Tyrer of Chester, cordwainer.

,, 7 John Williams, butcher, s. of Thomas Williams of Chester, cordwainer, deceased.

,, 9 Charles Haswell, cordwainer, s. of Jonathan Haswell of Chester, cooper.

,, 9 Joseph Hyde, cordwainer, s. of Thomas Hyde of Chester, glover, and p. of John Jones of Chester, cordwainer.

,, 9 James Allcock, tailor, s. of James Allcock of Chester, deceased.

,, 9 Joseph Lloyd, tanner, p. of Joseph Weigh of Chester, tanner.

,, 10 Maurice Briscoe, smith, s. of Maurice Briscoe of Chester, smith, deceased.

,, 10 Peter Olliver, tailor, s. of James Olliver, late of Chester, cordwainer, deceased.

,, 10 Jonathan Litler, cordwainer, s. of James Litler the younger of Chester, cordwainer.

Apr. 12 Thomas Walton the younger, glazier, s. of Thomas Walton of Chester, glazier.
,, 13 Alban Price, yeoman, s. of Edward Price of Chester, cordwainer.
,, 14 John Lawrenson, cooper, s. of James Lawrenson of Chester, yeoman.
,, 14 James Halliwell, cordwainer [staymaker, M.B.], s. of George Hallewell of Chester, tailor, deceased.
,, 14 Peter Boden, cordwainer, s. of John Boden of Chester, slater.
,, 14 Thomas Jones, pipemaker, s. of John Jones of Chester, pipemaker.
,, 14 James Conway, hornbreaker, s. of Thomas Conway, late of Chester, slater, deceased.
,, 16 Gamaliel Hawkins, slater, p. of John Maddock of Chester, slater.
,, 17 John Yates, butcher, s. of Samuel Yates of Chester, yeoman, deceased, and p. of Samuel Tonna of Chester, butcher.
,, 17 George Eaton, mason, s. of Hellen Eaton, widow, and p. of George Price of Chester, mason.
,, 18 Thomas Tilley the younger, wetglover, s. of Thomas Tilley of Chester, feltmaker, and p. of Andrew Duke of Chester, wetglover.
,, 18 Joseph Richardson, linencloth-weaver, s. of William Richardson of Chester, staymaker, and p. of John Calley of Chester, linencloth-weaver.
,, 19 Samuel Bevan, baker, s. of Richard Bevan of Stoak, co. Chester, and p. of William Briscoe of Chester, baker.
,, 19 Daniel Porter, brewer, s. of Daniel Porter of Chester, gentleman, and p. of Alderman John Warrington of Chester, brewer.
,, 19 John Edwards, cabinetmaker, s. of John Edwards of Chester, gentleman, deceased, and p. of Joseph Burrows of Chester, cabinetmaker.
,, 25 Edward Carey, feltmaker, p. of James Walley of Chester, feltmaker.
May 2 Stephen Hyde the younger, baker, p. of John Pyke of Chester, baker.
June 12 John Taylor, yeoman, s. of George Taylor of Boughton, yeoman.
July 14 Edward Farrell, vintner, p. of James Croxton of Chester, merchant and vintner.
,, 14 *Lawrence Smith, yeoman.
,, 21 *Thomas Pemberton, yeoman.
Sep. 15 *John Atkinson, gentleman.

Sep. 24 Jeffrey Edwards, flaxdresser, s. of Moyndeg Edwards of Chester, labourer, and p. of Joseph Ratcliffe of Chester, flaxdresser.
„ 28 *James Johnson, yeoman.
Oct. 11 Charles Woolham, hosier [" hosier " underlined, and " mercht." added in another hand].

1744–5 [18–19 G. ii.] THOMAS MADDOCK, Esquire, Mayor.

Nov. 5 Samuel Weigh, tanner, s. of Samuel Weigh of Higher Kinnerton, co. Flint, yeoman, and p. of Joseph Weigh of Chester.
„ 5 ‡Samuel Boswell, baker, s. of John Boswell of Chester, baker, deceased.
„ 5 Charles Parry, feltmaker, s. of Peter Parry, late of Chester, alderman, deceased.
„ 10 Thomas Randles, ironmonger, s. of Richard Randles of Allington, co. Denbigh, yeoman, and p. of Thomas Harvie, of Chester, ironmonger.
Dec. 31 Joseph Jordan, slater, s. of Francis Jordan of Chester, slater, deceased.
Jan. 7 Edward Chevers, butcher, s. of Philip Chevers of Chester, yeoman, deceased, and p. of Philip Chevers of Chester, butcher.
Feb. 4 John Williams, bricklayer, s. of Thomas Williams of Soughton, Northop parish, co. Flint, carpenter, deceased, and p. of John Meredith of Chester, bricklayer.
Apr. 6 The Hon. Arthur Barry, esquire, s. of the Right Hon. James, Earl of Barrymore, in the kingdom of Ireland.
„ 6 *Thomas Walley, gentleman.
„ 24‡*John Pakeman.
May 11 James Pennington, cordwainer, s. of John Pennington of Chester, labourer, and p. of John Jones the younger of Chester, cordwainer.
„ 20 Thomas Hitchcock, linendraper, s. of Thomas Hitchcock of Boughton, co. Ches., merchant, and p. of John Orange of Chester, linendraper.
„ 20 Thomas Speed, yeoman.
„ 24 Robert Cummins, saddler, s. of Josiah Cummins of Chester, yeoman, and p. of William Wilbraham of Chester, saddler.

May 27 Richard Ledsham, joiner, s. of Thomas Ledsham of Chester, tailor.
 „ 27 Isaac Hitchins, feltmaker, s. of Isaac Hitchins of Chester, weaver, and p. of William Pemberton of Chester, feltmaker.
 „ 31 Peter Ellames the younger, druggist, s. of Peter Ellames of Chester, alderman.
June 8‡*Ellis Bushell.
 „ 19 *Edward Davies, yeoman.
 „ 29 William Penkett, merchant, s. of Richard Penkett of Chester, ironmonger, deceased.
July 6 Thomas Towsey, feltmaker, s. of John Towsey of Chester, feltmaker.
 „ 13 John s. of Benjamin Peeres of Cholmondeley, co. Ches., blacksmith, and p. of Hugh Hand the younger of Chester, joiner.
Aug. 17 William Wrench, watchmaker, s. of Richard Wrench of Chester, gentleman, deceased.
 „ 24 Thomas s. of John Bevan of Pulford, co. Ches., yeoman, and p. of Calveley Calveley of Chester, joiner.
 „ 24 *Jonadab Vernon, gentleman.
 „ 26 *John Brerewood, esquire.
 „ 26 Richard Ledsham, apothecary, s. of Benjamin Ledsham of Chester, slater, deceased.
 „ 30 *Joseph Crewe, clerk.
 „ 30 *Randle Crewe, clerk.
Oct. 9 John Maddock, fisherman, s. of Joseph Maddock of Holt, co. Denbigh, labourer.

1745-6 [19-20 G. ii.] HENRY RIDLEY, Esquire, Mayor.

Oct. 28 Joseph Crew, p. of John Parker of Chester, apothecary.
Dec. 12 *Clear Saunders, victualler [yeoman, M.B.].
 „ 23 Paul Pyke, maltster [cordwainer, M.B.], s. of Robert Pyke of Chester, baker, deceased.
Jan. 20 Thomas s. of Edward Astle, late of Frodsham, co. Ches., yeoman, and p. of Edward Bromley of Chester, cabinetmaker, deceased.
 „ 20 John Salladine p. of Thomas Dutton of Chester, brewer.
 „ 25 Thomas Griffith, patternmaker, s. of William Griffith of Chester, labourer.
Mar. 1 William Gamon, yeoman [husbandman, M.B.], s. of John Gamon of Churton, co. Ches., husbandman.

Mar. 5 Edward Warrington the younger, carpenter, s. of Edward Warrington of Chester, carpenter.
Apr. 5 Christopher s. of William Hyde of Chester, cordwainer, deceased, and p. of John Phythian of Chester, cordwainer, deceased.
June 25 John Hughes, brewer, s. of Thomas Hughes of Cork, in the kingdom of Ireland, brewer, and late of Chester, ironmonger.
July 5 William Johnson, chandler, s. of Thomas Johnson of Neston, co. Ches., yeoman, deceased, and p. of Roger Wilbraham of Chester, tallowchandler and soapboiler.
„ 9 Henry Hesketh, merchant, s. of Sarah Hesketh of co. Lanc., widow, and p. of Henry Bennett, late of Chester, alderman, deceased.
*Samuel Johnson, yeoman.
*William Simpson, draper.
*Joseph Beckett, victualler.
John s. of Sarah Hignet of Rowton, co. Ches., widow, and p. of Thomas Massey of Chester, linendraper.
Henry Dyson, otherwise Dawson, wetglover, p. of Charles Cottingham of Chester, wetglover, deceased.
John Dicas, surgeon, s. of John Dicas of Chester, barber, deceased.
Joseph Holland, baker, } ss. of William Holland of
William Holland, butcher, } Chester, baker.
*The Hon. Richard Barry, esquire, } ss. of the Right Hon. James,
*The Hon. James Barry, esquire, } Earl of Barrymore, in the kingdom of Ireland.

1746 [20 G. ii.] EDWARD YEARSLEY, Esquire, Mayor.

William s. of John Palin of Farndon, co. Ches., yeoman, and p. of John Boswell, late of Chester, baker.
Joseph Rylands the younger, baker, s. of Joseph Rylands of Chester, baker.
*John Dutton, victualler.
Samuel s. of John Brooks of Chester, feltmaker, and p. of Thomas Jones of Chester, feltmaker.
George Jackson, p. of Joseph Sorton, wetglover.
Richard s. of Richard Jackson of Allington, co. Denbigh, yeoman, and p. of Robert Barrett of Chester, baker.

1746-7 [20-21 G. ii.] EDWARD NICHOLS, Esquire, Mayor.

- William s. of Thomas Morphett of Chester, husbandman, and p. of Thomas Wilkinson of Chester, coachmaker.
- John Hiccocke, tanner, s. of Thomas Hiccocke of Chester, alderman.
- William Broadbent, "upholder," s. of John Broadbent, late of Nantwich, co. Ches., silkstocking-weaver, and p. of Ralph Bingley of Chester, embroiderer and "upholder."
- James Seller, brewer, s. of William Seller of Chester, brewer, defunct.
- John Vernon, apothecary ["gent." added in another hand on roll], s. of Thomas Vernon of Chester, apothecary, deceased.
- Robert Lloyd, linendraper, } ss. of John Lloyd of Caerwys, co. Flint, gentleman.
- William Lloyd of Holywell, co. Flint, gentleman,
- John Rogers, yeoman, s. of Richard Rogers of Chester, joiner.
- Richard s. of Edward James of Llansemffraid parish, co. Montgomery, yeoman, and p. of Robert Cowdock of Chester, smith.
- Thomas Chapman, baker, s. of John Chapman of Chester, baker, deceased.
- Samuel s. of Samuel Nichols of Gresford parish, co. Denbigh, cordwainer, and p. of Richard Backarn of Chester, carpenter.
- Thomas Chaloner, cordwainer, } ss. of John Chaloner of Holt, co. Denbigh, periwigmaker.
- Timothy Chaloner, barber,
- William s. of Thomas Harrison of Chester, flaxdresser, deceased, and p. of Gerrard Jordan of Chester, slater.
- John s. of Morgan Shaw of Chester, deceased, and p. of Robert Cowdock of Chester, smith.
- Jonathan Roberts, joiner, s. of William Roberts of Chester, joiner, deceased.
- Charles Pigot, esquire, s. of Robert Pigot, esquire, alderman of Chester.
- Richard Allen, apothecary, s. of William Allen of Chester, alderman, deceased.

Thomas Harvey, bricklayer, s. of Edward Harvey of Chester, bricklayer, deceased.

Roger Comberbach the younger, esquire, s. of Roger Comberbach of Chester, esquire.

Calveley Speed of Churton, co. Ches., yeoman, s. of Calveley Speed of Chester, ironmonger, deceased.

Thomas Jones, carpenter, s. of Thomas Jones of Chester, yeoman.

Edward Davies of Nantwich, wheelwright, s. of Thomas Davies of Chester, innholder.

Thomas Sewell, gentleman, s. of Joseph Sewell of Chester, gentleman, deceased.

Thomas Jones, cordwainer, s. of John Jones of Chester, cordwainer.

Thomas Johnson, slater, s. of John Johnson of Chester, slater.

William Griffith, periwigmaker, s. of William Griffith of Chester, innholder.

Benjamin Carter, cordwainer, } ss. of Thomas Carter of
John Carter, cordwainer, } Chester, cordwainer.

Joseph Ellis, glover, s. of Joseph Ellis, late of Chester, wetglover.

Thomas Lee, breechesmaker, s. of John Lee of Chester, yeoman.

John Woodworth, cabinet-maker, } ss. of John Woodworth
July 11 William Woodworth, baker, } of Chester, bricklayer.

" 11 William Jennions of Holywell, joiner, s. of Samuel Jennions of Holywell, joiner.

" 11 Jonathan Bramwell, currier, s. of Jonathan Bramwell of Chester, innholder, defunct.

" 11 William Griffith, cordwainer, s. of John Griffith of Chester, cordwainer.

" 11 John Jackson, yeoman, } ss. of Samuel Jackson of
" 11 Henry Jackson, butcher, } Bebington, co. Ches., joiner.

" 11 Charles Price, tailor, s. of John Price of Chester, tobacconist.

" 11 John Davies, mason, s. of Thomas Davies of Chester, mason, deceased.

" 11 Benjamin Huntington, smith, s. of William Huntington of Chester, baker, deceased.

" 11 Samuel Parsonage, plumber, s. of Richard Parsonage of Allington, plumber, deceased.

" 11 Orian Adams, printer, s. of Roger Adams of Chester, printer, deceased.

July	11	Richard Richardson, chandler, s. of William Richardson of Chester, goldsmith.
,,	11	Charles France, plasterer, s. of Thomas France of Chester, labourer.
,,	11	Thomas Peeres, cordwainer, s. of John Peeres of Chester, yeoman, deceased.
,,	11	Thomas Andrew, bricklayer, s. of Esau Andrew of Chester, slater.
,,	11	John Bayley, feltmaker, s. of James Bayley of Chester, feltmaker.
,,	11	John Boxley, carpenter, s. of Henry Boxley of Chester, plasterer.
,,	11	John Roydon of Graisbey, yeoman, s. of Joseph Roydon of Chester, bricklayer.
,,	11	Jonathan s. of Thomas Cokeley of Chester, cordwainer.
,,	11	Thomas Prestbury, labourer, s. of Jonathan Prestbury of Chester, smith.
,,	11	William Meakin, pipemaker, s. of Samuel Meakin of Chester, pipemaker.
,,	11	Peter Ratcliffe, cordwainer, s. of William Ratcliffe of Chester, cordwainer.
,,	11	John Joynson, feltmaker, s. of Randle Joynson of Chester, tailor.
,,	11	John Jones, cordwainer, s. of Peter Jones, woolcomber.
,,	11	Nathaniel Bathoe, cordwainer, s. of Henry Bathoe of Bebington, cordwainer.
,,	11	James Percivall, baker, s. of James Percivall of Holywell, glazier, deceased.
,,	11	William Roberts, corkcutter, s. of Robert Roberts of Chester, wine cooper, deceased.
,,	11	John Ryley, corkcutter, s. of Charles Ryley of Chester, pipemaker, deceased.
,,	11	Robert Prichard, mason, s. of John Prichard of Chester, mason.
,,	11	Phillip Downes, butcher, s. of Phillip Downes of Chester, innholder, deceased.
,,	11	James Hampton, cordwainer, s. of Thomas Hampton of Chester, cordwainer, deceased.
,,	11	Timothy Jones, cordwainer, s. of Peter Jones of Chester, woolcomber.
,,	11	John Bellis, carpenter, s. of Edward Bellis of Chester, hornbreaker.
,,	11	Thomas Woodward, barber, s. of Peter Woodward of Chester, innholder, deceased.
,,	11	Benjamin Boxley, cordwainer, s. of Henry Boxley of Chester, plasterer.

THE ROLLS OF THE FREEMEN OF [1747

July 11 William Crane, corkcutter, s. of Francis Crane of Chester, corkcutter, deceased.
,, 11 Dawson Wallworth p. of Ephraim Bardsley of Chester, baker, deceased.
,, 11 William s. of Peter Jones of Chester, woolcomber, and p. of Matthew Sharp of Chester, pipemaker.
,, 11 James Peers, tailor, s. of Thomas Peers of Chester, tailor.
,, 11 William Rider, mariner, s. of George Rider, late of Nesson, mariner, deceased.
,, 11 Thomas Prichard, sawyer, p. of Thomas Bennion of Chester, timber merchant.
,, 11 John Horton p. of Thomas Yates of Chester, bricklayer.
,, 11 John s. of John Welsh of Chester, yeoman, and p. of Thomas Wrench of Chester, joiner.
,, 11 Ralph Boden the younger p. of Thomas Wright of Chester, cordwainer.
,, 11 Edward Hawkins p. of John Golborne of Chester, cordwainer, deceased.
,, 11 Joseph Ordain p. of Robert Ordain of Chester, bricklayer.
,, 11 George Yould p. of John Stubs of Chester, bricklayer.
,, 13 George Ball, gentleman, s. of George Ball of Chester, gentleman, deceased.
,, 13 Charles Townsend, gentleman, s. of Gerrard Townsend of Chester, esquire, deceased.
,, 13 Edward Orme, painter, } ss. of Charles Orme of
,, 13 Ambrose Orme, painter, } Chester, painter, deceased.
,, 13 Charles Parker, apothecary, s. of John Parker of Chester, alderman.
,, 13 Arthur Parker, upholsterer, s. of Richard Parker of Chester, innholder.
,, 13 John Lawton, stationer, s. of John Lawton of Chester, innholder.
,, 13 George Boswell the younger, pavier, s. of George Boswell of Chester, pavier.
,, 13 Daniel s. and p. of John Williams of Chester, carpenter.
,, 13 James s. of John Whitbey of Chester, innholder, deceased.
,, 13 Thomas s. of George Linney, weaver, and p. of Christopher Gill of Chester, cordwainer.
,, 13 Kenrick s. of Kenrick Eyton of Chester, gentleman, deceased, and p. of John Hiccocke of Chester, barber.
,, 13 John s. of Thomas Handley, and p. of John Davies of Chester, cordwainer.

1747]   THE CITY OF CHESTER   331

July 13 John Hewitt, cordwainer, s. of Edward Hewitt of Chester, cordwainer.
 ,, 13 John Almond, feltmaker, s. of Richard Almond of Chester, feltmaker.
 ,, 13 Robert s. of George Walker, and p. of Noah Golborne of Chester, pipemaker.
 ,, 13 Joseph Coleclough, carpenter, s. of John Coleclough of Chester, carpenter, deceased.
 ,, 13 John s. and p. of George Pickford of Chester, bricklayer, defunct.
 ,, 13 John s. of Anne Jones, and p. of Thomas Withers of Chester, pattenmaker, deceased.
 ,, 13 David Roberts, shipcarpenter, s. of Griffith Roberts of Chester, innholder.
 ,, 13 Robert Aldersey, draper, s. of Daniel Aldersey of Chester, draper, deceased.
 ,, 13 Wainwright Croughton, linendraper, s. of William Croughton of Chester, linendraper, deceased.
 ,, 13 Charles Goodwin, ironmonger ["esquire" added on roll], s. of William Goodwin of Chester, ironmonger.
 ,, 13 Richard Moulson, tobacconist, s. of Richard Moulson of Chester, tobacconist.
 ,, 13 John Brandrett, barber, s. of John Brandrett of Chester, barber, deceased.
 ,, 13 Thomas Ashton the younger, esquire, s. of Thomas Ashton of Ashley, co. Ches., esquire.
 ,, 13 William Spence p. of John Cotgreave of Chester, cordwainer.
 ,, 13 George s. of Robert Parry, and p. of Jonathan Whittle of Chester, ropier.
 ,, 13 William s. of Peter Dannatt, and p. of John Tyrer of Chester, cordwainer.
 ,, 13 Joseph s. of James Newell, and p. of William Adshead of Chester, cordwainer.
 ,, 13 Andrew s. of John Hall, and p. of John Tyrer of Chester, cordwainer.
 ,, 13 John s. of Roger Francis, and p. of Jonathan Whittle of Chester, ropier.
 ,, 13 Ely s. of Moses Poynton, and p. of Thomas Pratchett of Chester, stockingweaver.
 ,, 13 William Smith p. of Samuel Smith of Chester, glassgrinder.
 ,, 13 Thomas Rowland p. of Henry Couldock of Chester, slater.
 ,, 13 Thomas s. of Samuel Lawrence, and p. of Thomas Corbin of Chester, joiner.

July 13 Richard Clerkson, carpenter, s. of Richard Clerkson of Chester, carpenter, deceased.
,, 13 John s. of Samuel Starkey, and p. of William Carter of Chester, cordwainer.
,, 13 Charles s. of John Taylor, and p. of Joseph Ratcliffe of Chester, flaxdresser, deceased.
,, 13 Thomas s. of Samuel Nevitt, and p. of Richard Sneyd of Chester, cooper.
,, 13 Thomas s. of Thomas Dawson, and p. of John Maddock of Chester, slater.
,, 13 Thomas s. of Thomas Hughes, and p. of John Sayer of Chester, plumber, deceased.
,, 13 John s. of Henry Thornton, and p. of John Parry of Chester, carpenter.
,, 13 Christopher Leak p. of Richard Griffith of Chester, pavier.
,, 13 John s. of Hugh Shannan, and p. of Peter Hickson of Chester, cordwainer.
,, 13 Charles Powell p. of James Macquien of Chester, pipe-maker.
,, 13 Joseph s. of Elizabeth Lightfoot, and p. of Arthur Mercer of Chester, brewer, deceased.
,, 13 Robert Hincks, merchant, s. of Edward Hincks of Chester, linendraper, deceased.
,, 13 George Spurstow, apothecary, s. of John Spurstow of Chester, merchant.
,, 13 Jonathan Goldson the younger, feltmaker, s. of Jonathan Goldson of Chester, feltmaker.
,, 13 Edward Platt, gentleman, s. of Richard Platt of Chester, gentleman, deceased.
,, 13 Charles Wrench, gentleman, s. of Richard Wrench of Chester, gentleman, deceased.
,, 13 Charles Croughton, linendraper, s. of William Croughton of Chester, linendraper, defunct.
,, 13 Thomas s. of Thomas Grace, gentleman, and pp. of James Wilkinson of Chester, ironmonger, deceased.
,, 13 John s. of Margaret Smathers,
,, 13 George s. of George Wright, and p. of John Sant of Chester, butcher.
,, 13 Thomas s. of Aquila Davenport, and p. of Ormson Calley of Chester, slater.
,, 13 Thomas Harvey, carpenter, s. of George Harvey of Chester, bricklayer.
,, 13 William Stout, slater, s. of Joseph Stout of Chester, butcher.
,, 13 William Cross, cabinetmaker, s. of John Cross of Chester, barber.

July 13 Thomas Price, carpenter, s. of Joseph Price of Chester, carpenter.
,, 13 Hugh Thomas, slater, s. of Hugh Thomas, and p. of Joseph Tellett of Chester.
,, 13 Samuel s. of John Odier, and p. of Gerrard Jordan of Chester, slater.
,, 13 Robert s. of Owen Owens, and p. of Joseph Dennell, of Chester, glazier.
,, 13 Edward Lewis, tanner, s. of John Lewis of Chester, pipemaker, deceased.
,, 13 John Prestbury, husbandman, s. of Jonathan Prestbury of Chester, smith.
,, 13 John Cross the younger, barber, } ss. of John Cross of
,, 13 Francis Cross, glazier, } Chester, barber.
,, 13 John s. of Thomas Price, and p. of Charles Buckley of Chester, barber.
,, 13 John s. and p. of Thomas Hales of Chester, innholder, deceased.
,, 13 Thomas Hales, currier, s. of above Thomas Hales.
,, 13 Robert s. of Robert Leicester, and p. of John Golborne of Chester, cordwainer, deceased.
,, 13 Thomas Duke, wetglover, s. of Bartholomew Duke of Chester, goldsmith, deceased.
,, 13 Thomas s. of John Griffith, and p. of William Crooke of Chester, cutler.
,, 13 Edward s. of Humphrey Edge, and p. of Richard Gough of Chester, carpenter, deceased.
,, 13 John s. of Mary Joynes, and p. of John Kirkes of Chester, upholsterer.
,, 13 Thomas Pulford, tailor, s. of Robert Pulford of Chester, butcher, deceased.
,, 13 Edward Pover p. of Randle Sorton of Chester, wetglover.
,, 13 Frederick Brown, blockmaker, s. of Thomas Brown of Liverpool, officer of the customs.
,, 13 Thomas Hunt, labourer, s. of George Hunt of Chester, labourer, deceased.
,, 13 William Revington, cordwainer, s. of William Revington of Chester, baker, deceased.
,, 13 Thomas Humphreys, combmaker, s. of Richard Humphreys of Chester, hornbreaker.
,, 13 Joseph s. of Joseph Moores, and p. of Peter Hickson of Chester, cordwainer.
,, 13 Richard s. of Charles Whitehead, and p. of Thomas Weigh of Chester, currier, deceased.
,, 13 Randle Lee p. of Henry Bennion of Chester, cooper, deceased.

July 13 Philip Guile, cooper, s. of William Guile of Chester, cooper.
„ 14 James Adams, clerk, s. of Richard Adams of Chester, gentleman, deceased.
„ 14 William Nicholls, clerk, } ss. of Peter Nicholls of
„ 14 Benjamin Nicholls, clerk, } Chester, tanner, deceased.
„ 14 George Bennion p. of Thomas Calkin of Chester, cabinetmaker.
„ 14 James s. of John Leigh, and p. of John Kirkes of Chester, upholsterer.
„ 14 John Spurstow, chapman, s. of John Spurstow of Chester, merchant.
„ 14 George s. of David Ruscoe, and p. of Samuel Maddock of Chester, tailor.
„ 14 James Prince the younger, cordwainer, s. of James Prince of Chester, cordwainer.
„ 14 John Palin, p. of Peter Hale of Chester, butcher.
„ 14 John Crewe, slater, s. of Thomas Crewe of Chester, slater, deceased.
„ 14 John s. of Thomas Cope, and p. of John Crane of Chester, cordwainer.
„ 14 Theodore Aldcroft, chapman, s. of John Aldcroft of Manchester, fustianmaker.
„ 14 William s. of Robert Vernon, and p. of Samuel Tonna of Chester, butcher.
„ 14 Charles Cookson p. of Edward Bateman of Chester, butcher, deceased.
„ 14 Ralph Cartwright p. of John Adshead of Chester, barber, deceased.
„ 14 John s. of Thomas Evans, and p. of Charles Price of Chester, joiner.
„ 14 John Bayley p. of Edward Litherland of Chester, tailor.
„ 14 Nathaniel Jones, bookkeeper [No description given in M.B.], p. of Matthew Bayley of Chester, merchant.
„ 14 Thomas Mather, esquire, } ss. of Thomas Mather,
„ 14 Richard Mather, gentleman, } esquire, deceased.
„ 14 Paul Patton, butcher, s. of William Patton of Chester, tanner.
„ 14 Roger Eaton, labourer, } ss. of Roger Eaton of Manley,
„ 14 Richard Eaton, labourer, } co. Ches., yeoman.
„ 14 James Almond, labourer, s. of John Almond of Chester, cordwainer, deceased.
„ 14 Edward Evans, glazier, s. of Edward Evans of Chester, glazier, deceased.
„ 14 James s. of Nathan Artingstall, and p. of Joseph Stout of Chester, butcher.

July	14	George Hastings, tinplateworker, s. of John Hastings of Chester, turner.
,,	14	William s. of Richard Vernon, and p. of John Briscoe of Chester, barber.
,,	14	Edward s. of Peter Bowden, and p. of William Harvey of Chester, bricklayer, deceased.
,,	14	Joseph Gilbert, maltster, s. of James Gilbert of Chester, chandler, deceased.
,,	14	George Molyneux, joiner, s. of John Molyneux of Chester, cordwainer.
,,	14	John s. of Thomas Read, and p. of William Cooke of Chester, printer, deceased.
,,	14	John s. of George Spensley, and p. of Charles Moulson of Chester, chandler.
,,	14	William Bennion, butcher, s. of Bulkley Bennion, and p. of Joseph Stout of Chester, butcher.
,,	14	John Tylston, merchant, s. of John Tylston of Chester, merchant, deceased.
,,	14	Hugh Jones the younger, joiner ["mercht." added in another hand on roll], s. of Hugh Jones of Chester, joiner.
,,	14	Robert Bromley, butcher, } ss. of William Bromley
,,	14	Richard Bromley, pavier, } of Tarvin, co. Ches., pavier, deceased.
,,	14	Edward s. of John Lloyd, and p. of James Almond of Chester, butcher, deceased.
,,	14	William s. of John Wilcock, and p. of Thomas Harrison of Chester, cooper, deceased.
,,	14	Thomas s. of Thomas Eccleston, and p. of John Croughton of Chester, cordwainer.
,,	14	Samuel s. of John Hewitt, and p. of Henry Bennion of Chester, cooper, deceased.
,,	14	Aaron s. of Moses Poynton, and p. of Thomas Pratchett of Chester, stockingweaver.
,,	14	Joseph Bennett p. of Randle Wrench of Chester, butcher.
,,	14	John Crane, slater, s. of Thomas Crane of Chester, slater.
,,	14	Hugh Walters, p. of Charles Boswell of Chester, pavier.
,,	14	Henry s. of Richard Jackson, and p. of William Cartwright of Chester, butcher.
,,	14	Thomas Wilkinson, baker, } ss. of William Wilkin-
,,	14	Edward Wilkinson, yeoman, } son of Little Stanney, co. Ches., surgeon.
,,	14	John s. of Richard Bruce, and p. of Thomas Mulleneux of Chester, cordwainer.

July 14 Edward Buckley, smith, s. of Randle Buckley of Chester, smith.
,, 14 John Challoner p. of Henry Orum of Chester, slater.
,, 14 William Gregg, cordwainer, s. of Robert Gregg of Chester, cordwainer, deceased.
,, 14 Charles s. of Lewis Bruen, and p. of Thomas Crooke of Chester, carpenter, deceased.
,, 14 William s. of William Taylor, and p. of Richard Burrowes of Chester, carpenter, deceased.
,, 14 Thomas s. of William Bushell, and p. of John Tomlinson of Chester, wheelwright.
,, 14 William s. of Samuel Jones, and p. of Richard Carr of Chester, flaxdresser.
,, 14 William s. of John Griffith, and p. of William Sherman of Chester, staymaker, deceased.
,, 14 Joseph s. of Patrick Fitzgerald, and p. of John Sharp of Chester, pipemaker.
,, 14 John s. of John Cooke, miller, and p. of William Huntington of Chester, baker, deceased.
,, 14 John Elliston p. of Joseph Avern of Chester, corkcutter.
,, 14 Charles Cowdock, smith, s. of Richard Cowdock of Chester, smith.
,, 14 Joseph Porter p. of Griffith Biggins of Chester, upholsterer, deceased.
,, 14 George Biggins, tailor, s. of John Biggins of Chester, innholder, deceased.
,, 14 Thomas Eaton, cordwainer, s. of Roger Eaton of Manley, co. Ches., yeoman.
,, 14 John s. of John Hill, and p. of John Johnson of Chester, slater.
,, 14 Joseph s. of Joseph Mullineux, deceased, and p. of William Adshead of Chester, cordwainer.
,, 14 Thomas s. of Lawrence Nevitt, and p. of Peter Whittaker, of Chester, butcher.
,, 14 Thomas Brown, ropier, s. of Thomas Brown of Parkgate, co. Ches., cordwainer.
,, 14 Edward Mainwaring, clerk, s. of James Mainwaring, esquire, alderman.
,, 15 Richard s. of Richard Oakes, and p. of Thomas Carter of Chester, cordwainer.
,, 15 James Tylston, yeoman, s. of Thomas Tylston of Chester, bricklayer.
,, 15 John Denson p. of Michael Bromley of Chester, butcher.

July 15   Isaac Prestbury, tailor, s. of Jonathan Prestbury of Chester, smith.
„   15   Peter Capper, turner, s. of James Capper of Chester, carpenter, deceased.
„   15   William Waters, cordwainer, s. of Thomas Waters of Chester, tailor.
„   15   Thomas s. of Samuel Prichard, and p. of William Peyton of Chester, linendraper.
„   15   Robert Caulton, wine cooper, s. of Joseph Dyson of Chester, merchant, deceased.
„   15   Thomas s. of Thomas Bennett, and p. of Samuel Nicholls of Chester, butcher.
„   15   John Bellward p. of William Skellington of Chester, tailor.
„   15   James s. of John Sinclair, and p. of John Stubs of Chester, bricklayer.
„   15   Robert Murrey, clerk, s. of Robert Murrey of Chester, merchant, deceased.
„   15   John Hincks, merchant, s. of Edward Hincks of Chester, linendraper, deceased.
„   15   Edward Calley the younger, weaver, s. of Edward Calley of Chester, weaver.
„   15   Thomas Orme, barber, s. of Charles Orme of Chester, painter, deceased.
„   15   James s. of John Weaver, and p. of William Hill of Chester, carpenter, deceased.
„   15   Peter Fitzgerald p. of Gawen Richards of Chester, pipemaker.
„   15   John Backarn, carpenter, s. of Richard Backarn of Chester, carpenter, deceased.
„   15   John Croughton, cabinetmaker, s. of Henry Croughton of Chester, glover, deceased.
„   15   Sir Peter Warburton, baronet.
„   16   Edward s. of George Walker, and p. of James Golding of Chester, pipemaker.
„   16   John Bennett, yeoman, s. of John Bennett of Chester, tanner, deceased.
„   16   Thomas Bennett, yeoman, s. of John Bennett of Willaston, co. Ches., yeoman, deceased.
„   16   William s. of William Jones, and p. of Henry Pemberton of Chester, ropier.
„   16   John Pemberton, mariner, s. of John Pemberton of Chester, chandler, deceased.
„   16   Joseph s. of John Smith, and p. of George Juckle [or Inckle] of Chester, mason, deceased.
„   16   James s. of Philip Ardern, and p. of Ralph Probert of Chester, feltmaker.

July 16 John Wright, ironmonger, s. of Nathan Wright of Chester, alderman.
,, 16 Robert Davies, draper, s. of Thomas Davies of Chester, alderman.
,, 16 Thomas Bingley p. of William Harvey of Chester, bricklayer.
,, 16 Charles s. of John Jackson, and p. of Richard Rogers of Chester, joiner.
,, 17 William Bridge, gentleman, s. of Thomas Bridge of Chester, feltmaker, deceased.
,, 18 *Robert Foulkes, esquire.
,, 18 John Bennett, barber, s. of William Bennett of Chester, barber, deceased.
,, 18 John Bennion, yeoman, } ss. of Randle Bennion of Caldecott, co. Ches., yeoman.
,, 18 William Bennion, yeoman, }
,, 18 John Bennion, yeoman, s. of John Bennion of Chalton, co. Ches., yeoman, deceased.
,, 18 Daniel Craven the younger, yeoman, s. of Daniel Craven of Bunbury, co. Ches., yeoman.
,, 18 George Maddock, mariner, s. of Benjamin Maddock, "late a soldier in Gibraltar," deceased.
,, 18 John Peers, tailor, s. of Thomas Peers of Chester, tailor.
,, 18 Thomas Sparkes p. of Thomas Sefton of Chester, mariner.
,, 18 John Wheawell the younger, yeoman, } ss. of John Wheawell, of Chester, yeoman.
,, 18 William Wheawell, yeoman, }
,, 18 James Lyttler, cordwainer, s. of Thomas Lytler of Chester, cordwainer, deceased.
,, 18 Thomas s. of Richard Lowndes, and p. of John Parker, mercer, of Chester, alderman, deceased.
,, 18 Samuel Duke, clerk, s. of Thomas Duke of Chester, alderman.
,, 18 John Cotgreave the younger, chapman ["gent." added on Roll], s. of John Cotgreave of Chester, alderman.
,, 18 Thomas Cooke the younger, brewer, s. of Thomas Cooke of Chester, tailor.
,, 18 John Ellis, otherwise Foulkes, yeoman, s. of —— Foulkes of Hope, co. Flint, yeoman.
,, 18 Joseph s. of Thomas Tylston, and p. of John Dyson of Chester, tinplateworker, deceased.
,, 18 John Dennill, gentleman, s. of Joseph Dennill of Chester, glazier.
,, 18 John Wright, carpenter, s. of John Wright of Chester, brewer.

July	18	Daniel Newell p. of Thomas Hope of Chester, cordwainer.
,,	18	George Holland, cordwainer, s. of Joseph Holland of Chester, flaxdresser, deceased.
,,	18	Richard s. of Richard Linsdale, and p. of John Golding of Chester, pipemaker.
,,	18	Thomas Stones, saddler, s. of William Stones of Chester, saddler.
,,	18	John Bramwell, yeoman ["gent." added on Roll], s. of Jonathan Bramwell of Chester, innholder, deceased.
,,	18	James Johnson, cordwainer, ss. of William Johnson of Chester, cordwainer, deceased.
,,	18	Thomas Johnson, cordwainer,
,,	18	John Carter, cordwainer, s. of William Carter of Chester, cordwainer.
,,	18	James s. of John Beech, and p. of Thomas Pratchett of Chester, framework-knitter.
,,	18	William Baddiley p. of Robert Cowdock of Chester, smith.
,,	18	Hugh Hayward, esquire, s. of Robert Hayward of Chester, gentleman.
,,	20	John Poole, checkman, s. of John Poole of Chester, barber, deceased.
,,	20	James Halliwell, currier, s. of Hugh Halliwell of Manchester, cordwainer.
,,	20	Thomas Smith, cabinetmaker, s. of Thomas Smith the younger of Chester, sawyer, deceased.
,,	20	Daniel Young, yeoman, s. of Daniel Young of Bunbury, co. Ches., yeoman.
,,	20	William s. of John Holt, and p. of William Hill of Chester, carpenter, deceased.
,,	20	Thomas s. of Thomas Peers, tailor, and p. of Samuel Maddock of Chester, tailor.
,,	20	Thomas Wetherall, mariner, s. of Thomas Wetherall of Chester, wetglover, deceased.
,,	20	Charles Mechaughan p. of Thomas Hope of Chester, cordwainer.
,,	20	Jeffrey s. of Thomas Ashmull, and p. of Christopher Gill of Chester, cordwainer, deceased.
,,	20	Richard s. of Humphrey Edwards, and p. of William Wright of Chester, flaxdresser.
,,	20	Elias s. of William Foster of Bolton, co. Lanc., cordwainer.
,,	20	Matthew Whitney, yeoman, s. of Thomas Whitney of Chester, feltmaker, deceased.
,,	20	Thomas Barrow, barber, s. of John Barrow of Manchester, co. Lanc., feltmaker, deceased.

July 20 Peter Woodward, joiner, s. of Peter Woodward of Chester, innholder, deceased.
,, 20 Thomas Cope p. of Joseph Woodward of Chester, joiner, deceased.
,, 20 Peter Young, yeoman, s. of Daniel Young of Bunbury, co. Ches., yeoman.
,, 20 Thomas Conway, slater, s. of John Conway of Chester, slater.
,, 20 *Ellice Wynne, clerk.
,, 20 Robert s. of Robert Bartlam, and p. of William Cotton, of Chester, carpenter, deceased.
,, 20 Joseph Adams, yeoman, s. of Richard Adams of Hope, co. Flint, yeoman, deceased.
,, 20 John Briscoe, gentleman, s. of John Briscoe of Woodbank, co. Ches., gentleman.
,, 20 James Walker p. of Hugh Jones of Chester, joiner.
,, 20 Joseph Hayes, brewer, s. of Samuel Hayes of Great Neston, co. Ches., mariner, deceased.
,, 20 *Francis Price, esquire.
,, 21 *Robert Pigot of Chetwynd, esquire.
,, 21 *Sir Thomas Longueville, baronet.
,, 21 *Mathew Lyon, gentleman.
,, 21 *Francis Lloyd of Crossmere, esquire.
,, 21 *Edward Moreton of Elsmere, clerk.
,, 21 *Robert Ellis of Cross Newydd, esquire.
,, 21 *Thomas Ravenscroft of Pickhill, esquire.
,, 21 *Robert Banks of Winstanley, esquire.
,, 21 *Alexander Holford of Moolton, esquire.
,, 21 *Miles Lonsdale, esquire.
,, 21 *Richard Clayton, esquire.
,, 21 *John Parker of Fallowes, esquire.
,, 21 *Evan Vaughan of Bodidrist, esquire.
,, 21 *John Mostyn of Segroit, esquire.
,, 21 *Robert Booth of Salford, esquire.
,, 21 *John Salusbury of Denbigh, gentleman.
,, 21 Edward Ley, cordwainer, s. of Edward Ley of Chester, barber, deceased.
,, 21 Samuel Maddock the younger, gentleman, s. of Samuel Maddock of Chester, innholder.
,, 21 Hugh Topping of Liverpool, apothecary, s. of Hugh Topping of Chester, barber, deceased.
,, 21 Thomas s. of Thomas Rippington of Chester, innholder, deceased.
,, 21 *Thomas Edwards of Wrexham, clerk.
,, 21 *John Leche of Carden, esquire.

July	21	David ap Hugh, gardener, s. of David ap Hugh, and p. of William Littleton of Chester, gardener.
,,	21	William Maddocks of Nantwich s. of Simon Maddocks, deceased, and p. of Jonathan Whittle of Chester, ropier.
,,	21	Timothy Parsonage, yeoman, s. of Richard Parsonage of Allington, co. Denbigh, plumber, deceased.
,,	21	Robert Poynton, cordwainer, s. of William Poynton of Liverpool, co. Lanc., butcher.
,,	21	*Francis Elcock of Poole, esquire.
,,	21	James Bowen, painter, s. of John Bowen of Salop, painter, deceased.
,,	21	John Shone, collier, s. of Thomas Shone of Hawarden, collier.
,,	21	Cornelius Hayes, tobacconist, s. of Daniel Hayes of Chester, draper, deceased.
,,	21	John Evans p. of Hugh Hand of Chester, joiner, deceased.
,,	21	Thomas Griffith, mariner, s. of David Griffith of Chester, inkhorn-turner, deceased.
,,	21	George Hancock, mariner, s. of John Hancock of Parkgate, mariner, deceased.
,,	21	John Ormes, cabinetmaker, s. of Richard Ormes of Chester, pipemaker, deceased.
,,	21	Thomas Walters, cordwainer, s. of Thomas Walters of Chester, tailor.
,,	21	James s. and p. of Joseph Wilkinson, wheelwright.
,,	21	George Grason, pipemaker, s. of Jonathan Grason of Chester, pipemaker, deceased.
,,	21	John Larden, yeoman, s. of John Larden of Tattenhall, co. Ches., deceased.
,,	21	Samuel Kirkes, upholsterer, s. of Hamnett Kirkes of Chester, upholsterer, deceased.
,,	21	Peter s. of Peter Dutton, and p. of Thomas Hankey of Chester, saddler, deceased.
,,	21	*Cawley Humberston Cawley, esquire.
,,	21	Thomas Moyle of Nantwich, innkeeper, s. of Thomas Moyle of Chester, saddler, deceased.
,,	21	Samuel Harvey, bricklayer, s. of Edward Harvey of Chester, bricklayer, deceased.
,,	22	Richard Jones, pipemaker, s. of Peter Jones of Chester, woolcomber.
,,	22	Thomas Doland of Coventry, cordwainer, p. of Roger Griffith of Chester, cordwainer, deceased.
,,	22	John Halliwell, cordwainer, s. of Hugh Halliwell of Manchester, cordwainer.

July 22 Henry s. of Joshua Latham, and p. of Jonathan Haslow of Chester, cooper, deceased.
,, 23 James Hawkins, upholsterer, s. of Edward Hawkins of Chester, upholsterer.
,, 23 Richard Venables, bricklayer, s. of William Venables of Chester, bricklayer.
,, 24 James Wright, grocer, s. of James Wright of Chester, innholder, deceased.
,, 24 *Edward Lloyd of Horsley, esquire.
,, 24 John Bellin, barber, s. of Robert Bellin of Chester, cooper.
,, 25 *Robert Hyde, esquire.
,, 25 *George Kennion, esquire.
,, 25 *Sir Thomas Standish, baronet.
,, 25 Richard Twist, yeoman, p. of William Cotton of Chester, innholder.
,, 25 Thomas Hayes, doctor of physick, s. of Samuel Hayes of Great Neston, co. Ches., brewer, deceased.
,, 25 *William Price of Vaynol, esquire.
,, 27 *Robert Wynne of Garthewin, esquire.
,, 27 *Peter Bold of Bold, esquire.
,, 27 *Robert Price of Bathavarn, esquire.
,, 28 Joseph Tellett the younger, slater, s. of Joseph Tellett of Chester, slater.
Aug. 13 *The Right Hon. Charles, Lord Boyle, s. of Right Hon. Earl of Orrery.
,, 13 *John Hill of Sontley, esquire.
,, 13 *John Witter.
Sep. 5 John Price, baker, s. of Charles Price of Chester, innholder, deceased.
,, 15 *Thomas Slaughter, esquire.
,, 19 *John Amson, esquire.
,, 29 *Sir Richard Brooke, baronet.
,, 30 Robert s. of Thomas Dickson ["Dicken" on Roll] of Backford, co. Ches., deceased, and p. of Arthur Mercer of Chester, brewer, deceased.
Oct. 1 *Thomas Dod, esquire.
,, 1 *Randle Dod, gentleman.
,, 3 *John Egerton the younger of Broxton, esquire.
,, 3 *Thomas Hughes of Halkin, esquire.
,, 3 *Peter Davies of Chester, esquire.
,, 3 *George Ravenscroft of Wrexham, gentleman.
,, 10 *John Brooke, esquire.
,, 10 *William Hanmer of Iscoyd, esquire.
,, 10 *Thomas Worsley, yeoman.
,, 12 *The Reverend John Davie, clerk.

Oct. 12 *The Reverend James Stones, clerk.
„ 13 *Hugh Whishaw the younger, gentleman.
„ 14 *The Reverend Thomas Wrench, clerk.
„ 14 *Thomas Pennant of Downing, esquire.
„ 15 *The Reverend Thomas Parry, clerk.
„ 15 *Sir William Duckenfield Daniel, baronet.
„ 16 *Charles Fletcher of Whitchurch, gentleman.
„ 16 *Orlando Fletcher of Whitchurch, gentleman.
„ 16 *The Reverend Francis Gastrell, clerk.
July 21 *Robert Wynne of Plas Newydd, esquire.

1747-8 [21-22 G. ii.] WILLIAM EDWARDS, Esquire, Mayor.

Oct. 6 *Humphrey Read, gentleman.
Nov. 10 Thomas Croughton, draper, s. of William Croughton of Chester, linendraper, deceased.
Jan. 30 James Roberts, barber, s. of Griffith Roberts of Chester, innholder.
Mar. 28 Thomas Boswell, barber, s. of George Boswell of Chester, pavier.
Apr. 2 Thomas s. of Robert Mann of Marton, co. Ches., yeoman, deceased, and p. of John Dutton of Chester, butcher.
„ 9 Robert s. of Robert Hassall of Chester, yeoman, and p. of Thomas Goolding of Chester, wheelwright, deceased.
May 21 *George Wilson, yeoman.
„ 21 *Josiah Griffis, yeoman.
„ 21 Thomas s. of Samuel Rathbone of Chester, carpenter, and p. of John Williams of Chester, carpenter.
„ 28 *John Ellis, corkcutter.
[1747]
July 24 *William Wynne, clerk.
June 18 *William Bradshaw, clerk.
„ 25 *Thomas Store, gentleman.
„ 25 *Ralph Griffith, gentleman.
July 21 John Gaulter, linendraper, s. and p. of John Gaulter of Chester, innholder, deceased.
Sep. 10 Randle Dicas, tallowchandler, s. of Randle Dicas of Chester, tallowchandler, deceased.
Oct. 1 Charles Smith, flaxdresser, s. of Nathaniel Smith of Chester, feltmaker, deceased.

344 THE ROLLS OF THE FREEMEN OF [1748-9

Oct. 8 Hamnett Dobb the younger, s. of Hamnett Dobb the elder of Chester, gardener.
„ 13 *Thomas Edwards, maltster.
„ 14 *John Sefton, victualler.

1748-9 [22-23 G. ii.] EDWARD GRIFFITH, Esquire, Mayor.

Oct. 22 *Richard Surridge, esquire.
„ 22 *John Daniel, esquire.
Nov. 5 Francis Davies, slater, s. of John Davies of Chester, slater, deceased.
„ 10 Richard s. of John Barrow of Boughton, co. Ches., barber, deceased, and p. of Charles Adshead of Chester, barber, deceased.
Dec. 3 *John Tompkinson, yeoman.
„ 15 Christopher Bennett, barber, s. of John Bennett of Chester, yeoman, deceased, and p. of George Brown of Chester.
Jan. 7 John s. of John Martin of Eastham, co. Ches., yeoman, deceased, and p. of Alderman Charles Bingley of Chester, tallowchandler, deceased.
Mar. 4 John Taylor, slater, s. of Timothy Taylor of Chester, ropier.
May 20 John s. of Andrew Potter of Little Neston, co. Ches., mariner, and p. of Joseph Wilkinson of Chester, baker.
July 4 Giles Minshull, linendraper, s. of Thomas Minshull of Chester, silkweaver, deceased.
„ 12 Thomas s. of William Lawton of Chester, deceased, and p. of Edward Middlehurst of Chester, barber.
Aug. 18 William Martin p. of Arthur Mercer of Chester, brewer, deceased.
„ 28 *John Miller, maltmaker.
„ 28 *Joshua Wild, yeoman.
„ 28 *Thomas Kirkes, gentleman.

1749-50 [23-24 G. ii.] THOMAS BINGLEY, Esquire, Mayor.

Oct. 14 Francis Walley, feltmaker, s. of James Walley of Chester, feltmaker.
Dec. 2 Thomas Patton, tanner, s. of William Patton of Chester, tanner.

1750-1]   THE CITY OF CHESTER   345

Jan. 10   James Selby, butcher, s. of William Selby of Chester, butcher, deceased.
Feb. 26 *Edward Linke, wheelwright.
Mar. 9 *James Pardoe, merchant.
  ,,   9   Philip Prestbury, cabinetmaker, s. of Samuel Prestbury of Chester, wetglover, deceased.
  ,, 19 *William Cotterell, yeoman.
  ,, 19 *Charles Bridge, gentleman.
  ,, 21   Daniel Jennions, barber, s. of Joseph Jennions of Chester, barber, deceased.
  ,, 23   John Leadbeater, brewer, s. of John Leadbeater of Chester, brewer, deceased.
  ,, 26   Michael Cooper, shipwright, s. of William Cooper of Ewloe, co. Flint, deceased, and p. of Thomas Bennion of Chester, merchant.
Apr. 27   Thomas s. of Sarah Higginson of Chester, widow, and p. of John Cotgreave of Chester, cordwainer.
May 30   Thomas Marsden, merchant ["esq." added on Roll], s. of John Marsden of Chester, alderman, deceased.
Aug. 6   John Williams the younger, carpenter, s. of John Williams of Chester, carpenter.
Sep. 17   Thomas Bowers, linendraper, s. of Robert Bowers of Chester, linendraper, deceased.
Oct. 8   John Hickson the younger, tailor, s. of John Hickson of Chester, tailor.
  ,,   8 *William Watkins, distiller.
  ,,   9   Thomas Bateman, butcher, s. of Edward Bateman of Chester, butcher.
  ,, 10   James Poole, feltmaker, s. of John Poole of Chester, deceased.

1750-1 [24-25 G. ii.] JOHN HALLWOOD, Esquire, Mayor.

Nov. 21   John Egerton, brewer, s. of John Egerton of Chester, brewer, deceased.
Feb. 4   John Lumber, cutler, s. of James Lumber of Chester, yeoman.
  ,,   8   Ralph Tushingham, cooper, s. of Jonathan Tushingham of Great Boughton, co. Ches., yeoman, deceased, and p. of Richard Sneyd of Chester, cooper and fishmonger.
Apr. 23   John Wilkinson, grocer, s. of James Wilkinson of Chester, grocer.

May 6 Robert Price, butcher, s. of John Price of Chester, butcher.
June 4 John s. of John Robin of Shotwick Lodge, co. Ches., yeoman, and p. of Henry Bushell of Chester, wetglover.
„ 5 Thomas s. of Robert Fernall of Lea, co. Ches., yeoman, and p. of Robert Fernall of Chester, butcher.
„ 9 John s. of Jeremiah Lawrenson of Frodsham, co. Ches, cordwainer, and p. of John Hale of Chester, butcher.
July 23 Richard Crachley, brewer, s. of Robert Crachley of Broad Lane, co. Flint, gentleman.
Aug. 16 William Powell, barber, s. of Benjamin Powell of Chester, barber.
Sep. 7 Ralph Wilkinson, grocer, s. of James Wilkinson of Chester, grocer.
„ 9 Perry Dawson, wetglover, s. of Perry Dawson of Chester, wetglover.
„ 27 Ralph Bellin, cooper, [? s.] of Robert Bellin of Chester, cooper.
Oct. 7 William s. of William Roberts of Holywell, co. Flint, yeoman, and p. of Jane Pyke of Chester, baker.
„ 7 Thomas s. of John Powell of Chester, cordwainer, and p. of William Brown of Chester, cordwainer.

1751–2 [25–26 G. ii.] RALPH PROBERT, Esquire, Mayor.

Oct. 29 John Mort p. of Richard Orme of Chester, tailor.
Jan. 18 Samuel Hodgson p. of John Egerton of Chester, brewer, deceased.
Mar. 14 Anderson Davies, victualler, s. of Thomas Davies of Chester, alderman and draper.
Apr. 1 Charles Jordan, slater, s. of Gerrard Jordan of Chester, slater.
„ 1 Thomas s. of Peter Hopkins of Middlewich, co. Ches., baker, and p. of Samuel Price of Chester, bricklayer.
„ 6 Thomas Harrison, cooper, s. of Thomas Harrison of Chester, cooper.
„ 7 John s. of Richard Massey of Nether Whitley, co. Ches., yeoman, and p. of Richard Massey of Chester, baker, deceased.
Apr. 30 George Gethley, barber, s. of Matthew Gethley of Chester, cordwainer.

1752]   THE CITY OF CHESTER   347

May   9   George Trelford, victualler, s. and p. of James Trelford of Chester, innholder.
  „   9   William s. of Joseph Ratcliffe of Chester, flaxdresser.
  „ 26   Thomas s. of Lawrence Corles of Chester, wetglover.
  „ 26   John Thomas, pewterer, s. of Hugh Thomas of Hawarden, co. Flint, and p. of Alderman Thomas Brock, brazier.
June 1   John Sorton, wetglover, s. of Randle Sorton of Chester, wetglover.
  „   5   *Ralph Vernon, gentleman.
July 6   Charles Holland, merchant, s. of Robert Holland of Chester, linendraper, deceased.
Aug. 3   *Thomas Cholmondeley, esquire.
  „ 22   Thomas Pickmore, tailor, p. of Christopher Gill of Chester, staymaker.
  „ 27   Richard Grosvenor, esquire, s. of Sir Robert Grosvenor, baronet.
  „ 29   *Peter Leadbeater, brewer.
  „ 29   *James Glasiour, gentleman.
  „ 29   *Gabriel Smith, watchmaker.
  —   2   Thomas Grosvenor, esquire, [?s.] of Sir Robert Grosvenor, baronet.
Sep. 14   Robert Hickman p. of Thomas Hickman of Chester, brewer.
  „ 14   Hugh Bennett p. of James Calveley of Chester, flaxdresser.
  „ 18   Thomas Woodcock, feltmaker, s. of John Woodcock of Chester, feltmaker.
Oct. 2   *Richard Wareing, gardener.
  „   6   *William Thompson, watchmaker.
  „   6   *James Stubbs, druggist.
  „   7   Thomas Pate, butcher, s. of John Pate of Chester, butcher.
  „   7   *Jonathan Lewis, tobacconist.
  „   9   Thomas Lumber, barber, s. of James Lumber of Chester, yeoman.

1752-3 [26-27 G. ii.] THOMAS BROSTER, Esquire, Mayor.

Nov. 3   Samuel Bagnall, tea merchant, s. of Thomas Bagnall of Chester, grocer.
  „   3   Daniel Pemberton, carpenter, s. of Daniel Pemberton of Chester, carpenter.

—	7	Thomas Leadbeator, mason, [? p.] of Samuel Davies of Chester, ——.
Dec.	12	John Culm p. of Christopher Gill of Chester, tailor.
Feb.	6	John Price, butcher, s. of John Price of Chester, butcher.
,,	9	Richard Shone, butcher, s. of Daniel Shone of Chester, yeoman, deceased.
,,	15	Arthur Tushingham p. of Thomas Patton of Chester, currier.
Feb.	19	Ralph Wilkinson, yeoman, s. of Thomas Wilkinson of Chester, chandler, deceased.
Mar.	24	Hugh Rowe p. of William Cartwright of Chester, butcher.
,,	26	John Wilkinson, wine cooper, s. of John Wilkinson of Chester, wheelwright, deceased.
,,	28	William Rogers, butcher, s. of Samuel Rogers of Chester, deceased.
,,	31	John Yates, bricklayer, s. of Thomas Yates of Chester, bricklayer.
Apr.	16	William Porter, brewer, s. of Daniel Porter of Chester, gentleman.
May	7	George Smith, innholder, s. of William Smith of Chester, alderman.
,,	23	Thomas Plumbley, barber, s. of William Plumbley of Chester, flaxdresser, deceased.
June	18	William Hale, butcher, s. of William Hale of Chester, butcher, deceased.
,,	23	John s. of Thomas Pemberton of Chester, husbandman, and p. of Samuel Price of Chester, bricklayer.
July	2	*Edward Richardson, yeoman.
,,	21	*Joseph Betteley, yeoman.
,,	21	Edmund Warrington, baker [" malster " added on Roll], s. of Silvester Warrington of Puddington, co. Ches., yeoman, and p. of Mary Aires of Chester, widow, baker.
,,	26	John s. of Thomas Wright of Chester, maltster, and p. of William Dicas of Chester, barber.
,,	26	Benjamin s. of Benjamin Batho of Boughton, co. Ches., wheelwright, and p. of Robert Tapley of Chester, glazier.
Aug.	16	Robert Bower, linendraper, s. of Robert Bower of Chester, linendraper, deceased.
,,	16	Samuel Croughton, apothecary, s. of William Croughton, linendraper, deceased.
Sep.	15	Thomas s. of Richard Backarn, carpenter, deceased.
,,	23	John Hayes, cordwainer, s. of John Hayes, baker.

Oct. 6 *Thomas Griffith, yeoman.
„ 6 *John Short, gentleman.
„ 16 *Isaac Huntington, yeoman.
„ 17 *John Cheers, yeoman.

1753-4 [27-28 G. ii.] EDMUND BOLLAND, Esquire, Mayor.

Nov. 1 Thomas Shephard, beerbrewer, p. of John Saladine, brewer.
„ 12 William Monk, printer, p. of Roger Adams, deceased.
Dec. 18 Thomas Price, butcher, s. of John Price, butcher.
„ 19 *Thomas Adams, gentleman.
Jan. 6 *William Lewis, grocer.
Feb. 4 Daniel Lowndes p. of Samuel Sawyer, tin plate worker.
„ 9 *John Evans.
Mar. 2 John Lloyd the younger, staymaker, s. of John Lloyd, ————.
„ 2 George Bingley, glazier, ————.
Apr. 29 John Minshull, chandler, s. of Thomas Minshull, silk-weaver.
June 15 Robert Jones, pipemaker, s. of John Jones, pipemaker.
„ 20 Charles Parker, mariner, s. of Richard Parker, innholder.
„ 21 John Starkey, vintner, p. of James Croxton, merchant.
July 20 William Hall, p. of John Crane, cordwainer.
„ 20 James Butler, cutler, ————.
„ 20 William Turner, tanner.
„ 20 Joseph Dyson, merchant ["gent." added on Roll].
Aug. 15 Robert Harrison of Chester, tailor, s. of Thomas Harrison, tailor.
„ 17 *Daniel Smith of Chester, innholder.
„ 17 *George Eaton of Chester, mason.
„ 17 *William Coy of Chester, mason.
Aug. 22 *Edward Boodle, gentleman.
Sep. 7 John Jones p. of Charles Hitchins of Chester, butcher.
„ 28 William Bromley of Chester, butcher, s. of Michael Bromley, butcher.
Oct. 1 *Samuel Seller of Littleton, co. Ches., yeoman.
„ 1 Evan Jones of Chester, grocer, p. of Alderman Edward Griffith.

1754-5 [28-29 G. ii.] WILLIAM COWPER, Esquire, Mayor.

Nov. 9 John Gamon of Farndon, co. Ches., yeoman, s. of John Gamon of Churton, co. Ches., yeoman.
,, 23 *Roger Wilbraham of Chester, esquire.
— — Lively Oldham p. of ——— Jones, barber.
— — William Rathbone of Chester, cordwainer, p. of John Harrison, cordwainer, and assigned to Peter Hickson, cordwainer.
,, 26 Charles Hughes of Chester, p. of William Palin, baker.
Dec. 7 John Drake, mercer, p. of Alderman Edward Yeardsley, and assigned to Alderman Edmund Bolland of Chester, mercer.
,, 21 John Jones of Chester p. of Edward Powell, mason.
,, 28 John Salisbury of Chester, mariner, s. of Charles Salisbury, mariner.
Jan. 13 John Buckley, bookseller, ———.
,, 27 *William Robinson of Whatcroft, co. Ches., esquire.
,, 30 Philip Egerton of Chester, druggist, s. of John Egerton, brewer.
Feb. 6 John Davies of Chester, plumber, s. of Alderman Thomas Davies.
,, 11 Thomas Wynne of Chester, glover, s. of Humphrey Wynne, grocer.
,, 11 John Totty of Chester, whitesmith, s. of George Totty, whitesmith.
,, 11 William Briscoe, smith, ———.
,, 11 Peter Heath, cordwainer, s. of George Heath of Chester, cordwainer.
,, 11 Robert Maddock, cordwainer, s. of Robert Maddock, tanner.
,, 15 Thomas Kelley, barber, s. of Thomas Kelley, tailor.
,, 15 John Lawrence p. of John Maddock, slater.
,, 15 Lawrence Gother, tailor, s. of John Gother, weaver.
,, 20 John Mostyn, yeoman, s. of Rowland Mostyn, woolcomber.
Mar. 15 Thomas Griffith, grocer ["mercht." added on Roll], p. of Thomas Bennion, merchant.
Feb. 21 Hill Panton, tanner, s. of William Panton, tanner.
,, 22 Thomas Sproston, mariner, s. of John Sproston, cooper.
,, 22 John Jones, yeoman, s. of Thomas Jones, yeoman.

1755] THE CITY OF CHESTER 351

Feb. 22 John Sproston, cooper, s. of John Sproston, cooper, deceased.
,, 22 Thomas Phillips, plumber and glazier, } ss. of John Phillips, baker.
       John Phillips, baker,
,, 22 Peter Carter, cordwainer, s. of William Carter, cordwainer.
— — William French, pipemaker, s. of Thomas French, yeoman.
,, 24 Richard Whitehead p. of Peter Hickson, cordwainer.
,, 24 Samuel Waterwoods,   } pp. of John Maddocks, slater.
,, 25 James Parry [corkcutter, Roll],
,, 27 John Whitehead p. of Henry Owen, slater.
,, 27 Charles Holt, shipwright, s. of John Holt, carpenter.
,, 28 Owen Jones p. of Joseph Ratcliffe, flaxdresser.
,, 28 Joseph Ratcliffe, flaxdresser, s. of Joseph Ratcliffe.
— — William Cross, tailor, s. of William Cross, cordwainer.
Mar. 15 Thomas Griffith, shipwright, p. of Thomas Bennion, merchant.
,, 22 Richard Boulton, joiner, s. of Nathaniel Boulton, bricklayer.
,, 22 Thomas Dickens, } pp. of Joseph Witter of Chester, wetglover.
,, 22 John Moores,
,, 24 John s. of John Hunt of Chester, weaver, and p. of James Bayley of Chester, feltmaker.
,, 24 John Meredith, bricklayer, s. of John Meredith of Chester, bricklayer, deceased.
,, 24 John Edge,   } pp. of Samuel Price of Chester, bricklayer.
,, 24 John Brookes,
,, 24 John Reece, ropier, s. of John Reece of Chester, butcher.
,, 25 John Chapman, baker, s. of John Chapman, baker, deceased.
,, 28 John Hand p. of Alderman Henry Pemberton, ropier.
,, 28 James Bayley [Bailey, M.B.], ropier, s. of Henry Bayley, hatter, deceased.
,, 28 Robert Carter p. of John Croughton, cordwainer.
,, 28 Thomas Roden p. of William Smith of Chester, carpenter.
,, 29 Joseph Bedward, joiner, s. of John Bedward of Chester, mason.
Apr. 1 Samuel Hope, cordwainer, s. of Thomas Hope of Chester, cordwainer.
,, 1 Benjamin Culm p. of Arthur Culm of Chester, pipemaker.

Apr.	1	Samuel Henley, tailor, s. of Samuel Henley of Chester, tailor.
,,	1	Thomas Jones p. of John Tyson [Tyrer ?] of Chester, cordwainer.
,,	7	William Francis, gentleman.
,,	7	William Coy p. of William Coy, mason.
,,	7	William Brown p. of William Brown, cordwainer.
,,	7	John Davies, wetglover, s. of John Davies, wetglover.
,,	19	Dean Harding p. of Henry Bennion, cooper, deceased.
,,	19	Charles Robinson p. of Joseph Butler, bricklayer.
,,	21	Joseph Crosby, cordwainer, s. of Joseph Crosby, cordwainer.
,,	25	John Gother, mariner, s. of John Gother, weaver.
,,	28	John Yerwood p. of John Peers, silkdyer.
May	16	John Meredith, weaver, ⎫ ss. of William Meredith,
,,	16	Peter Meredith, sawyer, ⎭ sawyer, deceased.
,,	17	John Huntington, smith, s. of William Huntington, smith, deceased.
,,	17	Benjamin Lewis p. of John Stubbs, bricklayer.
,,	17	Thomas Maddock, cordwainer, s. of Thomas Maddock, slater.
,,	17	Richard Baxter p. of William Witter, wetglover, deceased.
,,	19	Thomas Thornley, flaxdresser, s. of Hugh Thornley, hornbreaker, deceased.
,,	24	Thomas Davies, yeoman, s. of John Davies, wetglover.
,,	24	Nathaniel Dewsbury, feltmaker, s. of Richard Dewsbury, feltmaker.
,,	24	William Francis p. of Alderman James Walley, feltmaker.
[1754] June	20	William Turner p. of Samuel Weigh, tanner.
[1755] June	6	Joseph Ordain, bricklayer, s. of Robert Ordain.
[1757] June	12	John Simpson, wine cooper.
[1755] June	20	John Axon.
July	16	Thomas Coppack p. of John Bowden, slater.
July	24	The Reverend Saml. Peploe, L.B.
,,	29	Thomas s. of Richard Moulson, tobacconist.
Oct.	1	Pusey Brooke, esquire.
[1754] Aug.	15	Joseph Dyson, merchant.

1755-6 [29-30 G. ii.] JOHN PAGE, Esquire, Mayor.

Oct. 27 Joseph Snow, merchant, s. of Joseph Snow, merchant.
,, 27 William Bingley, ironmonger, s. of Thomas Bingley, alderman.
Nov. 7 William Venables, carpenter, s. of William Venables, carpenter.
,, 29 Joseph Critchley, engraver, s. of Benjamin Critchley, goldsmith.
,, 29 Thomas Pennington, yeoman.
Dec. 4 John Bird, innholder.
Jan. 10 John Edwards, baker, p. of Robert Robinson, baker.
,, 17 John Maylor p. of Robert Hassall, wheelwright.
,, 31 Timothy Dayley the younger p. of Ralph Dutton, saddler, and assigned to Thomas Stones, saddler.
Mar. 10 Thomas Dewsbury, barber, s. of Richard Dewsbury, feltmaker.
,, 10 Samuel Tunna the younger, glover, s. of Samuel Tunna, butcher.
,, 27 Thomas Lightfoot p. of William Brown, cordwainer.
Apr. 6 ‡Samuel Adams, barber, s. of Philip Adams, cordwainer.
,, 9 George Owens p. of Peter Hale, butcher.
May 1 John Walters p. of Richard Brown, barber.
,, 21 Job Maddock p. of Samuel Tuna, butcher, and afterwards assigned over to William Cartwright, butcher.
,, 29 Charles Kearney p. of James Fletcher, cordwainer.
June 26 John Lockley p. of John Dutton, butcher.
,, 30 William Seller p. of Thomas Hickson, brewer.
July 17 Richard Thornton p. of John Boden, slater.
Sep. 1 John Bennion, cordwainer, p. of Seth Harrison, cordwainer, and by him assigned to John Tyrer.
,, 3 Thomas Edwards p. of William Irish, innholder.
,, 15 Thomas Farrington, gentleman, s. of William Farrington, merchant.
,, 17 Thomas Brock, gentleman, s. of Richard Brock, cheesefactor.
,, 28 Henry Huxley, yeoman.
Oct. 1 James Bailey p. of James Golding, pipemaker.
,, 7 Robert Whey, mariner.
,, 16 Hugh Speed, gentleman, s. of William Speed, surgeon.
,, 16 John Usherwood p. of Randle Wrench, butcher.
,, 18 William Briscoe, smith, s. of William Briscoe, smith.
,, 21 John Dewsbury, woollen draper, s. of Peter Dewsbury, alderman.
,, 21 John Newell, yeoman ["innholder" added on Roll].

1756-7 [30-31 G. ii.] PETER DEWSBURY, Esquire, Mayor.

Oct. 23 Thomas Hickson, cordwainer.
Dec. 1 Edward Woodfin p. of William Woodfin, joiner.
Jan. 15 John Goostrey p. of Randle Ley, cooper.
Feb. 5 William Jordan, carpenter, s. of Gerrard Jordan, slater.
,, 5 John Ordain, carpenter.
,, 7 Joseph Sidebotham, innholder.
,, 8 William Ratcliffe, cordwainer, s. of William Ratcliffe, cordwainer.
,, 12 John Shone p. of Edward Warrington, carpenter.
Mar. 19 Peter Pemberton, silversmith, s. of Peter Pemberton, silversmith.
,, 26 Robert Jones p. of Richard James, blacksmith.
,, 28 Roger Parry p. of Robert Dickson, brewer.
Apr. 6 John Turner p. of Thomas Crane, cordwainer.
,, 9 Thomas Penson, gardener.
,, 18 Thomas Powell p. of John Bridge, upholsterer.
,, 28 Thomas Powell, ship carpenter.
,, 28 James Rose, mariner.
May 14 Thomas Rathbone ["carpenter" added on Roll].
,, 14 John Hughes, bricklayer.
,, 16 Robert William [sic] p. of Randle Sorton, wetglover.
,, 26 Joseph Brown p. of Henry Aspinwall, tallow chandler.
June 11 Cotton Probert, haberdasher ["hatter" added on Roll], p. of Alderman Ralph Probert, haberdasher.
†John White, barber.
July 23 John Edwards p. of John Williams of Chester, carpenter.
Aug. 5 John Stringer, upholsterer.
Sep. 3 Thomas Woodworth, cabinet maker.
Oct. 3 John Dutton p. of Thomas Bennett, linendraper.
,, 7 The Right Rev. Father in God Edmund Keene, Lord Bishop of Chester.
,, 18 William Johnson p. of Christopher Gill, staymaker.
,, 19 *John Swinnerton, turner.
,, 19 Fisher Tench, gentleman, "chosen Mr. Mayor's Freeman."
,, 20 William Smith the younger, carpenter, s. of William Smith, carpenter.
,, 19 Edward Rippington, cordwainer.

1757-8 [31-32 G. ii.] RICHARD RICHARDSON, Esquire, Mayor.

Oct. 29 Thomas Davies p. of Samuel Dicas, tailor.
Nov. 7 *James Golborne, coal merchant.
„ 7 Benjamin Jones, slater, s. of William Jones, slater.
„ 26 James Jourdan p. of Samuel Lea, barber.
Jan. 7 Joshua Latham, grocer, p. of Mr. Tho. Marsden, merchant.
„ 7 Thomas Weigh, currier, s. of Thomas Weigh, currier.
Feb. 10 Benjamin Jordan, carpenter and joiner, s. of Francis Jordan, slater.
Mar. 2 Thomas Lea ["Lay," M.B.] p. of John Wilkinson, grocer and tobacconist.
Apr. 13 *William Evans, ironmonger and grocer.
„ 13 Peter Jackson p. of Michael Cooper, ship carpenter.
„ 22 Joseph Powell, perukemaker, s. of Benjamin Powell, perukemaker.
„ 22 John Broughton p. of Robert Cowduck, blacksmith.
„ 28 *Henry Hegg, druggist.
„ 28 Thomas Amery p. of Charles Croughton, linendraper.
„ 28 *Thomas Evans.
„ 28 Edward Williams p. of Richard Orme, tailor.
May 6 Edward Johnson, chandler, s. of Charles Johnson, dyer.
„ 9 *James Pickering, saddler.
„ 15 *John Lloyd, innholder.
„ 15 John Bennett, wine merchant, s. of John Bennett.
„ 19 William Corles, skinner, s. of Laurence Corles, skinner.
June 17 *Thomas Billington, cooper.
July 10 Humphrey Sharp, staymaker, s. of Mathew Sharp, pipemaker.
„ 15 George Fothergill p. of Joseph Burrows, joiner and cabinetmaker.
Oct. 11 William s. of Robert Williams.
„ 14 Samuel Sharp, grocer and mercer, s. of John Sharp, pipemaker.

1758-9 [32-33 G. ii.] THOMAS COTGREAVE, Esquire, Mayor.

Nov. 3 John Acton, butcher, p. of Michael Bromley.
„ 22 Randle Bennion, yeoman, s. of Randle Bennion of Caldecott, co. Ches., yeoman.

Nov.	28	Robert Richardson, tailor, s. of Francis Richardson, tailor.
,,	30	Edward Jones p. of James Roberts, barber.
Dec.	12	James Broadhurst p. of George Glover, apothecary.
Jan.	6	Edward Ball, yeoman, p. of Peter Morgan, esquire.
,,	20	Bennett Williams, esquire, s. of John Williams, esquire.
Feb.	10	William Seller the younger, cordwainer, s. of William Seller, cordwainer.
,,	10	Thomas Roberts, skinner, p. of Mr. Alderman Duke.
,,	10	John Sanders p. of Thomas Brown, cordwainer.
,,	10	Theodocius Moore p. of Thomas Moore, cooper.
,,	10	Thomas Meakin, pipemaker, s. of Randle Meakin, pipemaker.
,,	10	Charles Chesters p. of John Croughton, cabinetmaker.
,,	10	William Barber p. of Matthew Sharp, pipemaker.
,,	10	John Lloyd p. of George Eaton, mason.
,,	10	John Nicholls, corkcutter, s. of Paul Nicholls, corkcutter.
,,	10	Richard Sands p. of Gerrard Jordan, slater.
,,	10	John Griffith p. of William Smith, carpenter.
,,	10	John Jones, bricklayer, s. of John Jones, bricklayer.
,,	10	John Johnson p. of Samuel Ley, barber.
,,	12	William Williams, beerbrewer, s. of John Williams, carpenter.
,,	12	John Reece, butcher, s. of William Reece, butcher.
,,	13	John Frodsham p. of William Peyton, linendraper.
,,	13	Benjamin Hickson, tailor, s. of Peter Hickson, tailor.
,,	14	John Joynson p. of Thomas Harrison, cooper.
,,	15	John Brown the younger, yeoman, s. of John Brown, yeoman.
,,	15	Thomas Edge p. of Henry Perkins, merchant.
,,	15	Robert Hewitt, tobacconist, s. of Edward Hewitt, cordwainer.
,,	15	Benjamin Kennerley p. of Thomas Jellico, cordwainer.
,,	16	Thomas Whittle, silkdyer, s. of John Whittle, silkdyer.
,,	17	John Williams p. of John Gough, carpenter.
,,	17	Andrew Littler p. of Edward Warrington, carpenter.
,,	17	William Trevor, skinner, s. of William Trevor, skinner.
,,	17	Gerrard Jordan the younger, slater, s. of Gerrard Jordan, slater.
,,	17	Abel Andrew, slater, s. of Esau Andrew, slater.
,,	19	Jonathan Taylor, combmaker, s. of Jonathan Taylor, combmaker.
,,	22	Thomas Edwards p. of Thomas Randles, grocer and ironmonger.

Feb.	26	Charles Francis p. of Thomas Aldersey, woollendraper.
,,	28	John Edwards p. of Jeffrey Edwards, flaxdresser.
Mar.	29	Thomas Massey, mariner, s. of Thomas Massey, linendraper.
Apr.	12	Thomas Cooper, bricklayer, s. of Nicholas Cooper, cooper.
May	2	Thomas s. of William Smith, carpenter.
,,	21	James Cottingham, mariner, s. of James Cottingham, skinner.
July	7	Robert Johnson p. of Thomas Stringer, baker.
,,	14	William Somner p. of Joseph Wright, grocer.
,,	14	Henry Pate, mariner, s. of John Pate, butcher.
,,	19	Thomas Roberts p. of Thomas Harvie, grocer.
,,	19	Thomas Jones p. of Holme Burrows, cutler.
Aug.	29	*John Hart, innholder.
,,	29	Thomas Cowper, gentleman, s. of Edmund Cowper, gentleman.
Sep.	11	*William Beasley, esquire.
,,	28	Ralph Wilkinson, baker, s. of John Wilkinson, apothecary.
,,	28	*Thomas Parker, jeweller.
Oct.	20	*John Golborne, gentleman.

1759-60 [33-34 G. ii.] Sir RICHARD GROSVENOR, Baronet, Mayor.

Oct.	27	Hinton Maddock, gentleman, s. of Thomas Maddock, alderman.
Dec.	3	William Walley, baker ["malster" added on Roll], p. of Edmund Warrington, baker.
,,	3	*William Stonehewer, yeoman.
,,	3	*Daniel Chatterton, victualler.
May	8	James Roberts, tailor, s. of William Roberts, tailor.
,,	12	William Parker p. of Edward Chevers, butcher.
,,	12	John Leach p. of Charles Dicas, tallow chandler.
,,	12	John Gorton, butcher, s. of Daniel Gorton, yeoman.
July	14	Richard Humphreys, combmaker, s. of Samuel Humphreys, combmaker.
,,	14	Thomas Gamon, yeoman, s. of Thomas Gamon, yeoman.
,,	14	William Northover, confectioner, p. of James Glazier.
,,	14	William Peover p. of Robert Price, butcher.
,,	19	*William Falconer, victualler.
,,	19	Richard Case p. of Thomas Walton, baker.

358 THE ROLLS OF THE FREEMEN OF [1760-2

Aug. 9 John Dymock Griffith, merchant, s. of Edward Griffith, alderman.
,, 9 Charles Broster, cutler, s. of Thomas Broster, alderman.
,, 9 John Kerry p. of Richard Brock, brazier.

1760-1 [1-2 G. iii.] THOMAS GROSVENOR, Esquire, Mayor.

Nov. 19 Rowland Jones p. of Thomas Stones, saddler.
Dec. 13 George Lowe p. of James Mottershead, baker.
,, 20 Peter s. of Joseph Snow, stuffweaver.
,, 26 Roger Mostyn, clerk.
Mar. 25 *Richard Wilbraham Bootle, esquire.
,, 25 *Richard Chrichley, yeoman.
,, 25 John Hodskinson p. of Edmund Warrington, baker.
Apr. 7 John Arderne p. of John Palin, butcher.
May 5 Richard Vernon p. of Thomas Price, butcher.
July 14 *Joseph Reece, yeoman.
Aug. 3 Thomas Page, tanner, s. of William Page, blacksmith.
,, 22 John Townshend, esquire, s. of John Townsheud, esquire.
,, 22 John Jones p. of William Wrench, watchmaker.
,, 22 James Jones, cordwainer, s. of James Jones, bricklayer.
,, 24 William Presbury, skinner, s. of William Presbury, skinner.
Oct. 19 *Trafford Barnston, esquire.
,, 22 John s. of ——— Richardson.
,, 22 William Hasler, barber [perukemaker, M.B.], s. of William Hasler, cordwainer.
,, 22 Thomas Shaw p. of Jane Weigh, widow, currier.

1761-2 [2-3 G. iii.] THOMAS CHOLMELEY, Esquire, Mayor.

Oct. 24 Edward Leadbeater p. of Peter Leadbeater, brewer.
Jan. 2 Henry William Keay, grocer, s. of Randle Keay, grocer.
,, 2 George Walker p. of Henry Bushell, skinner.
,, 2 Richard Baker, butcher, s. of Richard Baker, carpenter.
,, 13 John Gibbons p. of James Selby, butcher.
,, 13 Thomas Garratt p. of Harwar Garratt, upholsterer.
,, 13 Richard Parry p. of Randle Ley, cooper.

1762] THE CITY OF CHESTER 359

Jan.	13	Lawrence Lawrenson p. of Samuel Humphreys, hornbreaker.
,,	13	Edward Thomas p. of Thomas Evans, glazier.
,,	13	Hamnett Gregg s. of Robert Gregg, gardener.
,,	13	Thomas s. of Robert Gregg, cordwainer.
,,	13	William Johnson, cordwainer, s. of William Johnson, cordwainer.
,,	13	Samuel Davies, butcher, s. of Samuel Davies, glazier.
,,	13	Robert Dutton, butcher, } ss. of Robert Dutton,
,,	13	Jacob Dutton, butcher, } butcher.
,,	13	George Pickford, joiner, s. of George Pickford, bricklayer.
,,	13	Bradford Jones, ropemaker, s. of William Jones, cordwainer.
,,	13	John Davies p. of John Shone, carpenter.
,,	13	William Hobrow, writing master, s. of Cornelius Hobrow, feltmaker.
,,	13	Richard Coppock, slater, s. of Richard Coppock, slater.
,,	13	Thomas Amery p. of Randle Wrench, butcher.
,,	13	John Taylor p. of Richard Sneyd, cooper.
,,	13	George Whitehead, slater, s. of Thomas Whitehead, slater.
,,	14	Hamnett Garratt p. of John Cotgreave, beer brewer.
,,	14	James Clutton p. of Richard Shone, weaver.
,,	14	William Dobb, cordwainer, s. of James Dobb, butcher.
,,	14	Thomas Williams, glazier, s. of David Williams, innholder.
,,	14	John Bateman, butcher, s. of Edward Bateman, butcher.
,,	14	Richard Bazine, joiner, s. of Richard Bazine, joiner.
,,	14	Robert Jones, cordwainer, s. of John Jones, cordwainer.
,,	14	Richard Brock, brushmaker, s. of George Brock, scalemaker.
,,	14	James Lumber, watchmaker, s. of James Lumber of Chester, porter.
,,	14	William Handley p. of Samuel Coy, tailor.
,,	14	Matthew Brown, upholsterer, s. of Matthew Brown, innholder.
May	11	Pattison Ellames, druggist, p. of Peter Ellames the elder, alderman.
,,	11	Edward Jones p. of William Hale, butcher.
,,	11	Robert Whitehead, slater, s. of Thomas Whitehead, slater.
,,	31	William Stones, currier, s. of William Stones, saddler.
,,	31	William Faulkner p. of John Egerton, brewer.

May 31 *Hugh M'Millan, linendraper.
July 19 Thomas Wright, dyer, s. of John Wright, dyer.
Sep. 4 Thomas Edwards p. of Thomas Jones, hatter.
Oct. 16 Robert Cawley, watchmaker, s. of Robert Cawley, watchmaker.
„ 16 Francis Smedley p. of Thomas Griffiths, grocer.
„ 21 *Randle Podmore.

1762-3 [3-4 G. iii.] HENRY HESKETH, Esquire, Mayor.

Oct. 25 Robert Evans p. of Arthur Culm, pipemaker.
Jan. 1 Neville Noble p. of John Hignett, linendraper.
„ 17 *Isaac Badger, vintner.
„ 18 *Thomas Barnes, plumber and glazier.
„ 29 *Thomas Jenkins, yeoman.
Feb. 2 John Fearnall p. of John Salisbury, mariner.
„ 2 John Williams p. of Zachariah Nicholls, cordwainer.
„ 5 *Francis Mesham, victualler.
„ 12 *George Smith, blacksmith.
Apr. 20 *John Eltoft, toyman.
May 4 *John Whitbey, maltster.
„ 4 *William Ridgway, maltster.
„ 21 *George Griffith, mercer.
June 6 William Bailey, ropemaker, s. of Henry Bailey, feltmaker.
July 2 Thomas Robinson, tanner, s. of Robert Robinson, tanner.
„ 29 Bartholomew Dillon p. of John Jones, cordwainer.
„ 29 Robert Williams p. of John Lawrenson, butcher.
„ 29 Thomas Hubbert, mariner, p. of Robert Caulton, vintner.
„ 30 Edward Townshend, gentleman, s. of John Townshend, esquire.
Oct. 15 *Abraham Kirkham.
„ 20 Edward Hincks, gentleman, s. of Thomas Hincks.
„ 21 *Daniel Coleclough.

1763-4 [4-5 G. iii.] HOLME BURROWES, Esquire, Mayor.

Oct. 29 William s. of George Smith.
Nov. 5 George Linney p. of Richard Cottingham, cabinetmaker.
Dec. 31 John s. of Thomas Harvey, grocer.

1764-5] THE CITY OF CHESTER 361

Jan. 14 John Cooke p. of Philip Presbury, cabinetmaker.
Feb. 8 *David Hughes.
 „ 18 John Linney p. of Phillip Presbury, cabinetmaker.
Mar. 3 Henry Pemberton, gentleman, s. of Henry Pemberton, alderman.
Apr. 21 Peter s. of John Thomas.
June 16 George Johnson, cabinetmaker, s. of Thomas Johnson, carpenter.
July 21 *John Doyle, cooper.
Oct. 6 *John Whitehead.
 „ 6 *John Ratcliffe, watchmaker.
 „ 6 *Edward Adams, victualler.

1764-5 [5-6 G. iii.] EDWARD BURROWES, Esquire, Mayor.

Nov. 3 William Cornelius, staymaker, s. of John Cornelius, mason.
Feb. 12 John Page p. of Michael Bromley, butcher, and afterwards of John Palin, butcher.
Mar. 30 James s. of Mr. Daniel Porter.
Apr. 6 Benjamin Saunders p. of Mr. Thomas Bennion, and afterwards of Edward Warrington, carpenter.
 „ 6 Thomas Brown, feltmaker, p. of Mr. Mayor.
 „ 19 John Monk p. of Mr. William Monk, printer.
 „ 24 William Massey, clerk, s. of Roger Massey, late of Chester, linendraper.
May 20 Peter Corles p. of John Hickson, tailor.
June 22 *John Gresty.
 „ 22 *Alexander Forrest, victualler.
 „ 22 *Henry Matthews, victualler.
 „ 29 *Samuel Taylor, wheelwright.
Aug. 17 Thomas Hankey, victualler, s. of Robert Hankey, innholder.
Sep. 28 *William Rowlands, gardener.
 „ 28 *Peter Davies, victualler.
Oct. 1 Charles Wright, mercer, s. of Thomas Wright, tailor.
 „ 12 John s. of Randle Keay, grocer.
 „ 21 John Hallwood the younger, grocer, s. of Mr. Alderman Hallwood. "The same day said John Hallwood the Younger was sworn one of the forty or Common Council of this City."

1765–6 [6–7 G. iii.] RICHARD OLLERHEAD, Esquire, Mayor.

Nov. 2 George Hodson, chandler, p. of Charles Moulson, tallow chandler.
Dec. 3 Samuel Basnett p. of John Usherwood, butcher.
  „ 19 Robert Stringer, baker, s. of Thomas Stringer.
  „ 31 Joseph Thomas p. of Daniel Ledsham, baker.
Jan. 11 Charles Gill, blacksmith, s. of William Gill, mason.
  „ 25 *Vincent Evans, victualler.
  „ 25 *Thomas Soreton, victualler.
Feb. 8 *Thomas Dickenson, sievemaker.
  „ 21 John Clubbe p. of Joseph Clubbe, ironmonger.
  „ 28 Hugh Bennett [of Little Neston, Roll] s. of Hugh Bennett late of Little Neston.
Apr. 17 John Chamberlaine, merchant, s. of Joseph Chamberlaine, ironmonger.
June 6 Thomas Brown, watchmaker, s. of Thomas Brown, cordwainer.
  „   6 Peter Broster, stationer, s. of Thomas Broster, alderman.
Aug. 1 William Linney p. of Thomas Linney, cordwainer.
  „   2 Charles Snow, merchant, s. of Joseph Snow.
  „   2 *William Birch, woollen draper.
  „   2 *John Probert, victualler.
  „   2 Thomas Lightfoot p. of John Phillips, baker.
  „   5 *Henry Whitley, esquire.
  „   5 *Robert Cunliffe, esquire.
  „   6 *John Peers, victualler.
  „   8 *William Edmondson of Bridge Trafford.
  „ 14 *Thomas Horrop, brazier.
  „ 14 George Griffith, grasier, s. of George Griffith, plumber.
  „ 23 Thomas Melam, victualler.
Sep. 8 James Batho, yeoman [labourer, M.B.], s. of Nathaniel Batho, glazier.
  „ 13 John Poole, stationer, p. of Thomas Ledsham, bookseller.

1766–7 [7–8 G. iii.] THOMAS ASTLE, Esquire, Mayor.

Nov. 15 *Sir John Chetwode, baronet.
Mar. 28 *Edward Jones, whitesmith.
  „ 28 *Robert Hughes, victualler.

Mar. 28 *Thomas Davies, victualler.
„ 28 Francis Gibson p. of Henry Aspinwall, tallow chandler.
„ 28 *William Peers, victualler.
Apr. 23 Job Harrison p. of John Palin, butcher.
May 25 William Dale p. of Thomas Billington, cooper.
July 25 George Walker, silversmith, p. of Mr. Alderman Richardson.
Sep. 9 John Astle, cabinetmaker, p. of Mr. Mayor.
Oct. 3 *John Belward, sheriff's officer.
„ 3 *Robert Richards, victualler.
„ 3 *James Clingin, victualler.
„ 3 *Simeon Leete, victualler.
„ 8 *Thomas Faulkner of Waverton, co. Ches., yeoman.

1767-8 [8-9 G. iii.] JOHN KELSALL, Esquire, Mayor.

Nov. 3 *William Boult, grocer.
„ 6 *Thomas Sidebotham, grocer.
Dec. 5 Samuel Boswell, gentleman, s. of Samuel Boswell.
„ 10 Robert Harvey, bricklayer, s. of George Harvey, bricklayer.
„ 10 Edward Jones p. of Roger Dawson, blacksmith.
„ 11 John Edwards p. of George Price, mason.
„ 11 Samuel Latham p. of Peter Robinson, tanner.
„ 11 Robert Gregg p. of —— ——, gardener.
„ 11 Benjamin Aires, cordwainer, s. of Thomas Aires, gardener.
„ 11 Benjamin Posnett, feltmaker, p. of John Towsey, hatter.
„ 11 Samuel Webster, cordwainer, p. of Thomas Linney.
„ 11 Thomas Hewitt p. of William Brown, coach maker.
„ 11 John Smith, cordwainer, p. of William Adshead.
„ 11 William Jones, cordwainer, s. of William Jones, cordwainer.
„ 11 William Davies, carpenter, ⎫
„ 11 John Davies, cordwainer, ⎬ ss. of Joseph Davies,
„ 11 Joseph Davies, coachman, ⎪ cordwainer.
„ 11 Thomas Davies, mason, ⎭
„ 11 Peter Nailor, blacksmith, p. of Robert Yoxall, smith.
„ 11 John Tomlinson, pipemaker, s. of John Tomlinson, wheelwright.
„ 11 Edward Poole, hatter, p. of James Bayley, feltmaker.
„ 11 Robert Hough, pipemaker, p. of Arthur Culm.
„ 11 Samuel Catteral, perukemaker, p. of John Briscoe.
„ 11 John Davies, pipemaker, p. of Arthur Culm.

Dec. 11 William Edwards p. of John Brookes, bricklayer.
„   11 William Jones, mason, p. of Edward Powell.
„   11 Thomas Sparkes, wine cooper, s. of Thomas Sparkes, mariner.
„   11 John Trape [Drake, M.B.] p. of Francis Buckley, blacksmith.
„   11 Daniel Thornley, cordwainer, p. of William Ratcliffe.
„   11 Richard Jones p. of Richard Jones, pipemaker.
„   11 Thomas Linney p of Thomas Linney, cordwainer.
„   11 George Ashmull, woolcomber, p. of Susanna Saunders, widow.
„   11 Thomas Cappur p. of Thomas Jellico, cordwainer.
„   11 Thomas Speed, cordwainer, p. of Mr. Jellico.
„   11 Thomas Wright, cordwainer, p. of John Jones.
„   11 George Shannon p. of Peter Hickson, cordwainer.
„   11 Joseph Higginson p. of Thomas Higginson, cordwainer.
„   11 John Ithell,   ⎫ pp. of Joseph Carter, cord-
„   11 Thomas Rowlinson, ⎬   wainer.
„   11 Robert Huxley, cordwainer, p. of Joseph Carter.
„   11 Thomas Johnson, cabinet-maker, p. of John Croughton.
„   11 Benjamin Maddock, cordwainer, p. of George Hope.
„   11 Thomas Thornton p. of George Harvey, bricklayer.
„   11 Benjamin Finney p. of Peter Heath, cordwainer.
„   11 George Hiccock, cordwainer, s. of Charles Hiccock, cordwainer.
„   11 Gabriel Evans p. of Arthur Culm, pipemaker.
„   11 Benjamin Hewitt p. of Thomas Hickson, cordwainer.
„   11 Richard Allenton p. of John Sharp, pipemaker.
„   11 John Oldham p. of George Gill, cordwainer.
„   11 Thomas Hill p. of Richard Billington, cooper.
„   11 George Hanley p. of Samuel Coy, tailor.
„   11 John Hall p. of Thomas Cliffe, pipemaker.
„   11 George Bradford p. of Richard Jones, pipemaker.
„   11 Owen Lloyd p. of Christopher Gill, tailor.
„   11 John Beckett, baker, s. of John Beckett, baker.
„   11 Samuel Aires, gardener, s. of Thomas Aires, gardener.
„   12 William Gibson, bricklayer, ⎫ pp. of John Pemberton.
„   12 Edward Peters, bricklayer, ⎬
„   12 Joseph Thornton p. of Richard Venables, bricklayer.
„   12 Thomas Phillips p. of William Pemberton, feltmaker.
„   12 Richard Gregg, coachman, s. of Robert Gregg.
„   12 Samuel Tilston, combmaker, s. of Samuel Tilston, slater.
„   12 James Meakin, pipemaker, s. of Randle Meakin, pipemaker.

Dec. 12 Samuel s. of Matthew Robinson.
,, 12 Richard Roberts p. of William Martin, beer brewer.
,, 12 James Bayley, feltmaker, s. of James Bayley, feltmaker.
,, 12 Thomas Jones, cordwainer, s. and p. of John Jones.
,, 12 Thomas Leadbeater, cordwainer, p. of John Jones.
,, 12 Robert Powell p. of Thomas Minshull, barber.
,, 12 John Bell p. of Thomas Vernon, gardener.
,, 12 Thomas Hill p. of Charles Parry, hatter.
,, 12 Joseph Forrest, blockmaker, p. of Thomas Bennion, shipbuilder.
,, 12 William Griffith, butcher,⎫ ss. of John Griffith, but-
,, 12 Thomas Griffith, butcher, ⎭ cher.
,, 12 Gilbert Inglish p. of Roger Maddock, cordwainer.
,, 12 John Maurice, glover, p. of Mr. Henry Perkins.
,, 12 John Parry, fisherman, s. of William Parry, butcher.
,, 12 John Jones p. of Thomas Pickmore, staymaker.
,, 12 Thomas Sidebotham, horse-hirer, s. of John Sidebotham, innholder.
,, 12 William s. of William Woodfin, carpenter.
,, 12 John Boden, slater, s. of Samuel Boden, slater.
,, 12 Jonathan Barnett, combmaker, p. of Edward Billis, and assigned to Mary Humphreys.
,, 12 William Taylor, cordwainer, s. of William Taylor, musician.
,, 12 John Jones, cordwainer, s. of John Jones, cordwainer.
,, 12 Henry Dutton, slater, s. of Thomas Dutton, tailor, deceased.
,, 12 George Baxter, ropemaker, p. of Samuel Harrison.
,, 12 Joseph Stout, slater, s. of Joseph Stout, butcher.
,, 12 Richard Frith, cordwainer, p. of William Fletcher.
,, 12 William Frith, cordwainer, p. of James Fletcher.
,, 12 Thomas Jennions p. of Charles Fletcher, cordwainer.
,, 12 William Davies, watchmaker, s. of William Davies, joiner.
,, 12 George Williams, combmaker, p. of Richard Humphreys.
,, 12 Richard Dutton, cordwainer, s. of Robert Dutton, butcher.
,, 12 William Brown, cordwainer, s. of George Brown, cordwainer.
,, 12 Joseph Walker, stockingweaver [framework-knitter, M.B.], p. of Thomas Pratchitt.
,, 12 Stephen Hyde the younger, cordwainer, s. of Stephen Hyde, baker.
,, 12 John Kearney, staymaker, p. of Thomas Pickford.

Dec. 12 Richard Archer, cordwainer, s. of Richard Archer, ropemaker.
" 12 Taylor Ratcliffe, cordwainer, s. of William Ratcliffe, cordwainer.
" 12 William Tyrer, cordwainer, s. of William Tyrer, tailor.
" 12 Charles Davenport, corkcutter, p. of Ralph Cartwright.
" 12 Thomas Maddock, beer brewer, s. of Edward Maddock.
" 12 Moses Poynton, leather-parer, s. of Aaron Poynton, stockingweaver.
" 12 John Barton, laceweaver, s. of John Barton, laceweaver.
" 12 William Warmingham, combmaker, s. of John Warmingham, tailor.
" 12 Robert Moulton p. of Robert Jones, cordwainer.
" 12 Joseph Maddock, corkcutter, s. of John Maddock, tanner.
" 12 Samuel Kelsall, cordwainer, s. of John Kelsall, corkcutter.
" 12 John Bayley, slater, s. of Henry Bayley, hatter.
" 12 William Baker, schoolmaster, s. of Richard Baker, carpenter.
" 12 Thomas Johnson, cordwainer, s. of Crispin Johnson, cordwainer.
" 12 John Adams, cordwainer, p. of Roger Maddock.
" 12 Thomas Cheswiss, hatter, p. of James Walley.
" 12 Thomas Hatherton p. of William Smith, carpenter.
" 12 Edward Povah, skinner, p. of Lawrence Corles.
" 12 William Hall p. of George Perkins, cordwainer.
" 12 John Walker p. of John Moors, cordwainer.
" 12 John Jones, wetglover, p. of Randle Sorton.
" 12 John Johnson, cordwainer, s. of John Johnson, cordwainer.
" 12 William Batho, cordwainer, s. of Richard Batho, barber.
" 12 Philip Presbury, flaxdresser, s. of William Presbury, skinner.
" 12 Thomas Sellers, combmaker, s. of William Sellers, mason.
" 12 Joseph Wilkinson, cabinetmaker, s. of Joseph Wilkinson, cabinetmaker.
" 12 Joseph Harrison, cordwainer, s. of William Harrison, cordwainer.
" 12 Thomas Hitchins p. of Peter Nicholls, corkcutter.
" 12 John Moffit, wheelwright, s. of William Moffit.
" 12 John Peacock, staymaker, p. of Christopher Gill.
" 12 George Allington p. of Thomas Jones, pipemaker.

Dec.	12	Peter Leadbeater p. of John Jordan, mason.
,,	12	Joseph Coleclough, carpenter, s. of Joseph Coleclough.
,,	12	Joseph Pattison, watchmaker, p. of Robert Cawley.
,,	12	Henry Hewitt, cordwainer, s. of John Hewitt.
,,	12	Joseph Coleclough, slater, s. of William Coleclough, tobacconist.
,,	12	Thomas Pritchard, tobacconist, s. of John Pritchard, slater.
,,	12	John Ashton, cordwainer, s. of John Ashton, tailor.
,,	12	Robert Lamb, butcher, s. of Robert Lamb, butcher.
,,	12	John Rogers, currier, s. of John Rogers, tanner.
,,	12	Nathaniel Bolton, bricklayer, s. of William Bolton, bricklayer.
,,	12	James Rathbone, cordwainer, p. of Richard Fitzgerrald.
,,	12	Richard Hayes, saddler, s. of John Hayes, beer brewer.
,,	12	Henry Maddock p. of John Maddock, slater.
,,	15	Thomas Jordan, slater, s. of Joseph Jordan.
,,	15	Edward Blackmore p. of Peter Jackson, shipwright.
,,	15	Joseph Tilston, cordwainer, s. of Thomas Tilston, cordwainer.
,,	15	James Meakin p. of Charles Jordan, slater.
,,	15	Richard Hawkins, cabinetmaker, s. of Edward Hawkins, upholsterer.
,,	15	James Mason, cordwainer, } ss. of John Mason, butcher.
,,	15	John Mason, cordwainer,
,,	15	George Williams p. of George Perkins, cordwainer.
,,	15	Mark Mears, tailor [Mark Taylor, M.B.], p. of Charles Price.
,,	15	Thomas Billington, cordwainer, p. of Roger Maddock.
,,	15	William Roach, patternmaker, p. of Thomas Griffith.
,,	15	John Hewitt p. of Randle Ley.
,,	15	John Overton, tailor, p. of Paul Maddock.
,,	15	John Bannister p. of Joseph Witter, skinner.
,,	15	John Edge, tailor, p. of John Hickson the elder.
,,	15	John Woods, glover, p. of Samuel Tonna.
,,	15	Thomas Evans, cordwainer, p. of John Ord.
,,	15	Thomas Hancock, cordwainer, } ss. of Henry Hancock, tailor.
,,	15	John Hancock, cordwainer,
,,	15	Samuel Joynson p. of William Crane, cordwainer.
,,	15	John Lawrence, cordwainer, p. of William High.
,,	15	Roger Woodfin, boatbuilder, p. of Michael Cooper.
,,	15	Richard Ralph, tanner, s. of Edward Ralph, sawyer.
,,	15	John Williams, staymaker, p. of Charles Dicas.
,,	15	Charles Hill, cordwainer, p. of Thomas Maddock.
,,	15	John Rimmer, mariner, p. of John Salisbury.
,,	18	Joseph Foulkes, ship carpenter, p. of Thomas Bennion.

368   THE ROLLS OF THE FREEMEN OF   [1767-9

Dec. 18 Charles McCans, cabinetmaker, p. of William Venables, joiner.
„ 18 Joshua Smith, feltmaker,⎫ ss. of John Smith, feltmaker.
„ 18 John Smith, cordwainer,⎭
„ 18 John Tilston, mason, s. of John Tilston, mason.
„ 18 John Roberts, hornbreaker, p. of Samuel Humphreys.
Jan. 2 Edward Morris p. of John Ords, cordwainer.
Mar. 17 Edward Harrison, ropemaker, p. of John Francis, ropier.
„ 17 *Thomas Walker, tailor.
Apr. 9 *Richard Griffith, carpenter.
„ 9 *Allen Mason, baker.
„ 9 *Thomas Fairclough, victualler.
„ 30 John Hughes p. of Joshua Bennion, cordwainer.
May 28 *Samuel Lea, victualler.
„ 28 William Davies, glazier, s. of Samuel Davies, glazier.
June 22 Henry Clubbe, linendraper, s. of Joseph Clubbe, ironmonger.
July 22 Richard Wright, woolcomber, s. of John Wright, woolcomber.
Aug. 18 Thomas Ince, esquire, s. of Thomas Ince, clerk.
„ 22 Robert Hesketh, merchant, s. of Henry Hesketh, esquire.
Oct. 1 William Morgan, skinner.
„ 11 Joseph Rawlinson of Dodleston, co. Ches., yeoman.

1768-9 [9-10 G. iii.] CHARLES BOSWELL, Esquire, Mayor.

Nov. 9 *John Rogers, oil merchant.
„ 19 John Chritchley, grocer, p. of Ralph Wilkinson, deceased.
Dec. 28 Robert Crosby, cordwainer, s. of Joseph Crosby, cordwainer.
„ 28 John Wilson p. of James Stubbs, druggist.
Jan. 7 *James Hughes, victualler.
„ 7 *Owen Thompson, grocer.
„ 7 *John Latham, gentleman.
„ 10 *Edward Jones, grocer.
Feb. 25 *George Bennion, victualler.
Apr. 15 Lewis Briscoe, linendraper, s. of James Briscoe, linendraper.
„ 25 Daniel Pickance, vintner, s. of Daniel Pickance, mariner.
„ 27 Thomas Jones p. of Thomas Griffith, grocer.
May 31 George Bowdon, slater, s. of John Bowdon.

June 3 Thomas Dean p. of Peter Capper, victualler.
 „   17 John Sefton p. of Richard Cave [? Case], baker.
 „   19 Andrew Davison p. of Mr. John Bennett, wine merchant.
 „   24 *John George the younger, victualler.
 „   24 Charles Crewe, carpenter and joiner, s. of Thomas Crewe.
July 13 Samuel Davies of Namptwich, co. Ches., hardwareman, s. of John Davies.
 „   13 William Dicas, gentleman, s. of William Dicas, barber and perukemaker.
Aug. 12 *John Wolfe, cabinetmaker.
Sep. 25 Jonadab Maddock, gentleman, s. of the late Alderman Maddock.
 „   25 Arthur Barber, esquire, s. of Nathaniel Barber, gentleman.
 „   22 Thomas Page, esquire, s. of Mr. Alderman Page.
 „   30 John Wright, grocer, s. of Joseph Wright, grocer.
 „   30 John Wilbraham the younger, grocer, s. of John Wilbraham.
Oct. 7 John Ireland p. of John Leadbeater, brewer.
 „   7 John Boden the younger p. of John Boden, slater.
 „   21 *John Seller, brewer.
 „   21 *Thomas Dean, tinman [tinplateworker, M.B.].
 „   21 *David Napier, brazier.
 „   21 *Anthony Guy.
 „   21 *John Jackson, barber.
 „   21 *Ambrose Davies, victualler.
 „   23 *Edward Fairbrother, tinman.
 „   27 Edmund Bushell, mercer.
 „   25 Samuel Bromfield, cutler, p. of Mr. Alderman H. Burrowes.
 „   26 James Kent, barber, s. of William Kent.

1769-70 [10-11 G. iii.] GEORGE FRENCH, Esquire, Mayor.

Oct. 28 William Bailey of Neston, cooper, p. of Thomas Harrison.
 „   28 Philip Bateman, butcher, s. of Edward Bateman, butcher.
Nov. 7 *Joshua Jones, tailor.
 „   11 Peter Bostock Heath, cordwainer, s. of George Heath, cordwainer.

Nov. 11 John Williamson p. of Thomas Croughton, linendraper.
„ 11 William Harrison p. of Thomas Craven, grocer.
„ 16 *Thomas Cowley, stationer.
„ 25 John Holland p. of Robert Brock, blacksmith.
„ 25 Thomas Hand, corkcutter, s. of James Hand, corkcutter.
Dec. 12 Robert Bigg p. of Mr. Samuel Bagnall.
„ 12 John Trevor, barber, s. of John Trevor, wetglover, deceased.
„ 30 Samuel s. of Shadrich Ball.
„ 30 William Read p. of William Monk, printer.
Jan. 4 Richard Maddock, gentleman, s. of Thomas Maddock, alderman.
„ 4 Samuel Swann p. of Charles Parry, hatter.
Feb. 10 Thomas Sadler of Tarvin, shopkeeper, s. of Thomas Sadler, late of Tarvin.
„ 17 Jarvis Holland p. of William Crane, bluemaker.
„ 26 Daniel Gorton, saddler, s. of Daniel Gorton.
Mar. 3 Charles Tomkinson of Gwersylt s. of John Tomkinson.
„ 27 William Vernon, tinman [tinplateworker, M.B.], s. of Thomas Vernon, gardener.
May 10 John Johnson, glover, s. of William Johnson of Chester, wetglover.
„ 19 William s. of Shadrach Ball, labourer.
„ 24 Bostock Jones, victualler, s. of William Jones, innholder.
„ 26 John Cooper p. of Edward Boden of Chester, bricklayer.
June 1 *George Cload, mariner.
„ 2 *John Williams, carpenter.
„ 2 *Thomas Bleades, victualler.
„ 2 *George Dimelo.
„ 2 *Thomas Adams.
„ 2 *Henry Rider the younger, merchant.
„ 2 *Job Hulse, victualler.
„ 4 John Posnett, cordwainer, s. of Thomas Posnett, cordwainer.
„ 8 *Edward Davies, breechesmaker.
„ 11 *Thomas Gresty of Christleton, victualler.
„ 12 *James Dixon, goldsmith.
„ 15 *Richard Jones, linendraper.
„ 15 James Tavo, glover and breechesmaker.
„ 19 Robert Robinson p. of Thomas Wilkinson, baker.
„ 23 *Thomas Latchford, cabinetmaker.
„ 23 *John Maurice, grocer.

1770-1] THE CITY OF CHESTER 371

June 25 *William Parry, flourman.
Sep.   3 ‡Edward Spencer, mason, s. of Thomas Spencer, mason.
  „   8 Samuel Walker p. of Thomas Rathbone, carpenter.
  „   26 Thomas Crane, grocer, s. of Thomas Crane, apothecary.
  „   28 John Davies p. of Thomas Higginson, cordwainer.
  „   29 Thomas Jackson p. of William Jordan, carpenter.
  „   29 Jonathan s. of John Brown.
Oct.   2 James Smith p. of Timothy Jones, cordwainer.
  „   19 Sir Watkin Williams Wynne, baronet, s. of Sir Watkin Williams Wynne, baronet, deceased.
  „   19 *Robert Howell Vaughan, esquire.
  „   20 *Samuel Butler.
  „   20 *John Ellis.
  „   23 Isaac Woodyer p. of William Howard, butcher.

1770-1 [11-12 G. iii.] JOHN LAWTON, Esquire, Mayor.

Oct. 27 *George Harding.
Nov. 24 *William Cole, carpenter.
         †Thomas Young, glover.
         †Edward Taylor, blacksmith.
Jan. 19 Richard Davies p. of Robert Richardson, currier.
  „ 19 *Samuel Moulton.
Feb. 2 *Richard Pritchard, joiner [carpenter, M.B.].
  „   9 Paschal Roberts p. of Thomas Harrison, cooper.
  „   9 Richard Powdrell p. of Thomas Amery, linendraper.
Mar. 9 John Cross p. of John Swinnerton, turner.
Apr. 3 Richard Walley p. of William Walley, baker.
         †John Moffitt, shipwright.
Aug. 31 William Sefton, brewer, p. of Thomas Sefton, mariner.
Sep. 25 Watkin Youd p. of Thomas Wilkinson, baker.
Oct. 23 William Pemberton, silversmith, s. of Samuel Pemberton, late of Chester, silversmith.
  „ 24 Thomas Farrington, victualler.

1771-2 [12-13 G. iii.] HENRY VIGARS, Esquire, Mayor.

Oct. 25 Benjamin Monk, stationer, s. of Mr. William Monk, printer.
  „ 25 William s. of Mr. Monk.
  „ 25 Thomas Dicas, cutler, s. of Mr. William Dicas, barber.
  „ 26 John Suddones, woollendraper, s. of Richard Suddones, schoolmaster.

Oct. 26 *Edward Rowland, mason.
,, 26 John Jones, cordwainer, s. of John Jones, cordwainer.
,, 26 Benjamin Bethell p. of John Spurstow, linendraper.
,, 26 Thomas Crane, corkcutter, s. of William Crane, corkcutter.
,, 26 Samuel s. of the above Mr. [William] Crane.
,, 26 Samuel Suddones, schoolmaster, s. of Richard Suddones, schoolmaster.
,, 26 John Jones, currier, s. of Robert Jones, cordwainer.
,, 26 Charles Hand, corkcutter, s. of James Hand, corkcutter.
,, 28 Thomas Crane, clerk, s. of Thomas Crane, cordwainer.
,, 28 Joseph Finchett, glover, s. of John Finchett, glover.
,, 28 William Holland, horse hirer, s. of William Holland, horse hirer.
,, 28 Richard s. of Richard Batho, barber.
,, 28 John Jowsey, hosier, s. of John Jowsey, feltmaker.
,, 28 Paul s. of Paul Pike, cordwainer.
,, 28 William Woods, mason, s. of William Woods, mason.
,, 28 Jacob Adams p. of Samuel Davies, mason.
,, 28 John Griffith, plumber, s. of George Griffith, plumber.
,, 28 Joseph Buckley, druggist, s. of John Buckley, stationer.
,, 28 Jeffrey Edwards, flaxdresser, s. of Jeffrey Edwards, flaxdresser.
,, 28 John Hostage ["gentleman" added on Roll] s. of Samuel Hostage, smith.
,, 28 Richard Roughley, grocer, s. of John Roughley, grocer.
,, 28 Edward Griffith, grocer, s. of John Griffith, butcher.
,, 28 Gabriel Simpson p. of John Simpson, vintner.
,, 28 John s. of John Pike, baker.
,, 28 John Taylor, gardener, s. of John Taylor, gardener.
†George Linney, cordwainer.
,, 28 Moses Millar, baker, s. of John Millar, innholder.
,, 28 Joseph Crane, grocer, s. of William Crane, grocer.
,, 28 James Golding, pipemaker, s. of James Golding, pipemaker.
,, 28 Charles Chevers, butcher, s. of Edward Chevers, butcher.
,, 28 John Thomas p. of John Dymocke Griffith, merchant.
,, 28 Samuel Boden, gardener, s. of Samuel Boden, slater and plasterer.
,, 28 Joseph Hand, slater, s. of John Hand, corkcutter.
,, 28 John s. of John Culm, staymaker.
,, 28 Edward Griffith, gentleman, s. of Edward Griffith, alderman.

[1771-3]   THE CITY OF CHESTER   373

Oct. 28   Richard Walley, baker, s. of George Walley of Tarporley.
 ,, 28   William Walley, maltster, s. of William Walley of Tarporley.
 ,, 28   Thomas Hatton p. of Thomas Crane, cordwainer.
 ,, 28   William Lowe, corkcutter, s. of Peter Lowe, corkcutter.
 ,, 28   Harwar Garratt p. of Thomas Shaw, currier.
 ,, 28   William Barlow p. of John Sorton, wetglover.
Nov. 4   Isaac Hallard p. of Thomas Humphreys, combmaker.
 ,, 21   *Samuel Jackson, gentleman.
 ,, 23   *John Perry, blacksmith.
 ,, 30   Hamnett Ley of Morley s. of Thomas Ley.
 ,, 30   Joseph Mostyn, cordwainer, s. of Rowland Mostyn, woolcomber.
Dec. 20   Thomas Smith p. of Thomas Weigh, currier.
Jan. 1   Joseph Beckett, upholsterer, s. of Joseph Beckett, innholder.
 ,, 18   *John Brett, victualler.
 ,, 18   *Thomas Langford, confectioner.
May   4   Thomas Vernon of Tushingham cum Grindley s. of Thomas Vernon, apothecary.
 ,,   6   Thomas Davies, wetglover, s. of John Davies, wetglover.
 ,, 29   William Beckett p. of Joseph Butler, bricklayer.
June 27   Peter Hale, butcher, s. of Peter Hale, butcher.
 ,, 27   William s. of John Salladine, brewer.
Aug. 29   Richard Crosby, cordwainer, s. of Joseph Crosby, cordwainer.
Oct. 22   *William Grahme, gentleman.

1772-3 [13-14 G. iii.] JOSEPH CREWE, Esquire, Mayor.

Oct. 24   *John Houghland, victualler.
 ,, 28   John Johnson, cabinetmaker, s. of Charles Johnson, dyer.
Nov. 3   Charles Wright, barber, s. of John Wright, woolcomber.
 ,,   7   *George Lloyd, victualler.
 ,, 16   *Thomas Smith, victualler.
 ,, 16   *Thomas Parry, gardener.
 ,, 19   *John Reader, mercer.
Jan. 23   Matthew Murphy p. of John Lawrenson, butcher.
 ,, 23   John Buckley, cordwainer, s. of Randle Buckley, whitesmith.

Jan. 23 Robert Wright p. of Thomas Buckley, innholder.
„ 30 Samuel Coulton p. of Robert Robinson, baker.
Feb. 2 John Linney, barber, s. of Thomas Linney, cordwainer.
Mar. 6 *Thomas Maning, saddler.
„ 27 *Joseph Brown, pavier.
Apr. 15 George Johnson, surgeon and apothecary, s. of Obadiah Johnson, gentleman.
May 15‡*Joseph Leech, barber.
„ 29 *Thomas Clayton, mayor's officer, "sworn one of the four Sergeants at Peace," &c.
June 5 Stephen Beckett, tailor, s. of John Beckett, baker.
„ 25 John Fox p. of Martha Hale, butcher.
July 17 Thomas Townshend, esquire, s. of John Townshend, esquire.
Aug. 21 *James Probert, sheriff's officer.
„ 21 *John Ellis, innholder.
„ 21 *William Edwards, grocer.
Sep. 1 Robert Whittell, ropier, s. of John Whittell, silk dyer.
„ 28 Peter Porter of Leeds, glover, s. of Thomas Porter, wetglover.
Oct. 9 George Sconce p. of George Walker, wetglover.
„ 16 Samuel Briscoe p. of Job Maddocks, butcher, and assigned to Hugh Rowe, butcher.

1773-4 [14-15 G. iii.] Sir WATKIN WILLIAMS WYNNE, Baronet, Mayor.

Oct. 23 James Bradford p. of Richard Case of Chester, baker.
„ 23 Francis Parry p. of Edmund Warrington of Chester, baker.
„ 25 Thomas Welchman Wynne, esquire, s. of Thomas Welshman [sic].
Apr. 12 John Penington, butcher, s. of John Penington, barber.
Aug. 22 Ralph Smith p. of Allen Mason, baker.
Sep. 14 *John Morgan, victualler.
„ 14 *Joseph Walker, victualler.
„ 14 Samuel Waterwoods the younger s. of Samuel Waterwoods, slater.
Oct. 21 *Thomas Carter, innkeeper.

1774] THE CITY OF CHESTER 375

Oct. 21 Peter Holland of Brist—, indigo blue-maker, p. of Mr. William Somner, grocer.
  „ 21 William s. of Thomas Massey, linendraper.
  „ 21‡*Henry Green, brazier.

1774-5 [15-16 G. iii.] JOSEPH DYSON, Esquire, Mayor.

Oct. 22 *Joseph Turner, architect.
  „ 22 *Edward Humphreys, carpenter.
  „ 22 *Robert Jones, victualler.
  „ 22 *Richard Lloyd, victualler.
  „ 22 *James Artingstall, cordwainer.
  „ 22 Thomas Jones, combmaker, s. of William Jones, cordwainer.
  „ 22 Thomas Saunders p. of William Brown, cordwainer.
  „ 24 *Thomas Poole, baker.
  „ 29 *John James, shopkeeper.
  „ 31 George Haswell, staymaker, s. of William Haswell, cordwainer.
  „ 31 Thomas Kent, coachman, s. of William Kent, victualler.
Nov. 14 Benjamin Jordan, barber, s. of Joseph Jordan, slater and plasterer.
  „ 19 John Millington p. of George Brown, barber.
  „ 19 John Ely p. of John Tonna, butcher.
  „ 23 George Holland p. of Henry Hegg, druggist.
  „ 26 *Charles Henchman, esquire.
Dec. 2 George Buckley, bookseller, s. of John Buckley, bookseller.
  „ 5 Benjamin Brassey p. of Thomas Croughton, linendraper.
  „ 5 John Meacock p. of Mr. Robert Maddock, linendraper.
  „ 5 George Rogers p. of George Geary of Chester, gardener.
  „ 5 Robert Brittain p. of Robert Aldersey, woollendraper.
  „ 5 Thomas Bennion, chandler, s. of John Bennion, chandler.
  „ 15 John Ridgway p. of William Ratcliffe, flaxdresser.
  „ 15 *Robert Davies, saddler.
  „ 17 Peter Foulkes, esquire, s. of Edward Foulkes, gentleman.
  „ 17 *Thomas Dickson, glazier and painter.
  „ 30 Thomas Ledsham, woollendraper, s. of Thomas Ledsham, stationer.

376   THE ROLLS OF THE FREEMEN OF   [1774-6

Dec. 31   George Boswell the younger s. of George Boswell of Parkgate, Custom House officer.
Jan. 14   *Thomas Woolwright, clerk.
Feb. 18   James s. and p. of James Pickering, saddler, deceased.
„ 18   John Davies, butcher, s. of Samuel Davies, glazier.
„ 23   Joseph Jones, cordwainer, s. of William Jones.
July 1   William Palin, cutler, s. of Thomas Palin, tailor.
„ 1   James Palin, laceweaver, s. of Thomas Palin.
„ 8   *John Dean, cabinetmaker.
„ 13   Joseph Hodkinson, baker, p. of John Hodkinson.
Aug. 1   *William Starkey, tailor.
„ 2   James Newell, barber, s. of Joseph Newell, cordwainer.
„ 3   *Samuel Vaughan, victualler.
„ 3   *Anderson Davies, pewterer and brazier.
„ 5   *John Probyn, baker.
„ 12   *George Groom, baker.
„ 30   William Shone p. of Joseph Thomas, baker.
„ 31   Peter Reece p. of Thomas Patton of Chester, currier.
Oct. 5   William Beavan p. of Robert Robinson, baker.
„ 7   John Poynton of Wimbolds Trafford, yeoman, s. of Charles Poynton.
„ 11   Benjamin Yoxall, saddler, s. of Robert Yoxall, smith.
„ 21   John Towsey, feltmaker, s. of Thomas Towsey, feltmaker.
„ 21   Thomas Denman p. of John Ratcliffe, watchmaker.
„ 27   *John Edmonds.
Aug. 26   Joseph Edwards p. of Mr. William Dicas, barber.

1775-6 [16-17 G. iii.] THOMAS GRIFFITH, Esquire, Mayor.

Oct. 28   Thomas s. of Thomas Harvie, late of Chester, grocer.
„ 31   Francis Wood, tinplateworker, s. of William Wood, late of Chester, mason.
„ 31   Richard Massey, stationer, s. of Richard Massey of Chester, baker.
Nov. 4   *Samuel Johnson, cabinetmaker.
„ 9   James Bacarn, perukemaker, s. of Richard Bacarn, carpenter.
„ 14   *Peter Hooley, victualler.
„ 23   *William Meredith, gunsmith.
„ 30   Samuel Mercer, cabinetmaker, s. of Ralph Mercer, cabinetmaker.
Jan. 20   John Lowe p. of Thomas Lea, tobacconist.

1776]   THE CITY OF CHESTER   377

Jan. 27 *Robert Meyrick, gentleman.
  „ 27 John Cartwright p. of John Clubbe, grocer.
  „ 27 *Thomas Lewis, victualler.
  „ 27 *John Edwards, Mr. Mayor's porter.
Feb. 9 Hedd Lloyd p. of William Wright, grocer.
  „ 24 William Turner p. of Christopher Bennett, barber.
Mar. 2 *Henry Thomas, tailor.
  „ 22 *John Richards, whitesmith.
  „ 23 *John Nichollson, carrier.
June 4 *James Standen of Poulton, co. Lanc., gentleman.
  „   6 Thomas Reece p. of Charles Francis, woollen-draper.
  „ 15 John Jones p. of John Meredith, bricklayer.
  „ 17 *Samuel Thomas, baker.
  „ 17 *William Blower, coachman.
  „ 19 *Charles Rackett, innholder.
  „ 19 William Jones, cordwainer, s. of William Jones, cordwainer.
  „ 19 *Robert Rogers, victualler.
  „ 19 *John Paul, victualler.
July 1 Thomas Nicholls, tanner, s. of William Nicholls of Chester, tanner, deceased.
  „   6 *Samuel Mason, innholder.
  „ 17 John Eaton, mason, s. of George Eaton, mason.
Aug. 5 *John Kenrick, grocer.
  „   5 *Jonathan Roberts, grocer.
  „ 28 *John Leatherbarrow, tinplateworker.
Oct. 2 John Larden, woollendraper, s. of John Larden of Tattenhall, gentleman.
  „   2 Stephen Palin, gentleman, s. of Thomas Palin.
  „   5 *William Wynne, grocer.
  „ 23 Thomas s. of Thomas Lumber, barber.

1776-7 [17-18 G. iii.] JAMES BROADHURST, Esquire, Mayor.

Nov. 2 *Thomas Whittell, brewer.
  „   4 Joseph Barlow p. of Thomas Williams, glazier.
  „   4 John s. of Charles Jackson.
  „   4 David Evans p. of John Shone, carpenter.
  „   4 John Goff p. of Charles Gill, blacksmith.
  „   5 Charles Griffith, mariner, s. of George Griffith, late of Chester, plumber.
  „   5 William Bellin, ship carpenter, s. of Robert Bellin, cooper.

Nov. 6 Laurence Welch p. of Thomas Powell, shipwright.
„ 6 John Dixon, baker, s. of Robert Dixon, late of Chester, brewer.
„ 7 John Dickens p. of William Jordan, carpenter.
„ 8 Thomas Newns p. of George Lindsey, afterwards assigned to Charles Crew, carpenter, and afterwards to John Griffith, carpenter.
„ 8 John Harrison the younger p. of Richard Griffith, carpenter.
„ 8 Edward Jones, brushmaker, p. of George French of Chester, alderman.
„ 8 Joseph Dickens, fisherman, s. of Thomas Dickens, wetglover.
„ 11 John Hale, butcher, } ss. of William Hale of Chol-
„ 11 William Hale, butcher,} ton, butcher.
„ 12 *John Ray, innkeeper.
„ 12 *William Tilston, cheesemonger.
„ 15 William Baxter, skinner, s. of Richard Baxter, skinner.
†John Bedward, joiner and carpenter.
„ 16 Henry Thomas, butcher, s. of Hugh Thomas, slater.
„ 18 Thomas Evans p. of John Sorton, wetglover.
„ 18 Thomas Davies p. of William Corles, wetglover.
„ 18 John Rowland, miller, s. of Thomas Rowland, slater and plasterer.
„ 19 Ralph Bellin, grocer, s. of Ralph Bellin, cooper.
„ 19 James s. and p. of James Clutton of Chester, grocer.
„ 19 Thomas Shepard, linendraper, s. of Thomas Shepard, grocer.
„ 21 *John Walker, joiner.
„ 23 Edward Roberts p. of William Stones, currier.
„ 26 Peter Belward, tailor, s. of John Belward.
„ 26 Joseph Ralphs p. of John Usherwood, butcher.
Dec. 7 James Mostyn, feltmaker, s. of Rowland Mostyn, jerseycomber.
„ 17 John Jameson p. of Richard Sneyd, cooper.
„ 23 Thomas Briscoe, mariner, s. of William Briscoe, mariner.
Jan. 7 Robert Allcock, whitesmith, s. of Thomas Allcock, whitesmith.
„ 10 Robert Hughes p. of John Totty, whitesmith.
„ 13 James Murphy p. of William Ratcliffe, flaxdresser.
„ 13 Thomas Ward p. of Timothy Jones, cordwainer.
„ 17 Zachariah Jones, cordwainer, s. of John Jones, cordwainer.
„ 17 Robert Roberts p. of John Jones, wheelwright.
„ 20 Robert Whitley p. of Thomas Jones, grocer.

[1777-8] THE CITY OF CHESTER 379

Jan. 21 John Shone p. of John Woodworth, and assigned to John Brookes, bricklayer.
„ 21 John Evans p. of John Pemberton, bricklayer, and assigned to John Meredith, bricklayer.
„ 28 *Zacheus Bartlem, fruiterer.
„ 28 Peter Meacock, tailor, s. of John Meacock, weaver.
„ 29 *Richard Denson, currier.
„ 29 *William Hughes, grocer.
„ 29 John Scully p. of John Shannon, cordwainer.
„ 29 *William Williams, victualler.
Feb. 1 *John Wildig, cheesemonger.
„ 1 James Taylor, slater, s. of William Taylor, slater.
„ 10 James s. of Richard Suddones, schoolmaster.
„ 10 *Jonathan Barth, victualler.
„ 10 *Samuel Peck the younger of Christleton, butcher.
„ 12 John Hassall p. of John Bennett, wine merchant.
„ 19 *John Davies, watchmaker.
Apr. 16 Samuel Lloyd p. of William Walley, and assigned to Richard Walley, baker.
May 3 William Bennion p. of John Swinnerton, turner, and assigned to John Cross, turner.
„ 10 Daniel Woolstanham p. of Thomas Rathbone, carpenter.
„ 24 William Cowdrey p. of John Monk, printer.
July 2 *John Wilding, cheesemonger.
„ 2 *Joseph Sinclair, victualler.
„ 24 *George Lowe, mercer.
„ 28 William Saunderson p. of George Walker, silversmith.
Aug. 21 James Jackson p. of John Pemberton, tailor.
Sep. 20 Joseph Wilkinson, baker, s. of William Wilkinson, surgeon.
Oct. 18 William Gamon, yeoman, s. of William Gamon, yeoman.
„ 18 Benjamin Clubbe, yeoman, p. of John Clubbe, grocer.

1777-8 [18-19 G. iii.] JOHN HART, Esquire, Mayor.

Oct. 31 Charles Williamson, wine merchant, p. of John Whitby, maltster.
Nov. 8 Samuel Reece p. of Robert Johnson, baker.
„ 22 Thomas Griffith, glovecutter, s. of Thomas Griffith, yeoman.
Dec. 10 John Littler p. of David Napier, brazier.
Jan. 24 Charles Price p. of Thomas Rathbone, carpenter.
Feb. 21 George Peck p. of Robert Lamb, butcher.

Mar. 7 Joseph Pemberton, hatter, s. of William Pemberton, hatter.
„ 18 Joseph s. of Thomas Moores of Chester, cooper, deceased.
„ 28 Thomas Williams, cordwainer, s. of Elias Williams of Chester, brazier, deceased.
Apr. 8 *Samuel Bullock, carpenter.
„ 11 *William Kendrick, carrier.
„ 11 *James Abbott, cabinetmaker.
„ 11 Robert Shearing p. of William Jordan of Chester, joiner and carpenter.
„ 13 *John Mainwaring, innkeeper.
„ 14 Richard } ss. of Nathaniel Dewsbury of Chester,
„ 14 Nathaniel }   feltmaker.
„ 20 William Posnett p. of John Towsey of Chester, feltmaker, and assigned to Thomas Towsey of Chester, feltmaker.
„ 21 *William Hassall, innholder.
May 9 John Barker p. of George Johnson of Chester, cabinetmaker.
„ 13 *Samuel Thomas, victualler.
„ 16 Daniel Smith, merchant, s. of Daniel Smith of Chester, deceased.
„ 22 *Joseph Moores, victualler.
June 10 *Henry Skeat, cabinetmaker.
„ 10 Edward Bateman, cooper, s. of Thomas Bateman of Chester, deceased.
„ 24 John Griffith, glover and breechesmaker, p. of Thomas Wynn of Chester, glover, deceased.
July 14 *Joseph Cooper, wheelwright.
Aug. 7. Edward Adams p. of Edward Adams of Chester, innkeeper, deceased.
„ 8 *Thomas Huxley, writing-stationer.
„ 8 *Charles Gregson, vintner.
„ 22 *Edward Powell, victualler.
„ 28 *John Rogers, pilot.
Sep. 5 John Thomas, glazier, p. of William Calkin of Chester, glazier and tallowchandler.

1778-9 [19-20 G. iii.] WILLIAM SELLER, Esquire, Mayor.

Nov. 24 William Lancaster p. of John Linney of Chester, barber.
Dec. 9 John s. of Robert Scasebrick of Chester, barber, deceased.

Dec.	28	Charles Hesketh, barber, p. of Christopher Bennett of Chester, barber and perukemaker.
Jan.	12	Samuel Parry p. of Joseph Clubbe of Chester, ironmonger and grocer.
,,	18	Thomas Meacock p. of Pattison Ellames of Chester, druggist.
Feb.	8	William Lewis, haberdasher, s. of William Lewis of Chester, gentleman, deceased.
Mar.	2	John Jones p. of Thomas Jones of Chester, cutler.
,,	4	*William Hancock, victualler.
,,	6	*Thomas Hayes, bricklayer.
,,	6	*Starkey Broadhurst, merchant.
,,	6	*Robert Evans, innkeeper.
,,	17	George Lighfoot, tea dealer, p. of John Hignett of Chester, linen merchant.
,,	25	*Thomas Jackson, innholder.
,,	25	Edward Harvey, scrivener, s. of Samuel Harvey, late of Chester, bricklayer.
Apr.	3	William Price the younger, p. of George Brown of Chester, barber.
,,	8	John Bailey, organist, s. of John Bailey of Chester, feltmaker.
May	1	*John Davies, victualler.
,,	8	*Richard Bradburn, victualler.
,,	15	Charles Lloyd p. of Richard Case of Chester, baker.
July	17	Charles Haswell, breechesmaker, s. of Charles Haswell of Chester, cordwainer.
Aug.	6	John Price, clerk, s. of Thomas Price of Chester.
,,	20	James Conway p. of Richard Richardson of Chester, silversmith.
,,	21	Joseph Barnes p. of Andrew Davison of Chester, wine merchant.
Sep.	17	Robert Williams, pattenmaker, p. of Mr. Alderman Wrench.
,,	29	Joseph Duke, silversmith, s. of Andrew Duke, late of Chester.
,,	29	Richard Richardson, silversmith, s. of Richard Richardson of Chester, alderman, deceased.
,,	29	Thomas Avern, corkcutter, s. of Thomas Avern of Chester, corkcutter.
Oct.	1	John Ratcliffe, cordwainer, s. of William Ratcliffe of Chester, cordwainer.
,,	6	Thomas Whitehead, slater, s. of Robert Whitehead, late of Chester.
,,	9	William Golding, carpenter, s. of James Golding of Chester, pipemaker.

Oct. 13 William Seller the younger, brewer, } ss. of Mr. Mayor.
„ 13 Samuel Seller, gentleman,
„ 16 William Hickson, slater, s. of Thomas Hickson, late of Chester, tailor.
„ 21 *Hugh Prince, cordwainer.
„ 21 John Hancock p. of Henry Hancock, tailor, and assigned to Benjamin Hickson of Chester, tailor.

1779-80 [20-21 G. iii.] GABRIEL SMITH, Esquire, Mayor.

Nov. 6 Thomas Totty, whitesmith, s. of George Totty of Chester, smith, deceased.
„ 30 *Peter Yoxall.
Dec. 6 Thomas Starkey, cordwainer, s. of John Starkey, deceased.
„ 11 William Corbin of Hawarden, yeoman, s. of William Corbin of Hawarden, gentleman.
„ 13 Michael Cowper the younger, shipwright, } ss. of Michael Cooper of Chester, shipwright.
„ 13 John Cooper, shipwright,
„ 23 John Shepherd p. of John Poole of Chester, bookseller.
Jan. 4 Ralph Eddowes p. of Thomas Moulson of Chester, tobacconist.
„ 4 Edward Moulson, gentleman, } ss. of Thomas Moulson.
„ 4 Thomas Moulson, tobacconist,
„ 29 John Herbert p. of Samuel Tonna of Chester, breechesmaker.
June 10 *Edward Evans, victualler.
„ 10 *George Randles, cabinetmaker.
„ 10 Samuel Dutton p. of William Cole of Chester, carpenter.
Aug. 19 Thomas s. of William Briscoe of Chester, smith, and p. of William Johnson of Chester, cordwainer, deceased.
Oct. 7 Thomas Nicholls, esquire, s. of the late William Nicholls, clerk.
„ 14 Ralph Jackson p. of John Jackson, barber, deceased, and assigned to William Turner, barber.
„ 21 *William Henderson, cabinetmaker.
„ 25 William Nicholls, grocer, s. of Rev. William Nicholls, clerk.

1780-1 [21-22 G. iii.] JOSEPH SNOW, Esquire, Mayor.

Nov. 1 Thomas Jones p. of John Massey, baker.
" 1 John Nicholls, tobacconist, s. of Rev. William Nicholls, clerk.
Dec. 11 Mason Barrow p. of Daniel Gorton, saddler, deceased, and assigned to Thomas Manning, saddler.
Jan. 13 *Joseph Moss, victualler.
" 13 John Carr p. of Richard Jones, pipemaker.
" 16 *William Hopson, innholder.
Feb. 3 William Darlington p. of Richard Ledsham, joiner.
" 10 *Simon Hawkins, victualler.
" 15 Roger Langshaw p. of John Spurstow, linendraper.
" 17 Nathaniel Warrington p. of Edward Warrington, and assigned to John Sefton, baker.
Mar. 6 *John Tamberlaine, victualler.
Apr. 21 Daniel Herbert p. of William Brown, cordwainer.
June 8 Thomas Haswell, barber, s. of Charles Haswell, cordwainer.
" 21 John Adams p. of Thomas Adams, carpenter.
" 22 Thomas Towsey, carpenter, s. of Thomas Towsey, hatter.
" 23 *Edward Lloyd, victualler.
July 7 John Crane, gentleman, s. of William Crane, deceased.
" 19 *John Davies, perfumer.
" 19 *Edward Jones, linendraper.
" 27 *William Nelson, clerk.
" 27 Charles Mytton, clerk, s. of Charles Mytton, wine merchant.
Aug. 2 *Richard Edwards, linendraper.
" 18 John s. and p. of John Jones, pattenmaker.
" 27 *The Right Reverend Bielby Porteous, Lord Bishop of Chester.
Sep. 11 John Denson p. of Robert Bowers, upholsterer, and assigned to Thomas Powell, upholsterer.
" 22 John Turner p. of James Jones, cordwainer.
Oct. 11 Thomas Roughley of Dublin, linen merchant, s. of John Roughley, grocer, deceased.

1781-2 [22-23 G. iii.] PATTISON ELLAMES, Esquire, Mayor.

Nov. 7 Thomas Bowers, linendraper, s. of Thomas Bowers of Chester, linendraper.
" 14 William Hale, butcher, s. of Peter Hale, late of Chester, butcher.

384 THE ROLLS OF THE FREEMEN OF [1781-3

Dec. 5 Ralph Lowe p. of Allen Mason of Chester, baker.
,, 19 Roger Ormes p. of Daniel Gorton of Chester, saddler, deceased.
,, 19 Ralph Wilcoxon p. of John Dutton of Chester, linen-draper.
,, 19 Samuel Witter, chandler, s. of John Witter, deceased.
Jan. 22 Charles Panton, banker, s. of Charles Panton.
Feb. 4 *John Williams, sheriff's officer.
Mar. 11 John Peers, silk dyer, s. of John Peers, deceased.
Apr. 24 Roger Dutton p. of Edmund Bushell, mercer.
,, 24 *Samuel Thring, victualler.
Aug. 28 John Spence, turner, s. of William Spence of Chester, cordwainer.
,, 29 *Jonathan Ordford, saddler.
Sep. 4 John Richards, tanner, s. of Thomas Richards of Chester, maltster.
,, 18 *Richard Ankers, victualler.
,, 25 *Joseph Hornby, linendraper.
,, 25 *Francis Lake, victualler.
Oct. 3 Robert Adams p. of Philip Presbury of Chester, cabinetmaker.
,, 22 *Jonathan Furber, victualler.
,, 23 John Taylor Newell, tanner, s. of John Newell of Chester.
,, 23 Robert Bowers, watchmaker, s. of Robert Bowers, woollendraper.
,, 23 *John Humphreys, victualler.

1782-3 [23-24 G. iii.] THOMAS PATTON, Esquire, Mayor.

Nov. 2 Thomas Maddock p. of Gamaliel Hawkins of Chester, slater.
,, 20 George Gregory p. of Francis Parry of Chester, baker.
,, 22 Samuel Meredith p. of George Lowe, miller and flour dealer.
,, 25 John Tapley, tailor, s. of John Tapley of Chester, tailor, deceased.
Mar. 1 Thomas Baccarn, carpenter, s. of Thomas Baccarn of Chester, butcher.
May 17 *Matthew Jones, beadle.
,, 21 *John Troughton, shipbuilder.
,, 21 *John Cheshire, victualler.
,, 21 *Thomas Gaulton, victualler.
,, 21 *Daniel Dod, pavier.

1783-4] THE CITY OF CHESTER 385

May 21 *James Huxley, victualler.
„ 23 *John Fleming, gardener.
„ 24 John Griffith, cabinetmaker, s. of John Griffith, late of Chester.
„ 24 Samuel Coy, tailor, s. of Samuel Coy, late of Chester.
June 15 William Wheawell, innkeeper, s. of William Wheawell, yeoman, deceased.
Sep. 2 Robert Oldham, barber, s. of Livesly Oldham of Chester, barber.
„ 6 John Huxley, mariner, p. of Charles Goodwin, esquire.
„ 6 Leenes Shone, corkcutter, s. of Joshua Shone, late of Chester, weaver.
„ 12 Thomas Rathbone, carpenter, s. of Thomas Rathbone of Chester.
„ 12 Thomas Steele p. of William Birch of Chester, woollen-draper.
„ 22 The Hon. Robert Grosvenor s. of Rt. Hon. Lord Grosvenor.
„ 22 Richard Grosvenor, esquire, } ss. of Thomas Grosvenor,
„ 22 Thomas Grosvenor, esquire, } esquire.
Oct. 8 *John Parry, yeoman.
„ 16 James Haswell of Liverpool, ironmonger, s. of Jonathan Haswell, late of Liverpool, whitesmith.
„ 16 *David Jones, innholder.
„ 20 Edward Astle, tanner, s. of Thomas Astle, late of Chester, alderman.
„ 22 Joseph Wright, tanner, s. of Joseph Wright of Chester, grocer.
„ 22 *Thomas Brown, painter.

1783-4 [24-25 G. iii.] THOMAS AMERY, Esquire, Mayor.

Nov. 1 Ellis Roberts p. of John Hodkinson of Chester, baker.
„ 3 *Paul Panton the younger of Plasgwyn, esquire.
„ 21 Aaron Miller, gentleman, s. of John Miller, late of Chester.
Dec. 13 William Huntington, cutler, s. of John Huntington.
Jan. 24 Hamnett Dobb, gentleman, s. of Hamnett Dobb of Mollington, gentleman.
Mar. 3 Hugh Rowe, butcher, s. of Hugh Rowe of Chester, butcher.
„ 3 Edward Maddock, butcher, s. of Job Maddock, late of Chester, butcher.
„ 6 Henry Tapley, cordwainer, p. of William Adshead, and assigned to William High.

Mar. 31 Roger Barnston, esquire, s. of Robert Barnston, esquire.
,, 31 John Brown, druggist, s. of William Brown, cordwainer.
,, 31 Henry Ridley Bennett, esquire, s. of Thomas Bennett of Chester, linendraper.
,, 31 Joseph Hincks, merchant, s. of Robert Hincks, merchant.
,, 31 John Miller p. of William Jones, pipemaker.
,, 31 Thomas High, staymaker, s. of William High, cordwainer.
,, 31 Richard Davenport p. of John Monk, printer.
,, 31 John Weaver, printer, p. of John Monk.
,, 31 David Martin p. of Thomas Plumbley, barber.
,, 31 Alexander Evans, p. of George Haswell, staymaker.
,, 31 George French, gentleman, s. of George French, alderman.
,, 31 John Jones p. of Lawrence Lawrenson, combmaker.
,, 31 George Salusbury Townsend, esquire, s. of John Townsend, esquire.
,, 31 Daniel Aldersey, woollendraper, s. of Robert Aldersey, woollendraper.
,, 31 Richard Boden, slater, s. of Samuel Boden, slater.
,, 31 Joseph Harrison p. of Edward Spencer, mason.
,, 31 John Nicholas p. of Thomas Golborn, barber.
,, 31 Ralph Crooks, carpenter, s. of Thomas Crooks, carpenter.
,, 31 John Lloyd p. of Thomas Maddock of Chester, cordwainer.
,, 31 James Nailor p. of Thomas Pickmore of Chester, staymaker.
,, 31 John Davenport p. of John Stringer of Chester, upholsterer.
,, 31 John Ruffell [? Russell] p. of James Jordan of Chester, barber.
,, 31 Roger Shone, painter, s. of Joshua Shone of Chester, weaver.
,, 31 Thomas Johnson p. of Jeffrey Edwards of Chester, flaxdresser.
,, 31 Thomas Jones p. of Jonathan Whittle of Chester, ropemaker.
,, 31 Ambrose Boden, staymaker, s. of Samuel Boden of Chester.
,, 31 William Shephard p. of Thomas Walker of Chester, tailor.
,, 31 Robert Parry p. of Benjamin Saunders of Chester, carpenter.

Mar.	31	John Baxter p. of Robert Whittle of Chester, ropier.
,,	31	Thomas Roberts p. of Philip Presbury of Chester, cabinetmaker.
,,	31	Nicholas Blake p. of John Shone of Chester, carpenter.
,,	31	Enoch Barnett p. of Richard Humphries of Chester, hornbreaker.
,,	31	John Key p. of John Croughton of Chester, cabinetmaker.
,,	31	Robert Lloyd p. of John Shone of Chester, carpenter.
,,	31	William Robinson, bricklayer, s. of Charles Robinson of Chester, bricklayer.
,,	31	John Rathbone, turner, s. of Thomas Rathbone of Chester, turner.
Apr.	1	John Dyke p. of Lawrence Corles of Chester, skinner.
,,	1	John Edson p. of William Corles of Chester, skinner.
,,	1	Josiah Meres p. of John Sorton of Chester, wet-glover.
,,	1	Edward Moreland p. of William Corles of Chester, skinner.
,,	1	John Lewis, bricklayer, s. of Benjamin Lewis of Chester, bricklayer.
,,	1	John Woodfin, slater, s. of Thomas Woodfin of Chester, bricklayer.
,,	1	Hamnett Holland, butcher, s. of William Holland of Chester, butcher.
,,	1	John Thornley, combmaker, s. of Hugh Thornley of Chester, hornbreaker.
,,	1	David Roberts p. of Thomas Lumber of Chester, barber.
,,	1	James Lumber, cooper, s. of Thomas Lumber of Chester, barber.
,,	1	Thomas Panton, tanner, s. of Paul Panton of Chester, tanner.
,,	1	Thomas Lloyd p. of George Whitehead of Chester, slater.
,,	1	John Manuel p. of Charles Haswell of Chester, barber.
,,	1	William Boden, slater, s. of Samuel Boden of Chester, slater.
,,	1	Joseph Pritchard, pump-borer, s. of John Pritchard of Chester, fisherman.
,,	1	James Fitzgerald, pipemaker, s. of Joseph Fitzgerald of Chester, pipemaker.
,,	1	Edward Hoy, tobacconist, s. of William Hoy of Chester, cordwainer.
,,	1	Thomas Shephard p. of John Hickson of Chester, tailor.

Apr. 1 John Coleclough, carpenter, s. of John Coleclough of Chester, carpenter.
,, 1 William Revington, carpenter, s. of William Revington of Chester, cordwainer.
,, 1 John Bennion, cordwainer, s. of John Bennion of Chester, cordwainer.
,, 1 Richard Randles p. of John Sorton of Chester, wetglover.
,, 1 John Edge, ropemaker, s. of Thomas Edge of Chester, ropemaker.
,, 1 John Spencer p. of John Sorton of Chester, skinner.
,, 1 Ralph Cotgreave, cordwainer, ⎫ ss. of Ralph Cotgreave
,, 1 Charles Cotgreave, cordwainer, ⎭ of Chester, almsman.
,, 1 James Ellson p. of Thomas Hand of Chester, corkcutter.
,, 1 Samuel Nield p. of Thomas Whittell of Chester, silk dyer.
,, 1 James Miller p. of Thomas Ley of Chester, tobacconist.
,, 1 John Venables, carpenter, s. of William Venables of Chester, carpenter.
,, 1 William Leeke, sawyer, s. of Christopher Leeke, pavier.
,, 1 John Meakin p. of John Millington of Chester, barber.
,, 1 Charles Broughton, blacksmith, s. of John Broughton of Chester, smith.
,, 1 John Harrison p. of Edward Harrison of Chester, ropemaker.
,, 1 William Smathers, butcher, s. of John Smathers of Chester, tobacconist.
,, 1 George Reece, ropemaker, s. of John Reece of Chester, ropemaker.
,, 1 Edward Cope p. of Thomas Bennett of Chester, feltmaker.
,, 1 William Leadbeater, mason, s. of Thomas Leadbeater of Chester, mason.
,, 1 William Corns p. of Benjamin Jones of Chester, slater.
,, 1 Charles Boxley, carpenter, s. of John Boxley of Chester, carpenter.
,, 1 John Fleming p. of Jonathan Whittell of Chester, ropier.
,, 1 John Smathers, carpenter, s. of John Smathers of Chester, ironmonger.
,, 1 Bartholomew Duke, cabinetmaker, s. of Thomas Duke, wetglover.

THE CITY OF CHESTER

Apr.	1	William Taylor } pp. of Thomas Harrop of Chester,
,,	1	Robert Jones } brazier.
,,	1	John Moss p. of James Smith of Chester, cordwainer.
,,	1	John Hughes p. of John Meredith of Chester, bricklayer.
,,	1	Thomas Duke, wetglover, s. of Samuel Duke of Chester, clerk.
,,	1	Abraham Hitchins p. of John Francis of Chester, ropemaker.
,,	1	Thomas Evans p. of Edward Boden of Chester, bricklayer.
,,	1	Edward s. of Edward Hawkins of Chester, cordwainer.
,,	1	Edward Hawkins, upholsterer, } ss. of James Hawkins
,,	1	James Hawkins, upholsterer, } of Chester, upholsterer.
,,	1	Thomas Andrews, labourer, s. of Thomas Andrews of Chester, bricklayer.
,,	1	William Harrison, carpenter, s. of William Harrison of Chester, slater.
,,	1	William Capper, carpenter, s. of Peter Capper of Chester, turner.
,,	1	Griffith Ellis, carpenter, s. of John Ellis of Hope.
,,	1	John Manuel p. of Michael Cooper of Chester, shipwright.
,,	1	Samuel Peers, staymaker, s. of James Peers of Chester, staymaker.
,,	1	John Hayes, breechesmaker, s. of John Hayes of Chester, barber.
,,	1	Sefton Carter, tobacconist, s. of Benjamin Carter of Chester, cordwainer.
,,	1	Thomas Jones p. of Thomas Griffies of Chester, heelmaker.
,,	1	David Powell p. of William Ratcliffe of Chester, flaxdresser.
,,	1	John Watson p. of John Dimock Griffith of Chester, ropemaker.
,,	1	Thomas Griffith } pp. of William Brown the younger
,,	1	George M'Kay } of Chester, cordwainer.
,,	1	Richard Williams p. of Abel Andrews of Chester, slater.
,,	1	Gilbert s. of John Wilkinson of Chester, wheelwright.
,,	1	James Price, butcher, s. of Thomas Price of Chester, butcher.
,,	1	Richard Leeke, bricklayer, s. of Christopher Leeke of Chester, pavier.

Apr. 1 George Gatley, plasterer, s. of George Gatley of Chester, barber.
,, 1 William Sorton, carpenter, s. and p. of Thomas Sorton.
,, 2 Thomas Minshall p. of Edward Boden of Chester, bricklayer.
,, 2 James Phenix p. of John Johnson of Chester, cabinet-maker.
,, 2 Richard Lewis p. of George Groom of Chester, baker.
,, 2 Thomas Nailor p. of William Cole of Chester, carpenter.
,, 2 Thomas Hodkinson p. of Richard Calley of Chester, weaver.
,, 2 John Bulkeley, whitesmith, s. of Edward Bulkeley of Chester, whitesmith.
,, 2 John Taylor, combmaker, } ss. of Jonathan Taylor of
,, 2 William Taylor, combmaker, } Chester, combmaker.
,, 2 John Meakin, slater, s. of William Meakin of Chester, pipemaker.
,, 2 John Axon, yeoman, } ss. of John Axon of Chester,
,, 2 James Axon, yeoman, } victualler.
,, 2 Thomas Lewis, pipemaker, s. of Edward Lewis of Chester, tanner.
,, 2 Samuel Hewitt p. of Arthur Culm of Chester, pipemaker.
,, 2 Charles M'Donald p. of John Saunders of Chester, cordwainer.
,, 2 William Ashmull p. of Roger Gill of Chester, cordwainer.
,, 2 Daniel Tasker p. of Thomas Adams of Chester, carpenter, and assigned to John Walker of Chester, carpenter.
,, 2 William Page, linendraper, s. of William Page of Chester, blacksmith.
,, 2 Hugh Sands, slater, s. of Richard Sands of Chester, slater.
,, 2 Henry Thornton, slater, s. of Richard Thornton of Chester, slater.
,, 2 William Hatton p. of Thomas Adams of Chester, carpenter.
,, 2 Richard Griffith, cordwainer, s. of Thomas Griffith of Chester, yeoman.
,, 2 Richard Dean p. of Cotton Probert of Chester, feltmaker.

Apr. 2 John Carter p. of Benjamin Carter of Chester, cordwainer.
„ 2 James Haswell, barber, s. of Charles Haswell of Chester, cordwainer.
„ 2 William Bartlam p. of Thomas Rathbone of Chester, carpenter.
„ 2 Richard Ellis p. of John Saunders of Chester, cordwainer.
„ 2 William Davies p. of Thomas Hand of Chester, corkcutter.
„ 2 Thomas Harrison p. of Robert Jones of Chester cordwainer.
„ 2 John Phillips p. of Richard Goulding of Chester, pipemaker.
„ 2 Samuel Nicholas p. of Robert Jones of Chester, cordwainer.
„ 2 John Briggs p. of Richard Cooper of Chester, shipwright.
„ 2 John Whitley } pp. of Thomas Jones of Chester,
„ 2 Joseph Holland } feltmaker.
„ 2 William Harrison, carpenter, s. of William Harrison of Chester, cordwainer.
„ 2 Charles Tylston, mason, s. of John Tylston of Chester, mason.
„ 2 William Hassall, blacksmith, s. of Robert Hassall of Chester, wheelwright.
„ 2 Edward Buckley p. of Peter Jackson of Chester, shipwright.
„ 2 George Bartlam, carpenter, s. of Robert Bartlam of Chester, carpenter.
„ 2 Thomas Harrison p. of Samuel Davies of Chester, mason.
„ 2 Charles Parry, tailor, s. of James Parry of Chester, corkcutter.
„ 2 Timothy Ollerhead p. of William Smith of Chester, carpenter.
„ 2 John s. of John Woodworth of Chester, cabinetmaker.
„ 2 John Brown p. of James Jordan of Chester, barber.
„ 2 Edward Powell, glover, s. of Edward Powell of Chester, mason.
„ 2 Charles Powell, pipemaker, s. of Charles Powell of Chester, pipemaker.
„ 2 Joseph Carter, cordwainer, s. of Benjamin Carter of Chester, cordwainer.
„ 2 James Harvey, bricklayer, s. of George Harvey of Chester, bricklayer.

Apr. 2 John Collins, glazier, s. of Samuel Collins of Chester, glazier.
„ 2 John Roberts p. of John Bulkeley of Chester, stationer.
„ 2 Arthur Culm, —— s. of John Culm of Chester, staymaker.
„ 2 John Jones, e—— s. of Samuel Jones of Chester, barber.
„ 2 Richard Baxter, skinner, s. of Richard Baxter of Chester, wetglover.
„ 2 Edward Lewis p. of William Nicholls, tanner.
„ 2 Joseph Shaw, blacksmith, s. of John Shaw of Chester, blacksmith.
„ 2 James Woodier p. of Isaac Woodier of Chester, butcher.
„ 2 Richard Crofts p. of John Yates of Chester, bricklayer.
„ 2 Samuel s. of William Daniel of Chester, mason.
„ 2 Thomas Darlington p. of Edward Boden of Chester, bricklayer.
„ 2 Charles Jordan, carpenter, s. of William Jordan of Chester, carpenter.
„ 2 William Jones, staymaker, s. of Thomas Jones of Chester, cordwainer.
„ 3 Thomas Coy, cutler, s. of Samuel Coy of Chester, tailor.
„ 3 John Cowduck, blacksmith, s. of John Cowduck of Chester, blacksmith.
„ 3 Randle Meakin, pipemaker, s. of Randle Meakin of Chester, pipemaker.
„ 3 Wilson Vizer, porter, s. of William Vizer of Chester, maltster.
„ 3 John Lloyd p. of Benjamin Saunders of Chester, carpenter.
„ 3 Samuel Burrowes, cooper, s. of Samuel Burrowes of Chester, baker.
„ 3 James Steens } pp. of Jonathan Whittell of Chester,
„ 3 Robert Challoner } ropier.
„ 3 George Barnett p. of Richard Humphries of Chester, combmaker.
„ 3 John Griffith p. of Richard Griffith of Chester, carpenter.
„ 3 Robert Hankey p. of Thomas Astle of Chester, cabinetmaker.
„ 3 Joseph Crofts p. of Thomas Speed of Chester, cordwainer.
„ 3 Samuel Hooley p. of Richard Walley of Chester, baker.
„ 3 John Parsonage p. of Samuel Coulton of Chester, baker.

[1784]   THE CITY OF CHESTER   393

Apr. 3 Richard Jackson, shipwright, s. of Peter Jackson of Chester, shipwright.
" 3 William Boyd p. of Charles M'Cans, and assigned to Thomas Rathbone of Chester, carpenter.
" 3 John s. of John Edwards of Chester, tailor.
" 3 William Holland, carpenter, s. of Mathias Holland of Chester, painter.
" 3 Richard Meakin, cordwainer, s. of Randle Meakin of Chester, pipemaker.
" 3 James s. of Edward Richardson of Chester, yeoman.
" 3 Hugh Thornley, cordwainer, s. of Hugh Thornley of Chester, hornbreaker.
" 3 Robert Williams, tobacconist, s. of David Williams of Chester, innholder.
" 3 Jonathan Brandrett p. of Thomas Golborne of Chester, barber.
" 3 John Hand, combmaker, s. of John Hand of Chester, ropier.
" 3 Richard Chamberlaine, gentleman, s. of Joseph Chamberlaine of Chester, grocer.
" 3 John Boxley, carpenter, s. of John Boxley of Chester, carpenter.
" 3 Charles Martin, cordwainer, s. of John Martin of Chester, tallowchandler.
" 3 William Stanton p. of Samuel Bagnall, and assigned to Thomas Grace of Chester, tobacconist.
" 3 George Richardson, butcher, s. of Edward Richardson of Chester, yeoman.
" 3 John Odier p. of Richard Goulding of Chester, and assigned to John Sharp of Chester, pipemaker.
" 3 John Stewart, tailor, s. of James Stewart of Chester, tailor.
" 3 John M'Gary, labourer, s. of Thomas M'Gary of Chester, weaver.
" 3 Charles Evans p. of Thomas Griffies of Chester, timber merchant.
" 3 Thomas Herbert p. of William Harrison of Chester, cordwainer.
" 3 John Wheawell, baker, s. of John Wheawell of Chester, yeoman.
" 3 Randle Batho, tanner, s. of Daniel Batho of Chester, currier.
" 3 John Welch, upholsterer, s. of Samuel Welch of Chester, maltster.
" 3 Jeremiah Smathers p. of Thomas Moulson of Chester, tobacconist.

Apr.	3	William Gibson p. of John Brooks of Chester, bricklayer.
,,	3	Peter Belward, weaver, s. of Peter Belward of Chester, tailor.
,,	3	Peter Hampton, printer, s. of James Hampton of Chester, cordwainer.
,,	3	James Hubbert p. of Thomas Hubbert of Chester, mariner.
,,	3	Joseph Odier, tinman, s. of Samuel Odier of Chester, slater.
,,	3	John Formstone p. of John Cooke of Chester, cabinetmaker.
,,	3	John Ingram p. of Gerrard Jordan of Chester, slater.
,,	3	William Gregg, cordwainer, s. of Robert Gregg of Chester, gardener.
,,	3	Benjamin Davies p. of John Brooks of Chester, bricklayer.
,,	3	William Pimblow p. of John Joynson of Chester, cooper.
,,	5	Thomas Wilson p. of John Wilson of Chester, druggist.
,,	5	Thomas Thompson p. of John Saunders of Chester, cordwainer.
,,	5	Christopher Owen, mason, s. of Richard Owen of Chester, glazier.
,,	5	John Ellis p. of John Shannon of Chester, cordwainer.
,,	5	John Linsdale, buttonmaker } ss. of Richard Linsdale of Chester, pipemaker.
,,	5	Richard Linsdale, buttonmaker
,,	5	Andrew Edge p. of Samuel Edge of Chester, butcher.
,,	5	Robert Jones p. of Edward Rowland of Chester, mason.
,,	5	Samuel Pemberton, weaver, s. of John Pemberton of Chester, bricklayer.
,,	5	John Hayes, breechesmaker, s. of John Hayes of Chester, cordwainer.
,,	5	William Panton, tanner, s. of Paul Panton of Chester, tanner.
,,	5	Edward Davies p. of John Brooks of Chester, bricklayer.
,,	5	James Peers, cabinetmaker, s. of James Peers of Chester, staymaker.
,,	5	Thomas Pownall, cordwainer, s. of Joseph Pownall of Chester, feltmaker.
,,	5	Henry Hancock, tailor, s. of Thomas Hancock of Chester, mason.

Apr.	5	Charles Dutton, linendraper, s. of John Dutton of Chester, linendraper.
,,	5	Ralph Meredith, breechesmaker, s. of William Meredith of Chester, sawyer.
,,	5	John Briscoe, smith, s. of Richard Briscoe of Chester, blacksmith.
,,	5	James s. of John Tylston of Chester, mason.
,,	5	John Allmond p. of Gerrard Jordan the younger of Chester, slater.
,,	5	George Smith, flaxdresser, s. of Charles Smith of Chester, flaxdresser.
,,	5	Thomas Mollinoux, cordwainer, s. of Thomas Mollinoux of Chester, cordwainer.
,,	5	Lumley Williams p. of Gerrard Jordan of Chester, slater.
,,	5	Humphrey Collins, hairdresser, s. of Samuel Collins of Chester, glazier.
,,	5	John Hollinshead p. of George Eaton of Chester, mason.
,,	5	Philip Bateman, carpenter, s. of Thomas Bateman of Chester, butcher.
,,	5	Thomas Dutton, butcher, s. of Robert Dutton of Chester, butcher.
,,	5	William Randles p. of Edward Warrington of Chester, carpenter.
,,	5	George Cooper, shipwright, s. of Michael Cooper of Chester, shipwright.
,,	5	John Ramsay p. of John Hiccock of Chester, barber.
,,	5	William s. of John Hand of Chester, ropemaker.
,,	5	John Davies p. of Richard Sneyd of Chester, cooper.
,,	5	James Johnson p. of Richard Humphries of Chester, hornbreaker.
,,	5	George Mooton p. of William Taylor of Chester, cordwainer.
,,	5	John s. of Thomas Jones of Chester, cordwainer.
,,	5	Samuel s. of Owen Jones of Chester, flaxdresser.
,,	5	Thomas Shannon p. of John Shannon of Chester, cordwainer.
,,	5	Richard Cowduck, musician, s. of Charles Cowduck of Chester, smith.
,,	5	James Hampton, cordwainer, s. of James Hampton of Chester, cordwainer.
,,	5	John Dickson, merchant's clerk, p. of Samuel Bagnall of Chester, tea dealer.
,,	5	Henry Forrester p. of Charles Whittell of Chester, cordwainer.

Apr. 5 William Hall p. of Robert Jones of Chester, cordwainer.
„ 5 John Leech p. of Edward Rowlands of Chester, mason.
„ 5 Samuel Coleclough, combmaker, s. of Thomas Coleclough of Chester, cordwainer.
„ 5 John Smith p. of John Green of Chester, staymaker.
„ 5 Thomas Skelleton, cordwainer, s. of Robert Skelleton of Chester, tailor.
„ 5 Matthew Conelley [Conally, M.B.] p. of Stephen Hyde, baker.
„ 5 Thomas Kirkham p. of Richard Goulding, pipemaker.
„ 5 Murray Hincks, gentleman, s. of Robert Hincks of Chester, merchant.
„ 5 William Heath, cordwainer, s. of Peter Heath of Chester, cordwainer.
„ 5 Thomas Shone, labourer, s. of John Shone of Chester, bricklayer.
„ 5 Benjamin Jones, bricklayer, s. of Benjamin Jones of Chester, slater.
„ 5 Peter Coleclough p. of Gamaliel Hawkins of Chester, slater.
„ 5 John Crosby p. of Robert Maddock of Chester, cordwainer.
„ 5 John Pate p. of Thomas Powell of Chester, upholsterer.
„ 5 Peter Capper p. of Joseph Jordan of Chester, slater.
„ 5 Joseph Thomas p. of Charles Woollam of Chester, flaxdresser.
„ 5 John Smith p. of Joseph Jordan of Chester, slater.
„ 5 Michael Gibson p. of Thomas Linney of Chester, cordwainer.
„ 5 Thomas s. of John Hunt of Chester, feltmaker.
„ 6 Thomas Bennion p. of Cotton Probert of Chester, feltmaker.
„ 6 John Norbury p. of George Johnson of Chester, cabinetmaker.
„ 6 John Gwinneth p. of William Linney of Chester, cordwainer.
„ 6 William Lewis, ship carpenter, p. of Thomas Bennion of Chester, merchant and shipwright.
„ 6 Joseph Gough, smith, p. of John Gough of Chester, blacksmith, and assigned to Charles Gill of Chester.
„ 6 James Palin, bookseller, s. of Thomas Palin, grocer.
„ 6 Jonathan Wilcoxon, chandler, p. of George Hodson of Chester, tallowchandler.

Apr.	6	William Tonna, gentleman, s. of Samuel Tonna of Chester, butcher.
,,	6	Thomas s. and p. of Thomas Latchford, cabinetmaker, and assigned to John Cooke of Chester.
,,	6	Hugh Jones, sailmaker, s. of Hugh Jones of Chester, broker.
,,	6	Henry Massey, watchmaker, s. of Thomas Massey of Chester, linendraper.
,,	6	John Jones, broker, s. of Hugh Jones of Chester, broker.
,,	6	Henry Thornton, cordwainer, s. of John Thornton of Chester, carpenter.
,,	6	Robert Bartlem, slater, s. of Robert Bartlem of Chester, carpenter.
,,	6	Robert Maddock, corkcutter, s. of Paul Maddock of Chester, tailor.
,,	6	Benjamin Peers, clockmaker, s. of James Peers of Chester, staymaker.
,,	6	Thomas Davies, tanner, s. of Thomas Davies of Chester, mason.
,,	6	George Hughes p. of Roger Maddock of Chester, cordwainer.
,,	6	John Brown, coachmaker, s. of William Brown of Chester, coachmaker.
,,	6	Daniel Jones, slater, s. of Benjamin Jones of Chester, slater.
,,	6	William Ratcliffe, corkcutter, s. of Peter Ratcliffe of Chester, cordwainer.
,,	6	Matthew Stubbs p. of Thomas Wynne of Chester, glover.
,,	6	Thomas M'Millan, bookseller, s. of Hugh M'Millan of Chester, linendraper.
,,	6	John Briscoe, mariner, s. of William Briscoe of Chester, mariner.
,,	6	William Pemberton p. of Joseph Ratcliffe of Chester, flaxdresser.
,,	6	George Edwards p. of Zaccheus Nicholls of Chester, cordwainer.
,,	6	John Griffith p. of Richard Griffith of Chester, carpenter.
,,	6	Joshua Cummins p. of Jeffrey Edwards of Chester, flaxdresser.
,,	6	William Edwards p. of John Taylor of Chester, cooper.
,,	6	John Butler, cutler, s. of James Butler of Chester, cutler.

Apr. 6 John Kendrick p. of Robert Jones of Chester, cordwainer.
,, 6 Charles Crewe, clerk, } ss. of Rev. Randle Crewe, clerk.
,, 6 Randolph Crewe, clerk,
,, 6 Offley Crewe, clerk,
,, .6 Joseph Crosby, cordwainer, } ss. of Joseph Crosby of Chester, cordwainer.
,, 6 William Crosby, cordwainer,
,, 6 Bagot Read, esquire, s. of Bagot Read, esquire.
,, 6 Edward Read, esquire, s. of said Mr. Read.
,, 6 James s. of Robert Evans of Chester, pipemaker.
,, 6 George s. of George Taylor of Chester, yeoman.
,, 6 John s. of Charles Powell of Chester, pipemaker.
,, 6 James Butler, cutler, s. of James Butler of Chester, cutler.
,, 6 John Longford Ball, esquire, s. of George Ball, esquire.
,, 6 John Griffith, mariner, s. of Thomas Griffith of Chester, shipwright.
,, 6 Richard Duke, schoolmaster, s. of Samuel Duke of Chester, clerk.
,, 6 James Hickson, barber, s. of Thomas Hickson of Chester, tailor.
,, 6 John Johnson p. of Edward Boden of Chester, bricklayer.
,, 6 Charles Woollam, merchant, s. of Charles Woollam of Chester, hosier.
,, 6 John Bakewell p. of Henry Hegg of Chester, druggist.
,, 6 Thomas Barnes, plumber, s. and p. of Thomas Barnes.
,, 6 Samuel Barnes, plumber, s. of said Thomas Barnes.
,, 6 Robert Price, butcher, s. of Robert Price of Chester, butcher.
,, 6 Thomas Amery the younger, linendraper, s. of Thomas Amery of Chester, esquire.
,, 6 Thomas Evans, druggist, s. of Thomas Evans of Chester, innholder.
,, 6 Thomas Penson, builder, s. of Thomas Penson of Chester, gardener.
,, 6 George Bingley, grocer, s. of William Bingley of Chester, grocer.
,, 6 William Baxter p. of John Wright of Chester, grocer.
,, 6 Thomas Weigh, currier, s. of Peter Weigh of Chester, currier.
,, 6 Joseph Allmark p. of Thomas Rathbone of Chester, turner.

Apr.	6	James Sumpter p. of John Brown of Chester, mariner.
,,	6	Gilbert Flint p. of John Shannon of Chester, cordwainer, and assigned to Joseph Carter of Chester.
,,	9	John Gill, farrier, s. of William Gill of Chester, mason.
,,	6	Jonathan Coleclough p. of George Boden of Chester, slater.
,,	6	John Fletcher p. of James Fletcher of Chester, cordwainer.
,,	6	Peter Betteley, musician, s. of Joseph Betteley of Chester, musician.
,,	6	Thomas Bennett, wine merchant, s. of John Bennett of Chester, wine merchant.
,,	6	Thomas Astle, cabinetmaker, s. of Thomas Astle of Chester, cabinetmaker.
,,	6	Robert Newell, skinner, s. of John Newell of Chester, innholder.
,,	6	John Baddeley, brewer, p. of Joseph Gilbert of Chester, maltster.
,,	7	Robert Higginson, watchmaker, s. of Robert Higginson of Chester, innholder.
,,	7	Robert s. of James Fletcher of Chester, cordwainer.
,,	7	Samuel Robinson p. of Robert Robinson of Chester, baker.
,,	7	William Rawlinson p. of Joseph Jones of Chester, cordwainer.
,,	7	Simon Faulkener p. of John Phillips of Chester, baker, and assigned to Thomas Lightfoot of Chester.
,,	7	John Dyson, druggist, s. of Joseph Dyson of Chester, esquire.
,,	7	John s. of Jonathan Haswell of Chester, wine cooper.
,,	7	John Tyrer, cordwainer, s. of John Tyrer of Chester, cordwainer.
,,	7	James Boden, bricklayer, s. of Peter Boden of Chester, cordwainer.
,,	7	Richard Spencer, mason, s. of Thomas Spencer of Chester, mason.
,,	7	John Stout, labourer, s. of Joseph Stout of Chester, butcher.
,,	7	Sylvan s. of William Robert of Chester, tailor.
,,	7	William Richards, gentleman, s. of Thomas Richards of Chester, maltster.
,,	7	John Brown p. of Richard Kelley of Chester, tailor.
,,	7	George Rawlinson p. of William Ratcliffe of Chester, flaxdresser, and assigned to Thomas Thornley of Chester.

Apr. 7 John Woollam, mariner, s. of Charles Woollam of Chester, hosier.
,, 7 Charles Chevers, butcher, s. of Philip Chevers of Chester, butcher.
,, 7 John Bazine, joiner, s. of Richard Bazine of Chester, joiner.
,, 7 Robert Fearnall, butcher, s. of Robert Fearnall of Chester, butcher.
,, 7 Joseph Starkey p. of Joseph Wright of Chester, tailor.
,, 7 Charles Hind p. of James Hind of Chester, cork-cutter.
,, 7 William Williams p. of Robert Jones of Chester, cordwainer.
,, 7 James Kinnaston p. of Charles Poynton of Chester, baker.
,, 7 James Hampton, plasterer, s. of Thomas Hampton of Chester, yeoman.
,, 7 Thomas Brock, brazier, s. of Samuel Brock of Chester, brassfounder.
,, 7 Thomas Davies p. of Charles Hitchens of Chester, butcher.
,, 7 Samuel Cleak p. of Gamaliel Hawkins of Chester, slater.
,, 7 Joseph Howard, skinner, p. of Thomas Duke of Chester, wetglover.
,, 7 Charles Joynson p. of Robert Richards of Chester, breechesmaker.
,, 7 Richard Chevers, butcher, s. of Philip Chevers of Chester, butcher.
,, 7 William Miller, bookbinder, p. of John Lawton of Chester, stationer, and assigned to Benjamin Monk of Chester.
,, 7 Thomas Massie, esquire, s. of Thomas Massie, esquire.
,, 7 Joseph Rollance p. of Joseph Butler of Chester, bricklayer.
,, 7 Charles Rowlands p. of Gamaliel Hawkins of Chester, slater.
,, 7 John Shone p. of John Shone of Chester, carpenter.
,, 7 William Hughes, bricklayer, p. of Thomas Cooper of Chester, deceased.
,, 7 Thomas Shone, carpenter, s. of John Shone, carpenter.
,, 8 John Mathews, mariner, s. of John Mathews of Chester, silkweaver.
,, 8 John Lewthwaite, anchorsmith, p. of John Manning of Chester, saddler.
,, 8 Richard s. of Thomas Walters of Chester, tailor.

Apr.	8	William Stout p. of Gamaliel Hawkins of Chester, slater.
,,	8	William Crosby p. of John Saunders of Chester, cordwainer.
,,	8	Nicholas Ball, esquire, s. of George Ball, esquire.
,,	8	Richard Sands, slater, s. of Richard Sands of Chester, slater.
,,	8	Thomas Shone, labourer, s. of Thomas Shone, late of Chester, collier.
,,	8	William Andrews, slater, s. of Esau Andrews of Chester, slater.
,,	8	William Boden, bricklayer, s. of Edward Boden of Chester, bricklayer.
,,	8	Abraham Chandler [Chantler, M.B.] p. of William Crane of Chester, corkcutter.
,,	8	Joseph Betteley, musician, s. of Joseph Betteley of Chester, musician.
,,	8	Lloyd Pate, butcher, s. of Thomas Pate of Chester, butcher.
,,	8	Edward Bailey, organist, s. of John Bailey of Chester, feltmaker.
,,	8	Thomas Swinnerton, turner, s. of John Swinnerton of Chester, turner.
,,	10	Calveley Speed, labourer, s. of Calveley Speed of Chester, yeoman.
,,	10	Jonathan Johnson, clerk, s. of William Johnson of Chester, wetglover.
,,	10	John Bennett, wine merchant, s. of John Bennett of Chester, wine merchant.
,,	10	William Kent, cordwainer, s. of William Kent of Chester, innkeeper.
,,	10	Thomas Roden p. of Peter Broster of Chester, bookseller.
,,	10	Thomas Duke, gentleman, s. of Thomas Duke of Chester, glover.
,,	10	James s. of Jonathan Bramwell of Chester, currier.
,,	10	Richard Rider p. of Robert Evans of Chester, pipemaker.
,,	12	Ralph Jackson, yeoman, s. of John Jackson of Chester, yeoman.
,,	12	Thomas Finchett, glover, s. of John Finchett of Chester, glover.
,,	12	William Jackson, smith, s. of John Jackson of Chester, yeoman.
,,	12	Gerard Townsend, gentleman, s. of Randle Townsend of Chester, grocer.

Apr. 12 John Finchett, gentleman, s. of John Finchett of Chester, glover.
,, 13 John Jones p. of Thomas Evans of Chester, glazier.
,, 13 Thomas Falconer, esquire, s. of William Falconer, esquire.
,, 14 Henry Hesketh, esquire, s. of Henry Hesketh of Chester, esquire.
,, 14 Benjamin Pemberton, linendraper, s. of Peter Pemberton of Chester, silversmith.
,, 16 Thomas Pierce p. of James Newall of Chester, barber.
,, 16 Joseph Steens ⎫ pp. of Gerrard Jordan of Chester,
,, 16 William Nield ⎭ slater.
,, 16 John Price p. of John Croughton of Chester, cabinetmaker.
,, 16 James Fletcher p. of James Fletcher of Chester, cordwainer.
,, 16 Robert Bartlam p. of Thomas Barnes of Chester, plumber.
,, 16 John Randles p. of John Sorton of Chester, skinner.
,, 16 John Clarke p. of John Saunders of Chester, cordwainer.
July 3 *John Howell, timber merchant.
,, 3 *John Hammond, innkeeper.
,, 3 *John Keeling, victualler.
,, 3 *John Hannah, victualler.
,, 3 *Edward James, victualler.
,, 3 *John Lloyd, esquire.
,, 3 *Joseph Davies p. of Joseph Ratcliffe, flaxdresser.
,, 7 William Sandland p. of Philip Presbury of Chester, cabinetmaker.
,, 10 George Ogden, gentleman.
,, 24‡*John Griffiths, victualler.
,, 17 *William Barlow, victualler.
,, 22 *William Thomas, victualler.
,, 23 William Rowland p. of John Saunders, cordwainer.
,, 31 *James Townley.
Aug. 7 *John Hughes, gentleman.
,, 7 George Green p. of George Bingley, glazier.
,, 26 *John Garner, gentleman.
,, 26 *Job Harrison, surgeon.
,, 26 *James Williamson, surgeon.
,, 26 *Richard Barker, gentleman.
,, 26 *George Bushell, gentleman.
,, 26 *George Whitley, gentleman.
Sep. 4 *John Legh, esquire.

1784-6]   THE CITY OF CHESTER   403

Sep.   6 *Paul Panton, esquire.
 „   15 Thomas Coppock, skinner, s. of Richard Coppock,
            slater.
 „   29 *Robert Williams Vaughan, esquire.
 „   30 *Edward Turner, gentleman.
Oct.   4 Thomas Shannon, cordwainer, s. of John Shannon,
            cordwainer.
 „   7 *Richard Cooile, tailor.
 „   9 *Thomas Hitchens, butcher.
 „   11 *William Amery of Caughall, gentleman.
 „   13 *John Hickman, victualler.
 „   16 *Daniel Widders, gentleman.

1784-5 [25-26 G. iii.] HENRY HEGG, Esquire, Mayor.
    Joseph Mostyn p. of Edward Spencer, mason.
    Richard Orme, tailor, s. of Richard Orme, tailor,
        deceased.
    *William Hall, gentleman.
    *Samuel Williams, victualler.
    *William Chrimes, victualler.
    James Faulkner p. of John Meredith, bricklayer.
    Benjamin Broughton, blacksmith, p. of John
        Broughton.

1785-6 [26-27 G. iii.] JOHN BENNETT, Esquire,
            Mayor.
    John Rowe, carpenter,   ⎫
    Thomas Rowe, butcher,   ⎬ ss. of Hugh Rowe, butcher.
    James Rowe, butcher,   ⎭
    John Wright, barber, s. of Richard Wright, wool-
        comber.
    *Charles Hawker, gentleman.
    ‡John Walley p. of Thomas Robinson, and assigned to
        Thomas Jenkins, tanner.
    *Edward Walmesley, victualler.
    Samuel Haswell, tailor, s. of Charles Haswell, cord-
        wainer.
    *Joseph Bage, papermaker.
    *Edward Phillips, yeoman.
    *Joseph Jones, yeoman.
    *Edward Jones, esquire.
    Timothy Dealey of London, saddler, s. of Timothy
        Dealey, saddler.

404 THE ROLLS OF THE FREEMEN OF [1786-7

Robert Ley, yeoman, s. of Thomas Ley, deceased.
Griffith ap Howell Vaughan, esquire, s. of Robert Howell Vaughan, esquire.
*Edward Williams Vaughan Salisbury, esquire.
*George Fairclough, esquire.

1786-7 [27-28 G. iii.] THOMAS EDWARDS, Esquire, Mayor.

Nov. 18 Thomas Pinington, yeoman, s. of Thomas Pinington, innholder.
Jan. 3 Thomas Prince, baker, p. of Thomas Langford, confectioner and baker.
„ 3 John Whitby, maltster, s. of John Whitby, late of Chester, maltster.
Feb. 22 Thomas Watmough of Bidstone, gentleman, s. of Thomas Watmough, deceased.
May 2 John Barnes, wine merchant, p. of William Ridgway of Chester, merchant, deceased.
June 2 *Benjamin Scott, victualler.
„ 2 *James Grey, victualler.
„ 2 *John M'Daniel, victualler.
„ 2 *Richard Smith, victualler.
„ 2 *John Sadler, yeoman.
„ 2 *David Roberts, victualler.
„ 2 *John Brittain, gentleman.
„ 8 *John Glegg of Withington, esquire.
„ 8 *Richard Mytton, esquire.
„ 8 *John Wilbraham, gentleman.
„ 13 *Thomas Price, victualler.
„ 15 *Joseph Boyer, innkeeper.
„ 15 *William Hartley, innkeeper.
„ 16 *John Jones, victualler.
„ 20 James Gill p. of Richard Venables, bricklayer.
„ 23 John Goff p. of William Shone, baker.
„ 23 William Barton, labourer [laceweaver, M.B.], s. of John Barton, laceweaver.
Aug. 7 *Daniel Roberts, victualler.
Sep. 15 Edward Bateman p. of Edward Chevers, butcher.
„ 19 Thomas Ledsham p. of John Hodkinson, baker, and assigned to Ellis Roberts, baker.
Oct. 7 *Thomas Ashley, victualler.
„ 25 John Dawson, baker, p. of Edward Spencer, mason.

1787-8 [28-29 G. iii.] JOHN HALLWOOD, Esquire, Mayor.

Oct. 31 *Thomas Duke, whipmaker.
Nov. 3 *Thomas Dixon, timber merchant.
„ 3 *Thomas Robinson, victualler.
Oct. 20 ‡John Price p. of Richard Tonna of Chester, beer brewer.
Nov. 7 John Meredith, bricklayer, s. of John Meredith, bricklayer.
Jan. 12 Charles Barnes p. of Allen Mason of Chester, baker, and assigned to Mary Chapman of Chester, widow.
„ 14 *Benjamin Capper, victualler.
„ 21 *Jervis Walker, victualler.
„ 21 *Absalom Ray, victualler.
„ 24 *John Williamson, joiner.
July 24 *John Golborne, liquor merchant.
„ 26 *Thomas Jonas, liquor merchant.
Aug. 15 *Foster Bower, esquire.
„ 23 Robert Jones, cordwainer, s. of Robert Jones, cordwainer.
Sep. 16 Thomas Griffith, silk mercer, s. of George Griffith, mercer.
„ 27 *Samuel Turner, innkeeper.
„ 27 *Thomas Williams, innkeeper.
Oct. 1 James Fox p. of John Tonna, butcher.
„ 1 *John Williams, grocer.
„ 1 *John Cleever, jeweller.
„ 21 *Titus Challoner, currier.

1788-9 [29-30 G. iii.] JOHN LEGH, Esquire, Mayor.

Nov. 12 Isaac Trevor p. of Thomas Eaton, mason, and assigned to Edward Spencer, mason.
Jan. 10 Charles Davison, vintner, p. of Andrew Davison, vintner, wine and spirituous liquor merchant.
„ 14 *John Smith, gentleman.
Feb. 28 John Webster p. of Thomas Edwards of Chester, grocer.
Apr. 11 Thomas Kay, victualler.
May 4 *John Beecroft, innholder.
„ 9 *John Parry, victualler.
„ 13 *Thomas Jones, victualler.
„ 13 William Hall p. of John Poole, printer.

406   THE ROLLS OF THE FREEMEN OF   [1789-90

May 13 *John Walley, innholder.
"   20 Charles Brown, yeoman, s. of George Brown, barber.
"   20 William Cunnah p. of Samuel Coulton, baker.
"   20 *John Lloyd, victualler.
"   20 *John Davies, victualler.
"   20 *William Dennis, victualler.
"   23 Thomas Smith, victualler, s. of Thomas Smith, victualler.
June 10 George Hastings, tinplateworker, s. of George Hastings, tinplateworker.
Sep. 4 *William Newell.
"   23 William Aldersey, woollendraper, s. of Robert Aldersey, woollendraper.
"   23 William Francis, woollendraper, s. of Charles Francis, woollendraper.
Oct. 21 *Edward Holt, esquire.

1789-90 [30-31 G. iii.] ROBERT HOWELL VAUGHAN,
                    Esquire, Mayor.

Oct. 24 *Peter Marcroft, victualler.
Nov. 5 Roger Parry, brewer, s. of Roger Parry, brewer.
"   11 Charles Worral Leadbeater, bookseller, s. of Edward Leadbeater, brewer.
"   11 John s. of Thomas Shepherd, beer brewer.
"   18 William Gamon of Brewers' Hall, farmer, s. of John Gamon, yeoman.
"   18 *William Beck, brewer.
Dec. 12 John Palin of Llay, gentleman, s. of Thomas Palin.
"   23 William Leicester p. of John Poole, stationer.
Feb. 25 Alexander Forrest, bricklayer, s. of Alexander Forrest, deceased.
Apr. 3 *Francis Tuck, victualler.
"   3 *Thomas Boteoyle, victualler.
"   19 *James Lewthwaite, victualler.
May 7 John Holland Pemberton of Liverpool, merchant, s. of Henry Pemberton, esquire.
"   19 *Charles Lloyd, victualler.
"   19 *Thomas Jones, innkeeper.
"   26 *Thomas Tamberlin, innkeeper.
"   28 John Dodd, skinner, p. of William Corles, wetglover.
"   29 Lloyd Price, butcher, s. of Robert Price, butcher.
June 19 Edward Ommaney Wrench, esquire, s. of Rev. Thomas Wrench.
"   24 Edmund Monk, printer, s. of John Monk.

THE CITY OF CHESTER

July 7   James Gardner p. of John Cooke, cabinetmaker.
Aug. 4   Daniel Mason, baker, s. of Allen Mason, baker.
„ 14   Thomas Pemberton p. of John Meredith, bricklayer.
Sept. 4 Thomas Willoughby Egerton, mariner, s. of Philip Egerton, druggist.
„ 11   *David Francis Jones, gentleman.
„ 11   John s. of Jonathan Brown, deceased.

1790-1 [31-32 G. iii.] THOMAS POWELL, Esquire, Mayor.

Oct. 30 Charles Lumber, upholsterer, s. of Thomas Lumber, barber.
Nov. 6   Thomas Denson p. of Thomas Bennion of Chester, chandler.
„ 27   *Wolrad Foepel, victualler.
Dec. 4   *James Parry, hosier.
„ 8   William Dawson, mercer, s. of Perry Dawson, wetglover.
„ 8   *Thomas Jones, linendraper.
„ 11   William Ball p. of Nathaniel Warrington, and assigned to Richard Case, baker.
„ 11   *John Smith, victualler.
„ 21   *William Dodd, perfumer.
„ 21   *William Wilkinson, linendraper.
„ 21   *Joseph Lawrence, innkeeper.
„ 21   *John Jones, currier.
„ 21   *John Stannier, clockmaker.
„ 21   *George Preston, tailor.
„ 21   *John Smith, victualler.
Jan. 4   *Robert Hoakesley, merchant.
„ 4   *John Davies, tailor.
„ 4   *Joseph Gresty, victualler.
„ 4   *Watkin Parry, victualler.
„ 8   *Thomas Parry, chandler.
„ 15   *William Coker, gentleman.
„ 20   The Rev. Thomas Maddock, clerk, s. of the Rev. Thomas Maddock, clerk.
Feb. 1   George Lowe, silversmith, s. of George Lowe.
„ 9   Thomas Bushell p. of Robert Robinson, baker.
„ 21   William Newell, merchant, s. of John Newell, gentleman.
„ 21   William Suddones, cordwainer, s. of Richard Suddones, schoolmaster.
„ 21   *Edward Rowlance, victualler.

May 27 *Robert Hodgson, esquire, s. of Joseph Hodgson, bookseller, deceased.
June 1 *Peter Wilkinson, apothecary.
July 21 *James Williams, woollendraper.
 „ 21 *David Hughes, linendraper.

1791–2 [32–33 G. iii.] PETER BROSTER, Esquire, Mayor.

Oct. 24 Samuel [John, M.B.] Bennett, ⎫ ss. of John Bennett of
        wine merchant,   ⎬ Chester, wine mer-
 „ 24 Daniel Bennett, druggist,   ⎭ chant.
Nov. 3 ‡Moses Ithell p. of Robert Jones, cordwainer.
 „ 16 Edward Repington, tanner, s. of Edward Repington, cordwainer.
 „ 22 John Chesters p. of John Totty, whitesmith.
 „ 25 Thomas Hall, tailor, s. of William Hall, cordwainer.
 „ 14 *John Mellor, plumber.
 „ 14 John Montgomery p. of John Sproston, cooper.
 „ 28 Thomas Smith of Marford, co. Flint, cooper, s. of William Smith, feltmaker, deceased.
Feb. 22 *William Moss, yeoman.
 „ 27 *Hugh Lloyd, druggist.
Mar. 16 *Richard Buckley, liquor merchant.
 „ 16 *William Jones, flaxdresser.
 „ 16 *Robert Denson, victualler.
 „ 16 *Robert Jones, victualler.
 „ 16 *John Moulton, victualler.
Apr. 4 *Richard Pritchard, grocer.
 „ 4 *Edward Price, victualler.
 „ 18 *John Ellaby, victualler.
 „ 18 William Walker p. of William Linney, cordwainer.
 „ 24 Joseph Hayes p. of John Davies, butcher.
May 5 Thomas Hanley, tailor, s. of William Hanley, tailor.
 „ 21 Samuel Crosby p. of Samuel Davies, butcher.
June 23 Joseph Boden, joiner, ⎫ ss. of Edward Boden, brick-
 „ 23 John Boden, bricklayer, ⎭ layer.
July 11 John Grimes p. of Joseph Ralphs, butcher.
Aug. 7 Peter Ellis, cutler, s. of John Ellis of Chester, wine merchant.
Oct. 17 *George William Prescott, esquire.
 „ 19 John Broster, stationer, s. of Peter Broster, esquire.
 „ 19 John Dutton, linendraper, s. of John Dutton, linendraper.
 „ 24 William Pinnington, carpenter, s. of Thomas Pinnington, innholder.

Oct. 24   William Minshull, printer, s. of Giles Minshull, linendraper.
"   19   William Hankey p. of John Trevor, barber.
"   26   Thomas Minshull, bookseller, s. of Giles Minshull,
linendraper.
July 4   William Bowers, linendraper, ⎱ ss. of Thomas Bowers,
"   4   Henry Bowers, druggist,   ⎰   linendraper.

1792-3 [33-34 G. iii.] JOHN WRIGHT, Esquire, Mayor.

Nov. 1   *Paul Hewitt, victualler.
"   9   John Williams, esquire, s. of Bennett Williams, esquire.
"   19   Richard Griffith, hairdresser, s. of Jo―――― Griffith of
Chester, carpenter.
"   28   *William Garratt, victualler.
"   28   *John Wright, victualler.
"   30   *Robert Wilkinson, brewer.
"   30   *William Tomlinson, victualler.
"   30   *Thomas Bradford, linendraper.
Dec. 31   Thomas Taylor, combmaker, s. of Jonathan Taylor,
combmaker.
Jan. 7   Thomas Crewe Dod of Edge, esquire, s. of Thomas
Dod, esquire.
"   30   Stephen Hickson, proctor, s. of John Hickson, tailor.
Mar. 13   Mathias Holland, cabinetmaker, s. of Mathias Holland,
painter.
May 23   Simeon Leete, mariner, s. of Simeon Leete, victualler.
"   23   George Coppock, barber, s. of George Coppock,
slater.
June 12   Thomas Bolland, gentleman, s. of Edmund Bolland,
alderman, deceased.
"   19   Edward Lowe, clock and watch maker, s. of George
Lowe.
July 14   Gerrard Jordan, slater, s. of Gerrard Jordan, slater and
plasterer.
"   31   *Richard Amery, tanner.
"   31   John Amery, gentleman, s. of Thomas Amery, alderman.
Aug. 8   *Robert Williams, grocer.
"   8   *Thomas Hodson, chandler.
"   26   *George Moyle, watchmaker.
"   26   *Robert Roberts, glass dealer.
"   28   *Daniel Gibson, victualler.
Sep. 11   *John Davies, grocer.

Sep. 11 *Joseph Vaughan, baker.
„ 14 Robert Boden, slater, s. of John Boden, slater.
„ 14 *William Pownall, victualler.
„ 18 *John Thomas, victualler.

1793-4 [34-35 G. iii.] THOMAS RICHARDS, Esquire, Mayor.

Nov. 5 *Edward Javo [Tavo, M.B.], instrument maker.
„ 9 Edward Woodfine, joiner, s. of Edward Woodfine, joiner, deceased.
„ 27 *Joseph Jones the younger, carter.
„ 27 Edward Hodkinson p. of John Walker, house carpenter and joiner.
Jan. 15 Richard Brown, cordwainer, s. of William Brown, cordwainer.
Apr. 15 ‡John Egerton of Oulton, esquire, s. of Philip Egerton, esquire.
May 4‡*John Harbridge, victualler.
„ 21 *John Owen, liquor merchant.
„ 21 *William Davies, victualler.
„ 21 *Richard Milner Smaithwaite, victualler.
„ 21 *James Hall, hairdresser.
„ 21 John Spencer, victualler, p. of Robert Davies of Chester, saddler.
„ 23 *George Holmes, victualler.
„ 23 *Joseph Richards, victualler.
„ 28 Thomas Lockley, butcher, s. of John Lockley, butcher, deceased.
„ 28 John Edwards, hatter, s. of Thomas Edwards, hatter, deceased.
June 4 *William Saunders, victualler.
„ 13 John s. and p. of Thomas Jones, cordwainer.
„ 28 Joseph Turner p. of Samuel Mercer, cabinetmaker.
July 3 John Moss p. of Philip Presbury, cabinetmaker.
„ 3 John Johnson, wine merchant, } ss. of John Johnson,
„ 3 William Johnson, wine merchant, } wine merchant.
„ 3 Perry Dawson, cabinetmaker, s. of Perry Dawson, skinner, deceased.
Oct. 23 John Swarbreck Rogers, merchant [skinner, M.B.], s. of John Rogers, merchant.

1794-5 [35-36 G. iii.] GEORGE BINGLEY, Esquire,
    Mayor.

Oct. 29 *John Hincksman, silkmercer.
 ,, 29 *Henry Johnson, victualler.
 ,, 29 *Thomas Ackers, victualler.
 ,, 29 *Thomas Marsh, victualler.
Nov. 7 Samuel Adshead, yeoman, s. of William Adshead of Hatton, co. Ches., yeoman.
 ,, 8 Thomas Lowe p. of William Meredith, gunsmith.
Dec. 27 Thomas Gamon, yeoman, s. of John Gamon of Farndon, co. Ches., yeoman.
 ,, 27 Thomas Gamon the younger of Pickton, s. of Thomas Gamon of Pickton, co. Ches., yeoman.
Jan. 21 John Hall, carpenter, s. of William Hall of Chester, cordwainer.
Feb. 14 *Jonathan Jones, victualler.
 ,, 14 *Daniel Chesters, whitesmith.
July 16 William Hickson, cordwainer, s. of Thomas Hickson, cordwainer.
 ,, 16 *John Evans, yeoman.
Feb. 18 John Johnson, gentleman, s. of John Johnson late of Scolecroft, near Middleton, co. Lanc., fustian manufacturer.
Mar. 4 *George Topham, yeoman.
 ,, 5 *Joseph Bozley of Chester, gentleman.
 ,, 19 Anthony Rowland p. of Edward Thomas of Chester, glazier.
 ,, 20 *Jonathan Passingham, esquire.
Apr. 2 Peter Ellames of Liverpool, esquire, s. of Pattison Ellames of Chester, alderman.
 ,, 4 *Hugh Leycester, esquire.
 ,, 27 William Hall, joiner and carpenter, s. of William Hall of Chester, cordwainer.
 ,, 30 *Joseph Garner, victualler.
May 20 James Peacock p. of George Bingley of Chester, glazier.
 ,, 20 *Thomas Davison, victualler.
 ,, 22 Edward Bennett, wine merchant, s. of John Bennett, alderman.
 ,, 27 John Sorton Hughes, merchant, } pp. of John Sorton.
 ,, 27 Thomas Hughes, merchant,
June 20 Thomas Poole, stationer, s. of John Poole of Chester, stationer.

412   THE ROLLS OF THE FREEMEN OF   [1795-6

June 20   Robert Simcock, bookbinder, p. of Peter Broster of Chester, bookseller.
  „   20   Benjamin Prince, bookbinder, p. of John Poole, stationer.
  „   22   Charles Broster, stationer, s. of Peter Broster of Chester, stationer.
  „   25   William Stanton p. of John Poole, stationer.
  „   27   Samuel Wainwright p. of Samuel Coulton, baker, of Chester.
July   1   *Samuel Broadhurst, gentleman.
  „   4   Thomas Boden of Manchester, stationer, s. of Edward Boden of Chester, bricklayer.
  „   27   *John Clayton, gardener.
  „   27   *Thomas Rogers, victualler.
  „   27   *Stephen Chadburn, victualler.
  „   27   *William Cunna, brandy dealer.
  „   27   *William Twemlow [Twamlow, M.B.], victualler.
Aug.   5   *Edward Lloyd, wine merchant.
  „   7   *Robert Littler, victualler.
Sep.   4   *Pierce Davies, tea merchant.
  „   9   William Ralphs p. of Richard Case, baker.
Oct.   3   John Reece of Trafford, gentleman, p. of Roger Dutton, silkweaver.
  „   7   John Price of Liverpool, butcher, s. of Thomas Price of Chester, butcher.
  „   10   Thomas Parsonage of Allington, co. Denbigh, yeoman, s. of Timothy Parsonage, late of Allington.
  „   20   Charles Gill p. of John Shone of Chester, bricklayer.
  „   21   *Henry Nevitt, yeoman.
  „   21   *Edward Barlow, breechesmaker.
  „   21   *Samuel Ball, victualler.
  „   22   Richard Gorst p. of Thomas Astle of Chester, cabinet-maker.
  „   22   *Richard Christopher, victualler.

1795-6 [36-37 G. iii.] WILLIAM HARRISON, Esquire, Mayor.

Nov.   7   John Watmough of Neston, brewer, s. of Thomas Watmough, late of Bromborow.
Jan.   6   Joseph Scott p. of Johua [sic] Jones of Chester, tailor.
  „   6   Thomas Williams p. of John Palin of Chester, butcher.
Feb.   5   *William Waters, gentleman.
  „   13   *Benjamin Bond, victualler.
  „   16   Benjamin Ellis, ironmonger, s. of John Ellis, wine merchant.

Mar. 5 Richard Joynson p. of ———— Charles of Chester, baker.
"   26 Samuel Sidebotham of Farndon, co. Ches., gentleman, s. of Richard Sidebotham, late of Wynnstay.
Apr. 2 John Bannister, carpenter, s. of John Bannister of Chester, skinner, deceased.
July 6 William Bellin the younger, plumber, p. of Thomas Barnes and Samuel Barnes of Chester, plumbers.
Aug. 27 Peter Shone p. of Joseph Carter of Chester, carpenter.
Sep. 7 John Rogers p. of Samuel Woolley of Chester, baker.
Oct. 18 *John Harrison of Alford, gentleman.
"   18 *John Hassall, wine merchant.
"   19 *John Ball, victualler.
"   19 *John Bedson, victualler.
"   19 *John Power, victualler.
"   19 *Hugh Edwards, victualler.
"   19 *Mark Topham, victualler.
[1795]
Dec. 22 John Harrison, grocer, s. of William Harrison of Chester, grocer, deceased.

1796-7 [37-38 G. iii.] THOMAS BARNES, Esquire, Mayor.

Nov. 9 Joseph Trape, hairdresser, s. of John Trape, late of Chester, blacksmith.
"   9 Samuel Thornley, staymaker, s. of Daniel Thornley of Chester, cordwainer.
"   12 James Harrison, slater, s. of William Harrison, late of Chester, slater.
"   28 Charles s. of Charles Wright of Chester, barber.
"   28 Charles Wright, dyer, s. of Thomas Wright of Chester, dyer.
Dec. 3 *George Ankers, whitesmith.
"   8 William Cole the younger, carpenter, s. of William Cole of Chester, carpenter.
Jan. 14 Thomas Jenkins the younger, tanner, s. of Thomas Jenkins of Chester, tanner.
Feb. 23 *James Parry, innholder.
Apr. 15 Thomas Stringer Langford p. of John Stringer of Chester, upholsterer.
May   5 Sir Watkin Williams Wynn, baronet. } ss. of Sir Watkin Williams Wynn, baronet.
"   5 Charles Watkin Williams Wynn, esquire,

414 THE ROLLS OF THE FREEMEN OF [1797–8

May	10	Joseph Wooding p. of Thomas Whittell of Chester, dyer.
,,	25	*Joseph Roberts, innkeeper.
,,	25	*John Haywood, victualler.
,,	25	*Thomas Sadler, victualler.
,,	25	*James Baker, victualler.
,,	25	Samuel Ellis, victualler.
,,	25	John Worrall p. of Thomas Manning, saddler.
June	13	Benjamin Barnes, plumber, s. of Thomas Barnes, esquire.
,,	13	William Davies, whitesmith, s. of William Davies, late of Chester, whitesmith.
,,	21	Richard Bromfield, cutler, s. of Samuel Bromfield, cutler, deceased.
July	6	*The Right Reverend Father in God [Cleever] Lord Bishop of Chester.
,,	8	Thomas Harrison of Tilston, co. Ches., butcher, s. of Job Harrison, butcher.
,,	15	George Lloyd, cabinetmaker, s. of George Lloyd, victualler, deceased.
Aug.	2	Thomas Cholmondeley of Vale Royal, esquire,
,,	2	Charles Cholmondeley of Vale Royal, esquire, } ss. of Thomas Cholmondeley of Vale Royal, esquire, deceased.
,,	2	Hugh Cholmondeley of Vale Royal, esquire,
,,	5	Charles Smith p. of William Adshead, cordwainer.
,,	9	*Thomas Faulkner, liquor merchant.
Sep.	2	*Peter Patten, esquire.
,,	2	Thomas Cooke, victualler.
Oct.	18	George Huxley p. of Ralph Lowe, and assigned to Allen Mason, baker.

1797–8 [38–39 G. iii.] ROWLAND JONES, Esquire, Mayor.

Oct.	8	Joseph Artingstall, cordwainer, s. of James Artingstall, butcher, deceased.
Nov.	3	Thomas Lewis of London, merchant, s. of William Lewis of Chester, grocer, deceased.
,,	20	Thomas Richards, tanner, s. of Thomas Richards, alderman.
Dec.	20	George Owens, butcher, s. of George Owens, butcher, deceased.
Jan.	19	Thomas Smith, gentleman, s. of Mr. Alderman Smith.

THE CITY OF CHESTER

Feb. 14   Charles Davies p. of John Goff of Chester, baker.
Mar. 14   *Charles Shaw, victualler.
Apr. 13   Hugh Dean p. of Rowland Jones, saddler.
June 2   John Edmondson of Liverpool, merchant, s. of William Edmondson of Trafford, gentleman, deceased.
„ 27   John Edwards, grocer, p. of Benjamin Clubbe, grocer and ironmonger.
Aug. 16   *Robert Goff, victualler.
„ 25   *William Pode, victualler.
Sep. 5   *Thomas Jones, victualler.
„ 17   Thomas Denson p. of Thomas Poole, baker, and assigned over to Thomas Langford, baker.
„ 26   *John Salusbury, victualler.
Oct. 16   *Samuel Strettell of Chester, linendraper.
„ 19   William Kendrick the younger, husbandman, s. and p. of William Kendrick, husbandman.
„ 24   Joseph Johnson, wine merchant, s. of John Johnson, wine merchant.
„ 24   John Lowe the younger, tobacconist, s. of John Lowe, tobacconist.
„ 24   John Paul the younger, coachmaker, s. of John Paul, innkeeper.
„ 26   John Bramwell p. of John Bedward of Chester, carpenter.

1798-9 [39-40 G. iii.] JOHN BRAMWELL, Esquire, Mayor.

Oct. 27   James Forest p. of Gilbert Inglish, cordwainer.
„ 27   James s. of Martha Walker, and p. of Peter Broster of Chester, bookseller and printer.
Nov. 21   *Joseph Leigh, huckster.
„ 21   Joseph Pearson of Chester, ironfounder, p. of William Harrison of Chester, ironfounder and grocer.
Dec. 6   John Fearnall p. of Robert Johnson of Chester, baker, and assigned to John Dawson of Chester, baker.
Oct. 24   Samuel Humphreys, gentleman, s. of Richard Humphreys, deceased.
„ 24   William Howard, druggist, s. of William Howard, butcher, deceased.
Dec. 10   John Pugh Conway } pp. of Richard Jones of Chester,
„ 10   John Jones   } linendraper.
„ 10   Thomas Francis, clothier, s. of Charles Francis of Chester, clothier.
„ 10   *John Evans of Chester, silk mercer.

Dec. 10 *John Dodd of Chester, flour dealer.
„ 31 William Massey of Chester, druggist, s. of John Massey of Chester, baker.
Jan. 14 *Joseph Clubbe of Chester, brewer.
„ 14 *Robert Pearce [Pierce, M.B.] of Chester, cheese factor.
„ 14 *Joseph Bellis of Chester, grocer.
„ 14 *George Teggin of Chester, hosier.
„ 14 *Bartholomew White of Chester, tailor.
„ 14 *John Davies of Chester, grocer.
„ 14 *Thomas Pleavin of Chester, tailor.
„ 14 Thomas Coathup p. of Andrew Davison of Chester, liquor merchant.
„ 23 *William Barth of Chester, linendraper.
„ 23 William Harrop, brazier, s. of Thomas Harrop of Chester, brazier.
„ 23 *Samuel Davies of Chester, upholsterer.
Feb. 25 John Rowland p. of Gerrard Jordan, slater.
„ 25 *Valentine Williams of Chester, blacksmith.
„ 25 *Thomas Hussey of Chester, baker.
Mar. 23 *George Walker, liquor merchant.
„ 23 George Walker the younger, silversmith, s. of George Walker, silversmith.
Apr. 6 Richard Powdrell of Farndon, gentleman, s. of Richard Powdrell, late of Chester, linendraper.
May 8 The Rev. Thomas Edwards of Alford, A.M., s. of Thomas Edwards of Chester, alderman.
„ 15 John Weigh, musician, s. of Thomas Weigh of Chester, currier.
„ 15 George Boden, carpenter and joiner, s. of George Boden of Chester, slater, deceased.
Apr. 25 *Charles Tomlinson, beer brewer.
„ 25 *Peter Stamford, soapboiler.
„ 25 *William Crofts, soapboiler.
„ 25 John Charles Smith, cordwainer, s. of John Smith of Chester, cordwainer.
June 1 Charles Pover, wetglover, s. of Edward Pover of Chester, wetglover, deceased.
„ 19 *Edward Thomas, victualler.
„ 19 *Samuel Sproston, victualler.
„ 19 *William Smith, victualler.
„ 19 *Robert Knowles, victualler.
„ 19 John Hughes, victualler.
„ 19 William Taylor p. of William Harrison of Chester, shoemaker, deceased.
July 4 *Daniel Williams, innkeeper.
Oct. 23 *Samuel Ackerley, victualler.

1799-800]   THE CITY OF CHESTER   417

Oct. 23 *James Shaw, hatter.
 ,, 23   James Austin p. of John Hughes of Chester, cordwainer.
 ,, 23   William Thring, victualler, p. of George Hastings of Chester, tinman.
 ,, 23   Charles Ellson p. of Robert Robinson of Chester, baker.
 ,, 23 *Charles Bebbington, tailor.
 ,, 23   Daniel Smith, cordwainer, s. of John Smith of Chester, cordwainer.

1799-800 [40-41 G. iii.] DANIEL SMITH, Esquire, Mayor.

Nov. 13 John Hobson p. of Samuel Davies of Chester, butcher.
Dec. 18 *Thomas Cropper, tobacconist.
 ,, 18 *John Harvey, butcher.
 ,, 18 *Albin Minshull, butcher.
 ,, 18 *Peter Laroux, staymaker.
 ,, 18   Joseph Reynoldson p. of Daniel Bennett of Chester, druggist, deceased.
 ,, 18   John Powell, upholsterer, s. of Thomas Powell of Chester, upholsterer.
 ,, 24 *William Richards, gentleman.
Jan. 24 *Richard Yoxall, broker.
 ,, 24   William Lloyd, stationer and bookbinder, s. of George Lloyd of Chester, victualler.
Mar. 15 John Duckers p. of Samuel Bullock of Chester, carpenter, deceased.
 ,, 15   John Davies p. of Samuel Woolley of Chester, baker.
 ,, 15 *John Foulkes, victualler.
 ,, 24 *Thomas Swanwick, tobacconist.
 ,, 24 *John Baker, cordwainer.
Apr. 1   Ralph Tushingham of Boughton, seedsman, s. of Ralph Tushingham of Boughton, cooper, deceased.
May 26 *John Parsonage, victualler.
 ,, 30 *Richard Young, glover.
 ,, 30   Joseph Harrison, stationer and bookbinder, p. of Peter Broster of Chester, alderman.
 ,, 30   George Topham p. of James Haswell and his assignee John Millington, both of Chester, hairdressers.
 ,, 31   Richard Whitehead the younger s. of Richard Whitehead of Chester, cordwainer, deceased.
June 14 Nathaniel Batho, cabinetmaker, s. of James Batho of Chester, cabinetmaker.

June 14 Thomas Mooton, cordwainer, p. of William Taylor of Chester.
Aug. 11 William Brown, innkeeper, s. of Thomas Brown of Chester.
„ 11 John Monk, printer, s. of John Monk of Chester, printer, deceased.
„ 11 William Bedward, joiner, s. of Joseph Bedward of Chester, joiner.
„ 20 *John Tomlinson, surgeon.
„ 20 Richard Littler p. of William Henderson of Chester, carpenter.
„ 20 James Bennett, druggist, s. of John Bennett of Chester, alderman.
Oct. 16 *William Henry [Majendie], Lord Bishop of Chester.
„ 18 *John Harrison, captain.

1800-1 [41-42 G. iii.] JOHN MEACOCK, Esquire, Mayor.

Oct. 31 *Joseph Ridgway, fringeweaver.
„ 31 *Joseph Munnerley, victualler.
„ 31 *Thomas Norton, victualler.
„ 31 *James Parry, victualler.
Nov. 1 *John Woolliscroft, victualler.
„ 3 *Robert Fletcher, watchmaker.
„ 3 *John Owens, victualler.
„ 8 William Palin of Aldford, maltster, s. of Thomas Palin of Chester, grocer.
„ 8 Joseph Edmondson of Bridge Trafford, gentleman, s. of William Edmondson, late of Bridge Trafford, gentleman.
„ 8 William Gamon of Chester, maltster, s. of Thomas Gamon of Chester, yeoman.
„ 19 Thomas Shuttleworth p. of Charles Barnes of Chester, baker.
Mar. 21 Robert Tushingham of Chester, skinner, s. of Arthur Tushingham, " one of the almsmen " of Chester.
May 19 John Beavan p. of William Turner of Chester, barber.
„ 19 *Matthew Garner of Chester, victualler.
„ 22 William Eltoft of Chester, liquor merchant, s. of John Eltoft of Chester, toyman.
„ 27 John Williams of Chester, stone and marble mason, p. of Joseph Turner of Chester, architect.

June 8 James Cooke of Chester p. of Samuel Robinson of Chester, baker.
„ 20 Charles Parry, baker, s. of Francis Parry of Chester, baker.
„ 22 John Massey of Chester, baker, } ss. of John Massey, late of Chester, baker.
„ 22 Francis Massey of Chester, tinman,
July 4 *John Whitebrook of Chester, cordwainer.
„ 9 *Richard Simcock of Chester, victualler.
„ 9 *John Charles of Chester, cordwainer and victualler.
„ 9 *Jonathan Green of Chester, butcher and victualler.
„ 19 Daniel Harrison of Chester, stonemason, p. of Edward Spencer of Chester, stonemason.
Sep. 5 John Johnson of Chester, baker, s. of Robert Johnson of Chester, baker.
„ 29 George Harrison of Chester, ironfounder, s. of William Harrison of Chester, alderman.
Oct. 17 *William Meacock of Stanney, gentleman.
„ 19 John Craven of Chester p. of John Meredith of Chester, bricklayer.

1801-2 [42-43 G. iii.] JOHN LARDEN, Esquire, Mayor.

Nov. 13 *William Connah of Chester, surgeon.
„ 13 *Thomas Davies of Chester, grocer.
„ 13 *Samuel Huntington of Chester, broker.
„ 13 John Cooper of Chester p. of Robert Brittain of Chester, woollendraper.
Dec. 2 John Orford of Chester p. of Jonathan Orford of Chester, saddler, deceased.
„ 2 Joseph Grace of Chester p. of Thomas Edwards of Chester, grocer, deceased.
„ 2 John Davies of Chester, druggist, s. of William Davies of Chester, glazier, deceased.
„ 2 Thomas Thompson of Chester, druggist, s. of Owen Thompson of Chester, grocer.
„ 2 John Cross of Chester, toyman, s. of John Cross of Chester, turner, deceased.
Jan. 8 James Moore of Chester, cooper, s. of Theodosius Moore of Chester, cooper.
„ 8 Thomas Taylor of Chester, cooper, s. of John Taylor of Chester, cooper, deceased.
„ 8 Thomas Bateman of Chester, cooper, s. of Edward Bateman of Chester, cooper.

Jan. 8 John Taylor of Chester, cabinet-maker, } ss. of John Taylor, cooper.
,, 8 Richard Taylor of Chester, upholsterer,
,, 8 John Percivall, cooper, s. of James Percivall of Chester, baker.
,, 8 *Ellis Roberts of Chester, grocer.
,, 8 *Thomas Richards of Chester, victualler.
,, 8 *Edward Evans of Chester, grocer.
,, 8 *Richard Taylor of Chester, toyman.
,, 8 Daniel Humphreys of Chester p. of John Montgomery of Chester, cooper.
,, 8 John Williams of Chester p. of John Sproston of Chester, cooper.
,, 22 *Richard Walford of Chester, porter brewer.
Feb. 1 *William Nicholls of Chester, esquire.
,, 1 *Timothy Whitby of Eccleston, esquire.
,, 5 John Johnson of Chester, innkeeper,' p. of Samuel Tonna of Chester, breechesmaker.
,, 5 *Edward Matthews of Chester, saddler.
,, 5 *John Ankers of Chester, whitesmith.
,, 5 *Charles Colton of Chester, seedsman.
,, 5 *Robert Topham of Chester, skinner.
,, 5 Richard Weigh of Chester, carpenter and joiner, s. of Thomas Weigh, late of Chester, currier.
,, 5 Richard Dutton of Chester, tinplateworker, s. of Richard Dutton of Chester, cordwainer.
,, 5 William Taylor of Chester, cooper, s. of John Taylor of Chester, cooper, deceased.
,, 6 Thomas Lightfoot of Aldersey, co. Ches., farmer, s. of Thomas Lightfoot, cordwainer.
,, 6 *Thomas Rowe of Caldecot, co. Ches., farmer.
,, 24 *Jonathan Colley of Chester, tanner.
,, 24 Thomas Paul of Chester, druggist, s. of John Paul of Chester, innkeeper.
,, 24 John Healey of Chester, butcher, s. of John Healey of Chester, butcher.
,, 24 Charles Whittell of Chester, druggist, s. of Robert Whittell of Chester, ropier.
,, 24 *Samuel Nevitt Bennett of Chester, gentleman.
,, 27 Isaac Hope of Chester p. of Henry Hegg of Chester, druggist, deceased.
Mar. 16 William Griffith of Chester, currier, s. of John Griffith of Chester, victualler, deceased.
,, 16 Joseph Griffith, cordwainer, s. of John Griffith.
,, 16 Joseph Ackerley p. of John Littler, brazier.

1802]   THE CITY OF CHESTER   421

Mar. 16   Thomas Artingstall p. of Richard Vernon, butcher.
„   16   John Herbert p. of Daniel Herbert, cordwainer.
„   16   Charles Scott p. of Edward Bateman, cooper.
„   16   Thomas Ellis of Chester, currier.
„   16   William Ollerhead, huckster, p. of Thomas Palin of Chester, tailor.
„   16   Robert Fearnall the younger p. of Robert Fearnall, butcher.
„   25   *Thomas Walshman, hairdresser.
„   25   *Charles King, pawnbroker.
„   25   *Thomas Williams, cheesemonger.
„   25   *William Hall, flour dealer.
„   25   *Anthony Holly, victualler.
„   25   *Richard Wright, mugman.
„   27   Samuel s. of George Harding, labourer.
Apr. 22   *William Cortney, shipbuilder.
„   22   *James Voice, flour dealer.
„   22   *William Jones, huckster.
„   25   *William Catheral, huckster.
„   25   *James Jeffery, whitesmith.
„   25   *William Turner of Chester, brewer.
„   25   *George Elliott of Chester, cordwainer.
„   22   *Edward Jones, victualler.
„   22   *Edward Titley, druggist.
„   22   *James Hassell, wine merchant.
„   22   *Richard Conyers, painter and glazier.
„   22   *William Hassell, victualler.
„   22   *Samuel Maddock, flour dealer.
„   22   *William Davies, flour dealer.
„   22   *Peter Sadler, glazier.
„   22   *Richard Sinker, victualler.
„   22   *Humphrey Hodson, victualler.
June 26   *James Hughes, gardener, s. of James Hughes, late of Chester, gardener.
„   29   *Richard Holmes, victualler.
„   29   *Robert Roberts, victualler.
„   29   *Ralph Hassall, victualler.
„   29   *William Davies, victualler.
„   29   *Henry Doughty, blockmaker.
„   29   Charles Griffith, glazier, s. of John Griffith of Chester, plumber.
July 3   James Wilkinson, cooper, s. of ——— Wilkinson, late of Chester.
„   3   *Samuel Nickson, cabinetmaker and upholsterer.
„   3   John Walker, cordwainer and farmer, p. of ———.
„   3   *John Minshull, block and pump maker.

July 10 William Faulkner, cabinetmaker, s. of William Faulkner of Chester, deceased.
Aug. 11 Charles Hall, bookbinder, s. of William Hall of Chester, cordwainer.
,, 11 *Richard Edwards, broker.
,, 28 James Kennerley, sugar baker [gentleman, M.B.], p. of Robert Hesketh, late of Chester, sugar baker.
Sep. 24 *Charles Harding, saltman.
,, 24 *Joseph Roberts, carter.
,, 24 *James Harrison, flour dealer.

1802–3 [43–44 G. iii.] ROBERT HODGSON, Esquire, Mayor.

Jan. 19 *Thomas Randles, victualler.
,, 19 *Benjamin Adams, carpenter.
,, 19 *William Roberts, innkeeper.
,, 20 George Walker p. of James Jones of Chester, cordwainer.
Feb. 7 Edward Rowland p. of John Harrison of Chester, ropemaker.
,, 26 David Evans p. of William Pennington of Chester, carpenter.
,, 26 Thomas Evans of Saltneyside, farmer, s. of David Evans of Chester, carpenter.
,, 26 John Leatherbarrow, tinplateworker, s. of John Leatherbarrow, late of Chester, tinplateworker.
Apr. 29 John Stewart Hughes p. of John Hughes of Chester, merchant, deceased.
May 25 John Finney, cordwainer, s. of Benjamin Finney of Chester, cordwainer.
,, 26 *Abraham Jones, cordwainer [victualler, M.B.].
,, 26 Joseph Weigh, painter, s. of Thomas Weigh of Chester, currier.
Sep. 23 *John Kendrick, carter.
,, 23 *Thomas Lunt, bricklayer.
,, 23 *Joseph Rigby, innkeeper.
,, 23 *John Sayer, victualler.
,, 23 *John Topping, blacksmith.
,, 23 *William Evans, victualler.
,, 23 *John Pearson, victualler.
,, 23 *William Maylor, victualler.

1803-4 [44-45 G. iii.] EDMUND BUSHELL, Esquire,
MAYOR.

Feb. 9 *Thomas Porter, plumber.
„   9 Thomas Huxley of Chester, stationer, s. of Thomas Huxley of Chester, stationer, deceased.
Mar. 16 John Roberts of Chester, sugar baker, s. of Thomas Roberts of Chester, grocer, deceased.
„   16 John Owen of Chester, brazier, s. of George Owen of Chester, butcher.
„   16 John Arrowsmith of Chester p. of William Edwards of Chester, grocer.
May 23 *Samuel Sandars of Chester, victualler.
„   23 *William Thomas of Chester, victualler.
„   23 *William Nicholas of Chester, victualler.
„   23 *Peter Hughes of Chester, victualler.
„   23 *John Brittain, victualler.
„   23 *George Bailey of Chester, tobacconist.
„   23 Edward Davies of Chester p. of John Millington of Chester, perukemaker.
„   23 Joseph Ashton of Chester p. of John Joynson of Chester, cooper.
„   23 John Podmore of Chester, yeoman, s. of ———.
July 14 George Hall of Chester, joiner, } ss. of William Hall of Chester, cord-
„   14 Edward Hall of Chester, joiner, } wainer.
„   14 Thomas Bellis of Chester p. of Edward Morris of Chester, cordwainer.
Aug. 29 William Adams of Chester, carpenter and joiner, s. of John Adams of Chester, carpenter.
Oct. 19 *Owen Foulkes, wine merchant.

1804-5 [45-46 G. iii.] WILLIAM EDWARDS, Esquire,
MAYOR.

Oct. 31 Peter Jameson p. of ———.
Dec. 10 Thomas Dyke p. of Thomas Crane of Chester, corkcutter.
„   10 John Moors p. of John Dawson of Chester, baker.
Mar. 26 William Bage p. of Joseph Bage of Chester, papermaker.
Apr. 1 *James Okell of Chester, surgeon.
„   1 Richard Edwards of Chester, liquor merchant, s. of William Edwards, grocer, mayor of the city.

May 27 *Nathaniel Bevan, victualler.
June 5 *Joseph Faulkner, victualler.
 „   5 *Robert Foulkes, liquor merchant.
 „   5 *Robert Morris, painter.
Aug. 5 William Lloyd Wilbraham, linendraper, s. of John
         Wilbraham, keeper of the Northgate Gaol, and
         formerly a grocer.
 „   5 John Woolley p. of Thomas Edwards of Chester,
         feltmaker, deceased.
 „   5 *Joseph Jarvis, victualler.
 „   5 *Joseph Lyster, victualler.

APPENDIX

The admissions here given are for years for which neither Rolls nor Mayors' Books are now to be found. They have been extracted from the series of Treasurers' Accounts referred to in Part I., page xi, and are valuable as helping to fill up the hiatus in the Rolls and Mayors' Books between 1616 and 1634.

1616–7 [14–15 Jas. i.] EDWARD BUTTON, Mayor.

(B) Edward s. of Edward Yonge, shoemaker.
Raphe Critchley p. of Thomas Revington, beer brewer.
(B) Richard s. of Robert Bennet, draper, defunct.
(B) John s. of William Andrew.
(B) Edward s. of David Evans the elder, pewterer.
(B) Robert s. of Richard Wright, baker.
(B) Edward s. of Richard Roberts, butcher.
John Maddock p. of John Maddock, tanner.
William Hawton.
William Jones p. of Mr. William Gamull, alderman.
(B) Humphrey s. of Robert Phillips, hatmaker.
John Glegge p. of Henry Anyon, tanner.
John Warrington p. of Roger Kinge, baker.
(B) Pawle s. of John Johnson, silkweaver.
John Souch p. of Mr. Randle Holme, "deputy of ye office of Armes" [added in another hand].
(B) William s. of Thomas Halliwell, webster.
John Stringer p. of William Butlar, ———.
Thomas Wealch p. of Mr. Thomas Weston.
(B) Thomas } ss. of William Alcock, innholder.
(B) Raphe }
(B) Richard s. of Richard Roberts, butcher, defunct.
(B) Robert s. of Mr. Thomas Anyon, innholder.
(B) Richard s. of Anthony Warmisham, sadler.
(B) Hugh s. of John Mowson, tanner.
(B) Alexander s. of Thomas Burde, tanner.
(B) John s. of William Whittell, tanner.
Peter Warburton.
Hugh Cappur p. of Mr. Richard Leicester, mercer.
Richard Cappur p. of Mr. Alderman Litlor.
Thomas s. of Thomas Prickett, ymbroderer.

1617-8 [15-16 Jas. i.] CHARLES FITTON, Mayor.

Raphe Heapie p. of Mr. Sutton, beer brewer.
John Seller p. of Lewis Jones, silkweaver.
Samuel Robinson p. of John Phillips, merchant.
Hugh Usher p. of Richard Shurlock, shoemaker.
Richard Hughes [p.] of Mr. Thomas Harvye, glover.
(B) Thomas Kettell.
John Johnson p. of Thomas Goose, draper.
(B) Edward s. of David Allen, shoemaker.
*Randall Hall, "the citties mazon," admitted as an apprentice.
*Hugh Davemporte.
Thomas Peckow p. of Thomas Fisher, butcher.
(B) Thomas s. of Thomas Case, tallow chandler.
Thomas Cooper p. of Edward Wall, ironmonger.
Oliver Stranke p. of Rowland Johnson, ironmonger.
(B) Raphe s. of Laurence Burde, tanner.
Thomas Morris p. of John Willson, smith.
*Edward Lewis, as an apprentice.
*Robert Fisher, as an apprentice.
(B) Raphe s. of William Bird, tanner.
(B) John s. of Robert Oullerhead, hatmaker.
John Leighe p. of William Skellington, slater.
(B) Samuel s. of William Butler, slater.
(B) William s. of John Hall, baker.
William Ince p. of Mr. Raphe Finchett, shereman.
Richard Gascoyne p. of William Smallshaw, slater.
(B) Raphe s. of Raphe Hilton, shoemaker.
(B) George Eaton, mariner, s. of John Eaton, defunct.
(B) Thomas Cowper, shoemaker, s. of Raphe Cowper, hooper.
John Adamson p. of Richard Hinde, tallow chandler.
Richard Tellett p. of William Butler, slater.
(B) John s. of Thomas Rider, shoemaker.
Thomas Coulter p. of Thomas Holbrooke, butcher.
(B) Thomas s. of Thomas Weston, glover.
(B) Richard } ss. of William Locker *alias* Richardson.
(B) William }

1618-9 [16-17 Jas. i.] RANDLE MAINWARING, Mayor.

Hugh ap Robert p. of Mr. Thomas Harvie, late alderman of the city, defunct.
George Deane p. of Roger Kinge, baker.

APPENDIX

(B) Thomas Harrison.
Raphe Davies p. of John Wilding, tailor.
John Farrall p. of Mr. Robert Berry, merchant.
Raphe Bennett p. of Tho. Benyson, brewer.
Thomas Johnson p. of Hugh Whicksteed, glover.
Thomas s. of Richard Tilston, citizen and shoemaker of Chester.
Laurence Wilcockson p. of Arthur Figes, citizen and ironmonger.
William Prymate p. of Richard Prymate, citizen and beer brewer.
John s. of John Sproson, feltmaker.
Thomas Burrowes } pp. of Roger Burrowes.
Robert Burrowes }
Richard Hill p. of Henry Tilston, feltmaker.
Robert Pemberton p. of Richard Fletcher.
John s. of Urian Rider, blacksmith.
Joh. s. of Richard Wright, baker.
Owen Jones p. of Peter Drinkwater.
Robert Fletcher p. of William Wilson, sherman.
*Charles Walley, gentleman.
Piers Vaughan.
(B) David s. of Robert Hatton, butcher.
William Barlowe p. of Edmund Challoner, tanner.
John Crew p. of Thomas Marston, beer brewer.
(B) John Waade.
John s. of Nicholas Hallwood, barber.
Thomas s. of Edward Smith.
Thomas Knowles p. of Griffith Jones.
David Robenson p. of [blank].
Peter Hawkin p. of Thomas Eaton, smith.
*John Savage, esquire.
Gawyn Hudson p. of William Fisher, innholder.
Robert Ensdale p. of Richard Taillor, clothier.
Richard s. of William Mercer, tallow chandler.
Peter s. of Paul Coulton.
William s. of Laurence Johnson, tanner.
William s. of Henry Anyon, tanner.
Thomas Madocke p. of John Maddocke.
Henry Handcock p. of Richard Spon, tanner.
Henry Totty p. of Ralph Wilson, tanner.
Edward Barnes p. of Hugh Jones, tailor.
Richard Williams, free born and p. of William Hand the elder.
Raphe Howell p. of Peter Goose, draper.

1626–7 [2–3 C. i.] NICHOLAS INCE, Mayor.

James s. of Robert Ridley.
James s. of James [Banister ?].
———————————
———————————
[William ?] s. of Roger Kinge.
William s. of William Modsley.
William Selsbye p. of his brother Robert Selsbye.
John [Steell ?] p. of John Smyth, feltmaker.
Thomas s. of [Peter ?] Bennett, innholder.
John s. of John Basford, saddler.
James s. of John Fletcher.
Robert Shone p. of Richard Shone.
George s. of George Bellin.
Richard Thomason p. of John Blanshed.
John s. of Peter Fletcher.
William Allen p. of John Hallywell.
Rondull s. of John Asbrocke.
John s. of John Harper.
Roger Morris p. of Thomas Fisher.
John s. of John Seall.
Mr. Edward s. of Mr. Edward Savage.
Thomas Joynson p. of Paul Coultone.
William s. of William Wilsone.
Roger Younge p. of Rondull Finchett.
Richard Cowop p. of William Booth.
William } ss. of Roger Kinge the younger.
Richard }
John s. of Roger Kinge the elder.
Richard Tottye p. of Thomas Farington.
Thomas Lyneger p. of Nicholas Cowper.
Rondull Henshaw p. of Thomas Aldersey.
Thomas Bennett p. of Richard Walker.
John s. of Robert Boydle.
Mr. William Brooke of Uptonne.
Mr. Tho. Gamull } ss. of Mr. William Gamull, alderman.
Mr. William Gamull }
Robert Dean p. of Ralph Minshull, shoemaker.
Peter s. of Richard Snead.
Henry s. of William Meeshame, sherman.
Robert Morris p. of Thomas Morris, sherman.
Thomas s. of John Garnett.
Thomas s. of James Byram.
Richard Willsone p. of Rondall Smyth, clothyer.

William s. of Richard Meacock, pewterer.
John Smyth p. of David Evans, pewterer.
Henry Owen p. of Mr. William Edwards.
Laurence Younge p. of William Orton, glover.
Hugh Handes p. of Richard Bridges, dyer.
John Blease } ss. of Mr. Robert Blease, alderman.
Robert Blease }
Mr. John Asbrooke, preecher, made free grates.
Edward s. of Mr. John Cooke, glover.
John s. of Mr. John Aldersey, ironmonger.
Will Ince } ss. of Mr. Robert Ince, draper.
Rondull Ince }
Daniel Leigh p. of Michell Sheppard.
John s. of John Eaton, officer.
Peter Leigh p. of William Ley.
Henry Hasloe p. of Tho. Taylor, smith.
George s. of John Harper, ironmonger.
Richard Deane p. of William Hignett, butcher.
William Bradborne p. of Peter Drinkwater, alderman.
Richard s. of William Wolfe, baker.
Thomas s. of William Kinge, baker.
Daniel Croxson p. of Robert Kerkman.
Richard Cooke p. of Richard Molenex, weaver.
Rondull } ss. of Rondull Fernall.
Richard }

INDEXES

I

OF CHRISTIAN NAMES AND SURNAMES

Names with varied spelling have been indexed as far as possible under the modern equivalent; but occasionally, owing to dropped aspirates and other causes, the modern equivalent is doubtful. In such cases the original spelling appears in its lexicographical order. Generally, the variants have been cross-indexed.

Where a surname has an *alias*, each form of surname is indexed under its initial letter.

[——] signifies the Christian name has either been omitted or is illegible in the original manuscript.

The asterisk following a page number denotes that the name appears more than once on the page in question.

A

Abbott, James, 380; Nicholas, 4; Roger, 13, 78; William, 18
Abraham, William, 29
Ackerley, Joseph, 420; Samuel, 416
Ackers, Thomas, 341, 370, 383, 390*; Welton, John, 423
Adam, Edward, 25
Adams, Benjamin, 422; Edward, 361, 380*; Jacob, 261; James, 334; John, 140, 156, 293, 360, 383, 423; Joseph, 160, 253, 340; Orian, 328; Philip, 266, 353; Richard, 150, 154, 172; Robert, 378, 425; Thomas, 341, 349; William, 185, 238, 254, 277, 302, 331, 336, 363, 385, 411, 414
Adamson, Donald, 10; John, 261; Peter, 331, 286; Robert, 304; Samuel, 201; Thomas, 12
Addison, Henry, 17
Adey, Thomas, 148
Adshead, Charles, 254, 344; John, 106, 215, 206, 277, 291*, 334; Randle, 75; Samuel, 411; Thomas, 307; William, 185, 238, 254, 277, 302, 331, 336, 363, 385, 411, 414
Agar, Adam, 15; Thomas, 17
Ainscough. *See* Ascough and Askow
Ainsdale. *See* Aynsdale

Airey, Benjamin, 303; Mary, 348; Samuel, 217, 292, 364; Thomas, 209, 303, 364
Albright, Stephen, 79, 103, 119
Alcock (Allcock, Alcok), Adam, 75; Charles, 134; James, 124, 149, 250; Joseph, 300*; Peter, 177, 250; Raphe, 125; Robert, 378; Thomas, 31, 55, 69, 134, 282*, 318, 378, 425; William, 69, 144, 160, 201, 425
Alcoft, Joseph, 209
Aldcroft, Charles, 384; Theodore, 175, 119, 208, 310, 334; William, 159
Aldersey (Aldersaie), Benjamin, 271; Calcott, 400; Caldecott, 180; Daniel, 240, 275, 311, 331, 380
Alington, 75. *See* Allington, 15, 40, 87, 89, 91, 107, 113, 119, 429
Allen, David, 73, 420; Edward, 79, 118, 357, 428; William, 35, 39, 40*, 42, 45, 69, 74, 80, 89, 99, 100, 101, 108*, 113*, 400
Alington. *See* Allington
All, John, 202; Thomas, 202. *See also* Hall
Alleby, Richard, 224
Allen, David, 73, 420; Edward, 79, 118,

119, 426; Hugh, 112; John, 34, 42, 43, 46, 58, 62, 66, 68, 70, 79*, 97, 118, 120, 223, 226; Ralph, 57, 83, 120; Richard, 327; Thomas, 63, 122, 132, 223; William, 57, 79, 93, 102*, 112, 113, 116*, 119, 153*, 201, 202*, 223, 226, 327, 428
Allenson, John, 158, 200*
Allenton, Richard, 364
Allerton, Thomas, 55
Allington [Alington, Allyngton], George, 366; John, 34, 42, 82*
Allmark, Joseph, 398. *See also* Halmarke
Almond, James, 241, 272, 300, 334, 335; John, 222, 262, 286, 292, 297*, 331, 334, 395; Ralph, 130, 148; Richard, 292, 331; Thomas, 262, 300; William, 256, 286, 300
Amery [Amerie], John, 215, 314, 409; Robert, 24, 45*, 69, 76, 78*, 93; Thomas, 86, 355, 359, 371, 385, 398*, 409; William, 403
Amont, Cuthbert, 79
Amote, John, 84
Ampson [Amson], Hugh, 126; John, 104, 342; Richard, 79, 104
Ancocke, William, 29. *See also* Hancock
Anderson, John, 131, 194, 303; Robert, 173, 184
Anderton, Charles, 176; Hugh, 113, 131, 152; John, 173, 272; Matthew, 131, 161*, 184, 263; Nathaniel, 213; Randle, 32; Walter, 9; William, 244, 263
Andrew [Andrewe], Aaron, 301; Abel, 162, 185, 190, 301, 356; Asah, 141, 162; Esau, 185*, 247*, 329, 356; John, 31, 36, 57, 60*, 80, 85, 110*, 114, 425; Robert, 136; Thomas, 63, 103, 114, 119, 329; William, 66, 103, 136, 425
Andrews, Abel, 389; Esau, 401; Thomas, 389*; William, 401
Andsell, Samuel, 312
Anglizer, Richard, 66
Ankers [Anckers], George, 413; Hugh, 132; John, 420; Richard, 384
Anley, Samuel, 300. *See also* Hanley
Anningson, Peter, 25
Annion [Anion, Anneon, Annyon, Anyon], Edmund, 34, 44, 58, 66; Henry, 13, 28, 40, 42*, 43, 53, 58, 66, 425, 427; James, 71, 90, 115; John, 16, 25, 53, 58, 59, 61, 62, 83, 101, 105, 106, 128, 134*, 146*, 167, 184, 189, 210; Joseph, 189; Randle, 105, 137, 209, 223; Richard, 45, 62, 94, 110, 124; Robert, 31, 65, 425;

Thomas, 65, 66, 110, 115, 128, 139, 181, 425; William, 8, 23, 73, 427
Ansteed, John, 132
Antrobus [Anthrobus], George, 44; John, 86
Anwill, William, 267
Anyon. *See* Annion
Apperley, James, 314
Appleton [Apleton], James, 93, 128; Matthew, 138, 159; William, 113
Archer, Andrew, 290; Richard, 290, 366*
Arden, Phillip, 337
Ardern [Arderne], James, 337; John, 158, 358
Armstrong, Andrew, 194
Arnett, James, 265
Arrowsmith [Arrosmith], Gilbert, 21, 60; John, 423; Richard, 54; William, 60
Arthur, Hugh, 155; Thomas, 172
Artingstall, James, 334, 375, 414; Joseph, 414; Nathan, 334; Thomas, 421
Asalls [or Esalls], Aaron, 185
Ascough, Thomas, 174. *See also* Askow
Ashbrooke [Asbrooke, Asbruck, Astbrock], Daniel, 295; Edward, 13; John, 46, 71, 110, 111, 135, 428, 429; Nathaniel, 295; Randull, 428; Samuel, 186, 242*; Thomas, 110
Ashley, Thomas, 404
Ashmull, George, 364; Jeffrey, 339; Thomas, 339; William, 390
Ashton [Assheton], Benjamin, 171; Charles, 175; George, 7; Henry, 11; John, 73, 84, 106*, 110, 111, 138, 263, 295*, 367*; Joseph, 423; Peter, 10; Ralph, 110; Randle, 16; Richard, 110, 133, 154, 203*; Robert, 63, 144, 154; Thomas, 24, 133, 160, 166, 186, 232, 331*; William, 69, 111, 145*. *See also* Aston
Ashwood [Assherwod], John, 48
Askew [Askewe], John, 83; Robert, 83
Askow, Robert, 40. *See also* Ascough
Asley, Francis, 215
Asmore [Asmor], John, 33, 48, 61; Marmaduke, 114; Robert, 39; Thomas, 73, 114
Aspinall [Aspinwall, Aspenwall], Henry, 314, 354, 363; Samuel, 164, 258; Thomas, 118, 142
Aspshowe, Roger, 29; Thomas, 29
Assheton. *See* Ashton
Astle, Edward, 325, 385; John, 363; Thomas, 325, 362, 385, 392, 399*, 412

INDEXES

Astley. *See* Asley
Aston, Edward, 142, 161 ; Henry, 142 ; John, 110 ; Randle, 155, 187*, 202, 229, 236, 259 ; William, 89. *See also* Ashton
Atkinson, George, 168 ; John, 323 ; Joseph, 294 ; Michael, 294
Aubrey, Thomas, 309
Austin, James, 417
Avans, Edward, 221*. *See also* Evans
Avern, Joseph, 220, 320, 336 ; Thomas, 320, 381*
Axon, James, 390 ; John, 108, 222, 352, 390* ; Ralph, 108
Aynsdale, William, 27

B

Bacarn [Baccarn, Backarn, Bakern], James, 376 ; John, 243, 337 ; Richard, 243, 327, 337, 348, 376 ; Thomas, 283, 348, 384*
Back, Christopher, 160
Bacon, John, 39
Baddeley [Baddiley, Badeley], John, 399 ; Richard, 23 ; William, 339
Badger, Isaac, 360 ; James, 113
Bafarn [Beforne], John, 144*, 281 ; William, 281
Bafron, Henry, 171. *See also* Balforn
Bage, Joseph, 403, 423 ; William, 423
Baghe [Bagh, Beigh], Edward, 89 ; John, 95, 224 ; Thomas, 89, 97 ; William, 95
Bagnall, John, 229, 234 ; Ralph, 243 ; Randle, 243 ; Samuel, 234, 347, 370, 393, 395 ; Thomas, 229, 242, 277, 317
Bagot, Charles, 314 ; George, 120 ; (Sir) Walter Wagstaff, 313
Baguley, James, 162, 298 ; John, 7 ; William, 148, 162
Bailey, Catherine, 257 ; Charles, 212 ; Edward, 401 ; George, 423 ; Henry, 360 ; James, 257, 353 ; John, 381*, 401 ; Richard, 84 ; William, 360, 369. *See also* Bayley and Bealey
Baines. *See* Banes
Baker, Elizabeth, 269 ; James, 414 ; John, 269, 285, 417 ; Richard, 283*, 358*, 366 ; Thomas, 149 ; William, 366
Bakern. *See* Bacarn
Bakewell, John, 398
Bakstove, William, 24
Baldwin, John, 317
Balforn, Henry, 218 ; William, 218. *See also* Bafarn and Bafron
Ball [Balle], Edward, 103, 356 ; George, 234, 330*, 398, 401 ; Henry, 9, 84 ;

Humphrey, 157 ; James, 54, 74, 103* ; John, 26, 91, 95, 103, 123, 136, 185, 217, 413 ; John Longford, 398 ; Nicholas, 401 ; Ralph, 42 ; Randle, 120, 158 ; Richard, 5, 62 ; Samuel, 370, 412 ; Shedrach, 256, 370* ; Thomas, 11, 13, 42, 51, 60, 116, 127, 139, 150, 184, 185, 249* ; William, 9, 21, 41*, 71, 82, 91, 97, 101*, 116, 154*, 158, 242*, 215, 250, 295, 370, 407
Bamber, James, 116 ; Richard, 103
Bamville [Bamvile], Francis, 29 ; Randle, 37, 43
Banes, James, 27
Banester. *See* Bannester
Banion. *See* Bannion and Bennion
Banks [Banckes, Bankes], Hugh, 122 ; John, 101 ; Robert, 340 ; William, 310
Banner, Charles, 162, 210*, 259 ; John, 174, 180
Bannester [Banester, Bannister], Edward, 103 ; Hugh, 62 ; James, 33, 42, 48, 95, 428* ; John, 132, 367, 413* ; Nicholas, 56, 83 ; Richard, 55, 83 ; Thomas, 95 ; William, 29, 62, 96
Bannion [Banian, Bannyon], George, 184 ; James, 48 ; John, 125, 151, 158, 172 ; Randle, 176 ; Samuel, 158 ; Thomas, 148, 182. *See also* Bennion
Bannister. *See* Bannester
Barber [Barbor], Arthur, 369 ; Nathaniel, 315, 369 ; Roger, 10 ; William, 356
Bardsley, Ephraim, 175, 204, 242*, 268, 279, 330 ; John, 268
Bargeley, John, 98
Barker, Charles, 317 ; David, 53 ; John, 7, 15, 53, 76, 121, 158, 380 ; Peter, 155 ; Richard, 7, 14*, 15, 33, 86, 126, 402 ; Robert, 317 ; Thomas, 37, 75, 280 ; Valentine, 75
Barkley [Barkeley], Hugh, 137 ; John, 145 ; Matthew, 133 ; William, 145
Barlow [Barlowe], Edward, 412 ; George, 169 ; Henry, 17 ; John, 74, 134, 173 ; Joseph, 377 ; Ralph, 26, 51 ; Richard, 79, 302* ; Roger, 17* ; William, 134, 373, 402, 427
Barnand, Christopher, 100
Barnard, Richard, 271
Barnes, Benjamin, 414 ; Charles, 405, 418 ; Edward, 105, 147, 427 ; John, 32, 42, 65, 68, 80*, 92, 93, 404 ; Joseph, 381 ; Richard, 48, 65, 77 ; Robert, 147 ; Roland, 48, 69, 92 ; Samuel, 398, 413 ; Thomas, 360, 398*, 402, 413*, 414 ; William, 62, 162

Barnett, Enoch, 387; George, 392; John, 215; Jonathan, 365
Barnston, Robert, 316, 386; Roger, 316, 386; Trafford, 358
Barow. *See* Barrow
Barratt, Robert, 225, 291; William, 225, 291
Barrett, Robert, 277, 326; William, 215
Barrow [Barrowe, Barow, Barowe], Benjamin, 191; Charles, 23; James, 123; John, 3*, 7, 10, 17, 224, 299*, 339, 344; Lawrence, 110; Mason, 383; Ralph, 310; Richard, 18, 73, 84, 344; Robert, 11, 16, 40; Roger, 17, 93; Thomas, 7, 11*, 13, 19*, 23, 38, 40, 90, 93, 224, 339; William, 191, 299
Barry, (Honble.) Arthur, 324; (Honble.) James, 326; John, 9; (Honble.) Richard, 326
Barrymore, James, Earl of, 269, 324, 326
Barth, Jonathan, 379; William, 416
Bartlam, George, 391; Robert, 340*, 391, 397*, 402; William, 391
Bartlem, Zacheus, 379
Barton, Charles, 322; Francis, 164; George, 322; Henry, 110; John, 26, 41, 43, 112, 116, 229, 233, 315, 366*, 404; Richard, 20, 38; Robert, 24, 41, 85; Thomas, 161, 197*, 233, 280; William, 41, 126, 229, 404 [——], 1
Basfeild, John, 189; William, 189, 193*
Basford [Basforde], John, 29, 78, 80, 138, 428*; Richard, 100; Robert, 78, 141; Roger, 18, 42*, 100; William, 80, 141
Basnet [Basnett, Bassenet, Bassinet], John, 173; Joseph, 159, 205, 233*, 273; Nathaniel, 133, 166; Robert, 62, 76; Samuel, 362. *See also* Bassett
Bassano, Francis, 230
Basseen, Mary, 283; Richard, 283
Bassett, Henry, 109; John, 109. *See also* Basnet
Bastwell, John, 25, 53*, 58, 117, 136*; Samuel, 84, 117; Thomas, 58, 125; William, 30
Batchelor, Robert, 222
Bate, William, 140, 151
Bateman, Edward, 276, 334, 345, 359, 369, 380, 404, 419, 421; James, 237; John, 24, 359; Phillip, 216, 237, 276, 369, 395; Thomas, 237, 345, 380, 395, 419
Bather [Batho, Bathoe, Bathowe], Benjamin, 348*; Daniel, 163, 184, 211, 283, 393; David, 103, 133; Edward, 70, 93, 98, 105, 127, 228; George, 316; Henry, 226, 236, 329; Jabez, 176, 201, 217, 219, 228, 231, 236, 238, 281; James, 286, 362, 417; John, 101; Nathaniel, 161, 166, 208, 217, 226, 236, 263, 275, 329, 362, 417; Ralph, 130; Randle, 133, 186, 211, 234, 283, 393; Richard, 208, 255, 257, 260, 265, 269, 275, 284*, 286, 297, 316, 366, 372*; Thomas, 126, 238; William, 139, 166, 217, 264, 281, 366; [——], 204
Battrich [Battriche], James, 33, 98, 104, 117; John, 56; Oliver, 237*; Richard, 56; Robert, 300; Rowland, 194*
Battridge, Thomas, 182
Baugh, Hugh, 47; John, 117; Thomas, 117
Baunt, Richard, 22*
Bavand [Bavant], Charles, 164; Daniel, 100, 128; Jane, 75; John, 69, 112, 290*; Michael, 84; Randle, 75, 112; Richard, 33, 46, 55, 55 *n.*, 56, 69*, 75*, 81, 84, 94, 100, 142, 163, 185, 222*; Robert, 55 *n.*, 112; Thomas, 19, 33, 44, 45, 111, 120, 146*, 165, 185, 200, 208, 225; William, 19, 83, 112, 125. *See also* Bevand
Bavin, Richard, 220; William, 220. *See also* Bevan
Baxter, George, 365; Henry, 106; John, 387; Ralph, 34; Randle, 141; Richard, 352, 378, 392*; William, 44, 57, 378, 398
Bayledonne, Robert, 16; Thomas, 16
Bayley [Baylie, Bayly, Baylye], Henry, 113, 288, 351, 366; James, 308, 329, 351*, 363, 365*; John, 329, 334, 366; Matthew, 308, 334; Peter, 142; Richard, 115*; Thomas, 320*; William, 100. *See also* Bailey and Bealey
Bazine, John, 400; Richard, 359*, 400
Bealey [Bealy], James, 190; John, 190; Thomas, 151. *See also* Bailey and Bayley
Beasley, William, 357
Beavan. *See* Bevan
Bebbington [Bebington, Bebinton, Bebynton], Charles, 417; Henry, 3; John, 1, 3, 51; Richard, 43, 65; Thomas, 24, 43, 56
Beck [Bek], Thomas, 20; William, 406
Beckenshaw. *See* Bekenshaw
Beckett, Arthur, 196*; John, 277,

INDEXES

364*, 374; Joseph, 326, 373*; Stephen, 374; William, 373
Beddow, John, 121
Bedford, Henry, 70
Bedson, Elizabeth, 146; George, 146; John, 413; Thomas, 203. *See also* Betson
Bedward, John, 255, 351, 378, 415; Joseph, 351, 418; William, 124, 126, 418
Beeby, John, 302; Thomas, 271, 302
Beech, James, 339; John, 269, 317*, 318, 339
Beecroft, John, 405
Beedle, Thomas, 89, 99*
Beevan. *See* Bevan
Beforne. *See* Bafarn
Beigh. *See* Baghe
Bek. *See* Beck
Bekenshaw [Beckenshawe], Henry, 5; Thomas, 9
Bekyngsam, William, 18
Belin. *See* Bellin
Bell, John, 365; Peter, 178; Richard, 10; Roger, 55; Thomas, 258*; William, 95
Bellard, Peter, 148
Bellerby, Robert, 10
Bellet, John, 9; Thomas, 9
Bellin [Belin, Bellen, Belyn], George, 27, 62*, 428*; John, 7, 51, 261, 342; Joseph, 193, 250, 261, 294*, 307; Ralph, 146, 193, 225, 250, 346, 378*; Randle, 61; Robert, 174, 193, 239*, 386, 307*, 342, 346, 377; Thomas, 40, 51, 61, 146, 225; William, 307, 377, 413
Belling, John, 217
Bellingham, John, 28. *See also* Billingham
Bellis [Billis], Edward, 259, 269*, 329, 365; John, 268, 329; Joseph, 416; Peter, 263; Thomas, 423; William, 177, 214, 263, 268
Bellward [Belward], John, 337, 363, 378; Peter, 260*, 378, 394*
Bellyn. *See* Bellin
Benison, Thomas, 427
Bennett [Benet, Bennet], Arthur, 54, 241; Charles, 169; Christopher, 135, 344, 377, 381; Daniel, 408, 417; David, 33, 51, 71; Edward, 53, 75, 76, 158, 169, 197, 411; Enoch, 241; Ephraim, 167, 219; Francis, 154; George, 133, 155; Hamnet, 96, 121, 154; Hamon, 51; Henry, 70, 112, 125, 139, 158*, 194, 196, 203, 225*, 238, 291, 308, 316, 326; Henry Ridley, 386; Hugh, 129, 179, 230, 264, 347, 362*; James, 418; John, 5, 48, 90, 106*, 112, 116, 118, 129, 141, 157*, 170, 179, 193, 198, 221, 230, 250, 254*, 258, 264, 268, 282*, 286*, 310, 337*, 338, 344, 355*, 369, 379, 399, 401*, 403, 408*, 411, 418; Joseph, 143, 195, 198*, 202, 250, 260, 264, 300, 335; Miles, 121; Peter, 49, 77, 83, 106, 114, 133, 163, 175, 185, 194, 195, 212*, 428; Raphe, 427; Randle, 30, 110, 130, 148*, 161, 259; Rice, 60; Richard, 63*, 77, 79, 83, 113, 124, 128, 130*, 155, 167, 184, 185, 425; Robert, 71, 110, 135, 161, 167, 221, 425; Samuel, 87, 112, 114, 181, 191, 219, 258*, 291, 408; Samuel Nevitt, 420; Thomas, 29, 31, 61*, 106*, 113, 135, 167, 182, 221, 230*, 233, 260, 264, 268, 273*, 337*, 354, 386, 388, 399, 428*; William, 73, 90, 98, 100*, 111, 115, 116, 121, 131, 134, 135, 140*, 141, 143, 148, 156, 171, 182, 190, 197, 198, 204, 215, 219, 274, 280*, 338; [——], 131
Bennion [Bennyon], Bulkeley, 335; George, 190, 223, 242*, 251, 255, 259, 275, 334, 368; Henry, 237, 316, 333, 335, 352; John, 199, 248*, 251, 319, 338*, 353, 375, 388*; Joshua, 368; Randle, 141, 251, 254*, 338, 355*; Thomas, 199, 237, 251*, 255, 319, 330, 345, 350, 351, 361, 365, 367, 375, 396*, 407; William, 335, 338, 379. *See also* Bannion
Bent, John, 13
Bentley, John, 179, 219
Benyson, Thomas, 427
Berchleye. *See* Birchley
Berdeshyll, Robert, 4
Bernard, Christopher, 119
Bernard, Thomas, 4
Berry, Robert, 84, 107, 427
Berscowe, John, 83
Beswick. *See* Bexwick
Bethell, Benjamin, 372; John, 312; William, 267. *See also* Bithell
Betley, John, 276. *See also* Betteley
Betson, Thomas, 63; William, 77. *See also* Bedson
Betteley, Joseph, 348, 399, 401*; Peter, 399; Richard, 161; William, 131, 161. *See also* Betley
Bettie [Betty], Adam, 148; Andrew, 207*, 301; James, 301
Bevan [Beavan, Beevan], John, 157, 209, 321, 325, 418; Nathaniel, 134, 192, 424; Richard, 178, 248, 307, 323; Samuel, 323; Thomas, 248, 321, 325; William, 285, 307, 376. *See also* Bavin
Bevand, Thomas, 229. *See also* Bavand

Bewley, Richard, 21
Bexwick, Richard, 25 ; William, 23
Bibby, Henry, 214 ; Thomas, 160
Bickerton, John, 120, 133 ; Thomas, 133
Bickley, Geoffrey, 34
Bigg, Robert, 370
Biggens [Biggins], Griffith, 299, 336 ; George, 336 ; John, 232, 299, 315, 336 ; Thomas, 177, 189*, 218, 232, 234 ; William, 234
Bildon, Hugh, 39 ; Robert, 29 ; Thomas, 31
Billinge, Benjamin, 251 ; John, 175, 192* ; Thomas, 192, 226, 230, 240, 242, 270, 280 ; William, 168, 251*
Billingham, Phebian, 177, 194. See also Bellingham
Billington, Fabian, 268 ; John, 255 ; Joseph, 157 ; Richard, 318, 364 ; Samuel, 268 ; Thomas, 136, 152, 162, 355, 363, 367 ; William, 151, 255
Billis, Edward, 365. See also Bellis
Bingley [Byngley], Charles, 228, 318, 320, 344 ; Edward, 276 ; Gabriel, 225 ; George, 178, 349, 398, 402, 411*; John, 16, 26, 59, 72*, 94, 161, 186, 188, 201, 202*, 208, 225, 228, 242 ; Matthew, 136 ; Moses, 196 ; Ralph, 137, 242, 327 ; Randle, 59, 94, 109, 137, 146, 161, 167*, 188*, 196, 202, 227, 231, 242, 263* ; Samuel, 167 ; Thomas, 263, 321, 338, 344, 353 ; Uriah, 188 ; William, 353, 398
Birch, Daniel, 227 ; Joseph, 227 ; Richard, 27 ; William, 362, 385. See also Burch
Birchall, Richard, 128
Birchenhead. See Birkenhead
Birchenshaw [Birchenshagh, Byrchenshagh, Byrchenshaw], Henry, 1 ; John, 1 ; Thomas, 49
Birchley [Berchleye, Bircheley, Byrchley], George, 42, 77, 80 ; Hugh, 80 ; Richard, 77
Bird [Burde, Byrd], Alexander, 425 ; Charles, 196 ; Edward, 72 ; George, 72, 92, 174, 196 ; John, 22, 67, 125, 353 ; Lawrence, 426 ; Ralph, 66, 426*; Richard, 34, 62, 92, 106, 123, 137, 150, 217, 269* ; Thomas, 59, 70, 73, 100, 106*, 112, 114, 137, 315, 425 ; William, 33, 54, 59, 66, 67, 72*, 76, 94, 151, 217, 426. See also Brid
Birkenhead [Birchenhead, Birchened, Birkenhed, Birkhened], Edward, 17 ; Henry, 189 ; John, 25, 30, 70, 216 ; Ralph, 9, 55 ; Robert, 22 ; Thomas, 40, 70, 115, 197, 270
Birth, John, 27, 51, 62 ; Thomas, 62

Birtles, William, 84
Bithell [Bythell], Evan, 196* ; John, 7, 70 ; Ralph, 52, 70 ; Richard, 7, 86. See also Bethell
Blackmore [Blakemore], Edward, 367 ; Francis, 239 ; John, 307 ; William, 194, 264*
Blacon, Edward, 62, 103
Blagg [Blagge, Blag], Ralph, 171, 187, 195, 224 ; Richard, 63, 112
Blake, Nicholas, 387 ; Peter, 73
Blakemore. See Blackmore
Blakey, Peter, 73
Blanchard [Blanshed], John, 37, 62, 68, 75, 98, 99, 112, 114*, 115, 130, 428 ; Robert, 112 ; Thomas, 37, 75 ; William, 42, 123
Bland, Brian, 47
Bleades, Thomas, 370
Blease [Blaze, Bleas, Bles, Blis], Adam, 36, 45, 68, 79 ; Benjamin, 158 ; Christopher, 92, 106, 113 ; John, 429 ; Ralph, 92 ; Randle, 79 ; Richard, 177, 197, 219, 260 ; Robert, 68, 92, 104, 107, 122, 429*; Thomas, 79, 122
Blessinge, Thomas, 133
Blethin [or Plethin], Thomas, 41
Blinston, Edward, 75 ; George, 81 ; Richard, 139
Blith [Blythe], Thomas, 25, 37
Blound, John, 1
Blower, Thomas, 321 ; William, 377
Blundell, William, 129, 145, 151, 154, 159, 229
Blythe. See Blithe
Boden, Ambrose, 386 ; Edward, 370, 389, 390, 392, 398, 401, 408, 412 ; George, 399, 416*; James, 399 ; John, 318*, 323, 353, 356*, 365, 369*, 408, 410 ; Joseph, 408 ; Peter, 323, 399 ; Ralph, 256, 330 ; Richard, 386 ; Robert, 410 ; Samuel, 365, 372*, 386*, 387 ; Thomas, 256, 412 ; William, 387, 401. See also Bowden
Bodvell, Peter, 155
Boidell. See Boydell
Bokeley, William, 18. See also Buckley, and Bulkeley
Bold [Bolde], Hugh, 15 ; John, 1* ; Peter, 342 ; Randle, 3 ; Richard, 3
Bolland, Arthur, 92, 157, 189, 194, 213, 259 ; Brian, 148 ; Bryan, 225*, 265 ; Edmund, 298, 349, 350, 409 ; Henry, 282 ; James, 138 ; John, 35, 184, 200 ; Mathias, 309 ; Richard, 35, 148 ; Samuel, 189, 263*; Thomas, 125, 144, 153, 157, 160*, 200, 212*, 216, 250, 272, 273*, 282, 298, 299*, 409 ; William, 138, 188*, 225, 250
Bolton, Henry, 132 ; Nathaniel, 237,

INDEXES

367; Thomas, 108; William, 108, 181, 237, 367. *See also* Boulton
Boman, Thomas, 15
Bond, Benjamin, 412
Boodle, Edward, 349. *See also* Bootle
Booer, Thomas, 96. *See also* Bore
Boote, John, 140
Boothe, George, 171; John, 95, 148, 162; Lawrence, 309; Rice, 95; Richard, 70, 190; Robert, 125*, 167, 340; Thomas, 55, 133, 169, 191, 260, 309, 313; William, 79, 95, 128, 428
Bootle, Richard Wilbraham, 358; Thomas, 313. *See also* Boodle
Borden, Richard, 235; Thomas, 235
Bore, Daniel, 111; John, 253; Philip, 170, 253; Robert, 121. *See also* Booer
Borrows [Borowes], Joseph, 355; Randle, 82*. *See also* Burrowes, and Burroughs
Bosley. *See* Bozley
Bostock, Charles, 13; Edward, 98; Francis, 193; John, 50, 86, 182, 193, 230, 272; Jonathan, 201, 224, 264*, 292; Mary, 272; Peter, 162, 182, 217, 219, 230; Phillip, 292; Ralph, 25, 61; Randle, 34; Richard, 264; Thomas, 29, 76, 154; William, 61, 74, 217
Boswell, Andrew, 187; Charles, 171, 197*, 209, 269, 300, 335, 368; George, 216, 259, 295, 330*, 343, 376*; John, 209, 291, 293, 324, 326; Richard, 269; Samuel, 324, 363*; Thomas, 343
Boteoyle, Thomas, 106
Botiler [Botyler], Henry, 3; Thomas, 3; John, 6*
Boult, William, 363
Boulton, Henry, 153, 217, 266; Nathaniel, 284, 351; Ralph, 189*; Raphe, 153; Richard, 217, 351; William, 153, 266, 284. *See also* Bolton
Bourne, Thomas, 156
Bowcock, Richard, 210, 298*
Bowden [Bowdon], Edward, 335; George, 368; John, 257, 352, 368; Peter, 257, 335. *See also* Boden
Bowell, John, 8; William, 7
Bowen, James, 341; John, 219, 341
Bower, Foster, 405; James, 11; John, 7; Ralph, 20; Robert, 7, 348*
Bowers, Henry, 409; Robert, 276, 345, 383, 384*; Thomas, 202, 224, 252*, 345, 383*, 409*
Bowes, George, 71
Bowier. *See* Bowyer
Bowker, John, 230, 278; Joseph, 230, 278; Thomas, 186, 202; William, 278
Bowman. *See* Boman
Bowyer [Bowier], Philip, 238; Robert, 238, 303; Thomas, 52
Boxley, Benjamin, 329; Charles, 388; Henry, 256*, 329*; John, 329, 388, 393*
Boyd, William, 393
Boydell [Boidell, Boydle], John, 63, 428; Richard, 26, 49, 50*, 61*, 79; Robert, 79, 123, 428
Boyer, Joseph, 404; Thomas, 86
Boyle, Lord Charles, 342; William, 321*
Bozley, Joseph, 411
Braband, Richard, 63
Brabant, Thomas, 44
Brackley, William, 239
Bradburne [Bradbourne, Bradburn], John, 19; Nathan, 158, 188, 208, 225; Richard, 381; Samuel, 225, 307, 313; Thomas, 19; William, 429
Bradbury, Robert, 314; Thomas, 224
Braddock, Samuel, 221, 281; Thomas, 281
Bradford, George, 364; James, 374; Thomas, 409
Bradley, John, 117, 134; Thomas, 111, 134, 143
Bradshaw [Bradshawe, Bradsha], Edward, 106, 130, 135, 161; James, 161; John, 44, 132, 202; Joseph, 136, 230; Richard, 118, 130, 181; Robert, 9; Roger, 37; Thomas, 106, 172; William, 106, 112, 118, 139, 163, 343
Bramhall. *See* Bromhall
Bramwell, James, 401; John, 339, 415*; Jonathan, 239, 328*, 339, 401
Brandred, Henry, 222; Hugh, 216; Samuel, 172, 222
Brandrett, John, 269, 331*; Jonathan, 393; William, 155
Brandritt, Hugh, 233; John, 233
Brandwood, John, 181
Branie, Robert, 86
Brassy [Brassey], Benjamin, 375; Hamon, 18; Richard, 34; William, 16
Brech, William, 13
Breck, Robert, 188
Breese [Breeze], Richard, 150; Robert, 150
Breides, Richard, 86
Bremes, Nicholas, 46
Brereton [Brerton], Edward, 170, 243, 281; George, 232; John, 98, 178, 281; Joseph, 109; Richard, 165,

INDEXES

232; Roger, 141; Thomas, 142, 243; William, 2. *See also* Brureton
Brerewood [Brerewod, Brerewode], James, 23; John, 14, 19, 59, 98, 102, 325; Peter, 19; Richard, 21; Robert, 14, 19*, 23, 32, 46, 58, 59, 64, 75, 76, 82, 83, 89, 102, 204; Thomas, 42
Brethwood, Josiah, 284; William, 284
Brett, John, 210, 373; Richard, 118, 146, 158, 210
Brewer, Jonathan, 186
Brewster, Richard, 11. *See also* Broster, and Browster
Brian. *See* Brine, and Bryan
Brice, Robert, 210
Brickhill, Hugh, 56
Brid [Bridd], Edward, 34, 54; George, 44; John, 52; Lawrence, 53; Richard, 53; Robert, 24; William, 30, 44*, 53. *See also* Bird
Bridge [Brydge], Benjamin, 236; Charles, 345; Edward, 117, 154, 161, 162, 236, 297; George, 251; Humphrey, 129; John, 131, 134, 154, 191, 268, 297, 354; Ralph, 228; Randle, 121, 146*; Richard, 38, 98, 106, 127, 132, 134, 150, 172, 191, 209, 223, 268; Thomas, 132, 154, 179, 188, 197*, 204, 213, 251, 257, 258, 288, 297*, 303, 338; William, 128, 161, 209, 338
Bridges, Richard, 73, 100*, 429
Bridgewood, Lawrence, 268; William, 268
Briggs [Brigges], John, 391; Thomas, 8
Brine [Bryne], John, 55; Randle, 85; Richard, 37, 43, 51, 61; Robert, 5; Roger, 24, 46, 59, 63, 74; Thomas, 54, 66; William, 135. *See also* Bryan
Briscoe, Edward, 214; James, 320, 368; John, 215, 217, 245, 253, 297, 320, 335, 340*, 363, 395, 397; Lewis, 368; Maurice, 201, 237, 253, 255, 257, 322*; Richard, 157, 303, 321*, 395; Samuel, 263, 374; Thomas, 255, 289, 319, 378, 382; William, 156, 201, 214*, 215, 243, 255, 257, 299, 303, 307, 321, 323, 350, 353*, 378, 382, 397
Briscowe [Briscow], John, 185; Richard, 223; William, 185, 223
Bristoe, John, 299; William, 299
Bristowe [Bristow], John, 103, 163, 218, 232; Peter, 232; William, 147, 218
Brittain, John, 404, 423; Robert, 375, 419
Broadbent, John, 327; William, 327

Broadfeld [Brodfeld], John, 9
Broadhurst, James, 356, 377; Samuel, 412; Starkey, 381
Brock [Brocke], Charles, 190; Edward, 72; George, 169, 252, 359; John, 132, 203, 260, 261, 296; Phillip, 142, 163, 190*, 197, 266; Richard, 180, 190, 243*, 249*, 252, 261, 266, 292, 353, 358, 359; Robert, 35, 65, 72*, 84, 94, 188, 250*, 370; Samuel, 292, 400; Thomas, 197, 261, 296*, 347, 353, 400; William, 72, 203, 250, 269. *See also* Brook
Brodfeld, John, 9
Brodrick, James, 278*
Brome, Robert, 27. *See also* Broome
Bromfield [Bromefeld], James, 107; John, 214; Richard, 45, 414; Samuel, 369, 414; William, 107, 131. *See also* Broomfield
Bromhall, Thomas, 117
Bromley [Bromeley], Edmund, 83; Edward, 113, 124, 133, 168, 235*, 241, 258, 296, 305, 318, 325; James, 296; John, 181, 319; Michael, 137, 168*, 225, 241, 295, 319*, 336, 349, 355, 361; Ralph, 30, 44; Randle, 65; Richard, 44, 96, 335; Robert, 174, 335; Roger, 235; Thomas, 36, 65, 178, 204, 305; William, 133, 168, 216, 258, 335, 349. *See also* Brumley
Brook [Brooke], Adonijah, 254; George, 91; John, 98, 119*, 343; Peter, 309; Pusey, 352; Richard, 254, 342; Thomas, 277, 308; William, 428. *See also* Brock
Brooks [Brookes], John, 284, 310, 326, 351, 364, 379, 394*; Randle, 284, 291; Richard, 47; Samuel, 291, 326
Broome, Thomas, 122; William, 134. *See also* Brome
Broomfield, Richard, 89; William, 89. *See also* Bromfield
Broster, Charles, 135, 166*, 171, 248, 297*, 358, 412; Edward, 90, 185; Hugh, 23; James, 68; John, 126, 177, 408; Peter, 362, 401, 408*, 412*, 415, 417; Richard, 50*, 90, 126, 135*, 145, 147, 177, 258*; Samuel, 135; Symon, 185; Thomas, 126, 248, 347, 358, 362. *See also* Brewster, and Browster
Brotherton, Henry, 102; Joseph, 176, 202
Broue, Robert, 13
Broughall, Samuel, 185
Broughton, Benjamin, 403; Charles, 388; Edward, 115; John, 355, 388, 403; Valentine, 40, 60, 67, 68, 83

INDEXES

Brown [Browne], Andrew, 163; Anthony, 222, 293, 322; Charles, 178, 306, 406; Daniel, 159; Frederick, 333; George, 54, 161, 210, 266, 277, 306, 344, 365, 375, 381, 406; Hans, 260, 266; John, 45, 196, 210, 223, 275, 277, 284, 356*, 371, 386, 391, 397, 399*, 407; Jonathan, 371, 407; Joseph, 354, 374; Lawrence 35, 196; Matthew, 150, 209*, 284*, 359*; Ralph, 196, 227; Richard, 62, 353, 410; Samuel, 312, 318; Thomas, 71, 123, 163, 196, 217, 260, 293, 333, 336*, 356, 361, 362*, 385, 418; William, 27, 39, 146, 150, 311, 322, 346, 352*, 353, 363, 365, 375, 383, 386, 389, 397, 410, 418

Brownet, Christopher, 132, 163; John, 139; Thomas, 173

Browster, Richard, 23. See also Brewster, and Broster

Bruce, John, 275, 335; Richard, 335; Thomas, 63. See also Bruse

Bruen [Bruyn], Andrew, 274; Calvin, 104, 116; Charles, 336; John, 13, 104, 199, 205, 274; Jonathan, 214; Joseph, 122, 234; Lewis. 336; Nathaniel, 234; Richard, 20*, 157; Robert, 21; Thomas, 120, 142, 199; William, 24

Brulle, William, 30

Brumley, William, 180. See also Bromley

Brundrett. See Brandred, Brandrett, and Brandrith

Brureton, Randle, 115. See also Brereton

Bruse, Thomas, 31. See also Bruce

Bryan [Bryen], Joseph, 222; Philip, 304; William, 222. See also Brine

Brydge. See Bridge

Bryne. See Brine, and Bryan

Buck [Bucke], John, 145, 172; Samuel, 113, 136, 145, 148, 152; Thomas, 148; William, 85

Buckley, Charles, 233, 275, 333; Edward, 293, 336, 391; Francis, 296, 297*, 364; George, 233, 375; John, 218, 233, 271, 282, 350, 372, 373, 375; Joseph, 175, 293, 372; Matthew, 219, 220; Matthias, 180; Phillip, 220; Randle, 336, 373; Richard, 408; Thomas, 233, 296, 312, 374; Timothy, 127; William, 185, 271, 312. See also Bulkeley, and Bokeley

Bucksey. See Buxy

Buckton, George, 281

Bulkeley [Bulkley], David, 175; Edward, 205, 390; Francis, 200; George, 7, 9, 112; Henry, 219; Jo., 205; John, 159, 181, 249, 390, 392; Joseph, 205, 227; Matthew, 249; Ralph, Raphe, 156, 200, 246; Randle, 36, 227; Richard, 165; Robert, 178, 223, 239, 312; Samuel, 165; Thomas, 150, 159, 223*, 239, 249; William, 41*, 171, 239. See also Buckley, and Bokeley

Bullen, Nathaniel, 156, 237

Bullock, John, 308; Samuel, 380, 417

Bummer, James, 215

Bunbury [Bunbery], Charles, 276; Dutton, 118; George, 71; (Sir) Henry, 207, 276, 280; Richard, 71, 72; Thomas, 7, 81; William, 216, 280; [——], 81

Bunnell, George, 125, 149; Nathaniel, 166; Ralph, 143, 172

Burch, Benjamin, 256; Daniel, 256. See also Birch

Burchett, Stephen, 245

Burde. See Bird, and Brid

Burgall, George, 277

Burgeny, William, 42

Burgess, Edward, 55; Francis, 130, 191*; Michael, 101; Robert, 26; Thomas, 43, 50*, 62, 108; William, 108

Burgeye, Roger, 6

Burnet, John, 73

Burroughs [Burroughes], Edward, 160*, 164, 193, 201, 289; Henry, 197; James, 219; John, 187, 195*, 219; Owen, 201; Ralph, 148, 187, 194*; Richard, 147, 197, 287*, 289; Robert, 159*; Samuel, 287; Thomas, 194. See also Borrows, and Burrowes

Burrowes [Burrows], Edward, 127, 202*, 264, 278, 296, 361; H——, 369; Henry, 267, 296; Holme. 316, 357, 360; Isaac, 214; John, 156, 253; Joseph, 276, 323; Randle, 214, 316; Richard, 127, 253, 336; Robert, 427; Roger, 116, 427; Samuel, 170, 392*; Thomas, 278, 427. See also Borrows, and Burroughs

Burrs, Roger, 89

Burscowe [Berscowe], John, 83

Burstow, Robert, 35

Burton, John, 45, 66, 95*, 100, 292; Thomas, 292

Bushell [Busshell], Edmund, 369, 384, 423; Ellis, 325; George, 271, 402; Henry, 271, 346, 358; James, 10, 303; John, 18, 129; Richard, 149, 194*, 219, 303*; Samuel, 219; Thomas, 117, 336, 407; William, 41, 336

Butler, Edward, 174, 190, 203; James, 349, 397, 398*; John, 397; Joseph,

275, 352, 373, 400; Samuel, 371, 426; William, 67, 88, 93, 425, 426*
Button, Edward, 65,111,425; Richard, 63; Thomas, 45, 65; William, 111
Buxy [Bucksey], George, 35, 40*, 71, 80; John, 71; Mark, 118; Nicholas, 52, 65; Peter, 52, 74; Richard, 71; Robert, 80
Byngley. *See* Bingley
Byram, James, 428; Richard, 46; Thomas, 428
Byrchenshaw. *See* Birchenshaw
Byrchley. *See* Birchley
Byrd. *See* Bird, and Brid
Byrom [Byrome], James, 9, 93; John, 91; Richard, 91, 93; William, 87
Bythell. *See* Bithell

C

Caddicke, Humphrey, 133; John, 149
Caddocke, Humphrey, 199; John, 124, 160; Robert, 115; William, 156, 199
Cadel, Thomas, 56
Caerlyle. *See* Carlyle
Calcen, George, 180
Calcot [Calcott], Edward, 96, 290; George, 45, 74, 87; John, 155, 210*, 290; Richard, 87, 120; Roger, 38, 46; Thomas, 74, 125
Caldey [Caldy], Richard, 27, 44; William, 27
Caldwall [Caldwell], George, 99; Thomas, 99; William, 15
Calkin, Thomas, 308, 313, 334; William, 49, 238, 313, 380; ——, 308
Callame, William, 24. *See also* Culm
Calley [Callie, Cally, Calye], Edward, 204, 230, 249, 250, 256, 290, 337*; George, 94; Hugh, 33, 71; John, 124, 137*, 152*, 194, 234, 243, 248, 250, 288, 323; Ormson, 215, 284, 332; Richard, 24, 37, 66, 96, 207, 230, 234, 255, 289, 290, 390; Robert, 62; Thomas, 6, 195, 248, 249; William, 35, 49, 194, 195, 255, 274*, 288. *See also* Kelly
Callister, Dannold, 71
Calveley, Calveley, 247, 325; George, 265; Hugh, 194, 247*, 265; James, 247, 347; Ralph, 29, 57, 61, 66
Cane, Adam, 82
Cany, Thomas, 12
Capenhurst, John de, 1
Capper [Cappur], Benjamin, 405; Hugh, 425; James, 227, 337; John, 204; Peter, 308, 337, 369, 389, 396; Richard, 425; Thomas, 364; William, 137, 142, 389
Carden, John, 145; Richard, 9, 111, 122, 145, 180, 249*; Roland, 303; Samuel, 179; Thomas, 9, 49, 67
Caren, Robert, 43
Carey [Cary], Edward, 323; Henry, 256; John, 256, 314
Carigge, Richard, 85
Carlyle [Caerlyle, Carlille], Hugh, 3; John, 5, 11; Richard, 3, 11
Carman, George, 176
Carr [Carre], Christopher, 216; John, 383; Paul, 256; Richard, 222, 236, 256*, 280*, 287, 308, 336
Carrier, Robert, 31*
Carrington [Carington]. Richard, 62, 97; Robert, 182, 195, 201, 224; Thomas, 144, 308; William, 144
Carrok, John, 5*
Carter, Benjamin, 328, 389, 391*; Fulke, 60; Henry, 146; Jacob, 104; John, 11, 32*, 103, 209*, 233, 282, 328, 339, 391; Joseph, 300, 364*, 391, 399, 413; Peter, 351; Richard, 48; Robert, 159, 351; Sefton, 277, 389; Thomas, 51, 59, 68, 104, 146, 219, 246, 260, 277, 282, 285*, 328, 336, 374; William, 212, 246*, 332, 339, 351
Cartmell, Thomas, 119
Cartwright, John, 13, 178, 313, 377; Peter, 263; Ralph, 334, 366; Richard, 316; William, 316, 335, 348, 353
Case, Peter, 97; Richard, 32, 64, 81*, 357, 369, 374, 381, 407, 412; Thomas, 64, 78, 90, 426*; William, 98
Catell, William, 14. *See also* Kettle
Catherall [Catterall], John, 188*, 196, 202; Richard, 36, 72*; Robert, 56; Samuel, 363; William, 106*, 111, 115*, 116, 421
Catterowe, Robert, 90, 91; William, 90, 91
Caulton, Robert, 337, 360
Cauncefeld, Robert, 9
Cause, William, 12
Cave, Richard, 369
Cawdie [Cawdey], Richard, 54, 76; Robert, 76; William, 54
Cawley, Cawley Humberston, 341; John, 212, 251; Jonathan, 273; Joseph, 251, 273; Richard, 275; Robert, 276, 360*, 367; Thomas, 275
Cawllame [Callame], William, 24
Cayne [Cane], Adam, 82
Cellars, Samuel, 136. *See also* Sellers
Chadburn, Stephen, 412
Chaddick, John, 188

INDEXES

Chaddock, Thomas, 225
Chalenor [Calnor, Challoner, Chalner, Chaloner, Chalnor], Christopher, 72, 91; Daniel, 102; David, 40; Edmund, 85, 427; Gitten, 9; Henry, 12; John, 40, 72, 91, 255, 327, 336; Robert, 14, 20, 59, 392; Thomas, 14, 59, 69, 78, 102, 175, 327; Timothy, 214, 255, 327; Titus, 405
Chamber. See Chambre
Chamberlain [Chamblayne, Chamblen], George, 136; James, 18; John, 362; Joseph, 298, 362, 393; Richard, 393; Robert, 34, 136, 149; Thomas, 173, 223, 298
Chambre [Chaumber], John de, 3; William, 10
Chandler, Abraham, 401
Chantrell [Chauntrell], Arthur, 40, 88, 90; John, 95; Paul, 37, 48, 51, 58, 60, 69, 92; Richard, 85, 99; Robert, 88, 102, 104; Roger, 48, 95
Chapman, John, 195, 197, 282*, 327, 351*; Mary, 405; Samuel, 318; Thomas, 146, 195, 212, 327
Charles, John, 419; [——], 413
Charleton, Thomas, 224
Chatterton, Daniel, 357
Chauntrell. See Chantrell
Cheers [Chears], Geoffrey, 207; John, 349; William, 207
Cheshire, John, 384
Chester, Bishop of, 57, 81, 88, 354, 383, 414, 418; Philip, 311
Chesters, Charles, 356; Daniel, 411; John, 408
Chesway, Charles, 192
Cheswis [Cheswiss], John, 113; Thomas, 366
Chetam, John, 24*; Henry, 24
Chetwode [Chetwood], (Sir) John, 362; Richard, 103; William, 233
Chevers, Charles, 372, 400; Edward, 324, 357, 372, 404; Philip, 281*, 324*, 400*; Richard, 311, 400
Child, William, 29
Chipyngdale, Thomas, 15
Cholle, John, 6
Cholmondeley [Cholmeley], Charles, 309, 414; (Earl) George, 272; (Lord) Hugh, 212, 414; Thomas, 347, 358, 414*
Chorlston, George, 19
Chrachley. See Crachley and Critchley
Chrimes, William, 403
Christian, Charles, 152; John, 96; Thomas, 60; William, 35, 60*, 64, 76, 152
Christleton. See Criscilton
Christopher, Richard, 412
Chritchley. See Crachley, and Critchley

Church, Robert, 53
Churton, John, 51; William, 46
Clappam, Edward, 70
Clarke [Clerc, Clerk], Hugh, 12; Isaac, 143; John, 402; Joseph, 172; Maurice, Son of Stephen, the, 1; Nathaniel, 138; Stephen, the, 1; Thomas, 3, 12, 155; William, 3, 11.
Clarkson [Clerkson], Richard, 182, 235*, 292, 298, 332*; Robert, 298
Claver. See Cleaver
Clay, Reginald, 269
Clayton [Cleaton], John, 182, 188*, 212, 219, 247, 301, 412; Mathias, 301; Richard, 340; Thomas, 374; William, 211, 247, 306
Cleak, Samuel, 400
Cleaver [Claver, Cleever], John, 405; Thomas, 27
Clerk, Maurice, Son of Stephen, the, 1
Clews [Clues], James, 216; Richard, 165
Cliffe [Clyffe, Clyff], John, 5, 11; Roger, 235; Thomas, 262*, 235, 283, 364; William, 27
Clifton, Laurence, 218
Clingin, James, 363
Clive [Clyve], Richard, 7
Cload, George, 370
Clough [Cluff], Adam, 267, 271; Henry, 69; Richard, 51; Robert, 271; William, 37, 45*, 69, 72*
Clubbe, Benjamin, 379, 415; Henry, 368; John, 208, 233, 282, 299, 362, 377, 379; Joseph, 208, 275, 299, 362, 368, 381, 416
Clues [Clews], James, 216; Richard, 165
Cluff. See Clough
Clutton, Henry, 288; James, 359, 378*; Thomas, 288
Conson, John, 147; Richard, 147
Coathup, Thomas, 416
Cockaine [Cockayne, Cokaine, Cokayne, Cookaine], Benjamin, 187, 243, 277; John, 213; Nathaniel, 181; William, 172, 195, 203, 212, 277, 306
Coddington, Edward, 114; John, 84, 124, 291; Richard, 45, 91; Robert, 91, 114, 137; William, 291
Coe, Thomas, 156, 168, 179, 205*, 230, 240
Coitmore [Coytmore], Rice, 68; Richard, 82, 311; William, 76
Cokayne. See Cockayne
Coke. See Cooke
Cokeley, Jonathan, 329; Thomas, 329
Coker, William, 190, 210*, 235, 407
Coldocke [Coldok, Couldock], Henry, 331; John, 117; Ralph, 42; Richard,

29, 42, 57, 81*, 82, 116 ; Robert, 82, 121 ; William, 57, 91*, 116, 117
Cole, William, 371, 382, 390, 413*
Colecliffe [Colecligh], John, 229, 291*; Thomas, 230, 322 ; William, 229, 322, 330
Coleclough, Charles, 262 ; Daniel, 360; John, 230, 331, 388* ; Jonathan, 250, 399 ; Joseph, 331, 367*; Josiah, 263 ; Peter, 396 ; Samuel, 208, 230*, 250, 262, 263, 281, 396 ; Thomas, 317, 396 ; William, 317, 367
Coleman. *See* Colman
Coleson, Henry, 212 ; Richard, 261 ; Samuel, 261. *See also* Colson, Coulson, and Cousson
Colley [Collie, Colly], Henry, 125 ; Hugh, 196 ; Humberston Colley, 311 ; Jonathan, 157, 420 ; Richard, 31 ; Samuel, 137 ; William, 73 ; [——], 196
Collier [Coleor], John, 23
Colling, Humphrey, 203
Collins, Humphrey, 229, 237, 263, 293, 294, 395 ; John, 392 ; Samuel, 294, 392, 395 ; Thomas, 293
Colly. *See* Colley
Colman, Peter, 32
Colmashe, Phillip, 29
Colson, Daniel, 159, 183 ; John, 193 ; Richard, 179; Samuel, 176; William, 183. *See also* Coleson, Coulson, and Cousson
Colton, Charles, 420 ; Paul, 94 ; Richard, 75 ; Thomas, 75. *See also* Coulton
Comberbach, James, 210, 275*, 276 ; John, 238 ; Robert, 192 ; Roger, 182, 192, 231*, 328*. *See also* Cumberbach
Comes, George, 76
Cona, Robert, 10. *See also* Connah, and Cunnah
Conally, Matthew, 396*
Congley, Robert, 26 ; William, 25, 52, 56
Conilow, John, 118 ; Otes, 64
Conley, Richard, 38
Connah [Conner], John, 317; William, 419. *See also* Cona, and Cunnah
Conniley, Luke, 108 ; Oates, 108. *See also* Conally, Conley, and Conilow
Consterdine. *See* Costerdyne
Conway [Conwaie], Charles, 197 ; Christopher, 59, 92 ; Frederick, 122; Hugh, 162, 180, 186, 197 ; James, 323, 381; John, 179, 186, 223, 237, 258, 340; John Pugh, 415 ; Peter, 19, 59 ; Richard. 237 ; Thomas. 223, 258, 323, 340; William, 94
Cony, Thomas, 128 ; [——], 128

Conyers, Richard, 421
Cooe, Henry, 93; Richard, 93
Cooile, Richard, 403
Cooke [Cocke, Coke, Cook, Coock, Coocke], Edward, 429 ; Geoffrey, 17, 52, 117; James, 419 ; John, 23*, 37, 74, 97, 117, 336*, 361, 394, 397, 407, 429 ; Jonathan, 140; Joseph, 246 ; Josiah, 176, 227, 229, 241 ; Miles, 103, 130; Nathaniel, 127; Peter, 121 ; Richard, 28, 30, 47, 74, 136, 429 ; Robert, 52, 141, 241 ; Samuel, 173, 220, 234*, 246; Thomas, 63, 110, 114, 220, 227, 288, 338*, 414 ; Tobias, 308 ; William, 87, 229, 255*, 293, 317, 335
Cookson [Cooxen], Charles, 334 ; Thomas, 139
Cooper, Edmund, 305 ; George, 395; John, 269, 273, 305, 370, 382, 419 ; Joseph, 380; Michael, 345, 355, 367, 389, 395; Nicholas, 168, 288*, 357; Nicholls, 232; Phillip, 214, 308*; Richard, 214, 312, 391 ; Thomas, 232, 286, 357, 400, 426 ; William, 141, 142, 345. *See also* Cowper
Coorke, John, 49
Cooxen. *See* Cookson
Cope, Edward, 388 ; John, 334 ; Jonathan, 181; Joseph, 140 ; Richard, 136, 143 ; Thomas, 334, 340; William, 136
Copland, Thomas, 238
Coppock [Coppack], George, 315, 409*; Richard, 359*, 403 ; Thomas, 135, 214, 352, 403
Corbin, John, 252, 278 ; Richard, 100; Thomas, 93, 278, 331 ; William, 93, 134, 252, 382*
Corbishall, Francis, 173
Corbishley. *See* Curbisley
Cordrey. *See* Cowdrey
Corkill, William, 46
Corles, Lawrence, 200, 347, 355, 366 387 ; Peter, 361 ; Thomas, 347 ; William, 355, 378, 387*, 406
Cormishe. *See* Cowmishe
Corne, John, 47, 68
Cornelius, John, 278, 320, 361 ; Peter, 278, 280*; William, 361
Cornell, Daniel, 141 ; James, 35 ; Robert, 11
Corns, William, 388
Cortney, William, 421
Corvell, Richard, 126
Cosson, Richard, 146 ; Thomas, 146
Costerdyne, John, 20 ; William, 33
Cotes, Alexander, 55 ; Peter, 32
Cotgreave [Cotgreve], Benjamin, 171, 307 ; Charles, 388 ; John, 15, 38, 142, 153, 154, 164, 183, 184*, 197,

219*, 228, 290, 291, 307, 312, 320, 331, 338*, 345, 359; Jonathan, 154, 184, 188, 192, 301; Joseph, 192; Peter, 122; Ralph, 207, 228, 291, 388*; Reece, 153; Robert, 143, 184, 197; Samuel, 301; Thomas, 17, 207, 320, 355; William, 26, 42, 64, 67
Cotterell [Cotterill, Cottrell], Charles, 280; Joseph, 280; Peter, 93; Roger, 20; William, 345
Cottingham [Cotyngham], Charles, 261, 326; James, 157, 357*; John, 308; Philip, 76, 95; Richard, 229, 250, 360; Thomas, 6, 180, 204, 234, 250, 261
Cotton, George, 65, 138; Hector, 286; John, 113, 132, 314; Paul, 94; Richard, 45, 94; Robert, 145*, 278; Samuel, 137; Thomas, 130, 169, 234; William, 214, 254*, 278, 286, 340, 342
Coughton, John, 241
Coulson [Couldson], David, 189; Henry, 189, 223; John, 174, 201; Jonathan, 171; Richard, 148; Samuel, 189; Thomas, 201. See also Coleson, Colson, and Cousson
Coulter, Thomas, 426
Coulton, Paul, 123, 131, 427, 428; Peter, 131, 427; Samuel, 374, 392, 406, 412. See also Colton
Courtney, William, 421
Cousson, Henry, 233. See also Coleson, Colson, and Coulson
Coventry, Edward, 84; Thomas, 47, 85; William, 46
Cowap, Richard, 428
Cowdock [Cowduck], Charles, 336, 395; Henry, 286; Hugh, 184, 260*; John, 250, 392*; Richard, 104*, 218, 336, 395; Robert, 168, 218, 263, 276, 327*, 339, 355; Thomas, 162, 199*, 218, 250, 256, 257, 286
Cowdrey, William, 379
Cowen, Henry, 156
Cowes, George, 107; Launcelott, 114; Matthew, 140; William, 107
Cowles, John, 117; Robert, 218
Cowley, Edward, 288; George, 282*, 288; John, 103; Richard, 76; Thomas, 46, 370
Cowmishe, Phillip, 59; Thomas, 59
Cowop, Richard, 428
Cowper, Edmund, 357; George, 46; James, 18; John, 23, 24, 36, 48, 50, 56, 65, 87, 119, 194, 269*, 283; Michael, 382*; Nicholas, 139, 161, 175, 189, 428; Peter, 14, 39, 79, 305; Ralph, 33, 56, 65, 74, 426; Richard, 13, 23, 33, 123; Robert, 25, 44, 69, 75, 79, 95; Roger, 18; Thomas, 43, 74,
124, 128, 152, 153*, 194*, 243*, 283, 357, 426; William, 119, 269, 304, 350. See also Cooper
Cowton, Richard, 34
Coy, Samuel, 283, 359, 364, 385*, 392; Thomas, 283, 392; William, 279*, 283, 352*, 349
Coytmore. See Coitmore
Coz, Henry, 52
Crachley [Chrachley], John, 310; Richard, 346; Robert, 282*, 346; Thomas, 310; William, 245, 311. See also Critchley
Cracknell, John, 124; Thomas, 132
Cradock, William, 33
Cragge, Robert, 10; Thomas, 191*
Crance, Francis, 330
Crancke. See Cranke
Crane, Edward, 293; John, 222, 256, 259, 265, 290, 293, 334, 335, 349, 383; Joseph, 372; Michael, 259; Ralph, 39; Richard, 129, 159; Samuel, 207, 372; Thomas, 259, 290, 335, 354, 371*, 372*, 373, 423; William, 159, 207, 222, 293, 330, 367, 370, 372*, 383, 401
Cranke [Crancke], Edward, 161; Francis, 161; John, 141, 171; William, 81. See also Cronke
Cranwall, Thomas, 211
Cranwell, William, 306
Craven, Daniel, 223, 294, 338*; John, 223, 294, 306, 321*, 419; Thomas, 370; William, 318
Crawford. See Crowfoot
Crewe [Crue], Charles, 309, 369, 378, 398; Edward, 256; John, 104, 113, 276*, 334, 427; Joseph, 325*, 373, Offley, 398; Randle, 28, 193, 325, 398; Randolph, 398; Samuel, 275; Thomas, 193, 256, 334, 369; William, 8, 104, 155, 201, 222*, 293*
Crier, John, 102
Crimes, John, 408
Criscilton, Roger, 12
Critchley [Chritchley], Benjamin, 140, 239, 353; John, 143, 172, 179, 314, 368; Joseph, 353; Raphe, 425; Richard, 102, 358; Thomas, 132, 173, 189, 224*, 239; William, 189. See also Crachley
Crocket, Robert, 29
Crofte, Peter, 5; William, 112
Crofts, Daniel, 124; Edward, 98; John, 118; Joseph, 392; Richard, 392; Thomas, 98, 111, 118, 134; William, 129, 416
Croke. See Crooke
Crompe, Hugh, 53, 122; John, 81. See also Crump

INDEXES

Crompton, Geoffrey, 26; Henry, 145; James, 136; Robert, 194*; Thomas, 136; William, 131, 145*
Cronke, William, 121. *See also* Cranke
Cronry, Simon, 77
Crooke [Croke], George, 189; Jenkin, 9; John, 9, 318; Josiah, 224, 287, 318; Lawrence, 94; Thomas, 336; William, 224, 287, 333
Crookes [Crooks], Edward, 109; George, 109, 227, 249*, 294; John, 102; Lawrence, 104; Ralph, 386; Thomas, 211, 229, 243, 249, 273*, 283, 292, 294, 386; William, 292
Cropper, James, 204; Thomas, 417
Crosby [Crosbie], George, 194; Henry, 78, 139, 180, 183, 194, 241, 262; John, 396; Joseph, 311*, 352*, 368, 373, 398*; Richard, 373; Robert, 178, 226, 262, 368; Samuel, 408; William, 398, 401
Crosley, Robert, 239
Cross [Crosse], Brian, 134; Daniel, 128, 163, 184, 194, 201, 224, 236, 241*; Francis, 333; Giles, 93; Isaac, 155, 193, 209; John, 137, 209, 236, 271, 332, 333*, 371, 379, 419*; Jonathan, 139; Margerie, 193; Peter, 96; Ralph, 23, 63; Richard, 15; Robert, 15, 34, 100, 193; Stephen, 19; Thomas, 19, 94, 110, 115, 116, 139, 177, 224, 238; William, 29, 39, 41, 47, 93, 94, 100, 106, 165, 241, 332, 351*
Crosson, William, 48
Croston, Brian, 112; William, 50
Croughton, Charles, 168, 201, 203, 231, 234, 265, 267*, 270, 273, 279, 332, 355; Edward, 131, 166, 174, 204, 207, 209, 228; Henry, 270, 337; Isaac, 164, 234; John, 93, 125, 136, 149, 164, 168, 209, 244, 277, 288, 335, 337, 351, 356, 364, 387, 402; Michael, 167, 188, 307; Richard, 20, 124; Robert, 273; Samuel, 240, 348; Thomas, 99, 203, 243, 343, 370, 375; Wainwright, 331; William, 33, 39, 87, 124, 131, 164, 167, 198, 231, 248*, 270, 307, 331, 332, 343, 348
Crowfoot [Croefoote], Edward, 138; Joseph, 170
Croxton [Croxon], Daniel, 429; George, 281; Hugh, 168, 281; James, 272, 323, 349; John, 312; Robert de, 1; Thomas, 145, 250; Wareing, 266; William, 18, 172, 178, 250, 266; William de, 1
Crue. *See* Crewe

Crump [Crumpe], Hugh, 100, 102*; John, 132, 168*. *See also* Crompe
Cryer. *See* Crier
Crymes. *See* Crimes
Cudworth, Thomas, 164
Culleigne, Robert, 82
Culm, Arthur, 285, 351, 360, 363*, 364, 390, 392; Benjamin, 310, 351; John, 285, 348, 372*, 392. *See also* Callame
Culmer, Richard, 2
Cumberbach, Roger, 160. *See also* Comberbach
Cummins, Joshua, 397; Josiah, 324; Robert, 324
Cunliffe, Ellis, 317; Foster, 239; Robert, 362
Cunnah [Cunna], William, 406, 412. *See also* Cona, and Connah
Curbisley, William, 100
Curmyne, Guy, 37; G—, 77; Henry, 25; William, 23
Currier, Edward, 65
Cutler, Richard, 57
Cuxton, Arthur, 51

D

Daggott, Thomas, 129
Dainteth. *See* Denteth
Dalby, Dalbie, Edward, 80; Moises, 96; Moses, 107; Thomas, 73, 140
Dale, Humphrey, 77; William, 363
Damport. *See* Davenport
Dandey, John, 216
Daniel [Danyel], John, 309, 344; Nicholas, 4*; Peter, 273; Samuel, 392; William, 392; (Sir) William Duckinfield, 343
Dannald [Dannold, Danold], Christopher, 95, 131, 204; David, 42; Edward, 131, 147; John, 34, 65, 70, 81, 99, 111, 113*, 188, 245; Joseph, 204; Randle, 95, 178, 193; Richard, 46, 70, 113; Robert, 81; Samuel, 190, 229*; Thomas, 46, 95, 99, 102, 123, 128, 156, 165, 166, 188, 189, 204*; William, 44, 95, 113. *See also* Donald
Dannatt [Dannott], Christopher, 159; Edward, 169; John, 225, 295*; Moses, 170, 225; Peter, 331; Samuel, 169; Thomas, 151; William, 331
Danne, Thomas, 13
Dannold. *See* Dannald, and Donald
Dannott. *See* Dannatt
Darby. *See* Derby
Darbyshire [Darbishire, Darbyshier],

INDEXES

Ferdinand, 106; John, 36, 106; Roger, 85
Darlington [Derlington], Arthur, 318; John, 1, 173, 216, 302*; Thomas, 392; William, 383
Darwall, Henry, 91; John, 128; Richard, 30, 44, 64, 97, 117; Robert, 44; Roger, 44, 91; Thomas, 117
Darwell, Charles, 161, 221; Henry, 143; John, 221, 293; Peter, 221, 288, 293; Richard, 284*; Thomas, 152, 178; William, 143, 221
Davenport [Damport, Davemport]. Arthur, 236*; Aquila, 283*, 284, 307, 332; Charles, 366; Edward, 15; Hugh, 198, 426; John, 386; Ralph, 7, 10, 12, 15, 133, 179; Richard, 121, 309, 314, 386; Roger, 31; Samuel, 284; Thomas, 47, 140, 162, 186*, 198, 332; Vivian, 140
David, Edward, 76; Edward ap, 51; Edward ap, Thomas ap, 56; Evan ap, 52; Henry ap, 17; Hugh, 47; Hugh ap, 82; John, 8*, 19; John ap, 63; Lawrence, 8*; Richard, 113; Robert, 39, 57; Thomas, 8
Davidson [Davison, Davyson], Andrew, 369, 381, 405, 416; Charles, 405; John, 7; Robert, 61; Thomas, 411; William, 11, 16
Davie [Davy], Hugh, 27; John, 51 (Rev.), 312; Nicholas, 12; William, 9, 17*, 121
Davies, Ambrose, 369; Anderson, 346, 376; Barton, 273; Benjamin, 208, 236, 280, 394; Charles, 415; Daniel, 222; David, 198, 302; Edward, 99*, 173, 200, 202, 219, 220, 230, 247*, 281*, 299, 303, 305*, 325, 328, 370, 394, 423; Francis, 344; Hugh, 238; Humphrey, 280; John, 101, 114*, 124, 129, 136, 139, 162, 169, 174, 181, 184, 193, 194, 196*, 199, 200, 201*, 208, 216, 224*, 235*, 236, 240, 242, 247, 250, 256*, 258, 260, 262, 263, 264, 288, 299, 302, 307, 316, 318*, 328, 330, 344, 350, 352*, 359, 363*, 369, 371, 373, 376, 379, 381, 383, 395, 406, 407, 408, 409, 416, 417, 419; Joseph, 208, 286, 299, 365*, 402; Peire, 146; Peter, 342, 361; Pierce, 412; Ralph, 84, 139, 162, 204, 208, 427; Randle, 138; Richard, 145, 148, 184, 200, 371; Robert, 116, 181*, 241, 245, 266, 314*, 321, 338, 375, 410; Roger, 86, 273; Rowland, 69; Samuel, 185, 199, 202, 223, 238*, 244*, 247, 287, 308, 311, 348, 359*, 363, 368, 369, 372, 376, 391, 408, 416, 417; Solomon, 193; Thomas, 95, 123, 142, 145, 156, 175, 193, 199*, 202, 214, 215, 219, 229, 239*, 247, 250, 269, 277, 280, 281, 307, 308, 312*, 319, 321, 328*, 338, 346, 350, 352, 355, 363*, 373, 378, 397*, 400, 419; Timothy, 136, 262; William, 121, 153*, 186, 224, 240, 262*, 321, 363, 365*, 368, 391, 410, 414*, 419, 421*
Davison. *See* Davidson
Davy. *See* Davie
Dawby, Edmund, 44, 67; Richard, 44, 46*
Dawson, Charles, 289; Henry, 326; James, 92; John, 132, 159, 178, 404, 415, 423; Jonathan, 167, 223; Josiah, 173; Parry, 258; Perry, 217*, 346*, 407, 410*; Peter, 83; Robert, 121; Roger, 289, 363; Thomas, 55, 103, 140, 332*; William, 82, 103, 223, 407
Daxon, Edward, 201, 211; John, 201; William, 211. *See also* Dickson
Day, Robert, 312
Dayley, Timothy, 353. *See also* Dealey
Dayner, Richard, 15
Deadwood. *See* Dedwodde
Dealey, Timothy, 403*. *See also* Dayley
Deane, Benjamin, 145; Charles, 281; Edward, 195; George, 426; Hugh, 415; John, 47, 72, 103*, 148, 178, 194, 376; Nathaniel, 135, 190*, 260*; Ralph, 195; Richard, 33, 60, 82*, 124, 148, 390, 429; Robert, 113, 428; Samuel, 135, 168*, 210, 212, 281; Thomas, 14, 47, 48, 49, 54, 59, 60, 90, 98, 99, 106, 114, 121, 145, 185, 199, 203, 209, 218*, 220, 243, 273, 369*; Timothy, 158, 209; William, 90
Dedwodde, John, 8
Deeley. *See* Dayley, and Dealey
Delahey, John, 25
Delamaine, John, 163
Denevet, David, 78; Evan, 41
Denman, Thomas, 376
Dennall, Samuel, 222
Dennell, Joseph, 229, 333
Dennett. *See* Dannatt
Dennill, John, 338; Joseph, 283, 304*, 315, 338; Samuel, 256, 265, 294, 309; William, 294
Dennis, William, 406
Denson, George, 249; John, 154*, 169, 265*, 268, 336, 383; Joseph, 169, 200, 272; Richard, 121, 154*, 200, 272, 379; Robert, 119, 136, 154, 408; Thomas, 19, 85, 130, 153,

182, 249, 268, 407, 415; William, 34, 53
Denteth, Robert, 143*, 163, 213*
Denton, Alexander, 192*, 230, 241, 270, 301*; Arthur, 301; Samuel, 275
Denwall, Humphrey, 115; Robert, 118; William, 66, 83, 87, 99, 100, 118
Derby, Charles, Earl of, 156; Elizabeth de, 2; William de, 2; William, Earl of, 211
Derlington. *See* Darlington
Dewe, David, 3
Dewsbury [Dewesbury, Dewsbery, Dewsburie], George, 102; James, 188, 224, 255, 264, 284, 288; John, 52, 65, 76, 102, 111, 170, 187, 217, 219, 222, 225, 255, 262*, 296, 353; Nathaniel, 352, 380*; Peter, 131; 268, 353, 354; Richard, 111, 131, 138, 148, 178, 195, 218, 221, 225, 245, 262, 289, 352, 353, 380; Thomas, 86, 148, 188, 218, 264, 353; Titus, 184, 225, 265, 268
Diason, Hugh, 301; John, 301; Samuel, 301. *See also* Dyason, and Dyson
Dicas [Dicus], Charles, 240, 318, 357, 367; George, 80, 249; John, 23, 222, 240, 318*, 326*; Ralph, 54; Randle, 166, 232, 318, 343*; Richard, 80, 139, 185, 193, 211, 249; Samuel, 222, 232, 318, 355; Thomas, 371; William, 166, 203, 211, 318, 348, 369*, 371, 376
Diccon [Dycon, Dykyn], John, 5; Nicholas, 6
Dickens, John, 378; Joseph, 378; Thomas, 351, 378
Dickenson, Richard, 115, 130; Thomas, 130, 149, 362
Dickley, Thomas, 20
Dickson [Dixon], James, 370; John, 378, 395; Robert, 342, 354, 378; Thomas, 342, 375, 405. *See also* Daxon
Dillon, Bartholomew, 360
Dimelo, George, 370
Dimmock. *See* Dymocke
Dio, William, 15
Ditchfield, Lawrence, 78
"Do," William, 81
Dobbe [Dob], Hamnett, 246, 320, 344*, 385*; James, 264, 278*, 359; John, 33, 98, 173, 177, 211, 222, 257, 259, 260, 291*, 311; Jonathan, 222; Joshua, 291; Richard, 129, 267; Robert, 184; Samuel, 170, 267, 320; Thomas, 21, 40; William, 200, 359

Dobbs, Richard, 167
Dobson, William, 137
Doby, Richard, 38
Dod [Dodd], Benjamin, 190; Charles, 235, 297; Daniel, 384; Edward, 81, 164, 304, 309; Griffin [Gruffin], 29, 60, 70, 89; Hugh, 70, 138, 171; John, 81, 89, 94, 118, 223, 406, 416; Joseph, 179; Joshua, 235, 297; Owen, 258*; Ralph, 42, 73; Randle, 62, 89, 342; Richard, 54, 72, 107, 195; Robert, 55; Sarah, 158; 223; Thomas, 48, 94, 128, 161, 195, 304, 342, 409; Thomas Crewe, 409; William, 23, 31, 37, 40, 42, 53, 60, 67, 87, 107, 140, 154, 309*, 315, 407
Doe, James, 187, 248; Richard, 141, 187, 214, 248; Thomas, 316, 341
Dolbie [Dolbye], Edward, 125; Moses, 128, 260
Doley, William, 141
Domvyle, Randle, 21
Donald [Downald], John, 7; William, 9. *See also* Dannald
Done, John, 30, 221; Phillip, 90; Ralph, 60, 182, 221; Samuel, 181, 266; William, 98, 266. *See also* Donne
Donne, Richard, 7
Doole, John, 74
Doughty, Henry, 421
Douglas [Duglas], Richard, 36
Dowby, William, 52
Downes, John, 107; Lancelot, 120; Phillip, 230, 329*; Robert, 259; Sarah, 230; William, 107
Downham [Downeham, Downam], James, 73, 95, 111; Peter, 156; Ralph, 141, 159; Robert, 126; Thomas, 111
Downton, Richard, 29
Doyle, John, 361
Drake, John, 350
Draycote, Roger de, 2*
Drew, Robert, 165
Drihurst, Richard, 69
Drinkwater [Drinckwater], Charles, 220; John, 62, 102; Jonathan, 257; Nathaniel, 128, 156; Peter, 77, 110, 118, 427, 429; Robert, 110; Thomas, 110, 137, 257; William, 102, 120, 118
Duccar, William, 47
Duckers, John, 417
Duggan, Thurstan, 117
Duke, Andrews, 239, 295, 323, 381; Bartholomew, 237, 333, 388; Joseph, 381; Mr., 356; Richard, 303, 398; Samuel, 338, 389, 398; Thomas, 18, 228*, 237, 239, 303*, 317, 333, 338, 388, 389, 400, 401*, 405

INDEXES

Dunbabin [Dunbaben], Peter, 177, 246; Richard, 246; Thomas, 221, 230, 313
Dunbavin, John, 182; Thomas, 183
Dunderdale, Thomas, 16; William, 16
Dunham, Geoffrey, 4
Dunne. *See* Donne
Dunstan, Joseph, 210
Durbar, John, 307; Thomas, 287*
Dutton, Charles, 395; Edward, 59, 87, 101, 109, 114, 312; Foulk, 16, 21, 27, 30, 42; Henry, 84, 365; Jacob, 359; John, 42, 114, 115, 201*, 209, 253, 263, 276, 277, 288*, 295, 326, 343, 353, 354, 384, 395, 408*; Jonathan, 204, 265, 277; Joseph, 209, 238, 253; Peter, 15, 341*; Ralph, 145, 160, 263, 295, 353; Richard, 28, 40, 46, 59, 109, 113, 365, 420*; Robert, 30, 306, 359*, 365, 395; Roger, 384, 412; Samuel, 382; Thomas, 128, 142, 170, 270, 276, 306, 318, 325, 365, 395; William, 101, 153, 265, 270
Dyas, Thomas, 111
Dyason, John, 306; Richard, 203, 306; Samuel, 203, 307; William, 307. *See also* Diason, and Dyson
Dycas, Daniel, 173; George, 158; Richard, 158; Samuel, 165
Dycon. *See* Diccon
Dye, John, 4; Ken, 4; Richard, 4; Thomas, 4
Dyerson, Richard, 157
Dyke, Henry, 5; John, 387; Thomas, 423
Dykyn. *See* Diccon
Dymocke [Dimmocke], Anthony, 118; David, 64; George, 113; Humphrey, 134; John, 314; Randle, 101; William, 26, 43*, 101, 113, 134
Dyson, Henry, 326; John, 232, 338, 399; Joseph, 179, 212*, 232, 283, 337, 349, 352, 375, 399; Thomas, 212. *See also* Diason, and Dyason

E

Eakin, Christopher, 187; Rowland, 113, 176
Eakins, Christopher, 245
Eardley. *See* Erdeley
Earle, Adam, 127
Earnshaw. *See* Ernshaw
Easom, John, 315
Eason, James, 240*
Eaton, Charles, 23; Edward, 91, 129, 163; George, 177, 267, 310, 323, 349, 356, 377, 395, 426;

Gilbert, 83, 102, 105*, 112, 114, 115, 205; Helen, 323; John, 31, 32, 59, 61*, 63, 377, 426, 429*; Joseph, 203; Nathaniel, 173*; Obadiah, 148; Randle,34; Richard, 38, 172, 175, 265, 334; Robert, 33; Roger, 265, 334*, 336; Samuel, 169; Thomas, 23, 61, 77*, 83, 99, 112, 115*, 119, 125, 336, 405, 427; William, 46, 99. *See also* Eton, and Eyton
Eccles, James, 55; John, 312
Eccleston, John, 99; Richard, 122; Thomas, 335*
Eddes, William, 110
Eddowes, Nathan, 172; Ralph, 382
Edge, Andrew, 394; Edward, 149, 217, 288, 333; Humphrey, 288, 333; James, 310; John, 351, 367, 388; Ralph, 51, 103*, 166, 167, 287; Randle, 174; Samuel, 287, 394; Thomas, 138, 217, 288*, 356, 388; William, 112
Edgesley, Francis, 179
Edmond, Robert, 67
Edmonds, John, 376; Richard, 84; Thomas, 70
Edmondson [Edmundson], John, 415; Joseph, 418; Robert, 124; William, 362, 415, 418
Edson, John, 387
Edward, David, 24, 73; John, 114; Robert, 64; Thomas, 16
Edwards, Ambrose, 164; Cadwallider, 115; David, 87, 155; (Sir) Francis, 312; George, 397; Griffin, 92, 261; Griffith, 133; Henry, 99, 177; Hugh, 413; Humphrey, 339; Jeffrey, 324, 357, 372*, 386, 397; John, 32, 81*, 83, 92, 110*, 119, 122, 226, 244, 277, 278, 323*, 353, 354, 357, 363, 377, 393*, 410, 415; Jonathan, 139; Joseph, 376; Kadwallader, 102, 108; Moyndeg, 324; Owen, 223; Peter, 117, 119, 133, 172*, 175, 186, 190, 261; Richard, 123, 229*, 281, 339, 383, 422, 423; Robert, 49, 265, 285; Samuel, 190; Thomas, 38, 138, 177, 181, 240, 245, 300, 340, 344, 353, 356, 360, 404, 405, 410, 416*, 419, 424; William, 62, 101, 104, 118, 119, 127*, 130, 153, 240, 278, 285, 309, ·343, 364, 374, 397, 423*, 429
Egerton, John, 212, 270, 309*, 313, 342, 345*, 346, 350, 359, 410; Phillip, 309, 315, 350, 407, 410; Ralph, 57; Thomas, 57, 58, 270; Thomas Willoughby, 407
Elcocke, Epham, 176; Francis, 310,

II.   Q

341; John, 129, 208, 250*, 288; Samuel, 129
Ellaby, John, 408
Ellam [Ellom, Ellome], Henry, 4; John, 18; Ralph, 73; Thomas, 35, 48; [——], 6
Ellames [Ellomes], Hugh, 14; Pattison, 359, 381, 383, 411; Peter, 227*, 311, 325*, 359, 411; Richard, 280
Elliott, George, 421
Ellis [Ellice], Anne, 144; Benjamin, 412; David, 95; Edward, 203, 261, 283*, 294; Griffith, 389; Henry, 322; Humphrey, 73; John, 86, 172, 181, 247, 261, 338, 343, 371, 374, 389, 394, 408, 412; Joseph, 224, 328*; Matthew, 158; Owen, 45, 95, 114, 133, 145*, 166, 182*, 201*, 261; Peter, 408; Richard, 391; Robert, 170, 201, 224, 247, 322, 340; Samuel, 414; Thomas, 24, 133, 144, 178, 247*, 289*, 308, 421; William, 86, 207*, 236, 294
Ellison, William, 286
Elliston, John, 163
Ellock, William, 163
Ellom. *See* Ellam
Ellson, Charles, 417; James, 388; John, 226; William, 226
Elrington, John, 318
Eltoft, John, 360, 418; William, 418
Ely, John, 375
Eminall, Richard, 262
Emley, Alexander, 255; Thomas, 255
Englefeld, John, 72. *See also* Inglefield
English. *See* Inglish
Ennion. *See* Annion
Enowe, Anthony, 56
Ensdale, John, 168, 186; Robert, 427
Erdeley, Richard, 14, 19; William, 19
Ernshaw, Abraham, 284; John, 284
Esalls [Asalls], Aaron, 185
Eton, Charles, 11; Robert, 7*. *See also* Eaton, and Eyton
Evan, Kenrick ap, 76
Evans, Alexander, 286; Ambrose, 215, 296; Charles, 393; David, 52, 90*, 91, 106, 162, 262, 320, 377, 422*, 425, 429; Edward, 129, 275, 276, 296, 334*, 382, 420, 425; Evan, 181; Gabriel, 364; Griffin, 58; Henry, 122; Hugh, 45; James, 140, 173, 398; John, 144, 313*, 320, 334, 341, 349, 379, 411, 415; Matthew, 45; Morgan, 144; Richard, 149; Robert, 36, 46, 50, 62, 106, 152, 360, 381, 398, 401; Thomas, 123, 255, 275, 334, 355, 359, 367, 378, 389, 398*, 402, 422; Vincent, 362; William, 355, 422. *See also* Avons
Evanson, Richard, 54
Evered, William, 310
Ewede, James, 302; Roger, 163. *See also* Yewd, and Youd
Ewley, Hugh, 49; Robert, 49
Ewlowe, John de, 2; Randle, 41
Eyton, George, 138; Gilbert, 137; Kenrick, 330*; Nathaniel, 138; Samuel, 128; Thomas, 309; William, 138, 172. *See also* Eaton, and Eton

F

Fairbrother, Edward, 369
Faircliff, John, 17
Fairclough, George, 404; Thomas, 368
Falconer, Thomas, 402; William, 308, 357, 402
Falker, Francis, 265
Falkner. *See* Faulkner
Fallowes, Thomas, 25
Falynbron, Robert, 5
Farrall, John, 427
Farbour. *See* Furbarr
Farrar, Edward, 96; John, 57, 174
Farrell, Edward, 323
Farrington [Farington, Faryngton], Charles, 262; Edward, 7; Hugh, 301; James, 224; John, 235; Jonathan, 127; Randle, 105; Robert, 61, 94, 105, 126, 172, 185, 235, 248, 262, 269, 301, 302; Samuel, 178, 228, 302; Thomas, 94, 112, 248, 353, 371, 428; William, 181, 224, 228, 269, 272, 353
Farshaw, William, 181. *See also* Forshall
Faulke, Randle, 156
Faulkner [Faulkener], Isaac, 234, 293, 308; James, 403; Joseph, 424; Simon, 399; Thomas, 363, 414; William, 293, 359, 422*
Fazakerley [Phasackerley], Edward, 91; George, 123; John, 74, 102; Joseph, 78; Robert, 48, 71, 78*, 121; Roger, 74*; Samuel, 132; William, 102
Fearnell, Evan, 200; Francis, 128, 156, 264; George, 168, 207, 221*; John, 121, 158, 198*, 200*, 226, 360, 415; Nathaniel, 183; Randle, 89; Robert, 126, 264, 318*, 346*, 400*, 421*; Samuel, 226; Thomas, 171, 194, 200, 346. *See also* Fernall
Feilding. *See* Fielding

INDEXES 449

Fells, Henry, 72
Femey, Robert, 35
Fenton, Henry, 6, 12; Hugh, 5; John, 6, 12; Ralph, 220; Thomas, 6
Fernall, Richard, 429; Rondull, 429. *See also* Fearnell
Fernihaugh [Fernaugh, Fernough], George, 98; John, 78, 182, 218; Phillip, 272; Randle, 71; Thomas, 127, 172*, 182, 218; William, 174, 190, 191, 202, 218*
Feror [Ferrour], David, 8; Thomas, 8, 12
Fichecale-hill, Edward, 98
Fichet, Thomas, 8
Fielding [Feilding], Bernard, 211, 272; William, 272
Figes, Arthur, 85, 100, 131, 427
Filkin, Samuel, 210
Filston, Robert, 25
Finch, Robert, 17
Finchett [Finchatt, Finchet, Fynchet], Henry, 26, 37, 74; James, 251; John, 94, 165, 207, 251, 252*, 280, 294, 304, 372, 401, 402*; Joseph, 372; Ralph, 51, 92, 94, 104, 157, 426; Randle, 101, 428; Richard, 74; Robert, 294; Thomas, 160, 280, 304, 401
Finley, John, 87; Thomas, 87
Finlow, George, 165, 187; John, 120, 129, 136, 158; Robert, 129; Samuel, 156, 228*; Thomas, 34, 64; William, 174
Finney, Benjamin, 364, 422; John, 422
Fisher, Edward, 116*, 121, 134, 251; Hugh, 13; John, 35; Joseph, 168, 251; Michael, 282; Ralph, 23; Richard, 31, 36, 134, 165; Robert, 23, 28, 52, 297, 321, 426; Roger, 295; Thomas, 25, 30, 49, 51, 58, 83, 94, 98, 111, 116, 157, 216, 426, 428; William, 83, 126, 270, 427
Fitchett, Matthew, 320
Fithian, John, 211, 280. *See also* Phithian
Fitton [Fytton], Charles, 84, 110, 118, 426; Edward, 91, 102, 123; John, 42, 68, 71, 76, 91*; Nicholas, 2; Thomas, 118
Fitzgerald, James, 387; Joseph, 336, 387; Patrick, 300, 336; Peter, 337; Richard, 300, 367
Fleete, John, 112, 113, 119; Peter, 137; William, 87, 112
Fleming, John, 385, 388; Thomas, 81
Fletcher, Aldersey, 321; Charles, 107, 286, 306, 343, 365; Edward, 122; George, 111; Hugh, 59; James, 15, 75, 100, 107, 111*, 132, 274, 353,

365, 399*, 402*, 428; John, 35, 66, 69, 75, 92, 111*, 115, 116, 118, 132, 140, 142, 143, 147, 155, 162*, 169, 170, 183, 184*, 238, 248*, 256, 286, 288, 310, 399, 428*; Lawrence, 92, 96, 127, 169; Orlando, 343; Peter, 37, 46, 48, 73, 118, 147, 428; Ralph, 62, 104*; Richard, 39, 70, 75, 99, 106*, 107, 111, 136, 161, 179, 427; Robert, 69, 85, 86, 99, 109*, 116, 118, 119, 132, 141, 147, 150, 190, 215, 274, 286, 399, 418, 427; Samuel, 155, 172, 180, 184, 238, 321; Thomas, 15, 18, 28, 37, 43*, 47, 71, 78, 79, 86, 99, 105, 106, 111, 115, 119, 120, 143, 168, 170, 183, 228, 235*, 238; Valentine, 87; William, 15, 16, 18, 23, 29, 30, 31, 37, 43*, 44, 45, 46, 47*, 61, 75, 79, 87*, 91, 95, 99, 109, 110, 115, 138, 141, 161, 173, 306, 365
Flint, Gilbert, 399
Flowers, David, 113; George, 64, 113
Floyd, John, 33. *See also* Lloyd
Foepel, Wolrad, 407
Fogg, Lawrence, 276
Folloyn, James, 30
Foote, Gower, 308
Ford, Richard, 318
Foreackers, Christopher, 290*
Formby [Formeby, Forneby, Fornibie, Forniby], Frances, 127; Richard, 7, 166
Formstone, John, 394
Fornibie. *See* Formby
Forrest, Alexander, 361, 406*; James, 415; Joseph, 365
Forrester, Archibald, 286; Henry, 395; John, 286
Forshall, Edward, 262; William, 155, 262. *See also* Farshaw
Forster, Ralph, 58; Robert, 17; William, 67
Fossey, John, 315
Foster, Elias, 263, 339; John, 132; Ralph, 29, 162; William, 58, 263, 339
Fothergill, George, 355
Foulke. *See* Faulke
Foulkes, Charles, 245; David, 193; Edward, 226, 305*, 375; Ellis, 193; 250; Hugh, 245; James, 310; John, 181, 250, 273, 306, 338, 417; Joseph, 367; Owen, 423; Peter, 375; Randle, 214, 251, 302, 306; Robert, 283, 302, 308, 338, 424; Samuel, 283; Thomas, 174, 251, 290*; [——], 338
Fovell, William, 155
Fox [Foxe, Foxse], Edward, 174; Henry, 14; Ignatius, 271; James,

405; John, 157, 162, 172, 180, 374; Lawrence, 21; Richard, 175; Thomas, 4, 41, 175, 199, 238*; Walter, 27
Foxall, John, 48, 59; Randle, 59; Robert, 54, 65
Foxcroft, George, 20
Foxley, Daniel, 255; Richard, 47; Samuel, 255
Framall [Frammall, Fromall], John, 92*; Thomas, 97; William, 26
Framway [Fromway], John, 16, 55; William, 16
France, Charles, 329; Thomas, 272, 329
Frances [Francis, Fraunces, Frauncis, Fraunceys], Benjamin, 265; Charles, 357, 377, 406, 415; David, 129; John, 20, 57, 75, 94, 99*, 101, 134, 241, 242*, 299, 331, 368, 389; Nicholas, 11; Richard, 62, 94, 134, 135, 146, 265; Robert, 99; Roger, 331; Thomas, 79, 415; William, 6, 84, 214, 239*, 280*, 352*, 406; [——], 318
Fregret, John, 4; William, 4
French, George, 308, 369, 378, 386*; John, 281; Joshua, 281; Thomas, 179, 180, 210, 351; William, 351
Frer, Hugh, 4
Frith, Richard, 365; William, 365
Frodsham [Froddesham], Henry, 212*, 307; John, 356; Peter, 277; Ralph, 5; Robert, 307; Thomas, 277
Fromall. *See* Framall
Fromway. *See* Framway
Frost, William, 219, 279, 312
Fryer. *See* Frer
Fulin, John, 39
Fulloon. *See* Folloyn
Furbarr [Farbour, Furbur], Jonathan, 384; Robert, 87; Thomas, 12
Fytton. *See* Fitton

G

Gaiton, Daniel, 116
Gamon, John, 242, 325, 350*, 406, 411; Jonathan, 311; Richard, 209, 261, 321; Thomas, 357*, 411*, 418; William, 242, 261, 325, 379*, 406, 418. *See also* Jaman
Gamull, Andrew, 101; Charles, 157; Edmund, 54, 62, 79; Francis, 111, 116, 164; Richard, 186; Thomas, 84, 155, 192, 276, 428; Valentine, 155; William, 79, 95, 101, 105*, 112, 155, 186, 192, 210, 305*, 425, 428*
Gardner [Gardiner], Christopher, 91; Henry, 150; James, 407; John, 56, 104, 119; Robert, 248; Thomas, 50, 70, 119, 150, 261; Timothy, 202, 248, 259, 261, 305*
Garfield [Garfild], John, 102, 122; Richard, 63, 102; William, 33, 80
Garland, Stephen, 172
Garner, John, 85, 402; Joseph, 411; Matthew, 418
Garnett, John, 85, 108, 428; Thomas, 428; William, 56
Garrard. *See* Gerrard
Garrat [Garrot], George, 29; Hamnett, 359; Harwar, 358, 373; Randle, 123; Richard, 26; Thomas, 358; William, 66, 130, 409
Garsey, Nicholas, 80
Gascoyne, Richard, 426
Gaskin, Richard, 113; Thomas, 113
Gastrell, Edward Peregrine, 308; (Rev.) Francis, 343; Peregrine, 308
Gatcliffe, Peter, 237; William, 237, 283. *See also* Gatliffe
Gateley, Ellis, 225
Gatgley, James, 12
Gatley, George, 390*
Gatliffe, Jo—, 112. *See also* Gatcliffe
Gaulter [Gawlther], James, 188; John, 184, 188, 211, 255, 266, 343*; Lawrence, 192*, 208; Richard, 85; William, 201, 208, 266. *See also* Gwalter
Gaulton, Thomas, 384. *See also* Gorton
Gaunt, Henry, 2; Richard, 2
Gawen, Lucas, 272
Gawne, Thomas, 102; William, 120
Gayton. *See* Gaiton
Geary, George, 315*, 375
Gee, Edmund, 28; Henry, 20, 22
Gell, Francis, 202. *See also* Gill
George, John, 369
Gerrard [Garrard, Gerarde], Charles, 187, 207, 241*, 277; Cuthbert, 60; Davies, 240; Gilbert, 60, (Sir), 67, 67; James, 191; John, 96; Joshua, 191; Mary, 204; Nicholas, 14; Peter, 14, 204; Samuel, 138, 152, 187, 207, 277; Thomas, 207, 274*, 307; William, 30, 47, 60*, 67, 239
Gervis, Robert, 181; Samuel, 175, 194. *See also* Jervis
Gest, Henry, 74; John, 48, 57, 68; Richard, 55; Roger, 45, 68, 74*; Thomas 31; William, 59, 66, 73. *See also* Gueste
Gethley, George, 346; Matthew, 256, 346; Thomas, 256
Gibbon, William, 117
Gibbons, John, 142, 183, 358; Peter, 225; Thomas, 122, 151*, 183, 194,

INDEXES

225, 226, 263, 267; William, 194, 239

Gibson, Daniel, 409; Francis, 363; Michael, 398; William, 364, 394

Giell, William, 47

Gilbert, Daniel, 124; James, 204, 211*, 295*, 335; Joseph, 335, 399; Thomas, 99, 134*, 295

Gilbody, Abner, 305; Hamlet, 305; Jonathan, 218, 305*

Gill, Charles, 362, 377, 396, 412; Christopher, 266, 280*, 330, 339, 347, 348, 354, 364, 366; Edward, 39, 149; George, 364; Henry, 185, 232, 239*; James, 404; John, 43, 132, 399; Joseph, 159; Peter, 260; Richard, 123, 124, 130, 149; Robert, 50; Roger, 3, 312, 390; Thomas, 43, 159, 170, 183, 220, 235, 244, 260, 271, 278; William, 285, 362, 399. *See also* Gell

Gillam, Foulk, 76; Gesper, 51; Hugh, 21; Luke, 143*, 151; Robert, 151; Thomas, 21, 76, 97

Gilson, Edward, 79

Girdler, William, 145*

Gitten [Gitton], James, 33; Richard, 43, 57*; William, 22, 73; [——], 22. *See also* Gutten

Gittens, Richard, 35. *See also* Gyddinges

Glasior [Glaseor, Glascour], Henry, 47; Hugh, 76, 86; James, 38, 347, 357; Thomas, 28; William, 19, 28, 38, 54

Gleave. *See* Gleive

Glegg [Gleg, Glegge], Edward, 226; John, 35, 404, 425; Robert, 237; Silvan, 115; Thomas, 87, 134; William, 100, 114, 128, 134, 226, 243

Gleive, John, 10

Gleyse, William, 17

Glidall, Robert, 9

Glover, Benjamin, 266, 309; Edmund, 241; George, 280, 356; John, 37, 280; Randle, 85; Richard, 41; Robert, 50, 85; Roger, 21; Thomas, 309; William, 66

Glyne, John, 2, 65; (Sir), 310; William, 68, 82

Goddman [Godeman, Godemon], Adam, 41; Hamon, 14; Richard, 10, 11, 16*; Robert, 14; William, 5, 14*, 19. *See also* Goodman

Godfrey, William, 141

Godlof, Francis, 39

Godwin, Arthur, 220; Henry, 220. *See also* Goodwin

Goff, John, 377, 404, 415; Robert, 415. *See also* Goughe

451

Golborn [Golborne, Golburn, Goulborn], George, 257; James, 355; John, 90, 156, 168, 190, 202, 274, 276, 302*, 330, 333, 357, 405; Noah, 227, 291, 331; Ralph, 50, 90, 99; Richard, 119, 166, 227, 257*, 259, 274; Robert, 63; Thomas, 14, 166, 202, 278, 291, 317, 386, 393; William, 31, 99, 317

Golbornes, John, 179

Golding [Goulding], James, 171, 337, 353, 372*, 381; John, 234, 267, 289, 339; Mary, 191; Peter, 314; Richard, 191, 216, 234*, 255, 259, 260, 262, 285, 289, 294, 391, 393, 396; Thomas, 317; William, 381. *See also* Goolding

Goldson [Gouldson], Francis, 131; John, 127, 253, 311; Jonathan, 127, 199, 224, 243*, 253, 255, 258, 262, 286, 307 332*

Goodacre [Goodaker], Joseph, 265; William, 184, 265, 302*

Goodicar, Robert, 83

Goodman [Gudman], Adam, 21, 36; Christopher, 55; Elizabeth, 41; Hugh, 24; Ralph, 22*, 26, 38; William, 20, 21, 28, 36, 53. *See also* Goddman

Goodwin, Charles, 331, 385; William, 231*, 278, 306, 331. *See also* Godwin

Goolding, James, 294; John, 294; Thomas, 343. *See also* Golding

Goose, Peter, 74, 108, 114, 427; Richard, 43, 74, 77*, 114, 129; Thomas, 56, 87, 112, 129, 426

Goostrey, John, 354

Goret, Thomas, 45

Gorse, Josiah, 174; Richard, 82; Roger, 148

Gorst, Ralph, 245; Richard, 412

Gorstilow [Gorstellow], Thomas, 22

Gorton, Daniel, 315, 357, 370*, 383, 384; John, 357. *See also* Gaulton

Gother, John, 246*, 350, 352*; Lawrence, 217, 239, 240, 269, 271, 280, 350; Thomas, 239

Goughe, John, 144*, 161, 277, 283*, 356, 396; Joseph, 396; Mary, 297; Nathaniel, 318; Richard, 103, 241, 277, 316, 333; Robert, 161; Thomas, 103, 106, 297, 316; William, 184. *See also* Goff

Goulborn. *See* Golborn

Goulding. *See* Golding, and Goolding

Gouldson. *See* Goldson

Gower, (Right Hon Lord) John, 314; William, 160*; (Hon.) William Leveson, 314

Goyton, Daniel, 106; Symon, 106

Goz, George, 22; Thomas, 22
Grace, Joseph, 419; Thomas, 332*, 393
Grafton, William, 71
Grahme, William, 373
Granno, Geoffrey, 42
Grantham, Geoffrey, 188; Henry, 188, 253*; Leonard, 229; Wilfrid, 275
Granwall, Jeffray, 111; John, 73; Richard, 31, 59; William, 59, 111, 122
Grason, George, 238, 341; Jonathan, 238, 341
Gratbach, Daniel, 107; Rowland, 107. *See also* Greatbach
Gratrex, John, 320*
Graunge, Ralph, 88
Gray, Alban, 162, 196, 204, 211, 221, 223, 264, 267; Edward, 132, 159, 162; Roger, 13. *See also* Grey
Grayson. *See* Grason
Greag [Greage], Henry, 110; Robert, 110. *See also* Gregg
Greasty, Samuel, 216. *See also* Gresty
Greatbach, Daniel, 146; William, 146. *See also* Gratbach
Greaves. *See* Greves
Green [Greene], Edward, 107, 309, 315; George, 402; Henry, 375; John, 68, 90, 91, 221, 265, 279*, 396; Jonathan, 419; Randle, 188; Richard, 130; Robert, 87, 111*; Rowland, 107; Thomas, 22, 38, 53; William, 35, 68, 125, 221
Greenholgh, Benjamin, 289; John, 226, 289*
Gregg, Hamnett, 359; Richard, 364; Robert, 211*, 241, 266, 290, 291*, 322, 336, 359*, 363, 364, 394; Thomas, 359; William, 336, 394. *See also* Greag
Gregory [Gregorie], George, 384; Hugh, 17; John, 70, 178; Richard, 73; Robert, 119; Thomas, 122; William, 92, 129, 166; [——], 3
Gregson, Charles, 380
Gremditch. *See* Grimsditch
Grenefield, William, 76
Gresty, John, 361; Joseph, 407; Thomas, 370. *See also* Greasty
Greves, Richard, 67
Grey, Clement, 32; James, 404; Richard, 22; Roger, 22*; Thomas, 171. *See also* Gray
Grice [Grise, Gryce], John, 35, 87, 111, 115; Joseph, 287; Richard, 28, 123; Robert, 56, 80, 87, 120; Roger, 41, 80, 87; Thomas, 223; William, 18, 130, 143, 155, 223
Griff, Hugh, 65; Llewelyn ap, 48; Richard, 72. *See also* Gruff

Griffies, George, 261, 282, 312; John, 282, 292, 294; Josiah, 343; Richard, 294; Robert, 292; Thomas, 389, 393; William, 261. *See also* Griffiths
Griffin, David, 106
Griffith, Charles, 173, 274, 377, 421; David, 103, 202, 226, 341; Edward, 68, 93, 108, 129, 135, 233, 260, 308, 344, 349, 358, 372*; George, 210, 222, 360, 362*, 372, 377, 405; Hugh ap, 69; Jo—, 409; John, 72, 91, 117, 129, 142, 147, 162, 175, 208, 225, 256*, 264, 288, 289, 314, 328, 333, 336, 356, 365, 372*, 378, 380, 385*, 392, 397, 398, 420*, 421; John Dymock, 358, 372, 389; Joseph, 420; Lawrence, 199, 248, 256, 276, 284; Mark, 217; Perseus, 270; Peter, 149, 261*, 288, 289; Ralph, 222, 288, 343; Richard, 133, 162, 208, 217, 295, 332, 368, 378, 390, 392, 397, 409; Robert, 186, 233, 248, 264; Roger, 341; Samuel, 302; Thomas, 97, 110, 153, 185, 259, 260, 274, 302, 325, 333, 341, 349, 350, 351, 365, 367, 368, 376, 379*, 389, 390, 398, 405; William, 32, 82, 226, 238, 241, 266, 285, 288, 320*, 325, 328*, 336, 365, 420. *See also* Gruffuth
Griffiths, John, 402; Lawrence, 285; Thomas, 360. *See also* Griffies
Grimsditch [Gremeditch, Gremsdich, Grimsdich, Grymsdiche], Anthony, 50; Henry, 37; Hugh, 47, 90; James, 52, 66; John, 38, 152; Lawrence, 61; Richard, 19*, 43*, 50, 61, 90; Robert, 39; Thomas, 38, 97; William, 31, 73, 127, 152
Grindley, Richard, 195; Samuel, 195
Gromwall, Geoffrey, 42; [——], 42
Grono, Geoffrey, 14; John, 14; Richard, 11
Groom, George, 376, 390
Grosby, Henry, 226; Robert, 212
Grosvenor, John, 207*; Randle, 126; Richard, 133, 141, 150, 226, 237, 347, 357, 385; Robert, 238, 314, 347*, 385; (The Right Hon. Lord), 385; Thomas, 95, 166, 176, 179, 226, 234*, 238, 347, 358, 385*, 310
Gruff [Gruffe], David ap, 15; Edward, 54; Henry, 14; Hugh, 54; John ap, 20; Lewis, 10; Richard, 26; Thomas, 23, 35; William, 35. *See also* Griff
Gruffeth, John, 77; Robert, 65*. *See also* Griffith

INDEXES

Grundy, James, 301 ; Richard, 163, 301
Gueste, Edward, 88, 116, 121 ; George, 210* ; John, 121 ; Robert, 116 ; Roger, 88. *See also* Gest
Guile [Guyle, Gyle], Phillip, 334 ; Robert, 85 ; Thomas, 233 ; William, 12, 103*, 233, 334.
Gutten [Guttyn], John, 19 ; Richard, 21. *See also* Gitten
Guy, Anthony, 369
Guyle. *See* Guile
Gwalter [Gualter], James, 157 ; John, 146 ; Lawrence, 146 166 ; William, 169. *See also* Gaulter
Gwinneth, John, 396
Gwynn [Gwynne], John, 158 ; Robert, 85
Gyddinges, [——], 3. *See also* Gittens
Gyle. *See* Guile

H

Hackley, Randle, 282
Hackney, Randle, 270
Haddock, Thomas, 163 ; William, 175
Hadley, William, 306
Hale, John, 17, 47, 164, 182, 184, 242, 312, 319*, 346, 378 ; Martha, 374 ; Peter, 291, 334, 353, 373*, 383 ; Richard, 11, 13* ; Roger, 47 ; Thomas, 11, 17, 205, 229, 283 ; William, 102, 155, 184, 191*, 205*, 242, 244*, 291, 319, 348*, 359, 378*, 383
Hales, John, 333 ; Thomas, 272, 333*
Halewood, Thomas, 118
Halfeild, Thomas, 316
Halkyn, Edward, 1
Hall [Halle], Andrew, 187, 233, 258, 331 ; Benjamin, 161, 221* ; Charles, 422 ; Edward, 70, 423 ; George, 423 ; Henry, 130, 157*, 161, 189, 204, 207, 225 ; James, 410 ; John, 37, 73, 110, 119, 180, 223, 225, 258, 331, 364, 411, 426 ; Nathaniel, 204 ; Peter, 295, 318 ; Randle, 77, 128,426 ; Richard, 87*,110 ; Robert, 44, 86, 89, 102, 142 ; Samuel, 318 ; Thomas, 180, 233, 275, 311, 313, 408 ; William, 32, 70, 77, 130, 189, 223, 349, 366, 396, 403, 405, 408, 411*, 421, 422, 423, 426
Hallard, Isaac, 373
Hallett, Joseph, 222, 257, 306 ; Randle, 306
Hallewell [Halliwell], George, 100, 112, 165, 323 ; Hugh, 109, 175, 339, 341 ; James, 323, 339 ; John, 46, 132, 176, 192, 341, 428 ; Moyses, 135 ; Nicholas, 44 ; Thomas, 128, 160, 425 ; William, 71, 109, 137, 175, 425 ; [——], 188
Hallwall, Richard, 64
Hallwood [Hallwod, Hallwoode, Hallwood], Christopher, 100 ; Edward, 198 ; John, 67, 80, 110, 141, 199, 279, 345, 361*, 405, 427 ; Mr., 361 ; Nicholas, 59, 100, 427 ; Ralph, 59 ; Richard, 37, 59 ; Robert, 61 ; Thomas, 61, 198, 279 ; William, 100
Halmarke, Thomas, 184, 197. *See also* Allmark
Halsall, Edward, 71
Hamilton, Edward, 322
Hamlin [Hamlyn], James, 87, 110
Hammond, Edward, 207, 227, 294 ; James, 207 ; John, 402 ; Robert, 294 ; Thomas, 204
Hamnet, Edmund, 16 ; Henry, 52, 74, 81, 99 ; John, 224 ; Richard, 224 ; Robert, 16 ; Thomas, 26 ; William, 14, 53, 65, 99
Hampson. *See* Ampson
Hampton, James, 329, 394, 395*, 400 ; John, 299 ; Peter, 394 ; Thomas, 212, 292*, 329, 400 ; William, 158
Hancock [Hancocke, Hancok, Handcock], Edward, 33 ; George, 341 ; Gilbert, 53, 76 ; Henry, 105, 249, 367, 382, 394, 427 ; John, 56, 105, 155, 160, 173, 211, 215, 239, 341, 367, 382 ; Prenton, 306 ; Robert, 24, 61* ; Roger, 85 ; Thomas, 27, 132, 138, 160, 183, 221, 249*, 256, 367, 394 ; William, 31, 53, 75*, 100, 105, 211, 306, 381
Hand, Charles, 372 ; Henry, 182 ; Hugh, 182, 247, 266, 307, 325, 341 ; James, 122, 247, 370, 372 ; John, 254, 266, 294*, 351, 372, 393*, 395 ; Joseph, 372 ; Stephen, 182, 247*, 254, 307* ; Thomas, 105, 140, 141, 142, 153, 209, 236, 370, 388, 391 ; William, 58, 82, 86, 96, 102, 105, 115, 116, 236, 395, 427
Handcock. *See* Hancock
Handley, John, 330 ; Randle, 197, 204 ; Robert, 197 ; Thomas, 330 ; William, 359. *See also* Anley, and Hanley
Hands, Hugh, 136*, 235*, 429 ; John, 170
Hankey [Hankie, Hanky], Anthony, 40 ; Henry, 257 ; Hugh, 45, 91 ; John, 22, 40, 44, 68, 123, 155, 166, 208, 256, 257, 273 ; Randle, 45 ; Robert, 148, 208, 268, 304, 361, 392 ; Thomas, 121, 136, 156, 161,

183, 191, 271*, 273, 304, 341, 361; William, 409
Hanley, George, 364; John, 193; Randle, 160; Thomas, 408; William, 10, 408. *See also* Anley, and Handley
Hanmer, Edward, 29; Richard, 55; William, 342
Hannah, John, 402
Harbotle, Thomas, 60
Harbridge, John, 410
Harding, Charles, 422; Dean, 352; George, 371, 421; Joseph, 210; Samuel, 421
Hardware, Henry, 25, 35, 49, 57*, 81
Harefinch, Peter, 194
Hargreve, Thomas, 15
Harker, Richard, 16
Harper [Harpur], George, 66, 79, 92, 429; Henry, 43, 48, 152, 171, 172, 215, 254*; John, 4, 11, 19, 79, 152*, 428*, 429; Richard, 11, 30; Thomas, 13, 19
Harrington, (Sir) Henry, 70
Harris [Harries, Harryes, Harrys], Edward, 109, 110, 119; Henry, 61; Owen, 100
Harrison [Harison, Harresone, Harrisone, Harryson], Alexander, 47; Anthony, 191, 307; Arthur, 86; Christopher, 156; Daniel, 419; Edward, 368, 388; George, 419; Griffith, 191; James, 413, 422; Job, 363, 402, 414; John, 44, 47, 68, 72, 73, 84, 95, 109, 122, 144*, 152, 159, 176, 198, 210*, 213, 221, 227, 251, 286, 313, 322, 350, 378, 388, 413*, 418, 422; Joseph, 198, 199, 251, 283, 366, 386, 417; Nathaniel, 200; Philip, 68; Ralph, 44; Randle, 135; Richard, 43, 79, 118, 154, 166*, 190; Robert, 349; Samuel, 181, 252, 365; Seth, 252, 353; Simon, 170; Thomas, 8, 79, 83, 105, 114*, 119, 122, 138, 154, 210, 254, 256, 276, 300, 308, 327, 335, 346*, 349, 356, 369, 371, 391*, 414, 427; William, 8, 39, 93, 105, 129, 148, 167, 194, 199*, 200, 207, 221, 254, 283, 287*, 308, 327, 366, 370, 389*, 391*, 393, 412, 413*, 415, 416, 419. *See also* Henrison
Harrop, Thomas, 389, 416; William, 416. *See also* Horrop
Harry [Harrie], Edward, 102; Griffin ap, 75; Owen ap, 68
Hart, John, 357, 379; Thomas, 320
Hartford, Richard, 38
Hartley, William, 404
Harvey [Harvie, Harvy, Hervy], Arthur, 136, 292; Charles, 253; Edward, 227, 292, 300, 328, 341, 381; George, 131, 143, 150*, 152, 190, 199, 247, 332, 363, 364, 391; Harwar, 313; Hugh, 77*, 149; James, 391; John, 26, 46, 49*, 50*, 77*, 98, 117, 134, 142, 217*, 360, 417; Lawrence, 185; Lucretia, 313; Richard, 117, 166; Robert, 26, 76, 99, 122, 131, 150, 166, 236, 242, 300, 363; Samuel, 242, 284, 313, 341, 381; Thomas, 63, 85, 96, 99, 117, 131, 184, 224, 227, 236, 240, 262, 288, 308*, 324, 328, 332, 357, 360, 376*, 426*; William, 16, 51, 67, 76, 128, 169, 199, 247, 253, 265, 287, 335, 338
Harwar, Thomas, 30
Harwarden. *See* Hawarden
Harwood, Edward, 271
Haslehurst [Hasselhurst], John, 108; William, 108
Hasler, William, 358*
Haslewall [Haselwall, Hasellwall], Richard, 47, 102*; Thomas, 18, 39
Haslow, Henry, 181, 182, 429; Jonathan, 342; Richard, 182; Thomas, 136
Hassell [Hassall], James, 421; John, 379, 413; Ralph, 421; Robert, 343*, 353, 391; Thomas, 139, 152, 167, 172, 174, 190; William, 380, 391, 421
Hastings, George, 192, 227, 229, 335, 406*, 417; Hugh, 322; John, 229, 274, 285, 322, 335
Haswell, Charles, 322, 381*, 383, 387, 391, 403; George, 285, 375, 386; James, 385, 391, 417; John, 399; Jonathan, 216, 285, 297*, 322, 385, 399; Samuel, 403; Thomas, 383; William, 218, 285, 375
Hatfield [Hatfeild], Thomas, 183, 276, 366
Hatton, David, 115, 427; James, 44; John, 38, 101, 115, 169, 201, 254, 321; Joseph, 201, 214, 254, 279*; Peter, 100, 184; Robert, 15, 23, 26, 49, 78, 94, 148, 184, 427; Thomas, 23, 44, 83, 115, 228, 302, 321, 373; William, 228, 302, 390
Haughton, James, 35; Thomas, 202. *See also* Hawton
Hawarden [Harwarden], Robert, 13; William de, 2
Hawborne, Samuel, 178
Hawkart, John, 148; Thomas, 148
Hawker, Charles, 403
Hawkin, Peter, 427
Hawkins, Edward, 275, 330, 342,

367, 389*; Gamaliel, 323, 384, 396, 400*, 401; James, 342, 389*; Richard, 367; Simon, 383
Hawkshaw, John, 140; Richard, 124; Samuel, 149; Thomas, 93, 149, 156
Haworth, Charles, 231, 236; John, 231; Josiah, 236
Hawton, William, 425. *See also* Haughton
Hay [Haye], John, 171; Richard, 3; Robert, 70. *See also* Hei and Hey
Hayes, Cornelius, 341; Daniel, 216, 341; John, 116, 216, 261, 275, 318, 348*, 367, 389*, 394*; Joseph, 340, 408; Mathias, 303*; Richard, 318, 367; Samuel, 183, 261, 340, 342; Thomas, 342, 381; William, 126, 216*
Haylen [Heylin], Gregory, 222; John, 231; Richard, 222; Sarah, 231. *See also* Helin
Haynes, Samuel, 303*
Haythorn, Henry, 200
Hayward [Haywarde, Haywart, Haywood], Edmund, 94; Hugh, 339; John, 414; Jonas, 156; Robert, 228, 339; William, 14
Heald, William, 149*. *See also* Hield
Healey, John, 420*
Heapie, Raphe, 426
Heath, George, 57, 252, 253*, 254, 319*, 350, 369; John, 140, 254; Peter, 350, 364, 396; Peter Bostock, 369; Richard, 139; Robert, 36, 57, 65, 77, 132, 153; Samuel, 156, 210; Thomas, 52, 66, 130, 142, 144, 187, 252; William, 396
Heathley, Abraham, 151, 185, 260
Heaton. *See* Heyton
Hedwod, Ralph, 75
Hegg, Henry, 355, 375, 398, 403, 420
Hei, Matthew, 322; William, 322. *See also* Hay, and Hey
Heighfield, John, 114; Richard, 112; William, 127
Held, James, 184; Thurstan, 55. *See also* Heald, and Hield
Helds, William, 107
Heley [Helley, Helly, Heyley], John de, 1; Robert, 212; Thomas, 196; William, 65, 155, 196, 212
Helin [Heylin, Heylyn], Henry, 18; Hugh, 21; John, 20; Richard, 45. *See also* Haylin
Helsby [Hellesby], Richard, 7
Hemingway, 55 n., 140 n.
Henchman, Charles, 375
Henderson, William, 382, 418
Henley, Samuel, 352*
Henrison, George, 15; John, 12, 15, 26. *See also* Harrison

Henshawe, John, 39; Rondull, 428
Henson, Richard, 28
Henthorne, Huth, 180; John, 180; Thomas, 181
Her [——], John, 6; Thomas, 6
Herall, Richard, 109; Thomas, 109
Herbert, Daniel, 383, 421; John, 382, 421; Richard, 30; Robert, 310; Thomas, 393
Hert, John, 7*
Hertford, Richard, 15; Thomas, 15
Hervy. *See* Harvey
Hesketh, Charles, 381; Elizabeth, 279; Henry, 326, 360, 368, 402*; James, 279, 321; John, 320; Robert, 368, 422; Sarah, 326; Thomas, 129, 171, 310
Heskie, John, 127
Hestok, Michael, 21
Heuster, Robert the, 1
Heward, Robert, 69; Thomas, 36, 69
Hewitt, Benjamin, 364; Edward, 257*, 331, 356; George, 158, 215, 252, 296*; Henry, 367; Humphrey, 175; John, 224, 331, 335, 367*; Paul, 409; Richard, 89; Robert, 137, 356; Samuel, 335, 390; Thomas, 224, 363; William, 89, 146, 162*, 165, 224, 252. *See also* Huet
Hewson. *See* Hughson
Hewys, Peter, 74; William, 74. *See also* Hughes
Hey, Edward, 27; John del, 2; Lawrence, 70; Robert, 22, 136. *See also* Hay, and Hei
Heycock, John, 223, 290*; Matthew, 251; William, 223, 251, 254*
Heydock [Hedock], Edward, 63; Richard, 31
Heyley. *See* Heley
Heys [Heyes], Mathias, 136, 200*; William, 120, 156
Heyton, Charles, 19; Henry, 16; James, 20; Ralph, 19
Heyward, Thomas, 97
Heywood [Heywod], Peter, 126; Robert, 135; William, 136, 145
Hibbert, George, 264; John, 151; William, 151, 264. *See also* Hubbert
Hiccock [Hickcocke, Hicok], Charles, 132, 196, 286, 364; Edward, 191, 232, 286*; George, 118, 364; John, 7, 135, 141, 186*, 204, 225*, 294, 327, 330, 395; Michael, 242, 311; Richard, 103, 127, 144, 151, 191, 192, 196, 218; Robert, 264; Samuel, 170; Thomas, 121, 187, 192, 204, 218, 230, 264, 294, 300*, 327; William, 181

Hichon, Richard, 19
Hickman, Daniel, 211; John, 403; Robert, 347; Thomas, 319, 347; William, 211, 287, 311
Hicks, Thomas, 122
Hickson [Hicson, Hixon], Benjamin, 356, 382; George, 209; James, 222, 287, 293, 398; John, 4, 30, 39, 47, 54, 71, 201, 241, 247*, 250, 313*, 316, 345*, 361, 367, 387, 409; John Thomason, 275; Peter, 241, 311, 321*, 332, 333, 350, 351, 356, 364; Ralph, 159; Robert, 209; Stephen, 409; Thomas, 250, 293, 353, 354, 364, 382, 398, 411; William, 54, 159, 201, 222, 382, 411
Hield, Thurston, 95; William, 95. See also Heald, and Held
Higgen, John, 75
Higginbotham, John, 150
Higginson [Hegynson, Higgenson, Higinson], Edward, 129, 143, 219; Francis, 53, 135; Hugh, 118; John, 5, 117, 169, 186; Joseph, 364; Randle, 95, 111*, 124; Richard, 129, 134, 168, 181; Robert, 163, 203, 218, 275, 399*; Samuel, 155; Sarah, 345; Thomas, 117, 124, 129, 174, 203, 248*, 293, 345, 364, 371; William, 84, 94, 111, 117, 134, 136, 164, 218, 219, 293, 301*. See also Huggenson
High, Thomas, 386; William, 367, 385, 386
Hignett [Higgnett, Higinet, Hygynet], Cornelius, 237; Hamnet, 114, Hugh, 114; John, 93, 326, 360, 381; Sarah, 326; William, 142, 146, 429
Hill, Charles, 367; Henry, 25; James, 128; John, 27, 109, 123, 280, 336*, 342; Jonathan, 273, 280, 298; Peter, 23; Richard, 109, 136, 427; Robert, 27, 58, 71, 79, 136, 145; (Sir) Rowland, 310; Samuel, 204, 312; Thomas, 30, 51, 58, 364, 365; William, 19, 273, 337, 339; [——], 204
Hilton [Hylton], Christopher, 107; David, 4; George, 88*, 109, 112, 254; John, 120, 127; Ralph, 43, 101, 112, 150, 185*, 254, 426*; Robert, 20, 43, 84; Roger, 4; William, 106, 107, 120
Hinckley [Hinkley], George, 112, 163, 217*, 288*; James, 288
Hincks [Hinckes], Edward, 160, 198, 246, 298, 332, 337, 360; John, 337; Joseph, 160, 198, 240*, 386; Murray, 396; Robert, 332, 386, 396; Thomas, 298, 360; William, 73
Hincksman, John, 411
Hind [Hinde, Hine, Hyne], Alexander, 101, 115, 131*; Charles, 400; Hugh, 7, 29, 63, 93, 101, 123, 166; James, 112, 400; John, 52, 90, 115, 116, 137, 171; Ralph, 53, 66, 90, 97*; Randle, 112; Richard, 93, 114, 199, 426; Robert, 175; Thomas, 112; William, 54, 131, 152, 166, 180, 186, 199
Hinkley. See Hinckley
Hinton, John, 65, 90, 107, 177; Matthew, 279; Robert, 28, 264; Samuel, 184, 264*, 279; Thomas, 65, 107, 324*
Hitchens [Hitchins], Abraham, 389; Anthony, 127; Charles, 316, 319, 349, 400; Isaac, 325*; Thomas, 106, 366, 403
Hitchenson, John, 66
Hoakesly, Robert, 407
Hobrow, Cornelius, 278*, 359; William, 359
Hobson, John, 417
Hockenhull [Hocknell, Hokenhull], Henry, 49, 98; Ralph, 150; Richard, 6, 8; William, 45, 124
Hodgkin [Hogeskine], Francis, 86
Hodgskinson, Thomas, 305. See also Hodskinson
Hodgson, Joseph, 187, 240*, 408; Richard, 117, 134; Robert, 45, 408, 422; Samuel, 346; Thomas, 121; William, 46
Hodkinson, Edward, 410; John, 376, 385, 404; Joseph, 376; Thomas, 390
Hodskinson, John, 358. See also Hodgskinson
Hodson, George, 362, 396; Humphrey, 421; Robert, 46; Thomas, 409
Hoell, Evan ap, 52. See also Howell
Hogge [Hogg], John, 5; Richard, 38
Hoghton, Thomas, 11. See also Houghton
Hokes, John, 18; Stephen, 18
Holbrooke [Holbroke, Holbruck], Peter, 236*; Richard, 34; Thomas, 28, 42, 61, 426
Holcroft, Isaac, 224; John, 285; Robert, 285; Thomas, 224; William, 24
Holden, John, 140
Holding, Richard, 168
Holenbury, Stephen, 25
Holford [Houlford], Alexander, 340; John, 184; Thomas, 105; William, 105

INDEXES 457

Holker, John, 68; Richard, 37, 68
Holland [Holand], Charles, 347;
  George, 339, 375; Hamnett, 387;
  Jarvis, 370; John, 11, 26, 166, 192,
  198, 213, 303, 370; Joseph, 236,
  309, 326, 339, 391; Mathias, 393,
  409*; Peter, 375; Ralph, 300*,
  306; Richard, 25, 158, 213, 223;
  Robert, 269, 347; Samuel, 236;
  Thomas, 97, 165, 185, 187, 196,
  213, 219, 220, 269, 306*; William,
  52, 220, 243*, 259, 326* 372*, 387,
  393
Hollett, Thomas, 126
Hollingworth [Holynworth], James, 8
Hollins, George, 321*; John, 315
Hollinshead [Holynshede], John, 395;
  Peter, 4; Richard, 6; Thurstan,
  47
Holliwell [Holiewell, Holywell],
  George, 216; Hugh, 209, 253,
  264*; John, 94, 202, 253, 255;
  Richard, 202, 271; Robert, 85;
  Thomas, 142, 196; William, 90
Holly, Anthony, 421
Holmark. *See* Halmarke
Holme, Ralph, 102, 103; Randle, 126,
  140, 196*, 425; Richard, 123, 258;
  Thomas, 36; William, 140
Holmes, Adam, 128; George, 410;
  Ralph, 117; Richard, 421; Thomas,
  91
Holt, Charles, 351; Edward, 406;
  John, 259, 339, 351; Thomas, 255,
  259; William, 255, 276, 339
Holve, Roger, 32
Holwood, Thomas, 142. *See also*
  Hallwood
Holywell. *See* Holliwell
Hoo, John, 77
Hoole, Christopher, 78
Hooley, Peter, 376; Samuel, 392
Hoose, Robert, 97; Thomas, 141;
  William, 97
Hooton, John, 33. *See also* Hoton
Hope, Elias, 315; George, 310, 364;
  Isaac, 420; John, 3, 4, 315; Robert,
  30; Samuel, 239, 351; Thomas,
  18, 239, 275, 321, 339*, 351
Hoper, John, 29
Hopkins, Peter, 346; Thomas, 346
Hopkinson [Hopkynson], Nicholas, 6
Hopley, John, 310
Hopson, William, 383
Hornby, Joseph, 384
Horner, Henry, 313; John, 313
Horrop, Thomas, 362. *See also*
  Harrop
Horton, John, 11, 48, 330; Peter,
  210, 252, 260*; Ralph, 52;
  Richard, 15, 24; Roger, 24, 36;
  Samuel, 176, 260; Thomas, 15, 31,
  252; William, 116, 119. *See also*
  Orton
Hostage, Charles, 186; Daniel, 255;
  John, 372; Samuel, 255, 372
Hoton, Richard, 20; Robert, 15. *See
  also* Hooton, Hoghton, and Haughton
Hough, Gilbert, 200, 246; Godfrey,
  46; Henry, 304; John, 125, 145,
  158, 200, 246; Robert, 363
Houghland, John, 373
Houghton, Edward, 8; Henry, 38;
  John, 49; William, 22, 49. *See
  also* Hoghton and Hoton
Houlford. *See* Holford
Houseman, John, 191
How, Samuel, 194
Howard, Charles, 212, 258, 270*,
  322; Edward, 258; Joseph, 400;
  William, 322, 371, 415*
Howell, Edward, 58; George, 84;
  John, 24, 402; Mathew, 58;
  Raphe, 427; Richard, 55; Thomas,
  20, 173. *See also* Hoell
Howen, Ries ap, 38
Hoy, Edward, 387; William, 387
Hubbert, James, 394; Thomas, 360,
  394. *See also* Hibbert
Hudde, Nicholas, 4
Hudson, Gowen, 134*, 160, 427
Huet [Hughet], Edward, 53, 266;
  John, 122; Richard, 32, 47, 74;
  Samuel, 266; Thomas, 13; William,
  127. *See also* Hewitt
Huggenson, Robert, 96. *See also*
  Higgenson
Hugh [Hue], David ap, 85, 341*;
  Robert ap, 82, 110; Thomas ap,
  36; William ap, 82, 94
Hughes, Andrew, 271; Charles, 134,
  183, 350; David, 281, 361, 408;
  Edward, 119, 289; Ellen, 287;
  Ellis, 202, 243; George, 397;
  Henry, 150; Hugh, 115, 211, 227,
  302; Isaac, 138; James, 368, 421*;
  John, 67, 141, 149, 162, 189, 216,
  243*, 282, 283, 287, 326, 354, 368,
  389, 402, 416, 417, 422; John
  Sorton, 411; John Stewart, 422;
  Lewis, 265; Owen, 113, 133, 159*,
  196*, 228, 236, 282*, 296*, 302;
  Peter, 35, 119, 271, 423; Reginald,
  27; Richard, 272, 300, 426; Robert,
  149, 216, 362, 378; Rowland, 211;
  Samuel, 227; Theodore, 161;
  Thomas, 174, 189, 216, 259, 281*,
  283, 326, 332*, 342, 411; William,
  151, 160, 168, 184, 185, 189, 192,
  199*, 243, 244*, 252*, 276, 282,
  300, 379, 400. *See also* Hewys

Hughson [Huson], Ralph, 135*; Robert, 28, 118; Samuel, 203; Thomas, 35
Hull, Benjamin, 169; John, 144; Richard, 2; Thomas, 144
Hulme, Hugh, 20; Ralph, 78; Randle, 78, 107*; Thomas, 47, 54, 78; William, 70, 107
Hulmes, Thomas, 107
Hulse, Huen, 166; Job, 370; John, 166; Robert, 177; Thomas, 162; Yuan, 121
Hulton, Edward, 138, 231; George, 47; John, 50, 119, 132, 133, 145, 151, 173, 176, 268; Ralph, 43, 70, 106, 116, 158, 159, 185*; Robert, 48; Seth, 159; Thomas, 170, 313; William, 48, 125, 146, 174, 268
Humphrey [Humfrey], William, 7, 81
Humphries [Humfreyes, Humphreys], Daniel, 420; David, 117; Edward, 375; John, 317*, 384; Mary, 365; Peter, 176; Richard, 194, 222*, 257, 269, 283, 289, 296, 322*, 333, 357, 365, 387, 392, 395, 415; Samuel, 244, 357, 359, 368, 415; Thomas, 95, 117, 138, 312, 321, 333, 373
Humpston, Hugh, 115; Richard, 139
Hunt [Hunte], Adam, 2; George, 162, 180, 215, 289*, 333; John, 151, 172, 181, 200, 351*, 396; Michael, 134; Nicholas, 1; Richard, 10; Thomas, 2, 333, 396; William, 75, 81; [——], 129
Huntington, Benjamin, 328; Isaac, 349; John, 29, 352, 385; Richard, 137; Robert, 37, 80; Samuel, 419; William, 38, 61, 80, 97, 210, 222, 279*, 328, 336, 352, 385
Hurleston, Charles, 204*, 209; John, 213
Hurleton [Hurlton], Anthony, 21; Hugh, 9, 15*, 17; James, 7; Richard, 17; Roger, 5, 10; Thomas, 7
Hurst [Hurste], Humphrey, 62; William, 18, 45
Huson. See Hughson
Hussey, Thomas, 416
Hutchens [Hutchins], Anthony, 161; Charles, 238*; Daniel, 148; John, 74, 104; Ralph, 270; Thomas, 90, 152*, 213, 264*
Hutchinson, James, 156, 180, 214*, 251, 253*; Thomas, 251
Huxley, George, 414; Henry, 353; James, 385; John, 237, 270, 385; Jonathan, 237; Ralph, 26; Robert, 364; Thomas, 380, 423*. See also Hoakesley

Hyde, Christopher, 326; Joseph, 322; Robert, 309, 342; Stephen, 323, 365*, 396; Thomas, 322; William, 326
Hyklyng, Richard, 2
Hylton. See Hilton
Hyne. See Hinde

I

Ilyffe, John, 114
Ince, Charles, 302; David, 125; Edward, 226; John, 127, 157, 294; Nicholas, 71, 102, 112, 115*, 185, 262, 268, 428; Peter, 98; Randle, 34, 43, 58, 62, 65*, 67, 71, 77, 98, 104*, 112, 175, 226, 429; Richard, 62; Robert, 45, 76, 112, 116, 149*, 202, 429; Samuel, 116; Thomas, 13, 67, 96, 100, 104, 109, 268, 368*; William, 13, 62, 84, 97, 110, 112, 125, 146*, 149, 162, 167, 185, 202, 262, 302, 426, 429
Incle, George, 132, 337
Ingham, John, 305; Robert, 304; William, 185, 203, 304, 305. See also Ingram
Inglefield, Michael, 126; Thomas, 99. See also Englefeld
Inglish, Gilbert, 365, 415
Ingram, John, 394. See also Ingham
Irby, John, 44; William, 44
Ireland, Francis, 202, 260, 301; John, 129, 141, 149, 150, 184, 369; Mathias, 311; Richard, 67; Samuel, 311; Thomas, 66, 130, 150, 184; William, 149, 200, 202*
Irish, William, 353
Irrelle, Richard, 21
Ithell [Ithel, Ythell], George, 57; Hugh ap, 13; John ap, 12, 13*, 17, 364; Moses, 408; Nicholas, 16; Robert, 13; Thomas ap, 17, 43; Walter ap, 6, 12; William ap, 13

J

Jackson, Charles, 155, 185, 227, 244, 338, 377; Edward, 259; Francis, 126, 151, 158, 168*; George, 141, 326; Henry, 174, 226, 328, 335; Humphrey, 80, 132; James, 379; John, 145, 177, 237, 259, 311*, 328, 338, 369, 377, 382, 401*; Josiah, 189, 237; Peter, 187, 355, 367, 391, 393; Philip, 118, 130; Ralph, 382, 401; Richard, 151, 326* 335, 393; Robert, 281; Roger, 168; Samuel, 263, 290, 328, 373; Thomas, 62*, 111, 145*, 162, 180, 187, 189*, 226,

227, 281, 371, 381; William, 61, 118,
124, 149, 161, 179, 221, 223, 237*,
262, 297, 401
Jaman, Ralph, 41; Richard, 56. *See
also* Gamon
James, Edward, 327, 402; John, 375;
Richard, 16, 54, 67, 88*, 95, 327,
354
Jameson, John, 378; Peter, 423
Jankynsone. *See* Jenkinson
Jannion, and Janyon. *See* Jennion
Janson. *See* Jenson
Jarvis. *See* Garvis, and Jervis
Javo, Edward, 410
Jeffrey [Jeffery], James, 421; John,
39
Jeffryes, John, 106
Jein, Richard, 25
Jeinson. *See* Jeynson, and Joynson
Jeinns, William, 24
Jellicoe, Charles, 175, 220, 230; John,
219, 294; Mr., 364; Thomas, 215,
294, 256, 364
Jenin. *See* Jenyn
Jenins, Elene, 69; Griff, 34; Ralph,
69; Robert, 30. *See also* Jennings
Jenion. *See* Jennion
Jenkin, Hugh, 77; Peter, 106;
Thomas, 360, 403, 413*
Jenkinson [Jankynson, Jynkynson],
John, 9; Thomas, 9, 12; Richard,
15
Jennings, Henry, 192*; James, 255;
John, 228; Richard, 151, 281;
Roger, 227; Samuel, 183, 196, 255;
William, 227, 281, 283. *See also*
Jenins
Jennion [Jannion, Jenion, Jenyon,
Jhanion], Henry, 22, 144; John,
223; Joseph, 269; Randle, 78;
Richard, 88; Thomas, 139, 163,
223; William, 85, 151, 153
Jennions [Jennyons], Daniel, 345;
John, 178, 246, 303; Joseph, 345;
Richard, 246; Samuel, 245, 279,
328; Thomas, 365; William, 167,
328
Jenson [Janson], Edmund, 51; Edward, 67; Hugh, 28; John, 36,
185; Lawrence, 73; Ralph, 34;
Thomas, 37, 50, 77; William, 77
Jenyn, Robert, 23
Jervis [Jarvis], Joseph, 424; Samuel,
234*, 319. *See also* Garvis
Jevan, Griff ap, 5; Griffith, 104;
Jevan ap Griff ap, 5; Joseph ap,
100
Jevin [Jevyn], Robert, 23, 26, 85, 100;
Thomas ap, 102
Jevins, Griff, 34; Robert, 30; William,
24

Jewett, George, 86; William, 52
Jeyne [Jein], Richard, 25
Jeynson [Jeinson], John, 108; Richard,
25; Robert, 97, 115; Thomas, 108;
William, 91. *See also* Joynson
Jhanion. *See* Jennion
Joet, William, 25
John, David ap, 19; George, 361;
Robert ap, 18; Thomas ap, 44, 61;
William ap, 7
Johns [Johnes], Alexander, 109;
David, 37, 66; Edward, 104, 106;
Ellis, 46, 68; Evan, 120; Grifin, 72;
Henry, 44; Hugh, 83, 93, 100, 119;
Humphrey, 100; Jevan, 100; John,
68, 71, 94*, 100; Lewis, 95, 106,
109; Nicholas, 89; Owen, 68;
Randle, 39; Robert, 22, 37, 68;
Roger, 109; Thomas, 68, 82, 87, 90*,
95, 96, 106*, 104, 107; William, 37,
74, 87, 109. *See also* Jones
Johnson, Adam, 40, 94; Aston, 303;
Bartholomew, 152; Benjamin, 129;
Charles, 183, 251, 355, 373; Crispin,
292, 366; Edward, 65, 193, 204, 222,
296, 355; Francis, 181; George,
183, 188, 221*, 252, 236, 238, 301,
304, 308, 374, 380, 396; Hamnet,
40; Hamon, 20, 35; Henry, 139,
166, 185, 411; Hugh, 94; James,
26*, 106, 162, 324, 339, 395; John,
31, 36, 55, 62, 98, 101, 116, 123,
125, 127, 129, 132, 133*, 134, 142,
143, 145, 146*, 149, 152, 155, 160,
161*, 170, 173, 181, 193, 197*, 198,
199, 218*, 219, 220, 228, 229, 241,
242*, 252, 254*, 263, 276, 284, 289,
293, 296*, 303, 304, 328, 336, 356,
366*, 370, 373, 390, 398, 410*, 411*,
415, 419, 420, 425, 426; Jonathan,
401; Joseph, 415; Laurence, 427;
Matthew, 6, 185; Michael, 157,
203, 204, 211; Nicholas, 12; Obadiah, 221, 374; Paul, 82, 425;
Ralph, 28, 52, 67, 99, 101; Richard,
12, 28, 38, 92, 112, 113, 123, 133,
170, 222, 301; Robert, 53, 63, 108,
113, 145, 152, 183, 295, 357, 379,
415, 419; Rowland, 92, 112, 426;
Samuel, 152, 326, 376; Thomas, 19,
25, 72, 73, 87, 99, 108, 138, 183, 251,
252, 254, 295, 326, 328, 339, 361,
364, 366, 386, 427; William, 23, 33,
64*, 67, 77, 80, 84, 108, 119, 139, 142,
152, 160, 162, 198*, 200*, 220, 228,
229, 256, 257, 260, 274, 292*, 293,
294, 295, 296, 303, 315*, 326, 339, 354,
359*, 370, 382, 401, 410, 427; [——], 2
Jolly, Nathan, 166
Jonas, Thomas, 405
Jones, Abraham, 178, 195, 274, 422;

Anne, 331; Anthony, 127; Benjamin, 164, 355, 388, 396*, 397; Bostock, 370; Bradford, 359; Cadwallader, 156; Charles, 160; Daniel, 44, 215, 397; David, 167, 214, 217, 285, 286, 385; David Francis, 407; Ednevett, 232; Edward, 250, 308, 356, 359, 362, 363, 368, 378, 383, 403, 421; Evan, 115, 171, 202, 349; Francis, 116, 242; George, 115; Gerrard, 141, 146, 151, 190, 208; Griffith, 82, 427; Henry, 80, 106, 117, 174, 210, 262, 303; Hugh, 105, 115, 144, 147, 215, 242*, 270, 286, 335*, 340, 397*, 427; Humphrey, 128, 131, 318; James, 315, 358*, 383, 422; John, 30, 34, 111, 123, 131*, 133*, 135, 151, 160, 182, 190, 201, 216, 223, 228, 232, 233, 240*, 244, 251, 257*, 267, 277*, 278, 282, 284*, 287, 288, 303, 315, 316*, 322, 323, 324, 328, 329, 331, 349*, 350*, 356*, 358, 359, 360, 364, 365*, 366, 372*, 377, 378*, 381, 383*, 386, 392, 395, 397, 402, 404, 407, 410, 415; Johua, 412; Jonathan, 411; Joseph, 376, 399, 403, 410; Joshua, 369; Lewis, 71, 105, 106, 426; Luke, 147; Matthew, 178, 310, 384; Michael, 107, 114, 306; Nathaniel, 334; Owen, 151, 182, 315, 351, 395, 427; Peter, 143, 235, 246, 257, 272, 290*, 319, 329*, 330, 341; Randle, 127, 133, 167; Reece, 274; Richard, 121, 147, 198, 257, 262, 303*, 341, 364*, 370, 383, 415; Robert, 62, 114, 140, 182, 212, 233, 255, 276, 349, 354, 359, 366, 372, 375, 389, 391*, 394, 396, 398, 400, 405*, 408*; Roger, 138, 226, 244, 258, 262; Rowland, 358, 414, 415; St. John, 202; Samuel, 151, 183, 312*, 336, 392, 395; Thomas, 54, 72, 91, 112*, 118, 135*, 137, 153, 167, 168, 169*, 170, 178, 191, 213*, 222, 223, 226, 235*, 241, 250, 251*, 258, 270, 272, 280, 282, 287, 294, 306, 314, 316, 318, 319, 323, 326, 328*, 350, 352, 357, 360, 365, 366, 368, 375, 378, 381, 383, 386, 389, 391, 392, 395, 405, 406, 407, 410, 415; Timothy, 329, 371, 378; William, 80, 113, 115, 116*, 119, 144, 177, 198, 208, 229*, 242, 246, 251, 258, 285, 288, 319, 330, 336, 337*, 355, 359, 363*, 364, 370, 375, 376, 377*, 386, 392, 408, 421, 425; Zachariah, 378; [——], 317, 350. *See also* Johns, and Joynes

Jopson, Allen, 317; James, 317
Jordan, Benjamin, 355, 375; Charles, 346, 367, 393; Francis, 221, 292, 324, 355; Gerrard, 159, 221, 304, 327, 333, 346, 354, 356*, 394, 395* 402, 409*, 416; Hugh, 215, 256, 271, 287*, 320*; James, 355, 386, 391; John, 170, 320, 367; Joseph, 184, 314, 324, 367, 375, 396*; Thomas, 292, 367; William, 354, 371, 378, 380, 393
Jowsey, John, 372*
Joynes, John, 333; Mary, 333; Ralph, 319*
Joynson, Charles, 400; John, 115, 138, 161, 220, 290, 329, 356, 394, 423; Peter, 161, 230, 293*; Ralph, 133; Randle, 230, 311, 329; Richard, 413; Robert, 220; Samuel, 176, 367; Thomas, 428; William, 133. *See also* Jeynson
Joynston, John, 158
Juckle (*or* Inckle), George, 337

K

Kay, Thomas, 405. *See also* Keay, and Key
Kearney, Charles, 353; John, 365
Keay, Henry William, 358; John, 361; Randle, 358, 361
Keeling, John, 402
Keene, Right Rev. Edmund, 354
Kell, John, 290; Thomas, 290
Kelley [Kalley], Edward, 184; John, 196*, 200*, 293; Ormson, 273; Peter, 170; Richard, 37, 116*, 399; Robert, 81; Thomas, 246, 350*; William, 45, 246; [——], 81. *See also* Calley
Kelsall, John, 163, 182, 186, 195, 207, 267*, 268, 277, 302, 315, 363, 366; Joseph, 198; Randle, 83; Samuel, 148, 184, 289, 366; Thomas, 267, 302; William, 142, 195, 198, 268, 277, 289
Kelsey, John, 204; Nathaniel, 204
Kempe [Kemp], Adam, 97, 115, 128, 160, 202, 203, 208*, 225; James, 55; John, 20, 38, 49, 58, 225, 269, 293; Thomas, 41, 49, 127, 160, 202, 293
Kendrick, John, 245, 398, 422; William, 380, 415*. *See also* Kenrick
Kenion. *See* Kenyon
Kenkeat, Henry, 112
Kenna, James, 207
Kennant, James, 302*
Kennerley, Benjamin, 356; Edmund, 221; James, 303, 422; Samuel, 315; Thomas, 221
Kennion. *See* Kenyon

Kenrick, Hugh, 42, 48, 70; John, 377; Josiah, 210; Thomas ap David ap, 37. *See also* Kendrick
Kent [Kente], James, 228, 310, 369; John, 94; Thomas, 6, 94, 375; William, 39, 310, 369, 375, 401*
Kenyon [Kennion], George, 342; John, 86, Thomas, 190, 220, 257*
Kenyough, George, 76
Kerfoot, Martha, 277; Samuel, 295
Kerison, John, 165
Kerkham. *See* Kirkham, and Kirkman
Kerry, John, 358; William, 20
Kessack, John, 287
Ketley, John, 96
Kettle [Ketell, Ketle, Kettell], Edward, 162; John, 60, 142, 150; Nicholas, 12, 17, 23, 42; Randle, 23; Richard, 23; Thomas, 17, 42, 66, 125, 131, 162, 426; William, 60. *See also* Catell
Kewqnicke, Henry, 92
Key, Elizabeth, 282; James, 199, 218; John, 174, 208, 387; Peter, 218; Ralph, 55; Randle, 282; Richard, 153, 211; Robert, 168, 302*. *See also* Kay, and Keay
Kilshe, Edward, 79
Kilso, Edward, 56
Kinaston. *See* Kynaston
King [Kinge], Charles, 421; Daniel, 123; John, 58, 71, 93, 114, 135, 165, 168, 253, 428; Nathaniel, 163; Richard, 29, 108, 153, 214, 292, 428; Robert, 124; Roger, 65, 79, 108, 114, 425, 426, 428*; Thomas, 85, 93, 191, 429; William, 29, 52, 56, 58, 59, 65, 69, 78, 79, 87, 96, 103, 111, 114, 142, 146*, 148, 153, 165, 214, 253, 428*, 429
Kingsley. *See* Kynsley
Kinley, William, 121
Kinnaston. *See* Kynaston
Kinsey, Edward, 116, 157; [——], 129
Kirkham [Kerkham], Abraham, 360; John, 281; Ralph, 281; Robert, 429; Thomas, 396
Kirkman, Robert, 96. *See also* Kerkman
Kirks [Kirkes], Charles, 264; Daniel, 276; Hamnett, 129, 151, 234, 341*; John, 17, 147, 172, 184, 195, 217*, 227, 261, 279, 333, 334; Jonathan, 171; Nathaniel, 167; Robert, 167, 195, 261, 264; Samuel, 159, 194*, 234, 279, 299*, 341; Thomas, 184, 264*, 344; William, 35, 46*, 58, 61; [—]nett, 171
Kitchen, Edward, 78
Kneckell, William, 56

Knee, Barnard, 121; Richard, 40, 70; William, 87
Kney, Richard, 99, 101*; Thomas, 99, 121
Knight, John, 152, 168, 209*; William, 41
Knott, Edward, 143; William, 196, 227, 236, 238, 256; [——], 143, 196
Knowles [Knolles], Gilbert, 28, 44, 50, 57; Griffen, 184; Griffith, 164, 228, 271, 300; Hughe, 165; James, 88; John, 100, 113, 126; Nicholas, 159; Richard, 132; Robert, 416; Thomas, 88, 95, 117, 120, 162, 169, 234*, 270, 427
Knowsley [Knowlesley], James, 41, 140, 166; Robert, 9; William, 41
Kynaston [Kinnaston], Corbet, 312; Edward, 309; Humphrey, 243; James, 400; John, 166, 195, 218, 243
Kynsley, John, 56

L

Lace, Nicholas; 17; Robert, 11, 17
Lach [Lache], Humphrey, 142; John, 64, 123, 240; Thomas, 37, 138; William, 102
Lacy, John, 110; Richard, 110
Laghok, William de, 1
Lake, Francis, 384
Lamb, Pickering, 312; Robert, 288, 312, 367*, 379; Thomas, 256*, 288
Lambakin, John, 140
Lammas, William, 203
Lamplin, John, 313
Lancasher, Thomas, 43
Lancaster, John, 4, 123, 158; William, 380
Lancelot, William, 177
Langdale, John, 209, 285; William, 209
Langford, Thomas, 373, 404, 415
Langley, Thomas, 33
Langshaw, Roger, 383
Langton, John, 70; Paul, 70; William, 235
Lant, John, 312*
Larden, John, 170, 226*, 341*, 377*, 419
Large, Daniel, 195
Laronx, Peter, 417
Latchford, Thomas, 370, 397*
Latham [Lathom], Henry, 342; John, 368; Joshua, 342, 355; Samuel, 363; Thomas, 38
Lathe, William, 133

Laton, John, 66; Randle, 66*; William, 66
Laughton?, John, 106. *See also* Lawton
Lawler, Nicholas, 141
Lawrence [Lorawnce], John, 92, 350, 367; Joseph, 407; Richard, 207, 272, 306*; Robert, 286*; Samuel, 331; Thomas, 331; James, 222, 323; Jeremiah, 346
Lawrenson, John, 323, 346, 360, 73; Lawrence, 359, 386; Richard, 97
Lawson, Robert, 218; William, 270
Lawton, John, 243, 330*, 371, 400; Joseph, 318; Peter, 70; Randle, 29, 111; Robert, 30; Samuel, 164; Thomas, 28, 84, 344; William, 111, 243, 344. *See also* Laughton
Lay, John, 70; Thomas, 355
Layton, William, 170
Lea, Daniel, 97; Edward, 80; John, 68, 70, 238; Richard, 45, 103, 238; Robert, 39, 71, 217; Roger, 35, 49, 71, 87, 97; Samuel, 355, 368; Simeon, 148; Simon, 103; Thomas, 68, 355, 376; William, 53, 58*, 68, 80, 83, 92, 101*, 103, 118. *See also* Lay, Lee, Legh, Leigh, and Ley
Leach, John, 357. *See also* Leche
Leadbeater, Charles Worral, 406; Edward, 177, 190, 228* 358, 406; Hugh, 262; John, 262, 274, 345*, 369; Joseph, 170; Peter, 177, 229, 235, 242*, 274, 306, 347, 358, 367; Richard, 235; Samuel, 163; Thomas, 348, 365, 388; William, 388
Leak, Christopher, 332
Leatherbarrow, John, 377, 422*
Leathwaite. *See* Lewthwaite
Leche [Leech], Charles, 163, 180, 304; Francis, 176; George, 29; Henry, 29; John, 16, 20*, 59, 63, 97, 240, 340, 396; Joseph, 374; Randle, 33; Richard, 16, 31, 37, 46; Robert, 37, 81, 90; Samuel, 304; Thomas, 30, 36; William, 13, 20, 29, 81. *See also* Leach
Leconby [Lekonby], Henry, 156, 298; John, 119; Peter, 212, 298*, 305; Samuel, 305
Ledsham [Ledesham, Ledshame], Benjamin, 234, 325; Daniel, 318, 362; Edward, 129; Fulke, 55; John, 149, 250, 267; Randle, 113, 149; Richard, 10, 17, 39, 132, 181, 219, 226*, 234, 304, 325*, 383; Roger, 17, 21*; Thomas, 74, 90, 113, 143, 183, 209*, 221, 230, 250, 293*, 325, 362, 375*, 404; William, 221, 267, 291
Lee, John, 328; Peter, 288; Randle, 333; Richard, 244, 245, 255; Samuel, 255; Thomas, 328; William, 4, 307
Leech. *See* Leach, and Leche
Leeke, Christopher, 388, 389; Richard, 389; William, 388
Leene [Leyne, Lyne], Edward, 114; Henry, 77; John, 85; Joshua, 147; Robert, 62; William, 60
Leenes, Daniel, 143, 173; George, 134; John, 186; Samuel, 144, 222; Thomas, 144; William, 114, 134; [——], 186
Leete, Simeon, 363, 409*
Legh, John, 402, 405; Peter, 315. *See also* Lea, and Leigh
Leicester [Lecester, Leycester], Lawrence, 69, 136*; Hugh, 411; Peter, 164; Randle, 132, 170; Raphe, 171; Richard, 97, 108, 132, 425; Robert, 333*; William, 54, 91, 96, 406. *See also* Lester
Leigh [Leighe], Andrew, 226; Daniel, 131, 429; George, 281; Hugh, 98; James, 164, 334; John, 125, 226, 228, 240, 334, 426; Joseph, 100, 415; Josiah, 228; Peter, 136*, 139, 141, 145, 161, 176, 178, 297, 309, 429; Ralph, 128, 115, 197*; Richard, 45, 100, 141, 169, 190; Samuel, 139, 159, 117; Thomas, 132, 176, 201; William, 129, 193; [——], 129. *See also* Lea, Legh, and Ley
Leithwaite. *See* Lewthwaite
Leivesley [Leavesley], John, 92, 115*, 117; Randle, 117; Robert, 245, 248; Thomas, 120, 248. *See also* Livesley
Lelfwiche, Timothy, 315
Lemm [Lem], James, 157, 217*
Lenard [Leonard], Henry, 102; John, 53, 75, 84, 100, 127, 151; Thomas, 60, 102
Lench, Michael, 146
Lester, Jo, 109; Thomas, 109. *See also* Leicester
Letherbarrow. *See* Leatherbarrow
Leving [Levinge], Richard, 147, 172*, 179, 217*
Lewis [Lewes], Benjamin, 352, 387; Edward, 284, 333, 390, 392, 426; Elias, 167; Ellis, 105, 131*, 167, 201, 216; Evan, 114; Henry, 163; Humphrey, 157; John, 83, 105, 114, 142, 149, 160, 234, 257, 289*, 333, 387; Jonathan, 347; Lewis, 105; Richard, 85, 115, 157, 390; Robert, 21, 44; Roger, 135, 166;

Thomas, 32, 220, 234, 267, 284, 377, 390, 414; William, 114, 119, 267, 349, 381*, 396, 414; Williams, 113

Lewthwaite, James, 406; John, 400

Ley [Leye], Edward, 227, 302, 340*; Hamnett, 247, 373; John, 50, 238, 296; Randle, 354, 358, 367; Robert, 404; Richard, 135, 238; Roger, 14, 45; Samuel, 302, 356; Simon, 136; Thomas, 18, 112, 128, 135, 169, 193, 217, 227, 247, 296, 302, 306*, 373, 388, 404; Valentine, 222; William, 131, 429. *See also* Lea, Legh, and Leigh

Leycester. *See* Leicester, and Lester

Leyne. *See* Leene

Lightbound, William, 122

Lightfoot [Lightfoote, Lightfot, Lyghtefoote], Edward, 112; Elizabeth, 332; George, 13, 126, 381; James, 11; John, 55, 62, 258; Joseph, 199, 332; Nicholas, 11; Ralph, 98, 112, 210, 258; Richard, 47; Thomas, 353, 362, 399, 420*

Lilly, William, 6

Linaker [Linacre, Linager, Lynacar, Lynacre, Lynaker], Joseph, 236; Robert, 103; Thomas, 32, 60, 61*, 103, 104*, 121, 137, 190, 236, 428; William, 29, 43

Lindford, John, 286*. *See also* Linford

Lindsey, Edward, 314; George, 378

Linford, John, 231; Peter, 231. *See also* Lindford

Lingley [Lyngley, Lynley], Hugh, 28; Jacob, 105; John, 24, 38, 61, 67, 71*, 102, 105, 127; Joseph, 102, 115, 179, 135; Richard, 34, 67, 92; Roger, 21, 42

Liniall [Linall, Lyneall, Lyniall, Lynniall, Lynyall], Edward, 84; Humphrey, 83; John, 83; Richard, 120; Roger, 38, 101*, 134, 144; Thomas, 33, 50, 54, 69, 70, 73, 101, 112, 155, 299; William, 73, 89; [——], 299

Linke, Edward, 345

Linney, George, 330, 360, 372; John, 361, 374, 380; Thomas, 330, 362, 363, 364*, 374, 389; William, 362, 396, 408

Linsdale, John, 394; Richard, 339*, 394*

Linson, George, 24

Linton, William, 57

Lister, Richard, 313. *See also* Lyster

Litherland [Lytherland], Edward, 157, 198, 216, 221, 260, 299, 334; Henry, 103*; John, 25, 55, 198;

Peter, 30, 82, 83, 88; Richard, 31, 88, 122; Robert, 82; William, 21, 83, 125, 166, 191, 210, 221, 265, 299; [——], 157

Littlehales, John, 264

Littler [Littlor], Alderman, 425; Andrew, 356; George, 104; James, 187, 233*, 256, 257, 261, 270, 282, 284, 311, 322, 338; John, 58, 79, 88, 89, 104*, 379, 420; Jonathan, 270, 322; Richard, 113*, 243, 418; Robert, 412; Thomas, 197, 233, 261, 262, 297, 338; William, 243; [——], 97

Littleton, William, 267, 315, 341

Liverpoole [Lyverpole], William, 26, 54

Livesley [Leivesley], Charles, 134; Frances, 134; John, 134*; Robert, 147, 180. *See also* Leivesley

Lle, John ap, 11

Llen, Edward, 89; John, 95; Launcellot, 56; Roger, 85; Thomas, 89; William, 95

Llewelyn, Edward, 48; John, 37; John ap, 48; Thomas ap, 32, 36; William, 32

Lloyd [Lloid, Lloyde], Charles, 310, 381, 406; David, 43, 72, 79, 122; Edward, 50, 136, 150, 174, 259, 296, 335, 342, 383, 412; Ellis, 165; Eubule, 309; Francis, 340; George, 128, 373, 414*, 417; Giwn, 314; Griffin ap David ap, 46; Hedd, 377; Henry, 137, 165, 178; Hugh, 93, 103, 104, 110, 408; Humphrey, 97, 115, 118, 119; John, 59, 88, 94, 110, 135, 151, 167, 204, 239, 245, 271*, 281, 291, 304, 309, 310, 313, 327, 335, 349*, 355, 356, 386, 392, 402, 406; Joseph, 322; Marmaduke, 136; Owen, 364; Owen dd, 110; Owen Jo, 110; Paul, 103; Peter, 165; Randle, 33; Raph, 115; Richard, 102, 298, 375; Robert, 68, 327, 387; Salusbury, 304; Samuel, 379; Simon, 203, 296; Thomas, 27, 59, 104, 111, 116, 227, 275, 298*, 309, 313, 314, 387; Watkin, 239; William, 127, 193, 259, 327, 417. *See also* Floyd

Locker [Lokker], Edward, 15; John, 23, 82, 99, 101, 129*; Nicholas, 155; Peter, 57, 91; Richard, 15*, 26, 23, 41, 82, 91, 426; Thomas, 90*, 112; William, 24, 49, 57*, 112, 426*. *See also* Looker

Lockerley, John, 353. *See also* Lockley

Locket [Lockit], John, 191, 211, 225, 236, 257, 259, 260, 284, 297*; Peter, 257; Ralph, 284

INDEXES

Lockley [Lokley], John, 6, 410; Thomas, 410. *See also* Lockerley
Longton, Henry, 45; John, 39
Longueville, Sir Thomas, 340
Lonsdale, Miles, 340
Looker, John, 63, 99*, 124; Richard, 53, 68; Robert, 117; Thomas, 68, 81; William, 24. *See also* Locker
Loundes. *See* Lowndes
Lovet, John, 28, 46
Lowe, Edward, 409; George, 358, 379, 384, 407*, 409; John, 7, 32, 108, 125, 224, 376, 415*; Peter, 373; Ralph, 384, 414; Robert, 90, 107, 118, 224; Thomas, 85, 108, 114, 131, 143, 411; William, 61, 88, 373
Lowndes [Lownds], Benjamin, 190; Daniel, 349; John, 156; Richard, 338; Robert, 176, 303; Samuel, 303; Thomas, 338
Loy, John, 59
Lucas, Donald, 19; George, 29, 60; Henry, 14; John, 28, 60; Richard, 129; Robert, 288, 289; Thomas, 129
Ludman, Thomas, 176
Lumber, Charles, 407; James, 277, 345, 347, 359*, 387; John, 345; Thomas, 347, 377*, 387*, 407
Lunt, Anthony, 93; John, 79; Roger, 61; Thomas, 422
Lurtinge, John, 135; Richard, 147; William, 96, 105, 135
Lute, Richard, 23*
Lyalton, William, 3
Lymme [Lyme], Hugh, 25; Richard, 10, 23*
Lyne. *See* Leene
Lyneall. *See* Liniall
Lyngley, and Lynley. *See* Lingley
Lyon, John, 243; Mathew, 340
Lyster, Joseph, 424. *See* also Lister
Lyth, Robert, 4

M

Maccally [Mcally], Ralph, 10
Maccane, Thomas, 7
M'Cans [McCans], Charles, 368, 393
Macclesfield. *See* Maxfeild
M'Daniel, John, 404
M'Donald, Charles, 390
M'Gary, John, 393; Thomas, 393
Machell, Richard, 150. *See also* Matchell
M'Kay, George, 389
Macklin, Thomas, 172
M'Millan, Hugh, 360, 397; Thomas, 397

Macquien, James, 259, 332; Susan, 259
Macwyn, Donald, 12
Maddock [Maddocke, Madock, Madocke], Alderman, 369; Benjamin, 176, 186, 221, 248*, 260, 295, 304, 338, 364; David, 33; Edward, 294, 366, 385; George, 284, 338; Henry, 367; Hinton, 357; Hugh, 123, 144*, 145, 178, 230, 246*, 261, 312; James, 257, 294; Job, 353, 385; John, 63, 75, 81, 86, 88, 93, 99, 100, 111, 113, 116, 135, 148, 160, 165, 174, 195, 199, 220*, 227, 230, 237, 249*, 254, 260, 263, 287, 292, 294, 303*, 323, 325, 332, 350, 366, 367, 425*, 427; Jonadab, 369; Jonathan, 135; Joseph, 151, 160, 186, 197*, 220*, 237, 246, 249, 254, 259, 325, 366; Nathan, 187, 279, 284, 294, 304; Owen, 175; Paul, 169, 217*, 246, 248, 292, 319, 322*, 367, 397; Ralph, 32, 75; Richard, 130, 133, 142, 145, 187, 199, 263*, 370; Robert, 126, 249, 317*, 319, 350*, 375, 396, 397; Roger, 245, 257, 365, 366, 367, 397; Samuel, 158, 202*, 221, 223, 226, 246, 260, 288, 294, 311, 334, 339, 340*, 421; Simon, 246; Thomas, 112, 118, 147, 195, 204, 227, 244*, 248, 249, 257, 261, 286, 287, 311, 312, 324, 352*, 357, 366, 367, 370, 384, 386, (Rev.) 407*, 427; William, 26, 64*, 124, 171, 198, 263, 311
Maddocks, Daniel, 271; Job, 374; John, 108, 139, 351; Roger, 181; Simon, 341; William, 341
Mainwaring [Maynwaring, Maynwaryng], Edward, 309, 314, 336; George, 155, 174, 180, 187, 193, 199, 200, 262, 298; Henry, 33, 73, 269; James, 187, 224, 275, 298, 336; John, 172, 200, 267, 269, 380; Johnson, 245; Peter, 39; Randle, 18, 111, 426; Robert, 262, 298; (Sir) Thomas, 172, 267
Majendie, William Henry, 418
Makin. *See* Maykyn, and Meakin
Mal [――], Jeffery, 129
Malbon [Malbone], Charles, 202, 272*; Geoffry, 117, 182; George, 154, 168; Griffith, 201; Henry, 154; John, 104, 139, 201, 202, 211; Robert, 104; Samuel, 211; Thomas, 171
Malpas [Malpasse], George Lord, 272; Robert, 58, 88; Thomas, 32; William, 88
Manley, James, 9; John, 9; Richard, 267; William, 97

Mann, Robert, 343; Thomas, 343
Manning, John, 400; Thomas, 185, 241, 281, 374, 383, 414; William, 76
Manuel, John, 387, 389
Mapletoff, John, 309
Marbury. See Merbury
Marcroft, Peter, 406
Margarey, John, 289; Joseph, 277; Thomas, 289
Marks [Marckes, Markes], John, 125; Richard, 46, 116; Robert, 82; Thomas, 73, 83, 116
Marsden, John, 232, 308, 316, 345; Thomas, 345, 355
Marsh [Marshe, Merssh], George, 239, 282; John, 7, 27, 50, 101; Moses, 173, 209*, 239, 282, 307; Owen, 143; Richard, 30, 57, 60; Roland, 50; Samuel, 259, 307; Thomas, 86, 411
Marshall [Mareschall], Christopher, 5; John, 1, 10; Richard, 10; Thomas, 4; William, 5
Marsland. See Masland, and Mersland
Marston, Charles, 49; Thomas, 427
Marten [Martin, Martyn], Arthur, 52; Charles, 393; David, 386; Edward, 23, 43, 50, 51; Foulke, 104; George, 190; Henry, 51; John, 43, 47, 113, 149, 159, 190, 344*, 393; Peter, 110; Richard, 50; Robert, 28, 60, 104, 149, 181, 230*; Thomas, 15, 109, 122; William, 43, 159, 198*, 344, 365; [   ], 110
Marton. See Merton
Mascy. See Massey
Masland, Thomas, 112*
Maslen, Thomas, 109
Mason, Allen, 368, 374, 384, 405, 407, 414; Charles, 236; Daniel, 407; David, 163, 199; George, 199; Henry, 126, 218; James, 367; John, 14, 26, 215, 236, 279, 317, 367*; Ralph, 218, 279; Robert, 146; Samuel, 377; Thomas, 29, 146. See also Meason
Massey [Mascy, Massie, Massy], Edmund, 273; Edward, 95; Elias, 180, 214, 235; Elisha, 235, 258; Francis, 219, 296*, 418; George, 126, 227, 258; Henry, 397; Hugh, 7, 32; James, 64, 100, 124; John, 8, 32, 91, 118, 187, 214, 259, 295*, 296, 346, 383, 416, 419*; Joseph, 177; Lawrence, 86; Nicholas, 35, 44, 64, 65, 88, 91; Ralph, 185; Richard, 3, 8, 22, 35, 75, 151, 187, 258, 310, 314, 318, 346*, 376*;

Robert, 84, 297; Roger, 212, 218*, 273, 281, 282, 312, 361; Thomas, 21, 64, 88, 93, 100, 103, 110, 282, 326, 357*, 375, 397, 400*; Trafford, 212, 229, 239, 280, 281, 296, 297; William, 32, 68, 69*, 71, 72, 75, 95, 236, 258, 361, 375, 416
Master, Legh, 311
Matchell, Alexander, 235; Randle, 235. See also Machell
Mather, Richard, 334; Roger, 313; Thomas, 226, 313, 334*; William, 171
Mathews [Mathewes, Matthews], Edmund, 145, 182, 222, 235, 241, 257, 304; Edward, 259, 420; Eleanor, 229; Henry, 361: John, 107*, 203, 237, 400*; Maurice, 279; Richard, 229; Samuel, 270
Maudesley. See Mawdesley, and Modesley
Maughan, John, 147. See also Morgan
Maurice, John, 365, 370
Mawburne, Robert, 75
Mawdesley, Ralph, 25; Richard, 25; Robert, 25. See also Modesley
Maxfeild, William, 179, 268*
Maxland, Thomas, 113*
Maxy, William, 122
Maykyn, Thomas, 21. See also Meakin
Mayler [Mailer], John, 17, 353; William, 422
Mayo, Ralph, 34
Mayor, Mr., 361, 363, 382
Meacock [Meycock], George, 108, 131, 178; Henry, 236, 280, 297; John, 142, 175, 229*, 236*, 261, 287*, 375, 379, 418; Joseph, 171; Peter, 379; Ralph, 132; Richard, 52, 100*, 108, 159, 429; Robert, 147, 276; Thomas, 297, 381; William, 131, 418, 429
Meade. See Meide
Meadows [Meadowes], John, 213, 286; Samuel, 213, 286
Meakin [Meykin], James, 364, 367; John, 259, 388, 390; Randle, 259, 356, 364, 392*, 393; Richard, 393; Samuel, 329; Thomas, 31, 356; William, 329, 390. See also Maykyn
Menles, Richard, 36; William, 212
Meall, John, 48
Mears. See Meres
Meason, William, 114. See also Mason
Mechaughan, Charles, 339
Mee, Magnus, 19
Meide, Henry, 131
Meire, Thomas, 14

Meirick, Lawrence, 56. See also Meyrick
Meisam, William, 67. See also Mesham, and Messam
Melam, Thomas, 362
Melling, John, 241, 278
Mellor [Meller], John, 408; William, 3
Meo, William, 24, 44, 50, 57
Meols, John, 150, 161; Thomas, 41, 54*, 169; William, 24
Merbury, John, 10
Mercer, Alice, 110; Arthur, 213, 233, 262, 270, 332, 342, 344; Edward, 115, 146; James, 142, 317; John, 216, 305; Ralph, 317, 376; Richard, 110, 129, 144, 213, 238, 427; Robert, 12, 146*; Samuel, 238, 283, 376, 410; Thomas, 68, 106, 115, 192; William, 110*, 158, 192*, 210, 216, 308, 427
Meredith, Amos, 309; David, 15, 43; Edward, 76; George, 152; John, 33, 185, 204, 221, 240*, 244, 293*, 304, 324, 351*, 352, 377, 379, 389, 403, 405*, 407, 419; Joseph, 204, 255, 269, 280*, 315; Owen, 195*; Peter, 174, 221, 230, 252; Ralph, 395; Samuel, 384; Thomas, 304; William, 230, 352, 376, 395, 411
Meres [Mears], Josiah, 387; Mark, 367
Merrick. See Meirick, and Meyrick
Mersland, Thomas, 91, 104
Merton, Roger, 10
Mesham, Francis, 360; Henry, 428; William, 428. See also Meisam
Messam, William, 102
Meykin. See Maykyn, and Meakin
Meyrick, Robert, 377. See also Meirick
Michael, John, 263
Middlehurst, Edward, 276, 344; John, 306; Thomas, 306
Middleton [Medelton, Midleton, Myddelton], Andrew, 194, 249*, 279; David, 22, 73; John, 22, 31, 89, 309; Ralph, 12, 18, 22, 23; Randle, 89; Richard, 16, 18, 23, 122; Robert, 12*; William, 125
Midless, John, 292; Thomas, 292
Miller [Millar], Aaron, 385; James, 388; John, 49, 344, 372, 385, 386; Lawrence, 101; Moses, 372; William, 400. See also Milner
Millington, Edward, 118; George, 233; John, 168, 180, 208, 238*, 284, 375, 388, 417, 423; Robert, 96, 179, 216, 300; Thomas, 112, 140; William, 233
Milner [Millner], Henry, 200; John,

31, 51, 53, 78; Robert, 28, 90; Thomas, 78. See also Miller
Milton, William, 230, 279
Minor, John, 2; William, 102
Minshull [Minshall, Mynshall], Albin, 417; Andrew, 109; Edmund, 4; Francis, 177; Giles, 344, 409*; Henry, 262; John, 165, 179, 187, 211, 229, 229 n., 233, 252, 262*, 263, 286, 349, 421; Jonathan, 211 Mary, 211; Peter, 4; Ralph, 96, 147, 152, 428; Randle, 124, 158*, 211; Richard, 123, 140, 164, 211, 244; Samuel, 244; Thomas, 147, 177, 186, 192, 233*, 286, 318, 344, 349, 364, 390, 409; Urian, 132, 149, 153; William, 147, 192*, 252, 409
Mitchell, Alexander, 288*; Richard, 208*
Modesley, Hector, 77; John, 120, 125, 126, 133; Nicholas, 85; Ralph, 47, 64, 71, 90; Randle, 47, 115; Richard, 44, 50, 73; Robert, 45, 47; William, 54, 97, 105, 108, 137, 428. See also Mawdesley
Mody, William, 1
Moffit, John, 366, 371; William, 366
Moldesworth. See Mouldesworth
Moldinge, Thomas, 64
Molleaux, Richard, 119. See also Molyneux, and Mullenex
Molson, John, 58, 69; Ralph, 47. See also Molston, and Moulson
Molston, Robert, 47*. See also Molson, and Moulson
Molyneux [Mollinoux], George, 335; John, 335; Richard, 429; Thomas, 300, 395*. See also Molleaux, and Mullenex
Momford, David, 38, 110; Richard, 16; Simon, 18, 110
Moneley, Henry, 34
Monk, Benjamin, 371, 400; Edmund, 406; John, 361, 379, 386*, 406, 418*; Mr., 371; William, 349, 361, 370, 371*. See also Munk
Monkes, John, 265
Monksfield [Monkesfilde, Monxfield, Monxfild, Munkesfeld], George, 28, 98; Henry, 98; John, 77; Ralph, 12; Richard, 121; Robert, 6, 37; Thomas, 6, 49
Montgomery, John, 408, 420
Moody. See Mody
Moore, the Hon. and Rev. Dr. Henry, 310; James, 419; John, 36, 289; Phillip, 105; Theodocius, 356, 419; Theodore, 289; Thomas, 213, 356; William, 107, 213. See also More
Moores, John, 39, 126, 351, 366, 423; Joseph, 333*, 380*; Josiah, 191,

INDEXES

297; Phillip, 96; Robert, 310; Theodore, 253; Thomas, 144, 168, 191, 253, 262*, 265, 310, 380; William, 89, 176
Mooton, George, 395; Thomas, 418. See also Moulton
Moran, John, 89
More, George, 21; Hamlet, 119; Henry, 28; Phillip, 119. See also Moore
Moreland, Edward, 387
Moreton, Charles, 139; Edward, 155, 340; Eliner, 138; George, 266; John, 106, 138, 183, 185, 244*, 252, 265, 266; Richard, 123, Robert, 252; Thomas, 116, 265, 307; William, 164, 215, 260
Morgan, Edward, 126, 191, 272, 315; James, 314; John, 310, 374; Peter, 315, 356; Ralph, 101, 107, 121; Randle, 92, 134*, 152; Thomas, 49; William, 5, 368. See also Maughan
Morgell, Edward, 145; Ralph, 173, 212; William, 212
Morpeth, William, 10
Morphett, Thomas, 327; William, 327
Morrey. See Mory
Morris [Morres, Moris, Morrice], Canon, 55 n.; Charles, 183; Edward, 368, 423; George, 120, 143*, 237; Hugh, 139; John, 66, 119; Owen, 106; Ralph, 105; Richard, 150; Robert, 142, 176, 188, 424, 428; Roger, 428; Samuel, 137; Thomas, 56, 101, 119, 128, 145, 150, 159, 161, 181, 203*, 214, 237, 255, 259, 266, 305*, 426, 428; William, 110, 128, 146, 201*, 297; [——], 128. See also Morys
Mort, Jacob, 185; James, 171, 186; John, 346; Peter, 186; Ralph, 51
Morvill [Morveyll], Christopher, 30
Mory [Morrey], John, 109; Robert, 157, 160; Thomas, 80; William, 109
Morys, Gilbert, 11. See also Morris
Moscrofte, William, 79
Moscrop, John, 9
Moseley, Joseph, 158*; Matthew, 170; Ralph, 95; Randle, 170
Moss [Mosse], John, 389, 410; Joseph, 383; Ralph, 85, 101, 110, 116*, 246; Robert, 64, 137, 166, 189; Thomas, 31, 189; William, 110, 156, 183, 278*, 408
Moston, Charles, 45; Robert, 29; Thomas, 39
Mostyn, Henry, 259, 296; James, 378; John, 165, 340, 350; Joseph, 373;

403; Roger, 257, 259, 285*, 287, 358; Rowland, 257, 350, 373, 378; Samuel, 310; Thomas, 311; William, 287
Motterom, Hugh, 86
Mottershead, Albean, 136; James, 226, 279, 282*, 306, 317, 358; John, 136, 279, 280; Samuel, 291; Thomas, 115, 129, 136*, 189, 226, 280, 291
Mouldesworth, Edmund, 131
Moulsdale, John, 81
Moulson, Charles, 150, 209*, 219, 221, 278, 335, 362; Edward, 382; Hugh, 133*, 162, 167, 184, 187; John, 126, 171, 183, 233, 278; Marmaduke, 274; Peter, 221, 274; Richard, 235, 331*, 352; Robert, 166, 173, 221; Samuel, 221; Thomas, 162, 174, 193, 219, 227, 233*, 235, 237*, 278, 352, 382*, 393; Urian, 173; William, 184. See also Molson, and Molston
Moulton, John, 408; Robert, 366; Samuel, 371. See also Mooton
Mountford, David, 79; John, 98; William, 79
Mouson [Mowson], Hugh, 146, 147, 425; John, 114, 425; Robert, 114, 136*
Mowsdale, John, 94
Mowson. See Mouson
Moyle, Charles, 299; Edward, 111; George, 409; John, 63, 80, 88, 90, 133, 167, 194, 253; Phillip, 87; Randle, 201, 262*, 297, 299; Richard, 133; Thomas, 194, 253, 341*; William, 203, 297
Mullenex, John, 235; Joseph, 336*; Richard, 86; Thomas, 235, 335; William, 87. See also Molleaux, and Molyneux
Mulleney, John, 285; Thomas, 223, 244
Mumford. See Momford
Munk, Thomas, 242. See also Monk
Munnerley, Joseph, 418
Murphy, James, 378; Mathew, 373
Murrey [Murray], David, 240; John, 191; Peter, 240; Robert, 124, 153, 191*, 212, 220, 337*; Thomas, 220, 240
Mutchell [Muchill], James, 102; Richard, 181; Thomas, 124; William, 129
Mutton, Peter, 28; William, 31, 59. See also Mytton
Mycalbalgh [Mykelhalgh], Henry, 6; Peter, 5
Myddleton. See Middleton
Myers, John, 267*; Richard, 214

INDEXES

Mykelhalgh. *See* Mycalhalgh
Mytton, Charles, 277, 320, 383*; John, 312; Richard, 404. *See also* Mutton

N

Nailor, James, 386; Peter, 363; Thomas, 390
Napier, David, 369, 379
Nayle, Catherine, 257; Thomas, 257
Naylor. *See* Nailor
Neil [Neal, Neale], Martha, 321; Richard, 219, 247; Robert, 219, 247; William, 247, 248
Neild, John, 321; Robert, 219; Samuel, 137, 388; William, 402
Neileson, Patrick, 6
Nelson, William, 383
Neturfeld, Robert, 5
Nevitt, Henry, 412; John, 231*, 292, 320*; Lawrence, 336; Samuel, 332; Thomas, 315, 332, 336
Newall [Newhall], James, 402; John, 19, 25; Peter, 38, 41; Richard, 21, 34, 42*, 45, 86; Robert, 21; William, 21. *See also* Newell, and Nowell
Newas, Randle, 45; Richard, 69; Simon, 69
Newbot, Henry, 64
Newboulte, William, 79
Newby, Edward, 76
Newell, Daniel, 339; James, 309*, 331, 376; John, 353, 384, 399, 407; John Taylor, 384; Joseph, 331, 376; Robert, 399; William, 406, 407. *See also* Newall, and Nowell
Newhall. *See* Newall, and Nowell
Newhouse, Nicholas, 7; Richard, 13, 74; William, 74
Newman, John, 309
Newns, Thomas, 378
Newport, Henry, 117; Joseph, 314; Richard, 88, 110; Thomas, 52, 81, 88; William, 156
Newton, Gilbert, 274*; John, 4, 205, 229, 304; Jonathan, 229; Richard, 69; Thomas, 11, 34, 69; William, 86, 165
Niccoll. *See* Nicholl
Nicholas, John, 272, 386; Peter, 24; Robert, 33, 100*, 129; Samuel, 272, 391; Thomas, 129; William, 423
Nicholl [Niccoll, Nickoll, Nicol], Anthony, 116; John, 50, 100*, 103, 113, 137; Peter, 161; Richard, 103; Samuel, 176; Thomas, 79, 116
Nicholls, Anthony, 187; Benjamin, 334; Charles, 227; Edward, 270, 313, 327; Gabriel, 243; Hugh, 228; John, 176, 197, 232, 238, 241, 246, 248, 278, 295, 308, 356, 383; Mary, 270; Moses, 246; Paul, 295, 356; Peter, 138, 167, 197, 225*, 243, 295, 305, 334, 366; Richard, 167; Robert, 308; Samuel, 221*, 232, 246, 257, 278, 303, 305, 327*, 337; Thomas, 104, 153, 303, 377, 382; William, 104, 153, 245, 305, 334, 377, 382*, 383*, 392, 420; Zachariah, 360; Zaccheus, 238, 291, 397
Nicholson [Nichollasson, Nichollson], Henry, 17; John, 377; Joshua, 313; Stephen, 116; Thomas, 15, 35
Nickoll. *See* Nicholl
Nickson [Nixon], Edward, 178, 228; George, 149; John, 149; Samuel, 421; Thomas, 228
Nicoll. *See* Nicholl
Nield. *See* Neild
Nilley, William, 55
Nixon. *See* Nickson
Noble, Neville, 360
Norbury, John, 396
Norcot, Thomas, 46
Norley, Ralph, 12
Norman, John, 69; William, 7
Northover, William, 357
Norton, Thomas, 418
Nowell, Walter, 48. *See also* Newall, and Newell
Nugent, Simon, 27
Nutter, John, 55

O

Oakborne. *See* Okborne
Oakes. *See* Okes
Oakley. *See* Okeley
Occle, John, 68
Odcroft, William, 222
Odier, John, 333, 393; Joseph, 394; Samuel, 333, 394
Offley, Hugh, 55; John, 30; Richard, 55; Robert, 63; Thomas, 63; William, 55
Ogden [Ogdain], George, 402; Joseph, 269; Robert, 269, 290; Thomas, 187
Ogle, Cuthbert, 214
Okborne, Walter, 3
Okeley, William, 8
Okell [Okyll], Daniel, 243; James, 423; Rosingreave, 214, 243
Okes [Oakes], George, 69; Richard, 336*
Oldham [Oldome, Ouldham], John, 364; Livesey, 350, 385; Richard, 9, 96; Robert, 385; William, 150
Ollerhead [Owlerhead], John, 201, 223, 281*, 320, 426; Nicholas, 263; Richard, 320, 362; Robert, 46, 85,

112, 426; Thomas, 127; Timothy, 391; William, 56, 201, 275, 421
Olliver [Oliver], James, 266, 322; John, 212, 235, 266, 270, 308; Peter, 322; Simon, 213, 254*, 260; Thomas, 270, 317; William, 260
Olton. *See* Oulton
Orandale, Henry, 275
Orange, John, 299, 324; Samuel, 220, 299
Orbistone, Charles, 286; Thomas, 286
Ord, John, 367
Ordain, John, 354; Joseph, 330, 352; Robert, 330, 352
Ordes [Ords], James, 252; John, 277, 368; Ralph, 277; Richard, 146, 180, 219, 241, 252, 277*
Ordford, Jonathan, 384
Oreton. *See* Orton
Orford, John, 419; Jonathan, 419
Orme, Ambrose, 330; Charles, 245, 330, 337; Edward, 330; John, 253*; Richard, 286, 346, 355, 403*; Robert, 227; Thomas, 185, 227, 303*, 337
Ormerod, 55 *n*., 140 *n*.
Ormes, Francis, 213, 257, 284; James, 284; John, 185, 213, 242, 284, 341; Richard, 145*, 185, 198, 242, 257, 341; Roger, 384; Thomas, 185, 198*, 213*, 316; Timothy, 240
Ormeston, John, 97
Orrery, The Right Hon. Earl of, 342
Orton [Oreton], Edward, 21, 76; George, 140; John, 69, 76, 88, 93; Richard, 16, 28; Robert, 150; Thomas, 40, 68, 85, 93; William, 85, 88, 429
Orum, Edward, 257; Henry, 336
Otie [Ottie, Oty, Ottye], Henry, 25, 65; Ralph, 65
Oulf, John, 212, 292; Joseph, 290; Peter, 290; Robert, 212, 292, 303*. *See also* Owffe
Oullerhead. *See* Ollerhead
Oulton [Olton], Charles, 232; Edward, 142, 162, 172, 178, 203, 211, 232; George, 168; Humphrey, 259; John, 124, 175, 259; Matthew, 212; Randle, 101, 123, 143, 151, 154, 162, 166*, 168, 197*, 253; Richard, 157, 203, 207, 212, 230*, 253; Thomas, 235
Ouslecroft, William, 131
Overton, John, 367
Owen, Arthur, 310; Edward, 86; Fulke ap Richard, 29; George, 423; Griffith, 195; Henry, 351, 429; Hugh, 236; Humphrey, 175, 195; John, 67, 80, 95, 119, 129, 131, 137, 143, 144, 154, 410, 423; Owen ap John, 67; Richard, 38, 86, 111, 216,
394; Robert ap, 265; Steven, 125; William, 143, 216, 271*, 314
Owens, Christopher, 394; George, 353, 414*; John, 418; Matthew, 280, 316; Owen, 333; Richard, 212; Robert, 137, 333; Thomas, 130
Owffe, John, 121, 164; Joseph, 170. *See also* Oulf
Owlerhead. *See* Ollerhead

P

Pace, Robert, 297
Packe, Christopher, 186, 195
Packman. *See* Pakeman
Pady, John, 5
Page, Alderman, 369; Humphrey, 176, 220, 242; John, 149*, 189, 247*, 270, 300, 353, 361; Leigh, 242; Stephen, 170; Thomas, 358, 369; William, 142, 154, 183, 189, 270, 358, 390*
Painter, Richard, 106; William, 315
Pakeman, John, 324
Palin [Palyn], George, 172, 187, 198; James, 147, 376, 396; John, 154, 165, 184, 198, 230*, 259, 285, 290, 291, 326, 334, 358, 361, 363, 406, 412; Robert, 116; Stephen, 282*, 316, 377; Thomas, 134, 314, 316, 376*, 377, 396, 406, 418, 421; William, 326, 350, 376, 418
Palmer, Randle, 13
Panton, Charles, 290, 384*; Edward, 230, 290; Fulke, 230, 240; Hill, 350; Paul, 385, 387, 394, 403; Thomas, 387; William, 240, 350, 394. *See also* Paynton
Pantre, John, 8, 9; William, 9
Pardoe, James, 345
Pares, James, 157
Park, Christopher, 217
Parkensonn, John, 93
Parker, Arthur, 330; Charles, 330, 349; Edmund, 220; Edward, 89, 272; Gerrard, 263; James, 35; John, 201*, 216, 220, 231, 271, 272, 273, 274, 296, 310, 325, 330, 338, 340; Joseph, 231, 278; Richard, 19, 176, 244, 283, 295, 330, 349; Robert, 94; Roger, 295; Thomas, 89, 296, 315*, 357; William, 315, 357
Parkinson. *See* Parkenson
Parks, John, 141, 188, 301; Josiah, 173, 301; Robert, 155; Samuel, 173
Parlowe, Richard, 17
Parnell, Thomas, 153*, 177, 192, 209, 232; Tobias, 133

Parrat, Richard, 198
Parry [Parrie], Charles, 324, 365, 370, 391, 419; David, 182; Edward, 100*, 111*, 236, 296, 320; Francis, 374, 384, 419; George, 331; Henry, 242, 260; Humphrey, 234, 311; James, 351, 391, 407, 413, 418; John, 146, 194, 234, 242, 303, 317, 332, 365, 385, 405; Lewis, 155, 194, 203, 216; Owen, 216; Peter, 204, 220*, 234, 255, 276, 278, 282, 308, 314, 324; Richard, 25, 358; Robert, 331, 386; Roger, 320, 354, 406*; Rowland, 175; Samuel, 381; Thomas, 41, 141, 343, 373, 407; Watkin, 407; William, 100, 117, 194, 296, 317, 365, 371; [——], 204
Parsonage, Edward, 223; John, 162, 392, 417; Richard, 255, 283, 328, 341; Samuel, 255, 283, 328; Thomas, 94, 412; Timothy, 341, 412; William, 88, 115, 128, 162
Parsons, Richard, 163, 196, 249, 250*; Robert, 180, 249
Parte, Robert, 141
Partington, Edward, 162, 192, 196, 202, 215, 245; John, 142, 236; Puleston, 158, 179, 219; Richard, 71, 93; Thomas, 177, 227, 234*, 236
Partridge [Pattridge], Daniel, 287; David, 169; John, 169, 287; Samuel, 181; Thomas, 156, 183; William, 147
Pasmich, Richard, 22
Passingham, Jonathan, 411
Pate, Henry, 357; John, 244, 347, 357, 396; Lloyd, 401; Richard, 12; Thomas, 52, 177, 224, 231, 244, 298*, 401
Pater, Thomas, 347
Patrick, Robert, 274
Pattison, Joseph, 367
Patton, Edward, 317; Foulke, 164; Hugh, 216; Paul, 312, 334; Peter, 414; Robert, 299; Thomas, 188, 267, 299, 311, 317, 344, 348, 376, 384; William, 151, 188, 216, 267, 334, 344. See also Paynton, and Peyton
Pattridge. See Partridge
Paul, John, 377, 415*, 420; Thomas, 420
Payne, Richard, 283; Robert, 135; Thomas, 30, 283; William, 63
Paynton, Charles, 400; Thomas, 245. See also Panton
Payton, William, 246. See also Patton, and Peyton

Peacock [Peycock, Peakock], James, 411; John, 266*, 366; Richard, 62
Pearson, John, 422; Joseph, 415. See also Pierson
Peccowe [Peckow], John, 19; Thomas, 426
Peck, Christopher, 253; Daniel, 210; George, 379; John, 316*; Samuel, 379; William, 253
Peeres [Peers, Piers], Benjamin, 325, 397; Daniel, 258; Elizabeth, 311; James, 330, 389, 394*, 397; John, 210, 244, 277, 286, 289*, 311, 325, 329, 338, 352, 362, 384*; Joseph, 286; Peter, 103; Samuel, 258, 389; Thomas, 140, 248*, 329, 330, 338, 339*; William, 277, 363. See also Pierce
Peerson. See Pearson, and Pierson
Peever. See Peover
Pekkell, Hugh, 14; Thomas, 14
Pemberton, Benjamin, 181, 252, 402; Daniel, 223, 274, 280, 347*; Edward, 92; Elnathan, 249; George, 135; Henry, 43, 85, 127, 168, 184, 196*, 197, 234, 296, 337, 351, 361*, 406; John, 141, 145*, 175, 184, 185, 188*, 196, 220, 236, 255, 267*, 273*, 279, 280, 290, 296, 337*, 348, 364, 379*, 394; John Holland, 406; Jonathan, 163, 234, 249; Joseph, 173, 176, 380; Miles, 115, 136, 143, 156; Nicholas, 22; Peter, 166, 182, 212, 252, 263*, 354*, 402; Randle, 178; Richard, 13, 43, 92*, 112*; Robert, 66, 427; Samuel, 263, 371, 394; Thomas, 98, 125, 165, 182, 199*, 223, 315, 323, 348, 407; William, 66, 83, 212, 288*, 325, 364, 371, 380, 397
Pendlebury, Collins, 230, 296, 298*; Samuel, 296
Penketh, John, 163, 299
Penkett, Richard, 195, 218, 231, 299, 325; Thomas, 195; William, 325
Pennant, David, 310; Edward, 309; John, 310; Peter, 83, 309; Thomas, 343
Pennington, James, 324; John, 324, 374*; Thomas, 353; William, 212, 422. See also Pinnington
Penny [Peny], Jo., 110; Ralph, 74, 110; Richard, 27; William, 52
Pensell, Nicholas, 5
Penson, Thomas, 354, 398*
Penteny, Thomas, 46
Penwortham, Roger de, 1
Peover [Peever], John, 193; Robert, 93; William, 357

Peploe, (Rev.) Samuel, 352
Percivall [Percyvale, Percyvall, Persivall, Psyvall], George, 24; James, 238, 260, 319*, 329*, 420; John, 3, 18, 40, 171, 254, 260, 311, 429; Peter, 194, 254; Randle, 23, 53; Richard, 18; Robert, 14, 18*, 23, 24, 53; Thomas, 41, 102, 109; William, 254
Perkins, George, 256*, 366, 367; Henry, 276, 356, 365
Perrin, Benjamin, 235, 276
Perrison, Nicholas, 17
Perry, John, 373; Richard, 32; Thomas, 148; William, 227
Pert, William, 16
Pesaunt [Pessaunt], Gillam, 21*; Hugh, 21; William, 14
Peters, Edward, 364
Pety, Robert, 13
Peyton, William, 337, 356. See also Patton, and Payton
Phasackerley. See Fazakerley
Phenix, James, 390
Phillips [Phillippes]. Cornelius, 184, 266; David, 34; Edward, 114, 135, 403; Francis, 130; George, 37, 67; Henry, 80, 81, 114; Humphrey, 52, 71, 101, 130, 425; John, 91, 130, 147, 188, 266, 351*, 362, 391, 3-9, 426; Philip, 57, 81, 92, 142; Ralph, 184; Randle, 67; Richard, 301; Robert, 29, 44, 50, 57, 77, 88, 96, 272, 425; Thomas, 119, 188, 391, 351, 364; William, 88, 101, 109, 123, 272
Philpot [Phillpott], John, 244; Joseph, 201, 244, 298; Nathaniel, 298; Robert, 201, 244; William, 298
Phitheon [Phithian, Phythian]. Hugh, 185; John, 272, 326. See also Fithian
Phœnix. See Phenix
Pick [Picke], John, 129; William, 34; [——], 80. See also Pickes, Pike, and Pyke
Pickance, Daniel, 205, 368*
Pickavant [Pikyvanne], George, 119; John, 97, 119
Pickering, James, 355, 376*; Jonathan, 203*, 237, 267; Thomas, 127, 166
Pickes, John, 80
Pickford, Edward, 241, 285*, 295*; George, 295, 331, 359*; John, 331; Thomas, 365
Pickmeire, Randle, 157
Pickmore, Henry, 143; John, 291; Ralph, 207, 232, 239, 241; Randle, 207, 210, 222*, 313;

Samuel, 292; Thomas, 190, 263, 291, 292, 347, 365, 386; William, 222, 263
Pierce [Pearce], Robert, 416; Thomas, 402. See also Peeres
Pierson [Peereson, Peerson, Perrison, Person], John, 31, 59; Nicholas, 17; Phillip, 67. See also Pearson
Pigot [Piggott], Charles, 327; Henry, 51; Hugh, 217; Piercy, 234; Richard, 306; Robert, 201, 243, 270, 306, 327, 340; Thomas, 243; Walter, 243
Pike, George, 259; John, 372*; Joseph, 192; Paul, 372*; Ralph, 115; Robert, 227, 259; Samuel, 159, 259; Thomas, 192; William, 137. See also Pick, Pickes, and Pyke
Pilkington [Pylkynton], Thomas, 3, 112
Pillen [Pillin, Pyllyn], Henry, 29, 22; James, 41; John, 33, 41; Ralph, 22; Robert, 41; Thomas, 29, 40, 41*; William, 41
Pimblow, William, 394
Pimrose [Pymrose], Henry, 45; John, 80; William, 80
Pindar, Charles, 178; (Sir) Peter, 169
Pinnington, Thomas, 404*, 408; William, 408. See also Pennington
Pixley, William, 49, 50, 59
Platt, Edward, 332; John, 41, 215, 252, 290, 319; Peter, 160, 200*, 261, 268, 277*, 319; Richard, 271, 332; Thomas, 171; William, 215
Pleavin, Thomas, 416
Plethin [Plethyn], Ralph, 96; Thomas, 57, 91; William, 91
Ploughtin [Ploughin], John, 241
Plumbe [Plomb, Plombe], David, 101; John, 135; Phillip, 103, 218, 221*; Richard, 198; Thomas, 218; William, 61, 96, 103
Plumley, Richard, 173; Thomas, 170, 246, 259*, 348, 386; William, 134, 159*, 172, 227*, 246, 348
Plumpton, Richard, 11; William, 159
Pode, William, 415
Podmore, John, 423; Randle, 360
Poghton, John, 11
Pointon. See Poynton
Pollatt, William, 255
Poole [Pole], Barnabas, 52; Edward, 51, 363; Hugh, 309; James, 219, 345; John, 62, 101, 103*, 112, 124, 147, 148, 161, 167*, 232*, 339*, 345, 362, 382, 405, 406, 411, 412*; Ralph, 8, 163; Richard,

6, 12, 19, 38, 103, 156, 262; Robert, 47, 219; Thomas, 32, 37, 82, 262, 296, 375, 411, 415; William, 82, 97. 114, 135
Pooley, Thomas, 71
Pope, John, 42; Richard, 19, 34, 42
Port, Henry, 4
Porteous, (the Right Rev.) Bielby, 383
Porter, Daniel, 238, 274, 317, 323*, 348, 361; Henry the, 2; James, 361; John, 2, 251, 271, 295, 320; Joseph, 265, 336; Peter, 374; Richard, 159, 184, 251, 306, 307; Thomas, 295, 317, 374, 423; William, 348
Posnett, Benjamin, 363; John, 279, 370; Thomas, 222, 279, 300*, 370; William, 380
Postons, George, 268; Robert, 268
Potter, Andrew, 218, 344; Daniel, 192, 292*; John, 158, 192, 210*, 220, 302, 344; Peter, 180, 221*; Richard, 148; Robert, 93; Samuel, 139, 220, 266, 302; William, 131, 151
Pova [Pover, Povah], Charles, 416; Edward, 333, 366, 416; Robert, 26
Povall, John, 228, 301; Robert, 29; Thomas, 272; William, 301
Povey, Jane, 274; William, 274
Powdrell, Richard, 371, 416*
Powell, Benjamin, 247, 346, 355; Charles, 332, 391*, 398; David, 389; Edward, 58, 102, 130, 185*, 193*, 235, 252, 285, 303*, 350, 364, 380, 391*; Evan, 102; George, 249; Henry, 108; Isaac, 224; James, 233, 315; John, 35, 36, 73, 102, 104, 108, 170, 185, 225, 235, 242, 249, 315, 346, 398, 413, 417; Joseph, 355; Michael, 252; Richard, 65, 109; Robert, 33, 37, 365; Thomas, 18, 104, 233, 278, 285, 346, 354*, 378, 383, 396, 407, 417; Walter, 314; William, 185, 224, 247, 346; [——], 52
Pownall, John, 283; Joseph, 305; 394; Samuel, 163; Thomas, 283, 394; William, 410
Poynton [Pointon], Aaron, 335, 366; Charles, 317, 376; Ely, 331; John, 172, 261, 376; Leonard, 239; Moses*, 331, 335, 366; Randle, 220*, 274. 317; Robert, 341; William, 108*, 120, 169, 196, 228*, 261, 341
Pratchitt [Prachett], John, 321; Richard, 223, 273, 276; Thomas, 273, 321, 331, 335, 339, 365
Preece [Prees], Erasmus, 85; John,

70, 272*; Richard, 149; Thomas, 27, 132
Prenton, John, 63, 75, 100*, 120; Richard, 28; Thomas, 66, 113; Urian, 66; William, 73, 132
Prescot [Prescote], George, 238; George William, 408; Hugh de, 1; John, 308; Margaret, 256; Thomas, 308; William, 256, 316*.
Preson, William, 27. *See also* Preston
Prestaton, Hugh de, 3; Robert, 3; William de, 3
Prestbury [Presbury, Prestburie], Isaac, 265, 337; John, 244, 265, 333; Jonathan, 244, 329, 333, 337; Joseph, 176, 221, 253, 313; Philip, 253, 345, 361*, 366, 384, 387, 402, 410; Samuel, 221, 293, 316, 345; Thomas, 329; William, 293, 358*, 366
Preston, George, 407; John de, 2*; William, 2. *See also* Preson
Price, Alban, 323; Benjamin, 219; Charles, 245, 275, 328, 334, 342, 367, 379; Edward, 237*, 268, 285, 323, 408; Erasmus, 106, 133; Francis, 271, 340; George, 256*, 323, 363; Henry, 256; James, 314, 389; John, 106, 222, 251, 256*, 270, 298, 328, 333, 342, 346, 348*, 349, 381, 402, 405, 412; Jonathan, 158, 172; Joseph, 224, 333; Lloyd, 406; Mary, 219; Nathaniel, 271; Peter, 56, 103, 119, 124; Richard, 121, 148, 149*, 168, 213, 251, 266, 271, 285, 320; Robert, 155, 224, 225, 342, 346, 357, 398*, 406; Samuel, 271, 285, 346, 348, 351; Thomas, 95, 168, 174, 213, 237*, 268, 271, 311, 320, 333*, 349, 358, 381, 389, 404, 412; William, 256, 342, 381
Prichard. *See* Pritchard
Pricket [Prickett, Prycket], Arthur, 116; Joseph, 113; Ralph, 78, 97; Robert, 116; Theodore, 126; Thomas, 65, 78, 425*
Primatte. *See* Prymatte
Prince, Benjamin, 412; Francis, 125; George, 290; Hugh, 382; James, 217, 290*, 334*; John, 157, 217, 290; Thomas, 202, 404; William, 204
Pritchard [Prichard]. Edward, 72, 314; Henry, 70; John, 197, 252*, 284, 329, 367, 387; Joseph, 157, 197, 252, 387; Richard, 371, 408; Robert, 316, 329; Samuel, 284, 337; Thomas, 316, 330, 337, 367; William, 50
Probert, Cotton, 354, 390, 396;

INDEXES 473

James, 374; John, 362; Ralph, 244, 337, 346, 354
Probin [Probyn], Humphrey, 58, 67; John, 52, 376
Proby, William, 173
Proderough, David, 114; John, 114
Prymatte, Richard, 85, 427; William, 427
Pugh [Pue], David, 120; John, 188, 191*, 212, 216; Richard, 32; Robert, 120; William, 114*
Puleston, Edward, 179, 217, 240*; John, 310; Richard, 310; Thomas, 278
Pulford, Alexander, 186, 234, 266; George, 116, 226; John, 49, 50, 266, 293; Richard, 129, 224; Robert, 224, 293*, 333; Thomas, 118, 138, 226, 266, 333; William, 174
Pulton, William, 15
Pvall, Robert, 29
Pye, Christopher, 105; Henry, 74, 105
Pyke, George, 209; Jane, 346; John, 296, 323; Paul, 325; Robert, 209, 278*, 291, 296, 301, 325; Samuel, 209, 221. *See also* Pick, Pike, and Pickes

Q

Qua, William, 217*, 279
Quaile [Queile], John, 111, 140
Quick, George, 169; William, 177
Quirke, Gilbert, 23

R

Rabon, Richard, 106. *See also* Rathbone
Raborne, Henry, 32. *See also* Rathborne
Raburne, Richard, 36. *See also* Rathburne
Rackett, Charles, 377
Radcliffe [Radcliff, Radclive], Alderman, 104; Coldson, 104; John, 14, 23; Thomas, 23; William, 48. *See also* Ratcliffe
Radford, Daniel, 125; Foulk, 81; Henry, 20, 87; James, 64; John, 20; Nathaniel, 133; Ralph, 35, 40, 51, 93*, 99; Richard, 21; Robert, 63, 99, 133, 143, 182*, 203; Roger, 20, 40, 58; Samuel, 135, 172; Thomas, 35, 58; Walter de, 1; William, 31, 84; [——], 81
Radley, John, 30, 109; Richard, 31,

35, 67*, 109*; Thomas, 22; William, 15; [——], 22
Ralph, Edward, 275*, 367; Richard, 367
Ralphs, Joseph, 378, 408; William, 412
Ralphson, Richard, 278
Ralton, Adam, 22
Ramsay, John, 395
Ramsden, Henry, 94; William, 41, 94
Randle, Samuel, 215, 256*
Randles, George, 382; John, 402; Richard, 324, 388; Thomas, 324, 356, 422; William, 395
Ratcliff [Ratcliffe], Benjamin, 172, 246, 304; James, 217, 240, 279; John, 51, 66, 76*, 84, 94, 97, 99, 101, 103, 106, 107, 112, 114*, 115*, 118, 152, 161, 172, 304, 361, 376, 381; Joseph, 279, 324, 332, 347, 351*, 397, 403; Nicholas, 105; Peter, 329, 397; Richard, 161; Robert, 50, 77; Samuel, 120, 152; Taylor, 366; Thomas, 265; William, 77*, 152, 246, 265, 329, 347, 354*, 364, 366, 375, 378, 381, 389, 397, 399. *See also* Radcliffe
Rathbone, James, 367; John, 12, 89, 256*, 387; Lawrence, 89; Peter, 129; Ralph, 89; Richard, 21, 95, 129; Robert, 12, 23; Samuel, 343; Thomas, 343, 354, 371, 379*, 385*, 387, 391, 393, 398; William, 89, 114, 168, 299, 350. *See also* Rabon
Rathborne, Henry, 156; John, 123. *See also* Raborne
Rathburne, John, 34, 46, 61; Lawrence, 101; Ralph, 45, 56, 59, 66, 74; Richard, 44, 52, 68, 75*, 80. *See also* Raburne
Ravenscroft, Anne, 231; Charles, 150, 159; Daniel, 240; George, 62, 342; Hugh, 122; James, 136; John, 236, 300; Nicholas, 5, 9; Peter, 9, 236, 240; Ralph, 129, 151; Thomas, 231, 340; William, 181, 267; [——], 171
Ravenson, William, 4
Rawlin [Rowlin], George, 116; John, 62, 140
Rawlinson, George, 399; Joseph, 368; Lawrence, 46; William, 399. *See also* Rowlandson, and Rowlinson
Ray [Rea], Absalom, 405; John, 216, 298*, 378; Robert, 158
Raynald. *See* Reynolds
Rayne, Thomas, 245
Read [Reade], Bagot, 308, 315, 398*; Edward, 398; Humphrey, 343;

474   INDEXES

John, 185, 335; Mr., 398; Thomas, 335; William, 370
Reader, John, 373
Redich, William, 4
Redrope, John, 182; Richard, 263
Reece [Rees, Reice, Res, Ries], Egidius [Giles], 158, 180, 187: Elizabeth, 284; Ellis, 144; Fulke, 54; George, 170, 245, 287, 388; Giles, 210, 301; John, 27, 32, 51, 273, 284, 351*, 356, 388, 412; Joseph, 358; Nicholas, 135, 182, 233, 273; Peter, 376; Randle, 233; Richard, 151, 177, 186, 196, 251; Robert, 144; Samuel, 379; Thomas, 20, 112, 158, 194, 196, 212*, 251, 259, 260, 277*, 279, 301, 377; William, 140, 158, 170, 179, 279, 356. *See also* Rice
Reive, Anthony, 92, 115
Repington, Edward, 408*. *See also* Rippington
Revington. *See* Rivington
Reynolds [Raynald, Reignaldes, Reignolds, Renolds], Edward, 96, 115; Gilbert, 143, 298*; Humphrey, 37, 43, 298; Patrick, 9
Reynoldson, Joseph, 417
Rhoden. *See* Roden, Rowden, and Royden
Rhodes [Rodes], Hugh, 178, 235; Richard, 164
Rice, Richard, 60; William, 302. *See also* Reece
Richard, Edward ap, 40; Griffin, 55; Henry ap, 55; Thomas, 120; William, 50, 53
Richards, David, 53; Gawen, 337; Hugh, 27; James, 315; John, 34, 43, 53, 377, 384; Joseph, 246, 410; Robert, 363, 400; Thomas, 242, 319*, 384, 399, 410, 414*, 420; William, 29, 185, 242, 246, 399, 417
Richardson, David, 30, 57; Edward, 348, 393*; Francis, 227*, 356; Gawen, 260; Geoffrey, 15, 22; George, 117, 393; Hugh, 70; James, 393; John, 4, 10, 53, 76, 79, 139, 173, 180*, 185, 208, 211, 273, 296, 358; Joseph, 185, 260, 323; Josiah, 208, 273, 293*; Matthew, 91; Mr., 363; Peter, 15, 57; Ralph, 78, 106, 111; Randle, 150, 162; Richard, 26, 41, 55, 57, 70, 99, 106, 211, 283*, 329, 355, 381*, 426; Robert, 185, 356, 371; Simon, 57; Thomas, 15, 17, 19*, 22, 28, 49, 52, 54, 193, 296; William, 13, 14, 15, 17, 29, 36, 49, 57*, 68, 70, 75, 79, 83, 91, 99,

111, 117, 128, 136, 146, 155, 185*, 193, 245, 323, 329, 426; [——], 358
Richmond [Rycchemond], William, 5
Rider. *See* Ryder
Ridge, John, 134, 264; Jonathan, 127, 168*, 236*, 264; Robert, 139, 152, 154, 192*
Ridgway, John, 375; Joseph, 276, 418; William, 360, 404
Riding [Ridyng, Ryding], Charles, 18; Richard, 14
Ridley [Rydley], Alexander, 301; Henry, 195, 270*, 325; James, 285, 428; John, 34, 43, 62, 125, 145, 160; Robert, 59, 105*, 428; Roger, 12; Thomas, 195, 285, 286, 301; William, 63, 286
Rigby [Rigbye], Alexander, 158; Joseph, 422
Rigmarden [Rigmayden], John, 66, 94, 106
Riley. *See* Ryley
Rimmer [Rymer, Rymmer], Gilbert, 297; James, 283*; John, 149, 367; Peter, 305; Samuel, 141, 181, 192; William, 149, 192, 271, 305
Rippington, Edward, 354; Thomas, 272, 340*. *See also* Reppington
Riscoe, John, 224
Rivers, John, 265*
Rivington [Revington], George, 94, 137, 181; John, 94, 201, 288, 300, 302*; Samuel, 148, 180*, 201, 231, 264*; Thomas, 54, 83, 89, 92, 94, 102, 425; William, 231, 274, 333*, 388*
Rixon, Randle, 49; Thomas, 49
Roach, William, 367
Robert, Hugh ap, 426; Ingerham ap, 28; Sylvan, 399; Thomas, 96
Roberts, Daniel, 404; David, 93, 105, 331, 387, 404; Edward, 108, 116, 136, 269, 378, 425; Ellis, 385, 404, 420; Evan, 272; Francis, 244; Griffith, 266, 331, 343; Hugh, 108, 141, 154, 228, 244, 274; James, 218, 343, 356, 357; John, 98, 111, 113, 147, 153, 173, 192, 213, 218*, 225, 263, 269, 300, 368, 392, 423; Jonathan, 327, 377; Joseph, 414, 422; Lawrence, 162; Lewis, 60, 88, 94, 98; Margaret, 257; Owen, 128; Paschal, 371; Paul, 286; Richard, 73, 92, 102, 111, 257, 365, 425*; Robert, 90, 99, 146, 218, 274, 275, 329, 378*, 409, 421; Thomas, 106, 111, 126, 146, 151, 162, 186, 221, 225, 260*, 263, 285, 294*, 300, 356, 357, 387, 423; William, 102, 139, 225, 272, 287*, 327, 329, 346*, 357, 399, 422

INDEXES

Robertson, George, 273; John, 230*, 313
Robicoite, Nicholas, 8
Robin [Robyn], Edward, 36, 44; Humphrey, 44; John, 346*; Randle, 26
Robins, George, 76
Robinson [Robynson], Charles, 352, 387; David, 17, 105, 112, 151, 158, 427; George, 279*; Henry, 107; James, 110, 133; John, 10, 17*, 22, 33, 34, 35, 36, 66, 77*, 81*, 94, 101, 108*, 110, 133, 156, 174, 298; Jonathan, 236; Lawrence, 108; Matthew, 271, 365; Morris, 105; Peter, 221, 298, 363; Richard, 26, 36, 92*, 94, 101, 107, 117; Robert, 27, 122, 172, 221, 298, 321, 353, 360, 370, 374, 376, 399, 407, 417; Samuel, 115, 151, 290*, 365, 399, 419, 426; Thomas, 9, 16, 32, 55, 93, 97, 101, 112, 122, 131, 132, 174, 196, 261, 307, 308, 321, 360, 403, 405; William, 47, 139*, 151, 162, 185, 194*, 271, 350, 387
Roby, Edward, 166
Roden, Alexander, 258; Thomas, 351, 401. *See also* Rowdon, and Royden
Rodes. *See* Rhodes
Roe, John, 153
Rogers [Rodgers], David, 97; Francis, 124; George, 375; Henry, 255; John, 55, 61, 77, 145, 197, 239, 255, 268, 272, 274, 275, 304, 327, 367*, 368, 380, 410, 413; John Swarbreck, 410; Richard, 272, 285, 304, 327, 338; Robert, 77, 145, 224, 304, 377; Roger, 111; Samuel, 274, 348; Thomas, 55, 167, 197, 268, 285, 412; William, 239, 274, 348
Rogerson, Christopher, 14; Hugh, 26, 45, 53, 72; John, 3, 61; Peter, 22; Ralph, 22*, 35; Richard, 23, 54, 72; Robert, 5, 73; Thomas, 18, 39, 55; William, 3, 9, 22, 31, 45*, 61
Rollance, Joseph, 400
Rollinson, Thomas, 119
Rose, Edmund, 105; John, 354; Martin, 244; Stephen, 233; Thomas, 105
Rosingreve, John, 16, 39; Ralph, 36; Robert, 15; Seth, 21; William, 157
Roston, Charles, 289*
Rothe, William, 9
Rothwell [Ruthwell], Henry, 4; John, 178, 196, 221*, 259, 262, 267; William, 196*

Roughley, Henry, 164, 282, 313; John, 313, 372, 383; Lancaster, 205; Richard, 372; Thomas, 205, 216, 282, 297, 383
Rowdon, Alexander, 185. *See also* Roden, and Royden
Rowe, Charles, 278; Hugh, 348, 374, 385*, 403; James, 313, 403; John, 403; Thomas, 278, 403, 420
Rowlance, Edward, 407
Rowland [Roland], Anthony, 411; Edward, 372, 394, 422; James, 107; John, 115, 198, 378, 416; Philip, 107; Robert, 122; Thomas, 331, 378; William, 402
Rowlands, Charles, 400; Edward, 396; John, 312; Robert, 171; William, 361
Rowlandson, Thomas, 131, 143; William, 25. *See also* Rawlinson, and Rowlinson
Rowley, John, 257, 319; Roland, 257; Thomas, 240, 319
Rowlin. *See* Rawlin
Rowlinson, Abel, 317; Thomas, 364. *See also* Rawlinson, and Rowlandson
Rowney, Thomas, 314
Rowson, Nicholas, 31*
Royden, Alexander, 237; John, 329; Joseph, 237, 305, 329. *See also* Roden, and Rowdon
Roylands. *See* Rylands
Royle, John, 179
Ruffell [? Russell], John, 386
Rughe, John, 152
Rumer, Thomas, 104; William, 104
Runcorne, Richard, 9; William, 9
Ruscoe, David, 334; George, 334
Rushton, Charles, 249; James, 179, 249
Russell, John, 386
Rutter, Henry, 182; John, 285; Joseph, 260; Ralph, 139; Richard, 160; Robert, 88, 260, 285
Ryder [Rider], George, 239, 330; Henry, 370; John, 48, 84, 92*, 119, 214, 301*, 426, 427; Peter, 240; Richard, 101, 119*, 401; Thomas, 76, 100, 111*, 114, 119, 164, 426; Urian, 24, 78, 123, 145, 427; William, 79, 114, 120, 164, 180, 195, 214, 222*, 330
Ryding. *See* Riding
Rydley. *See* Ridley
Rylance, Elias, 213; Ellis, 250; Joseph, 213, 217, 233, 250; Richard, 233, 265; Samuel, 223, 307*; Thomas, 217
Rylands [Roylands], John, 202;

Joseph, 167, 202, 326*; Richard, 304; Thomas, 184
Ryley, Charles, 228, 329; John, 228, 284, 329; Walter, 284
Rymmer. *See* Rimmer

S

Sadler, John, 302, 404; Peter, 267, 421; Roger, 294; Samuel, 192, 281, 294, 302; Thomas, 163, 192, 267, 281, 370*, 414
Saint John, John, 153
Saladine [Salladine, Seladine], Charles, 176; George, 144; John, 325, 349, 373; William, 144, 373
Sale, John, 88; James, 58, 88; Richard, 66; William, 27, 53, 58. *See also* Seale
Salisbury [Salisburie, Salusbury], Charles, 224, 300*, 350; Edward Williams Vaughan, 404; Foulk, 94, 105, 300; George, 224, 300, 307; Henry, 170, 189*, 224, 284*; John, 181, 229, 340, 350, 360, 367, 415; Robert, 317; Thomas, 72; William, 72, 109
Salman, John, 155, 165
Salte, George, 83
Sampson, Thomas, 210, 297*
Sanders [Sandars], John, 356; Samuel, 423. *See also* Saunders
Sanderson, Thomas, 13. *See also* Saunderson
Sandford [Sanford], Thomas, 31; William, 44, 53, 58
Sandland, William, 402
Sands, Hugh, 390; Nicholas, 57; Richard, 356, 390, 401*; Robert, 161
Sanford. *See* Sandford
Sanky. *See* Sonky
Sant, Hugh, 257, 283; John, 283, 332; Thomas, 257
Santhey, George, 115
Saracold, John, 128
Sargeant, Randle, 131, 169
Sarrat [Serratt], John, 184, 238, 246*; Thomas, 238, 291. *See also* Sharrat, and Sherot
Sars, John, 56
Saunders [Sawnders], Benjamin, 361, 386, 392; Clear, 325; John, 166, 390, 391, 394, 401, 402*; Ralph, 70; Richard, 51, 64; Susanna, 364; Thomas, 70, 375; William, 64, 82, 102, 410; [——], 102. *See also* Sanders
Saunderson, Thomas, 166; William, 379. *See also* Sanderson

Savage, Christopher, 8; Edward, 8, 92, 428*; George, 8; Humphrey, 8; James, 8; John, 8*, 9*, 42, 49, 78, 81, 92*, 93, 111, 139, 427; Lawrence, 8; Richard, 8, 148; Robert, 33; Thomas, 92, 102; William, 8
Sawer, Richard, 11
Sawyer, Samuel, 349
Saxton. *See* Sexton
Sayer [Saer], Donald, 12; Francis, 189, 230, 234, 243*, 271, 273, 306; John, 230, 332, 422; Samuel, 273; Thomas, 86, 271
Scarisbrick [Scarsbrick, Scarsbridge, Scarsbrigg, Scarsbricke], Henry, 49*, 74, 90*; John, 380; Robert, 90, 380
Scarsbrocke [Scaisbrook], Robert, 232*, 321*
Scholefeild, John, 122
Scholes [Shcoles], Abner, 179, 202, 267*, 313
Sconce [Scons], Abraham, 78; George, 258, 284, 374; John, 20, 60, 88, 258; Richard, 56, 88, 187, 284; William, 86
Scott, Benjamin, 404; Charles, 421; Joseph, 412; Richard, 185, 307; Thomas, 307
Scully, John, 379
Seale [Seall], Henry, 161; John, 57, 72, 83, 101*, 114, 428*; Robert, 83, 114; William, 72, 114*, 134*, 161. *See also* Sale
Seavell, John, 122
Seddon, John, 260
Sedgewick, George, 33
Sefton, Edward, 58; Francis, 48; John, 344, 369, 383; Joseph, 179, 217; Richard, 50, 217; Samuel, 189; Thomas, 165, 276, 338, 371; William, 371
Sekerson, Ralph, 64
Selby [Selbie], James, 345, 358; Nathaniel, 184, 222, 239, 247; Robert, 103; Samuel, 155, 242; Thomas, 184, 232, 239; William, 170, 184, 192, 232, 247, 273, 345. *See also* Selsby
Seller, James, 327; John, 369, 426; Samuel, 272, 349, 382; William, 234*, 272, 287*, 319*, 327, 353, 356*, 380, 382
Sellers [Sellars], Jeremy, 284; John, 260; Thomas, 366; William, 183, 260, 284, 366. *See also* Cellars
Selsby [Selsbie], Robert, 428; Thomas, 123; William, 136*, 428. *See also* Selby
Selvy, Peter, 73
Sempole, John, 270

INDEXES

Sergeant. *See* Sargeant
Sevell, Robert, 80
Sewell, Joseph, 270, 271, 328; Thomas, 328
Sexton, Henry, 6; Thomas, 226
Shakerley, Peter, 186, 311, 314
Shalcrofte, George, 32
Shale, Charles, 207, 218
Shalleross. *See* Shawcross
Shand, John, 196
Shannon [Shannan], George, 364; Hugh, 332; John, 332, 379, 394, 395, 399, 403; Thomas, 395, 403
Shard, John, 168, 182, 192, 232*, 280, 312*
Sharman, William, 203. *See also* Sherman
Sharp [Sharpe], Azariah, 256; Humphrey, 185, 227, 253, 254, 355; Isaac, 187; John, 13, 198, 254, 336, 355, 364, 393; Joseph, 256; Matthew, 253, 330, 355, 356; Richard, 4, 12; Samuel, 355; Thomas, 12
Sharples, Ralph, 115
Sharrat, John, 291; Thomas, 291, *See also* Sarrat, and Sherott
Shaw [Shawe], Charles, 415; Ellis, 30, 53; Henry, 53; Hugh, 134, 145; James, 16, 417; John, 182, 327, 392; Joseph, 392; Morgan, 327; Peter, 190, 258*; Richard, 186; Thomas, 159, 358, 373; William, 16, 22*
Shawcross [Shawcrosse], Francis, 304; Ottiwald, 261; Ottiwell, 152, 203; Robert, 203, 261, 304
Sheale, Charles, 177; James, 123
Shearing, Robert, 380
Shelley, John, 156, 282; Robert, 282; Sampson, 120; William, 304
Shepheard [Shephard, Shepperd], Francis, 160, 188; John, 159, 382, 406; Michael, 97, 429; Richard, 22, 42; Thomas, 349, 378*, 387, 406; William, 42, 188, 233*, 299, 386
Sherington, Lawrence, 27, 60
Sherlock. *See* Shurlock
Sherman [Shermon], John, 3, 250; Nicholas, 7, 12; Robert, 12; Roger, 3; William, 224, 250, 278, 292*, 336. *See also* Sharman
Sherott, John, 106; Thomas, 106. *See also* Sarrat, and Sharrat
Sherrard, Thomas, 199
Sherrington, Randle, 153*
Sherwood [Schirwod, Shirrewod], Thomas, 14, 17; William, 17
Shettles, John, 217
Shevington, Foulk, 80; Richard, 51; Thomas, 97; William, 37, 80

Shewton, Richard, 311
Shoar, Richard, 171
Shocklach [Shekelach], Thomas, 14, 164
Shone, Bennedict ap, 69; Daniel, 245, 265, 348; Edward, 257; George, 207, 252, 292; John, 52, 76, 204*, 207, 248*, 250, 257, 291, 293, 341, 349, 354, 359, 377, 379, 387*, 396, 400*, 412; Joshua, 252, 385, 386; Leenes, 385; Owen, 154, 187, 188; Peter, 291, 413; Richard, 78, 167*, 197, 293, 348, 359, 428; Robert, 167, 428; Roger, 386; Thomas, 213, 250, 286, 341, 396, 400, 401*; William, 286, 376, 404
Short, Hockenhull, 272; Richard, 13; Valentine, 142
Shrigley [Shridgley], John, 239; Thomas, 183, 239, 275
Shurlache, William, 14
Shurlock [Shurlocke], George, 169; John, 38, 59, 66, 83; Richard, 60, 83, 183, 426; Robert, 50, 66, 105*, 124, 154; Thomas, 172; William, 37, 60, 120
Shuttleworth [Shotleworth], Thomas, 31, 418
Siddall [Seddall, Sidall, Sydall], John, 101, 118*, 131; Roger, 38, 66, 101; William, 131
Siddons. *See* Suddons
Sidebotham [Sidebothom], John, 314, 365; Joseph, 354; Richard, 314, 413; Samuel, 314, 413; Thomas, 312, 363, 365
Sidney, (Sir) Henry, 78
Sier [Syer], John, 103; Thomas, 112
Silvester, James, 244
Sim. *See* Sym
Simcock [Symcocke], Anthony, 79; John, 185; Richard, 419; Robert, 412; Thomas, 36, 79; William, 26
Simmons, John, 186, 254*. *See also* Symonds
Simson [Sympson], Gabriel, 372; Herbert, 226; John, 112, 352, 372; Samuel, 207; Thomas, 137, 163, 178, 226, 267; William, 267, 326
Sinclair, James, 337; John, 337; Joseph, 379
Singleton, John, 274; Thomas, 138
Sinker, Richard, 421
Sirard, Thomas, 7
Skeat, Henry, 380
Skelberne [Skellorne], Francis, 136, 167, 168, 182, 185, 200; John, 123, 131, 136, 143, 168, 200; Joseph, 295; Richard, 185; Thomas, 177, 198, 254*, 295
Skelleton, Robert, 396; Thomas, 396

Skellington, Robert, 290; Thomas, 254, 158; William, 85, 102, 158, 184, 246*, 254, 290, 337, 426
Skinner [Skynner], David the, 2; Hugh, 55; John, 39
Slaughter, Thomas, 342
Smaithwaite, Richard Milner, 410
Small, Joshua, 274
Smalshaw, John, 156; William, 93, 106, 426
Smarley, John, 63
Smathers [Smethers], Jeremiah, 393, John, 332, 388*; Margaret, 332; Richard, 19; Thomas, 19; William, 388
Smedley, Francis, 360
Smith [Smyth], Benjamin, 226; Charles, 343, 395, 414; Christopher, 30, 53, 66; Daniel, 237, 349, 380*, 417*; David, 5; Edmund,17, 36; Edward, 21, 56, 71, 98, 139, 317, 427; Fulke, 51; Gabriel, 347, 382; George, 199, 203, 258*, 272, 281, 348, 360*, 395; Hammet, 40; Hamon, 16; Hugh, 195, 264; James, 78, 117, 233, 371, 389; Jesse, 60; John, 10, 21, 25, 31, 40, 55, 68, 70, 77, 78, 84, 92, 100, 115, 119, 137, 156, 194, 203, 207*, 215*, 226, 231, 237, 243, 251*, 252, 256, 267, 285, 286*, 294, 337; 363, 368*, 396*, 405, 407,* 416, 417, 428, 429; John Charles, 416; Joseph, 214*, 231, 257, 294, 299*, 337; Joshua, 368; Lawrence, 22*, 24, 34, 37, 42, 43, 258, 323; Lewis, 6; Matthew,107*; Michael, 38, 77; Mr., 414; Nathaniel, 181, 217, 231, 276, 279, 304, 343; Oliver, 26, 60; Peter, 11, 19, 23, 46, 98; Ralph, 14, 23, 42, 100, 374; Randle, 14, 84, 116,428; Richard, 5, 34, 38, 75, 78, 93, 147, 209*, 281, 404; Robert, 25, 42, 44, 75, 82*, 83, 92, 104*, 124, 195; Roger, 42*; (Captain) Samuel, 133, 154, 199, 218, 225, 233*, 255, 294, 331; Simon, 52; Solomon, 51; Stephen, 151; Thomas, 11, 12, 15, 17*, 18*, 19*, 20*, 22, 29, 36, 42*, 56, 65, 76, 77, 91, 102, 107, 140, 144*, 208, 230, 241*, 252*, 256, 267, 276, 294, 300*, 312, 339*, 357, 373*, 406*, 408, 414, 427; Timothy, 156; Tobias, 97; William, 7, 18, 21, 34, 98, 115, 141, 149, 174, 188, 211, 216, 232*, 243, 251*, 255, 267, 299, 331, 348, 351, 354*, 356, 357, 360, 366, 391, 408, 416
Snagg, Robert, 41
Snape, Thomas, 117

Snead [Snede, Sneyd, Sneyde],Christopher, 135; Francis, 149; George, 37; Nicholas, 11; Peter, 119, 428; Ralph, 37; Richard, 20, 24, 74, 105*, 149, 175, 242*, 332, 345, 359, 378, 395, 428; Thomas, 11; William, 5, 11*, 18, 20, 24, 39, 140, 151
Snow, Charles, 362; John, 276; Joseph, 272, 276, 322, 353*, 358, 362, 383; Peter, 358
Soane. See Sone
Solden [Soden], Thomas, 191; Vaughan, 191
Somner, Miles, 92; William, 257, 375
Sone, Stephen, 219, 255, 281, 302*, 306
Sonky, Roger, 31
Soones, Paul, 127
Sorocold. See Saracold
Sorton [Soreton, Sowrton], Alice, 217; Charles, 193; John, 347, 373, 378, 387, 388*, 402, 411; Joseph, 202, 228, 245, 258, 290, 295, 326; Randle, 258, 333, 347, 354, 366; Richard, 152; Thomas, 202, 217, 362, 390; William, 258, 390
Souch, John, 425
South, John, 118
Southern [Sothorne], Hamon, 51; John, 48; Thomas, 48. See also Suthern
Southworth [Sotheworthe, Sowthorthue, Sowthworth], John, 5, 6, 48; Thomas, 48
Sownds, Griffin, 50
Spanne, Edward, 131
Spark [Sparke], Hugh, 36; John, 113, 138, 216, 290; Justician, 30; Robert, 165, 204, 218, 226; Thomas, 114; William, 86, 101, 113*, 119
Sparks [Sparkes], Samuel, 290; Thomas, 338, 364*; [——], 140
Sparrow [Sparowe], John, 190*, 228, 300; Randle, 7
Speed, Calveley, 209, 248, 328*, 401*; Hugh, 353; John, 264, 287; Mary, 277; Thomas, 287, 324, 364, 392; William, 248, 264, 277, 353
Spele, William, 7
Spence, Andrew, 321; John, 384; Thomas, 321; William, 331, 384
Spencer, Edward, 371, 386, 403, 404, 405, 419; John, 267, 314, 388, 410; Joseph, 300; Richard, 39, 256, 316, 399; Thomas, 39, 124, 300, 316, 371, 399
Spenne, William, 76
Spensley, George, 335*
Spicer, Nicholas, 7

Sponne, Richard, 42, 72, 81*, 109, 105, 427; Thomas, 86
Spragge, Roger, 17; Thomas, 14, 17
Sproson [Sproston, Sprowson, Sprowston], John, 63, 82, 111*, 114, 121, 125, 160*, 168, 199*, 249*, 350, 351*, 408, 420, 427*; Peter, 130; Phillip, 111; Richard, 114, 129; Robert, 96, 115, 121, 148*, 257; Samuel, 416; Thomas, 257, 350; William, 104, 111, 168
Spruce, Samuel, 295*
Spurstow, George, 332; John, 236, 332, 334*, 372, 383
Stacey [Stacye], William, 159*
Stamford, Peter, 416
Standen, James, 377
Standish, Daniel, 161; Henry, 195; Phillip, 136; Thomas, 342
Stanley [Stannley], Richard, 84; William, 6*
Stanmere, William, 3
Stanney, John, 78
Stannier, John, 407; Thomas, 78
Stansfild, Robert, 3
Stanton, Abraham, 316; Charles, 283; Joseph, 283; Thomas, 316; William, 393, 412
Stanway, Randle, 208, 260; Samuel, 260
Staples, John, 47
Stapleton, Thomas, 64, 186, 301*
Starkey [Starkie], Edward, 142, 179, 193, 197*, 214; Elizabeth, 259; George, 134*; Hugh, 151, 172, 179*, 183, 199*, 200, 208, 212; John, 200, 241, 320, 332, 349, 382; Joseph, 400; Matthew, 122; Peter, 156, 172, 199*, 241, 247*; Robert, 183; Samuel, 332; Thomas, 382; William, 144, 227*, 259, 376; [———], 144
Staut, Thomas, 319
Staynor, Nicholas, 8
Stede, John, 122
Steele [Steale], John, 128; Richard, 163; Thomas, 385; William, 33
Steens, James, 392; Joseph, 402
Stephens, John, 215
Stephenson, James, 313
Ster, Donald, 11; Robert, 11
Stevens, Robert, 40. See also Stephens
Stevenson [Steevenson], John, 32; Richard, 177, 218, 273, 274, 303; Thomas, 86, 218, 303; William, 50. See also Stephenson
Steward, Duncan, 256; Thomas, 25, 70, 256
Stewart, James, 321, 393; John, 393; Thomas, 321
Stiles [Styles], John, 63, 64, 101;

Mark, 77; Stephen, 101; William, 57, 63, 64, 77
Stirropp, William, 117
Stockton, Hugh, 28, 58, 75, 113; John, 97; Randle, 67; Richard, 58, 108, 138, 160; Simon, 75, 113; Thomas, 108, 128, 184; William, 16, 215
Stoke, Nicholas, 3
Stokes, William, 33, 42, 48, 49
Stole, Dannold, 27
Stone, Thomas, 343
Stonehewer, William, 357
Stoneley [Stonnley], Edward, 83
Stones, (Rev.) James, 343; John, 340; Thomas, 339, 353, 358; William, 245, 311, 339, 359*, 378
Stonier, John, 65
Stoppord, Thomas, 182, 198
Stot, John, 200
Stout, John, 399; Joseph, 179, 246, 332, 334, 335, 365*, 399; William, 135, 332, 401
Strange, Lord, 64; Lord Fardinando, 63
Stranke, Oliver, 426
Street [Streete, Strete], George, 119, 134; Humphrey, 115; John, 239; Peter, 17, 56; Richard, 123, 164, 193, 239; Thomas, 153; William, 19, 128*, 134, 143, 153, 176, 180, 252*; [———], 171
Stretch, John, 63, 298
Strettall, John, 184
Strettell, Samuel, 415
Stretton, Thomas, 10*
Strettwell, John, 247; Thomas, 247
Stringer, Francis, 156; Hugh, 147, 152; John, 111, 169, 179, 231, 232, 244, 354, 386, 413, 425; Peter, 126, 144*, 199*, 276; Richard, 139; Robert, 362; Thomas, 149, 177, 234, 244, 246*, 256, 284, 357, 362, 413
Stuart. See Steward, and Stewart
Stubbs [Stobbes, Stubbes], James, 347, 368; John, 109*, 213, 255*, 284, 330, 337, 352; Matthew, 397; Richard, 162, 200, 213, 284; Robert, 31; Thomas, 200
Suddons [Suddones], James, 320, 322*, 379; John, 371; Ralph, 322; Richard, 322, 371, 372, 379, 407; Samuel, 372; William, 407
Sudlow, Benjamin, 296; John, 16, 151, 168, 177, 184, 198, 238; Ralph, 198, 231; Robert, 223; Samuel, 164, 223; Thomas, 274; William, 184, 238, 296
Suker, Randle, 107; Thomas, 107
Sumner. See Somner

Sumpter, James, 399
Surridge, Richard, 344
Suthern [Suthorn], 225, 257; John, 257; Ralph, 193, 225, 241*, 246; Thomas, 246. *See also* Southern
Sutton, John, 165, 256; Mr., 426; Thomas, 78; William, 119
Swann, Samuel, 370
Swanwick, Thomas, 417
Swarbeck, Lawrence, 202
Swetenham [Swetnam], George, 125; Nicholas, 6, 9; William, 9
Swift, Abraham, 163; Isaac, 197; Richard, 197; William, 176
Swinnerton, John, 354, 371, 379, 401; Thomas, 401
Swinton, John, 136*, 189*, 269*, 305; Samuel, 305
Sydall. *See* Siddall
Syer. *See* Sier
Sylk, William, 5
Sym [Syme], John, 1; Robert, 69
Symon, Rice, 217*
Symonds, John, 36. *See also* Simmonds
Synot, Nicholas, 27

T

Tagg, Thomas, 228
Taite. *See* Tayte
Talbot, David, 6
Tamberlaine, John, 383; Thomas, 406
Tapley, Henry, 193, 250, 293, 385; John, 281, 295, 384*; Jonathan, 140, 193, 213*, 295; Robert, 281, 348; Thomas, 250; William, 134, 293, 322
Tarbock. *See* Torbock
Tarleton, John, 39; Thomas, 39, 72; William, 72
Tasker, Daniel, 390; John, 33, 82*
Tassie, Robert, 100
Tate. *See* Tayte
Tatton, John, 12; William, 8
Tavo, James, 370
Taylor [Tailer, Taillior, Tailor, Tayler], Andrew, 28, 82; Bartholomew, 35; Charles, 332; Daniel, 159, 212, 253, 281; Edmund, 77; Edward, 59, 140, 371; Elizabeth, 262; Ferdinand, 106; Francis, 110; George, 169, 188*, 214*, 216, 243*, 248, 252, 288, 297, 323, 398*; Gilbert, 23; Hamnett, 129; Henry, 77; Hugh, 90, 96; J., 110; James, 370; John, 10, 16, 17, 27, 30, 38, 43, 49, 52, 56, 73, 75, 84, 89, 90, 100, 103, 106, 107, 122, 124, 146*, 151*, 189, 190*, 193, 248, 253, 318, 323, 332, 344, 359, 372*, 390, 397, 419, 420*; Jonathan, 252, 356*, 390, 409; Joseph, 164; Joshua, 124, 169*, 197, 253, 268; Mark, 367; Peter, 82, 86, 143, 183, 204; Ralph, 20; Richard, 20, 55, 89, 93, 95, 99, 101, 105, 108, 113, 131, 134, 144, 150, 160*, 169, 179*, 187, 188, 189, 193, 203, 420*, 427; Robert, 125, 164, 215; Roger, 10, 20*, 49, 59, 85, 98; Samuel, 175, 187, 192, 207, 212, 318, 361; Thomas, 21, 43, 77, 93, 96, 107, 127, 144, 169*, 196*, 258, 268, 281, 409, 419, 429; Timothy, 253, 344; William, 34, 36, 46, 71, 87, 95, 137, 146, 193, 197, 262, 309, 336*, 365*, 379, 389, 390, 395, 416, 418, 420
Tayte, John, 1
Teggin, George, 416; Joseph, 85
Tellet, Ewan, 94; John, 97; Joseph, 275, 333, 342*; Richard, 426
Tench, Fisher, 354
Termond, Robert, 81
Tetley, John, 96
Tetlowe, Henry, 57; Thomas, 30, 57, 63
Thatcher, Edward, 32
Thickins, William, 56
Thomas, Arthur, 82; David, 48, 81; Edward, 48, 319, 359, 411, 416; Evan, 71; Griffin ap, 63; Henry, 377, 378; Hugh, 32, 333*, 347, 378; Isaac, 90, 176, 306*; John, 37, 46, 64, 169, 233, 236, 240, 280, 296, 298, 347, 361, 372, 380, 410; Joseph, 362, 376, 386; Peter, 361; Robert, 27; Samuel, 377, 380; Thomas, William, 64, 92, 270, 402, 423
Thomason [Thomasson], Benjamin, 199; George, 138; Hugh, 4, 300; John, 148, 183, 195*, 203*, 209, 223, 226, 231, 270, 284, 303; Patrick, 61; Randle, 199; Richard, 148, 182, 228, 296, 304, 428; Robert, 90, 108; Roger, 147; Thomas, 108, 137, 182, 211, 213, 236, 262, 296, 303; William, 13, 139, 160, 195
Thomlinson [Tomlinson, Tomblinson, Tomlynson], Benjamin, 285; Charles, 149, 416; John, 291, 336, 363*, 418; Joseph, 78; Ralph, 36, 100; Randle, 149; Richard, 26; Samuel, 285; Theodore, 78; Thomas, 29, 63, 78, 92*, 94; William, 100, 216, 291, 295*, 409
Thompson [Thomson, Thomsson, Tumson], Edmund, 22; Edward, 27,

103, 112, 113, 161, 184, 185, 198, 200, 259; James, 183; John, 159; Owen, 368, 419; Phillip, 159; Raphe, 134*; Richard, 18, 198, 217; Simon, 259; Thomas, 200, 394, 419; William, 153, 189*, 259, 347
Thorneley [Thornly], Daniel, 364, 413; Hugh, 130, 166, 215, 233, 266, 287, 288*, 291, 352, 387, 393*; John, 166, 210*, 249, 287, 387; Ralph, 98; Robert, 36, 90, 103, 112, 210, 249; Samuel, 413; Thomas, 162, 291, 352, 399
Thornton [Thorneton], Henry, 49, 332, 390, 397; John, 17, 30, 32, 44, 56, 332, 397; Joseph, 364; Ralph, 18, 28, 65, 98; Richard, 33, 34, 353, 390; Robert, 91; Thomas, 9, 13, 17, 18, 65, 121, 190, 364; William, 30
Thralfell, William, 149
Thring, Samuel, 384; William, 419
Throp [Thropp, Throppe], Barnett, 135; Bernard, 160; Bradford, 74, 107, 149, 193, 200; Daniel, 90, 105; Edward, 71, 109*, George, 183; John, 52, 72, 79, 94, 125, 158; Randle, 56, 113; Richard, 107, 117, 147, 149; Samuel, 175; Thomas, 28, 49, 71, 72, 74, 102, 109*, 113, 120, 145, 150, 160, 183, 255; William, 49, 77, 85, 90, 103, 115, 125, 136, 137, 158, 169, 170, 187, 215, 218*, 273*
Ticer, Thomas, 56
Tildesley, Henry, 8; John, 8; William, 8
Tilley, Thomas, 255, 323*
Tilston [Tylston], Charles, 391; Christopher, 98, 116, 132; Henry, 88, 427; James, 336, 395; John, 21, 32, 39, 42, 45, 53, 58*, 65*, 67, 74, 79*, 82, 91, 113, 165, 191, 193, 200*, 223, 265*, 272, 279, 290, 305, 335*, 368*, 391, 395; Joseph, 367; Modland, 193; Peter, 73, 113; Ralph, 38, 67; Richard, 27, 42, 49, 52, 88, 91, 114, 141, 427; Samuel, 191, 321, 364*; Thomas, 58, 67, 79, 121, 200, 285*, 290, 305, 321, 336, 338, 367, 427; William, 52, 378
Tirell. See Tyrell
Titley, Edward, 421. See also Tytlen
Tomkins. See Tompkins
Tomkinson. See Tompkinson
Tomlinson. See Thomlinson
Tompkins, John, 267; Thomas, 267
Tompkinson [Tomkinson], Charles, 370; John, 344, 370
Tonge, Ralph, 37, 80*

Tonna, Bradford, 183; Edward, 104; George, 183; John, 102, 319, 375, 405; Richard, 319, 405; Samuel, 231*, 295, 319, 323, 334, 367, 382, 397, 420; William, 397. See also Tunna
Tonnay, David, 87
Tony, John, 75
Topham, George, 411, 417; Mark, 413; Robert, 420
Topping, Hugh, 234, 240*; John, 422; Thomas, 234
Torbok, Thomas, 10
Tottie [Totty], Edward, 205, 268; George, 268, 350, 382; Henry, 70, 103, 105, 106, 427; John, 102, 103, 110, 205, 266, 268, 287, 350, 378, 408; Richard, 94, 115, 133, 177, 203, 428; Robert, 287; Roger, 26; Thomas, 141, 147*, 209, 287, 382; [——], 105
Touchett, Francis, 174, 196
Towers, Edward, 96; Thomas, 34
Townend, Richard, 118; Thomas, 117
Townley, James, 402
Townsend [Townesend, Townshend], Charles, 330; Edward, 360; George Salusbury, 386; Gerrard, 205, 280, 305, 330, 401; John, 274, 305, 314, 358*, 360, 374, 386; Randle, 315, 401; Richard, 149, 204; Robert, 159, 205, 280; Thomas, 374
Towsey, Jane, 257; John, 257, 305, 325, 363, 376, 380; Thomas, 325, 376, 380, 383*
Trafford [Traford], Henry, 25, 54, 56, 77, 97; Nicholas, 29; Richard, 106, 153; Thomas, 157
Trallock, Robert, 48; William, 48. See also Trollock
Trape, John, 364, 413; Joseph, 413
Traver, William, 215
Travers, Charles, 266; John, 152; Thomas, 266
Tregorne, Griffith, 155. See also Trygarn
Trelford, George, 347; James, 317, 347
Trevers, Ebenezer, 186; John, 131, 182, 186; Samuel, 182; Tyrall, 182
Trevis, Francis, 97; Henry, 138
Trevor, Arthur, 223; David, 82; Edward, 42; Isaac, 405; John, 42, 240*, 292, 370*, 409; Peter, 292; Ralph, 32; Richard, 30; Roger, 223; William, 275, 292, 356*
Tristram, Ebenezer, 273; John, 231, 273, 299; Sarah, 231, 273; William, 299

Trollock, Robert, 67, 84. *See also* Trallock
Troughton, John, 273*, 384
Trowtbeck, Roger, 30
Trueman, Matthew, 220
Trussell, Gilbert, 1
Trygarn, Griffith, 224. *See also* Tregorne
Tuck, Frances, 406
Tuder [Tudder], Griff, 41; Gruff, 21; John, 19, 201, 274*; Richard, 201
Tuleton, Joseph, 338
Tunna [Tuna, Tunnar, Tunnea], Randle, 171; Samuel, 353*; William, 139. *See also* Tonna
Tunnall, George, 213*, 217; John, 213, 232, 243, 301, 303, 305
Turner, Edward, 403; George, 150; Henry, 48, 185; John, 136, 185, 186, 251, 354, 383; Joseph, 375, 410, 418; Randle, 115, 174; Robert, 48; Samuel, 164, 405; Thomas, 167, 251; William, 131, 164, 167, 186, 251, 349, 352, 377, 382, 418, 421
Tushingham, Arthur, 348, 418; Francis, 241; Jonathan, 345; Ralph, 241, 345, 417*; Robert, 418
Twanbrook, Edward, 203*, 210, 255; Thomas, 210
Twemlow, Job, 164; Joseph, 162; Mathew, 173, 180; William, 412
Twie, Richard, 27
Twis [Twisse], John, 12, 26, 49, 84; Richard, 60; Robert, 108; William, 31*, 108, 152
Twist, Richard, 342
Tyddar, Richard, 162
Tylston. *See* Tilston
Tynsdale, Thomas, 210
Tyrell [Tirell], John, 16; Richard, 13
Tyrer [Tyrerer], Edward, 120; George, 120; Henry, 111; John, 89, 280, 322, 331*, 353, 399*; Richard, 36, 89; William, 280, 287*, 366*
Tyson, John, 352
Tytlen, Henry, 98

U

Underwood, James, 275
Urian, Thomas, 201*; William, 119
Urmeston, Arthur, 84; John, 147, 286; Richard, 111, 147, 166; Robert, 31, 70; Samuel, 225; Stephen, 218; Thomas, 166, 225, 286; William, 70
Usher, Hugh, 217, 426; James, 219;
John, 200, 256, 298, 301; Thomas 217, 269*, 300*, 301
Usherwood, Hugh, 56; John, 353, 362, 378

V

Valentine, John, 215, 237
Vaughan, Evan, 340; Griffith ap Howell, 404; Jane, 260; Joseph, 410; Lewis, 260; Piers, 427; Robert Howell, 371, 404, 406; Robert Williams, 403; Samuel, 376; William, 312
Vawdrey, Samuel, 128
Vawse [Vaws, Vawes, Vos, Vouse], George, 103, 128, 172, 189, 199*; Gilbert, 117; John, 216; Oliver, 32, 54; Proby, 317; Randle, 103, 165, 180; Richard, 54, 67; Thomas, 95, 245, 317
Venables, John, 200, 238, 249*, 388; Peter, 165, 203; Randle, 125, 145, 182; Richard, 342, 364, 404; Samuel, 200; Thomas, 79; William, 167, 238, 342, 353*, 368, 388
Vernam, Thomas, 52
Vernon, Charles, 233; George, 21*; John, 327; Jonadab, 325; Ralph, 23, 47, 347; Richard, 174, 229, 233, 335, 358, 421; Robert, 321, 334; Thomas, 47, 245, 309, 327, 365, 370, 373*; William, 245, 334, 335, 370
Vigars, Henry, 315, 371
Villam, William, 39
Vincent, George, 289; Thomas, 228; 289
Vizar, Edward, 275; William, 308, 392; Wilson, 392
Voice, James, 421
Vrane, Robert, 3
Vuldre [Vuldur], Gervase de, 8*

W

Wade, Edward, 79; Ellis del, 3; Francis, 121, 155; George, 24; John, 51, 106, 121, 427; Richard, 85, 103; Thomas, 158; William, 143, 178
Waine. *See* Wayne
Wainwright [Wainewright, Waynewright, Waynwright], Edward, 157; Lawrence, 74; Robert, 105; Samuel, 412; Thomas, 117, 132; Walter, 9
Waite, Thomas, 40. *See also* Weite
Wakefield, John, 290; Thomas, 164, 198*, 283*, 290

Walford, Richard, 420
Walker, Christopher, 31, 64, 70, 104, 107; Edward, 122, 130, 135, 337; Elizabeth, 259, 265; George, 331, 337, 358, 363, 374, 379, 416*, 422; James, 320, 340, 415; Jervis, 405; John, 64, 83, 107, 265, 284, 320, 366, 378, 390, 410, 421; Joseph, 365, 374; Martha, 415; Phillip, 16, 38, 119, 159; Randle, 70, 101, 104, 105, 114*, 125, 155; Reginald, 27; Richard, 86, 428; Robert, 75, 331; Samuel, 125, 165, 371; Thomas, 104, 105, 141, 259, 368, 386; William, 107, 408
Wall [Walle], Edward, 96, 259, 426; Ralph, 96, 113; Richard, 97, 112; Robert, 38, 61, 66, 78, 87, 97; Thomas, 34, 35, 259; William, 33, 61, 63, 87*, 301
Walley [Waley], Arthur, 121, 143, 145; Charles, 119, 126, 130, 175, 218, 231, 295, 427; Francis, 344; George, 297, 373; Henry, 305; Humphrey, 173, 282; James, 187, 222, 246, 273*, 311, 323, 344, 352, 366; John, 8, 10, 24, 48, 162, 198, 203, 231, 246, 247*, 252, 295, 297, 403, 406; Joseph, 226, 282; Matthew, 252; Raphe, Ralph, 175, 211, 283, 285*, 305; Richard, 10, 25, 316, 371, 373, 379, 392; Robert, 5, 8, 223, 283, 311, 313; Samuel, 165; Thomas, 25, 155, 168, 175, 185*, 198, 203, 223, 226, 240, 310, 316, 324; William, 357, 371, 373*, 379
Wallworth. See Walworth
Walmsley [Walmesley], Edward, 133, 164, 198, 214*, 293*, 403; George, 58, 71; John, 306; Samuel, 200, 235*, 306; Thomas, 58, 166, 186, 216
Walsh [Walshe], Donald, 9; James, 99; John, 2, 9, 69; Robert, 13; Thomas, 67, 94, 103*; William, 56, 69, 99, 165*. See also Welsh
Walshman, John, 64; Thomas, 421. See also Welshman
Walter. See Gaulter, and Gwalter
Walters, Hugh, 335; John, 353; Richard, 490; Thomas, 341*, 400
Walthew. See Wathew
Walton, Adam, 17; Edward, 132, 161, 210, 274, 301; Hugh, 122; John, 108; Richard, 8, 17, 108; Robert, 24; Roger, 9; Samuel, 220, 274, 301; Thomas, 10, 161, 210, 216, 220, 235, 254, 274, 323*, 357; William, 24*, 254. See also Wareton, Warton, and Waulton

Walworth [Wallworth], Dawson, 330; Thomas, 185, 294*
Warburton [Werburton], (Sir) George, 271; Hugh, 8; Peter, 59, 78, 337, 425; Phillip Henry, 369
Ward, Andrew, 122; John, 157; Richard, 197, 299*; Thomas, 177, 194*, 197, 378
Wareing, George, 284; Peter, 284; Richard, 347
Wareton, Geoffrey, 76; Henry, 105*; Richard, 28; Robert, 76, 92, 120; Thomas, 98. See also Walton, and Warton
Warmingham [Warmincham, Warminsham, Wermynsham, Warmisham, Warmyncham], Antony, 66, 88, 101, 425; Charles, 176, 209, 211, 228, 244, 304; Christopher, 12, 23*; George, 213; Henry, 6; Isaac, 91, 116, 154, 161, 180, 182, 195, 203, 208, 224, 228, 237*; James, 7; John, 178, 291, 304, 366; Joseph, 247; Lawrence, 24, 53*; Peter, 304; Ralph, 41, 66, 88; Richard, 51, 105, 115, 181, 425; Robert, 148, 179, 195, 235, 247; Roger, 6, 7; Stephen, 7, 12; Thomas, 19, 39, 53, 91, 101, 115, 116, 123, 131, 135, 136*, 138, 161, 178, 195, 219, 228, 244, 253, 255; William, 105, 164, 176, 213, 219, 235, 249, 253, 259, 263, 267, 291, 356; [——], 154
Warner, John, 4
Warre, Thomas, 314
Warrington, Charles, 181; Edmund, 348, 357, 358, 374; Edward, 235*, 284, 320, 326*, 354, 356, 361, 383, 395; George, 109, 130, 142, 261; Henry, Earl of, 187; John, 175, 216, 261, 279*, 283, 298, 313, 320, 323, 425; Nathaniel, 383, 407; Samuel, 313; Silvester, 348; William, 130, 298
Warton, John, 27, 47, 50; Robert, 62, 115; Thomas, 82; William, 56, 82. See also Walton, and Wareton
Washington [Wesshynton], Robert de, 2; William de, 2
Wastenburye, John, 13
Water, Thomas, 225*
Waters, John, 316; Peter, 293; Thomas, 293, 316, 337; William, 337, 412
Waterwoods, John, 223, 311; Joseph, 285; Samuel, 351, 374*; Thomas, 311; William, 285
Wathew, William, 291*
Watkins [Wattkynes], John, 64, 76; Thomas, 78; William, 345

Watkinson, John, 50
Watmough [Watmoughe, Wattmouth], John, 412 ; Nathaniel, 133 ; Thomas, 171, 208*, 295*, 404*, 412 ; William, 109, 116
Watson, John, 389 ; Thomas, 67
Watt [Watte], Arrat, 78 ; Henry, 108, 152 ; John, 112, 129 ; Thomas, 108, 129, 145, 158*
Waulton [Waverton], John, 20. *See also* Walton, Wareton, and Warton
Wayne, Richard, 149 ; Robert, 149
Weatherby, John, 236*
Weaver [Weever, Wever], Charles, 126 ; Francis, 139 ; Gabriel, 101, 114, 119 ; James, 337 ; John, 337, 386 ; Richard, 55, 101, 105 ; Thomas, 105
Webster, John, 9, 23, 32, 40*, 110, 405 ; Samuel, 363
Wedderley, Nicholas, 20
Wederall, Thomas, 25
Weeran, Richard, 96
Weigh [Weight], Jane, 358 ; John, 416 ; Joseph, 322, 324, 422 ; Peter, 228, 273, 320*, 398 ; Richard, 420 ; Samuel, 324*, 352 ; Thomas, 273, 333, 355*, 373, 398, 416, 420, 422
Weite, George, 40* ; Raffe, 40 ; Robert, 40. *See also* Waite
Weld [Welde], Joseph, 236, 238 ; Nathaniel, 150. 166, 190, 220 ; Richard, 37 ; Samuel, 222, 236 ; William, 275. *See also* Wild
Welley, Geoffrey of, 3 ; John, 3
Wells, Joseph, 137 ; Richard, 49
Welsh [Welch, Welshe], Anthony, 106 ; John, 110, 126, 244, 330* ; 393 ; Joseph, 182 ; Lawrence, 378 ; Nicholas, 106, 121 ; Richard, 130 ; Robert, 190, 244, 255*, 290 ; Samuel, 290, 393 ; Thomas, 108, 125, 415. *See also* Walsh
Welshman [Welchman, Welsheman], Edward, 161 ; Ephraim, 179 : John, 94*, 110 ; Peter, 121 ; Samuel, 134, 163 ; Thomas, 116, 130*, 134, 149, 276, 374 ; William, 110, 124, 126, 150, 161, 224, 238. *See also* Walshman
Wenseley [Wynsley], John, 5 ; Robert de, 3
Werden, (Sir) John, 315 ; Robert, 158 ; Thomas, 43, 62, 72
Werdes, Thomas, 74
Wervin. *See* Wirvin
Weston, Humphrey, 35, 54, 69, 74 ; James, 20 ; John, 10, 49*, Peter, 196 ; Richard, 74 ; Robert, 36 ; Samuel, 165 ; Thomas, 69, 99, 103, 106, 108, 114, 177, 190, 425, 426* ; William, 81*
Wetherbey, John, 222
Wetherell, Thomas, 257*, 339*
Wethynse, William, 16
Wettenhall, Gabriel, 309 ; John, 219 ; Richard, 198 ; William, 199
Whatton, Roger, 48 ; William, 18
Whawell [Wheawell], Ambrose, 212, 222, 236 ; John, 204*, 212, 228, 251, 312, 338*, 393* ; Joseph, 261 ; Peter, 251 ; Thomas, 183, 228, 261 ; William, 338, 385*
Whey, Robert, 353
Whishaw, Hugh, 310, 343
Whitaffe, Thomas, 229, 231, 260*
Whitasse, Thomas, 217
Whitby [Whitbey, Whitbie, Whitbye], Edward, 99 ; George, 245 ; James, 330 ; John, 83, 95, 109, 112, 115, 168, 222, 232, 305*, 330, 360, 379, 404* ; Jonathan, 136, 164, 168, 179, 232 ; Randle, 38, 67, 96 ; Richard, 18 ; Robert, 85, 91, 93, 98, 99*, 127 ; Thomas, 60, 91 ; Timothy, 420 ; William, 11, 18, 107
White, Bartholomew, 416 ; John, 16, 30, 35, 36, 54, 61*, 311, 354 ; Nicholas, 32 ; Ralph, 33 ; Richard, 202 ; Thomas, 21, 36, 211
Whitear, William, 226
Whitebrook, John, 419
Whitehall, Broughton, 309
Whitehead [Whitehed, Whithed], Charles, 243, 285, 287, 333 ; George, 359, 387 ; Gilbert, 23, 40 ; John, 26, 34, 44, 107, 133, 170, 171, 174, 248, 351, 361 ; Josiah, 249, 291 ; Richard, 23, 41, 170, 243, 249, 333, 351, 417* ; Robert, 26, 42 ; 64, 84, 106, 107, 313, 359, 381 ; Roger, 12, 16, 90 ; Samuel, 235 ; Thomas, 94, 170, 185, 232*, 235, 248, 285, 287*, 291, 359*, 381 ; William, 41, 84, 132, 249
Whitelegg [Whitlegg], Richard, 35
Whitemore [Whytemore], John, 2
Whiteside [Whitside], John, 120 ; Thomas, 181
Whitfield, James, 214, 231, 299 ; Robert, 214 ; William, 299
Whitle. *See* Whittle
Whitley [Whittley], George, 402 ; Henry, 362 ; John, 391 ; Morgan, 192 ; Peter, 173 ; Ralph, 158 ; Robert, 6, 378 ; Roger, 172, 187, 189, 191, 192, 193 ; Thomas, 172, 265, 310
Whitney [Whittney], James, 174 ;

Matthew, 329 ; Samuel, 287 ; Thomas, 216, 287, 339
Whitoff [Whitaffe, Whitcof, Whytoffe], George, 36 ; John, 86 ; Thomas, 180, 203
Whittaker, Daniel, 224 ; George, 223, 273* ; John, 260 ; Paul, 251 ; Peter, 221, 336 ; Reginald, 186, 221, 251, 260 ; William, 224, 228
Whittakers [Whitakers, Wittacres], James, 90 ; Ralph, 140
Whittingham [Whityngham], Ralph, 313 ; Richard, 279 ; William, 14, 140
Whittle [Whitill, Whitle, Whittell, Whytle, Whyttle], Charles, 318, 395, 420 ; Christopher, 7 ; Elizabeth, 192 ; John, 127, 136, 140, 157, 167, 304, 356, 374, 425 ; Jonathan, 282, 331*, 341, 386, 388, 392 ; Joseph, 167, 218*, 282, 289, 301*, 304 ; Josiah, 171 ; Randle, 289 ; Robert, 103, 307, 374, 387, 420 ; Thomas, 80, 112, 157, 356, 377, 388, 414 ; William, 68, 88, 93, 99*, 101, 104, 107*, 112, 192, 425
Wiatt. See Wyatt
Wiche. See Wyche
Wicherley. See Witcherley
Wickstead [Whickstead, Wicksteed, Wikstad, Wiksted], Henry, 7 ; Hugh, 89, 111, 112, 117*, 120, 253, 427 ; John, 275 ; Richard, 164, 253, 275, 288* ; Thomas, 6, 111
Widders, Daniel, 403
Wiggen, Hugh, 127
Wigh [Wighe], Joseph, 177 ; William, 27
Wignall, Peter, 80
Wilberforce, John de, 1
Wilbraham, John, 224, 276, 309*, 404, 424 ; Randle, 311, 317 ; Richard, 166, 268 ; Robert, 268 ; Roger, 117, 195, 224, 230*, 298, 308, 317, 326, 350 ; Thomas, 298, 300 ; William, 156, 229, 311*, 324 ; William Lloyd, 424
Wilcock [Wilcok, Wilcocke, Willcock, Willcocke], Benjamin, 155 ; George, 212 ; John, 70, 335 ; Paul, 180, 231, 234 ; Randle, 157 ; Robert, 8 ; Samuel, 270 ; Thomas, 75*, 138, 157, 162, 212, 268* ; William, 30, 157, 335
Wilcockson, Laurence, 427
Wilcoxon, Jonathan, 396 ; Ralph, 384
Wild, Joshua, 344. See also Weld
Wildig, John, 379

Wild [igge ?], James, 98
Wilding [Wildinge, Wyldinge], Alexander, 40*, 62, 74, 109, 113* ; Edward, 111, 133, 144 ; James, 109 ; John, 48, 82, 108, 116, 128, 134, 218, 379, 427 ; Richard, 22, 74, 122 ; Robert, 38, 74, 100, 109, 218 ; William, 46, 85, 109, 111*, 113
Wildon, John, 54
Wilkinson [Wilkynson], Edward, 264, 320, 335 ; Gilbert, 389 ; Hugh, 61 ; James, 252, 278, 318, 332, 341, 345, 346, 421 ; John, 175, 195, 227, 230*, 242, 252, 264, 270, 278, 279, 282, 288, 306, 318, 345, 348*, 355, 357, 389 ; Joseph, 271, 282, 318*, 341, 344, 366*, 379 ; Nicholas, 7 ; Olfley, 182 ; Peter, 408 ; Ralph, 270, 279, 346, 348, 357, 368 ; Richard, 6, 193, 216, 251* ; Robert, 10, 409 ; Roger, 88 ; Samuel, 314 ; Stephen, 191, 258, 306 ; Thomas, 242*, 258, 259, 288, 327, 335, 348, 370, 371 ; William, 227, 305, 335, 379, 407 ; [———], 421
William [Guilliam], Gruff ap, 20 ; Lawrence, 4 ; Robert, 13 ; Stephen, 44 ; Thomas ap, 20
Williams, Alice, 244 ; Arthur, 280 ; Benjamin, 219 ; Bennet, 356, 409 ; Charles, 167 ; Daniel, 330, 416 ; David, 166, 219, 220, 278, 359, 393 ; Edward, 96, 125, 197*, 244, 297, 299, 302, 309*, 355 ; Elias, 278, 389 ; Ellis, 82, 93 ; Foulk 82 ; Geofrey, 312 ; George, 365, 367 ; Griffith, 104, 143, 186, 215, 233, 278 ; Henry, 143, 153, 159 ; Hugh, 33, 57*, 94, 102, 112, 152, 245, 278 ; Humphrey, 221 ; James, 170, 408 ; John, 53, 68*, 74, 94, 101, 120, 126, 130*, 133, 146*, 162, 164, 167, 177, 178, 190, 201, 232, 233, 236*, 245, 247*, 258*, 275, 280, 302, 306, 312, 322, 324, 330, 343, 345*, 354, 356*, 360, 367, 370, 384, 405, 409, 418, 420 ; Joseph, 185 ; Kenricke, 141 ; Kyfflin, 245 ; Lewis, 72, 93, 153, 167, 172 ; Lumley, 395 ; Martha, 257 ; Morgan, 105 ; Nicholas, 131, 143, 173, 219, 226, 280 ; Owen, 64, 137 ; Percival, 120 ; Peter, 54, 153, 174 ; Phillip, 151 ; Powell, 176 ; Ralph, 261, 300 ; Reece, 134 ; Richard, 7, 105, 131, 245, 314, 389, 427 ; Robert, 71, 109, 123, 164, 212*, 245, 259, 269, 279, 311, 313, 354, 355, 360, 381, 393, 409 ; Roger, 264, 289*

Rowland, 41; Samuel, 201, 403; Thomas, 73, 88*, 94, 101, 102, 111, 112*, 176, 215, 219, 221, 226, 230, 232, 257, 269, 270, 274, 279, 300, 322, 324, 359, 377, 380, 405, 412, 421; Valentine, 416; Watkin, 240; William, 111, 125, 144, 154, 179, 190, 240, 269, 270, 307, 320, 355, 356, 379, 400

Williamson, Charles, 379; Edward, 80, 140, 154, 173; Henry, 178; Hugh, 80, 104, 106; James, 266, 402; John, 39, 46, 47, 80, 111*, 170, 179, 259, 370, 405; Jonathan, 266; Nathaniel, 151, 186; Ralph, 51; Randle, 36; Richard, 56, 150, 181, 305*; Robert, 56, 135, 160, 200*; Thomas, 96, 97, 106, 115, 144, 183; William, 21, 115, 139, 144

Willme. *See* Wilme

Willolugh, Thomas, 125

Willoughby [Willoughbie, Wiloughby], Isaac, 169; John, 278; Phillip, 241; Thomas, 136, 143, 271; William, 136, 184*, 241, 278, 313; [———], 271

Wills, William, 186

Wilme [Willme, Wylme], John, 165; William, 143, 172

Wilson [Willson], Arthur, 118, 182, 255; Benjamin, 308; Daniel, 175; Edward, 131, 159; George, 150, 245, 343; Henry, 61; James, 107, 131; John, 88, 103, 136, 230, 308, 368, 394, 426; Joseph, 315; Nicholas, 191*; Philip, 119, 174; Ralph, 89, 105, 111, 112, 119, 159, 230, 268,* 427; Randle, 139, 221*; Richard, 60, 126, 428; Robert, 39, 47, 88, 107; Thomas, 50, 183, 225, 232, 265, 290, 394; William, 92, 104, 110, 133, 147, 150, 155, 159, 162, 177, 182*, 198*, 225, 232, 255, 280, 290, 303*, 427, 428*

Winchester [Wynchester], Thomas, 13

Winnington, Robert, 208; Thomas, 164, 208, 223*, 225, 256, 259

Winstanley [Wynstanley], Henry, 126, 152, 263; Thomas, 7, 230; William, 230, 263

Wirrall [Weyrehall, Wirrell, Wyrall, Wyrehall, Wyrrehall], John, 13, 154; Moses, 154; Peter, 108; Randle, 9; Richard, 10, 11, 14, 188; William, 240*. *See also* Worrall

Wirvin [Wervin, Wyrvyn], Nicholas, 2; [———], 2

Wiswall, Thomas, 28; William, 207

Witcherley [Wicherley], John, 248; Richard, 244; Thomas, 244; William, 161, 215, 244*, 248

Withers, Robert, 219; Samuel, 262; Thomas, 208, 262, 331

Witten, William, 54, 66

Witter, John, 127, 136, 151, 168, 213*, 299, 342, 384; Joseph, 131, 136, 164, 213, 303, 351, 367; Richard, 208; Samuel, 136, 384; Silvan, 150; Thomas, 299; William, 163, 208, 213*, 239, 240, 271, 299*, 303, 352

Wodhop, Edward, 19

Wolfe, John, 369; Richard, 28, 47, 429; William, 47, 429

Wombe, George, 8

Wood, Francis, 376; Geoffrey, 16; John, 123; Michael, 219; Peter, 144, 258; Ralph, 228; Thomas, 144, 177; William, 28, 376

Woodcock [Woodcocke, Woodcok], Henry, 129, 231; John, 231, 347; Richard, 37, 53, 116; Robert, 51, 96, 113, 129; Thomas, 347

Woodfen [Woodfin], Edward, 222, 289, 354, 410*; John, 248, 252, 267, 277, 387; Richard, 215, 288; Roger, 297, 367; Samuel, 229, 289; Thomas, 118, 215, 267, 275, 320*, 387; Uriah, 198, 236, 275, 277, 289; Urian, 246; William, 188, 191*, 198, 210, 222, 229, 252, 288, 289*, 354, 365*

Woodier. *See* Woodyer

Wooding, Joseph, 414

Woods [Woodes], Charles, 199*; Daniel, 116, 162, 194, 198*, 259*, 287; Francis, 185; George, 68, 178, 253*; John, 51, 69, 98, 144, 162*, 264*, 367; Peter, 214, 222, 297; Reginald, 148, 199; Reignold, 168*; Robert, 38, 75; Roger, 306; Stephen, 38; Thomas, 74, 65, 306; William, 144, 185*, 194, 196*, 198, 199, 220, 221, 256, 300*, 372*

Woodward [Wodward, Wodwerde], George, 52; John, 9, 154, 209, 315; Joseph, 304, 340; Nathaniel, 86; Peter, 245, 329, 340*; Robert, 2; Thomas, 304, 329; William, 2

Woodworth, John, 183, 210, 241*, 260, 264, 328*, 379, 391*; Joseph, 210; Peter, 147; Thomas, 354; William, 328

Woodyer [Woodier], Isaac, 371, 392; James, 392

Wooley. *See* Woolley
Woolham, Charles, 324
Woollam, Charles, 396, 398*, 400; John, 400
Woolley [Wooley], Hugh. 204*, 241; John, 424; Samuel. 413, 417
Woolliscroft. John, 418
Woolstanham, Daniel, 379
Woolwright, Thomas, 376
Worger, Richard. 203
Worrall, John. 144*, 168, 211*, 231, 414; Moses, 187; Robert, 124; Samuel, 137, 168. *See also* Wirrall
Worsley, Thomas, 342
Wotton, John 3; Thomas, 3
Wrench, Alderman, 381; Charles, 332; Edward, 245; Edward Ommaney. 406; Ellen, 152; John, 185, 214 239, 253, 298; Joshua, 173; Peter. 185, 232, 235, 236*, 248, 253, 254, 292, 304; Randle, 232, 278, 312, 335, 353, 359; Richard, 228, 254, 292, 298, 325, 332; Robert, 188, 218, 233, 269, 275, 317; Thomas, 152, 175, 188, 218, 248, 275, 330, 343, 406; William, 239, 269, 299, 325, 358
Wrenchall, Jonathan, 178, 199
Wright [Wrighte, Wryghte], Charles, 361, 373, 413*; Daniel, 97, 110; Edward, 31, 49, 67, 102, 174, 204; George, 89, 160, 247*, 332*; Humphrey, 137; Isaac, 113; James, 197, 238, 248, 255, 342*; John, 6, 11, 18, 24, 30, 44, 51, 55, 59, 70, 75, 89, 102, 107*, 112, 113, 154, 178, 180, 219, 220*, 227, 229*, 247, 262, 293, 313, 338*, 348, 360, 368, 369, 373, 398, 403, 409*, 427; Joseph, 139, 167*, 183, 185, 204, 223, 229, 241*, 247, 295*, 319*, 357, 369, 385*, 400; Matthew, 172; Nathan, 227, 296, 338; Nathaniel. 316; Nicholas. 32, 48, 59, 64*; Peter, 32, 49, 57, 59, 65, 69, 168, 241; Ralph, 18, 40, 44, 75, 167, 261; Richard, 6, 25, 29, 34, 49, 54, 64, 89, 99, 120, 147, 163, 164, 190, 202, 209*, 238, 368, 403, 421, 425, 427; Robert, 10, 13, 39, 57, 89, 123, 128, 170, 374, 425; Samuel. 172; Thomas, 14, 37, 48, 64, 65, 88*, 89, 93*, 95, 99, 104, 118, 130, 139, 170, 172, 180*, 197, 202, 219, 220*, 225, 276*, 278, 283, 293, 297*, 315, 321, 330, 348, 360, 361, 364, 413; William, 14, 19, 45, 59, 66, 127, 129, 138, 168*, 169, 255*, 296,
309, 318, 339, 377; Zaccahary, 174, 248
Wyatt [Wiatt, Wyat]. Edward, 130; John 121, 162; Thomas 85, 119*, 162; [——], 130
Wyche, Lawrence 13
Wykes, Thomas. 50
Wynn [Win], Charles Watkin Williams, 413; Edward. 181, 273; Ellice, 349; Godfrey, 58, 106; Henry. 271; Hugh, 85, 112*, 153; Humphrey. 273, 350; Jane, 120, 188; Morrice, 177; Ralph, 231; Richard, 182; Robert, 128, 342, 343; Thomas, 261, 359, 380, 397; Thomas Welchman, 374; (Sir) Watkin Williams, 313, 371*, 374, 413*, William 188, 343, 377
Wynsley. *See* Wenseley

Y

Yale, David, 68
Yardley, Robert, 24
Yarworth. *See* Yerworth
Yate, William, 26
Yates, Catherine. 226; Henry. 166, 200; John, 323, 348, 392; Peter, 226; Richard, 134, 155, 160, 166, 167, 200, 214; Samuel, 323; Thomas, 160, 200, 235*, 330, 348
Yeaman [Yeamon], John. 211, 229, 240, 271
Yearsley. Edward, 272, 326, 350; Robert, 272
Yeomans, John, 178
Yerwood, John, 352
Yerworth, Dudley, 65; John, 32, 65
Yewd. Roger, 219, 224*; Thomas, 231, 293; William, 217*, 219, 231, 292*, 293, 321. *See also* Ewde, and Yond
Ykin [Eakin]. Rowland, 113
Yockinge [Yoken]. Richard, 39; Thomas, 26
Yockson, John, 214; Joshua. 214
Yoken. *See* Yockinge
Yorke, Robert, 21
Youd [Yowd]. John. 215; Watkin, 371. *See also* Ewde, and Yewd
Yould George, 330
Younge [Yonge] Daniel, 266, 339*, 340; Edward, 49, 57, 69, 115, 425*; Henry, 50, 72, 90, 118, 133, 143, 148, 153, 165, 176, 192; Humphrey, 63; John, 10, 15, 17, 84, 116, 140, 143, 148, 165, 179, 222; Joseph, 163, 272; Josiah. 181; Lawrence,

119, 429; Peter, 163, 266*, 340;
Ralph, 57; Randle, 215, 292;
Richard, 10, 22*, 96, 183, 417;
Robert, 185, 211, 234, 237; Roger,
428; Samuel, 153, 266, 270; Simon,
245, 270; Thomas, 57, 127, 153,
163, 165, 167*, 182, 184*, 211*,
231, 242, 371; William, 86, 90,
116*, 143, 170, 292
Yoxall, Benjamin, 376; Peter, 382;
Richard, 417; Robert, 319, 363,
376; Thomas, 319

II

QUALITY, TRADES, PROFESSIONS, OCCUPATIONS

A

Alderman, 17, 20, 22*, 36*, 37, 38, 40*, 41, 42*, 43*, 45*, 46, 48, 49*, 50*, 53*, 57, 59*, 61*, 64, 67*, 68, 69*, 70, 71*, 72*, 75*, 76*, 77*, 78, 79*, 81, 82*, 83, 87*, 88, 89*, 91*, 92*, 94*, 95, 97*, 98, 99*, 100, 101*, 103, 104, 106*, 107*, 109*, 110, 111, 112*, 113*, 114*, 115*, 117, 118*, 119*, 136, 145*, 146*, 148, 149, 151, 153, 159, 160*, 161, 162*, 166*, 167, 168, 172, 182, 183, 185, 187*, 190*, 193, 195*, 197, 200*, 202, 203*, 204, 211, 212*, 217, 218, 219, 220*, 223, 225*, 226, 227, 230*, 231, 232, 234, 235, 236, 239, 240*, 242, 243*, 244, 253, 261, 262, 263, 267, 268, 271, 273, 278, 280, 282, 296*, 298*, 301, 302, 306, 308, 320, 324, 325, 326, 327*, 330, 336, 338*, 345, 346, 348, 353*, 357, 358*, 359, 361*, 362, 370, 372, 378, 381, 385, 386, 409*, 411*, 414, 416, 417, 418, 419, 425, 426, 428, 429*

Alderman of the Art or Mystery of the Butchers, 270

Almsman, 388, 418

Anchor Smith, 400

Apothecary, 45*, 68*, 85, 93, 95, 107, 117, 123, 127, 129, 133*, 135, 136*, 142*, 147, 150, 151, 154*, 156, 158, 159, 164, 166, 168*, 171, 173*, 174, 177, 179, 182, 184*, 187, 188, 190, 192, 195, 196*, 198*, 201, 202, 213, 214, 216, 218, 224, 227, 231, 232*, 238, 239, 243*, 245*, 264*, 267, 271, 273*, 274, 277, 278*, 279*, 280, 282, 286, 287, 296*, 299*, 301, 303, 306, 312, 313, 320, 325*, 327*, 330, 332, 340, 348, 356, 357, 371, 373, 374, 408. See *also* Druggist

Architect, 375, 418

Armes, Deputy of the Office of, 425

B

Baker, 3*, 6*, 8*, 9*, 10, 11*, 12, 13, 14*, 15*, 17*, 18*, 19, 20*, 22, 24*, 25*, 26*, 27*, 28, 29*, 30, 32*, 33*, 34*, 35*, 37*, 39, 41*, 42*, 44*, 45*, 46, 47*, 48, 50*, 51, 52*, 53*, 54*, 55, 57*, 58, 59*, 60, 62*, 63, 64*, 65*, 66*, 68*, 69*, 70*, 73*, 75*, 77*, 78*, 79*, 80, 81*, 85*, 87*, 90*, 91, 94*, 95*, 96, 97*, 98*, 99, 100*, 101, 102*, 103, 105, 106*, 107*, 108*, 109, 110*, 111*, 112*, 113*, 114*, 115*, 116*, 118*, 119, 120, 121*, 122, 124*, 126*, 127*, 128*, 129*, 131*, 132*, 133*, 135*, 137*, 138, 139, 141*, 142*, 143*, 144, 145,* 146, 147*, 148, 149*, 150, 151, 154, 155, 156*, 157, 158*, 159, 160*, 161*, 162, 164, 165*, 167*, 168*, 169*, 170*, 174, 175*, 176, 180, 184, 186*, 188*, 192*, 195, 196*, 197*, 198*, 199*, 200, 201, 202*, 203*, 204*, 205, 208*, 209*, 210*, 212*, 213, 215*, 217, 218, 220*, 222, 223, 224, 225*, 226, 227, 230, 231, 232, 235, 237, 238*, 242*, 243, 246, 247*, 249*, 250, 251, 252, 253*, 254*, 255, 258, 259, 260, 261, 264, 265*, 268*, 272*, 274*, 275, 277*, 278, 279*, 282*, 286, 287*, 289, 290, 291, 292, 293, 294*, 295, 296*, 297*, 299*, 303, 304, 305*, 308, 311, 317*, 318*, 320, 321*, 323*, 324*, 325, 326*, 327*, 328*, 329, 330, 333, 335, 336, 342, 344, 346*, 348*, 349, 351*, 353*, 357*, 358*, 362*, 364*, 365, 368, 369*, 370, 371*, 372*, 373, 374*, 375, 376*, 377, 378, 379*, 381, 383*, 384*, 385, 390, 392*, 393, 396, 399*, 400, 404*, 405, 406, 407*, 410, 412*, 413*, 414, 415*, 416*, 417*, 418, 419*, 420, 423, 425*, 426*, 427, 429*. See *also* Sugar, Baker, and Baxter

Banker, 384
Barber, 3*, 8, 11*, 12, 14, 16*, 17*, 18, 19, 21, 22, 26, 27, 29, 30, 32, 34, 36, 37*, 40, 41, 46*, 55, 59*, 61, 75, 81*, 82, 90, 92*, 97, 100*, 103, 114, 118, 120, 124, 130, 131*, 133, 134*, 135*, 137, 140*, 156, 161, 165, 169*, 176, 178*, 180, 185, 186, 187, 189*, 190, 192, 195, 196, 199, 204*, 207, 210, 212, 218, 219*, 220*, 222, 223, 225, 232*, 233*, 234, 235, 236*, 238, 239, 240, 241, 242, 245*, 246, 247, 248, 249, 250, 251*, 252*, 254*, 261*, 268, 269*, 271, 272, 273, 275, 276*, 277*, 278, 279*, 280*, 281, 282*, 286*, 289*, 291*, 292, 293, 294*, 297, 298, 300*, 301*, 304*, 305, 306*, 312, 314, 316*, 317, 318*, 321*, 326, 327, 329, 330, 331*, 332, 333*, 334, 335, 337, 338*, 339*, 340*, 342, 343*, 344*, 345*, 346*, 347, 348*, 350*, 353*, 354, 355, 356*, 365, 366, 369*, 370, 371, 372, 373, 374*, 375*, 376*, 377*, 380*, 381*, 382*, 383, 385*, 386*, 387*, 388, 389, 390, 391*, 392, 393, 395, 398, 402, 403, 406, 407, 409*, 413, 418, 427
Barber-chirurgeon, Barber-surgeon, 68*, 102, 112, 124, 142, 146*, 147*, 150, 151*, 154*, 155, 159*, 160*, 162, 163, 164, 168, 170, 171, 172*, 173, 175*, 176*, 178, 179, 186, 188*, 190, 192*, 193*, 195, 196*, 198*, 200, 201, 202*, 207, 208, 209, 212*, 217, 227*, 228*, 229, 230, 238, 240*, 245, 254, 305, 315, 320*
Barber - chirurgeon and Wax - chandler, 146
Barber-chirurgeon, Wax-chandler, and Painter, 131, 154*
Barber-surgeon, Wax and Tallow-Chandler, and Innholder, 320
Barber and Periwigmaker, 316, 317
Barber and Perukemaker, 369, 381
Barker, 5, 7*, 9*, 11* 12* 13, 14*, 15, 16*, 17, 18*, 19*, 20, 21, 22, 25
Baronet, 144, 150, 166, 169, 172, 176, 179 190, 207, 226*, 229, 234*, 237, 238, 240, 247*, 269, 271, 276, 280, 308, 310*, 312, 313, 314*, 315, 337, 340, 342*, 343, 347*, 357, 362, 371*, 374, 413*
Baxter, 5, 6*, 8. *See also* Baker
Beadle, 384
Beam-maker, 190

Beer-brewer. *See* Brewer
Blacksmith, 96, 108, 119, 121, 125, 128*, 130*, 132, 135, 136, 137, 138*, 139*, 140, 142*, 143, 144*, 145*, 147, 148, 150, 152*, 154, 155, 156*, 157, 160*, 161, 163*, 164, 165, 166, 168*, 169, 170, 171*, 173, 175, 177*, 178, 185*, 187, 188, 189, 193, 197, 201, 214, 263, 274, 325, 354, 355, 358, 360, 362, 363*, 364, 370, 371, 373, 377, 388, 390, 391, 392*, 395, 396, 403*, 413, 416, 422, 427
Block and Pumpmaker, 421
Blockmaker, 333, 365, 421
Bluemaker, 370, 375
Boatbuilder, 367
Boatman, 73
Bodymaker, 151
Bookbinder, 39, 400, 412*, 417*, 422
Bookkeeper, 334
Bookseller, 155, 168, 176, 240, 293, 319, 350, 362, 375*, 382, 396, 397, 401, 406, 408, 409, 412, 415
Bookseller and Printer, 415
Bowier, Bowyer, Booer, 3, 7, 8, 11, 13, 19*, 22, 25, 30, 32, 35, 48, 51, 53*, 64*, 89, 99
Brandy Dealer, 412
Brassfounder, 292, 400. *See also* Founder
Brazier, 105, 163, 178, 202, 347, 358, 362, 369, 375, 376, 379, 380, 389, 400, 416*, 420, 423
Brazier, and Pewterer, 202
Breechesmaker, 328, 370*, 380, 381, 382, 389, 394, 395, 400, 412, 420
Brewer, Beerbrewer, 21, 31*, 32, 33*, 43*, 50*, 53, 61, 62*, 64*, 66*, 72* 74* 76*, 78, 79, 83*, 84, 85*, 87, 89, 92, 94*, 95, 96*, 98*, 99, 102*, 103, 104*, 105, 106, 108*, 109*, 110*, 112*, 113, 114*, 115*, 116, 118*, 119*, 120, 121, 122, 123, 124*, 125*, 126, 127*, 128*, 129, 130*, 132, 134*, 135*, 136*, 137*, 138*, 139*, 142*, 143*, 144, 147, 148*, 149*, 150, 153*, 154*, 155, 156*, 157*, 161, 162*, 163*, 164*, 165*, 166, 167*, 168, 169*, 170, 171*, 172*, 173*, 174*, 175*, 176*, 177*, 178*, 179, 180*, 182, 184*, 185, 186, 188, 189*, 190*, 191, 192, 193*, 194*, 195, 197*, 200*, 201, 203*, 207, 208, 209, 210, 211, 213, 214*, 215*, 218, 219*, 220, 221, 222, 225, 226, 229, 230*, 232*, 233, 234*, 235, 236, 241*, 242, 247*, 249, 251*, 253, 254, 258, 259*,

INDEXES

260*, 262, 263, 264, 266*, 270*, 271, 272*, 274*, 275, 278, 281, 282, 284, 296, 301, 302, 304, 306, 307, 313, 318, 319*, 323, 325, 326*, 327*, 332, 338*, 340, 342*, 344, 345*, 346*, 347*, 348, 349*, 350, 353, 354, 356*, 359*, 365, 366, 367, 369*, 371, 373, 377, 378, 382, 399, 405, 406*, 409, 412, 416*, 420, 421, 425, 426, 427*

Bricklayer, 98, 105, 125, 128, 131*, 141, 143, 145, 150*, 151*, 152, 159*, 160*, 161*, 162*, 163, 168, 170*, 171*, 172, 179*, 184, 185, 190, 196, 198, 199*, 200*, 208*, 209, 211, 215*, 216, 217, 221*, 223*, 224, 227*, 228, 235, 236*, 237*, 238, 240, 241*, 247*, 249, 252*, 253*, 254, 255*, 256*, 257, 258, 260*, 261*, 262, 263, 264*, 265*, 267*, 268, 269, 271, 275*, 278, 284*, 285*, 286*, 287*, 288, 290*, 291, 292*, 295*, 296, 297*, 300*, 305, 311*, 312, 315*, 318, 320*, 321, 324*, 328*, 329*, 330*, 331, 332, 335, 336, 337, 338, 341*, 342*, 346, 348*, 351*, 352*, 354, 356*, 357, 358, 359, 363*, 364*, 367*, 370, 373, 377, 379*, 381*, 387*, 389*, 390, 391*, 392*, 394*, 396*, 398, 399, 400*, 401*, 403, 404, 405*, 406, 407, 408*, 412*, 419, 422

Bricklayer and Linen-draper, 128, 150*, 160

Brickmaker, 316

Brickman, 13, 59*, 66*, 69

Bridlecutter, 243

Broderer (sic), 20. See also Embroiderer

Broker, 397*, 417, 419, 422

Brushmaker, 359, 378

Builder, 398

Butcher, 2, 6, 7*, 11*, 12*, 13*, 14*, 15, 17*, 18*, 19, 20*, 21, 22*, 24*, 27, 28, 29, 30*, 31, 32*, 33, 35, 36, 37*, 42, 43*, 44*, 46*, 49, 50*, 51*, 54*, 55, 56, 57, 58*, 59, 61*, 62*, 63*, 64*, 65*, 66*, 67*, 70, 73*, 74*, 78*, 81*, 85, 86*, 88*, 92, 94*, 95, 96*, 98, 99, 100, 102, 103*, 106*, 110, 111*, 113, 114, 115, 116*, 117*, 121*, 122, 123*, 126*, 127*, 129, 130*, 131*, 134*, 136*, 137, 138, 139, 140, 142, 143, 146*, 148*, 149*, 150, 151, 153, 155*, 156, 157*, 159, 161*, 162, 163, 164, 168*, 170, 171*, 174, 176, 177*, 179, 182, 184*, 185*, 186, 191*, 192, 193, 194, 202, 205*, 207*, 209, 210, 213, 218, 219, 221*, 222*, 224, 226, 229, 231, 232*, 237, 238, 239*, 241*, 242*, 244*, 245, 246*, 247*, 251*, 253*, 257, 258, 260*, 264, 266, 270, 272, 273, 274*, 275, 276, 278*, 279*, 280, 281, 283, 287, 290*, 291*, 293*, 295*, 298, 300*, 303*, 306, 307, 308, 312*, 314, 315*, 316, 317*, 318, 319*, 322*, 323*, 324*, 326, 328, 329, 332*, 333*, 334*, 335*, 336*, 337, 341, 343, 345*, 346*, 347*, 348*, 349*, 351, 353*, 355, 356*, 357*, 358*, 359*, 360, 361*, 362, 363, 365*, 367*, 369*, 371, 372*, 373*, 374*, 375, 376, 378*, 379*, 383*, 384*, 385*, 387*, 388, 389*, 392, 393, 394, 395*, 397, 398*, 399, 400*, 401*, 403*, 404, 405, 406*, 408*, 410*, 412*, 414*, 415, 417*, 419, 420*, 421*, 423, 425*, 426*, 427, 429. See also Flesher

Butcher and Victualler, 419

Button-maker, 158*, 170, 189, 198, 226, 304, 394*

C

Cabinetmaker, 185, 203*, 224, 235, 250*, 255, 276, 287, 292, 298, 301, 304*, 305*, 307, 308*, 310, 318, 323*, 325, 328, 332, 334, 337, 339, 341, 345, 354, 355, 356, 360, 361*, 363, 364, 366*, 367, 368, 369, 370, 373, 376*, 380*, 382*, 384, 385, 387*, 388, 390, 391, 392, 394*, 396, 397, 399*, 402*, 407, 409, 410*, 412, 414, 417*, 420, 421, 422

Cabinetmaker and Upholsterer, 421

Candlemaker, 27, 95, 96

Capper, 5, 12, 28, 50, 65, 91

Captain, 418

Cardmaker, 14, 24, 29*, 38, 40*, 53*, 66*, 97, 106, 121, 141, 161*, 171, 252, 253, 254

Carpenter, 6, 14*, 16, 21, 22, 26, 83, 91, 95*, 96, 106, 108, 110*, 116, 120, 124, 128*, 131, 132, 134, 135, 139*, 141, 145, 146, 148, 155, 162*, 167, 169, 170*, 174*, 175, 176, 178, 180, 182, 185*, 188, 190, 192, 202, 203, 208, 211, 212*, 216, 217, 218*, 220, 221, 223, 227, 229*, 230*, 231, 232, 235*, 237, 241*, 242*, 243, 247, 248*, 249*, 250*, 251*, 254*, 257, 259, 260*, 262*, 267, 273*, 274, 275, 277, 279, 280*,

283*, 284, 287*, 290, 291*, 292*, 293, 294, 298*, 301, 306, 307, 311, 313*, 316*, 317, 320, 321*, 324, 326*, 327, 328, 329*, 330, 331*, 332*, 333*, 336*, 337*, 338, 339, 340, 343*, 345*, 347*, 348, 351*, 353*, 354*, 355, 356*, 357, 358, 359, 361*, 363, 365, 366*, 367, 368, 369, 370, 371*, 375, 376, 377, 378*, 379*, 380*, 381, 382*, 383*, 384, 385, 386*, 387*, 388*, 389*, 390*, 391*, 392*, 393*, 395, 397*, 400*, 403, 408, 409, 410, 411*, 413*, 415, 416, 417, 418, 420, 422*, 423*
Carpenter and Joiner, 355, 369, 416, 420, 423
Carpenter and Sawyer, 241
Carrier, 47, 88, 377, 380
Carter, 21, 410, 422*
Carver, 26, 142, 173, 175, 193, 199, 202, 214, 223, 238, 239, 263, 272, 279, 305, 308
Carver and Mason, 279
Castor-maker, 199
Chandler, 29, 46, 52, 53, 55, 63, 70*, 83, 103, 110, 131, 137, 138, 146, 154, 180, 186, 188*, 192*, 195, 197, 201, 202*, 204, 208, 209, 210, 211, 213*, 214*, 220, 221*, 224, 225*, 228, 229, 230*, 232*, 233, 235, 236, 242*, 245, 246, 247, 254, 268, 273, 274, 278, 279, 286, 287, 295*, 298, 301*, 304, 307, 314, 315, 317, 318*, 319, 320*, 326, 329, 335*, 337, 348, 349, 355, 362, 375*, 384, 396, 407*, 409. *See also* Tallow Chandler
Chapman, 44, 144, 152*, 334*, 338
Chaunsler (*sic*), 130
Checkman, 339
Cheese-factor, 190, 210, 238, 244*, 353, 416
Cheese-monger, 233, 378, 379*, 421
Chirurgeon, Surgeon, 47, 85, 86, 100*, 122, 124*, 125, 180*, 135, 187, 190, 211, 216, 236, 242, 244, 252, 264*, 271, 273, 274, 289, 297, 300*, 301, 302*, 304, 307, 326, 335, 353, 374, 379, 402*, 418, 419, 423
Clerk, 35, 63, 67, 73, 82, 93, 128, 133, 134, 139, 153, 155, 167, 189, 196, 201, 209, 210*, 211, 218, 224, 230, 232, 235, 240*, 244, 258, 262*, 267, 268, 269*, 270, 273, 280, 283, 297, 305*, 307, 308*, 309*, 310*, 312*, 314*, 317, 325*, 334*, 336, 337, 338, 340*, 342, 343*, 358, 361, 368, 372, 376, 381, 382*, 383*, 389, 395, 398*, 401, 407*
Clerk of the Pentice, 82, 91, 93*, 133, 298, 313
Clerk in Holy Orders, 229, 343*
Clerk and Tailor, 35
Cliderall-haberdasher (*sic*), 27
Clockmaker, 99, 118, 120, 123, 157, 165, 170, 266, 397, 407, 409
Clock and Watch maker, 409
Clocksmith, 85
Clothier, 50, 70, 93*, 98, 104, 105*, 106, 110, 113, 117, 125, 131*, 132, 137, 155, 173*, 198, 313, 415*, 427, 428
Cloth Printer, 195
Clothworker, 41, 56, 89, 94, 95, 99, 100*, 101*, 102*, 104*, 106, 107, 108*, 109*, 110*, 113, 114*, 115, 116, 117, 119, 121*, 122, 123, 124*, 126, 128, 129*, 130, 132, 135, 137, 138*, 140, 141*, 143, 144, 145, 149, 153*, 154*, 155, 156, 158*, 160, 163, 165, 167*, 168*, 169, 173, 176, 187, 192, 199, 214, 218, 219, 224*, 230, 236, 237, 240, 267, 271, 302, 305*, 306*
Coachmaker, 322, 327, 363, 397*, 415
Coachman, 273, 363*, 375, 377
Coal Merchant, 355
Collier, 250, 341*, 401
Combmaker, 174, 218, 250*, 252, 288*, 322*, 333, 356*, 357*, 364, 365*, 366*, 373, 375, 386, 387, 390*, 392, 393, 396, 409*
Confectioner, 156, 207, 210, 218, 270, 305*, 357, 373
Confectioner and Baker, 404
Cook, 13, 14, 37, 49, 69, 72, 79*, 91, 93, 121, 142, 166, 271, 313
Cooper, Cowper, 2, 11, 12, 14, 17, 18*, 19, 25, 26*, 28*, 29*, 32*, 36*, 37, 38*, 44*, 46, 47*, 50, 51, 52*, 55, 56*, 58*, 59, 60*, 61*, 63*, 66*, 67*, 70, 73*, 75, 78, 82*, 83*, 84, 86*, 87, 88, 90, 91, 92*, 94, 103*, 104, 106, 108, 113, 114, 116*, 117*, 121, 125, 126*, 129*, 132*, 134, 139, 140, 141*, 146, 148*, 150, 152, 154, 155, 157, 158, 159*, 163, 164, 165*, 167*, 173, 174, 175, 190*, 193*, 199*, 200, 201, 213*, 216*, 218, 221, 225*, 233, 234*, 236, 237*, 239, 242, 243, 245, 246, 249*, 250*, 251, 253*, 254*, 258*, 265, 270, 273, 275, 278, 283, 285, 286*, 287*, 288*, 289, 293*, 297, 302, 307*, 312, 315, 316, 318, 322, 323, 332,

INDEXES

333, 334*, 335*, 342*, 345*, 346*, 350, 351*, 352, 353, 355, 356*, 357, 358, 359, 361, 363, 364, 369, 371, 377, 378*, 380*, 387, 392, 394, 395, 397, 408*, 417, 419*, 420*, 421*, 423
Cooper and Fishmonger, 146, 148, 174, 190, 193, 216, 225, 234, 345
Cordiner, 177*, 178*, 179*. *See also* Cordwainer
Cordwainer, 31, 32, 33, 178, 180, 183, 184*, 185*, 186, 187*, 192, 193, 194*, 196, 198*, 199*, 200*, 202*, 203, 207, 208*, 209*, 211*, 212*, 213*, 215*, 217*, 218, 219*, 220*, 221*, 222*, 223*, 224, 225, 226, 227, 228*, 230, 231, 232*, 233*, 235, 236*, 237, 238*, 239, 240*, 241*, 242*, 243, 244*, 245, 246*, 247*, 248*, 249*, 250*, 251*, 252*, 253*, 254*, 255*, 256*, 257*, 258*, 259*, 260*, 261*, 262*, 263*, 264, 265*, 266*, 267, 268*, 270*, 271, 272, 274*, 275, 276*, 277*, 278, 279*, 280*, 281, 282, 283*, 284*, 285*, 286*, 287, 288*, 289*, 290*, 291*, 292*, 293*, 294*, 295*, 296*, 297*, 298*, 299*, 300*, 301*, 302, 303*, 304*, 305, 306, 307, 310, 311*, 312*, 315*, 316, 318, 319*, 320*, 322*, 323*, 324*, 325, 326*, 327*, 328*, 329*, 330*, 331*, 332*, 333*, 334*, 335*, 336*, 337, 338*, 339*, 340, 341*, 345, 346*, 348, 349, 350*, 351*, 352*, 353*, 354*, 356*, 358, 359*, 360*, 362*, 363*, 365*, 366*, 367*, 368*, 369*, 370*, 371*, 372*, 373*, 374, 375*, 376*, 377*, 378*, 379, 380, 381*, 382*, 383*, 384, 385, 386*, 387*, 388*, 389*, 390*, 391*, 392*, 393*, 394*, 395*, 396*, 397*, 398*, 399*, 400, 401*, 402*, 403*, 405*, 407, 408*, 410*, 411*, 413, 414*, 415, 416*, 417*, 418, 419*, 420*, 421*, 422*, 423*. *See also* Corviser and Shoemaker
Cordwainer and Farmer, 421
Cordwainer and Victualler, 419
Cork-cutter, 220, 241, 247*, 248*, 254, 266*, 271, 273, 277, 282, 288*, 289, 295*, 302, 307, 319, 320*, 329*, 330*, 336, 343, 351, 356*, 366*, 370*, 372*, 373*, 381*, 385, 388, 391*, 397*, 400, 401, 423
Corviser, 2, 6*, 7*, 9, 10, 11*, 13*, 14, 16*, 17, 18*, 24*, 34, 35*, 36, 151*. *See also* Cordwainer and Shoemaker
Coryer, 30*

Currier, Corier, 24, 31, 53, 58, 61*, 94*, 105, 112, 118, 129, 141, 148, 153, 159, 163, 168, 178, 180, 208, 228, 233*, 238, 273, 289, 304, 312, 317, 320*, 328, 333*, 339, 348, 355*, 356, 359, 367, 371, 372, 373*, 376, 378, 379, 393, 398*, 401, 405, 407, 416, 420*, 421, 422
Custom House Officer, 376 ; Officer of Customs, 333
Cutler, 57*, 70*, 75, 82*, 90*, 91*, 93, 98, 99, 101, 112*, 113, 124, 125, 132, 134*, 139, 145, 163, 172, 211, 214, 225, 227, 234, 237, 269, 271, 292, 293, 316*, 333, 345, 349, 357, 358, 369, 371, 376, 381, 385, 392, 397*, 398*, 408, 414*

D

Dancing Master, 226
Distiller, 157, 194, 217, 249, 317, 345
Ditcher, 31
Doctor of Medicine, 178, 192, 233, 265, 272*, 308, 310*, 314
Doctor of Physick, 176, 342
Draper, 3, 4, 7*, 8, 9*, 10, 12*, 15*, 16*, 18, 19, 20*, 21*, 24, 25*, 26*, 27, 28*, 29*, 31, 33, 34*, 35, 37, 41, 43*, 44*, 45*, 46*, 50*, 51*, 52*, 53*, 54*, 55*, 58*, 59*, 60*, 61, 62, 63*, 64*, 65*, 66*, 69*, 71*, 72*, 73*, 74*, 76, 77*, 79*, 80*, 81*, 83*, 87*, 88*, 89*, 90, 91*, 94, 95, 96, 97*, 98*, 99*, 100, 101*, 103, 104, 105*, 106*, 108, 110*, 112*, 113*, 114*, 115, 116*, 117, 118*, 119*, 123, 124, 125*, 126, 127*, 128*, 129*, 130, 131*, 133*, 134, 136, 137*, 138, 140*, 142, 144*, 146*, 148, 150, 151*, 152, 153, 156, 158, 163, 164, 166, 167*, 168, 169, 172*, 173*, 178*, 186, 187*, 188, 189, 192, 194, 198, 201, 212, 213, 216*, 218, 224, 230, 239*, 240, 254, 270, 275, 277, 278, 282*, 300, 303, 306, 326, 331*, 338, 341, 343, 346, 425, 426, 427, 429*. *See also* Linen-draper and Woollen-draper
Draper and Hosier, 119*, 123
Drawer and Upholsterer, 171
Drawer in Dee, 187
Drover, 15, 229
Druggist, 313, 319, 325, 347, 350, 355, 359, 368, 372, 375, 381, 386, 394, 398*, 399, 407, 408*, 409, 415, 416, 417, 418, 419*, 420*, 421. *See also* Apothecary

Dry-glover, 192. *See also* Glover and Wet-glover
Dyer, 5, 11, 18, 27, 33, 36, 41*, 42, 60*, 62, 63, 66*, 67, 73, 75*, 77, 79*, 81*, 85, 91, 94, 98*, 100*, 108, 119, 120, 121, 127, 128, 129, 131, 132*, 134, 136, 137, 139, 140*, 141, 148, 149, 150, 153, 162*, 163, 164*, 172, 174, 176, 179, 191, 192, 200*, 209, 212, 217*, 221*, 223*, 227, 229, 233*, 241, 251*, 252, 254, 259, 267, 276, 278, 288, 290, 295, 306, 355, 360*, 373, 413*, 414

E

Earl Barrymore, Ireland, 269, 324, 326
Earl Cholmondeley, 272
Earl of Warrington, 187
Embroiderer, 30, 33, 37, 42*, 52, 63, 65, 76*, 78*, 86*, 95, 97, 102*, 113, 129 135, 327; Ymbroderer, 425. *See also* Broderer
Embroiderer and Upholsterer, 327
Engraver, 353
Esquire, 6*, 11, 15, 16, 20, 24*, 25, 30, 37*, 38, 47, 48, 54, 58*, 59, 60*, 65, 67, 71, 72, 76*, 79, 81, 84, 86, 87, 91, 92, 99, 100, 102*, 104, 116, 127, 133, 134, 135, 137, 138, 139, 140, 141*, 142, 145, 146, 147*, 148*, 150, 151*, 152*, 153, 154*, 157*, 158*, 159, 160, 161*, 163*, 165*, 167, 169, 171*, 172*, 173*, 174, 175, 176, 177, 178*, 179*, 180*, 181, 182, 186*, 187, 189, 190, 191, 192*, 193, 195, 196, 201, 202*, 203*, 204*, 207*, 208*, 209*, 210, 211, 212, 213, 214, 215, 216*, 217*, 218, 219, 220, 224, 226*, 227, 229, 231, 232*, 234*, 238*, 240*, 241*, 242, 243*, 244*, 245*, 265, 266, 267, 268, 269*, 270, 271*, 272*, 273*, 274*, 275, 276*, 277*, 278, 279, 280*, 281, 296, 297, 304*, 305*, 308*, 309*, 310*, 311*, 312*, 313*, 314*, 315*, 316*, 317, 318, 319, 321, 324*, 325*, 326*, 327*, 328*, 330, 331*, 334*, 336, 338, 339, 340*, 341*, 342*, 343*, 344*, 345*, 346, 347* 349, 350*, 352, 353, 354, 355*, 356*, 357, 358*, 360*, 361, 362*, 363, 368*, 369*, 371*, 373, 374*, 375*, 376, 377, 379, 380, 382*, 383*, 384, 385*, 386*, 998*, 399, 400*, 401*, 402*, 403*, 404*, 405*, 406*, 407, 408*, 409*, 410*, 411*, 412, 413*, 414*, 415, 417, 418, 419, 420*, 422, 423,* 427

F

Farmer, 406, 420*, 421, 422. *See also* Husbandman
Farrier, 77, 293, 399
Feltmaker, 99, 100, 103, 104*, 105, 108, 109*, 111*, 112*, 113*, 114*, 115*, 116*, 117*, 118*, 120*, 121*, 122*, 123, 124*, 125*, 126*, 127*, 128*, 130*, 131*, 132*, 133*, 134*, 135*, 136*, 137*, 138*, 139*, 141*, 143*, 144*, 147*, 148*, 149*, 151*, 153, 154*, 155*, 156, 158*, 159*, 160*, 161, 162*, 164*, 165*, 167*, 168*, 169*, 170*, 171*, 177, 178*, 185, 186, 187, 188*, 189*, 190, 191, 193*, 194*, 195, 197*, 198, 199*, 200, 201, 204, 209, 212*, 213*, 214*, 215*, 216, 217*, 218, 219, 221*, 222*, 223*, 224*, 225*, 226*, 228, 231, 233, 234, 235*, 236, 239*, 241*, 243*, 244*, 245, 246*, 247*, 248*, 251*, 252*, 253*, 254*, 255*, 257*, 258*, 260, 262*, 263*, 264*, 266*, 267*, 268*, 273*, 276*, 278, 282*, 284, 285, 286*, 288*, 289, 290, 291, 292*, 293*, 294, 296*, 297*, 299*, 302*, 303*, 304, 305, 307, 308, 311, 321*, 323*, 324, 325*, 326*, 329*, 331*, 332*, 337, 338, 339*, 343, 344*, 345, 347*, 351, 352*. 353, 359, 360, 363*, 364, 365*, 368*, 372, 376*, 378, 380*, 381, 388, 390, 391, 394, 396*, 401, 408, 424, 427*, 428
Fisher, 7
Fisherman, 254, 284, 325, 365, 378, 387
Fishmonger, 6*, 10, 22, 26, 31, 35*, 37, 38*, 51, 52, 53, 57*, 64*, 78, 80, 87, 103*, 104, 106, 116, 117*, 121, 128, 137, 142, 146*, 148, 165, 174, 175, 180, 188, 190*, 193, 216, 225, 231, 234, 316, 345
Flaxdresser, 222, 236, 246*, 247, 256*, 260, 279, 280, 284, 286*, 287*, 294*, 304*, 307, 308, 309, 315, 324*, 327, 332, 336, 339*, 343, 347*, 348, 351*, 352, 357, 366, 372*, 375, 378, 386, 389, 395*, 396, 397*, 399, 402, 408
Flesher, Flechier, Fletcher, 1*, 2, 7, 8*, 10, 12, 14, 15, 18, 28, 29, 33, 36, 43, 52, 65, 78, 88, 100, 109*, 139, 175, 242. *See also* Butcher

INDEXES

Flour Dealer, 384, 416, 421*, 422
Flourman, 371
Founder, 16, 17, 18, 20, 31, 38, 44*, 50*, 54, 57*, 79*. *See also* Brass founder and Iron-founder
Framework-knitter, 339, 365
Fringeweaver, 418
Fruiterer, 379
Furbur, 2, 14, 15, 41, 49, 52
Furrier, 190, 273
Fustianmaker, 268, 305, 334
Fustian Manufacturer, 411
Fustian weaver, 89

G

Gaol keeper, 424
Gardener, 189*, 193, 208, 214, 217, 219, 222, 224, 237, 238, 243, 244, 252, 253, 255, 256, 258, 266, 267, 271*, 276, 284, 291, 292*, 309*, 312, 315, 320*, 321, 341*, 344, 347, 354, 359, 361, 363*, 364*, 365, 370, 372*, 373, 375, 385, 394, 398, 412, 421*
Gentleman, 8*, 12, 17, 20, 24, 29, 30, 31*, 32, 33*, 35, 38, 39, 41*, 42, 43, 45, 47, 50, 52, 54*, 55*, 56*, 59, 60, 63*, 64, 69, 71*, 72, 76*, 78, 82*, 84*, 85*, 89, 91*, 92, 93*, 97*, 98*, 101*, 102*, 105*, 107, 108*, 110, 112, 113*, 114*, 117, 118*, 119*, 120*, 122, 123*, 128*, 132*, 133*, 134*, 136, 137, 138, 139, 140, 141, 142, 145*, 146*, 147*, 148, 149*, 150*, 151, 152*, 154, 155*, 156, 157*, 158*, 159, 161*, 163*, 164*, 165, 166*, 167, 168, 169*, 171, 174*, 176*, 178*, 179*, 182*, 183, 184, 185, 187*, 188, 189, 190, 191*, 192, 193*, 194*, 195, 196, 197*, 199, 201, 202*, 203*, 204, 205, 208, 210*, 212*, 213, 214, 216*, 217, 218*, 219, 223*, 224, 225, 226*, 227*, 228*, 229*, 230, 231*, 233, 234*, 235, 236*, 237*, 239*, 240*, 242, 243*, 244, 245*, 246, 250, 252*, 253, 254, 261, 262*, 263*, 265*, 266*, 267*, 268*, 269*, 270*, 271*, 272*, 273, 274*, 275*, 276*, 277, 278*, 279*, 280*, 281*, 282*, 283*, 294*, 296, 297*, 298*, 299*, 300*, 301*, 302*, 303*, 304, 305*, 307, 308*, 309*, 310*, 311*, 312*, 313*, 314*, 315*, 316*, 317*, 318*, 320*, 321, 323*, 324, 325*, 327*, 328*, 330*, 332*, 334*, 338*, 339*, 340*, 342*, 343*, 344, 345, 346, 347*, 348, 349*, 352, 353*, 354, 357*, 360*, 361, 363, 368, 369*, 370, 372*, 373*, 374, 375, 377*, 381, 382*, 383, 385*, 386, 393, 396, 397, 399, 401*, 402*, 403*, 404*, 405, 406, 407*, 409*, 411*, 412*, 413*, 414, 415*, 416, 417, 418*, 419, 420, 422, 427
Girdler, Gurdeler, 10, 29, 77, 104
Glaiser. *See* Glazier
Glassdealer, 409
Glass-grinder, 270, 282, 296, 307, 331
Glazier, Glasier, 12, 38, 44*, 46*, 64*, 67*, 80*, 85, 96, 107*, 117, 119, 121, 125, 128, 130, 131, 140, 142, 160*, 162*, 175, 176*, 177, 179, 188*, 203, 215, 216, 221*, 227, 229, 230, 237, 238, 245, 246*, 253, 257, 260, 262, 263, 268, 275*, 276, 281, 283, 288, 293, 294*, 296*, 301*, 304, 313, 315, 323, 329, 333*, 334*, 338, 348, 349, 351, 359*, 360, 362, 368*, 375, 376, 377, 380*, 392*, 394, 395, 402*, 411*, 419, 421*
Glazier and Fishmonger, 188
Glazier and Painter, 375
Glazier and Plumber, 266, 268
Glazier and Tallow chandler, 380
Glove cutter, 379
Glover, 1, 2, 6, 7*, 10*, 11*, 12, 13*, 14*, 15, 16, 17*, 18*, 19*, 21*, 22*, 23, 24, 25*, 26*, 27*, 28*, 29*, 30, 32*, 34*, 35*, 36*, 37*, 38, 39*, 40*, 41*, 42, 43*, 44*, 45*, 46*, 47, 48*, 50*, 51, 52*, 53, 54*, 55, 56, 57*, 59*, 60, 61*, 63*, 64*, 68, 69*, 70*, 71*, 72, 74*, 75*, 76*, 77*, 80*, 81, 82*, 84*, 87*, 88*, 89*, 90, 91*, 92*, 93*, 94*, 95*, 96*, 97*, 98*, 99*, 100*, 102*, 103*, 104*, 105*, 106*, 107, 108, 109, 111*, 112*, 113, 114*, 115*, 116*, 117*, 119*, 120*, 121, 122*, 123, 124, 125*, 127*, 128*, 129*, 130, 131*, 132, 133, 134*, 136*, 137*, 139, 141*, 142*, 143*, 145*, 149*, 152*, 153, 155*, 156*, 157, 159*, 161*, 162*, 164*, 165, 167, 170*, 171*, 174, 178, 189*, 198*, 202, 203, 208*, 211, 217*, 221*, 222, 224, 226, 227, 228*, 229, 231, 239, 240, 242, 245, 253, 257*, 270, 274, 276, 280, 284, 291*, 295, 301, 319, 322, 328, 337, 350, 353, 365, 367, 370*, 371, 372*, 374, 380*, 391, 397, 401*, 402, 417, 426*, 427, 429*. *See also* Dryglover and Wetglover

II.   T

Glover and Breechesmaker, 370, 380
Goldsmith, 1, 10, 11, 12, 19*, 21, 23, 24, 25, 30*, 31, 32, 42*, 59*, 71*, 73, 82, 92*, 95, 102, 105*, 115*, 133*, 146, 148, 151*, 156, 166, 168, 172, 173*, 174, 175, 177, 182, 186, 190*, 196, 202, 211, 212, 234, 236, 237*, 239, 244, 245, 248, 252*, 259, 261*, 263*, 266, 276, 278, 283*, 285, 290, 297, 303, 305, 329, 333, 353, 370
Governor, 2
Grasier, 362
Grocer, 33, 55, 98, 174, 178*, 180, 191, 202*, 255, 299*, 302, 306, 342, 345*, 346*, 347, 349*, 350*, 355*, 356*, 357, 360*, 361*,363*, 368*, 369*, 370*, 371, 372*, 374, 375, 376, 377*, 378*, 379*, 381, 382, 383, 385, 393, 396, 398*, 401, 405*, 408, 409*, 413*, 414, 415*, 416*, 418, 419*, 420*, 422, 423*, 424
Grocer and Ironmonger, 356, 415
Grocer and Mercer, 355
Grocer and Tobacconist, 355
Gunsmith, 249, 272*, 376, 411

H

Haberdasher, 27, 32, 34, 55, 58, 65, 66*, 70, 118, 130*, 134*, 140*, 143, 147, 155*, 156, 166, 167, 171*, 177, 179, 188, 202*, 203, 226, 231, 232, 307, 354*, 381
Hairdresser, 395, 409, 410, 413, 417*, 421
Hardwareman, 4, 369
Hatmaker, 28, 38, 39*, 45, 46*, 50*, 56, 57, 58*, 62, 63, 65*, 66*, 68, 69, 71, 73*, 74*, 78, 79*, 80*, 81*, 82*, 83, 84*, 85*, 86*, 87, 88*, 89*, 90, 91, 93*, 94, 96*, 97*, 98*, 100, 101*, 103*, 109, 121, 425, 426
Hatter, 54*, 57, 62, 65*, 68, 77*, 351, 354, 360, 363*, 365, 366*, 370, 380*, 383, 410*, 417
Hedmaker, 24
Heelmaker, 389
Herald Painter, 196*
Hewster, 4, 5, 9, 10*, 12, 14, 15, 16, 26, 39
Hewster and Smith, 39
Honourable, 314, 324, 326
Honourable and Revd., 310
Hooper, 19, 31, 34, 43, 115, 116, 126, 130, 420
Hornbreaker, 158, 170, 179, 194, 222, 223, 257, 259, 260, 269*, 283, 289, 296, 306, 322*, 323, 329, 333, 352, 359, 368, 387*, 393, 395
Hornbreaker and Combmaker, 322*
Horse-hirer, 365, 372*
Hosier, 61*, 66, 82, 87, 113, 114, 116, 119*, 123, 167, 175, 277, 280, 320, 324*, 372, 398, 400, 407, 416
House carpenter and Joiner, 410
House-wright, 76
Huckster, 415, 421*
Husbandman, 2, 105*, 107*, 108, 109*, 144*, 145*, 146*, 147, 149*, 169, 190, 194, 203, 204, 207, 210, 214, 219, 220, 221*, 226, 227, 233, 234, 237*, 257, 284, 285, 287*, 289*, 294, 322, 325*, 327, 333, 348, 415*. See also Farmer

I

Ilarchus (sic), 127
Indigo blue-maker, 370, 375
Inkhorn maker, 226
Inkhorn-turner, 202, 341
Innholder, Innkeeper, 26, 31, 32, 35, 39, 42*, 48, 49*, 54, 61*, 63, 64, 70, 75, 80, 83*, 84, 96*, 111, 113, 114, 115*, 117, 119*, 122, 128*, 130, 131*, 133*, 134*, 136, 138*, 139*, 141, 143*, 146*, 147*, 148, 152, 155*, 156, 157, 158*, 160*, 161*, 162, 163*, 164, 165, 171, 173*, 175*, 177, 178, 179*, 185*, 187, 188, 189*, 190, 191, 193, 194*, 195*, 196, 197, 201, 202, 203*, 207, 214, 215*, 218*, 219, 221, 223, 224, 226, 228, 231, 232*, 234, 235, 236, 238*, 240, 241, 242, 243*, 244, 248, 251, 258, 262, 263*, 266, 267, 268, 269, 271*, 272, 274, 275*, 278, 279, 280, 281*, 285, 286, 290, 291*, 292, 293, 299, 301*, 302*, 304, 305, 312, 317*, 318, 319*, 320*, 328*, 329*, 330*, 331, 333, 336, 339, 340*, 341, 342*, 343*, 347, 348, 349*, 353*, 354, 355, 357, 359*, 361, 365, 370, 372, 373, 374*, 377*, 378, 380*, 381*, 383, 385*, 393, 398, 399*, 401, 402, 404*, 405*, 406*, 407, 408, 413, 414, 415, 416, 418, 420*, 422,* 425*, 427, 428
Instrument-maker, 117, 157, 410
Iron Founder, 415*, 419. See also Brass founder and Founder
Iron Founder and Grocer, 415
Ironmonger, 9, 11, 12, 13, 14, 16*, 18, 19*, 22*, 23, 24, 25*, 26, 29*, 30, 31*, 32*, 33*, 34, 35*, 36, 37,

INDEXES

38*, 39*, 41, 42*, 44*, 45*, 46*,
48*, 49*, 50, 51, 52, 54, 55*, 56,
57*, 58*, 60*, 61*, 62*, 63, 65,
66*, 67*, 68*, 69*, 71*, 74, 75*,
76*, 77*, 78*, 79*, 81, 82*, 84,
85*, 86*, 87, 88*, 89*, 91*, 92,
93*, 94*, 95*, 96*, 98*, 99, 100*,
101*, 102*, 103*, 105, 107, 110,
112, 113, 115, 116*, 117*, 118*,
119*, 120*, 122*, 123*, 126, 127*,
128*, 130, 131*, 133, 134*, 136*,
137*, 139*, 140*, 141*, 142*,
143*, 145*, 146*, 147*, 148*, 149,
150*, 151, 152*, 153*, 155*, 156*,
158*, 159*, 161, 162*, 163*, 164*,
165*, 166, 167*, 168*, 169*, 170,
172*, 173*, 174*, 175*, 177*, 180,
182, 186*, 188*, 189*, 190*, 191*,
192*, 194*, 195*, 196, 197*, 200*,
201, 202*, 203*, 205, 208*, 209*,
210, 211*, 212*, 213, 214*, 215,
216*, 218*, 220, 222, 223*, 224*,
225*, 227, 228*, 229*, 231*, 232*,
233*, 234*, 237*, 239*, 240, 242*,
245*, 246*, 248*, 249, 252, 253,
255, 260, 261*, 263*, 264*, 267*,
268, 269*, 271*, 273, 275, 277*,
278*, 279, 280, 281*, 282*, 283,
288, 292, 293*, 294*, 296, 298,
299*, 302*, 304, 306*, 307, 308,
312, 313, 314, 315, 318*, 321*,
324*, 325, 326, 328, 531*, 332,
338, 353, 355, 356, 362*, 368, 381,
385, 388, 412, 415, 426*, 427, 429*
Ironmonger and Grocer, 355, 381

J

Jail Keeper, 424
Jerseycomber, 257, 306, 378
Jeweller, 250, 305, 357, 405
Joiner, 5, 31, 33*, 42*, 44, 48*, 49*,
50*, 51*, 55, 61*, 63, 70*, 71, 72,
74*, 75*, 79, 80*, 82*, 84, 87, 88,
89*, 90*, 94, 95*, 102, 105, 106,
109, 110, 111, 114, 115*, 116, 117,
120, 123, 125*, 134, 135, 138, 139,
141*, 142, 144*, 146*, 148*, 150,
153, 155, 156, 157, 160*, 161, 163,
165, 166*, 167*, 169*, 170, 173*,
177*, 178, 180, 184, 185, 186,
188*, 189, 191, 192, 193*, 194,
196, 199, 201*, 203, 208, 209*,
210*, 211*, 212, 216*, 217, 220,
222, 224*, 225, 233, 235*, 237,
238, 241, 242*, 244, 245, 246,
247*, 250*, 251, 252, 255, 258*,
263, 265*, 266, 268*, 269*, 271,
272, 275*, 277, 278*, 279, 282*,
283, 284, 288*, 289*, 290, 292,
295*, 297, 299*, 300, 304*, 307*,
311, 312*, 313, 317*, 320*, 321*,
325*, 327*, 328*, 330, 331, 334,
335*, 338, 340*, 341, 351*, 354,
355, 359*, 365, 368, 369, 371,
378*, 380, 383, 400*, 405, 408,
410*, 411, 416, 418*, 420, 423*.
See also Carpenter
Joiner and Cabinetmaker, 355
Joiner and Carpenter, 378, 380, 411
Joiner-carver, 193
Joiner, Carver, and Turner, 142, 173

K

Knight, 8*, 9*, 22*, 34, 37, 38 39,
42, 43, 49, 60, 67*, 70, 78, 81, 92*,
93, 102*, 107, 111, 144, 158, 190
Knight and Baronet, 190

L

Labourer, 32, 103, 140, 146, 147,
159, 160, 166, 170*, 191, 201, 204,
207, 215, 220, 221*, 223*, 224,
225*, 232, 233, 235, 236, 238*,
240, 241, 243, 246, 255, 256*,
257*, 259, 260*, 261, 262*, 265*,
268, 271, 274, 275, 280, 282, 283,
284*, 285*, 286, 287*, 288, 289,
297, 302, 305, 315*, 316, 320*,
324*, 325*, 329*, 333*, 334*, 362,
370, 389, 393, 396, 399, 401*, 404,
421
Lace Weaver, 366*, 376, 404*
Lastmaker, 196, 322
Leather parer, 366
Leatherseller, 285, 301, 305*
Leavelooker, 180*
Linencloth-weaver, 323*
Linen-draper, 26, 44, 51, 57, 64, 94,
112*, 115, 116, 123, 125, 128*,
135, 140*, 142*, 143, 144*, 150*,
151*, 154, 155*, 156, 157, 159,
160*, 162, 164, 165*, 166*, 169,
172*, 173*, 174, 175*, 177*, 180,
182, 186, 187, 188, 189, 196*, 198,
199*, 200, 203, 204, 207, 215, 216,
218, 219, 220, 226, 231, 240, 241,
243, 246, 249*, 268, 269, 270,
273*, 274, 276, 282, 296, 298, 299,
302, 312, 317, 320, 324*, 326, 327,
331*, 332*, 337*, 343*, 344, 345*,
347, 348*, 354, 355, 356, 357,
360*, 361, 368*, 370*, 371, 372,
375*, 378, 383*, 384*, 386, 390,
395*, 397*, 398, 402, 407*, 408*,
409*, 415*, 416*, 424. *See also*
Draper

Linen-draper and Milliner, 144*
Linen merchant, 381
Liquor Merchant, 405*, 408, 410, 414, 416*, 418, 423, 424
Locksmith, 119*, 297
Long cutler, 145. *See also* Cutler
Lord Bishop, 354, 383, 414, 418
Loriner, 79, 118
Lynner, 133

M

Macebearer, 7, 176
Maltmaker, 145, 266, 344
Maltster, 83, 98, 102, 116, 132, 144, 153, 157, 168, 170, 177, 178, 191, 217, 244, 251, 255, 265, 275, 290, 291, 299, 307, 310, 325, 335, 344, 348*, 357, 360*, 373, 379, 384, 392, 393, 399*, 404*, 418*
Marble Mason, 418
Mariner, 17, 27*, 32, 47*, 48*, 61, 66, 72*, 77*, 78, 83, 85, 101, 103, 117, 120, 138*, 165, 172, 175, 177, 195, 196, 201, 202, 203*, 204*, 205, 216, 217*, 218*, 225, 229, 236, 238, 239*, 240*, 245*, 249*, 250, 251, 254, 257*, 258, 261*, 262, 264*, 266, 268, 270*, 271, 272, 273, 275, 276*, 277, 281, 289*, 300*, 301*, 302*, 304*, 306*, 307*, 308*, 309, 311, 312, 313, 318, 322, 330*, 337, 338*, 339, 340, 341*, 344, 349, 350*, 352, 353, 354, 357*, 360*, 362, 364*, 367, 368, 370, 371, 377, 378*, 385, 394, 397*, 398, 399, 400*, 407, 409, 426. *See also* Sailor
Mason, 7, 15, 16, 102, 121, 134, 141, 144*, 151, 156, 159, 161, 162, 167, 171, 173, 178*, 185*, 186, 196*, 197*, 198, 199, 204, 209*, 212, 217*, 218, 219, 220, 221*, 222, 228, 230, 233, 238, 240*, 243, 244*, 247*, 248*, 249*, 250, 252, 255, 256*, 258, 265, 269, 270, 278, 279*, 280, 281, 282, 284*, 285*, 287*, 288*, 290, 291*, 294*, 300, 304, 306, 309, 316*, 320*, 323*, 328*, 329*, 337, 348, 349*, 350, 351, 352, 356, 361, 362, 363*, 366, 367, 368*, 371*, 372*, 376, 377*, 386, 388, 391*, 392, 394, 395*, 396, 397, 399*, 403, 404, 405*, 418, 419*
Master of the Rolls at Westminster, 67
Mayor, most of the Pp. 1 to 428
Mayor's Officer, 21, 374
Mayor's Porter, 377

Mercer, 1, 2, 4, 5, 6, 7, 8*, 9*, 10, 11*, 12, 16, 17*, 18*, 19*, 20, 23*, 24*, 27*, 32, 33*, 34, 35*, 36, 37*, 38*, 39, 40*, 41, 42*, 45*, 48*, 50*, 51, 52*, 53*, 54*, 55, 57, 58*, 59*, 60*, 61*, 63, 64*, 67*, 68*, 69*, 74*, 79*, 80*, 81, 82*, 83, 85*, 86*, 89, 91, 92*, 94, 95, 97*, 98*, 101*, 104, 108, 116, 118, 120, 121, 122, 124, 127, 129, 130*, 135, 136, 138, 140*, 141, 142, 145, 148, 150*, 151*, 157*, 162, 163, 166*, 173, 176*, 177*, 180, 182, 195, 196, 201*, 202*, 203, 220, 231, 243, 245, 260, 261*, 262, 265, 267*, 272*, 281, 282, 287, 298, 300, 302, 303*, 304, 305, 307, 311, 317, 338, 350*, 355, 360, 361, 369, 373, 379, 384, 405, 407, 425. *See also* Silk-mercer
Merchant, 5, 8, 12, 13, 14*, 15*, 16*, 19*, 20*, 21*, 22*, 23*, 24, 25, 27*, 28, 29*, 30*, 32*, 33*, 34*, 35*, 36, 37, 38*, 39*, 40*, 41*, 42*, 43, 44*, 45*, 46, 48, 49, 50*, 51*, 55*, 56*, 57*, 58, 59, 60, 61*, 62, 63*, 65*, 67, 68*, 69*, 70*, 71*, 72*, 74, 75, 76*, 77*, 78, 79*, 80, 82*, 83, 84*, 86, 87*, 89*, 91, 92, 93, 94*, 95*, 97, 98, 99, 100, 101, 103, 107*, 109, 112, 113, 114, 115, 117*, 118*, 119*, 120, 122*, 124, 125*, 128*, 129, 130, 133, 134*, 136*, 137*, 138*, 142, 143, 145, 146*, 151, 153, 155*, 158*, 163*, 164, 167*, 168*, 172, 173, 174, 175*, 176, 179, 180, 184, 185*, 186, 187, 193, 194, 196*, 197, 202, 203, 204, 205, 207, 210*, 211, 212*, 213*, 214, 215, 216, 223, 225, 227, 232*, 235, 236*, 239, 240, 241, 251, 253, 265, 267*, 268*, 272, 273, 275, 276*, 277, 280, 281*, 283, 298*, 305*, 306*, 308*, 310*, 311, 312, 316*, 317, 320*, 323, 324*, 325, 326, 330, 332*, 334*, 335*, 337*, 345*, 347*, 349*, 350*, 351, 352, 353*, 355*, 356, 358, 362, 368*, 370, 372, 380, 381, 386*, 393, 396*, 398, 402, 404, 405*, 406, 407*, 410*, 411*, 412, 414, 415, 422, 426, 427. *See also* Wine Merchant
Merchant and Draper, 41, 128, 167, 173
Merchant Draper and Hosier, 167
Merchant and Ironmonger, 119
Merchant and Shipwright, 396
Merchant and Vintner, 323
Merchant's Clerk, 395

INDEXES

Miller, Milner, 9, 10, 31, 32, 38, 57, 63, 86, 91, 98, 131*, 136, 211, 280, 291, 297, 336, 378, 384
Miller and Flour Dealer, 384
Milliner, 85, 144
Millioner (sic), 103*
Minstrel, 224
Mugman, 421
Musician, Musitioner, 94, 117, 133*, 137, 196, 201, 234, 365, 395, 399*, 401*, 416

N

Nailer, 261, 284, 306
Needleman, 189
Northgate Gaol, Keeper of the, 424

O

Officer, 49*, 429
Officer of the Customs, 333; Custom House Officer, 376
Office of Armes, Deputy of, 425
Officiar, 71
Oil Merchant, 368
Organist, 381, 401
Organmaker, 20
Ostler, 47

P

Painter, 20, 34, 37*, 41, 78, 82, 102, 107, 118*, 131, 140, 154*, 169, 222, 245, 271*, 306, 330*, 337, 341*, 375, 385, 386, 393, 409, 421, 422, 424
Painter and Barber, 41, 118
Painter and Glazier, 421
Papermaker, 209, 248, 393, 423
Parish Clerk, 14
Pattenmaker, 331, 381, 383
Pattern-maker, 9, 259, 262, 267, 272, 325, 367
Pavior, 171, 197, 209, 259, 269*, 282, 295, 300, 330*, 332, 335*, 343, 374, 384, 388, 389
Pawnbroker, 421
Peddler, 45
Perfumer, 383, 407
Periwig-maker, 203, 210, 214, 219*, 223, 224, 229, 255, 264, 280, 284, 284*, 286, 297, 302*, 305, 306*, 311, 316*, 317, 319, 327, 328
Perukemaker, 355*, 356, 363, 369, 376, 381, 423
Pewterer, 7, 9, 11, 12, 13, 21*, 27, 28, 30, 34, 39*, 45*, 52*, 57, 64, 69*, 70, 81, 83, 84, 88, 90*, 91, 93, 98, 99, 100, 102, 106, 108, 119, 123, 131*, 132, 137, 141, 142, 159, 169, 171, 176, 177, 190*, 197*, 202, 230, 243, 268*, 347, 376, 425, 429*
Pewterer and Brazier, 376
Picture-drawer, 157
Pilot, 380
Pinner, 14, 17, 44, 54
Pipemaker, 161, 162, 166, 170, 180, 185*, 191, 198*, 214, 227*, 228, 234*, 235*, 238*, 240, 249, 251*, 252, 253, 254*, 257*, 258, 259*, 260, 262, 267, 268, 275, 277, 283*, 284*, 285, 289*, 290*, 291*, 294*, 295*, 296, 323*, 329*, 330, 331, 332, 333, 336, 337*, 339, 341*, 349*, 351*, 353, 355*, 356*, 360, 363*, 364*, 366, 372*, 381, 383, 386, 387*, 390*, 391*, 392*, 393*, 394, 396, 398*, 401
Plasterer, 67, 134, 149, 159, 162*, 164*, 174, 185, 189, 193, 194, 198*, 201, 208*, 216, 223, 225, 228, 246, 250, 256, 258, 259, 262, 264*, 315, 320*, 322, 329*, 372, 375, 378, 390, 400, 409
Plumber, 9, 37, 44*, 45, 56, 82, 83, 103, 124, 140*, 149*, 174, 189, 194, 210, 225, 248, 261*, 262, 264*, 268, 280, 282*, 292, 294, 306, 315, 328*, 332, 341, 350, 351, 360, 362, 372*, 377, 398*, 402, 408, 413*, 414, 421, 423
Plumber and Glazier, 351, 360
Portator (sic), 197, 200
Porter, 1, 134, 224, 359, 377, 392
Porter Brewer, 420
Preacher, 55, 98, 429
Printer, 233, 293, 328*, 335, 349, 361, 370, 371, 379, 386*, 394, 405, 406, 409, 415, 418*
Printer of Cloth, 195
Proctor, 409
Public Notary, 24, 48
Pumpborer, 387
Pumpmaker, 421
Pursuivant, 51, 91

R

Recorder, 47, 172, 179, 190, 231, 313; (Deputy Recorder), 186
Rector of Llanymonthy, 229
Right Honble., 342*
Ropemaker, 125, 221, 253, 359, 360, 365, 366, 368, 386, 388*, 389*, 395, 422
Ropier, 45*, 57, 68*, 73, 74*, 88, 94, 116, 121, 124, 196, 197, 220*, 231, 236, 255, 256, 273, 276, 282, 290,

308, 331*, 336, 337, 341, 344, 351*, 368, 374, 387, 388, 392, 393, 420

S

Saddler, 2, 7, 10*, 14, 15, 16*, 17, 19, 24*, 26, 29, 30, 34, 37*, 38, 39, 41*, 44*, 51, 53*, 56, 62, 66*, 75*, 76*, 79*, 80, 88, 89, 90, 91, 94, 96, 97, 101, 102, 107, 109, 111, 114, 123, 124, 129, 133, 140*, 141, 142, 155*, 161*, 169, 170, 171, 174, 177, 178*, 195, 204, 208, 210, 224, 228, 233, 236, 245, 253, 258, 263, 271, 277, 280, 281*, 286, 295, 296*, 298, 302, 303, 307, 311, 312, 316, 318, 324*, 339*, 341*, 353*, 355, 358, 359, 367, 370, 374, 375, 376*, 383*, 384*, 400, 403*, 410, 414, 415, 419, 420, 425, 428
Sailmaker, 397
Sailor, 7, 103
Salter, 13, 35
Saltman, 422
Sawyer, 61, 208, 230, 241, 242, 251, 255, 276, 283, 293, 315, 330, 339, 352*, 367, 388, 395
Scalemaker, 359
Schoolmaster, 242, 366, 371, 372*, 379, 398, 407
Scrivener, 80, 154, 381
Sculptor, 102
Seedsman, 417, 420
Sergeant (sic), 19, 21
Sergeant-at-Law, 58, 78
Sergeant-at-Peace, 374
Sergeant of the Keys, 47, 49, 60, 64, 71, 74, 81
Servant, 38, 47, 48, 50, 70, 77, 78, 82, 91, 99, 105*, 136
Servant of the Queen, 47
Sheriff, 19, 71, 92, 179*, 211, 235
Sheriff's Officer, 363, 374, 384
Sheriff's peer of the City, 107
Sherman, 1, 4, 7, 10, 13*, 14*, 15, 16*, 17*, 18*, 20*, 21, 22, 23, 24*, 25, 26*, 27*, 28*, 29, 30, 31, 33*, 36*, 37*, 38*, 39, 40*, 42*, 43*, 45*, 47*, 49*, 50, 51*, 52*, 54*, 56, 59*, 61*, 62, 64*, 65, 66*, 67*, 70*, 71*, 72*, 73*, 74*, 79*, 82*, 84*, 88*, 89*, 90*, 91*, 92, 94*, 95, 97, 104, 112, 120, 426, 427, 428*
Shipbuilder, 363, 384, 421
Ship-carpenter, 23, 212, 331, 354, 355, 367, 377, 396
Shipman, Shipmon, 1, 3
Shipwright, 249, 345, 351*, 367, 371, 378, 382*, 389, 391*, 393*, 395*, 396, 398
Shoemaker, 9, 13, 19*, 20*, 21*, 23*, 25*, 26*, 27*, 28*, 29*, 31*, 32*, 34*, 36, 37*, 38*, 39*, 40*, 41, 42*, 43*, 45*, 46*, 47*, 48*, 49*, 50*, 51, 52*, 53*, 54*, 57*, 58*, 59*, 60*, 61*, 62*, 63*, 65*, 67*, 68*, 69, 70*, 71*, 72*, 73*, 74*, 75*, 76*, 77*, 79*, 80*, 81*, 82*, 83*, 84*, 85, 86*, 87*, 88*, 89*, 90*, 91*, 92*, 94*, 95, 96*, 97*, 98*, 100*, 101*, 102*, 103*, 104, 105, 107*, 109*, 110*, 111*, 112*, 113*, 114*, 115*, 116*, 117*, 118*, 119*, 120*, 121*, 122*, 123*, 124*, 125*, 126*, 127, 128, 129*, 130*, 131*, 132*, 133, 135*, 136*, 138*, 139*, 140*, 141*, 142, 143*, 144*, 145*, 147*, 148, 149*, 150*, 151, 152*, 153*, 154*, 155*, 156*, 157*, 158*, 159*, 161*, 162, 163, 164*, 165*, 166*, 167*, 168*, 169*, 170*, 172, 173*, 174*, 175, 176*, 177, 178*, 190*, 191*, 194, 197*, 198*, 200, 222, 226, 228, 230, 235, 237, 264, 298, 416, 425, 426*, 427, 428. *See also* Cordwainer and Corviser
Shopkeeper, 370, 375
Sievemaker, 194, 362
Silk-dyer, 269, 304, 311, 318, 352, 356*, 374, 384, 388. *See also* Dyer
Silk-mercer, 405, 411, 415. *See also* Mercer
Silk Stocking Weaver, 223, 273, 276, 327
Silk-weaver, 55, 58, 71, 95, 97, 105, 106, 109, 117, 125*, 131*, 136*, 139, 140*, 143, 148, 149, 156, 160, 161, 162, 163, 165, 167*, 168*, 169, 170*, 171, 173, 175*, 176, 177*, 178, 180, 186, 189, 191, 194*, 197*, 198, 201, 203, 207*, 213, 217, 221, 231, 232, 233*, 234*, 240, 243, 249*, 251, 252, 265, 266, 267, 270, 286*, 288, 294, 298, 308, 311, 315, 320, 344, 349, 400, 412, 425, 426. *See also* Weaver
Silversmith, 354*, 363, 371*, 379, 381*, 402, 407, 416*
Singer, 48
Singingman, Syngyngman, 25
Skinner, 2*, 7, 12*, 16, 21, 31*, 37, 39, 40*, 46*, 49*, 51, 56, 77*, 80, 85, 90, 102, 103, 115, 116, 127, 132, 137, 141, 165, 169, 174, 177, 180, 185, 187, 197*, 202, 208*, 209, 221, 226*, 272, 320, 355*,

INDEXES

356*, 357, 358*, 366*, 367, 368,
378*, 387*, 388, 392, 399, 400,
402, 403, 406, 410*, 413, 418, 420
Slater, Sclater, Sklater, 11, 24, 34,
55*, 56*, 67*, 69*, 71*, 78*, 84,
85, 86, 88, 93, 96, 99, 102, 105,
106, 110, 111, 113, 114, 117, 118,
122, 123, 124, 129, 133*, 134, 135,
141, 146, 149*, 151, 155, 159, 161,
162*, 164, 166, 174*, 179, 185,
188, 191*, 194, 196, 198*, 199*,
200*, 210, 214*, 215*, 218*, 219,
220*, 221, 222, 226, 227, 229, 232,
234, 235*, 236, 237, 242, 243, 246,
247, 248*, 250*, 252*, 254*, 256*,
257, 258*, 259*, 260*, 262, 263,
269, 273, 275*, 277, 283*, 284*,
285, 286*, 287*, 288, 289*, 290*,
292, 293, 296, 304, 306, 315, 316,
318*, 321, 323*, 324*, 325, 327,
328*, 329, 331, 332*, 333*, 334*,
335*, 336*, 340*, 342*, 344*,
346*, 350, 351*, 352*, 353, 354,
355*, 356*, 359*, 364, 365*, 366,
367*, 368, 369, 372*, 374, 375,
378*, 379*, 381, 382, 384, 386*,
387*, 388, 389*, 390*, 394*, 395*,
396*, 397*, 399, 400*, 401*, 402,
403, 409*, 410*, 413*, 416*, 426*
Slater and Plasterer, 315, 372, 375,
378, 409
Smith, 7, 11, 13*, 14*, 15, 17, 20,
21, 22*, 24*, 26*, 28*, 29*, 32*,
33*, 34*, 35, 36*, 37, 38*, 39, 44,
46*, 47*, 49*, 52, 54, 56*, 58*, 60,
61*, 63, 64*, 67*, 70*, 71, 74*, 75,
77*, 78*, 79*, 84, 85*, 87, 88*,
91*, 96*, 101, 102*, 103*, 104,
107, 108*, 111, 112*, 115*, 116,
119, 122*, 123, 126, 128*, 166*,
175, 185*, 195*, 198, 199, 200*,
201*, 203, 205*, 209*, 210*, 214*,
215, 218*, 220, 222, 223, 226,
227*, 233, 237, 244, 247, 248,
250*, 252*, 253*, 255*, 257*,
266*, 268*, 269*, 270*, 273, 279,
282*, 285*, 287*, 288*, 289*,
291*, 293, 294, 297, 300*, 301,
303*, 313, 319, 321*, 322*, 327*,
328, 329, 333, 336*, 337, 339, 350,
352*, 353*, 363, 372, 376, 382*,
388, 395*, 396, 401, 426, 427, 429
Soapboiler, 157, 318, 326, 416*
Soapmaker, 176, 251
Soldier, 338
Solicitor, 58
Spurrier, 103, 130, 141, 176, 216
Spycer, 1
Stationer, 70, 117, 124, 137, 138,
147, 165, 179, 187, 211*, 218, 317,
330, 362*, 370, 371, 372, 375, 376,
380, 392, 400, 406, 408, 411*,
412*, 417*, 423*
Stationer and Bookbinder, 417*
Staymaker, 285, 318, 319, 323*, 336,
347, 349, 354, 355, 361, 365*, 366,
367, 372, 375, 386*, 389*, 392*,
394, 396, 397, 413, 417
Staynor, 8
Stockingweaver, 305, 321, 331, 335,
365, 366. *See also* Weaver
Stonemason, 419*
Stone and Marble Mason, 418
Stringer, 2, 18, 25, 26, 39, 45*, 52
Stuff-weaver, 322*, 358
Sugar-baker, 178, 180, 422*, 423.
See also Baker
Surgeon. *See* Chirurgeon
Surgeon barber. *See* Barber Chirurgeon and Barber Surgeon, &c.
Surgeon and Apothecary, 374. *See also* Chirurgeon and Apothecary
Swordbearer, 319

T

Tailor, 1*, 7*, 9, 10*, 11, 13*, 14,
16*, 18*, 19, 21*, 22*, 23*, 26*,
27*, 29*, 30*, 31*, 32*, 33*, 34,
35*, 36*, 38, 39*, 41*, 42*, 44,
45, 46, 47*, 48*, 49*, 50*, 51, 52*,
53*, 54*, 55, 56*, 57*, 58*, 59*,
61*, 62*, 63*, 64, 66*, 67*, 68*,
69*, 71*, 72*, 73, 74*, 75, 78, 79*,
80*, 81*, 82*, 84*, 85*, 86, 87*,
90*, 92, 93*, 94*, 96*, 97, 100*,
101*, 102, 103*, 104*, 105*, 106*,
108*, 109*, 110*, 111*, 112*, 113,
114*, 115*, 116*, 119*, 120, 122*,
123, 124, 127*, 129*, 130, 131*,
132, 133, 134*, 135, 136*, 138*,
139*, 141, 142, 143*, 144*, 145,
147*, 149*, 150, 151*, 152*, 154*,
156*, 157*, 158*, 159*, 160*, 162,
163, 164*, 165*, 166, 168*, 169,
170*, 171, 172*, 173*, 176*, 177,
178, 179*, 180*, 185*, 186*, 187,
188, 189*, 190*, 192*, 193*, 195*,
196, 198*, 200, 201*, 203*, 207*,
208, 209, 210*, 211, 213*, 214*,
215*, 216*, 217*, 218, 219*, 220*,
221*, 222*, 224, 225*, 226, 227*,
229, 230*, 232*, 234*, 235*, 238*,
241*, 242*, 246*, 247*, 248*,
249*, 250*, 251*, 252*, 253*, 255*,
256, 260, 261*, 264, 265*, 266*,
267*, 268*, 271*, 272*, 273*,
274*, 276, 277, 278*, 279*, 280*,
281, 282*, 283*, 284, 286*, 287*,
288*, 289*, 290*, 291*, 292*, 293*,
294, 295*, 297*, 298*, 299*, 300*,

INDEXES

301*, 302*, 304*, 306, 311*, 312, 313, 315, 316*, 318, 319*, 321*, 322*, 323, 325, 328, 329, 330*, 333, 334*, 336, 337*, 338*, 339*, 341, 345*, 346, 347, 348, 349*, 350*, 351, 352*, 355*, 356, 357*, 359, 361*, 364*, 365, 366*, 367*, 368, 369, 374, 376*, 377, 378, 379*, 382*, 384*, 385, 386, 387, 391, 392, 393*, 394*, 396, 397, 398, 399*, 400*, 403*, 407*, 408*, 409, 412, 416*, 417, 421, 427*
Tallow Chandler, 24, 29, 31, 34, 35, 39, 53, 63, 68*, 78*, 81*, 90*, 92, 93, 99*, 101*, 106, 113, 114, 115*, 117*, 119*, 123, 124, 129*, 131*, 133, 135, 137*, 140, 142, 146, 148, 150, 152, 153*, 155, 156, 158, 161*, 163, 166*, 167, 168*, 171, 173, 177, 179*, 186, 211*, 216, 217*, 231, 318, 326, 343*, 344, 354, 357, 362, 363, 380, 393, 396, 426*, 427. *See also* Chandler
Tallow Chandler and Soapboiler, 318, 326
Tanner, 22, 25*, 27*, 28, 29, 30*, 32, 33*, 34*, 35, 37, 38*, 42*, 43*, 44*, 46, 48, 49, 50*, 51*, 52, 53*, 55, 56*, 57*, 58*, 59*, 61*, 62*, 63*, 64*, 65*, 66*, 67, 68*, 70*, 72*, 73*, 75*, 76*, 77*, 79, 80, 81*, 82, 83*, 84*, 85*, 87, 88*, 89*, 90*, 91, 92*, 93, 94, 96, 97, 99*, 100*, 101*, 103*, 104, 105*, 106, 107*, 111*, 112*, 114*, 116, 117*, 118,* 120, 122, 123*, 124*, 125*, 126*, 127*, 130*, 132, 133*, 134, 135*, 136*, 137*, 138, 139*, 140, 141, 142*, 143*, 144*, 145, 146, 147*, 148*, 150*, 155, 157*, 160*, 161, 162, 163*, 164, 166*, 167*, 169, 170*, 171*, 172, 173, 174*, 177, 178*, 179, 182, 184*, 185*, 186, 187, 191, 195*, 199, 200*, 201, 202, 204*, 207*, 209*, 211*, 213, 215, 216, 217*, 218, 219*, 221*, 223*, 224*, 225*, 226, 228*, 229, 230*, 231*, 233, 234*, 235, 236, 237*, 238, 240, 241, 243, 245, 246*, 248, 249*, 250, 252, 260, 261*, 264*, 269, 281*, 283, 294*, 295*, 297, 298*, 303*, 312, 320, 322*, 324, 327, 333, 334*, 337, 344*, 349, 350*, 352, 358, 360*, 363, 366, 367*, 377*, 384*, 385*, 387*, 390, 392, 393, 394*, 397, 403, 408, 409, 413*, 414, 420, 425*, 426*, 427*
Tapemaker, 264
Tea Dealer, 381, 395
Tea Merchant, 347, 412

Threadmaker, 87
Timber Merchant, 275, 330, 393, 402, 405
Tinman, 369*, 370, 394, 417, 419
Tinplate worker, 179, 212*, 232, 243, 273, 274, 277, 293, 317, 335, 338, 349, 369, 370, 376, 377, 406*, 420, 422*
Tobacco-cutter, 192, 198, 222*, 259, 266, 303, 311, 317, 320, 322
Tobacconist, 175, 198, 213, 236, 245, 254, 256, 285, 292, 328, 331*, 341, 347*, 352, 355, 356, 367*, 376, 382*, 383, 387, 388*, 389, 393*, 415*, 417*, 423
Toyman, 282, 360, 418, 419, 420
Treasurer, 113
Turner, 75*, 86, 96, 120, 124, 127, 138, 142, 148*, 155, 159, 162*, 165, 169, 171, 173*, 175*, 177, 208, 210, 211, 225, 229, 246, 247*, 248, 251*, 254, 256, 274, 281, 285, 298, 303, 306, 307, 321, 322*, 335, 337, 354, 371, 379*, 384, 387*, 389, 398, 401*, 419

U

"Upholder," 327
Upholsterer, 22, 145, 147, 158, 159, 171, 172, 173, 178, 179*, 194*, 202, 209, 231, 234, 239, 242, 244, 250, 264, 266, 267*, 274, 275, 278, 279*, 297, 299*, 304, 306, 313, 318, 327, 330, 333, 334, 336, 341*, 342*, 354*, 358, 359, 367, 373, 383*, 386, 389*, 393, 396, 407, 413, 416, 417*, 420, 421

V

Victualler, 251, 315, 325, 326*, 344, 346, 347, 356, 357, 360, 361*, 362*, 363*, 368*, 369*, 370*, 371, 373*, 374*, 375*, 376*, 377*, 379*, 380*, 381*, 382, 383*, 384*, 385, 390, 402*, 403*, 404*, 405*, 406*, 407*, 408*, 409*, 410*, 411*, 412*, 413*, 414*, 415*, 416*, 417*, 418*, 419*, 420*, 421*, 422*, 423*, 424*
Vintner, 3, 8, 89, 102, 114, 121, 122, 133, 136*, 137, 139, 145, 150, 151, 152, 154, 158, 159*, 163, 171, 192, 198, 203, 217, 224, 227, 230*, 233, 263, 279, 294, 302*, 323*, 349, 360, 368, 372, 380, 405*
Vintner and Merchant, 172

INDEXES

W

Walker, 10, 12, 15, 22
Warehouse-keeper, 293
Watchmaker, 158*, 172, 175, 179, 185, 194, 214*, 230, 239*, 241, 276, 278, 292, 293, 294, 298, 300, 305, 312, 319, 320, 325, 347*, 358, 359, 360*, 361, 362, 365, 367, 376, 379, 384, 397, 399, 409*, 418
Water-leader, 31, 48, 110
Wax Chandler, 131, 146, 154*, 320. *See also* Chandler and Tallow Chandler
Weaver, Webster, 2, 3, 6, 7*, 8, 9, 10, 11, 12*, 13*, 14*, 15*, 19, 20, 22, 25, 27*, 28*, 30, 31*, 32, 34*, 35, 36, 38, 39, 41*, 42, 45*, 46*, 47*, 48*, 49*, 50, 51, 52, 54*, 55*, 56, 59*, 60*, 61, 62, 68*, 71*, 72*, 75*, 76*, 80*, 86*, 87*, 89, 90, 91*, 92, 93*, 95, 96, 101*, 102, 103, 109, 111, 112*, 114, 115, 119, 121, 123, 126*, 129*, 132*, 137*, 139, 141, 142, 146, 147, 151, 158, 164, 171, 173, 175, 191, 204, 207, 223, 229*, 230, 233*, 234*, 236*, 240, 241, 245, 246, 248*, 249*, 250*, 251*, 252*, 253, 255*, 256, 261*, 266, 272, 273, 275, 276*, 280, 287, 288, 289*, 290*, 291, 292, 293, 297, 299, 301*, 302, 307, 316, 317, 322, 323*, 325, 327, 330, 337*, 350, 351, 352*, 359, 366*, 376, 379, 385, 386, 390, 393, 394*, 404*, 418, 425, 429. *See also* Silk-weaver
Weaver and Linen-draper, 146
Webster. *See* Weaver
Wet-glover, 118, 147*, 150, 154*, 158*, 161, 162, 164, 165, 173, 175, 176*, 179, 187, 189, 192, 215, 226, 230*, 236, 237, 239, 240*, 241, 242, 244*, 246, 247*, 248*, 250*, 253*, 258*, 259, 260*, 261, 263, 269, 270*, 271*, 275, 277, 279, 280, 281*, 282*, 283, 286, 289, 290, 292*, 293*, 294, 295*, 296*, 298, 299*, 303*, 307*, 315*, 316*, 318, 323*, 326*, 328, 333*, 339, 345, 346*, 347*, 351, 352*, 354, 366, 370*, 373*, 374*, 378*, 387, 388*, 389, 392, 400, 401, 406, 407, 416*. *See also* Dry-glover and Glover
Wheelwright, 48, 65, 242, 244, 265, 271, 282, 288, 290, 291, 293, 295, 316, 328, 336, 341, 343, 345, 348*, 353, 361, 363, 366, 378, 380, 389, 391

Whipmaker, 303, 405
Whitesmith, 306, 318, 350*, 362, 373, 377, 378*, 382, 385, 390*, 408, 411, 413, 414*, 420, 421
Widow, 144, 145, 146, 152, 188, 191, 192, 193, 204, 211, 217, 219, 226, 229, 230, 231*, 241, 242, 244, 257*, 259*, 262, 265, 269, 270, 272, 273, 277*, 279, 283, 284, 287, 297, 311, 313, 321, 323, 326*, 345, 348, 358, 364, 405
Wigmaker, 189*. *See also* Periwig-maker and Perukemaker
Wine-cooper, 125, 142, 162, 193, 322*, 329, 337, 348, 352, 364, 399
Wine-merchant, 355, 369, 379*, 381, 383, 399*, 401*, 404, 408*, 410*, 411, 412*, 413, 415*, 421, 423. *See also* Merchant
Wine and Spirituous liquor Merchant, 405
Wood-comber (*sic*), 164
Wood-comber, 290, 295, 313, 319, 329*, 330, 341, 350, 364, 368*, 373*, 403
Woollen-draper, 140, 175, 179, 182, 253, 311, 353, 357, 362, 371, 375*, 377*, 384, 385, 386*, 406*, 408, 419. *See also* Draper
Woollen-draper, Hosier, Innholder, and Merchant, 175
Wright, 4*, 10, 22, 56, 60, 62, 65, 66, 70, 73, 78*, 82, 83, 100. *See also* House-wright and Wheelwright
Writing Master, 322, 359
Writing-stationer, 380. *See also* Stationer

Y

Yeoman, 25*, 26, 31*, 32*, 34, 36, 39*, 42, 45, 46*, 47, 48*, 51, 52*, 53, 54*, 55*, 56*, 58*, 59, 62*, 63*, 64, 65, 68*, 69*, 70*, 73*, 76, 77*, 78*, 79, 81, 82*, 83*, 84*, 85*, 86*, 87*, 88, 89*, 90*, 91, 92*, 93*, 95*, 98, 99, 101, 104*, 105*, 106, 107*, 108*, 109, 110, 114, 117, 118, 120, 122*, 128*, 130, 131, 132*, 134, 135, 136*, 137*, 138*, 142, 143*, 144*, 145*, 146*, 147, 149*, 150*, 153*, 154*, 156, 157, 160*, 162, 164*, 166, 167, 168, 171*, 180, 185, 188*, 190, 191, 192*, 193*, 195*, 196*, 201*, 204*, 205*, 207*, 208*, 209*, 210*, 211*, 212*, 213*, 214*, 216*, 217, 218, 219*, 220, 221, 223*, 224*, 225, 226*, 228*, 229*, 230, 231*, 233*, 234,

235*, 236, 237, 238*, 239*, 240, 243*, 245*, 246, 248, 249, 251*, 252*, 254*, 255, 256, 258*, 260, 261*, 264*, 265*, 266*, 267*, 268*, 269, 270*, 271*, 272*, 273, 274, 275, 276*, 277, 278*, 279*, 280*, 281*, 282, 283*, 285, 286, 287, 288*, 289, 290*, 291*, 292*, 293, 295*, 296*, 297, 298, 299*, 300*, 301*, 303, 304*, 305, 306*, 307*, 308, 309*, 311*, 312*, 313, 314, 316, 317*, 318*, 319*, 320* 321*, 322*, 323*, 324*, 325*, 326*, 327*, 328*, 329*, 330, 334, 335, 336*, 337*, 338*, 339*, 340*, 341*, 342*, 343*, 344*, 345*, 346*, 347, 348*, 349*, 350*, 351, 352, 353*, 355*, 356*, 357*, 358*, 360, 362, 363, 368, 376, 379*, 382, 385*, 390*, 393*, 398, 400, 401*, 403*, 404*, 406*, 408, 411*, 412*, 418, 423

III

PLACES

The place names are generally indexed under their modern form; the chief variations in the spelling, as they appear in the Mayor's Books, being shown after in brackets. It should, however, be noted that a few of the places have not been identified.

A

Abergele [Abbergelly], 146
Abram [Abra], 108
Adlington, 322
Aldersey, 231, 279, 283, 420
Aldford [Alford], 220, 224, 293, 296, 413, 416, 418
Alkington, 261
Allington, 244, 324, 326, 328, 341, 412
Allostock, 272
Alpraham [Alperom], 82
Altrincham, 236
Alvanley [Orvenley], 143, 261
Anglesey, 67; Co., 191, 211, 306
Ashley, 331
Ashton, 104, 229, 241
Aston, 144, 217, 231, 233, 252, 266
Audlem [Auldem], 190

B

Backford, 211, 342
Baddiley [Baddeley], 266
Bangor, 267, 273, 290
Barrow, 194, 207, 244, 254, 265, 266, 295, 300
Barton, 231, 262, 295
Bathavarn, 342
Beaumaris [Beumaris], 191, 303
Bebington, 262, 328, 329; Higher, 214, 263
Beeston, 262*
Belgrave, 195, 295
Bickerton, 239, 278
Bidston, 145, 404
Birkenhead [Beckett], 295
Birmingham, 145, 306*, 307
Bodidris [Bodidrist], 340
Bold, 342
Boles, 219
Bolin [Bollin], 283

Bolton, 339
Boughton, 47, 48, 144, 214, 228, 281, 284, 323, 324, 344, 348, 417*; Great, 319, 345; Spital, 48
Bredford, 209
Bretton, 230
Brewers' Hall, 408
Bridgenorth, 48
Bridge Trafford, 57, 242, 261, 362, 418*
Brimstage, 295
Bristol, 306, 307*
Broad Lane, 63, 217, 252, 278, 290, 296, 310, 346
Bromborough, 229, 234, 298, 412
Broughton, 105, 224, 243, 287, 296, 306, 318
Broxton, 196, 309, 342
Brynford [Brinford], 268
Bryngriffith [Bringriffith], 246
Budworth, 105
Bulkeley, 223, 239
Bunbury, 266*, 294, 338, 339, 340
Burland Green, 195
Burton, 106, 197*, 193, 217, 237, 255, 258, 269, 300, 301

C

Caerfallwch [Caervallough in Northop], 281, 283*
Caergwrle [Cargurley], 225
Caerwys, 204, 327
Calcot, 145
Caldecott, 338, 355
Caldy [Cauldy], 145
Capenhurst, 279
Carden, 340
Carnarvon [Caernavon], 60, 195; Co., 143
Catspole, 246
Caughall [Coughall], 264, 403
Celyn [Kelin], 272

506   INDEXES

Cheaveley [Cheweley], 110
Chelsea, 302
Chester and Co. Chester are not indexed, as they occur on practically every page
Chester, Gloverstone, 192, 272, 297; Boughton, 47, 48, 144, 214, 228, 281, 284, 323, 324, 344, 348, 417*; Boughton Great, 319, 345; Handbridge, 15, 46, 47*, 58, 76*, 91, 108, 144, 201, 227, 287*, 288, 289, 291, 320; Northgate Gaol, 59; St. John's Lane, 2; Spital Boughton, 48; The Bars, 47*
Chetwynd, 340
Childer Thornton, 147, 242
Cholmondeley, 325
Chorlton [Charlton, Chalton, Chaulton, Cholton], 145, 201, 338, 378
Christleton, 90, 154, 230, 823, 305, 306, 370, 379
Church Minshull, 307
Churton, 45, 191, 222, 280, 325, 328, 350
Cilcen [Kilkin], 147
Clive, 149
Clotton, 208
Clutton, 212
Coddington, 201, 211, 262*, 274, 289
Conway, 143, 278
Coolane, 191
Cork, 326
Cornist, 283, 294
Cotton, 270; Edmunds, 233
Coughall. *See* Caughall
Coventry [Couyntrie], 2, 341
Crewe, 264
Croesnewydd [Cross Newydd], 340
Crossmere, 340
Croughton, 238
Crowton [Croton], 154, 313

D

Daniel's Ash, 310
Daresbury, 304
Denbigh, 340; Co., 146, 188, 193*, 202, 209, 217, 229, 237, 239, 243, 244, 251, 255, 258, 268, 269, 270, 274*, 275, 286, 289, 290, 297, 298*, 300, 301, 316, 317*, 324, 325, 326, 327*, 341, 412*
Derby Co., 148, 209
Dodleston, 260, 368
Dolgan, 236
Dolgelly [Dolgethly], 195
Dongray, 273
Downing, 343
Drogheda, 2

Dublin, 202, 232, 268, 302, 304, 305, 322, 383
Dunham-on-the-Hill, 108, 167
Dymeirchion, 268

E

Eastham, 149, 344
Eaton, 243, 267, 271*, 278
Eccleston, 235, 289, 305, 420
Edge, 309, 409
Edge Lane, West Derby, 146
Edgmond [Edgemont], 315
Ellesmere [Elsmere], 264, 304, 340
Elton, 104, 143, 144, 227, 260, 277
Estin, 234
Ewloe, 283, 345

F

Fallowes, 340
Farndon, 224, 268, 299, 326, 350, 411, 413, 416
Farne, 211
Flint [Flynt], 1, 255, 261; Co., 93, 144, 147, 149, 151, 167, 192, 194, 196, 204, 205, 217*, 219, 221, 223, 224, 225, 231, 233*, 234, 238*, 240, 243, 251, 252*, 263*, 264, 266, 267, 268*, 269, 270, 271, 272, 273*, 278, 281, 282, 283*, 287*, 290*, 292, 294*, 295, 296*, 297, 302, 303, 316, 318, 320*, 321, 324*, 327*, 338, 340, 345, 346*, 347, 408
Flixton, 271
Flookersbrook, 59
Foulke Stapleford, 188, 201, 231, 240. *See also* Stapleford
Frankby, 106, 192
Frodsham [Frodesham], 3, 109, 201, 295, 298, 318, 325, 346

G

Gadlys [Gadlis], 264, 297
Garston [Garstoune], 109
Garthewin, 342
Gibraltar, 338
Gloverstone, 190, 272, 297
Golbourn David, 313
Grange, 191
Greasby [Graisbey, Gresebie, Grisby], 105, 263*, 329
Great Barrow, 319
Great Boughton, 319, 345. *See also* Boughton
Great Budworth. *See* Budworth
Great Marton [Great Mortin], 146

INDEXES

Great Neston, 195, 342. *See also* Neston
Great Saughall, 221, 273
Great Sutton, 107, 270, 271, 278, 279
Greencaugh,
Greenfield, 205
Gresford, 113, 274, 290, 298, 327
Grindley [Tushingham - cum - Grindley], 373
Guilden Sutton [Gilden Sutton], 108, 129, 231
Gwersyilt, 370

H

Halkin, 342
Halton [Haleton], 3
Hampton, 309
Handbridge, 15, 46, 47*, 58, 76*, 91, 108, 144, 201, 227, 287*, 288, 289, 291, 320
Handley, 243, 292
Hanmer, 107
Hargrave [Hargreve], 107, 308; Stubbs, 58
Hartford, 278
Hassall, Little, 268
Hatherton, 109, 219
Hatton, 15, 241, 411
Havyndon, 3
Hawarden [Harwarden, Hawardyn], 3, 101, 113, 199, 238*, 240, 242, 251*, 252*, 259, 262, 264, 268, 269, 292, 295, 316, 341, 347, 382*
Heath, Little, 190
Helsby [Hellesby], 104
Hendrebiffa [Hendre befay], 149
Heswall [Haswell], 265
Higher Kinnerton, 324. *See also* Kinnerton
Hilcot [Hillcott], 145
Hodnet, 264
Hollinwood, 321
Holt, 107, 193, 251, 268*, 294*, 325, 327
Holyhead, 396
Holywell, 287, 296*, 302, 327, 328*, 329, 346
Houston. *See* Onston
Hoole, 319
Hooton [Hoton], 6*
Hope, 148, 193, 204, 221, 250, 338, 340
Horsley, 342
Hugmer [Hugmoore], 108
Hull, 300
Hulme [Holme], 295
Hunsterson [Hunsterston, Hunpsterston], 202
Huntington, 208
Huxley, 107, 237

I

Ince, 251, 294
Ireland, 3, 106, 269, 324, 326
Iscoyd, 105, 342
Isle of Man, 64, 152, 217

K

Kailin, 239
Kanufud. *See* Llanyfud
Kelin. *See* Celyn
Kelsall, 280
Kelsterton, 265
Kelston, 271
Kent, 109
Kilkin. *See* Cilcen
Kingsley, 233. *See also* Kinsley
Kinnerton, 194, 264, 295, 297; Higher, 324; Lower, 190, 266
Kinsley, 108. *See also* Kingsley
Knutsford [Knottesford], 136, 147, 264, 269, 305, 307

L

Lache, Marlston-cum-, 311
Lanc. Co., 146, 153, 188, 193, 204, 205, 216, 229, 234, 267*, 268*, 271, 273, 299, 302, 305*, 306, 308, 313, 321, 326, 339*, 341, 377, 411
Landican [Lancan], 108
Lea, 223, 231, 318, 346
Lea Newbold, 145
Ledsham, 195, 329
Leeds, 374
Leeswood, 321
Leftwich, 152
Leighton, 192
Leitrim Co., 191
Lichfield [Litchfield], 231
Litherland [Liverland], 153
Little Hassall, 268
Little Heath, 190
Little Mancot, 151
Little Neston [Little Nesson], 254, 258*, 264*, 290, 344, 362*
Little Stanney, 335
Little Sutton, 321
Littleton, 349
Liverpool, 105, 188, 216, 261*, 264, 265, 267*, 268, 273, 296, 298, 299, 301, 302, 305*, 306, 313, 333, 340, 341, 385*, 406, 411, 412, 415
Llanddaniel-Fab [Llandaniell], 211
Llandysilio in Yale [Llandesillo in Yale], 104
Llanegryn [Llanegrin], 152
Llanfair [Llanvaior], 114

Llangollen [Llangullan], 67, 298
Llansaintffraid [Llansemffraid], 327
Llanyfud [Kanufud], 188
Llanymowddwy [Llanymonthy], 229
Llay, 275, 405
Llwynegrin [Lloynegrine], 196
London, 61*, 67, 134, 137, 166, 189*, 196, 300, 301*, 302*, 303*, 304*, 305*, 306*, 310, 403, 414
Lostock, 227
Lower Kinnerton, 190, 266. *See also* Kinnerton
Lyme, 228, 309

M

Macclesfield, 288
Macefen, 193
Malpas [Malpasse], 107, 267, 285, 315
Manchester, 227, 260, 264, 268, 281, 294, 295, 301, 305*, 334, 339*, 341, 412
Mancot, 151
Manley, 209, 265, 334, 336
Mannor, Parish of Hawarden, 242
Marford, 408
Marlston-cum-Lache, 311
Marple, 318
Marston, 106
Marton, 343
Merioneth Co., 152, 195, 229, 236, 239
Mickle Trafford, 203, 204, 237, 263, 285. *See also* Trafford
Middleton, 411
Middlewich, 195, 232, 283, 294, 297, 298*, 303, 305, 318, 346
Milton Green, 287
Minshull [Church Minshull], 307
Mold [Mould], 263, 294, 296, 303
Mollington [Molington], 211, 260, 385
Montgomery Co., 327
Moore, 144, 264
Moreton [Morton], 109
Morley, 195, 373
Mortin, Great. *See* Great Marton
Mostyn, 223, 320
Mouldsworth, 104
Moulton [Moolton], 340

N

Nantwich [Namptwich, Wyco Malby], 2, 3, 108, 195, 239, 270, 284, 292, 302, 303, 316, 327, 328, 341*, 369
Nerquis, 309
Ness, 294
Neston [Nesson], 146, 195, 295, 326, 330, 340, 369, 412; Great, 195, 342;
Little, 254, 258*, 264*, 290, 314, 362*
Nether Leigh, 237
Netherley, 153
Nether Poole, 275
Nether Whitley, 346
Newcastle, Staffs., 303
Newcastle-on-Tyne, 303
Newton, 79, 136, 204, 208, 228
Northop, 282
Northwich, 59, 224, 231, 269, 296, 316, 317

O

Onston [Honston], 2
Oswestry, 282
Oulton, 261, 410
Over, 267, 268
Over Kellet, 308
Overton, 209
Oxton [Oxen], 105

P

Parkgate, 202, 286, 300*, 306, 313, 336, 341, 376
Peckforton, 107, 223
Peele, 172, 218
Pemberton, 305
Pentre, 320
Pentrehobin, 310
Peover, 172, 267, 269; Little, 144
Pickhill, 340
Pickton, 107, 110, 195, 204, 232, 411*
Plasgwyn, 385
Plas Newydd, 343
Plymouth [Plimouth], 304*
Plymyard [Plimyard], 297
Poole, 341 ; Nether, 275
Poulton [Poolton, Pulton], 9, 107, 150, 252, 231, 295, 377
Prenton, 259*
Preston, 304*
Preston-on-the-Hill, 221
Puddington [Podyngton], 3, 294, 348
Pudleston, 227
Pulford, 210, 321, 325
Pulton. *See* Poulton

R

Raby [Rabie], 146
Rhyding, 270
Ridley, 258
Rock Savage, 92
Roe Wen [Roe], 269, 279

Rossett, 249
Rowton, 326
Ruabon [Rhuabon], 316
Rudheath, 2
Rushton, 234
Ruthin, 265

S

Saighton [Saughton-on-the-Hill], 104, 214, 226*
Salford, 349
Salop, 2, 224, 230, 341; Co., 48, 136, 149, 191, 227, 231, 234, 267, 273, 281, 282*, 288, 298, 303, 307, 315
Saltneyside, 422
Sandbach [Sanebach], 264*, 268, 272, 317
Sandiway, 266
Saughall [Soughall], 258*, 298; Great, 221, 273
Saughall-Massey, 105, 106, 220
Saughton-on-the-Hill. *See* Saighton
Scolecroft, 411
Sconder, 167
Seacombe, 105, 225
Segrwyd [Segroit], 340
Shocklach [Shocklidge], 262, 274, 296, 299
Shotwick, 146*, 295
Shotwick Lodge, 346
Shrewsbury, 49, 231, 303, 306
Simons Woods, 234
Siverfield, 243
Somerset Co., 211
Sontley, 342
Soughall. *See* Saughall
Soughton, 324
Sound [Soond], 196
Speke, 1
Spital Boughton, 48
Stafford Co., Staffs. Co., 145, 218, 231, 234, 303, 306, 307, 313
Stanlow House, 231
Stanney, 239, 204, 311, 419; Little, 335
Stapleford, 281. *See also* Foulke Stapleford
Stoak [Stoke], 201, 312, 323
Stone, 307
Stretton, 251, 254, 277, 303
Sutton, 205, 207*, 235, 258; Great, 107, 270, 271, 278, 279; Little, 321; Guilden, 108, 129, 231

T

Tamworth, 313
Tarporley [Tarpourley], 226, 252, 297, 373*

Tarvin, 144, 153, 204, 217, 237, 238, 243, 253, 258, 261*, 262, 281, 294, 302*, 335, 376*
Tattenhall, 225, 238, 241, 259, 272, 341, 377
Tatton, 309
Thornton, 212, 219; Childer, 147, 242; Hough, 146, 250*, 294, 307
Thornton-le-Moors, 321
Tilston, 414
Tiverton, otherwise Turton, 213, 261
Trafford [Troghford], 231, 412, 415; Bridge, 57, 242, 251, 362, 418*; Great, 3; Mickle, 203, 204, 237, 263, 285; Wimbolds, 259, 376
Tushingham-cum-Grindley, 373

U

Upton, 196, 212, 235
Utkinton, 261

V

Vale, 145
Vale Royal, 414*
Vaynol, 342

W

Walbank, 203, 210
Wallasey, 107, 108*, 109, 126
Wardend [Warden], 307
Warrington, 188, 204, 216, 234, 267*, 299
Warwick, 304; Co., 145, 246, 307
Waverton, 237, 270, 276, 308, 313, 363
Weaverham [Waverham], 207*
Wednesbury [Wedgebury], 306
Welley, 3
Wenlock, 307
Werneth, 191
Wervin, 188
West Derby, 146, 214; Edge Lane in, 146
Westhoughton, 229
West Kirby, 233
Whatcroft, 350
Whitby, 154, 226, 279
Whitchurch, 107, 216, 261, 267, 273, 282, 288, 298, 343*
Whitegate, 300
Whitford, 82, 263
Whitley, Nether, 346
Whixhall [Whixa], 149
Wigan, 268

INDEXES

Willaston, 2, 145, 179, 216*, 221, 230, 254, 261, 262, 291, 306, 337
Wimbolds Trafford, 259, 276. *See also* Trafford
Winstanley, 340
Wirral [Werrall], 105, 221, 263*, 265, 270
Wistaston, 308
Wiswall [Wisewall], 82
Wollerts Hall, 154
Woodbank, 340
Woodchurch, 144, 270

Worthenbury, 192
Wrenbury [Renbury], 239
Wrexham, 109, 202, 212, 218, 229, 236, 239, 243, 263, 270, 274, 286, 289, 297, 303, 317, 340, 342
Wynnstay, 413

Y

Yale, 104
York, 3, 313
Ystin Colwyn, 309

THE END

Printed by BALLANTYNE, HANSON & Co.
Edinburgh & London

THE RECORD SOCIETY

FOR THE

PUBLICATION OF ORIGINAL DOCUMENTS

RELATING TO

LANCASHIRE AND CHESHIRE

COUNCIL, 1907-8

Sir GEORGE J. ARMYTAGE, Bart., F.S.A., Kirklees Park, Brighouse, President.

G. E. COKAYNE, M.A., F.S.A., Clarenceux King of Arms, Heralds' College, London, E.G., Vice-President.

Lieut-Col. HENRY FISHWICK, F.S.A., The Heights, Rochdale, Vice-President.

JOHN PAUL RYLANDS, F.S.A., Highfields, Bidston Road, Birkenhead, Vice-President.

HENRY BRIERLEY, Thornhill, Wigan.

The Council deeply regret to announce the death of the Rev. Canon STANNING, which has occurred since the printing of this Report.

Willaston, 2, 145, 179, 216*, 221, 230, 254, 261, 262, 291, 306, 337
Wimbolds Trafford, 259, 276. *See also* Trafford
Winstanley, 340
Wirral [Werrall], 105, 221, 263*, 265, 270
Wistaston, 308
Wiswall [Wisewall], 82
Wollerts Hall. 154
Woodbank, 340
Woodchurch, 144, 270

Worthenbury, 192
Wrenbury [Renbury], 239
Wrexham, 109, 202, 212, 218, 229, 236, 239, 243, 263, 270, 274, 286, 289, 297, 303, 317, 340, 342
Wynnstay, 413

Y

Yale, 104
York, 3, 313
Ystin Colwyn, 309

THE END

THE RECORD SOCIETY

FOR THE

PUBLICATION OF ORIGINAL DOCUMENTS

RELATING TO

LANCASHIRE AND CHESHIRE

COUNCIL, 1907-8

Sir GEORGE J. ARMYTAGE, Bart., F.S.A., Kirklees Park, Brighouse, *President*.

G. E. COKAYNE, M.A., F.S.A., Clarenceux King of Arms, Heralds' College, London, E.C., *Vice-President*.

Lieut.-Col. HENRY FISHWICK, F.S.A., The Heights, Rochdale, *Vice-President*.

JOHN PAUL RYLANDS, F.S.A., Highfields, Bidston Road, Birkenhead, *Vice-President*.

HENRY BRIERLEY, Thornhill, Wigan.

THOMAS H. DAVIES-COLLEY, M.A., Newbold, near Chester.

WILLIAM FARRER, Hall Garth, Carnforth.

Colonel PARKER, F.S.A., Browsholme, Clitheroe.

R. D. RADCLIFFE, M.A., F.S.A., Old Swan, Liverpool.

The Rev. Canon STANNING, M.A., The Vicarage, Leigh, Lancashire.

CHARLES W. SUTTON, M.A., Free Reference Library, Manchester.

WM. ASHETON TONGE, Staneclyffe, Disley.

HONORARY TREASURER

JOHN PAUL RYLANDS, F.S.A., Highfields, Bidston Road, Birkenhead.

HONORARY SECRETARY

WM. FERGUSSON IRVINE, F.S.A., 56 Park Road South, Birkenhead.

RULES

1. That the Society shall be called the RECORD SOCIETY, and shall have for its object the transcribing and publishing of Original Documents relating to the Counties of Lancaster and Chester.

2. That the affairs of the Society shall be governed by a Council consisting of a President and twelve Members, the former of whom shall be *annually* elected by the Council.

3. That three Members of the Council shall form a quorum.

4. That the subscription of Members of the Society shall be £1, 1s. per annum, which shall entitle them to the publications for the year; but any Member whose subscription shall be two years in arrear shall thereupon be removed from the Society, and shall not be re-admitted until all arrears have been paid. The number of Members is limited to 350.

5. That the subscriptions shall be due in advance on the 30th of June in each year, and that no work shall be issued to any Member whose subscription is in arrear.

6. That an Annual Meeting of the Society shall be held in the month of October, of which due notice shall be sent to all the Members. At this meeting a Report of the work of the Society, with a Statement of the Income and Expenditure, shall be presented. These shall be annually published, together with a List of Members and the Rules of the Society.

7. That so long as the funds of the Society permit, two volumes at least shall be issued to the Members in each year.

8. That no copies of the publications of the Society shall be sold to non-members, except at an increased price to be fixed by the Council.

9. That no payment shall be made to any person for editing any work for the Society, but that the Editor of each Volume shall be entitled to twenty copies of the work so edited by him.

10. That the Treasurer's Accounts shall be audited by two Members of the Society, who shall be elected at the Annual Meeting.

11. No alteration shall be made in any of the above Rules except at the Annual General Meeting. Notice of any proposed alterations must be sent to the Hon. Secretary a month before such General Meeting.

12. That a meeting of the Council of the Society shall be called by the Hon. Secretary at least once in every three months.

The Annual Subscription of £1, 1s., entitling the Members to all the Volumes issued for that year, may be paid to the Hon. Treasurer, or to the credit of the Society at their Bankers, the Manchester and Liverpool District Banking Company, Limited, at any of their branches.

RECORD SOCIETY OF LANCASHIRE AND CHESHIRE

REPORT FOR THE YEAR 1906-7

Read at the Annual Meeting held in the Audit Room of Chetham Hospital, Manchester, 4th December 1907.

SINCE the Annual Meeting, held on the 6th November 1906, one volume has been issued to the Members. This is Volume 53, being Abstracts of Marriage Licences granted within the Archdeaconry of Chester (including Lancashire south of the Ribble). This volume, the first, it is hoped, of a long series, covers the period from 1606 until 1616. It has been edited by the Honorary Secretary.

The second volume for the year should have been the fifth volume of the Royalist Composition Papers, and was being edited by Canon Stanning. The Council very much regret that, owing to ill-health, Canon Stanning found that he was not able to proceed with the work, and after a portion had been printed off the volume has been postponed until a later date. Its place has been taken by a second volume of Lancashire Inquests and Feudal Aids, edited by Mr. Farrer, to whom the Society is indebted for a gift of the transcript. The volume is now all printed, and only awaits the completion of the index before being issued to the Members.

For the current year the second part of the Freemen Rolls of the City of Chester (1700–1805), edited by Mr. J. H. E. Bennett, is already in type and in the hands of the indexer; and another volume of Marriage Licences has been sent to the printer.

REPORT OF THE SOCIETY

The Council wish to place on record their thanks to Mr. Farrer and to Mr. Bennett for generously presenting to the Society the transcripts of the above-named volumes.

Since the 30th June 1906 two new members have joined the Society. During the same period three members have died, viz.: Mr. Assheton of Downham, Mr. R. B. M. Lingard-Monk, and Sir David Radcliffe, and the name of one member has been removed from the list of members under Rule 4. The number of paying members of the Society now only stands at 148.

The following is a list of some of the volumes which are in progress, and which it is hoped to print shortly:—

The Visitation of Cheshire, 1613. By Sir George Armytage and Mr. Rylands.
The Chartulary of St. Werburgh's Abbey, Chester. By Mr. Powicke.
Lancashire Plea Rolls, 1500–1536. Part I. By Colonel Parker.
Lancashire Final Concords. Part IV. By Mr. Farrer.
A Complete Index to the Record Society's Publications (Vols. 1–50). By Mr. Henry Brierley.

A few sets of the Society's Publications are still on hand. Members can obtain the price of sets or of single volumes by applying to the Honorary Secretary.

The following is a complete list of the Society's Publications printed up to the present time:—

1878–79. { I. Commonwealth Church Survey.
         { II. Index to the Wills at Chester, 1545 to 1620.
1879–80. { III. Lancashire Inquisitions. Stuart Period. Part I. 1603 to 1613.
1880–81. { IV. Index to the Wills at Chester, 1621 to 1650.
         { V. The Register of Prestbury, co. Chester, 1560 to 1636.
1881–82. { VI. Cheshire and Lancashire Funeral Certificates, 1600 to 1678.
         { VII. Lancashire and Cheshire Records. Part I.
1882–83. VIII. Lancashire and Cheshire Records. Part II.

REPORT OF THE SOCIETY v

1883-84.
- IX. Preston Guild Rolls, 1397 to 1682.
- X. Index to the Lancashire Wills proved at Richmond, 1457 to 1680.

1884-85.
- XI. Exchequer Depositions, 1558 to 1702.
- XII. Miscellanies, Lancashire and Cheshire. Vol. I.

1885-86.
- XIII. Index to the Lancashire Wills proved at Richmond, 1680 to 1748.
- XIV. Annales Cestrienses.

1886-87.
- XV. Index to the Wills at Chester, 1660-1680.
- XVI. Lancashire Inquisitions. Stuart Period. Part II. 1614 to 1622.

1887-88.
- XVII. Lancashire Inquisitions. Stuart Period. Part III. 1622 to 1625.
- XVIII. Index to the Wills at Chester, 1681 to 1700.

1888-89.
- XIX. Civil War in Cheshire.
- XX. Index to the Wills at Chester, 1701 to 1720.

1889-90.
- XXI. The Register of Leyland, co. Lancaster, 1653 to 1715.
- XXII. Index to the Wills at Chester, 1721 to 1740.

1890-91.
- XXIII. Index to the Lancashire Wills proved at Richmond, 1748 to 1792.
- XXIV. The Royalist Composition Papers relating to Lancashire. Vol. I. A and B.

1891-92.
- XXV. Index to the Wills at Chester, 1741 to 1760.
- XXVI. The Royalist Composition Papers relating to Lancashire. Vol. II. C to F.

1892-93.
- XXVII. Lancashire Lay Subsidies, Henry III. to Edward I.
- XXVIII. Plundered Minister's Accounts, Lancashire and Cheshire. Part I. 1643-1654.

1893-94.
- XXIX. The Royalist Composition Papers relating to Lancashire. Vol. III. G and H.

1894-95.
- XXX. A Collection of Lancashire and Cheshire Wills.
- XXXI. Miscellanies, Lancashire and Cheshire. Vol. II.

1895-96.
- XXXII. Pleadings and Depositions in the Duchy Court of Lancaster. Part I.
- XXXIII. Miscellanies, Lancashire and Cheshire. Vol. III.

1896-97.
- XXXIV. Plundered Minister's Accounts, Lancashire and Cheshire. Part II. 1654-1660.
- XXXV. Pleadings and Depositions in the Duchy Court of Lancaster. Part II.

REPORT OF THE SOCIETY

1897–98.
- XXXVI. The Royalist Composition Papers relating to Lancashire. Vol. IV. I to O.
- XXXVII. Index to the Wills at Chester, 1761 to 1780. A to M.

1898–99.
- XXXVIII. Index to the Wills at Chester, 1761 to 1780. N to Z.
- XXXIX. Lancashire Final Concords. Part I. 1196 to 1307.

1899–1900.
- XL. Pleadings and Depositions in the Duchy Court of Lancaster. Part III.
- XLI. Lancashire Court Rolls, 1323–1324.

1900–01.
- XLII. Manchester Quarter Sessions Records. Part I.
- XLIII. Miscellanies, Lancashire and Cheshire. Vol. IV.

1901–02.
- XLIV. Index to the Wills at Chester, 1781–1790.
- XLV. Index to the Wills at Chester, 1791–1800.

1902–03.
- XLVI. Lancashire Final Concords. Part II. 1308 to 1377.
- XLVII. Lancashire Assize Rolls. Part I. 1202–1281.

1903–04.
- XLVIII. Lancashire Inquests, Extents, &c. Part I. 1205–1307.

1904–05.
- XLIX. Lancashire Assize Rolls. Part II. 1284–1285.
- L. Lancashire Final Concords. Part III. 1377–1509.

1905–06.
- LI. Chester Freemen Rolls. Part I. 1392–1700.
- LII. Miscellanies, Lancashire and Cheshire. Vol. V.

1906–07.
- LIII. Chester Marriage Licences. Part I. 1606–16.

☞ The Council must again refer to Rule 5, under which no volume can be delivered to any Member whose Subscription is in arrear.

The Record Society of Lancashire and Cheshire

Receipts and Expenditure from 1st July 1906 to 30th June 1907.

Dr.

	£	s.	d.
Balance (Bank-book) 30th June 1906	282	15	6
Subscriptions paid, July to December 1906	118	15	0
Subscriptions paid, January to June 1907	48	6	0
Books sold	6	17	3
Waste-paper sold	1	3	3
Bank Interest	6	3	6
	£464	**0**	**6**

Cr.

		£	s.	d.	£	s.	d.
PRINTING:—							
Ballantyne & Co., Vol. 51		63	9	6			
Pollard & Co., Vol. 52		63	8	3			
Brakell & Co., Circulars		0	10	4	127	8	1
SUNDRIES:—							
Mr. Fazakerley, Binding Copies of Volumes presented to Probate Registry					1	12	0
Mr. Mason, Rent of Stock-rooms, Dec. 1905 to Dec. 1906		8	10	0			
Mr. Mason, brown paper, packing, postages, &c.		3	15	9			
Mr. Mason, taking care of Stock		2	2	0			
Mr. Mason, expenses and remuneration for destroying Surplus Stock of Volumes		3	3	0			
Hon. Treasurer and Hon. Secretary, Incidentals					17	10	9
Alliance Assurance Co., Fire Insurance of Stock					20	0	0
Cheque Book					0	12	0
Bank Commission					0	5	0
Balance (Bank-book) 30th June 1907					0	12	2
					296	0	6
					£464	**0**	**6**

Examined and found correct.
(Signed) R. D. RADCLIFFE, } Auditors.
WILLIAM E. GREGSON, }

1st August 1907.

(Signed) J. PAUL RYLANDS,
Hon. Treasurer.
29th July 1907.

LIST OF MEMBERS

Corrected to 31st December 1907.

AMHERST OF HACKNEY, The Lord, Didlington Hall, Northwold, Stoke Ferry, S.O., Norfolk.
Antiquaries, The Society of, Burlington House, London, W.
Armytage, Sir George J., Bart., F.S.A., Kirklees Park, Brighouse.
Ashton, T. Gair, 36 Charlotte Street, Manchester.
Aspinall, Colonel R. J., Standen Hall, Clitheroe.
Athill, Charles H., Richmond Herald, Heralds' College, London, E.C.

BAILEY, Sir W. H., Sale Hall, Cheshire.
Beazley, F. C., Fern Hill, Oxton, Birkenhead.
Bennett, John H. E., 66 Cambrian Crescent, Chester.
Bispham, William, 12 West 18th Street, New York.
Bostock, R. C., Beddgelert, Grove Road, Ramsgate.
Bramwell, W. H., Bow, Durham.
Brierley, Henry, Thornhill, Wigan.
Bromley, James, The Homestead, Lathom, Ormskirk.
Brooke, Sir Thomas, Bart., F.S.A., Armitage Bridge, Huddersfield.
Burke, H. Farnham, C.V.O., Somerset Herald, Heralds' College, London, E.C.

CARINGTON, H. H. Smith, Grangethorpe, Rusholme, Manchester.
Chippindall, Colonel W. H., 12 Oaklands Road, Bedford.
Chorlton, Thomas, 32 Brazenose Street, Manchester.
Cokayne, G. E., M.A., F.S.A., Clarenceux King of Arms, Heralds' College, London, E.C.
Crofton, H. T., Oldfield, Maidenhead, Berks.
Crompton, John, High Crompton, Oldham.
Cross, The Viscount, G.C.B., Eccle Riggs, Broughton-in-Furness.
Cross, James, Great Ness, Baschurch.
Crossley, E. W., Dean House, Triangle, Halifax.
Cunliffe, Walter F., 12 Stanley Crescent, London, W.

DAMES, R. S. Longworth, 21 Herbert Street, Dublin.
Davenport, The Rev. G. H., M.A., Foxley, Hereford.

LIST OF MEMBERS

Davies-Colley, Thomas H., M.A., Newbold, near Chester.
Derby, The Earl of, K.G., G.C.B., Knowsley, Prescot.
Dixon, Colonel George, Astle Hall, Chelford, Cheshire.

EAGLE, George, 37 Brown Street, Manchester.
Earle, T. Algernon, 90 King Street, Manchester.
Edge, Sir John, Waverley Court, Camberley, Surrey.
Ellis, T. Ratcliffe, 18 King Street, Wigan.

FARRALL, The Rev. L. M., M.A., 12 Stanley Place, Chester.
Farrer, William, Hall Garth, Carnforth.
ffarington, Lieut.-Colonel R. A., Mariebonne, Wigan.
Fishwick, Lieut.-Colonel Henry, F.S.A., The Heights, Rochdale.
Fletcher, J. S., Merlewood, Virginia Water, Surrey.
Ford, John Rawlinson, Yealand Conyers, Carnforth.
Frost, F. A., Grappenhall Hall, Warrington.

GAMON, G. P., 52 Grafton Street, Fitzroy Square, London, W.
Gladstone, Robt., Jun., M.A., B.C.L., Woolton Vale, Liverpool.
Gregson, W. E., 43 Moor Lane, Great Crosby, Liverpool.

HARRISON, Henry, 47 Magdalen Road, Wandsworth Common, London, S.W.
Healey, C. E. H., C.B., K.C., Chadwyck, 119 Harley Street, London, W.
Heape, Charles, Hartley, High Lane, Stockport.
Holland, Walter, Carnatic Hall, Mossley Hill, Liverpool.
Holme, Colonel Arthur Hill, 6 Gambier Terrace, Liverpool.
Hovenden, R., F.S.A., Park Hill Road, Croydon, Surrey.
Hughes, H. R., Kinmel Park, Abergele.
Hulton, Arthur Hyde, LL.B., Wood Bank, Macclesfield.
Hyde, The Hon. John, F.R.G.S., F.S.S., Lanier Heights, Washington, D.C.

IRVINE, Wm. Fergusson, F.S.A., 56 Park Road South, Birkenhead.

KELSALL, John, The Cottage, East Sheen, London, S.W.

LEVER, W. H., M.P., Thornton Manor, Thornton Hough, Cheshire.
Library, Free Public, Accrington.
   ,,   Free Public, Ashton-under-Lyne.
   ,,   Free, Barrow-in-Furness.
   ,,   Free, Birkenhead.
   ,,   Central Free, Birmingham.
   ,,   Free Public, Blackburn.
   ,,   Public, Bolton-le-Moors.

REPORT OF THE SOCIETY

Library, British Museum, care of Dulau & Co., 37 Soho Square, London, W.
,, University, Cambridge.
,, Free Public, Chester.
,, Chapter, Chester.
,, Chester and North Wales Archæological Society, Grosvenor Museum, Chester.
,, Free Public, Chorley.
,, Free, Edinburgh.
,, Free Public, Heywood, Lancashire.
,, The Storey Institute, Lancaster.
,, Leyland, Hindley, near Wigan.
,, Public, Leeds.
,, Free, Leigh, Lancashire.
,, Historic Society of Lancashire and Cheshire, Royal Institution, Liverpool.
,, Athenæum, Liverpool.
,, Free Public, Liverpool.
,, College of Arms, London, E.C.
,, Guildhall, London.
,, Inner Temple, London.
,, Lincoln's Inn, London.
,, St. George's, Hanover Square, Buckingham Palace Road, London.
,, Sion College, Victoria Embankment, London, E.C.
,, Public Record Office, care of Wyman & Sons, Fetter Lane, London, E.C.
,, Chetham, Manchester.
,, Free Public, Manchester, C. W. Sutton, M.A., Chief Librarian. (*Two Subscriptions.*)
,, Public, Moss Side, Manchester.
,, John Rylands, Manchester.
,, Lancashire College, Whalley Range, Manchester.
,, Cathedral, Manchester.
,, Incorporated Law Library Society, Kennedy Street, Manchester.
,, Owens College, Manchester.
,, Portico, Mosley Street, Manchester.
,, Free, Nottingham.
,, Bodleian, Oxford.
,, Dr. Shepherd's, Preston.
,, Free Public, Rochdale.
,, Royal Free, Peel Park, Salford.
,, Central Free, Sheffield.
,, Free, Southport.
,, Free Public, St. Helens.
,, Museum and, Warrington.
,, Free, Wigan.

LIST OF MEMBERS

Library, Melbourne Free, care of Agent-General of Victoria, 142 Queen Victoria Street, London, E.C.
,, Bibliothèque Nationale, Paris.
,, Athenæum, Boston, U.S.A. ⎫ per Kegan Paul, Trench,
,, Public, Boston, U.S.A. ⎬ Trübner & Co., Dryden
,, Harvard College, U.S.A. ⎪ House, 43 Gerrard Street,
,, Worcester Free, Mass., U.S.A. ⎭ Soho, London, W.
,, New York State, Albany, New York, U.S.A. ⎫ per G. E. Stechert,
,, Columbia University, New York City, U.S.A. ⎬ 2 Star Yard, Carey Street, London, W.C.
,, Public, New York, U.S.A.
,, Newberry, Chicago, Illinois, U.S.A.
,, New England Historic-Genealogical Society, Boston, U.S.A. ⎫ per B. F. Stevens and Brown, 4 Trafalgar Square, London, W.C.
,, New York Historical Society.
,, Public, Detroit, Michigan, U.S.A.
,, Pennsylvanian Historical Society, Philadelphia, U.S.A.
,, Company, Philadelphia, U.S.A. ⎫ c/o E. G. Allen, King Edward Mansions, 14 Grape Street, Shaftesbury Avenue, London, W.C.
,, Yale University, New Haven, Conn., U.S.A.
,, Congress, U.S.A.
,, Cornell University, Ithaca, New York, U.S.A.
,, The Watkinson Hartford, Conn., U.S.A.
,, State Historical Society of Wisconsin, U.S.A., c/o H. Sotheran & Co., 140 Strand, London, W.C.
,, New Hampshire State, Concord, New Hampshire, U.S.A.
Literary and Philosophical Society, Newcastle-upon-Tyne.
Lockett, Richard Cyril, Clonterbrook, St. Anne's Road, Aigburth, Liverpool.
Longstaff, G. B., M.A., Highlands, Putney Heath, London, S.W.

MARSHALL, Isaac, Sarnesfield Court, Weobley, R.S.O.

NEWBIGGING, Thomas, C.E., Ardwell, Delahays Road, Hale, Cheshire.
Nicholson, Major, 16 Pulteney Street, Bath.
North, Colonel Bordrigge N., Newton Hall, Kirkby Lonsdale.

PARKER, Colonel John, F.S.A., Browsholme Hall, Clitheroe.
Parr, J. Charlton, Grappenhall Heyes, Warrington.
Pemberton, Major-General, C.S.I., 13 Cresswell Gardens, South Kensington, London, S.W.
Pink, W. D., Winslade, Lowton, Newton-le-Willows.

Radcliffe, R. D., M.A., F.S.A., Old Swan, Liverpool.
Ridgway, T. J., Wildersmoor House, Lymm, near Warrington.
Rigg, Henry, 49 Gordon Road, Ealing, London, W.
Roper, W. O., F.S.A., Yealand Conyers, Carnforth.
Roscoe, James, M.A., Oatlands, Harrogate.
Royden, E. B., Blyth Lodge, Bromborough, Birkenhead.
Rylands, John Paul, F.S.A., Highfields, Bidston Road, Birkenhead.
Rylands, W. Harry, F.S.A., South Bank Lodge, Campden Hill Place, London, W.

Sanders, Rev. F., M.A., F.S.A., The Vicarage, Hoylake, Birkenhead.
Sephton, The Rev. J., M.A., 90 Huskisson Street, Liverpool.
Smith, J. C. C., F.S.A., care of Miss Wood, Whitchurch, Reading.
Stanning, Rev. Canon, M.A., The Vicarage, Leigh, Lancashire.
Stewart-Brown, Ronald M.A., of Fairoaks, Bromborough, Cheshire.
Swettenham, Sir Alexander, K.C.M.G., Bellevue, Gordontown, Jamaica.

Tatton, E., Wythenshawe, Northenden.
Taylor, Henry, 8 John Dalton Street, Manchester.
Tempest, Mrs., Broughton Hall, near Skipton.
Thornely, Samuel, Hatfield, Norton, near Worcester.
Threlfall, Henry S., 1 London Street, Southport.
Tonge, W. Ashton, Stoneclyffe, Disley, Cheshire.
Toulmin, John, *Guardian* Office, Preston.
Tweedale, John, The Moorlands, Dewsbury.
Twemlow, Lieut.-Col. Francis R., D.S.O., Peatswood, Market Drayton.

Wagner, Henry, M.A., F.S.A., 13 Half Moon Street, London, W.
Weldon, W. H., C.V.O., Norroy King of Arms, Heralds' College, London.
Wilkinson, William, M.A., Middlewood, Clitheroe.
Wilson, Colonel Edmund, F.S.A., Denison Hall, Leeds.
Woodcock, F. A., 8 St. James' Square, Manchester.
Worsley, P. J., Rodney Lodge, Clifton, Bristol.

www.ingramcontent.com/pod-product-compliance
Ingram Content Group UK Ltd.
Pitfield, Milton Keynes, MK11 3LW, UK
UKHW010808010725
6642UKWH00083B/824